MASTERING TRIAL ADVOCACY

Second Edition

■ ■ ■

Charles H. Rose III
Dean and Professor of Law
Ohio Northern University Pettit College of Law

Laura Anne Rose
Assistant Professor of Law
University of South Dakota School of Law

AMERICAN CASEBOOK SERIES®

WEST
ACADEMIC
PUBLISHING

American Casebook Series is a trademark registered in the U.S. Patent and Trademark Office.

© 2014 LEG, Inc. d/b/a West Academic
© 2020 LEG, Inc. d/b/a West Academic
    444 Cedar Street, Suite 700
    St. Paul, MN 55101
    1-877-888-1330

West, West Academic Publishing, and West Academic are trademarks of West Publishing Corporation, used under license.

Printed in the United States of America

ISBN: 978-1-68467-121-2

Dedication:

For Ms. Erika McArdle - the consummate coach, teacher, and trial lawyer.

Dean Charles H. Rose III

Dedication:

For Professor Lee Coppock - the only professor in law school who shone so brightly I had to wear sunglasses to class! PC, I cannot express how much being your TA and a member of your trial team means to me. I hear your voice every time I teach.

Prof. Laura Anne Rose

Some Thoughts on Learning

"[W]e shall be better and braver and less helpless if we think that we ought to enquire, than we should have been if we indulged in the idle fancy that there was no knowing and no use in seeking to know what we do not know;– that is a theme upon which I am ready to fight, in word and deed, to the utmost of my power."

Plato, mathematician and philosopher, (427?–347 BC)

"In seeking wisdom, the first step is silence, the second listening, the third remembering, the fourth practicing, the fifth—teaching others."

Ibn Gabirol, poet and philosopher (AD 1022–1058)

"If you hold a cat by the tail you learn things you cannot learn any other way."

Mark Twain, author and humorist (1835-1910)

Contents

Acknowledgments...xvii
Preface...1

Chapter 1: How Trials Work
    A. Introduction...5
    B. Forming the Attorney Client Relationship.................8
    C. Case Analysis & Preparation....................................10
    D. Pretrial Practice..11
    E. Jury Selection...13
    F. Preliminary Matters..15
    G. Opening Statements..16
    H. Prosecution/Plaintiff's Case in Chief......................17
    I. Motions at Close of Plaintiff's Case........................19
    J. Defendant's Case in Chief.......................................20
    K. Motions at Close of Defendant's Case.....................22
    L. Plaintiff's Rebuttal & Defendant's Surrebuttal........22
    M. Motions at the Close of All Evidence.....................23
    N. Closing Argument & Jury Instructions....................24
    O. Deliberations & Verdict...26
    P. Post-Trial Motions & Appeals..................................27
    Q. Conclusion...28

Chapter 2: Case Analysis & Preparation
    A. Introduction...29
    B. Creating the Litigation File and Trial Notebook.....32
        1. The Litigation File...............................32
        2. The Trial Notebook.............................33
    C. Organizing the File..36
    D. Developing the Legal and Factual Theory..............38

       1. Identify the Available Facts..............................39

   E. Analyzing the Case....................................42

       1. The Rule of Threes...............................43

       2. The Three Primary Steps.......................45

   F. Finding the Story.....................................48

   G. Preparing for Trial...................................49

       1. Closing Argument................................50

       2. Case-in-Chief.....................................51

       3. Opening Statements.............................52

       4. Bringing it All Together........................53

   H. Examples of Case Analysis.......................56

   I. Conclusion………………………………….63

Chapter 3: Jury Selection

   A. Introduction..65

   B. The Right to a Jury Trial..........................66

   C. Deciding if You Want a Jury.....................67

   D. How Jury Selection Works.......................68

       1. Jury Selection System..........................68

       2. Permissible Subjects............................70

       3. Legal Issues.......................................72

       4. How Challenges Work..........................74

   E. Purpose and Process of Jury Selection...................76

   F. Preparing for Voir Dire............................80

   G. Voir Dire..83

       1. Overview...83

       2. Making a Connection...........................85

       3. Managing Responses............................86

       4. Maintain Credibility............................87

       5. Challenges for Cause............................88

       6. A Suggested Approach..........................94

   H. Examples of Voir Dire Questions................96

Chapter 4: Opening Statements

   A. Introduction...113

   B. What the Jury Sees and Thinks....................114

   C. How the Law Impacts Openings...........116

    1. Overview...116
    2. Using Instructions...............................116
    3. Objecting During Openings...............119
  D. Creating the Opening............................122
    1. Introduction......................................122
    2. Relevant Story...................................125
    3. Preview the Hard Questions of Fact.................128
    4. Introduce Self, Bring Jury to Present............130
    5. Preview Relevant Legal Standard.................131
    6. Connect Law, Facts, Moral Theme..............133
    7. Forecast Prayer for Relief......................134
  E. Delivering the Opening............................136
    1. Beginning...137
    2. Using Body Language...........................140
    3. Verbal Keys......................................142
    4. Dangers of Improper Argument.................143
    5. A Call to Action.................................143
  F. Examples...144
  G. Checklist...163
  H. Evidentiary Rules to Consider.......................165
  I. Conclusion...166

Chapter 5: Direct Examinations
  A. Introductions..167
  B. How the Law Impacts Direct...............170
  C. Structuring the Direct............................172
    1. Identify Goals of the Direct...................172
    2. Prepare the Witness............................174
    3. Organizing.......................................177
  D. Asking Proper Questions........................179
    1. Headlines...180
    2. Open or Non-Leading Questions.............186
  E. Creating and Delivering the Direct..............189
    1. Factual Theory of the Case.....................189
    2. Legal Theory of the Case.......................190
    3. Moral Theme of the Case.......................190

      4. Outlining the Testimony.................................191

      5. Physicality..193

      6. Language...196

      7. Fundamental Techniques...............................198

  F.   Examples..202

  G. Checklist...217

  H. Evidentiary Rules to Consider.......................219

Chapter 6: Exhibits

  A. Introduction..221

  B. How the Law Impacts Exhibits...........................222

      1. Introduction..222

      2. Foundations...223

      3. Authentication...225

      4. Voir Dire & Objections................................226

  C. Admitting Exhibits..230

  D. Laying Foundations...232

      1. Admitting Diagrams.....................................233

      2. Admitting Photographs.................................235

      3. Admitting Non-fungible Evidence.................237

      4. Admitting Fungible Evidence........................239

  E. Persuasive Use of Exhibits..................................242

  F.   Sample Foundations...243

      1. Diagram Foundation.....................................244

      2. Photograph Foundation.................................246

  G. Foundation Checklists...248

      1. Diagrams..248

      2. Photographs...249

      3. Fungible Evidence..250

      4. Non-fungible Evidence.................................252

      5. Chain of Custody Documents........................253

      6. Chain of Custody Documents (Hearsay).........254

      7. Child Witnesses...256

      8. Spouse Witnesses...257

      9. Lay Witness with Personal Knowledge..........258

      10. Lay Opinions...259

      11. Expert Opinion...260

12. Bias..261

13. Habit..262

14. Reputation..263

15. Prior Bad Acts Resulting in Conviction..........264

16. Prior Bad Acts Not Resulting in Conviction....265

17. Other Crimes, Wrongs or Bad Acts................266

18. Character Trait of Untruthfulness.................267

19. Character Trait for Truthfulness...................268

20. Prior Inconsistent Statement........................269

21. Prior Consistent Statement..........................270

H. Evidentiary Rules to Consider.....................271

I. Conclusion..271

Chapter 7: Cross Examination

A. Introduction..273

B. How the Law Impacts Cross.........................274

C. Structuring the Cross..................................277

   1. Identify Goals of the Cross 277

   2. Organizing..283

D. Asking Proper Questions.............................285

E. Creating and Delivering the Cross.................289

   1. Creating the Cross................................289

   2. Delivering the Cross..............................296

F. Impeaching Witnesses................................303

G. Dealing with Difficult Witnesses...................304

   1. The Polite Approach..............................304

   2. The Polite but Firm Response...................305

H. Examples...307

I. Checklist..312

J. Evidentiary Rules to Consider.......................314

K. Conclusion...315

Chapter 8: Impeachment

A. Introduction..317

B. How the Law Impacts Impeachment...............320

C. Prior Untruthful Acts..................................322

D. Prior Convictions.......................................325

E.   Prior Inconsistent Statements..............................331

F.   Bias and Motive.....................................339

G.   Defects in Capacity................................344

H.   Impeachment by Omission...................................351

I.   Impeachment by Contradiction.........................357

J.   Checklist...358

K.   Evidentiary Rules to Consider.......................360

L.   Conclusion..361

Chapter 9: Advanced Direct & Cross

A.   Developing Superior Direct Examinations...........363

1. Start with the Fundamentals.......................363

2. Time...364

3. Location..365

4. Structure..365

5. Advanced Direct Examination Techniques......367

B.   Refreshing Memory......................................372

C.   Past Recollection Recorded.........................376

D.   Developing Superior Cross Examinations….........379

1. Getting Beyond the Fundamentals...............379

2. Advanced Cross Examination Techniques........382

E.   Planning Advanced Direct & Cross Examination...388

1. Direct Examination Plan...........................392

2. Cross Examination Plan….........................393

F.   Advanced Direct Examination Checklist…..........395

G.   Advanced Cross Examination Checklist...........398

H.   Conclusion..400

Chapter 10: Expert Witnesses

A.   Introduction...401

B.   How the Law Impacts Experts.....................403

1. Qualification to Form an Opinion................405

2. Proper Subject Matter...........................406

3. Basis for the Expert's Testimony................406

4. Relevance.......................................408

5. Reliability.......................................409

C.   Selecting and Preparing Experts...................410

1. Goal of the Expert Testimony..........................410
2. Dealing with Jury Expectations......................411
3. Selecting Experts...412
4. Preparing Experts..414

D. Structuring Direct Expert Testimony..................416
1. Why is the Expert Testifying....................417
2. Qualifications..417
3. Tendering the Witness................................420
4. Voir Dire for Purposes of Forming an
    Objection...421
5. Provide the Major Opinions.........................428
6. Basis for the Major Opinions........................430
7. Diffusing Weaknesses..................................432
8. Restating the Major Opinion.........................433

E. How to Cross Examine Experts........................434
F. Checklist..440
G. Evidentiary Rules to Consider........................442

Chapter 11: Closing Argument
A. Introduction..443
B. What the Jury Sees and Thinks..........................445
C. How the Law Impacts Closing...........................446
D. Creating the Closing...448
1. Case Analysis..448
2. Structure...450
    a. Theme...450
    b. Burden...452
    c. Elements...455
    d. Address the Opposition.........................458
    e. Prayer for Relief and Summation...........461

E. Delivering the Closing.......................................462
1. Themes..462
2. Argue...463

F. Rebuttal...466
1. Beginning...466
2. Common Mistakes..466
3. Sandbagging..467

      4. Control the Agenda...............................467

    G. Examples..470

      1. Defense Criminal Assault Closing...............470

      2. Defense Closing in a Civil Wrongful Death.....475

      3. Defense Closing in a Murder Case...............480

      4. Defense Closing in a Termination of Parental

        Rights Case.......................................485

      5. Portion of Defense Closing (State v. Simpson)..488

    H. Checklist..504

    I. Evidentiary Rules to Consider........................506

Chapter 12: Motions and Objections

    A. Motions...509

    B. How the Law Impacts Motions...........................512

    C. Drafting the Motion..................................514

      1. Balance the Law, Facts, and Moral Theory.......514

      2. Understanding the Legal Standard..................515

      3. Organize the Facts............................517

      4. Apply the Law to the Facts......................518

      5. Focus on the Judge............................518

    D. Arguing the Motion...................................520

      1. Introduction.................................520

      2. How the Law Impacts the Motion Argument...521

      3. Power of the Court............................523

      4. Identify the Audience.........................524

    E. Checklist - Writing Motions..........................525

    F. Checklist - Motions Hearings.........................526

    G. Objections...527

    H. How the Law Impacts Objections.......................528

    I. Planning Objections..................................529

    J. Making the Objection.................................534

    K. Offers of Proof......................................534

    L. Objections as to Form................................536

    M. Objections as to Substance...........................539

Chapter 13: Post Trial Matters

    A. Introduction...549

B.   Post Trial Matters - Pretrial.................................550
   1.   Motion for Summary Judgment......................550
   2.   Motions in Limine...552
C.   Post Trial Matters - Trial..................................554
   1.   Making the Record..554
   2.   Jury Selection...555
   3.   Evidentiary Issues...555
   4.   Proffers...557
   5.   Openings and Closings....................................558
   6.   Jury Instructions...558
D.   Preserving the Record - Post Trial.....................559
E.   Creating the Record Checklist...........................559

Chapter 14: Federal Rules of Evidence.........................563
Chapter 15:   Common Objections............................599
Chapter 16:   MacCarthy's Trial Advocacy....................603
Chapter 17:   Common Foundations...........................611
Chapter 18:   Delaware RPC...............................633

-Notes-

ACKNOWLEDGEMENTS
Advocacy Teachers

It is considered normal in texts such as this to identify the substantive law contained in appellate cases that are referenced in the following pages. This, however, is a book about oral advocacy, and it rests primarily on the foundations of my own experiences, the substantive procedural law, and the wisdom of those from whom we have learned. The book identifies the first two well, but is woefully meager in identifying the third. The following list, incomplete though it may be, is our small attempt to identify the many excellent friends whose ideas the we have used and teaching have admired. Those on this list helped to mold our advocacy, communication, and teaching in ways great and small, and we cannot thank you enough. If we left you off, please trust that it was not intentional. These are the true resources for anyone who practices the art of advocacy, may your list be as long some day.

LTC Jan Aldykiewicz

Mr. Bill Anderson

Professor Linda Anderson

Dame Ellish Angiolini

Mr. Joseph R. Bankoff

Mr. John Baker

Hon. Thomas Barber

Hon. Lamar Battles

Mr. Thomas G. Becker

Professor Chris Behan

Mr. Curtis Beem

Professor. A.J. Belido de Luna

Professor Pamela Bell-Cole

Professor Barbara Bergman

Mr. Chris Biggs

Professor G. Robert Blakey

Mr. Joseph Bodiford

Mr. Brandon Booth

Mr. George H. Brauchler

Ms. Ashleigh Brooks

Colonel Robert Burrell

Mr. Jude Borque

Mr. Brett Bayne

Mrs. Allana Forte Branch

Mr. Brandon Breslow

Mrs. Lara Breslow

Hon. Sandy Brook

Mr. Jeffrey Brown

Mr. Mark Caldwell

Professor Catherine Cameron

Professor. Megan Canty

Professor James P. Carey

Ms. Emily Carney

Mr. David Carlton

Professor Chrissie Cerniglia

Mr. Byron Cerrillo

Professor Meghan Chaney

LTG Dana Chipman

Mr. Kristopher M. Colley — *Hon. George Hanks*

Ms. Mary Commander — *Ms. Michelle T. Hannigan*

Professor Carlos Concepcion — *Professor Vic Hansen*

Mr. Dillon Cook — *Colonel Tyler Harder*

Ms. Ashley Crisafulli — *Ms. Brandi Hardin*

Professor Lee Coppock — *LTC Ernie Harper*

Mr. Nicholas Cox — *Hon. Alfred C. Harrell, Jr*

Hon. Shawn Crane — *MSG Matt Harris*

Mr. Roger Curlin — *Mr. Josh Harris*

Ms. Patricia L. Davis — *Mr. Jared Hatcliffe*

Hon. David Demers — *Mr. Joel Hayes*

Professor Susan Demers — *Mr. Peter A. Hedeen*

Mr. Bob Dillinger — *Ms. Abigail Heller*

Professor Mark M. Dobson — *Professor Peter Hoffman*

Ms. Christine Donoghue — *Colonel Keith Hodges*

Hon. Mark Drummond — *Professor Tom Horton*

Professor Catherine Dunham — *Ms. Lynne M. Hufnagel*

LTC Christina Ekman — *Mr. William Hyland*

Mr. Lucas Elsbernd — *Colonel Mackey Ives*

Colonel Bill Eleazer — *Mr. William W. Jack*

Mr. Ron Eide — *Mr. Joseph C. Jaudon*

Professor Steve Emens — *Professor Jeanne Jordan*

Hon. Dave Erikson — *Mr. Joshua Karton*

Mr. Todd Foster — *Professor Jerry Latimer*

Professor Rafe Foreman — *Professor Jay Leach*

Mr. Stuart Freeman — *Col. Cal Lederer*

Colonel James Garrett — *Hon. Lawrence Leffler*

Mr. Brian Garrity — *Mr. Thomas V. Linguanti*

Mr. Jason Goss — *Mr. Matthew Lucklum*

Professor Keri Gould — *Mr. Cecil Lynn*

Ms. Candice Gullickson — *Mr. Sean MacCarthy*

Ms. Christina M.Habas — *Mr. Terrance MacCarthy*

Ms. Lynn Haney — *Hon. Terrance MacCarthy Jr.*

Prof. Elizabeth Lippy Machovina

Mr. Jan Majewski

Hon. Lawrence Manzanares

Ms. Jessica Marichal

Ms. Megan W. Martinez

Hon. Michael A. Martinez

Mr. Mark Matthews

Mr. Julius Matusewicz

Professor Tom Mauet

Mrs. Erika McArdle

Mr. Patrick McArdle

Mr. Bernie McCabe

Mr. Sean MacCarthy

Mr. Terrance MacCarthy

Honorable Terrance MacCarthy Jr.

Ms. Norma McClure

Mr. James Lincoln McCrystal

Hon. Robert McGahey

Ms. Helen McKeown

Ms. Sarah Mieczkowski

BG John Miller

Ms. Tracy Miller

Mr. Rob Mitchell

Ms. Alexa Moeller

Professor Gillian More

Mr. Christian Myer

Mr. Adam Nate

Mrs. Kelly Navarro

Mr. Jared Nooney

Mr. Anthony Nunnally

LTC E.J. O'Brien

Professor Eddie Ohlbaum

Ms. Courtney Olivier

MAJ Mark Opachan

Dir. Ramon Ortiz

Hon. Bill Ossmann

Mr. Armando Padron Cruz

Mr. Lee Pearlman

Ms. Chantay Perry

Ms. Paige Petersen

Ms. Alexis Petrosino

Ms. Jeanne Philotoff

Professor Ellen Podgor

Mr. Cory Powell

1st Lt. Austin Printz

Professor David Raack

Mr. Nick Ramos

Mr. Mark Rankin

Mr. Justin Reininger

Ms. Judith Roberts

Hon. Jim Roberts

Ms. Melody Roberts

LTC Dave Robertson

Hon. Gilbert M. Roman

LTC John Saunders

Professor James Sheehan

Professor David C. Schott

Professor Nancy Schulz

Col. Craig Schwender

Professor Jim Seckinger

Mr. Ben Selbo

Professor Hugh M. Selby

LTC Keith Selene

Professor Adam Shlahet

Hon. Daniel Sleet

Professor Stacey-Rae Simcox

Professor Tom Singer

Ms. Rebecca Sitterly

Professor Reese Smith Jr.

Lt. Col. Mike Stahlman

Ms. Karen S. Steinhauser

Mrs. Gwen Roseman Stern

Mr. Jonathan Stien

Hon. Ralph Stoddard

Ms. Carolina Suazo

Mr. Thomas A. Swett

Mr. Eddie Tarbay

Mr. Jim Thaler

SGT Ed Thiel

Ms. L. Michaelle Tobin

Professor Jim Underwood

Mr. Michael Van Oyen

Ms. Danya Vargas

Professor Stephanie Vaughan

Professor Dave Velloney

Professor Louis Virelli

Mr. Tucker Volesky

Mr. Tyler Waugh

Ms. Erin Willadsen

Mr. Jared Williams

Hon. Michael Williams

Ms. Sara Williams

Dean Warren Wolfson

Preface, 2nd Edition

"Mastering Trial Advocacy" provides a particular methodology for learning and applying advocacy skills designed to help you become an attorney competent in preparing and trying cases. The text is based upon years of practice and teaching. It lays out the information in a straight forward fashion designed to immediately identify what is being taught, how you should do it, and why a particular methodology is preferable.

In this edition we have added a second author, Professor Laura Anne Rose. Professor Rose teaches evidence and trial advocacy at the University of South Dakota. She also runs their trial team. Our hope is to combine the voices of advocates from different generations, identifying the core concepts of trial advocacy which reach across barriers of age, race and gender.

The structure of this book fits the needs of anyone who wants to quickly and efficiently develop mastery over a particular trial advocacy skill. We designed this text to provide maximum flexibility for anyone who uses it. You can turn to any section in the book and begin to learn that skill immediately. Each section provides a template for how to proceed with examples from cases trial lawyers routinely encounter, creating an excellent baseline approach to learning advocacy.

 If you are interested in a discussion of learning trial advocacy skills in a more holistic fashion we suggest that you consider reading another Rose-Advocacy text, "Fundamental Trial Advocacy." It teaches advocacy holistically, discussing the law, skill and art in combination with one another. That approach may not be for everyone, but if you are drawn to learning the craft of our profession in such a fashion we recommend it to you.

This text is put together in a modular design. Each section is complete in and of itself, allowing you to turn to any portion and immediately begin to learn the identified skill. We have created a companion workbook for this text titled "Mastering Trial Advocacy: Cases, Problems, & Exercises." The examples provided through out this text are based in part on the case files and problems contained within the companion workbook.

While not every case goes to trial in our complex world, the ability to confront your accuser or to seek redress within a court of law when you have been wronged is a quintessential part of what it means to live in a democratic society. Trials are the template for all other dispute resolution forms and the skills necessary to competently prepare and to try a case are core competencies. Trial remains the template for our adversarial process, as well as the ultimate decision making structure for a civilized society. It is the only advocacy skill taught in law school guaranteed by the U.S. Constitution.

We must master the skills necessary to try cases if we are to effectively represent clients - even if we are part of the profession who never actually make it into the four walls of the local courthouse.

We wish to thank the many friends with whom we have taught advocacy, to include members of the U.S. Army JAG Corps, the National Institute of Trial Advocacy, an entire generation of Stetson trial team members, and our colleagues at Ohio Northern University College of Law and the University of South Dakota .

We also wish to thank the many attendees and presenters at Educating Advocates: Teaching Advocacy Skills. Each and every one of you has enriched our teaching, scholarship, and more importantly the quality of our lives. We look forward to many more conferences, competitions, and programs spent teaching each other the intricacies of the practice - both teaching and advocating.

No author scales the mountain of a book by themselves. We had two excellent "Tenzing Norgays" on this journey, Ms. Amanda Olson, a member of the ONU trial team, and Ms. Meaghan Janousek. Their invaluable work as our research assistants made this text possible.

The mistakes within, and we am sure that they are many, are of course our own.

Enjoy!

Charles H. Rose III
Laura Anne Rose
Fall 2019

Preface, 1st Edition

"Mastering Trial Advocacy" provides a particular methodology for learning and applying advocacy skills designed to help you become an attorney competent in preparing and trying cases. The text is based upon years of practice and teaching. It lays out the information in a straight forward fashion designed to immediately identify what is being taught, how you should do it, and why a particular methodology is preferable.

The structure of this book fits the needs of anyone who wants to quickly and efficiently develop mastery over a particular trial advocacy skill. I designed this text to provide maximum flexibility for anyone who uses it. You can turn to any section in the book and begin to learn that skill immediately. Each section provides a template for how to proceed with examples from cases trial lawyers routinely encounter, creating an excellent baseline approach to learning advocacy.

If you are interested in a discussion of learning trial advocacy skills in a more holistic fashion I suggest that you consider reading another text of mine, "Fundamental Trial Advocacy." In that book I teach advocacy holistically, discussing the law, skill and art in combination with one another. That approach is not for everyone, but if you are drawn to learning the craft of our profession in such a fashion I recommend it to you.

This text is put together in a modular design. Each section is complete in and of itself, allowing you to turn to any portion and immediately begin to learn the identified skill. I have created a companion workbook for this text titled "Mastering Trial Advocacy: Cases, Problems, & Exercises." The examples provided through out this text are based in part on the case files and problems contained within the companion workbook.

While not every case goes to trial in our complex world, the ability to confront your accuser or to seek redress within a court of law when you have been wronged is a quintessential part of what it means to live in a democratic society. Trials are the template for all other dispute resolution forms and the skills necessary to competently prepare and to try a case are core competencies. Trial remains the template for our adversarial process, as well as the ultimate decision making structure for a civilized society. We must master the skills necessary to try cases if we are to effectively represent clients - even if we never actually make it into the four walls of the local courthouse.

I wish to thank the many friends with whom I have taught advocacy through out my career, to include fellow members of the U.S. Army JAG Corps, the National Institute of Trial Advocacy, and my colleagues at Stetson University College of Law. This book is made possible by their generous scholarship grant program. I am particularly indebted to Shaun Cummings, Claudette Goyannes, Kristin Johnson, Khalil Madani, Diego Novaes, Laura Rose, Robert Seay, and Erika Wilson for their contributions.

I also wish to thank the many attendees and presenters at Stetson's Annual Conference Educating Advocates: Teaching Advocacy Skills. Each and every one of you has enriched my teaching, my scholarship, and more importantly the quality of my life. No author scales the mountain of a book by themselves. I had two excellent "Tenzing Norgays" on this journey, Ms. Victoria San Pedro, and Ms. Adrianna Corso. Their invaluable work as my research assistants made this text possible.

As always my work would be impossible without the love and support of my wife - Pamela. Like everything else this is for you.

The mistakes within, and I am sure that they are many, are of course my own.

Enjoy!

Charles H. Rose III
Fall 2013

Chapter 1: How Trials Work

A. Introduction 5
B. Forming the Attorney Client Relationship...................8
C. Case Analysis & Preparation 10
D. Pretrial Practice..11
E. Jury Selection 13
F. Preliminary Matters 15
G. Opening Statements 16
H. Prosecution/Plaintiff's Case in Chief.......................17
I. Motions at Close of Plaintiff's Case 19
J. Defendant's Case in Chief 20
K. Motions at Close of Defendant's Case 22
L. Plaintiff's Rebuttal & Defendant's Surrebuttal.........22
M. Motions at the Close of All Evidence 23
N. Closing Argument & Jury Instructions......................24
O. Deliberations & Verdict..26
P. Post-Trial Motions & Appeals 27
Q. Conclusion..28

A.   Introduction

A trial is an adversarial process overseen by an impartial judge where each side, referred to as a party, are directly adverse to one another. While most trials are similar, the type of case tried will bring to light some variations in the process. In a criminal case the prosecutor represents the people of the jurisdiction where the case is being tried. If it is in a state court, the prosecutor will represent the state. If it is in Federal Court, the prosecutor will represent the United States. The defendant in a criminal case is also represented by counsel during the proceedings. Counsel for the defense may either be appointed by the court at no cost to the defendant (when they qualify), or hired by the defendant. The prosecutor bears the burden of proof to

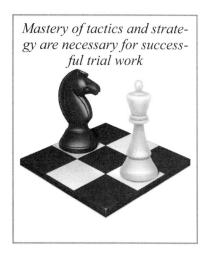

Mastery of tactics and strategy are necessary for successful trial work

---

Excerpt from Preliminary Instructions

....What is not evidence:

During the trial, you'll hear certain things that are not evidence and you must not consider them.

First, the lawyers' statements and arguments aren't evidence. In their opening statements and closing arguments, the lawyers will discuss the case. Their remarks may help you follow each side's arguments and presentation of evidence. But the remarks themselves aren't evidence and shouldn't play a role in your deliberations.

Second, the lawyers' questions and objections aren't evidence. Only the witnesses' answers are evidence. Don't decide that something is true just because a lawyer's question suggests that it is. For example, a lawyer may ask a witness, "You saw Mr. Jones hit his sister, didn't you?" That question is not evidence of what the witness saw or what Mr. Jones did unless the witness agrees with it....

Excerpt from preliminary civil jury instructions, 11th Circuit, 2013

---

the indictment, and it is normally a beyond a reasonable doubt standard.

Civil trials employ different terminology when referencing the parties engaged in the adversarial process. In a civil case, the side bringing the cause of action is referred to as the plaintiff. The party defending the action is referred to as the defendant, or the respondent. The plaintiff also bears the burden of proof in a civil case. However, unlike in a criminal trial, the burden of proof may shift to the defense in limited circumstances. The burden of proof in a civil trial is normally a preponderance of the evidence standard. Occasionally the burden of proof in a civil case may modify, based upon statutory law, but that is rarely, if ever, the case in a criminal proceeding.

In a jury trial the judge decides questions of law, and the jury decides questions of fact. In a bench trial the court serves as both the arbiter of law and the decider of fact. Bench trials are either authorized by statute, or occur at the request of the parties. The advocacy skills discussed in this text apply in both bench and jury trials, but there are some procedural differences between the two. The text will address primarily skills in the context of a jury, where appropriate it considers the differences between jury and bench trials, positing how advocacy skills should be adapted for judge alone trials.

---

3 Definition of "Reasonable Doubt"

The Government's burden of proof is heavy, but it doesn't have to prove a Defendant's guilt beyond all possible doubt. The Government's proof only has to exclude any "reasonable doubt" concerning the Defendant's guilt.

A "reasonable doubt" is a real doubt, based on your reason and common sense after you've carefully and impartially considered all the evidence in the case.

"Proof beyond a reasonable doubt" is proof so convincing that you would be willing to rely and act on it without hesitation in the most important of your own affairs. If you are convinced that the Defendant has been proved guilty beyond a reasonable doubt, say so. If you are not convinced, say so.

Reasonable Doubt Instruction from the 2011 Pattern Criminal Instructions for the 11th Circuit

---

In both jury and bench trials the actions of counsel, the judge, and the jury are controlled by the local rules of court, the applicable rules of procedure, and the rules of evidence. The rules of procedure and evidence are specific to the jurisdiction of the court. The examples within this text are based upon the Federal Rules of Evidence, Criminal Procedure, and Civil Procedure. Counsel practicing in a particular state court or other jurisdiction must familiarize themselves with the local rules and identify where they deviate from the federal standard. Counsel and the court are also bound by their applicable rules of professional conduct.

It is important for the trial attorney to understand not only the substantive law (the basis of the indictment, cause of action, or any affirmative defenses), but also the procedural and evidentiary law. Procedural law is made up of rules designed to control the process. Evidentiary law is designed the control the presentation of evidence. With this legal background in mind, the trial attorney may begin a case analysis.

Case analysis and preparation requires counsel to consider the law in light of the facts of each case. A thorough case analysis will allow the attorney to arrange and present the evidence in a way designed to persuade the fact

finder that your side's interpretation of the controverted facts is correct. Persuading the jury is the attorneys ultimate goal. It requires counsel to

Burden of proof:

[Name of plaintiff] has the burden of proving [his/her/its] case by what the law calls a preponderance of the evidence. That means [name of plaintiff] must prove that, in light of all the evidence, what [he/she/it] claims is more likely true than not. So, if you could put the evidence favoring [name of plaintiff] and the evidence favoring [name of defendant] on opposite sides of balancing scales, [name of plaintiff] needs to make the scales tip to [his/her/its] side. If [name of plaintiff] fails to meet this burden, you must find in favor of [name of defendant].

To decide whether any fact has been proved by a preponderance of the evidence, you may, unless I instruct you otherwise, consider the testimony of all witnesses, regardless of who called them, and all exhibits that the court allowed, regardless of who produced them. After considering all the evidence, if you decide a claim or fact is more likely true than not, then the claim or fact has been proved by a preponderance of the evidence.

Example of a Preponderance of the Evidence Standard taken from the 2013 Civil Jury Instructions for the 11th Circuit.

manage the facts, identify the law that admits, or excludes those facts, present those facts in an acceptable fashion, and then explain what they mean in a way that brings the jury to that side side. This text will explain how to master the discreet portions of the trial. The persuasive power of a case will be discussed in case analysis and preparation, but mastering the ability to persuade the jury is ultimately the lifelong pursuit of any competent advocate. That mastery will not be possible if counsel has not first developed competency with each discreet skill.

B.   Forming the Attorney Client Relationship

Almost every case begins with a prospective client making an appointment to seek counsel. This appointment may occur in a variety of

Counsel must always know who has the burden of proof to shift the scales of justice

ways, but there must always be an initial meeting where the scope of representation is established. The client sets
the objectives of the representation and
the advocate chooses the means necessary to achieve the clients objective.
Those "means" include tactical decisions at trial that are advocacy-based.
Although counsel will make these tactical decisions, it is imperative for the
attorney to continue to inform the
client of counsel's chosen means in
order to ensure no conflict with the clients objective.

*The Attorney-Client Relation-
ship is contractual*

This initial meeting determines whether any actual representation takes
place, and sets the tone of the relationship for the duration of the case.
During this meeting counsel will obtain the information necessary to identify potential conflicts of interest, form the attorney client relationship, and
begin to properly advise the client. There are a variety of practical and legal considerations that go into the formation of this relationship, many of
them outside the scope of this text. Counsel should review their responsibilities under the applicable rules of professional conduct and proceed accordingly. Any firm, agency or office should have a structured approach
when dealing with prospective clients.

Normally the attorney client relationship is contractual, with a clearly defined scope of representation set forth in the form of a retainer or fee
agreement. Fee agreements are sometimes required by law but are always
recommended. If the fee agreement is properly prepared and executed,
both counsel and the client will have a fairly clear idea of what is expected
from the representation. This allows for any possible future misunderstanding between counsel and the client to be minimized. This is a "best
practice" approach to beginning a healthy attorney client relationship, and
will pay huge dividends during case analysis and trial preparation.

This relationship is the door to the factual and emotional issues the jury
will turn to when deciding who wins at trial. For example, in the section
on Trial Preparation and Analysis, it will be shown how crucial this attorney client relationship will be while developing the factual and moral theory of the case. Counsel must understand all professional duties and responsibility in the jurisdiction where the proceeding takes place. Doing so
will outline for counsel how to properly communicate with both clients
and witnesses in a way that do not run afoul of those rules. These commu-

nications skills become even more important while analyzing cases, interviewing witnesses, and presenting testimony.

C.   Case Analysis & Preparation

The first time counsel are introduced to a case is crucial. At this point they will make certain decisions that have a long term impact on the way the case is ultimately resolved. Case analysis, preparation, and investigation does not end at this initial introduction, but must instead continue throughout the trial.

These initial decisions are brought about after a detailed analysis is conducted. This analysis will highlight the relevant facts and gives counsel the opportunity to identify the legal basis for admitting those facts at trial. These decisions are important because they will drive each step counsel takes during the proceeding.

Case analysis forces the attorney to identify the factual theory of the case —what counsel believes happened, the legal theory—how the law impacts the facts, and the moral theme—why counsel's side should win. A more thorough discussion of the mechanics of how to analyze a case and prepare a case analysis will be discussed later in this text. For now it is sufficient that counsel understand it is a continuing process that requires a lot of front-loaded work.

During case analysis the attorney will routinely review evidence, investigate issues, interview witnesses, prepare exhibits, and then compare the results of this work to see if they are on the right track. This process should be redone continuously until the case is complete, modifying as required based upon the portion of the trial in which counsel finds themselves. The goal is to develop a cohesive presentation supported by the legally admissible facts. Counsel will use the moral theory of the case to drive the presentation of the evidence and the law. The jury will adopt a moral theme and then accept the factual and legal theory supported by their moral theme. It is imperative that counsel's factual theory, legal theory, and moral theory do not create a sense of cognitive dissonance in the collective mind of the jury. Cognitive dissonance leads to a lack of credibility, loss of trust, and often a lost case.

Using these three elements of case analysis helps to prepare the case based upon identified targets that give the advocate the best chance for a successful outcome. Case analysis is an ongoing organic process, and is particularly important when counsel begin to develop directs, crosses, and plans the use of exhibits during witness testimony. It is also a crucial component that drives the jury selection process. While we will discuss case analysis

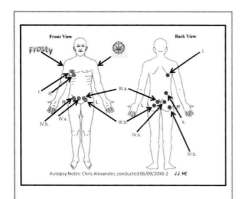

*Demonstratives are
effective Persuasion Tools*

and preparation at length in a separate section, counsel must internalize how case analysis is the driving force for every intelligent trial advocacy decision. Successful advocates proceed during each distinct portion of the trial in a specific fashion based upon their case analysis.

D.   Pretrial Practice

Entire books have been written about pretrial practice, and it is important to keep in mind that pretrial practice covers developing your case, filing motions, requesting preliminary instructions, and, when necessary, negotiating settlements in civil cases and plea deals in criminal cases. From a trial practice perspective, motions practice and preliminary instructions are important because they help to determine the relevancy and admissibility of evidence. Determinations on relevancy and admissibility impact what questions the advocate must ask their witnesses, and the order in which they are called to testify.

Motions practice is the vehicle trial advocates use to get a sense of how the judge will rule on specific legal issues. Case analysis assists in forming a legal theory of the case that is best for the advocates position based upon substantive, procedural and evidentiary law. The legal theory chosen by counsel must be supported by the law in that jurisdiction. The legal theory should also control how the judge rules on the admissibility of evidence, which instructions are given to the jury, and what the controlling law will be on substantive issues. Trial lawyers use motions practice to further refine their legal theories and to develop the greatest degree of determinacy when dealing with the unknowns of trial. Motions are required for some substantive issues, depending upon the jurisdiction, and the rules of procedure will identify

*Stipulations of Fact, and
Stipulations of Testimony,
are evidence*

which motions are effectively waived when not brought prior to trial. Counsel must check the applicable rules of procedure for the court and file your motions based upon the required or suggested timelines.

Superior motions practice turns cases into summary judgments, limits evidence that will be admissible against a client, or establishes precedents shaping the entire trial process in counsel's favor. Motions also allow the advocate to set the factual stage through the application of the law. While many facts may be logically relevant, they are not necessarily legally relevant and therefore not admissible. The extent to which counsel effectively learns how to use motions will impact their success at trial.

In addition to pre-trial motions, counsel will also have the ability to respond to issues at trial by making motions before the court when they occur during the proceedings. This may be as simple as requesting an advance ruling on evidentiary issues, or as complex as determining the admissibility of a key piece of evidence that may very well be case dispositive. Counsel will also have the opportunity to re-address motions filed prior to the start of the actual trial, but be advised that any attempt to re-litigate an issue previously decided must be made in light of the court's earlier ruling and the predicted impact of addressing that issue in the presence of the jury. Rulings on motions are important because they directly impact what evidence counsel may present to the jury. The superior advocate routinely uses motions to shape the courtroom battlefield

A side benefit of effective pretrial motions practice concerns preliminary instructions. In cases with complex or counterintuitive issues, motions practice can effectively identify areas where the court can be persuaded to provide preliminary instructions to the jury that are directly relevant to the theory of the case.

Motions are addressed to the judge - not to opposing counsel

This can serve to either highlight or draw the sting out of a particular piece of evidence, as well as to begin the education process of the jury before the case-in-chief begins. Additionally, certain preliminary instructions are provided as a matter of course at certain instances in the trial, such as when the jury is sworn, to set the stage and to provide structure for those involved. Once pretrial is concluded it is time to select the jury.

E. Jury Selection

Once you have completed pretrial matters it is time to begin jury selection. The process of selecting a jury is referred to as voir dire in most jurisdictions and encompasses pre-trial questionnaires, initial questions posed by the judge, and live questions by advocates in those jurisdictions allowing advocates to question jurors. Some juris-

Jury Selection is an Opportunity to connect to the Potential Jurors - use it!

dictions, most notably federal courts, no longer allow advocates to conduct voir dire and instead require all questions to be provided in writing to the judge, who in turn poses them to the potential juror pool. This is a local rule of court preference, and advocates always have the ability to request voir dire when necessary.

The court schedules the time and place for jury selection, and the process is controlled by the judge. Normally clients are present, along with other court personnel such as the court reporter and bailiff. If more than one jury is being chosen on a certain day, there may be several sets of litigants in the room who will wait in turn to pick a jury. Alternatively, counsel may need to pick a jury with the trial set to begin immediately after the jurors are chosen. The more complex or controversial the case, the more likely it is that jury selection will take an extended period of time.

When the jury selection process begins, advocates from each party will take their place at the table. In most jurisdictions, the party bearing the burden of proof is seated closest to the jury. When in doubt, observe what other advocates do in the courtroom, or ask the clerk of court. Once seated, the judge will call the court in order and ask both advocates if they are ready to proceed to trial. When counsel affirms that they are prepared the jury selection process will begin and the judge will then call in the prospective jurors.

The jurors will be brought by the bailiff, referred to as the venire, into the courtroom. It is common for each venire to number somewhere between 25 to 50 prospective jurors. The number is dependent on the local rules and the judge's instructions. Counsel should be advised that the judge may engage both parties in another attempt to settle the case before the jury selection process begins in earnest.

When the venire is present in the courtroom the judge will normally introduce themselves, the parties, and court personnel. The judge will explain how jury selection works in their jurisdiction, and may ask some preliminary questions designed to quickly and efficiently sort out any jury members with a conflict. Once the court is satisfied, the clerk of court swears the jury, and the process begins in earnest. In a few jurisdictions the court

- Will alternative jurors be required, and if so how many
- Acceptable reasons for "challenges for cause"
- The number of peremptory challenges available to each side
- How the challenge process works within the courtroom itself
- Acceptable topics when questioning prospective jury members
- How questioning will be conducted
- The use of questionnaires

allows the attorneys to make a short opening statement before beginning with jury selection, but most do not. Usually, initial questioning of the venire is done by the judge, with additional questions by the attorneys.

Jury selection is subject to the control of the court, based upon local rules, local practice, and any applicable statutes. It is very much a home grown process. These local rules and statutes define many different aspects of the jury selection process, to include:

- Process used to identify prospective jurors
- Qualifications for jury duty

How many jury members are necessary for a particular case (for example, in Florida a criminal case requires 6 jury members, unless it is a capital case, where 12 are required), to include:

Jurisdictions vary greatly in the actual process, and counsel would be well advised to spend some time in the courthouse where your jury will be selected prior to the day of selection. The process of interacting with the jury will be covered in greater detail later in this text.

Regardless of the format, jury selection is one of the first things the advocate will do during the trial, but along with closing arguments, is one of the last portions of the trial counsel will actually prepare. Jury selection involves identifying those members of the prospective jury counsel believe they will be unable to persuade to consider their evidence favorably. It is not about picking those that like the questioning attorney. Instead, it is about identifying those who do not like the advocate or the party and who will be unable to change their mind—those are the jurors that should be removed. Counsel is best situated to perform this complex task only after they are fully prepared for trial. The important thing to remember is that the advocate must identify jurors who are biased against the legal theory, factual theory, or moral theme of the case. Those who fundamentally oppose any of these areas must go.

F.   Preliminary Matters

After the jury is chosen and sworn, the judge will provide the preliminary instructions. These instructions include practical "this is how we will conduct business" information, as well as any particular limitations placed on the jury. It will normally include an admonishment not to investigate the case themselves, or to receive information from outside sources, which includes news media.

Internet access and the vast availability of information in the digital age is creating difficulties for the court in properly protecting the judicial process where juries are concerned. Preliminary instructions to the jury is one way the court can highlight the importance of refraining from improperly seeking extrajudicial information through the internet or communicating about the case on social media sites. Such instructions are a "best practice" and are becoming the norm in many jurisdictions.

Courts differ on what jurors may do when observing the trial. In some jurisdictions note taking is encouraged, in others it is forbidden. Some courts are even experimenting with providing tablet devices for the review of evidence and note taking. The same applies to the actual instructions process. In some jurisdictions printed copies of the instructions are provided to the jury, in others they are merely read. Counsel must be aware of local practices, and modify their advocacy techniques accordingly. This will be discussed in greater detain in the sections on openings, exhibits, and closings.

In addition to providing preliminary instructions to the jury the court will normally take the time, outside the presence of the jury, to address any last minute motions or other issues with counsel. Sometimes counsel will actually plea the case once the jury has been selected. In other instances counsel may see a last minute motion or a request for witness sequestration. When witnesses are sequestered they are not allowed to watch the proceedings prior to testimony, or after testimony if they are potentially going to be recalled by either side. Courts normally grant requests to remove the witnesses from the courtroom when asked by counsel, although in certain instances, such as close family members, the court may allow them to remain in the room. Once all of the final preliminary matters have been dispensed with the jury will be called and counsel proceed with opening statements.

G.   Opening Statements

After the jury has been selected, sworn, and instructed, the trial begins with an opening statement by both sides. Most jurisdictions allow the defendant or respondent to defer opening statement until the beginning of their case-in-chief, but it is usually a "best practice" not to defer. In some instances counsel may waive opening statement, but persuasion theory makes it clear that waiving opening is not in the best interests of the client.

Opening statements are not governed by the rules of evidence. In most jurisdictions the applicable law is either procedural or case law and varies substantively from state to state, as well as within the federal court system. Generally speaking, the court expects counsel to tell the jury what they intend to prove, preview the relevant law, and forecast why the jury should decide the case in their favor. Argument is not allowed in most jurisdictions, but local practice often blurs the line between acceptable storytelling and argument. Counsel should, whenever practical, observe trials within the relevant jurisdiction before crafting their opening statements.

The focus in most jurisdictions during opening statement is the description of what each side believes will be proved at trial. This description is usually referred to as the "story" of the case, and most jurisdictions expect that counsel will relate the story of what happened, from their client's perspective, and intimate how the law impacts that story, focusing the jury on the controverted issues of fact that will guide them in their decision. Acceptable opening statement persuasion techniques focus the jury by communicating the factual theory of the case (what happened), previewing the legal theory (what the law requires), and establishing a moral theme (why the jury should decide the case).

Judges have discretion in controlling the manner and substance of opening statements; they also instruct the jury about opening statements and explain what they mean and how to weigh them. Time limits for opening will vary by jurisdiction, and are based upon the complexity of the case. Openings can range from 10 minutes to an hour. The court controls the time limits for openings under local rules, and judges routinely limit the time allowed for openings and other portions of the trial.

Counsel should review standard jury instructions for the court where the case is called and fashion their presentations in a way to reflect the relevant standards within the jurisdiction. Pattern instructions embody the opinions and actions of the bench within that jurisdiction and provide the structure on how to address similar legal issues. They also serve as a repository for the culture of a particular bar, capturing the daily practice of the attorneys who appear using those instructions.

H. Prosecution/Plaintiff's Case in Chief

The party bearing the burden of proof presents evidence first. In a criminal case the prosecution will proceed with their case-in-chief. In a civil case usually the plaintiff bears the burden, except in those instances where the defense has admitted the basis for the plaintiff's cause of action but has raised an affirmative defense shifting the burden to the defense. Burden shifting normally does not occur in criminal cases because the United States Constitution requires the state to prove their case to a beyond a reasonable doubt standard.

During the case-in-chief evidence is submitted to the jury based on the questioning of witnesses by counsel during direct and cross examination. Every question that is asked on direct or cross examination is designed to admit evidence, exclude evidence, or explain the amount of weight that should be given to a particular piece of evidence. Evidence admitted during this process falls into several categories; testimonial, real evidence (either fungible or non-fungible), demonstrative evidence, and documentary evidence.

When a witness is first called to testify they are sworn by the clerk of court before taking the stand. Once the witness has either sworn, or affirmed, to tell the truth direct examination begins, with the attorney calling the witness conducting direct examination. After the attorney finishes with the direct the witness is "passed" to opposing counsel and cross examination begins. The rules of evidence control the form of questions during both direct and cross examination, and the rules give the court the authority to modify acceptable questioning techniques as needed.

Cross examination is conducted while examining an opposing counsel's witness. Cross examination normally takes place after the opposing counsel has completed their direct examination, but may occur during the direct examination when their is an adversarial relationship or a need to challenge the basis or qualifications of an expert's testimony. During cross the attorney is focused on establishing facts supporting their theory of the case, calling into question facts supporting the opposing counsel's theory, and attacking, when appropriate, the credibility of the witness. The focus of the cross examination is limited to those issues discussed on direct examination, but most courts grant a great deal of leeway into how wide the cross examination may be. If counsel can establish a viable relevancy theory the court will likely allow the inquiry on cross, particularly if it will save time.

Once cross examination is complete, redirect examination is allowed to address any issues discussed on cross examination. Counsel uses redirect to rehabilitate the witness or to explain how the inferences contained within the cross examination are not valid. After redirect most jurisdictions will allow recross as well, limited to the focus of the redirect. This process is controlled by the court, and jurisdictions, as well as individual judges, and the degree of leeway may vary greatly.

In some jurisdictions after counsel have completed direct and cross examination, the judge may pose questions to the witness. Some jurisdictions allow the jury to ask questions of the witness. Where jury questions are allowed there is a process that requires them to be posed in writing, reviewed by the judge, with potential objections made by counsel. Instructions on how to ask questions as a jury member are usually provided during preliminary matters.

The testimony of witnesses during the case-in-chief is evidence the jury may consider. Additionally, real evidence is admitted through the testimony of witnesses, once the appropriate foundation for the evidence in question has been laid. Real evidence is any evidence related to the cause of action or indictment. Examples include weapons, documents, substances, and digital media. Real evidence falls into two categories, fungible and non-fungible. One is not easily identifiable, the other is. The difference between the two will be discussed in the section concerning exhibits and foundations.

Witnesses may also provide demonstrative evidence designed to assist the jury in understanding the relevancy of their testimony. Demonstrative evidence can include diagrams, demonstrations, and in some instances digital media recreating events. Demonstrative evidence is admitted in tandem with the testimony of a witness. This is normally required to lay the appropriate foundation for the authenticity and relevancy of the demonstrative evidence. A discussion on how to use demonstrative evidence effectively will be done in subsequent sections.

Documentary evidence is usually introduced through the testimony of a witness laying the appropriate foundation. The court must ascertain that the document is what it purports to be and has not been fraudulently modified before admitting it. Often the witness is required to do this, except in those instances where the documentary evidence is accompanied by a self-authenticating attestation. How to lay the appropriate foundation, along with effective usage of this evidence, will be explained in subsequent sections of this text.

Occasionally in criminal cases, and frequently in civil cases, counsel will admit stipulations of fact and stipulations of expected testimony. Stipulations of fact identify factual issues that both sides agree are true. Stipulations of fact must be accepted by the court, and appropriate instructions concerning them are given to the jury prior to deliberations. Once a fact has been stipulated to it cannot be contested by the parties at trial. Although counsel agree to stipulations of fact, it must be with the consent and agreement of the parties. The judge should inquire to determine if the parties agree to any stipulations.

Stipulations of expected testimony are used to capture the testimony of witnesses that are not available for trial. The effect of a stipulation of expected testimony, when admitted by the court, is to place into evidence the testimony of the expected witness. This allows counsel to argue as true any facts contained within the stipulation of expected testimony. The parties must agree to the stipulation of expected testimony or the court will not accept it. Both types of stipulations are published to the jury, usually, but not always, by reading them.

Once the plaintiff or prosecution has presented their evidence they rest their case, subject to rebuttal. Normally at this point the jury is excused. Court and counsel should then address any relevant issues. It is common at this point for the party not bearing the burden of proof to make a motion for a directed verdict.

I.   Motions at Close of Plaintiff's Case

At the close of the plaintiff's case the jury is excused from the courtroom and the judge considers any relevant motions before the defense begins their case-in-chief. This is the point in the trial where the defense will normally file a motion to end the case. This motion has different names depending upon the jurisdiction where the case is being tried, and whether it is a civil or criminal proceeding. If it is a civil case in Federal District court it is called either a motion for a directed verdict or a judgement as a matter of law (JMOL). If it is a criminal case, it is referred to as a motion for a judgment of acquittal. A review of the relevant civil and criminal procedure rules in your jurisdiction will provide the specific names for these motions in your state court.

Under either motion the court considers the evidence presented in the light most favorable to the nonmoving party, in this instance the plaintiff or prosecution. If there is no evidence supporting the nonmoving party's case then the judge enters a judgment on behalf of the defendant and the case is dismissed in a civil case, or the judge enters a directed verdict in a criminal case. If there is a question of fact as to which side should prevail, then the court denies the motion and the defense proceeds with their case. Even if the court denies the motion they have the ability to reconsider it, upon request, after the defense rests their case.

The defense normally make the motion for a directed verdict or judgment as a matter of law, even if it is has very low chance of success. If the motion is made at the mid-trial point then it is possible to raise it again at the close of the defense's case-in-chief. Failure to make it after the plaintiff rests their case may constitute waiver of the issue at the close of trial. In those instances where the motion was made at the mid-trial point they can be renewed, even after the verdict is returned. These renewed motions are commonly referred to as a motion for a judgment notwithstanding the verdict, or J.N.O.V.

Judgments notwithstanding the verdict (non obstante veredicto) are only permitted if the motion for a directed verdict was made at the mid-trial point. Otherwise, the granting of a J.N.O.V. by the court would be a violation of the 7th Amendment to the U.S. Constitution. Technically speaking when the judge grants a J.N.O.V. at the close of trial they are reopening their decision on the mid-trial motion.

Once the mid-trial motion is made the judge has several different options. She may deny, grant, or reserve ruling on the motion. She also has the ability to deny it in part, or to grant it in part. For instance, if it was a civil action with several different potential causes the court could grant a motion for a judgment as a matter of law as to those causes of action that the plaintiff failed to prove during their case-in-chief. If the judge denies the motion or reserves ruling she can always take it up again at the close of trial. The same holds true for criminal cases.

J. Defendant's Case in Chief

If the mid-trial motion is denied the defendant proceeds with their case-in-chief. There are substantial differences in how the defense case-in-chief is normally approached, depending upon whether it is a civil or criminal case. The different approaches are based at least in part on the very real differences in the burden of proof and Constitutional constraints between civil and criminal cases.

In a civil case, the defense must deal with the plaintiff's case. They can offer evidence attacking, or refuting what the plaintiff has attempted to prove. Alternatively, they may have raised an affirmative defense, cross-claim or counter claim in their written responses.

If so, their case-in-chief is where they must provide evidence supporting their responses. There is an affirmative duty placed on the shoulders of the defense in a civil setting that is absent in a criminal case. If the plaintiff in a civil case presents evidence, evidentiary law concerning presumptions and burdens may very will shift the burden of proof to defense. Failure to meet that burden could result in an instruction from the judge at the close of trial almost guaranteeing a plaintiff victory. That does not happen in criminal cases.

In a criminal case, the burden of proof remains with the prosecution through out the trial. The defense may, under certain statutes, have a burden to produce evidence for certain defenses, but normally once they have raised such a defense through the presentation of evidence, or by giving notice to the state (depending upon the statute), the burden shifts to the state to disprove the affirmative defense to a beyond a reasonable doubt standard. The interplay between burdens of proof and the parties in a criminal case can be statutorily dependent, and counsel must carefully review the relevant statutes and standards before proceeding with an affirmative defense.

Although the defense does not have a burden in a criminal case, they may, nonetheless, choose to offer evidence of an alternative theory as to what happened. When doing so they do not assume a burden, but are instead offering their evidence to show how the state has failed to prove their case to a beyond a reasonable doubt standard. The unique nature of criminal cases creates different opportunities for advocacy in this regard, which we will discuss in detail on the section in the text dealing with closing arguments.

Structurally, the defense will call witnesses to testify on direct, they will then be cross examined by the plaintiff. Questions may be posed by the presiding judge, and in those jurisdictions allowing it the jury may pose questions as well. Redirect and recross are also treated the same during the defense case-in-chief. All evidentiary and procedural issues are identical.

Once the defense has completed their case they will "rest." This is usually a formal moment in the trial where the defense counsel states, on the record, "The defense rests." In some jurisdictions the defense may instead say something like "Subject to surrebuttal, the defense rests." Counsel should take the time to watch at least one trial in their jurisdiction to get a sense of how certain language approaches are preferred. This can vary from jurisdiction to jurisdiction, and while it does not normally have a legal significance, it helps to look like a local when trying a case in a particular jurisdiction.

After the defense rests, the judge normally excuses the jury and takes up any issues with counsel outside of the jury's presence. Such issues may include a discussion about potential rebuttal and surrebuttal witnesses, motions, or a meeting where the court and counsel discuss which instructions the court should use when charging the jury before their deliberations.

K. Motions at Close of Defendant's Case

Motions normally occur after the defense rests. These motions are heard by the court outside the presence of the jury. Usually the mid-trial motion for either a directed verdict or judgment as a matter of law is renewed. The court can grant the motion in whole or in part, or deny it. Normally they will not reserve ruling at this point, unless there is an anticipated rebuttal and surrebuttal case that will be substantive. The standard is the same as earlier, with the court considering the evidence in the light most favorable to the nonmoving party. If the court finds a failure of proof under this standard they will grant the motion in whole or in part.

Occasionally the legal or factual issues in the case may give rise to other substantive motions. The rules of evidence do not require counsel to raise objections or motions again when the court has ruled dispositively on them, but in certain situations, most notably when arguably new information was introduced at trial that could effect the court's earlier ruling, they can be raised again at this point in the trial. It is a "best practice" to ensure that all motions and rulings are clearly defined and dispositively addressed at trial. This maximizes their potential value on appeal.

L. Plaintiff's Rebuttal & Defendant's Surrebuttal

The trial process allows for the opportunity to present additional evidence in response to the defense's case-in-chief. This evidence is called rebuttal evidence, and must be narrowly tailored to address the evidentiary issue raised during the defense case. It may provide a defense to the counterclaims made by the defense during their case, or provide evidence specifically contradicting factual assertions with the defense's case-in-chief. In some instances the court may have initially prevented the plaintiff from addressing a particular piece of evidence, but the subsequent case presented by the defense now allows the plaintiff to provide that evidence to the jury. Counsel should offer rebuttal evidence when necessary. Normally rebuttal evidence will be factual in nature, and not opinion based. Counsel must be prepared to explain to the court the relevancy of the proffered rebuttal evidence. Sometimes the court will inquire as to why the evidence was not presented during the case-in-chief of the plaintiff. Plaintiff's counsel must be able to answer this question effectively, or they run the risk of not being allowed to introduce the evidence during the rebuttal case.

After the plaintiff has presented their rebuttal case the defense is allowed to present relevant evidence in surrebuttal. This evidence may only address the evidence provided during the rebuttal case.

M.   Motions at the Close of All Evidence

This is the final opportunity for counsel to address any motions with the court before the jury deliberates. They are free to again make motions for a directed verdict. The same standards of proof apply. While these motions are relatively pro forma, in some jurisdictions they must be made to preserve any appellate issues. Otherwise, the doctrine of finality will apply and the appellate court will not consider the issue during the appeal, unless the Constitution requires it. The goal in those jurisdictions is to push as much of the decision making process as possible down to the trial level and to prevent the appellate courts from being "clogged" with matters better addressed at the trial level. Counsel should make certain that they know the standard in their jurisdiction on this issue.

During this time period the court may, depending upon the jurisdiction, conduct a hearing about possible instructions to the jury. In other jurisdictions this occurs after closings. Most jurisdictions have a set of pattern instructions developed by the bench and bar. These instructions are designed to capture the application of substantive and procedural law to different factual scenarios arising at trial. They are based upon the law and the unwritten procedures of the bench. Pattern instructions are an excellent starting point when researching how the court may address certain issues during the trial. Some instructions are required, depending upon the type of case, while others are discretionary. Both sides are allowed to propose instructions to the court based upon case law and the circumstances of a particular case.

In some instances the parties and the court will agree on the proposed instructions, other times it is less collaborative, with the court eventually being forced to grant or deny specific requests for certain instructions. We will discuss the use of instructions in the sections on case analysis, opening statements and closing arguments. Instructions have multiple effective uses from an advocacy perspective and counsel should take the time to understand how they are captured, maintained, and applied in their jurisdictions.

N. Closing Argument & Jury Instructions

Counsel for both the plaintiff and defense give their closing arguments after final motions have been made. In some jurisdictions this is referred to as "summation" because the evidence is being "summed up" in a fashion designed to assist the jury. Most jurisdictions refer to it as "closings," or "argument." Regardless of the label, this is the final opportunity for both sides to address the legal, factual and persuasive theories of their case. The goal during closing argument is to clearly explain to the jury the substance of your argument in a way that emotionally appeals to them.

Persuasive closings combine the evidence at trial with the relevant law, and explain how the jury's understanding of human nature requires them to accept certain facts as having been proven, and sharing with them what the law now requires them to do. It is called argument for a reason, and counsel should spend the majority of their time drawing inferences from the controverted facts and explaining why the jury should consider their versions of the events to have been proven - and how opposing counsel failed to do so. This is the moment in trial where the advocate brings together everything that has happened. Exhibits, documents and evidence admitted over the course of the trial should be referred to, and where appropriate, used during the closing argument.

The court has the power to limit the amount of time for each side during closings. How much time is taken is very much a jurisdictionally dependent question, driven by local practice and the complexity, or simplicity, of the issues present in that particular case. Normally they last around an hour per side, but that is only a guideline. Attorneys want to take as much time as they need, and not a minute more. This can be a difficult balance to accomplish, and counsel may spend a great deal of time perfecting their closings. The side bearing the burden of proof argues first, followed by their opponent. After the party not having the burden of proof ends their closing argument the side bearing the burden of proof, usually the prosecution or plaintiff, is given an opportunity to argue last. This final argument is referred to as rebuttal argument and should focus on the specific issues raised by the defense during their argument, while also reiterating the key strengths of the advocate's case.

Counsel should use the instructions discussed earlier if there has been an instruction confer-

3.1 Introduction

UNITED STATES DISTRICT COURT
DISTRICT OF _____
_____ DIVISION

CASE NO. _____

_____,

Plaintiff,

vs.

_____,

Defendant.
/

COURT'S INSTRUCTIONS
TO THE JURY

Members of the jury:

It's my duty to instruct you on the rules of law that you must use in deciding this case.

When I have finished, you will go to the jury room and begin your discussions, sometimes called deliberations.

41

ence or hearing, or the prospective instructions they expect the court to give, when structuring their closing arguments. It is a "best practice" to rely upon the instructions when explaining the law because the court will use that same language when charging the jury. The court is required to instruct the jury, with some judges doing so before closing argument, and others after the closing argument. Some courts will split the instructions with them both before and after the closing arguments. The way in which the instructions are provided are also jurisdictionally unique. Some places provide a printed copy of all relevant instructions to the jury members for their use, others do not allow printed copies and read them out loud during the instructions phase of the trial. Counsel may modify their arguments in response to the way in which courts instruct. In jurisdictions where the instructions are only read, it is fairly common for counsel to provide a checklist taken from the instructions as a demonstrative aid during their closing. This serves to focus counsel, and hopefully the jury, on those legal issues believed to be not only relevant, but dispositive to the case.

Finally, the court will also provide a verdict form to the jury. The verdict form is based upon the specific causes of action, affirmative defenses, or indictment. It should be reviewed by both sides and agreed to before the court provides it to the jury. The amount of time taken to instruct the jury depends upon the length of the case and the complexity of the issues. Instructions are important both substantively and persuasively, counsel ignore their power at their peril.

O.   Deliberations & Verdict

After closing arguments are completed the judge charges the jury by instructing them on the law. The evidence is collected and the jury retires to deliberate. The deliberation process is addressed in the instructions provided by the court to the jury, which are standard in most jurisdictions.

They are instructed to begin by electing a foreperson to preside over deliberations. Jurors are also told they will be required to sign the verdict form once they are done. Beyond those instructions, the jury is free to organize and conduct itself as it sees fit.

The bailiff is responsible for assisting the jury by providing support during deliberations. They normally collect all of the evidence, bring it to the jury room, manage food and other requests, and ensure both the privacy and sanctity of the deliberation process. The bailiff will also communicate any questions or concerns that the jury has to the court. If a question arises the jury will write it down and the bailiff will bring it the judge, who will then decide what action to take. The court will confer with counsel for both sides before responding to the questions posed by the jury. Normally a response is prepared, the jury is called back into the courtroom, and the response is read to them, after which they retire again to deliberate.

Ultimately the jury must come to a decision that meets the requirements of that jurisdiction. In criminal cases that is normally a unanimous verdict for conviction, one or more against conviction for a hung jury, or an acquittal. In civil cases the standard is much less specific, with some jurisdictions requiring a two thirds majority on the jury for any decision. When the jury cannot reach a decision they will inform the judge, who normally brings them into open court to discuss their inability to reach a decision. Most jurisdictions have a process the court uses to attempt to force the jury to decide. In Federal Court it is often referred to as an "Allen" charge. If the jury is unable to reach a verdict the judge will dismiss them, and then address what to do with the case. In some instances, the process begins again, but in others the court may dismiss the case, either with or without prejudice. The system is designed to achieve a verdict, but is not always successful in doing so.

When jurors do reach a verdict they inform the court through the bailiff. The parties are summoned to the courtroom and the jury provides their verdict. The jury verdict can be published to the court in a variety of ways. Normally the bailiff will retrieve the verdict form, it will be appropriately marked for the record, the judge will review it for legal sufficiency, and then the clerk will announce it to the court. Some jurisdictions modify this process, but in all instances the verdict form must be accounted for, reviewed by the court, and published.

P.   Post-Trial Motions & Appeals

In civil cases the rules of civil procedure identify the process for post-trial motions and appeals. Normally they specify a period of time by which such motions or appeals must be made. After the specified time has elapsed the verdict of the jury is final. Criminal rules of procedure also identify timelines for required post-trial motions and appeals, but the Constitutional implications of criminal practice make it more problematic when enforcing timelines for the post-trial process on criminal defendants.

JNOVs, as discussed earlier, are commonly made during the post-trial phase. Such a motion asks the court set aside the jury's verdict and enter a decision for the side bringing the motion. If a JNOV motion was not made during the mid-trial and post-trial phases it may not be possible, in some jurisdictions, to request it during the post-trial phase. In civil cases, a JNOV is often accompanied by a request for a new trial by the losing party. The parties may also ask the court, through a motion, to reduce or increase the award made by a jury in a civil case where liability was found. The issue of who will pay attorney fees, when not covered by statute, is also routinely addressed during the post-trial process.

The court will consider any written or oral motions, and provide counsel time to file briefs when appropriate with follow on oral argument. The court will then consider the verdict of the jury, the motions made by counsel, and enter judgment in accordance with the verdict and the motions. This is the moment when the case becomes final, passing from the trial process to the appellate process.

Q. Conclusion

We have begun our time together in studying advocacy by reviewing the components of a notional trial. Every trial is somewhat unique, and the elements discussed here are provided as a starting point in your development as a competent advocate. The process of learning how to try cases requires counsel to connect with their humanity while developing and employing the necessary skills for mastering trial advocacy. It is important to remember that while trials normally follow a process similar to the one we have discussed here, they can vary a great deal depending upon the local rules of practice. Make certain that you have a complete understanding of what your jurisdiction expects and requires.

Chapter 2: Case Analysis & Preparation

A. Introduction 29
B. Creating the Litigation File and Trial Notebook......................32
C. Organizing the File 36
D. Developing the Legal and Factual Theory.............................38
E. Analyzing the Case...42
F. Finding the Story 48
G. Preparing for Trial 49
H. Examples of Case Analysis..56
I. Conclusion...63

A.   Introduction

There is nothing earth shatteringly unique about case analysis, it is the application of a process of organization to a series of factual and legal questions designed to identify the controverted questions of fact, and in some case law, that should resolve the disputed case. The difficulty comes in translating the data that has been acquired and analyzed into a presentation that persuades. To accomplish this counsel must connect the law and facts to a sense of justice that will move the jury.

Counsel must so understand their case as to be able to connect each individual fact, piece of testimony, or exhibit to the element of the charge, claim, or defense to be proven at trial. This requires a connection between persuasion theory, or morality, and substantive law and facts. It is in a very real sense a right brain and left brain activity.

Case Analysis Puts the Pieces Together

A proper structural approach is useful for attorneys who are confronted with the need to connect their analytical ability to their humanity. The case analysis suggestions contained within this section allows the attorney to become an advocate for their client by bringing into focus the connections between the law, the facts, and the moral question residing within them.

In this section we will identify a structure for conducting case analysis allowing counsel to focus their efforts on analyzing the legal and factual issues of the case using a methodology maximizing their persuasive power. This approach uses concepts of backwards planning familiar to most major entities, combining it with a persuasive structural analysis built upon time tested theories of rhetoric. Counsel adopting these techniques are better able to manage the process and find the most persuasive story for their client.

We will learn how to (1) perform case analysis, (2) understand a litigation file, and (3) conduct case preparation for trial. To accomplish these tasks counsel must choose an organizational construct that processes information, prioritizes the value of that information, and then identifies crucial legal and factual issues. It is truly a matter of preparation, preparation, and preparation. It is also a matter of personal preference. Counsel must find a way to properly aggregate and marshal the information in their case such that they can see the most persuasive litigation route laid before them. For the most part case analysis is data acquisition and management, a relatively mundane process constrained by the procedural rules of discovery and evidence, oriented towards a substantive question of law that is determined by the controverted facts.

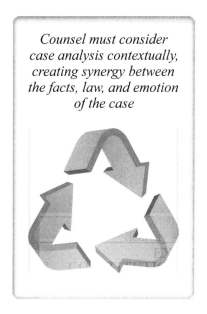

Counsel must consider case analysis contextually, creating synergy between the facts, law, and emotion of the case

Most law firms have an accepted process designed to address the flow of litigation, with hard copy files, notebooks and procedures that manage the life of a case from the moment the client walks in the door through resolution. These firms often use software platforms to accomplish these tasks. Major government agencies also have best practices that are preferred within their offices to manage litigation. Managing the litigation is not the same as preparing for trial. Keeping the file up to date with notes is not equivalent to the process of connecting the pieces of that file to the issues to be proven or fought against at trial. However, an organizational system that allows counsel to clearly understand when the evidence emerged in the life of the case, and gives them the ability to put hands on that evidence as quickly as possible is essential for successful litigation. The materials for trial flow out of the litigation file, but are more oriented towards the presentation of evidence and persuasion of the finder of fact. Systems to accomplish both, which complement one another by having both an organizational structure and schema that make the most sense to counsel, should be part of any competent case analysis and preparation methodology.

Proper case analysis has a direct and long lasting impact on the quality of any individual advocacy skill performed in the courtroom. These skills do not exist in a vacuum. Moreover, the individual facts of a case do not exist in a vacuum. Every fact, exhibit, and piece of testimony works in concert with each other to make up the entirety of a case, and counsel must develop a system that allows them to understand the interplay of these component pieces. Counsel's understanding of each of this interplay reflects an understanding of the relevant substantive and procedural law. Those facts necessary to tell a cohesive story explaining the client' position in light of the substantive law, and an emotional hook capturing the emotional intelligence of the jury - empowering them to interpret the law so that it favors the client. The importance of case analysis cannot be overstated. It is an overarching component of every thing counsel does, both in the courtroom, and out. A weak case analysis will lead to individual trial components that are weaker than what counsel could reach by spending the time doing the heavy prep work up front.

A superior case analysis:

(1) assists jurors in understanding the relevant legal and factual issues,

(2) brings clarity and focus to the issues the advocate wishes to emphasize, and

(3) provides a morally persuasive theme empowering the jury to decide the case in the client's favor.

Case analysis has long-term consequences for the clarity and persuasiveness of counsel's position at trial. Remember - even when the client is motivated to settle and there is no reason to suspect the case will linger to the point of trial, analyzing the case in terms of its trial potential benefits the client by posturing the case in the strongest possible position for resolution by any means. If counsel is ready from the very first stages of litigation to discuss all the issues of the case as if trial were in a matter of weeks, it heightens their bargaining power and position for their client.

B.   Creating the Litigation File and Trial Notebook

1.   The Litigation File

A litigation file's creation and appearance is a product of the organization's culture, defined by the firm or government entity representing the client. While each are somewhat unique, they do share certain commonalities. Sometimes counsel will be involved in the creation of the litigation file from the very beginning, creating the case file based upon their understanding of the legal and factual issues in a fashion that ensures all of the pertinent timelines, requirements, and issues are covered. More often, however, counsel will inherit a case file that is either incomplete, or instead created based upon another attorney's approach. The organization of a litigation file is often unique to the individual working it, and while picking up someone else's work can be difficult, the commonalities of the process are an excellent place for counsel to start.

Potential Trial Evidence

(Identified by Case Investigation and Discovery):

- Witness Statements
  - Handwritten
  - Typed
  - Depositions
  - Video
- Business Records (germane to the case)
  - Email
  - Letters
  - Policies
  - Correspondence
  - Contracts
  - Banking Records
- Public Records (germane to the case)
- Visual Evidence
- Digital Evidence
  - Smartphone Location Data
  - Text Messages
  - Call Records
  - Social Media Posts
  - Web Histories
  - App Use Information

At a minimum counsel should review the timelines contained within the file and compare them to the filing and reporting requirements for litigation in the jurisdiction where the case has been brought before beginning case analysis. This is both an internal and external requirement. Counsel should compare the timeline to any firm management metrics, and to the filing requirements of the clerk of court. Both of these contain procedural benchmarks and timelines that can derail the litigation if not properly dealt with. Once they are sure that all appropriate filing and management requirements have been met counsel can begin to analyze the case. When checking the materials counsel should expect to find on the previous page.

If the case is a criminal case counsel should look for the indictment or information, often referred to as the charge, any affirmative defenses that may have been raised, and potential related cases. In civil cases it is often helpful to create a document that contains the elements of the claims alleged and any affirmative defenses raises for ease of reference.

Attorney Work Product & Firm Internal Tracking Records:

- Chronology of the litigation (usually a timeline or matrix)
- Representation Agreement
- Retainer contract, billing, costs of litigation
- Correspondence sent during the representation
- Legal research
- Other materials that are case dependent

The litigation file is used to control work flow and to assist in analyzing the case, but is not normally used to actually try the case. Sections of the litigation file will be placed in the Trial file, commonly referred to as a trial notebook. The notebook is narrowly tailored to support trying the case. The documents and product within it start as part of the litigation file, but are transformed through the process of case analysis and preparation into a trial notebook. The information contained in the notebook is case specific, and remains in flux through out the trial.

2.   The Trial Notebook

The trial notebook is organized based upon the expected flow of legal issues and factual issues when the case goes to trial. It is a best practice to organize it in a modular fashion, building it around either witnesses, factual issues, or legal issues. The way the file is organized shifts depending upon the core issues that case analysis identified, and the visual presentation that makes the most sense to individual counsel. It comes as no surprise that different people have different ways of organizing information in life. Counsel should not be afraid to make alterations to the trial notebook where the intent behind doing so is to allow them to get to information faster than they otherwise might. The average trial notebook, contains some form of the following:

- **A Statement of the facts of the case:** This depends upon the jurisdiction and nature of the case. In a criminal case it might consist of a stripped down version of the indictment or affirmative defenses raised, in a civil case it is often a restatement of the facts alleged in the cause of action. Having the facts available in the trial notebook serves to focus the advocate during the process, keeping them on track. Counsel must be sure to review this document frequently in order to ensure that each fact is connected to some piece of testimony from a witness or an exhibit, and not merely the logical leaps counsel has made while spending so much time with the case file.

- **Court Documents tracking the litigation:** In this section of the trial notebook counsel place the pleadings, answers, interrogatories, motions and court orders. These are administrative materials identifying the flow of the litigation. Often counsel will include a timeline coversheet in the front of this section identifying who filed what action, who responded, and the court's ultimate decision. These documents can become necessary at trial if an issue of discovery, violations of discovery or trial by ambush becomes relevant. It is also useful to have the dates and times pre-trial motions were decided in the event opposing counsel attempts to relitigate the issue during the trial. By having the ability to point to the specifics of the prior hearing at a moment's notice, counsel enhances their credibility and believability with the judge. Preparing this section assists the advocate in making certain that all procedural and timing requirements for the litigation have been met.

- **Exhibits for use at trial:** Trial notebooks contain a section on exhibits, identifying each document or piece of evidence the advocate intends to reference or admit during the trial. One set can be found in the trial notebook, with additional individual copies of the exhibits available in separate binders or folders for use during the trial. The trial notebook contains the master copy, with the individual binders or folders containing the copy of the exhibit presented at trial. Some exhibits do not fit into folders or notebooks, but the trial notebook and folder should contain a short description of that exhibit, and a picture when appropriate. The goal is to identify, track, and manage the evidence that will be referenced through out the various stages of the trial. Many litigation management software applications are particularly excellent at this task.

- **Jury Selection Information:** This section of the trial notebook should contain the matrix used to record the responses of the potential jurors to voir dire questions. Counsel should also include their pre-trial jury research discussed in the section on jury selection. This section of the trial notebook is designed to connect the voir dire process to case analysis and jury research.

- **Opening Statement:** This section of the trial notebook contains the notes made by counsel in preparation of delivering the opening statement. Some attorneys will type out their entire opening statement, placing a copy in this section of the trial notebook. While that technique is acceptable, it is not recommended. The better practice is to ensure that the theme, or hook, of your opening is recorded, followed by a bullet point format of the information counsel intends to cover during the opening statement.

- **Plaintiff case-in-chief:** In this section counsel should place the materials they intend to use when examining the witnesses called during the plaintiff's case in chief. Plaintiff's counsel will include the outline of direct examinations, as well as any documents or exhibits specific to the witness. Defense counsel will include the outline of the cross examination of witnesses, with supporting materials for the crosses of the witnesses.

- **Mid-Trial Motions:** In this section counsel should place the governing standard for dismissal of the case based upon the failure of the state or plaintiff to meet the burden of proof sufficient to send the case to the jury. In most jurisdictions the court will decide this motion while considering the evidence admitted to that point in the light most favorable to the non-moving party. Failure to make this motion may prevent counsel from making a similar motion at the close of the evidence.

- **Defense case-in-chief:** In this section counsel should place the materials they intend to use when examining the witnesses called during the defense's case in chief. Plaintiff's counsel will include the outline of cross examinations, as well as any documents or exhibits specific to the witness. Defense counsel will include the outline of the direct examination of witnesses, with supporting materials.

- **End-of-Trial Motions:** In this section counsel should place a reminder to reiterate the mid-trial motion. Failure to raise the motion again can constitute waiver of the issue on appeal in many jurisdictions. The same legal standard applies.

- **Closings:** In this section counsel should include blank paper to make notations during the trial itself. Copies of the cause of action, defenses, or the elements of the offense should be found here as well. Finally a bullet outline of the subjects counsel intends to discuss should be provided.

- **Instructions:** In this section of the trial notebook counsel should place the instructions their case analysis supports. Most jurisdictions have pattern instructions that serve as the starting point for the court, but case law allows for the use of case specific instructions proposed by counsel, when the judge agrees.

- **Law:** In this section of the trial notebook counsel should place the relevant statutes, defenses, procedural rules and relevant case law. This section is used to place the law that must be available at counsel's fingertips through out the trial. Sometimes the legal issues are sufficiently complex that this section serves as an overview piece and table of contents identifying where the additional information is located.

In order to create an effective trial notebook counsel must work their way through the litigation file, applying a structured case analysis to ensure the most persuasive presentation at trial. The first step after the file has been assembled is to organize it around three overarching themes; the law, the facts, and the persuasive story of the case. The persuasive story of the case is of particular importance because it identifies the moral questions surrounding the case and provides a means to deal with them.

C.   Organizing the File

The degree of familiarity with the type of case file, and documents contained within, help determine the approach counsel should take when organizing their materials. If counsel is familiar with the system used by the firm, as well as the types of documents contained within the litigation file, they are capable of reviewing the file to make certain it is complete. On the other hand, if they are not familiar with the set up of the file or the materials contained within counsel should find someone within the firm, or outside the firm, to assist them in understanding the documents. Either way, counsel must break the file down into its component parts to determine if it is complete or incomplete, poorly developed, or improperly addresses the information it should contain.

A Large Part of Case Analysis Involves Reducing Material to its Core - Information Is Useless if You Cannot Find It When You Need it!

For the most part this process is one of document identification, review and management. The ability to identify the foundation for documents within the case, understand their legal significance, and properly manage them is a core concept in case analysis. Developing these skills sufficiently requires a knowledge of the business or organizational practices of the client, the evidentiary rules controlling the authenticity and admissibility of documents at trial, and the connection between these documents and witnesses. Once counsel has acquired the baseline knowledge necessary to know what a litigation file is and how to read it, the next step is to organize it with an eye towards performing case analysis. Counsel should begin by reading through the entire file without thinking about the law. This can be difficult to do, in that attorneys naturally filter information through their understanding of the law, jumping immediately to legal analysis. While such inclinations are helpful, it is not wise to begin reviewing the case file in that fashion. Initially counsel should read through the material, jotting down their initial impressions. Next they should ask themselves what factual questions are on their mind? Is there something they wish they knew? Have they formed initial opinions about the people involved in the case? What assumptions do they find themselves making? These questions are important. They represent the types of questions and reactions jurors will have when they hear the evidence at trial. At this point in the process counsel is as close to being a member of the jury as they will ever be.

Recording their initial reactions serve as an excellent starting point for interpreting the evidence, and works later as a gut check to ensure that the case has not gotten lost in the weeds of legal analysis. Counsel should write these questions down and refer to them throughout not only their case analysis, but in all other areas of trial preparation. Unless and until counsel believes they have done all they can to answer these questions, they are not sufficiently prepared for trial. But after they are initially recorded, counsel should set these observations aside and set about the business of organizing the materials they have read.

It is only after counsel gathers together all of the relevant documents, legal pleadings, and other information and organizes it in a systematic way, that they can see the "conceptual whole" of the case. This big picture understanding identifies strengths and weaknesses and potential moral themes and legal theories. The ability to correctly identify the underlying moral themes is crucial to discovering the winning persuasive theory for the case. In terms of legal theories, counsel should look to their local jurisdiction for any model jury instructions concerning the charges, claims or defenses to be litigated. While these model instructions may not precisely constitute what counsel will use at trial, they can serve as guiding posts in the overarching organization of the litigation.

The file must be broken down into its component parts and organized with an eye towards identifying the relevant legal standards and factual issues. Gather together all relevant documents and evidence, and organize the information. When doing so counsel should use the approaches discussed earlier, to include developing timelines and chronologies, checklists, witness folders, case management software and trial notebooks. The goal at this point is to identify potential legal and factual issues. In order to accomplish this each must be addressed separately, and then brought back together through analysis.

D.   Developing the Legal and Factual Theory

There are three primary sources of potential legal issues in a trial, substantive, procedural and constitutional. Each must be thoroughly identified and analyzed in light of the facts present in the case. Most analysis of the legal theory for purposes of persuasion will revolve around the substantive elements of the action and the controlling rules of evidence and procedure. The substantive law identifies what must be proven, while the procedural rules control the way in which it is proven. Normally constitutional issues come into play more often during motions practice, but they do impact standards of proof at certain points in the proceeding as well.

Counsel must review and develop their understanding of the substantive law, remembering always that a good faith based argument for a change to existing law is sufficient to allow bringing an action where the law is not in the client's favor. Connecting the facts to the relevant law is the core of effective case analysis. It is often helpful to begin with one category and then connect it to the other. It is not necessary to always start with the law, or to begin with the facts, counsel should decide where to initially focus on a case by case basis.

1.   Identify the Available Facts

Sometimes it makes sense to identify all of the facts present in the case file and list them out without regard for which side's legal position is supported. This is a brainstorming exercise designed to get all of the facts on the table where they can be identified by their source. This list of facts is then compared to the elements of the legal claim and sorted into two groups, controverted and uncontroverted.

Uncontroverted facts are those facts which both sides agree are true. These are the strongest facts available within the case, and if sufficient uncontroverted facts exist supporting every element of a counsel's claim the case will most likely not go to trial, unless a strong legal defense exists obviating the strength of the factual theory of the opposing side. Controverted facts are those facts where different sides have different versions of what happened, and admissible evidence supporting those multiple versions of events. The amount and nature of controverted facts directly impacts the likelihood the case goes to trial. It also increases the importance of proper case analysis. Once the controverted and uncontroverted facts have been identified, they are plugged into a proof chart where they impact the elements of the cause of action or indictment.

Example:The following facts have been extracted from a file in a local insurance defense attorney's office. They represent the local grocery store in a slip and fall case. The facts are as follows:

A busy parent is shopping for eggplant in the local grocery store. The produce section has an area of the floor that is covered in standing water. There is a full mop bucket beside the wet area, with a mop laying on the floor. The area is cordoned off with warning signs in multiple languages identifying the danger of the wet floor. It appears as though the water is coming from a pipe underneath the produce stand that is currently leaking. The store has also surrounded the wet area with shopping carts. The parent pushes the carts aside and carefully steps into the water, reaching for an eggplant. Unknown to the customer the water contains a solution normally sprayed on the plants that is slippery, and despite their best efforts the customer slips and falls, breaking an arm and suffering a mild concussion. Counsel has created the following chart identifying the facts, and indicated whether they are controverted or uncontroverted.

Fact	Status	Source
Floor is wet	Uncontroverted	Multiple Statements, accident report, emails
Store caused the leak	Controverted	Store admits in answer that the floor was wet, but alleges it is the result of a defective repair, the leak was subsequently repaired by a store employee
Substance in water made it more slippery	Controverted	Plaintiff expert says yes, defense expert says no, both reports are contained in the file
Plaintiff entered area that was wet	Uncontroverted	Multiple Statements, accident report, emails
Area was not properly controlled	Controverted	Warning signs present, no tape, mop left on the floor, shopping carts used to make a barrier

Counsel should notice that listing the facts in the left hand column require some degree of judgment as to what the facts mean. Those controverted facts will become the focus areas at trial. In the above example the experts will argue over the substances in the water and the actions of the grocery store to cordon off the area will be interpreted as both proper and improper, depending upon the side discussing it. Sorting through the existing known facts, and then attributing them to elements of the claim is the essence of case analysis.

In those instances where the uncontroverted facts heavily favor the opposing side, counsel will often turn to a theory of the case relying instead upon a friendly legal standard. An example of such a legal theory is contributory negligence, which bars the victim of a negligent act from recovering if they contributed to the act. This balance between legal theories of the case and factual theories of the case is driven by proper identification of all relevant facts, to include their authenticity and admissibility at trial.

The same slip and fall case can be analyzed initially from a legal theory instead. The first step identifies the elements of the cause of action in a civil claim or the elements of the crime in a criminal case by listing them out in a column, leaving room next to them for additional notations. Some of these additional columns can include one where each fact that supports the element that is listed, one where the location of those facts is listen for ease of retrieval, and one where any anticipated evidentiary law issues are contemplated. In this example, the column might list a statement from the grocery store clerk, give the page and line number of that portion of the clerk's deposition, and then contemplate what hearsay exception would be used to admit the evidence at trial. This is often referred to as a proof chart.

> *Example:*
>
> Plaintiff's counsel has brought a tortious claim against the defendant, a grocery store, for failure to keep the produce section of the store safe for customers shopping in the produce section. A customer was shopping for eggplants and slipped in a puddle of water found in the produce section. The grocery store has denied responsibility and put forth a counter claim of contributory negligence on the part of the customer, alleging that the water in the produce section was the result of a failed line recently installed by a private repair company. The grocery store further alleges that the wet area was clearly marked with the appropriate warning devices and that the customer moved those devices to reach the eggplants.

Legal analysis begins by reviewing the elements for the cause of action. Counsel should sort through all available documents, identifying where evidence exists supporting their ability to prove the elements. Those facts are then inserted into the proof worksheet as follows:

Elements of the Substantive Law	Facts Available to Prove the Elements
Duty	Grocery store controls the produce section, sells produce to the public
Breach	Floor was wet, still leaking
Causation	They knew it was leaking, tried to get it fixed, repair was faulty, did attempt to prevent access
Damages	Broken Arm, pain, loss of work, suffering

Next counsel must consider the impact of the counter claim of contributory negligence. In this jurisdiction the relevant law establishes that when an individual contributes, through their own negligence, to the cause of the injury, they will be barred from recovery. Legal analysis of the counterclaim would begin with the following chart:

Elements of the Counterclaim	Facts Available to Prove the Elements
Individual acted affirmatively	Moved carts, entered the area
In a negligent fashion	Saw signs, chose to enter
The act contributed to their injury	Did not have knowledge of substance in the water, too slippery, but did enter

Finally, counsel should consider the allegation that the line recently installed by the private repair company may provide another potential part to inter-plead into the case. Counsel would go to the appropriate rule of civil procedure for adding an additional party to the litigation, with a potential need to file an amended complaint. Having identified the elements for the cause of action, counsel go through the factual issues in the case to identify how the available facts support or weaken the claims and counter claims.

Counsel can begin with either the facts or the law, and still ultimately arrive at the same conclusion about the strengths and weaknesses of the case. The goal during this process is not to write the perfect brief or motion, but rather to understand the legal and factual issues present in the case.

E.   Analyzing the Case

Case analysis is the process of organizing information, applying specialized knowledge to that information, and then viewing the results of that process in light of the advocate's personal understanding of the moral values existing within the community where the case is tried. This is the point in the practice of law where an attorney melds their legal knowledge, common sense and world experience. This can be overwhelming, particularly in complex cases or when the advocate in inexperienced. Sometimes counsel find themselves wandering aimlessly through the case file, attempting to generate sufficient activity to feel as though you are accom-

plishing something. This is
rarely, if ever, successful, and
even when it is, it is not efficient.

Case analysis is an ongoing
process that begins as the client
walks in the door and ends
when the conflict is resolved.
The only way to overcome
what appears to be an overwhelming project is to begin. It
is a lot like eating an elephant—

*You view the world in three di-
mensions. Words and thoughts
reflecting a Rule of Threes organizational construct will ring true
in the minds of others. Failure to
properly organize your thoughts
impinges on the ability of your
audience to accept as true the
message you are presenting.*

you do it one spoonful at a time. Every attorney must develop the ability to
properly perform the tasks listed above, and develop them in a way that
best lays out the case for their interpretation and use. The use of rhetorical
constructs such as the Rule of Threes, in conjunction with an attorney's
heightened ability to logically reason, will help create persuasive trial presentations through a synergistic combination of the practical and the theoretical. This is the definition of what lawyers actually do, and it makes the
profession challenging and rewarding. The Rule of Threes is particularly
useful because it employs sound rhetorical, psychological, and physical
characteristics which make it effective when analyzing cases and making
persuasive presentations.

1.   The Rule of Threes

The Rule of Threes provides a common sense template to assist you in
case analysis. This section uses the Rule of Threes as an overarching structure for case analysis, suggests a series of common sense checklists applicable in most situations, and provides an analytical tool explaining how
the three main portions of any trial are connected during case analysis.

The Rule of Threes is an organizational construct used to communicate
ideas through the written or spoken word. It posits that when information
is organized in triplets human beings are more likely to accept and internalize the messages contained within those three-pronged packages. This
three-part harmony view of communication is a powerful tool if you accept its basic premise. Both Western and Eastern cultures have employed
the Rule of Threes. Using the Rule of Threes to conduct case analysis will
increase counsel's persuasive ability at trial.

The philosophy of the ancient world focused what it means to be an advocate on the three concepts of logos, pathos, and ethos. Other examples of
Trilogies using the Rule of Threes to persuade can be found across re-
markably different cultures, including the Judea-Christian traditions, the

When Used Properly The Rule of Threes Binds the Component Portions of the Case into a Persuasive Whole

mythology of ancient Greece, and the tenets of Hinduism.

It is not necessary, however, to rely upon religion or philosophy to support the use of this organizational approach. The Rule of Threes is grounded in humanity's physical ability to perceive the world around us. It is part and parcel of how the brain is wired, information is received, and thoughts processed. Human beings experience the world as a three dimensional place containing height, depth and width. These three dimensions form the boundaries of the physical world.

In the same way, words and thoughts that do not reflect a Rule of Threes organizational construct ring less than true in our minds, impinging on our ability to accept as true the message being presented. Using this rule as an advocacy approach creates an internal sense of believability and acceptance. When properly applied it can serve as a template for organizing, analyzing, and presenting a case.

The doctrine of primacy and recency is an excellent common sense example of an application of the Rule of Threes. Counsel are taught to put their best facts first and last, to not hide the weakness of their case, but to instead place that weakness strategically within their presentation so that its potential impact on the jury is minimized. Advocates use the doctrine of primacy and recency to (1) tell the jury what they are going to tell them (opening statement), (2) tell them (case-in-chief), and (3) then tell them what they told them (closing argument). This approach ensures that advocates start and finish strong.

The Rule of Threes is an excellent tool for breaking case files down into their component parts, with the goal of fully answering three primary of questions: (1) What is the strongest argument available, (2) What evidence must be presented through the available witnesses, and (3) what story should be told during openings? Proper case analysis using the Rule of Three's identifies and answers each of these core questions in the development and presentation of your case.

It is only after counsel gather together all of the relevant documents, legal pleadings, and other information and organize it in a systematic way, that they can see the "conceptual whole" of the case by using the Rule of Threes. This big picture understanding identifies potential moral themes that will carry the persuasive burden of the case. The ability to correctly identify the underlying moral themes is crucial. Morality, right and wrong, good and bad, yes or no—this is the language of the jury. People are fascinated with the process of assigning moral blame and imposing legal judgment. When looking to make use of this tool, counsel should focus in on what universal human truth is contained within the logic of their case, and build their client's story from there. If the client's story falls into an archetype the jury understands counsel will benefit immensely by harnessing the archetype and making it part of their moral theme.

2.   The Three Primary Steps

Counsel should begin by using the Rule of Threes to organize the information, identifying factual and legal issues and how they relate to one another. Organizing the information is the primary goal. Doing this systemically is the key to successfully understanding the case file, allowing the advocate to list the legal elements of the claims and defenses, analyze the legal principles and questions of the law, and then develop a legal theory for each persuasive question of fact. The three primary steps in case analysis are used for bench trials (judge alone), jury trials, arbitration panels, or any adversarial dispute resolution proceeding.

A complete case analysis applies these three steps to each component part of a trial or adjudicative proceeding, ensuring the case analysis is complete. Examples of where this happens includes identifying closing argument topics, preparing direct, cross and redirect examinations, conducting discovery, deposing witnesses, creating juror profiles, choosing jurors, and selecting opening statement topics. This list is not exhaustive, but it does provide a sense of the various portions of a trial where you must apply the three main steps of case analysis.

While performing the three primary steps of case analysis counsel must be aware of potential persuasive themes contained within the facts and law of their case. The persuasive theme, or moral theory, of the case provides coherence and continuity to the facts presented at trial and connects those facts to the legal issues in a way that demands victory. These three component pieces must remain in harmony throughout the trial process. When dissonance exists between the moral theory and the facts or law of the case, counsel must adapt and resolve it by discovering additional facts or law that support their position, modifying their theme and theory, or settling the case. Whenever the theme and theory changes they must also go back and reevaluate the previous case analysis in light of those changes.

A systematic approach is necessary to ensure counsel cover all of the possible legal issues. They should identify admissibility issues while substantively looking for strengths and weaknesses where the law intersects with the facts. This also includes properly crafted and considered jury instructions—if counsel does not know where they are ultimately headed, they cannot possibly plan for success. These substantive and procedural legal issues must be identified and explored so that proper motions, objections and responses can be properly prepared and presented.

Once counsel have identified the important legal theories their next step is to convince the judge their interpretation of the law applies in this particular instance. This occurs during pretrial motions or motions in limine. The arguments about which law applies are normally made by counsel before the judge and outside the presence of the jury. When the issue is solely a question of law, it may be possible to argue motions without the need for evidence, but that is rarely the case.

Identify & Analyze the Factual Issues:

List the contested claims and defenses, with the burden of proof. For each contested claim or defense identify:

- The contested legal elements
- The deciding questions of facts
- The persuasive legal theory for each deciding question of fact

Develop a plan for managing the source of facts, including:
- Creating chronological timelines
- Arranging documents systemically
- Listing and cataloging all available exhibits
- Listing all potential witnesses

Whenever the court is talking about evidence they are really talking about facts placed before the court through the testimony of a witness. During motions arguments about controverted questions of fact the court will ask for a proffer of proof supporting the representations made by counsel during motions argument. The first thing a good judge will ask counsel for when arguments about the law are being made is what facts support their position and what evidence will be offered for the judge's consideration. This is why case analysis that identifies where information is contained in the file is crucial. If counsel has done the detail work of the case analysis to be able to put their fingers on a fact's location as quickly as possible, it heightens their familiarity with the factual issue and how it interplays with the legal and moral issues of the case. This makes the overall argument more persuasive, and increases counsel's credibility with the judge hearing the motion.

Counsel can make a proffer of what the evidence will be, but that proffer is only counsel's opinion and not substantive evidence the judge may rely upon when ruling. Evidence may be actual testimony, previous stipulations, or previously admitted evidence. Trial judges in federal court are not bound by the normal hearsay rules when determining most motions and can rely upon written documents or other out-of-court statements for the limited purpose of ruling on a motion.

Counsel must develop the skill of identifying and analyzing the facts that are case dispositive. Dispositive facts are much more easily identifiable after completing an analysis of the appropriate legal issues presented in the case. The facts of the case will determine whether the law applied by the judge assists or hurts the theme and theory of the case. Counsel must fully develop the relationship between the facts and the law. The ability to identify the ruling legal precedent, develop case dispositive facts, and then explain their relationship to the jury using an appropriate moral theme and legal theory is the essence of trial advocacy.

> **Identify & Analyze Legal Issues:**
>
> - List the legal elements for the claims and defenses
>
> - Analyze the legal principles and questions of law
>
> - Develop a legal theory for each persuasive question of fact

We have identified three primary areas of case analysis that continuously shift in importance depending upon the situation. Counsel may have a preference for factual analysis, legal analysis, or moral issues, and can use that preference to choose the starting point for their case analysis. When doing so they must take care to ensure they do not allow their personal predilections to prevent them from seeing issues in areas that may not be their strongest suit. Following this process will assist counsel in discovering which facts must be admitted, and the legal rulings that will strengthen or weaken their position. This allows counsel to then file motions with the court to protect needed facts and apply preferred legal rulings for the case.

Once counsel have identified the legal issues and potentially admissible facts it is time to take the next step—creating a persuasive vehicle combining the law and the facts into a persuasive whole that will convince the jury to decide in their favor. A proper case analysis assists the advocate in choosing the correct moral theme and legal theory in light of the available facts. Failure to accomplish this results in a cognitive dissonance in the minds of the fact-finder. What comes out of the mouth of counsel does not match the facts as the jury sees them. If this happens they will conclude that counsel are either incompetent or lying. Either way they lose.

F.   Finding the Story

A legal theory is the application of the relevant law to the specific facts of the case. It forms the basis for the legal or procedural reasons that counsel should win. When done properly the legal, factual and moral theory of the case creates a framework the jury uses to decide the case, normally in favor of the side whose theory they have adopted as their own. A review of our earlier discussion lays out the relative ease with which counsel can identify each legal element of the offenses and potential defenses to identify possible legal theories. A presentation to the jury focused solely on the law creates difficulties from a persuasive standpoint.

The shipwrecked crew adrift in a lifeboat that kills and eats the weakest member of their group and is then later rescued is a classic example of the difficulties with a purely legal defense. A murder occurred and a potential legal defense of necessity, or justification, exists. That legal defense however, will only work if the accompanying moral theme excuses the otherwise criminal behavior in the minds of the jury. The story accompanying this legal defense is crucial in establishing the moral theme. How the decision was made to eat one of the party members might be crucial to the validity of the legal defense, as is the status of the one chosen to be eaten. The story told matters from a persuasive perspective, particularly when the legal defense allows someone who has committed an illegal act to not be held accountable. Counsel must square the requirements of the law with a story that allows the jury to enforce that law, especially in situations where the law requires deeper moral considerations.

It is often possible for valid legal theories to run into a lack of credibility when they require the jury to adopt an unpopular moral theme or to reject a cherished community belief. In either instance, counsel may find themselves with an excellent legal theory that will never

Apply the three primary steps when:
• identifying proper claims or defenses
• preparing and responding to discovery
• conducting depositions
• drafting mediation statements
• preparing motions
• preparing final pretrial statements.

carry the persuasive burden. Jurors are not lawyers and most trial attorneys would do well to remember that fact. Legal theories must be combined with a solid moral theme to succeed. If the jurors cannot reach a place of moral peace with the decision counsel is asking them to make, they are far less likely to find for counsel, regardless of what the law and facts might say.

The theme is the moral reason counsel should win. It is why the jury wants to decide the case in their favor. A good moral theme identifies an injustice that is being committed against the client and empowers the jury to right that wrong. Themes are as varied as the people, places, and situations they are designed to capture and represent. The theme provides the moral force breathing life into the case. A good theme not only gets the jury on your side, it creates a feeling of comfort within them about deciding things your way.

When searching for the moral theme that resonates within the case counsel should return to their initial review of the litigation file, where they jotted down their responses to their initial review of the materials. Their initial reaction to the story line of the materials is often an excellent starting point when searching for the moral theme of the case.

When counsel has difficulty finding the theme that will resonate with the jury, they should identify what it is about the case that seems unfair. Is there a wrong that was committed against the client that can be used to energize the jury to decide the case the right way? Classic themes include wrong person, wrong time, some one else did it, the other side was incompetent, never attribute to malice what can be explained through stupidity-the list is endless. The storylines are as varied and complex as the tales of humanity that surround us each day. They exist in our shared experiences as a members of the collective society represented by the fact-finder. But while they vary, they each connect back to a universal human truth that allows the jury to morally identify with counsel's argument, and gives them the harmony needed to act in accordance with the facts and the law. Counsel must stay in touch with these perennial themes of life. They are the vehicle through which advocates find the story to persuasively explain their case.

G.   Preparing for Trial

Once case analysis has been completed it is time to prepare for trial. Counsel should go back and review the initial impressions recorded when they read through the litigation file the first time. Does the current theme and theory of the case answer those questions sufficiently? Does it tell a story that resonates? Do the facts identified through case analysis reflect the earlier understanding of the case? If the answer to these questions are affirmative it is time to begin trial preparation. If not, counsel should go back and review the choices made during case analysis.

It may be that the case analysis is solid. Sometimes not all sides are equally arrayed in an adversarial proceeding and proper case analysis exposes the inequities of the case. While attorneys have an ethical duty to try as best they can to represent the client based upon the facts and the law available, bad facts rarely make for good cases, but they sometimes create excellent advocacy opportunities.

Once all legal, factual and thematic issues have been fully addressed it is time to bring it all together into a cohesive presentation. The Rule of Threes, used earlier to identify potential themes and theories, serves as an excellent tool to accomplish this task.

Trial is broken down into three primary sections: closing argument, case-in-chief, and opening statement. They are not listed chronologically because cases are not prepared chronologically, but rather in a logical fashion based upon the desired endpoint. Approaching trial preparation using this method allows counsel to use proof worksheets to develop the testimony of individual witnesses based upon case analysis.

1.   Closing Argument

Superior trial preparation methodologies begin with closing argument in order to take advantage of the backwards planning process. Trial preparation is a goal oriented endeavor, with the final destination the delivery of a closing argument combining the law, facts, and morality in a fashion designed to move the jury. Closings are the destination, the case-in-chief is the route taken to reach the destination, and the opening statement is the departure point. When done properly using this approach the closing argument contains the words empowering the jury to decide the case in the client's favor. It melds the facts and the law of the case, casting them in a moral light.

A good closing argument demands, sometimes loudly, sometimes quietly, sometimes reluctantly, but demands nonetheless, that the jury do nothing other than what counsel asks. How can an advocate take a jury to that place if they have never identified the destination? It is imperative that trial preparation begins with the closing argument—from that destination all other decisions must flow.

If the legal and factual issues have been correctly identified, and if counsel have chosen the right theme and theory, the closing argument will come as an organic expression of what the previous hard work has shown to be true. When the case has not been properly analyzed counsel will struggle to find a closing argument that makes sense, fitting the facts and the law of the case.

There is great danger in choosing a closing argument that does not organically spring from the facts and the law. Counsel may sound wonderful delivering it, but the jury will be left cold in the end and will turn to the side whose argument makes the most sense, both rationally and emotionally. Later in this text we will devote a considerable amount of time in the steps necessary to craft such closing arguments, for now counsel should internalize the belief that effective trial preparation requires beginning at the end, with closings. If counsel cannot see themselves standing before the jury in that moment, with those words, then they have not effectively analyzed the case and are not yet ready to truly prepare for trial. If they have, it is time to lay the groundwork for admitting the evidence by developing the testimony of witnesses during the case-in-chief.

2.   Case-in-Chief

Once the final destination is chosen, counsel must choose the route to get there. The testimony of witnesses is the primary means available to introduce evidence at trial. For every fact that the case analysis has identified that must be argued in the closing argument, a witness must be questioned to introduce that fact. The earlier case analysis established a legal theory and moral theme, during the case-in-chief counsel use them to determine which witnesses to call, and what to ask them.

Each witness is a piece of the puzzle counsel is building for the jury. This includes not only their own witnesses, but the opponent's as well. By connecting expected testimony to the closing argument, advocates increase the persuasive power of their case. This process is double edged. Not only should counsel identify the issues their witnesses will testify about, they should also identify issues to either introduce or buttress through the cross examination of opposing counsel's witnesses.

By taking the time to do this, counsel test the validity of their theme and theory and also identify crucial testimony that must be asked of witnesses on direct and cross. This type of case analysis produces a template that guides counsel in selecting, questioning, and preparing witnesses. The jury hears the witnesses testifying and supporting counsel's legal theory and moral theme. This is accomplished through the use of proof analysis worksheets during case analysis in order to further refine the presentation of witness testimony during trial.

The use of this process is not limited to factual issues for the case-in-chief. The judge will rule upon motions and objections during the trial. The ability to produce questions supporting the admissibility or suppression of testimony or physical evidence is critical. Knowing that certain instructions from the judge will be given to the jury before deliberations empowers counsel to make certain that the witnesses testify in a manner supporting the court's instructions on the impact of the law on the facts.

Consider the following scenario based upon the timeless bedtime story of Little Red Riding Hood. Counsel is defending the woodsman. The preparation of the proof analysis worksheet would begin as follows:

Proof Analysis Worksheet: State v. Woodsman Charge: Premeditated Murder		
Elements	**Method of Proof**	**Defect or Attack**
Certain person is dead That the death was the result of an oct or omission by the accused;	Coroner will testify that wolf died as a result of axe wounds Red Riding Hood will testify the wolf was in the closet when the huntsman killed it	Defense has potential necessity or defense of others defense. May also raise mistake of fact as to dangerous nature of the wolf Little Red Riding Hood will testify she was screaming, in fear for her life, and sobbing at the time the wolf was killed
That the killing was unlawful; That at the time of the killing the accused had a premeditated design to kill	Grandmother will testify that wolf did not eat her when he had the chance Wolf's mother will testify he was a pacifist and vegetarian	Huntsman can testify as to his state of mind if he takes the stand

Using this approach allows counsel to foreshadow the judge's instructions during their closing argument. The jury hears counsel discuss how the law works, and the judge confirms counsel's statements, increasing their credibility in the eyes of the jury by instructing the jury on the law in accordance with counsel's argument during closing. As a consequence, counsel appear fair, impartial, and correct. This makes them trustworthy in the eyes of the jury.

3.   Opening Statements

Opening statements are the first thing counsel do once the trial starts but the last thing counsel prepare. This is the beginning point in the journey with the jury. During opening statements counsel identify the final destination and explain the route the trial will travel to reach the destination. This allows them to tell the story of what happened and to then forecast the relevant law in light of the relevant legal issues.

Proper case analysis creates a persuasive opening statement that is not argumentative, but does persuade. Most advocates either descend into argument during their opening statement or spend a great deal of time explaining the process of what the jury can expect throughout the course of the trial. They do this because they have not connected the three main sections of trial together as described when the Rule of Threes is used to create coherence and persuasion.

A fact heavy storytelling approach to opening statements avoids the pitfalls of an argumentative objection and engages the emotional and intellectual reasoning capabilities of the jury appropriately. Practically speaking it does not make sense to argue about the case during the opening statement. The jury does not yet have any context in which to place argument, they simply do not know enough to reason their way through it.

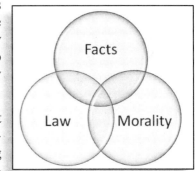

This is the time to tell the story of what happened so that the jury can begin to decide whose story makes sense. Opening statements are concerned with what happened—counsel will get a chance during closing arguments to tell the jury why it matters. Openings are the best chance to set the stage for the testimony and arguments that will follow. It is not, however, an appropriate time to argue what the evidence means - after all the jury has not heard any testimony at this point in the trial.

4. Bringing It All Together

The following series of diagrams explain how to cohesively prepare the case, regardless of its relative complexity or simplicity. It is a simple concept that builds off of the earlier work done using proof analysis worksheets by combining that work with an application of the Rule of Threes. Before counsel can work through this process they must first complete a proof analysis for each factual or legal issue they intend to address in the case.

The proof analysis worksheets identify the relevant evidence counsel will produce and the source of the evidence. This foundational work is crucial to properly prepare for trial. Often this additional work uncovers new legal theories or facts not available earlier in the life of the case. The completed proof analysis worksheets connect with the following explanation to provide a cohesive graphical method assisting in preparing the case for trial. The concept is deceptively easy, allowing for additional layers of complexity as needed. This type of analysis can be done with nothing more than a piece of paper and a pencil by drawing three columns and labeling them as follows:

Opening Statement	Case-in-Chief	Closing Argument

Think about the final destination. What is needed to bring the jury to the conclusions requiring them to find in the client's favor? How will the facts presented connect to the law and the sense of injustice captured by the moral theme? List those items in the Closing Argument column:

Now that counsel knows where they are going they have to choose the route to reach the destination. This guides the approach to both direct and cross examination. This allows them to identify the subject matter of each direct and cross examination they need to conduct based upon the argument that must be made during closings.

Each witness connects to a fact that will be discussed during the case-in-chief. Failure to identify evidence in this fashion directly impacts their ability to prove to the case. The beauty of this approach is that it provides them with a context for everything done at trial. In the diagram this can be represented as follows:

Opening Statement	Case-in-Chief	Closing Argument
		Moral Theme **Factual Theory** (evidence) 　facts 1, 2, & 3 **Legal Theory** (law) 　facts 4, 5, & 6

The connection between the moral theme, factual theory, and legal theory becomes obvious using this tool. If counsel want to talk about a fact or get a legal instruction from the judge in closing, they have to produce the fact through either their own witness or opposing counsel's. The same holds true for most persuasive facts and necessary legal rulings.

Laying out case preparation in this manner identifies substantive weaknesses in the case based upon a lack of legal precedent, a dearth of facts, or a moral theme simply comporting with the facts and the law. This is a warning bell to perform additional investigation until the dichotomies are resolved. If counsel cannot do so, it is time to settle this particular case if it is a civil matter, or plead it out if a criminal one.

Opening Statement	Case-in-Chief	Closing Argument
	Directs: W 1: facts (1) & (6) W 2: facts (2) & (5) **Crosses:** W 1: supporting fact W 1: credibility W 2: facts (3) & (4)	**Moral Theme** **Factual Theory** (evidence) facts 1, 2, & 3 **Legal Theory** (law) facts 4, 5, & 6

The last step in using this diagram is to list what is needed in the opening statement. Opening statements serve as the bookend for the closing argument. Openings and closings contain the same strands of law, facts and morality. The emphasis is different depending upon the timeline of the trial, but the core value remains the same throughout the trial. Analyzing the case in this fashion allows counsel to use persuasive teaching techniques that both science and experience tell us work.

Opening Statement	Case-in-Chief	Closing Argument
Moral Theme (hook) **Tell the story** (facts) facts 1, 2, 3 **Foreshadow the law** (instructions) facts 4, 5, 6	**Directs:** W 1: facts (1) & (6) W 2: facts (2) & (5) **Crosses:** W 1: supporting fact W 1: credibility W 2: facts (3) & (4)	**Moral Theme** **Factual Theory** (evidence) facts 1, 2, & 3 **Legal Theory** (law) facts 4, 5, & 6

Consider the relationships between the three basic portions of a trial created on the previous page. By viewing them in a connected way counsel can create a coherent message for the jury. Although it was planned in reverse by beginning at the end, it plays forward when presented. The jury hears where they are going to go and how they will get there in the opening statement. They are then transported to the final destination through the testimony and reminded of where they are and what that means during the closing argument. To the juror, counsel has told them what they are going to do, done it, and then reminded them while explaining what it all means.

Taking this approach creates credibility. The jury will view attorneys adopting this approach as an ethical, straight-shooter who they can trust. More importantly, counsel will actually be an ethical advocate that has done the ground work to ensure success.

We have spent a great deal of time discussing case analysis and preparation. The goal has been to identify the "what." By that I mean case analysis and preparation. Both help us to discover the evidence that must be admitted under the law to win the case. It is a process driven by both logical and creative thought. The final product is capable of being objectively tested to ensure the core concepts of the law, persuasion and professionalism are met.

Counsel must remember that methods used to perform case analysis are individual in nature, and each advocate must, to a certain extent, discover through practice the way that works best for them. The suggestions in this section are just that, suggestions. Each attorney will, over time, develop the approach that best suits their individual personality and the nature of their practice. The important point to take from this section is that, regardless of the process used, counsel must analyze their case from a moral, factual and legal perspective. Only by doing so will they be able to find their most persuasive voice.

H.   Examples of Case Analysis

In each of the following examples counsel have been given a case file and tasked to conduct case analysis for their senior trial attorney. The examples represent various ways that attorneys deal with case analysis, reflecting the elements based, or evidence based, approach discussed earlier. Counsel should review the suggested materials for potential ways to proceed when conducting their own case analysis.

Example:

The following chart was prepared to identify the location of specific pieces of evidence identified during case analysis. Counsel can use this sort of approach to build a graphical representation for the concepts discussed earlier in this section. This chart was produced by counsel preparing for trial in a child custody case. Note how counsel have used the good, bad, and neutral fact approach to identify relevant areas to consider in deciding how to try the case.

Statement	Pg; Ln	Good for ⊓	Good for Δ	Neutral
Name is Ryan Thomson	1:5			X
Specialization in family studies	1:7 / 2:5	Appropriate field to analyze this situation		
Degree in psychology from State College	1: 9	Can talk about psychology stuff		
M.S. in Behavior and Cognitive Neuroscience and a Ph.D. in Childhood Development from Tulane University	1:10	Can discuss this stuff		
M.S. program included study of brain and what makes humans behave in certain ways.	1:13	X		
Focused on neurodevelopment and ran studies about infant cognition	1:15	Understands how infants brain's work (attachment issues)		
Interned for non-profit, tutoring inner-city children who had just lost one or both parents	1:17	Practical experience in this field		
Interested in relationships between families and how that dynamic impacts children of all ages	1:19 -2:3	X		
Worked at an infant cognition lab in MA and stayed there an extra year after finishing Ph.D.	2:5	More practical experience that Defense Expert		
works as an assistant prof in Developmental Psychology department with focus on childhood development and familial studies	2:9	Academic study in the area		
Present at Joey Reynold's deposition	2:13			X

Statement	Pg; Ln	Good for ∏	Good for Δ	Neutral
Joey Reynolds is present at this deposition	2:15			X
Generally agree with Joey Reynolds	2:17			
Child should be placed with Roberta Seay	2:19	**Ultimate issue and our legal position**		
Relationship between child and biological mother is more significant than relationship between the twins	3:5	More important to keep Jr. with RS than keep Jr. with William		
Readily admit that this isn't perfect situation	3:5		X	
Given the choices, the child would thrive with R.S.	3:7	Good to keep Jr. with RS		
Met with R.S. for about 4 hours	3:11	Relatively long period of time		
During mtg talked about loss of husband, birth of twins, giving up William, surrogacy agreement, and how R.S. intended to raise baby Joey	3:13	Comprehensive evaluation performed (arguably)		
Reached conclusion that R.S. is a wonderful mother	3:19	Fit to be a mother		
Been through horrible few months, but she is grounded and knows what she wants	3:19 -4:3	Considered evidence that negatively impacts R.S., and still believes that RS is best place for Jr.		
Talked with Doris Presley (R.S.'s friend), and Peggy Gordon (R..S's cousin)	4:7			

Statement	Pg; Ln	Good for ∏	Good for ∆	Neutral
Presley and Gordon are supportive of R.S., and are willing to help in any way they can	4:10	Support system in place for RS		

You will note that this chart is a working document designed to identify in a quick and dirty fashion the relevant evidence, how it connects to the strength of the plaintiff or defense's case, and its location.

Example:

The following chart is based upon an element by element analysis of a charge in a criminal case. It is alleged that an individual assaulted Paula Osmer with a blunt instrument causing an injury that eventually resulted in her death. At issue in the case is the identify of the assailant, with other potential suspects identified but not investigated by the state.

PE 1 for ID

There are substantive bias issues between the witnesses, some degree of controversy about the ability of the witnesses to observe the events on the night of the assault, and the lack of physical evidence.

The charge reflected in the element chart that follows is:

Charge I: (1) That the defendant performed the acts that caused the death of Paula Osmer; and (2) that the defendant performed the acts that caused great bodily harm to Paula Osmer; and (3) he knew that his acts created a strong probability of death or great bodily harm to Paula Osmer

Element	Evidence	Location
That the defendant performed the acts that caused the death of Paula Osmer, and	"I can see two people in the alley, but it is not well lit. They are struggling."	1:38 911 Call KC
	"No, no - just one person. I think I know who. . ." Something about the way he was acting that night clued me in to his guilt....	1:38 911 Call KC
That the defendant performed the acts that caused the death of Paula Osmer, and	The voice of Mark Baer was also coming from the law office because I heard Paula say things like, "You got to give me my ticket," and "I am not putting up with the bullshit any more." She was obviously upset. I saw her start to cry when he raised his voice.....	April 13 statement to police Paragraph 1 First Page KC

Element	Evidence	Location
That the defendant performed the acts that caused the death of Paula Osmer, and	Then she went back into the office through the same alley door. Within a couple of seconds she came out again, and was tussling with someone who was wearing a black coat. I recognized that black coat, because it belongs to my roommate, and I see it all the time. There was a lot of movement.	April 13 statement to police paragraph 1 second page KC
He intended to kill or do great bodily harm to Paula, and	So I went back to bed. Then about a half hour later I woke up again. I could hear the shouting again, and Paula was yelling again. Then I heard her say, "Stay away!" and then I heard a scream. I am sure Paula was the one screaming. Then I heard nothing."	April 13 statement to police paragraph 1 second page KC
He intended to kill or do great bodily harm to Paula, and	Then Paula went down on the bricks in the alley. She did not seem to be moving, and I realized that there was someone still over her in the alley.	April 13 statement to police Paragraph 1 Second page KC
He intended to kill or do great bodily harm to Paula, and	I believe Mark took her money – her ticket – and would not return it to her. These rip-offs are happening all the time in this country.	Supplementary Interview Witness Report Paragraph 3 Seventh Page

Element	Evidence	Location
He knew that his acts created a strong probability of death or great bodily harm to Paula	So I went back to bed. Then about a half hour later I woke up again. I could hear the shouting again, and Paula was yelling again. Then I heard her say, "Stay away!" and then I heard a scream. I am sure Paula was the one screaming. Then I heard nothing."	April 13 statement to police paragraph 1 second page KC
	I heard a sound like a bat hitting a watermelon, then everything was silent.	Handwritten statement provided sua sponte by the witness to the ADA three days before trial

This chart is a section of a multiple element chart used to arrange the contents of the case file on an element by element analysis. It is a method of analysis discussed inter alia, and is a common approach, particularly in the office of many district attorneys.

Counsel should select a method of case analysis that is no more complicated than required to master the facts of the case while also being sufficiently comprehensive and sophisticated as to ensure that nothing is missed. This balancing act is a necessary component of case analysis, and is something that most attorneys learn by doing. When making decisions about how to proceed counsel should also consider what programs or approaches are available as part of the customs or processes of the firm or entity where they work.

Counsel will discover, over time, the degree of analysis they must conduct to become comfortable with the case and capable of navigating the substance of the factual and legal issues effectively during the compressed world of an actual trial. The degree of focus, and the nature of the focus, varies, and is influenced by the nature of the work, the quality of the attorneys, and the jurisdiction within which the case is tried. It is a best practice to over prepare when first starting developing case analysis skills. It is much easier to remove information counsel later decide is not relevant - it is difficult, if not impossible, to manufacture evidence or an understanding of the relevant law in the moment.

Once the case has been fully analyzed and the evidence prepared for presentation it is time to select the jury.

I. Conclusion

We have spent a great deal of time in this chapter learning case analysis and preparation. The goal has been to identify the "what." By that, we mean case analysis and preparation shows counsel what evidence must be admitted under the law to win their case. It is a process requiring logical thought and creativity. The final product is capable of being objectively tested to ensure that the core concepts of the law, persuasion, and professionalism have been met. At the same time, methods used to perform case analysis are individual in nature. Each attorney must discover through practice the way that works best for them.

We have focused on certain overarching themes in case analysis that relate back to concepts of pathos, ethos, and logos. Counsel should try them but not feel tied to them. The important thing is to develop a process analyzing the case from a moral, factual, and legal perspective in light of the issues the finder of fact must decide.

-Notes-

Chapter 3: Jury Selection

A. Introduction 65
B. The Right to a Jury Trial 66
C. Deciding if You Want a Jury 67
D. How Jury Selection Works 68
E. Purpose and Process of Jury Selection.............76
F. Preparing for Voir Dire 80
G. Voir Dire 83
H. Examples of Voir Dire Questions 96

A.   Introduction

Jury selection is a skill most attorneys routinely struggle with. It is both situationally and personality dependent, with multiple variables present each and every time a jury is chosen. Your best practice is to approach the process with clearly defined goals based upon the law and the facts of your particular case. This section reviews the process that many jurisdictions employ when selecting a jury, and then provides an approach to jury selection based upon experience, research, and common sense. When you are done with this section you should have a clear plan for how you will approach choosing a jury.

The primary purpose of jury selection is to obtain information about potential jurors so you can make intelligent decisions about whom to seat on the jury, an65d whom to excuse. We will discuss the legal basis for excusing jurors in this section, and then turn to the process for satisfying that legal basis.

Why Voir Dire?

- Identify jurors to challenge for cause
- Identify jurors to peremptorily challenge
- Educate potential jurors about facts in the case
- Educate potential jurors about the legal issues
- Eliminate shocks and surprises
- Obtain promises of fairness
- Develop rapport with the jury pool

When done properly, jury selection allows the parties to intelligently exercise peremptory challenges and challenges for cause; eliminating potential jurors who are prejudiced, biased, or inflexible. You will also use jury selection to properly educate potential jurors as to particular factual and legal issues in the case; eliminate shock and surprises; obtain promises of fairness; and develop a rapport with the jury pool. Many of the questions concerning fairness and transparency have a sound basis in persuasion theory, while others are nothing more than a representation of expected practices in that particular jurisdiction. From an advocacy perspective the process should be focused on "mindful" questioning designed to accomplish specifically identified goals.

B.   The Right to a Jury Trial

Our federal and state constitutions establish rights to a jury trial, a right frequently reinforced by statute. The United States Constitution guarantees the right to a jury trial in federal court for both civil and criminal cases. The right to a jury trial in state court for criminal cases is also guaranteed by the due process clause of the Fourteenth Amendment. The United States Supreme Court has built on these foundations to strengthen the role of the jury, particularly in criminal cases.

The right to a jury trial in criminal cases can be found in Article III, the Sixth Amendment, and the Due Process Clause of the United States Constitution. The right to a jury trial in civil cases at the federal level is found in the Seventh Amendment. In *Duncan v. Louisiana*, 391 U.S. 145, 88 S.Ct. 1444, 20 L.Ed.2d 491 (1968), the United States Supreme Court explained that the right to a jury trial prevents oppression by the government, protecting against unfounded criminal charges and judges that are too compliant to authority.

Our right to a jury trial reflects a fundamental decision about how we approach the power of the court—with fear. This fear of unchecked power, of overzealous prosecutors, or poor judges, led to the development of the right to a jury trial, particularly in criminal cases, along with the presumption of innocence.

The importance of preserving the right to a jury trial cannot be overstated. For many citizens jury duty is one of the few times in their adult life when they are fulfilling a civic duty. In a very real sense, the jury process is a promise to continue with our great democratic experiment.

The jury members represent the community, bringing community values to the decision making process. The presence of jurors who are not trained in the law has impacted the development of evidentiary and procedural law, as well as greatly influencing advocacy in the courtroom.

C.   Deciding if You Want a Jury

In most jurisdictions the right to a jury trial exists at both the state and federal level for criminal and civil cases. The decision on whether or not to exercise that right is an important choice made by the client. In many circumstances it may be in the client's best interest to waive the right to a jury trial and proceed on a judge alone basis, in others a jury may be the client's best opportunity for a favorable verdict.

When deciding whether or not to elect trial by jury, you should advise your client based upon an understanding of the factual, legal, and emotional issues in the case. Generally speaking, if the emotional and factual issues are repugnant, inflammatory, or not accepted as appropriate by society, it may be best to elect a judge alone trial and proceed on a legally based argument about the law—not the facts. Conversely, if the facts, and the emotional appeal of the case are in the client's favor, a jury is usually preferable.

Part of the thought process must include knowledge of the judge assigned to the case and the probable make up of potential juries. While the personal preferences or backgrounds of the court and jury should not matter, in fact they do—a great deal. A plaintiff friendly judge will see, on average, many more bench trials than a defense friendly judge. Why? Because the plaintiff, as the party with the burden of proof, usually chooses the forum. In a criminal setting, a defense friendly judge, either for sentencing or findings, will, all things being equal, see more bench trials than jury trials. The attitudes of the finder of fact matter, when they can be known. Judge's acquire a reputation over time in this regard. Competent counsel take the time to research prospective judges carefully and then include that knowledge in the choice of forum.

You should understand that choosing a jury or a judge alone forum is a decision best made once the attorney has analyzed the case completely. Attorneys often fear juries, bringing many of the prejudices about lay people to the jury selection process. This is unfortunate because a well chosen jury is often the best chance for an equitable balancing of justice and compassion. Decisions about whether or not to request a jury trial should be based on the issues within the case, and not your individual fears about your ability to properly sway a jury, or a judge.

D.   How Jury Selection Works

Jury selection is controlled by local custom, statutes, and practice rules, and varies from jurisdiction to jurisdiction. In federal courts, criminal cases have 12 jurors, civil cases have 6. In state court it varies from 6, 8 or 12 jurors in both civil and criminal cases.

The number of alternates is controlled by local rules or statute, with some degree of flexibility given to the court based upon the complexity of the issues, or degree of media interest in the case. The goal is to have enough alternate jurors to make it to the finality of a verdict, without wasting the time of potential jury members who might otherwise serve as voting members for another case.

You must check the appropriate governing practice rule or statute when proceeding. Most state courts require a 12 person jury in a capital case, and it is always a best practice to verify how many jurors will decide a particular issue. Once you know how many jury members will be selected, the next step is to actually choose them. In order to effectively select a jury, advocates must know going in the answer to some fundamental questions. Including:

- What jury selection system does the jurisdiction use

- The manner, type and permissible subjects when questioning potential jury members

- Legal issues present during jury selection

- How challenges are apportioned and utilized

1. Jury Selection System

You should remember that the system used depends upon the local practice rules, preferences of the judge and any applicable statutes. Attorneys must consult the applicable resources when selecting juries in a jurisdiction with which they are unfamiliar. This portion of the trial, more so than any other, is driven by local custom and judicial preference. A good starting point as a best practice is to watch someone else select a jury for a similar case in the same jurisdiction whenever possible.

The group of potential jurors assembled by the court are referred to as the venire. The venire is assembled based upon the local requirements, often being generated by either voter registration or some other neutral means acceptable to the court. Once the venire has been assembled at the courthouse, they are apportioned to various courts where the judge controls the questioning process by which potential jury members are taken from the venire and become members of a particular jury. The questioning process is called voir dire, and the pronunciation is those two words is different from place to place, and is an inside joke for many trial lawyers.

There are several different systems that a particular court or judge may use to control the voir dire process. Generally speaking, questioning is either controlled by the court, controlled by the attorneys, or some hybrid system that combines questions by the court with follow up questions by counsel. Some jurisdictions, most notably federal courts, have moved to a judge only approach, while allowing the attorneys to provide written questions the judge that the court may, or may not, put to the potential jurors.

In all three systems of questioning it has become relatively common to have jurors fill out questionnaires prior to voir dire. These questionnaires are used to address juror attitudes concerning potential lines of inquiry that advocates do not wish to ask face to face. Such lines of questioning might include bias issues, such as race, gender or sexuality.

Some cases concern causes of action or offenses that are either repugnant or run the danger of improperly inflaming the passions of the jury during jury selection. Questionnaires are a great way to identify issues that might otherwise destroy the potential impartiality of the venire if addressed during group questioning. If the court agrees for the need to ask the jury about those issues, the questions will be posed by the court to the jury. Using the judge to ask these type of questions can minimize the possibility of a particular attorney being associated with an idea or issue.

There are two types of challenges that remove potential jurors from a particular jury—challenges for cause and peremptory challenges. You can "challenge a prospective juror for cause" when their answers to voir dire questions establish they will not be able to serve as a fair and impartial juror in a particular case. Peremptory challenges are given to each side based upon the local rules of practice, local rules of court, or by statute. Peremptory challenges are subject to challenge by opposing counsel if they appear to have been racially motivated, and are finite in number. Challenges for cause, on the other hand, are not limited to a particular number, but are instead based upon the answers of the potential jurors to voir dire questions. They are theoretically infinite in number—subject to the trial judge's control of the process.

Challenges for cause are usually case dependent. For example, if a prospective juror's immediate family member was the victim of a sexual assault, they would most likely be challenged for cause if part of the venire for a sexual assault case. The case dependent nature of challenges for cause is one of the primary reasons for voir dire, it is often difficult, if not impossible, to properly identify issues that support a challenge for cause through questionnaires or group voir dire conducted by the trial judge.

Advocates use both challenges for cause and peremptory challenges to deselect those potential jurors they identify as objectionable. In a very real sense, the selection of a jury is actually the deselection of those jurors who cannot fairly and impartially decide the case. The preference, particularly in the 21st century, is for jurors who have not arrived at some predetermined opinion about the case as a result of exposure to the media coverage of the case.

2. Permissible Subjects

Historically courts provided a great deal of latitude during the jury selection process, with some jurisdictions allowing for complete attorney control of jury selection. The modern movement has been away from this approach. Most jurisdictions now allow questioning, but only under the control and direction of the trial judge. This attitude about who controls the questioning process has influenced not only how the questions are posed to the potential jurors, but what may be asked.

Generally speaking, the questions posed by counsel and the court are designed to identify reasons that a juror could not serve. The court will normally handle administrative reasons that might prevent the potential juror from serving. In most jurisdictions reasons that are accepted for excusal include financial hardship, inability to secure child care, predisposition concerning the case, or predisposition concerning the legal issues present in the case. These types of issues are often identified in the applicable local rule or statute covering jury selection.

The court has the ability, through rehabilitative questions, to legally cure some of these potential conflicts, and will often do so, thereby effectively preventing counsel from raising a challenge for cause. Consider the following situation where a potential juror has a predetermined strong opinion about the relevant legal statute.

Example:

> *Judge:* Do any members of the potential jury have a strong opinion concerning the Driving Under the Influence laws, commonly referred to as DUIs, in our state? If so please raise your right hand.

Judge: Potential juror number 6, I noticed that you raised your right hand. What is your opinion concerning these laws?

Juror 6: I think that you should not get a trial if you blow over the legal limit. It ought to be automatic. If you blow over the legal limit you should go directly to jail.

Judge: Potential juror 6, despite this personal opinion, do you promise to follow the instructions of this court?

Juror 6: Of course. You are the judge and I will do what you say.

Judge: Can you promise that you will set your personal opinion aside and apply the law as I instruct?

Juror 6: Yes.

Judge: (In those jurisdictions where the court allows questioning by counsel during jury selection) Do either counsel have any questions based upon my questions to the jury?

In the example above, the judge identified a potential viable issue that would support a challenge for cause, but then rehabilitated the potential juror so that they might continue to serve. Counsel for the defense would prefer to challenge this juror for cause, but that will be more difficult after the rehabilitation by the court. They may be forced to use a peremptory challenge to strike this juror, potentially losing the opportunity to strike someone else later.

If counsel for the defense still wants to make a challenge for cause, they should first try to reestablish the basis for a challenge for cause through questioning. If the jurisdiction does not allow counsel questioning, such as in federal court, the defense would be forced to use a peremptory challenge or accept the potential juror. It is through this fashion that the trial judge is able to control the jury selection process, eventually seating a jury, even in complex cases.

In most jurisdictions the court, at a minimum, handles preliminary issues of suitability for jury duty. In jurisdictions where counsel are allowed to question the potential jurors, issues normally associated with potential challenges for cause based upon the specific nature of the case are dealt with by counsel, and not the court. Most judges are careful to not address such case specific issues because of a fear that the judge's authority might inadvertently or improperly persuade jurors about the issues in controversy during jury selection.

3. Legal Issues

In *Batson v. Kentucky*, 476 U.S. 79 (1986), the United States Supreme Court applied the equal protection clause to an analysis of peremptory challenges by the prosecution in a criminal case. The Court established that once defense counsel makes a prima facie showing that there appears to be a pattern of racial discrimination to prosecutorial peremptory challenges, the burden shifts to the prosecution to establish a race-neutral reason for the challenge. This standard has been extended to gender and ethnicity as well. Counsel should note that the standard is not absolute, but at a minimum an understanding of this doctrine serves as an excellent starting point for counsel when selecting a jury.

A *Batson* Challenge is the most common legal issue raised during jury selection. Under *Batson*, peremptory challenges may not be used to remove individuals from the jury pool based solely upon their race—counsel must have a neutral reason other than race for their decision to strike a particular juror. Counsel should take note that *Batson* applies to peremptory challenges and not to challenges for cause. Challenges for cause are based upon the attitudes of the jury to issues relevant to the case, and are therefore less likely to be based upon racial bias. Nonetheless, counsel must be prepared to answer a *Batson* objection to the exercise of a challenge for cause if race is raised as an alternative reason for the challenge. Counsel are not allowed to exercise peremptory challenges in a discriminatory manner based on race or gender. This prohibition applies to both parties. It is not necessary for the defendant and the challenged potential jurors to be of the same racial group before a *Batson* challenge may be raised. In order to overcome a *Batson* issue counsel must articulate a neutral reason for the challenge.

For example, if the defense were to challenge, under *Batson*, the prosecution's peremptory challenge of a potential minority juror, the prosecutor would be required to provide the court with a race neutral reason for striking that potential juror. Counsel must articulate race or gender neutral reasons, depending upon the situation, that are unambiguous and supported by the record. Counsel must be prepared to articulate as many neutral reasons as possible in order to protect the record. Opposing counsel must force the challenging party to specify a race-neutral or gender-neutral reason for the challenge in order to preserve the issue for appeal.

Example: In the following case, the defense counsel has a client who is a member of a racial minority. The state has just used a peremptory challenge to remove a potential juror who is a member of the same racial minority as the defendant.

Defense: Your Honor, the defense objects to the prosecution's use of a peremptory challenge on potential juror 8. We ask that they be required to state a race neutral reason for the peremptory challenge, given that the potential juror in question is a member of a racial minority.

Judge: I agree. Does the State have a race-neutral reason for this challenge?

State: We do your Honor. While we acknowledge that potential juror 8 is a member of an ethnic minority, we are not using our peremptory based upon that fact. We are exercising our peremptory challenge based upon the physical actions of the potential juror during questioning.

Judge: How so counsel?

State: During questioning the juror in question gave off several different physical clues indicating his lack of comfort with counsel for the state. Those included crossing his arms, refusing to make eye contact with us, answering in one word answers, and occasionally snorting in response to our questions. Taken together these actions have created a sense on the state's part that this juror is not receptive to our position.

Judge: Counsel do you wish to challenge this juror for cause?

State: While we would like to do so your Honor, the juror's answers do not rise to that level. That is why we are using our peremptory challenge.

Defense: Your Honor, the arguments put forth by the state are not sufficient, and are in fact a subterfuge for what is clearly a racially motivated challenge, which is improper under *Batson*.

Judge: Counsel, I agree with the state and overrule your objection to their peremptory challenge. Your objection is noted for the record. Let's move on to the next potential juror.

The above is a clear example of how the defense should object when raising a *Batson* issue, and how the state should respond, with a proper ruling from the judge, based upon the actions of counsel.

4. How Challenges Work

Peremptory challenges are defined by statute or procedural rule, and grow out of the customary practice within the jurisdiction. They can vary from place to place, but a survey of most jurisdictions indicates that the number of peremptory challenges in civil cases generally falls in a range of 2 – 4, with 3 peremptory challenges being the most common number. Counsel should be aware that the number of challenges can be modified by the court. For example, in a case where there is one plaintiff and three co-defendants most rules allow the three co-defendants to each receive 3 peremptory challenges, totaling 9 for the defense side. In that instance, either by rule or through modification of the rule by the court, the plaintiff should normally also receive 9 peremptory challenges.

In criminal cases, the number of peremptory challenges is tied to the nature and complexity of the crime. Capital cases receive more peremptory challenges than other murder cases, with felonies receiving more peremptory challenges than felonies. Peremptory challenges in both civil and criminal cases are jurisdictionally dependent and it is counsel's responsibility to identify the approved number of peremptory challenges, as well as potential arguments that may be raised to expand that number.

It is generally accepted that the need for peremptory challenges comes from the traditions of the law, not from any constitutional requirement. The lack of constitutional underpinning for peremptory challenges allows each jurisdiction to deal with them as they see fit. In most cases, the number of peremptory challenges is influenced by case law. The development of *Batson* and its progeny has underlined how constitutional constraints may be placed on peremptory challenges.

Challenges for cause are based upon constitutional rights of due process, procedural rules, and by statute. A good example of a civil rule of civil procedure defining what constitutes a challenged for cause can be found in the Florida Rules of Civil Procedure. Rule 1.431(c) defines Challenges for Cause as follows:

> Florida Rule of Civil Procedure 1.431 (c) Challenge for Cause, providing that:
>
> (1) On motion of any party, the court shall examine any prospective juror on oath to determine whether that person is related, within the third degree, to (i) any party, (ii) the attorney of any party, or (iii) any other person or entity against whom liability or blame is alleged in the pleadings, or is related to any person alleged to have been wronged or injured by the commission of the wrong for the trial of which the juror is called, or has any interest in the action, or has formed or expressed any opinion, or is sensible of any bias or prejudice concerning it, or is an employee or has been an employee of any party or any other person or entity against whom liability or blame is alleged in the pleadings, within 30 days before the trial. A party objecting to the juror may introduce any other competent evidence to support the objection. If it appears that the juror does not stand indifferent to the action or any of the foregoing grounds of objection exists or that the juror is otherwise incompetent, another shall be called in that juror's place.
>
> (2) The fact that any person selected for jury duty from bystanders or the body of the county and not from a jury list lawfully selected has served as a juror in the court in which that person is called at any other time within 1 year is a ground of challenge for cause.
>
> (3) When the nature of any civil action requires a knowledge of reading, writing, and arithmetic, or any of them, to enable a juror to understand the evidence to be offered, the fact that any prospective juror does not possess the qualifications is a ground of challenge for cause.

Challenges for cause in criminal cases are more broadly defined that in civil cases, with the court having discretion to ensure that the constitutional right to a fair trial is preserved. The general qualifications to be a juror are found in the applicable state statutes, and a failure to meet those qualifications can form the basis for a challenge for cause.

Additionally, each jurisdiction has well developed case law concerning what constitutes a potential challenge for cause. Finally, counsel should consider it a best practice to carefully consider the legal, factual, and moral issues present in the case when identifying potential challenges for cause based upon the bias or prejudice of potential jurors.

E.   Purpose and Process of Jury Selection

The phrase jury selection is a misnomer. The actual process is better defined as jury deselection. The goal is to identify those jurors who are not able to fairly and impartially decide the case. You would be well advised to let go of the notion that you will be able to identify and select jurors that will decide the case your way. The best practice is to approach jury selection as an opportunity to identify potential jurors that are so biased against your case that they should be struck.

While this may seem like a paradigm shift, it actually comports with the law, and is a manageable goal during voir dire. Bias is easier to identify and query than friendship. When done properly voir dire is an excellent opportunity for counsel to get a sense of how individual jurors respond to questions designed to identify bias for or against their legal theory, factual theory, and moral theme. Bias against a fundamental concept upon which a particular side has built their case is a clear indicator that a particular juror should not be selected to serve on the jury.

Appropriate approaches to voir dire will be driven by the attitude of the court to the process. If the jurisdiction approaches voir dire in an open fashion, attorneys will be free to spend their time as they see fit during the voir dire process. While some jurisdictions still follow this approach, most are more restrictive in their approach to the process, forcing counsel to identify the reasons behind their lines of questioning.

It is a best practice for you to select voir dire questions carefully, refraining from asking questions insulting the intelligence of potential jurors. A good place to begin is by choosing topics for inquiry and presentation of questions which are carefully tailored to the facts of the case. When doing so, be sensitive to the education and experience level of potential jurors, as well as the practice requirements of the trial judge. Those practical requirements may address the use of questionnaires, providing the court with proposed questions, the use of group voir dire before individual voir dire, and the subject matter for potential lines questioning. You must know the preferences of the trial judge, and in those instances where the rights of their client are not affected, modify the questions accordingly. When justice require it, advocates must be prepared to establish with the court the basis for any line of questioning the court does not like, preferably with supporting case law when possible.

For example, some judges will agree to review written questions before trial, while others require written questions, especially in serious cases. There are some benefits to this approach in that it allows you to identify and resolve potential problem areas for voir dire outside the presence of the potential jury members. Most trial judges are protective of the jury and view voir dire as an opportunity for counsel to improperly educate the jury or even embarrass citizens attempting to perform their civic duty. In jurisdictions where judges are elected, voir dire is one of the few instances where judges are allowed to "campaign" their voting base. Be sensitive to this potential issue—when in doubt never embarrass a potential juror.

Sometimes, particularly in serious cases, the trial judge may allow questionnaires to the potential jurors. These questionnaires provide counsel with a great deal of information about the members before a single question is asked in court. Judges generally prefer questionnaires because they save court time and avoid embarrassing questions of the potential jurors. Also, jurors, being human beings, are more inclined to answer sensitive and personal questions candidly and honestly on a questionnaire than in the courtroom.

Most "group" voir dire questions can be asked in questionnaires. Often, the use of group questionnaires will identify potential areas of individual voir dire that would otherwise be missed during group questioning. When a juror answers a question that might call for individual voir dire, the court will normally make sure that counsel do not ask the follow up questions during the group voir dire. In many jurisdictions the applicable statute or procedural rule identifies the questioning process for voir dire to include the use of individual voir dire to avoid embarrassment to the potential jurors or inadvertently improperly tainting the venire on certain issues through group voir dire.

You should think of the voir dire process as an inverted triangle, a funnel if you will, going from broad general issues to narrow specific ones that are specific to a potential juror. This approach is often referred to as the "funnel" approach when taking depositions, and it works equally well in jury selection. Group voir dire identifies potential overarching non-bias based

Use the Funnel!

reasons to challenge potential jurors, as well as indicating potentially challengeable areas that are best addressed during individual voir dire.

Individual voir dire is better than group voir dire at identifying jurors that should be challenged for cause. The best practice is to craft questions appropriate to group voir dire that create a reasonable basis to request individual voir dire without embarrassing any individual potential juror. Consider the following exchange from a criminal case where the charged offense is sexual assault. Note how the group question allows the defense attorney to identify a potential challenge for cause without running the risk of embarrassing any member of the venire.

Example: in the following example the defense is conducting group voir dire in an attempt to establish rapport with the venire while beginning the process of identifying potential challenges for cause.

Defense: Members of the jury this case revolves around an alleged violent sexual assault. Because of the nature of this crime there are some questions that I must ask to see if you belong on this particular jury.

Defense: Let's begin with some questions for the group. I would ask that if the answer to my question is yes that you please raise your right hand. Will all of you be willing to do that? If your answer is yes please raise your right hand.

Defense: Thank you very much. Let the record reflect that all members of the venire have agreed to raise their hand if I ask a yes no question and their answer is yes.

Defense: Has anyone heard of this case in the news? (No one raises their hand)

Defense: Negative response from all members of the venire.

Defense: Please listen carefully to my question and only raise your hand if your answer to the question is yes. Has any member of the venire, their close family, or friends, been the victim of sexual assault? If so please raise your right hand.

Defense: Affirmative response from potential jurors 3, 6,
         and 8.

At this point the defense attorney has a choice—they can continue to question each juror about the nature of sexual assault in the group setting, they can change topics, or they can request individual voir dire on these jurors. Usually the court prefers that counsel ask all of their group identified voir dire questions before moving on to individual voir dire, but this is judge and jurisdiction dependent. In any event, because these potential jurors have identified that either they themselves, a family member, or a friend have been the victim of a sexual assault it is best to ask any follow up questions about that assault during individual voir dire. Sufficient basis has been laid to justify individual voir dire and the judge will not only allow it, but expect it for these potential jurors.

Group voir dire questions focus on basic information that allow counsel to identify problematic jurors. Some potential challenges for cause can be perfected during group voir dire, others require individual voir dire before a valid challenge for cause exists. The number and nature of group voir dire questions depend upon the complexity of the case.

Potential jurors are reluctant to answer questions of a sensitive or personal nature in front of others. Most judges now allow individual voir dire, especially after questionnaires have been circulated. Judges realize that many of the general questions asked during group voir dire have been covered by the questionnaires leaving the questions that probe information that could lead to challenges for cause for individual voir dire.

Individual voir dire should be conducted much like the deposition of a witness. Counsel should ask open-ended questions such as "what happened next..." and "how did that make you feel" and "explain that situation for us." The goal is to obtain as much information as possible about a potential disqualifying event or attitude. Understanding the what, when, where, why, and how of the event is normally sufficient to form a challenge for cause—if one exists. Counsel should enquire only to the point that the challenge for cause has been established and then move on.

In other words, counsel should know what happened, when it happened, where it happened, how it happened, why it happened, and what effect it had on the potential juror. When conducting individual voir dire, open ended questions are preferable.

 Open-ended questions let potential jurors answer questions in their own words and way of expression. This gives the court a better insight into their opinions. With that information counsel will be able to fully develop a factual basis to exercise challenges for cause when appropriate. It allows counsel to develop a gut instinct when deciding when and how to use peremptory challenges if a challenge for cause is not warranted.

In some jurisdictions the court will be willing to instruct the potential jurors about defenses or complicated issues of law if counsel requests the opportunity to voir dire in those areas. It is unwise to address legal issues within the case without first letting the judge know that such an inquiry is necessary. Judges are protective of their role as the ultimate arbiter of what the law means, and can become upset when an attorney attempts to instruct jurors about the impact of the law on this particular case.

Asking the judge to first instruct the potential jurors allows the judge to perform her role as the law giver in the trial. This saves time, and, more importantly, may deter the judge from interrupting counsel in front of the jurors when they try to explain an issue of law in order to conduct an effective voir dire.

F.   Preparing for Voir Dire

You should begin preparation for voir dire during the pre-trial litigation process, long before the actual day of jury selection, particularly given the more restrictive approach to jury selection preferred by many courts today. Taking the time to treat voir dire preparation with the same degree of care and consideration reserved for the rest of the trial process makes sense. Proper preparation for voir dire removes the mystery from the process, allowing you to approach jury selection systemically, maximizing the ability to identify and remove potential jurors identified as unacceptable based upon case analysis.

Advocates will always be constrained during jury selection by the judge's approach to the process. You cannot guarantee that sufficient time will be allowed to fully conduct voir dire, or even that the court will allow you to fully inquire into certain areas. While voir dire remains the primary process for jury selection, advocates can prepare to more effectively conduct voir dire by developing a pre-trial process when preparing for voir dire that assists in overcoming the limitations of the process in the courtroom.

The groundwork for sound jury selection occurs long before voir dire begins. It includes surveying the community from which the jury will be selected, conducting focus groups, and presenting the case, or portions thereof, to mock juries. Each of these allow you to not only hone the best theory of the case, they also provide a wealth of information concerning potential jurors that may respond in a similar fashion, based upon criteria they share with the community, focus group, and mock jury.

When you combine these approaches with a well researched and drafted pretrial questionnaire it can take a lot of the uncertainty out of the jury selection process. This becomes particularly important in those jurisdictions where the court has so constrained the jury selection process that it can longer be effectively used by counsel to identify potential jurors that should be removed under the law. As a best practice you should consider using the following tools during the pre-trial stages of jury selection:

- Community surveys - these can include questionnaires, interviews, and focus groups

- Analyzing the respondents - used to develop a "profile" for preferable jury members by comparing the analysis of the respondents to potential jurors

- Mock trials - conduct complete or partial mock trials to gage community reaction to the core issues within the case

- Venire review - once the venire is known counsel can investigate its members and match them to the developed preferred juror profile

- Juror Questionnaire - propose a questionnaire to the court for potential jurors before voir dire is conducted

- Employ a Jury Consultant - assists in developing themes and theories of the case, and provides support during both pre-trial voir dire preparation and jury selection. May also provide support in preparing witnesses to testify based upon the selected jury.

Each of the suggested approaches listed above are designed to inform counsel, providing information that can remove the sense of uncertainty inherent during jury selection. Many of them are both labor intensive and cost intensive, but the basis for doing them can be used by any attorney, regardless of resources, to develop a system approach to jury selection that takes into account the community from which the jury venire is drawn.

This information is needed to create jury profile charts and checklists that are used to screen the venire and to guide the voir dire process. Juror profiles are nothing more than a list of characteristics counsel believe will work in their favor.

Example: You represent the defendant in a wrongful death case where a 13 year old boy was crossing the street with his brothers and sisters in the dark, while not in a crosswalk. Your client was driving the car that struck them, killing two of them and injuring three more. The victims are all members of a minority, as is your client. Both liability and damages are at issue.

Issues to address with potential jurors

- Ever been involved in a car accident
- Attitudes towards traffic rules
- Parents leaving children alone
- Streetlights and traffic accidents
- Specific issues within your factual and moral analysis of the case

Good Jurors:
- College education
- Drivers
- Business owners
- Military Experience
- Preference for rule following
- Prefer structure

Bad Jurors:
- Single parents
- Latch key children
- Service industry
- Do not drive
- Free spirit
- Challenge authority

The creation of jury profile lists and checklists of potential issues serve as a starting point for developing specific lines of questioning, as well as working to keep you on track during the voir dire process. While these can be helpful, you must keep in mind that jury selection is an organic process requiring that you respond in the moment. Some attorneys create lists of characteristics to sort through potential jurors as quickly as possible. Often these lists are based upon factors that can be identified through the use of questionnaires when allowed by the court. While such lists are based in part upon a stereotypical approach to jury selection, they can assist an overworked attorney who must make jury selection quickly. The possible factor include:

- Age
- Education
- Work History
- Residence
- Marital Status
- Family
- Hobbies and Interests
- Media Habits
  - Video
  - Print
  - Internet
- Membership in Organizations
- Past Involvement with the Legal System
  - Prior Jury Duty
  - Involved in Lawsuits
  - Involved in Crime
  - Work for Insurance Company

The work done before voir dire allows you to focus on the questions asked and the answers received. When voir dire preparation is done properly, you will be able to remain "in the moment," maximizing the persuasive power voir dire allows.

G. Voir Dire

1. Overview

Your goal when conducting jury selection is to remove those potential jurors whose life experiences prevent them from fairly considering the case. The goal is to uncover a bias that makes the juror unfit to serve, while not simultaneously upsetting neutral potential jurors or identifying those potential jurors whom your pre-trial work indicates should consider the case in a favorable light, to opposing counsel so that they can strike them.

This process is implicitly judgmental, and no one likes to be judged, including potential jurors. The very nature of the jury selection process makes it difficult to get potential jurors to do what you most want them to do during this process—talk. It is important to begin well to accomplish this goal. Certain clues as to what is acceptable can be derived from watching voir dire in another case tried in the same jurisdiction, but a large part of this is personal.

You must create a sincere viable connection beginning with the process of making the jury receptive. Beginning well is of prime importance. The degree to which counsel will be allowed to establish rapport can shift from judge to judge, but introductory remarks built upon a culture of civility and respect not only build credibility with the court, but with the potential jury members. Done properly it begins the process of creating opportunities for true communication between the attorneys and potential jurors.

Example: Consider the following example of introductory remarks by plaintiff's attorney in a civil case involving a wrongful death claim in a car accident case.

Plaintiff: Good morning. My name is Marie Frost, and I represent Ms. Washington in this case. Judge Hodges just covered some fundamental questions with you, and now we have a chance to visit together. I'd like to start by making sure that everyone is ready to begin. If you are ready to listen to my questions and answer please raise your right hand.

Plaintiff: Let the record reflect that everyone has raised their right hand. It is important that the court is able to keep track of your responses to our questions during jury selection. To make that easier, would all of you be willing to raise your right hand whenever I ask a question of the group if your answer to the question is yes? If you are willing to do that please raise your right hand now.

Plaintiff: All members of the venire have complied with my request. Thanks for raising your hand. Let's begin with some preliminary issues that were not covered by the court.

Plaintiff: How many of you drive a car?

Plaintiff: Positive response from all venire members except for potential juror number 12.

Plaintiff: Of those of you who drive, how many have been involved in a car accident of some kind?

Plaintiff: Positive responses from potential jurors 3,5 and 7. Potential juror number 5, do you feel comfortable talking about the accident you were involved in?

Juror 5:   Sure. It was a minor fender bender. Someone rear ended me while I was stopped at a red light.

The attorney began here by taking control of the process, recognizing the authority of the court and connecting to the jury. She made everyone comfortable and provided the venire with an immediate way to communicate with her, and then made sure they did so. She next inquires about a potential issue in the case. Proceeding in this fashion has allowed her to connect to the venire and focus her inquiry. If additional time were available for voir dire, she could spend more time with pleasantries, but this approach works well when time is constrained.

The plaintiff's attorney above can now explore what happened to potential juror number 5 in greater detail, she could connect their experience to the current case, or move on to another line of questioning. She also has the option of going back and engaging the other juror's who indicated they had been involved in an accident. Taking the answers and connecting them to the theory of the case in a way designed to identify and either develop or neutralize a potential bias is the essence of effective voir dire.

2. Making a Connection

Voir dire is the first opportunity to make a good impression on the jurors who will decide the case. As advocates strive to make this impression, they must remember that every question posed must connect to one or more of the accepted purposes of voir dire. The same advocacy skills used to questions witnesses and communicate with groups work well here, with some slight modifications. For example, eye contact is important when creating rapport and credibility with an audience. When conducting voir dire, you should not read questions to the potential jurors without looking them in the eye. Doing so tells the audience that the written questions are

more important to the attorney than the physical and verbal responses of the potential jurors to those questions.

Eye contact while talking to the potential jurors has several benefits. It allows counsel to connect with the jurors and it provides an opportunity to read the responses of the potential jurors to the issue, including their body language. Body language and facial expressions are keys that the observant advocate can use to direct potential additional lines of inquiry. Counsel should watch for changes in facial expressions, body movements, avoidance of eye contact, hesitancy to respond, and other indications that a juror is uncomfortable or insincere in his or her response. Such indications should be noted and may serve as grounds the beginnings of a challenge for cause, the basis for a peremptory challenge, or to refute an allegation that a peremptory challenge violated the restrictions of *Batson*.

Your body language is also important. The use of a podium, crossing arms, looking away from the venire, and similar actions all have the ability to place a communications barrier between the lawyer and the potential jurors. Most of these communication techniques are well known and generally accepted, but counsel tend to forget them under the stress of trial.

You should also fully develop the ability to move between open and leading questions to maximize their ability to identify potential jurors to strike. The form of questions used during voir dire impacts the type and structure of the inquire. Close ended, otherwise known as leading questions, are an excellent form of question when conducting directed voir dire. Open ended questions designed to get the potential jurors talking are more appropriate when the goal is an undirected approach. Both forms of questioning have a valid purpose during voir dire, depending upon the time constraints and relevant issues. We will discuss each potential approach further later in this section.

3. Managing Responses

Before you can determine how and when to ask questions, you must first develop a method for accurately recording responses, particularly during group voir dire. The best questions in the world are useless if you cannot, in the moment of group voir dire, record answers in a way that helps determine whom to question during individual voir dire. You must be able to note answers and to follow up. In some instances it will not only be necessary to record the general response, but the specific words as well. A basis for challenge may also be found in not only the answer but the way in which it is given.

A variety of methods are available to track responses during voir dire, from a simple pad of paper, printed forms, computer programs, and even tablet applications. All of them work to record data in a way that makes it easily retrievable and usable. One acceptable method is to create a matrix containing the names of potential jurors, along with the relevant questions for voir dire, and then have co-counsel carefully record all responses from both parties and the judge. Use some type of shorthand and key so they can quickly record answers and decipher what is written. On those occasions where counsel do not have co-counsel, a matrix and seating chart is vital. Another option is to have a co-worker or other support personnel to sit in the gallery and take notes, sharing them with counsel as needed.

4. Maintain Credibility

During voir dire, advocates interact with the potential jurors in order to assess their attitudes about the case. The potential jurors understand the process, and while counsel are weighing and measuring them, they are weighing and measuring counsel, opposing counsel, and the case itself. This dynamic is present throughout the trial, and begins in earnest during voir dire, and is one of the primary reasons that you should refrain from using trick questions designed to catch potential jurors. It serves no useful purpose to alienate potential members of the jury. It creates distrust, leading them to root for the other side.

Advocates must be careful, for the same reason, to appropriately reference instructions during voir dire in the manner required by their jurisdiction. Some judges do not want attorneys talking to the jury about the law—period. When faced with that situation you should avoid the dynamic of attempting to discuss the instructions you expect the judge to give during the course of the trial. Failure to follow those restrictions can lead to an embarrassing moment in front of the venire and potential loss of credibility, not to mention drawing the ire of the court.

In those jurisdictions that do allow you to use instructions during voir dire, the judge will listen carefully, preventing counsel from misinterpreting the law when discussing it with potential jurors. Even with such oversight, advocates can use instructions to underline legal concepts favoring their position in the case to great effect. For example, in a case where accident may be raised as a defense, you could ask the jury the following question to drive the point home: "If the judge instructs you that the defense of accident is a complete defense to the indictment, please raise your hand if you can follow that instruction?"

When counsel choose to incorporate legal instructions or the substantive law during voir dire, the judge will pay close attention. The court will respond quickly to any misstatements of the law, correcting counsel and instructing the venire to disregard counsel's statements. This potential pitfall can be avoided by asking the court to provide instructions to the venire about any legal concepts counsel wish to discuss with them before beginning that section of the voir dire. Once the court has read the applicable instruction counsel should begin voir dire on the related issued, referencing back to the words of the judge as potential jurors are questioned. This gives counsel the ability to gage the receptiveness of potential jurors to the relevant legal standard identified through earlier case analysis.

Leading questions are the preferred questioning methodology when educating the jury on factual and legal concepts within the case. Counsel should be careful not to insult the intelligence of the potential jurors when doing so.

5. Challenges for Cause

One of the primary purposes of voir dire is to develop a challenge for cause. When developing challenges for cause, an advocate must be intimately familiar with the grounds for a challenge for cause and the potential juror's responses to the earlier written questionnaires. Previous involvement with any of the witnesses, parties, counsel, or judge in the case may support a challenge for cause. Too much exposure to media coverage, forming an opinion about the ultimate issue in the case prior to trial, or expressing an inability to follow the instructions of the court will also result in a challenge for cause.

This basis of knowledge, when combined with the following techniques, will assist you in developing strong challenges that will overcome opposing counsel's argument and sway the judge. Although challenges for cause are based upon the inability of the potential jurors to be fair in a particular case, you should take care to never use accusatory, reproaching or embarrassing questions, especially during group voir dire.

Before engaging in voir dire designed to perfect challenges for cause, counsel should begin by reviewing jury questionnaires to identify potential areas of bias that will support striking the potential juror. The potential issues identified in the questionnaires can be developed during voir dire through the judicious use of non-leading and leading questions used in combination with one another. While engaging in this interplay with an individual juror, you must be careful to avoid improperly tainting the rest of the venire.

There is an art to this process. Sufficient information must be placed before the court to support individual voir dire, but the questions posed during group voir dire should not be presented in a fashion that taints the group as a whole, unless counsel has a valid reason to suspect that the venire is already tainted on the issue being addressed. Practically speaking this can be a difficult line to walk. One technique is to use sufficiently tailored questions on potential areas of bias. By doing so, counsel maximize their opportunity to gain information without tainting the venire.

Sometimes it is advisable to use a response during group voir dire establishing a challenge for cause as a litmus test with the rest of the venire. To accomplish this, counsel should be careful during group voir dire, avoiding going into too much detail with a potential juror on an issue that could potentially ripen into a valid challenge for cause, while providing sufficient opportunity for potential jurors to provide information ultimately supporting individual voir dire and a subsequent challenge.

Example: group voir dire in a sexual assault case where the defense counsel is attempting to identify potential challenges for cause.

Defense: Has anyone heard of this case in the news? (No one raises their hand)

Defense: Negative response from all members of the venire.

Defense: Please listen carefully to my question and only raise your hand if your answer to the question is yes. Has any member of the venire, their close family, or friends, been the victim of sexual assault? If so please raise your right hand.

Defense: Affirmative response from potential jurors 3, 6, and 8.

Defense: You honor we request a brief recess for the venire to discuss some issues.

Judge: Okay. Members of the venire the bailiff will take you back into the waiting room while counsel and I discuss some administrative issues. We may call some or all of you back shortly so please do not leave the room without the bailiff's approval and knowledge. Thank you. (Venire leaves).

Judge: Okay counsel, what's up?

Defense: You honor we request individual voir dire of potential jurors 3, 6, and 8. Each has indicated that either they themselves, a family member, or close friend was a victim of sexual assault. Given the nature of this case a potential issue exists that would disqualify them from servicing on this jury.

Judge: Any objection from the state?

State: Your honor in this instance we agree with the defense and believe that individual voir dire is warranted.

Judge: Very well. Anything else?

Defense: Your honor the delicate of this issue might best be addressed by the bench during individual voir dire.

Judge: Very well. Bailiff please bring in potential juror number 3.

Once the potential juror is brought into the room and seated, individual voir dire begins. Usually the court will inform the potential juror about the reason, and, either sua sponte or on the request of counsel, may conduct the individual voir dire.

Judge: Potential juror number 3 please take a seat. I need to ask you some individual questions to make certain that this is the right jury for you to serve on. Okay?

Juror 3: Absolutely.

Judge: You indicated during group voir dire that you, a member of your family, or a close friend had been a victim of sexual assault. I wanted to ask you some questions about your earlier answer individually to ensure your privacy. Who exactly was the victim?

Juror 3: It was my sister. She was a victim of date rape at a frat party one night. She got drunk and passed out. When she woke up someone had had sex with her.

Judge: I see. Did they ever find who did this?

Juror 3: Not yet, but we are hopeful they will someday. It messed her up pretty bad.

Judge: Has this been hard on your family?

Juror 3: Incredibly. Things have never been the same since it happened.

Judge: Potential juror number 3 I am going to excuse you from service on this particular jury. The bailiff will escort you back to the clerk who will make arrangements for you to be considered for service on another venire. Thank you very much for your time.

The same ultimate result could be achieved through individual voir dire conducted by the defense counsel. Consider what might have occurred to the venire if defense counsel had to deal with this issue during group voir dire.

Example: group voir dire in a sexual assault case where the defense counsel is attempting to identify potential challenges for cause.

Defense: Please listen carefully to my question and only raise your hand if your answer to the question is yes. Has any member of the venire, their close family, or friends, been the victim of sexual assault? If so please raise your right hand.

Defense: Affirmative response from potential jurors 3, 6, and 8.

Defense: You honor we request a brief recess for the venire to discuss some issues.

Judge: Not now counsel. You may continue to inquire.

Defense: Yes your honor. Potential juror number 3, you answered yes to my last question. Are you comfortable discussing what happened?

Juror 3: Sure.

Defense: What kind of sexual assault was it?

Juror 3: Date rape.

Defense: Were you close to the victim?

Juror 3: Extremely. She is my sister.

Defense: I am sorry for what happened to you and your family.

Juror 3: I doubt that. All defense counsel are soulless people who put criminals back out on the street to hurt others. Happens all the time. The guy who raped my sister hired a good lawyer and never even went to trial. Just not fair.

This response creates a problem for counsel and the court. The judge did not allow individual voir dire, and the potential juror has now made comments about the legal system and defense attorneys that could taint the entire venire. If the court does not stop the inquiry now, the defense attorney must deal with this issue. One way to effectively do so is to use the words of the potential juror as a limit test for the rest of the venire, polling the rest of the group for their reaction. This is best done with a directed questioning approach.

Defense: Is there anyone here who did not hear what potential juror number 3 just said? Please raise your hand if you did not hear his comments?

Defense: Negative response from all potential jurors. Let's talk about it. If you agree with his statement that defense counsel put criminals back on the street to hurt others please raise your hand.

Defense: Affirmative response from potential jurors 11, 15, 23, and 9.

At this point, counsel has laid a sufficient foundation to challenge these jurors for cause. Alternatively, she could continue, shifting now to a non directed form of voir dire designed to get potential jury members talking to each other about the issues in the case.

> *Defense:* Potential juror number 4, I noticed that you did not raise your hand in agreement with potential juror number 3. Why not?

> *Juror 4:* I have my reasons.

> *Defense:* Would you please share them with us?

> *Juror 4:* (Sighs). Okay. My dad was accused of a crime he did not commit. The cops framed him and it took a criminal defense lawyer to keep him out of jail. That man saved my family.

> *Defense:* Potential juror number 3, how do you respond to what potential juror number 4 just shared?

> *Juror 3:* I never thought about it like that. I guess sometimes defense attorneys do good, I just know that my sister never got over what happened to her.

These examples showcase the relative strengths and weaknesses of both the directive and non directive approach to voir dire. Judges with a preference for tight control of the jury selection process will not appreciate the non directive method, and may in fact instruct counsel not to use it, or force them to justify each time they wish to ask an open ended question. Conversely, when used judiciously it creates a sense of community on the part of the potential jurors and allows the attorney to get the people who will actually decide the case talking to one another about the core issues they will deal with if seated as a jury.

If a response is general, voir dire clearly establishes a ground for a challenge for cause, counsel should then ask the other potential jurors if they agree with the response. If others agree, then the number of potential jurors that could be challenged for cause has increased. These potential jurors should be queried further during individual voir dire, if possible. During individual voir dire, counsel should consider shifting to the use of leading questions to nail down the potential challenge for cause identified during group voir dire.

One common source of potential challenges that counsel should pursue is whether any potential juror has had any previous contact with counsel, witnesses, or the defendant, or heard something about the case. Based upon this the potential juror may have either favorable or unfavorable opinions that could affect their ability to be fair and neutral.

Remember, just because they may have heard something about the case does not disqualify them per se. Instead, attorneys should focus on whether the potential juror can set aside what they heard and make their decision solely on the evidence presented in court. Counsel will need to get potential jurors to state on the record how they would be able to set aside what they heard earlier with sufficient specificity to overcome a challenge for cause. This can be particularly problematic in high profile cases, with the court often taking ownership of the questions relating to media coverage.

Finally, where a potential juror, or a family member or friend, has been accused or convicted of a crime, or was the victim of a crime, counsel needs to inquire into this area in individual voir dire. Again, counsel should not merely accept the assurances that the potential juror can set aside these facts and faithfully execute their duty as a juror. Counsel should seek to have them explain how they would do so. If a challenge for cause is denied in this area, counsel should generally exercise a peremptory challenge, stating on the record that but for the denial of their challenge for cause they would have saved the peremptory challenge for later use.

6. A Suggested Approach

Consider for a moment the situation you confront when voir dire begins. you find yourself standing before a group of individuals who are here because they have been told they have to be here. They have entered a world that is not normal for them. They know that it is your job to decide whether or not they are capable of being a jury member. The power dynamic is unbalanced, and the potential jurors are in an unfamiliar environment. A good way to start is to begin by giving them the authority and power to do something. It can be as simple as asking them to take an action in response to questions. You might begin as follows:

> *Q:* Good morning ladies and gentlemen. My name is
> _____ and I am the attorney for the plaintiff in
> this case. I will be asking a series of questions to-
> day some of which will require a yes or no answer.
> Could we all agree that if the answer to my question
> is yes you will raise your right hand? Why don't we

> try that out now? If you agree to answer yes by raising your right hand please do so? Let the record reflect that all prospective jury members have complied with my request and have raised their right hands.

> *Q:* Very good. Let's start with a couple simple questions, how many of you have served on a jury before? A positive response from number 16, number 23, and number 42.

> *Q:* Number 42. What did that case involve?

By beginning with a series of questions each requiring a 'yes' or 'no' answer, counsel very quickly get the jury involved in responding to your questions. This involvement requires them to actually listen to what is being asked, and to respond intelligently. Notice how the yes/no approach is followed by an open-ended question designed to get the potential jury member talking.

You should assume that most potential jurors watch television and have some idea of how this process is supposed to work. They should also realize that it is not human nature to have an open mind, nor is it human nature to admit when you are wrong. Nonetheless, advocates have to inquire. The questions must open up the jury members so that they feel comfortable talking. Some people use humor, others use sense of civic duty, and some just try to ingratiate themselves with the jury members. The first two or fine but the last one plays into stereotypical lawyer behavior and is not recommended. Imagine how potential jury members might respond to the following question:

> *Q:* How many of you looked at my client today and thought, 'that poor innocent boy'?

There is a nice bit of humor in that question, yet at the same time it points out a very difficult issue in criminal cases, the presumed innocence of the accused. You can follow up this sort of inquiry with additional questions about the right to remain silent, the right to confront your accuser, and the right to a fair trial.

Sometimes, in the press of criminal justice practice counsel find themselves without sufficient time to properly conduct jury selection. What to do? When running short on time, they can always consider the possibility of seeking general affirmations from the potential jurors. An example of that is found in the following:

> *Q:*   Members of the jury, can each of you promise me that you'll wait until I get a chance to present my case before you make up your mind about what happened?

One of the things you must do during jury selection is to educate the panel about potential legal or moral issues in your case. The law allows them to do this under the cover of searching for potential bias that would keep the potential juror from fairly deciding the case. One way to accomplish this is to ask pointed questions about the issue from the standpoint of bias. There is nothing wrong with this approach, but there is a better way. What would happen if you could get jury members talking to one another about an issue in the case? Consider the following illustrative example:

> *Q:*   How many members of the jury own a firearm? A positive response from jurors 23 and 42. Juror number 23, why do you own a firearm?
>
> *Q:*   Juror number 17, I noticed that you did not raise your hand when I asked if you owned a firearm. What did you think about the comments that juror number 23 made about why they own a weapon?
>
> *Q:*   Please explain to juror number 23 your concerns about firearms in the home.
>
> *Q:*   Juror number 23, how would you respond to juror number 17 about their concerns?

Note that these types of questions are designed to get the jury members talking to one another. When counsel can get discussions going between potential jurors about an issue they know is relevant to the case, magical moments in jury selection occur. It provides a chance to step back and see them interact with one another, much as they may do during deliberations

H. Examples of Voir Dire Questions

The following examples are provided as a starting point for voir dire questions addressing certain issues permeating trials. They are predominately criminal in nature, because the vast majority of issues that arise out of voir dire at the appellate level are tied to a criminal case, and these examples are taken from appellate cases identifying acceptable language on these issues. Consider how they might be properly modified so they accurately reflect the issues identified during case analysis.

This is a crucial point. Counsel must take the final step of making suggested voir dire questions their own. The only way to do this is to connect them to specific legal, factual, and moral issues identified as discussed during the section on case analysis and preparation. The selection of an appropriate legal theory, factual theory, and moral theme will assist counsel in finding not only the right voir dire questions substantively, but the best means of delivering them to the jury.

Location of Each Voir Dire Question by Subject Matter:

The Offense:
- You have all read the indictment. The judge told you that these alleged offenses are not evidence of guilt. Do you have a problem with that concept of the law?

- The offense alleged in this case is [offense]. Do you feel that the nature of the offense would make it difficult for you to render a fair and impartial verdict in this case?

- [Defendant's name] is charged with several different offenses. Does the mere fact that he is facing multiple allegations lead you to believe that he is probably guilty of some or all of them?

Jurors as Victims of a Crime:
- Have you, a close friend, or member of your family ever been the victim of a [similar] offense?

- Have you, a close friend, or any member of your family ever been a witness to an offense?

- Have you, a close friend, or any member of your family ever been accused of a [similar] offense?

Relationship with the Opposing Counsel:
- Do you know [insert name]? If yes, ask:
  - How do you know her? Professionally? Personally?
  - Do you rely on her for advice on legal matters?
  - Have you ever received any legal assistance advice from her?
  - How often do you consult with her?

- How long has she served as your legal advisor?

- Would you give her arguments more weight?

Knowledge of the Case:

- Other than what you have learned so far in court today, do you know anything about this case?

- Do you regularly review the community newspaper or watch local news? Do you recall seeing anything about this case?

Knowledge of Witnesses:

- During the course of the trial, we expect the following witnesses to be called. If you know any of these people, please raise your hand when the name is called. [Follow up during their individual voir dire.]

- Potential Juror #12, how do you know Witness Z?

- Do you believe that, by virtue of your relationship with Witness Z, you would give any greater or lesser weight to his testimony than to the testimony of a witness you did not know?

Knowledge of Location:

- The indicted offenses are alleged to have occurred at [location]. Are you familiar with [location]?

- How?

- If you were to receive testimony that [Defendant] was present at [location], would that fact alone lead you to draw any ideas about him?

Weight of Prosecution v. Defense Evidence:

- Do you believe that evidence presented by the prosecution is more reliable than evidence presented by the defense?

- If [Defendant] decides to call witnesses or present evidence in his behalf, will you weigh this evidence just as you would evidence presented by the prosecution?

Objections to Evidence:

- You are aware that trials are governed by certain rules, which are designed not only to assist you in reaching the truth, but also to ensure fairness to both sides. Can you accept this proposition?

- Would you agree that each side is entitled to have those rules enforced so that only proper matters are brought before you for consideration?

- Do you agree that the defense may properly object to evidence that the prosecution is trying to offer because that evidence does not comply with the rules governing trials?

- Would you hold it against the defense in your deliberations for attempting to prevent improper evidence from coming before you?

Burden of Proof:

- The judge will instruct (or has instructed) you that the government has the burden of proof in this case, the standard of proof is beyond a reasonable doubt, and the burden of proof never shifts to the defense. All elements of the crime charged must be proven beyond a reasonable doubt. If even one element is not proven beyond a reasonable doubt, you must vote not guilty. The defense need not introduce any evidence whatsoever.

- Do you have any problem with these legal concepts?

- Do you wish that the standard were less for the government?

- Do you believe that the defense should be required to answer the government's evidence, explain his case or present any evidence at all?

Indictment as Evidence of Guilt:

- Do you, right now, have an opinion as to whether [Defendant] is guilty of any of the offenses indicted?

- Do you believe that, because the government has indicted my client with an offense, he must be guilty of the crime?

Presumption of Innocence:

- The judge will instruct (or has instructed you) that the [Defendant] is presumed to be innocent of the charges the government has brought against him.

- Do you agree that the presumption of innocence means that [Defendant] remains an innocent man unless the prosecutor can prove guilt beyond a reasonable doubt?

Jury's Basis for a Decision:

- The judge will instruct you as to the law, but you are the sole and exclusive judges of the facts. Do you believe that the rule should be some other way? How would you do it?

Confidential Informant:

- [In a short two sentences explain how the confidential informant in your case began working for police, what the trouble the confidential informant was in and that he began working to get out of trouble—if all of this will come into evidence. If the evidence will not be admitted, you will not be able to explore this area. Explain in one sentence that the believability of the source is critical to the government's case (if this is true).]

- Do you believe that you should consider the motive of the confidential informant to help the government as a factor in weighing his credibility?

Confessions (as applicable):

- Do you believe everything that you read in newspapers or magazines, hear on radio or see on television?

- Do you agree that many words of the English language have various meanings?

- Do you agree that a word may mean one thing to one person and another thing to another person?

- Do you agree that just because an individual is an American that does not mean that he is able to read and write English?

- Have you heard from whatever source that hundreds of high school graduates every year cannot read or write?

- Do you agree that someone, whose native language is not English, may have a very difficult time understanding English?

- Have you ever known someone who took the blame for something he did not do so that he could protect a friend/individual?

- Do you agree that there are reasons why someone would take the blame for something they did not do? For example, maybe they were protecting a loved one?

- Can you agree that circumstances could exist where a confession would not be the truth? Or would not be accurate? In other words, can you agree that someone would confess to a crime they did not commit?

- Have you heard of individuals giving false confessions?

- Do you agree that there may be circumstances surrounding an interrogation of an individual where the individual would say anything just to end the interrogation?

- Do you agree that a person's breaking point varies from person to person? In other words, some people break easier under stress than others do?

- Would you agree that a statement taken after an individual has been interrogated for a long time, with little or no sleep, could have less reliability than a statement from an individual who is not tired?

- Would you agree that a statement given under stress could be unreliable or untrue?

- Have you ever signed a document, then later discovered that you had signed something other than you thought you were signing?

- Is it reasonable to assume that people sometimes sign documents without reading them carefully? Or without reading them at all?

Defense Theory of the Case:

- Do you disagree with the proposition of law [state defense theory of case, e.g., that a man who is threatened with deadly force is entitled to use deadly force in his own defense]? [NOTE: You may want to request that the judge give the jury the instruction prior to your voir dire.]

Defendant's Right to Plead Not Guilty:

- [If plea is not guilty, and conviction is likely] As you are aware, [Defendant] has pleaded not guilty to all the offenses. In the event that you were to find him guilty, would you in any way hold against him the fact that he pled not guilty?

Testimony of the Defendant:

- Do you agree that [Defendant] has no duty to present any evidence in trial to prove that he is innocent?

- If [Defendant] were not to testify in his own defense, would you draw any negative inference from that fact or consider his failure to testify as an indication of guilt?

- Do you agree that it is the prosecutor's duty to present evidence in this trial?

- Do you agree with the proposition of law that says the burden of proving the defendant guilty beyond a reasonable doubt rests with the prosecution, and that the defendant need not introduce any evidence whatsoever?

- Knowing this, you do realize that [Defendant] is not bound to explain his side of the case?

- Would you consider [Defendant]'s failure to testify as an indication that he is guilty?

- In a trial, a defendant has the right not to testify, to not take the witness stand. Do you believe that a defendant that does not testify is more likely to be guilty than a defendant that does testify?

- If the defense does not present any witnesses of their own, but relies solely on the cross-examination of government witnesses, would that cause you to conclude [Defendant] is guilty?

- If [Defendant] were to testify, would you be inclined to disbelieve him solely because the state has indicted him?

- If [Defendant] were to testify, would you listen to his testimony the same way that you would any other witness?

- Will you consider and judge [Defendant]'s testimony by the same rules and standards you would use in judging the testimony of any other witness in this case?

- Would the fact that [Defendant] was convicted of an offense in the past cause you to prejudge him and to disregard any of his testimony?

- Will you assume, because of his prior conviction, regardless of what his testimony is, that he is not telling the truth?

- You will be told that you can consider his prior conviction only in evaluating his credibility. Would you assume that because he has a prior conviction that he must be guilty of this offense?

Defendant's Relatives will Testify:
- You may hear from [Defendant]'s relatives when the defense has an opportunity to present evidence. Would any of you disbelieve these witnesses merely because they are related to [Defendant]?

- Do you believe that because [Witness] is the defendant's relative, his/her testimony is entitled to lesser belief than that of someone unrelated to the defendant?

Joint Trial:

- There is more than one person on trial here. The judge will tell you these individuals must be given separate consideration. Will you assume the evidence admitted against only one of the defendants should also be used against the others, just because they are being tried together?

- If the evidence convinces you of guilt beyond a reasonable doubt of one but not the other, will you have difficulty finding the other not guilty?

- Sodomy and Other Consensual Acts:

- Do you agree that the issue of consent is a very important factor to consider? Would you agree that consensual _____ sex is not necessarily indicative of a lack of moral character?

- Do you have religious or strong moral feeling against _____ sex?

- Do you believe that the only legitimate purpose of human sexual actions is to reproduce?

- Do you understand what a victimless offense is?

Interracial Issues:

- Do you believe that interracial dating is improper?

- Do you believe that interracial marriage is improper?

- Do you feel that you would be unable to impartially serve in a case where the defendant and the alleged victim are of a different race?

- Do you agree that an individual who pursues an interracial relationship may experience problems with prejudice in the community? Do you agree that prejudice can affect your judgment?

- Are you uncomfortable with the idea of interracial dating/marriage?

- Do you have religious or moral objections to interracial dating or marriage?

- Do you agree that any discomfort you may feel concerning interracial relationships must be set aside in order to give [Defendant] a fair trial?

Guns or Other Weapons:

- You will receive testimony in this trial that a [gun] [knife] was used in the alleged commission of this crime. Have you, your close friends or family members, ever had an experience with [weapon] that might make it difficult for you to sit on a case where [weapon] was involved?

- Do you actively participate in the debate over the issue of gun control?

- Would you be prejudiced against an individual merely because he had owned or carried a firearm?

- Are you a member of the National Rifle Association?

- Do you feel that the sale of handguns should be prohibited?

- Do you object to anybody keeping a firearm in his home for self-protection?

- Do you own a gun?

Cursing:

- You may hear swear or curse words in this trial. Would you be so uncomfortable after hearing these words in this courtroom that you would have difficulty in impartially weighing the evidence in this case?

Narcotics:

- You may receive evidence that on the day in question, [Defendant] used illegal drugs. Would this fact alone make it difficult for you to render a fair and impartial verdict?

Alcohol:

- Do you make it a point never to allow alcoholic beverages in your home?

- Do you have religious or moral beliefs against drinking alcoholic beverages?

- You will hear evidence that [Witness] is a chronic alcoholic. Is there any reason why you could not fairly judge the case of an individual who is an alcoholic?

Pornography:

- You may hear evidence concerning [Defendant] [use, possession, reading, and viewing] pornographic [movies, magazines, materials]. Do you have a religious or moral aversion to pornography?

- Should pornography be outlawed completely?

- Do you hold the belief that a person who [reads, possesses, watches] pornographic material is immoral?

- Do you believe that a person who [possesses, watches, reads] pornographic material is predisposed or inclined to commit [offense]?

- Do you feel that a person should be punished for [watching, possessing, and reading] pornographic material?

Publicity:

- Do you know anything about the facts of this case other than what you have heard in court today?

- Over the past several months there has been considerable publicity on television, radio, magazines, and newspapers concerning this [case] [type of offense]. What specific facts do you remember from what you saw, heard or read? Do you feel that you could not sit as a juror on this case in view of the publicity you have seen, heard or read?

  - Have you heard anybody discussing this case?

  - [If the juror has knowledge] What did you [read, hear, discuss]?

  - Have you formed an opinion as to the guilt or innocence of [Defendant] from what you [heard, discussed, read]?

  - In spite of what you have read or heard, do you think you could judge this case only on the facts that emerge in testimony and evidence in this courtroom, and not be influenced by anything you heard or read?

Emotional Issues/Abuse Case:

- Do you agree that a situation involving _____ can be a highly emotional situation?

- Do you agree that it is only human to have some type of emotional reaction to this type of case?

- Do you agree with the proposition that being emotional can have some impact on your ability to rationally and objectively evaluate the facts or make a rational decision?

- Can you agree to minimize, as extensively as possible, your emotional feelings about this case, to ensure that [Defendant] receives a fair and impartial trial?

- If the complaining witness takes the stand and becomes emotional, or even cries, while telling her story, would this fact, standing alone, convince you that she is telling the truth?

Adverse/Gruesome Photographs:

Photos – General Issues

- Do you agree with the proposition that, based on how they are taken or developed, photographs may not accurately depict the subject of the photo?

- Do you agree that the circumstances under which a photograph was taken are important? Such as lighting or weather conditions?

- Photographs only depict the scene shown in the photo. Do you agree that testimony must be heard to determine how serious an injury is? For instance, an injury can look serious in a photo, but not be serious?

Autopsy Photos

- You will see autopsy photographs today Have you seen an autopsy before or have seen photographs of an autopsy?

- Some of the photographs are very gruesome. This may cause some type of emotional response. [See Emotion line of questions.]

- Autopsies are done after a person's death and are an accepted medical procedure to determine the cause of death. Do you understand that [Defendant] did not cause this to be done to the body you see in the photos?

- Except for a medical opinion of the cause of death, do you agree that an autopsy is not reflective of what happened to the individual as is charged?

Photos – Bruises and Wounds

- You will see photos of [Victim]'s injuries. Do you agree that photographs cannot tell you how serious an injury is?

- Do you agree that, based on how a photograph is taken, it can distort or make the scene appear worse than it actually is?

- Do you agree that enlarging a photo would have a tendency to do this? In other words, enlargement makes a wound or bruise appear larger than is actually was?

Child Abuse – Sexual/Physical:

- The case involves [physical, sexual] abuse of a child. Do you agree that these types of cases can be very emotional? [See Emotion line of questions.]

- Do you feel any pressure to convict because this case involves alleged acts of violence and sexual misconduct with a child?

- Would you automatically believe the testimony of the alleged victim in this case merely because she is a child?

Parental Discipline:

- Do you believe that a parent has a right to use physical punishment in disciplining a child? Do you all agree that this could include spanking?

- Did you receive excessive punishment as a child?

Experts:

- What is your opinion of [name of profession]?

- Do you have training in, experience with, or interaction with someone in [area of expertise]?

- Can you accept the opinion of a psychiatrist, etc.?

- Will you consider the evidence given by [Expert] in the same light as other evidence received here today?

- Will you give the testimony presented by the government's expert witness any more credibility, just because it is coming from someone called an expert?

- Do you agree that, as a human being, an expert can make mistakes?

- Do you agree that [name of expertise] is not an exact science? That the opinion the expert gives is just that, an opinion?

- That this opinion may not be exactly accurate or correct?

- Do you agree that the expert's opinion may vary depending on the facts that form the basis for that opinion?

- Do you agree that it is important for an expert to have all the relevant facts surrounding a situation before forming an opinion?

Mistaken Identification:

- The defense in this case is one of mistaken identity. This is a proper and legitimate defense under the law. Do you have preconceived ideas that would make it difficult for you to consider a defense of mistaken identification?

- Do you agree that the identity of the person who commits a crime must be shown with such certainty as to eliminate any possibility of error?

- That is, it is not enough for the government to prove beyond a reasonable doubt that the offense was committed as alleged in the specification, but the government must also prove beyond a reasonable doubt that [Defendant] was the person who committed it?

- Do you agree that the most honest witness may be mistaken or inaccurate in his or her recollection? Will you consider the witness's opportunity to observe, the lighting conditions, the rapidity with which the offense occurred?

Self Defense:

- Do you disagree with the principle of law that says that a person is justified in injuring another human being if he believes that he is in actual danger of being seriously injured by his attacker?

- The defense in this case is self-defense. The judge will instruct you that if evidence of self-defense is present, the government must prove beyond a reasonable doubt that [Defendant] did not act in self-defense. Would you have difficulty returning a verdict of not guilty if they fail to prove beyond a reasonable doubt that [Defendant] did not act in self-defense?

- Do you feel that you would be unable to follow the judge's instructions on self-defense because of your personal views on the subject? For example, are you a pacifist or do you hold any religious beliefs that would prevent you from accepting the general principle of self-defense?

- Do you feel that self-defense can never justify the willful taking of a human life?

- The judge will instruct you that a person has a right to use a [knife, gun, etc.] under certain circumstances. Would the fact that [Defendant] used a [knife, gun] in self-defense make it difficult for you to return a verdict of not guilty if the government fails to prove beyond a reasonable doubt that [Defendant] did not act in self-defense?

- Do you have any feelings against a person who uses a [knife, gun] to protect himself [or his family]?

- Do you have feelings or convictions about possession of weapons that would make it difficult for you to consider a defense of self-defense in this case?

- There will be no question in this trial that [Defendant] [struck, stabbed, shot] [Victim]. To juror: Do you believe that a person is justified in [striking, stabbing] an attacker if she believes that she is in actual danger of being seriously hurt by the attacker?

Use of a Dangerous Weapon:

- Should the judge instruct you that if [Defendant] had a reasonable belief that he could use whatever force he believed necessary to stop the attack upon himself, to include [striking, stabbing, shooting] and not be guilty of the charge, would you be able to abide by that instruction?

- If the judge instructs you that a person has a right to use [knife, gun, etc] in self-defense under some circumstances, will you accept and follow this principle of law?

Insanity Defense:

- Are you aware that the law does not hold a person responsible for his act, if he was insane at the time he committed the crime? Do you disagree with that proposition of law?

- If you find [Defendant] was legally insane when he committed the crime, will you have any difficulty following the judge's instructions and rendering a verdict of not guilty?

- Do you feel that the insanity defense should be removed from our system?

- If a psychiatrist/psychologist testifies in this case, would you give less weight to his testimony merely because the defendant and his family retained and paid for his services?

Murder:

- Knowing that the charge against [Defendant] is murder; could you give him the same fair trial that you would give him if he were charged with a lesser crime?

- Have you had close family or friends who died as a result of foul play?

- If the spouse of the deceased were to testify, would that testimony so influence you that you could not give [Defendant] a fair trial?

- Can you accept the proposition that one person can accidentally kill another person without being criminally liable?

Rape:

- One of the offenses alleged in this case is rape. Do you feel that the nature of the charge itself would make it difficult for you to render a fair and impartial verdict in this case?

- Do you believe the law of rape is unfair to the woman who claims she was raped?

- The judge will instruct you that consent is a defense to rape, and requires a verdict of not guilty. Would you be reluctant to apply the principle of law that says consent is a defense to rape?

- The judge will instruct you that the law does not permit a conviction for rape unless the victim makes her lack of consent known by taking appropriate resistance under the circumstances. Would you have difficulty applying this principle of law?

- Do you feel pressure to convict the defendant of rape because this case involved alleged sexual misconduct with another man's wife?

Character Evidence:

- Witnesses will testify about the alleged victim's poor character for truth and veracity. Do you agree to consider this testimony in determining whether or not to believe the witness?

- If evidence of the defendant's good character for [insert relevant trait] is presented during the trial, are you willing to consider that evidence using the guidelines given to you by the Judge?

Driving While Under the Influence of Alcohol:

- In addition to the blood alcohol test, are you willing to consider the testimony of witnesses who observed the defendant on the night in question in determining whether or not the defendant was under the influence of alcohol?

Accomplice Testimony:

- Are you willing to find the defendant not guilty if he did not share the motive of the accomplice?

- Are you willing to find the defendant not guilty if he did not encourage or assist the accomplice?

- Can you agree that the mere presence at the scene of a crime is not a crime?

Closing questions:

- At this time would you, if you were in [Defendant]'s position, be satisfied to have your fate decided by a juror who had your frame of mind?

- Do you agree that you will be fulfilling your sworn duty if you find [Defendant] not guilty because the prosecutor failed to prove him guilty beyond a reasonable doubt?

-Notes-

Chapter 4: Opening Statements

A. Introduction..113
B. What the Jury Sees and Thinks 114
C. How the Law Impacts Openings................................116
D. Creating the Opening..122
E. Delivering the Opening...136
F. Examples 144
G. Checklist 163
H. Evidentiary Rules to Consider During Openings 165
I. Conclusion..166

A. Introduction

During openings counsel have their first opportunity to explain to the jury what happened, and why it matters. It is during openings that they get the opportunity to answer key questions placed in the minds of the jury during jury selection. These questions include: "Why are we here today?" and "What is it you want me to do about it?" This is an important persuasive moment in the trial, counsel must make it count. Openings are carefully constructed to highlight the relevant facts, foreshadow the law when appropriate, and to establish the moral imperative demanding justice for the client. The structure and nature of openings are controlled by the relevant rules of procedure, either civil or criminal, the local rules of court, and the unwritten local customs. Counsel must prepare openings with all three of these in mind.

The court normally instructs the jurors on their responsibilities as members of the jury before the trial begins. After initial instructions the court begins the first "formal" part of the trial - opening statements. Jurors' expectations about opening statements are driven by perceptions grounded in television, movies, and

The key to effective communication with the jury is focus.

What happened, How it happened, and Why it matters.

books. There is an unwritten desire for drama and conflict based on those expectations. Opening statements are the beginning of the story of the trial from a juror's perspective. From the attorney's perspective they are not only the "beginning" of the trial, but they are in a very real sense the end of the case preparation and analysis process.

Jurors are concerned with what happened, how it happened, and why it happened. Counsel providing answers to these concerns establish credibility with the jury and create interest in the rest of their case. Openings are promises to the jury members that counsel later keep through the direct and cross examination of witnesses. Closings are when counsel remind the jury of the promise they made in opening and then ask them to do something based upon the promise that has been kept. This approach is grounded in human nature, and can be quite effective. It engages our storytelling brain.

> *The opening statement is a promise made to the jury - everything else we do must be oriented towards keeping that promise. Everything.*

The opening statement is the first and best opportunity to influence the jury's decision-making process. Counsel should use openings to tell their relevant story of the case, based upon thorough case analysis and preparation. Proper openings provide a framework for the jury to conceptualize what is going to happen during the trial, as well as an outline making the testimony of witnesses more relevant. Stellar openings provide a roadmap for the jury to follow through out the course of the trial. It is not enough to merely present the information the jury will hear over the course of the trial. In a stellar opening, counsel will also spend time telling the jury that the power to do justice lies with them, and instruct them on how the verdict the facts, evidence and testimony they are about to review will lead them to the right verdict.

B. What the Jury Sees and Thinks

Once the jury has been selected and sworn the trial begins in earnest. The jurors are seated in the jury box, and some version of the following exchange takes place.

Example: The Court is prepared to begin openings in a criminal case.

Judge: State are you prepared to proceed?

State: The state is ready.

Judge: Defense are you prepared to proceed?

Defense: The defense is ready your honor.

Judge: *(Turning to face the jury)* Members of the jury we are now going to hear opening statements from the attorneys in this case. The openings should give you an overview of what the attorneys expect the evidence they will introduce will show. The opening statements themselves are not evidence, but merely counsel's expectation of what the evidence will be. The party bearing the burden of proof normally goes first. State you may proceed with opening statement.

State: Thank you. Your honor *(acknowledging the court)*, counsel *(acknowledging opposing counsel)*, *(Approaches the jury, centering herself on the jury box)*, members of the jury....

From this point onward the state delivers their opening, subject to objections by opposing counsel. It is important to remember that for the jury members this is a new and novel process. They normally experience some degree of anxiety about what they are supposed to be doing at this point, and that anxiety translates into an opportunity for counsel to establish themselves as the credible provider of truth. The jury wants to do their job properly, and this presents counsel with the chance to empower them to do that job. By constructing an opening informing the jury about why they are there and what counsel wants them to do about it, counsel can empower the jury in their decision making process. The members of the jury are looking for someone to trust, and they are both curious and worried about their ability to ultimately decide the case. When crafted correctly, the opening becomes the call to action that puts all of the power in the courtroom into the hands of the jury members. This reassures the jury as to their importance in the case, allowing counsel to become,

in the minds of the jur, the most credible source of information in the courtroom.

The tone and presentation of the opening statement establishes a relationship between the attorney and the jury that must be nurtured through out the trial to maximize the persuasive power of the case. To effectively deliver persuasive openings counsel must carefully structure and deliver their openings using a thoroughly developed knowledge of themselves, the case, and human nature.

C.   How the Law Impacts Openings

1.   Overview

In most jurisdictions the applicable law governing opening statements is either procedural or case law, and can vary substantively from state to state, as well as within the federal court system. That being said, there are certain fundamental concepts most jurisdictions not only accept, but expect when counsel deliver openings. Those include:

- Storytelling of the facts
- Structured to inform the jury
- Primacy and recency emphasize key points
- Focuses the jury on relevant facts
- Counsel use appropriate tone & pace
- Previews the law
- Set the stage for effective directs, crosses, and closings

These acceptable opening statement techniques focus the jury, bringing them to accept counsel's version of events by communicating a powerful factual theory, previewing relevant legal concepts, and establishing a moral imperative which requires the jury to decide the case in their favor. Counsel must remember to consider the local rules of court and review the relevant case law in the jurisdiction in which the case will be heard when creating their opening statements.

2.   Using Instructions

The standard instructions on the law in most jurisdictions require the judge to instruct the jury to not make any decisions about the case until it is time to do so during deliberations. This instruction is designed to ensure jurors maintain an open mind until all of the evidence has been heard and each side has been provided an opportunity to present their case. The ideas be-

hind such instructions are noble, but whether or not the jury can actually follow them is an open question. In reality human nature makes it almost impossible for jurors to listen to a story without beginning to place the information they are receiving in context. Neuroscience and psychology establish that once people begin to receive information about a subject, they start to draw conclusions based upon what they have learned up to that point, filling in the gaps with their versions of what they expect should happen next.[1]

Human beings do not record the information received from their senses and then later retrieve it. Instead they create narratives by focusing on certain portions of the information, highlighting some data and ignoring others, often based upon their own implicit bias. We do this to ensure the narrative remains coherent. This desire for coherence is how humans deal with a world saturated with data - when understood properly it serves to further emphasize the importance of openings. This is the first time counsel has the opportunity to answer the jury members' question of why they are there, to provide context as to what brought each individual into the courtroom that day. It is at this point in the trial that the jury begins to develop their "narrative of the case" in order to understand and deal with the information received. Since this is the first time they are hearing the story of the case, counsel has the greatest amount of influence on the development of the narrative. Once that narrative has been developed jurors act in accordance with it, often disregarding evidence that does not support the narrative they are using to create coherence. This is not a conscious attempt to modify the information, but a cognitive step human beings use when learning. Information received out of context with expectations is dismissed, ignored, or modified to fit the perceptions of the listener.

When you stop to think about this dynamic, it makes sense. As human beings, each of us weighs, measures, and categorizes our observations as they occur, and then reflect upon them afterwards. We are hardwired to take incomplete information and apply our paradigms to that information to create a cohesive and understandable whole. Jurors do the same thing when called to judge their peers. It would be hard to imagine them being

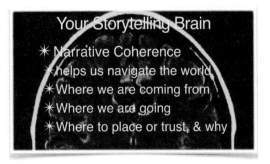

unable to do otherwise. It becomes imperative that counsel provide for the jury, as early in the process as possible, a logical and consistent framework that allows them to consider the evidence from the most persuasive perspective.

The court has a great deal of discretion in controlling the manner and substance of opening statements; they also instruct the jury about opening statements by letting them know what they mean and how to weigh them. In some jurisdictions these instructions are provided before the opening is heard, in others it comes immediately after the opening. Counsel can find examples of these instructions in the pattern jury instructions for those jurisdiction that have them.

Example: the following pattern instruction[1] addresses how the jury should address direct and circumstantial evidence during deliberations.

3.3 Consideration of Direct and Circumstantial Evidence; Argument of Counsel; Comments by the Court

As I said before, you must consider only the evidence that I have admitted in the case. Evidence includes the testimony of witnesses and the exhibits admitted. But, anything the lawyers say is not evidence and isn't binding on you.

You shouldn't assume from anything I've said that I have any opinion about any factual issue in this case. Except for my instructions to you on the law, you should disregard anything I may have said during the trial in arriving at your own decision about the facts.

Your own recollection and interpretation of the evidence is what matters. In considering the evidence you may use reasoning and common sense to make deductions and reach conclusions. You shouldn't be concerned about whether the evidence is direct or circumstantial.

"Direct evidence" is the testimony of a person who asserts that he or she has actual knowledge of a fact, such as an eyewitness.

"Circumstantial evidence" is proof of a chain of facts and circumstances that tend to prove or disprove a fact. There's no legal difference in the weight you may give to either direct or circumstantial evidence.Instructions like this should be used by counsel to identify the relevant law the court will apply to the proceedings. By identify-

---

[1] Taken from the 2013 11th Circuit pattern instructions.

ing the relevant law counsel can then properly forecast the language the court will use when instructing the jury, placing it where appropriate in their opening statements, witness examinations, and closing arguments.

Counsel must review the standard jury instructions to learn what the judge will tell the jury about opening statements. That knowledge should then be used to fashion a more effective opening statement. The jury instructions within a jurisdiction capture the local customs, rules, and relevant case law. Whenever counsel are pressed for time when preparing for trial the instructions are an excellent place to begin. They represent the opinions and actions of the bench within that jurisdiction and often provide the structure that the judge relies upon to identify and solve issues that have been dealt with by other judges. They serve as a repository for the culture of a particular bar, capturing a portion of the daily practice of the attorneys who appear using those instructions.

Counsel must also gain as much knowledge as possible on how the particular judge assigned to the trial views opening statements. While the jury instructions give a readable example of a particular jurisdictions culture, researching a particular judges' viewpoints provides the unwritten rules of a particular courtroom. Different judges have different preferences, and different view points on some of the shades of grey that are encountered in the rules of opening statements. These preferences can serve as guidelines for which persuasive tools counsel will be able to take the greatest advantage of, and which, if any, must be avoided at all costs. The learning of these preferences is best accomplished by maintaining a strong professional, collegial relationships with other members of the bar, and is something counsel must continually consider in their preparations not only for opening statements, but in all areas of trial.

While the court expects counsel to make powerful and persuasive opening statements relying upon the relevant facts, forecasting legal issues, and identifying potentially powerful moral questions, there is relatively little uniformity about the best way to proceed.

3.   Deciding to Object during Openings

Counsel have the right to object to any portion of opposing counsel's opening statement that violates the instructions of the court, local rules of practice, and the relevant rules of procedure. Unfortunately while counsel have that right, they rarely have the ability to object. In some jurisdictions there is almost a sub rosa agreement between counsel, a sort of "you don't object to me and I won't object to you" approach. This is a tactic grounded in fear, and not useful to advocates who are focused on proper openings.

Counsel should listen carefully when the opposition is opening. If the opening descends into argument, misstates the law, or makes an ad hominem attack then an objection is not only permissible, but warranted.

Most attorneys find it difficult to tell a story during opening without descending into argument, and arguing during opening statement is a violation of the rules in almost every jurisdiction. Argument is not appropriate during openings because the jury has not yet received any evidence.

Counsel often make this mistake because they have been living with the case for an extended period of time, and not only have a natural bias as to how things should turn out, but have done the case analysis to back that up. They begin to argue about what it all means during the opening, because they have the advantage of this complete picture in their minds. But the jury has yet to see any of the supporting information and evidence, and connecting dots may not only confuse them, but is objectionable as improper argument and when it occurs should be sustained by the court. The inability to identify and remove argument creates a tentativeness that has destroyed the effectiveness of more than one opening statement.

Experienced counsel are able to "sense" the wrongness of argument within an opening statement. To them something just does not sound or feel right about the presentation and the argumentative objection is made almost before opposing counsel has worked out why it was argument. Counsel can follow these three rules with some degree of confidence: (1) opposing counsel will usually allow you to state your theme and theory in your initial opening and end your opening with the same; (2) one sentence of argument in opening gets opposing counsel's attention, two sentences will cause their body to tense and three sentences strung together will have them on their feet; and (3) how much argument is allowed within the opening can vary greatly from one jurisdiction to another.

If opposing counsel is describing what happened in the present tense from the point of view of someone who was there or who will testify about what they observed after the event then it is not argument - even though it may be persuasive. Persuasive is not argumentative. The structure, form and delivery of the opening determines whether or not it will veer off into inadmissible argument. When counsel find themselves interpreting what the evidence means, assigning relative worth, or discussing how the law will apply to a particular set of facts, then they are arguing, not explaining. Let's take a look at some examples of opening statements, one that is argumentative, and one that relies up a storytelling structure to "argue" without being argumentative. The first is unacceptable, and the second is exactly what counsel should strive for.

Argumentative Opening Statement:

Members of the jury, you will learn that on the ninth of October the county school board negligently cared for Mary Lou because they placed an incompetent driver behind the wheel of a school bus and then gave him improper bus route information. These actions violated county regulations and are clear circumstantial evidence of their negligence in the wrongful death of this young lady. The decision made by the bus driver to park the bus and open the door is the "but for" causation factor that establishes their legal responsibility for Mary Lou's death. Don't let them get away with it.

The presence of legal terms such as "negligently," "clear circumstantial evidence," and "causation" are red flags indicating that counsel is arguing. Other red flags that counsel should be on the lookout for include hyperbole that exaggerates, extrapolates, or speculates. Argument is not effective in opening statement because the jury does not yet know the  facts of the case. The lack of context for the jury during opening statement renders argumentative openings ineffective. This makes sound logical sense—until the jury is presented with the fullness of available information, they cannot understand how each bit of information interacts individually and how those interactions effect the entirety of the case.

Counsel should object when an opening like this is being delivered by their opponent. Such presentations are sloppy, reflect a lack of focus on the part of opposing counsel, along with a lack of understanding about the superior persuasive value of a well told story. The better practice is to use the accepted legal principles of opening statements to craft an opening statement that persuades without arguing.

Proper Opening in a Civil Case:

They did nothing. On the ninth of October, Mary Lou gets off the elementary school bus just like she does every day. She did not know the new bus driver, but she was excited about getting home and playing with her new baby sister. Mary Lou leaves the bus and walks across the road, just like she did every day. But today was different because the bus was on the wrong street. Mary Lou looks around, unsure what to do when she sees six lanes of traffic. She walks to the median, making it safely across the three lanes of traffic stopped by the bus, while the bus driver watches. When she steps into the fourth lane, her world ends. A black SUV slams into Mary Lou, taking her life. They did nothing. But now is the time that you as a jury can do something, something to make it right.

This second example quickly and emotionally tells the story of what happened that day. It uses present tense and has the jury there at the time of death. It also utilizes the theory of primacy and recency while setting the moral theme—outrage at the unnecessary endangerment of a child by those responsible for ensuring her safety. It also highlights the grabber of the case, "They did nothing," while providing a call to do something now to make it better.

D.   Creating the Opening

1.   Introduction

The opening statement delivered in the courtroom before the jury must reflect the hard work done by counsel during case investigation, analysis, and preparation. It is controlled by the relevant legal standards, but must also be grounded in an understanding of how to tell a story in a way that grabs the jury's attention, holds their interest and makes them receptive to the evidence later admitted. In preparing the opening, counsel must consistently remind themselves that this is the first time the jury will learn of the events that make up their case, and great effort must be given to ensuring the story told is clear and understandable to these first time listeners.

One way to conceptualize the purpose of the opening statement is to think about them like movie trailers for anticipated summer blockbusters. These trailers give the viewer enough information to understand the basics of the story the movie presents, introduce the audience to the cast of characters they will see, and tug at the heartstrings of the audience in order to convince them to see the film. In an opening, counsel should present information sufficient so that the jury knows the basics of the story of their case, introduce the most relevant witnesses the jury will hear from, and conclude with the call to action that empowers the jury to make a decision.

Superior openings contain cohesive and complementary factual and legal theories developed using the techniques of case analysis previously discussed. The moral theme of the case should be readily apparent to anyone hearing the opening. It is often described as a "hook" or "grabber" capturing the essence of the case, why one side should win. These three elements of case analysis work together to create a narrative that the jury will adopt. Once the jury has adopted the narrative put forth in the opening statement counsel is well on their way to prevailing. A note of caution, counsel can snatch defeat from the jaws of victory if their opening statement creates a sense of cognitive dissonance or disbelief. Statements made to juries during openings are promises, and must be kept throughout the trial. The persuasive power of the opening will not matter if counsel fails to keep the promises made in it. The theme provides the moral imperative that moves the jury to emotionally accept the facts presented by counsel.

Often counsel will begin their opening with a thematic statement setting the stage for the story of the case. These thematic statements catch the jury's attention and focus them. They serve as an intellectual "shorthand" designed to connect the jury to whatever timeless human theme may be present in the case. Instead of beginning with "once upon a time," themes allow counsel to begin with the core concept of the case in way designed to grab the jury's attention.

Example: In the following case the criminal defense counsel represents a client charged with assaulting her husband. The defense intends to use a legal theory based upon battered spouse syndrome, while drawing attention to the failure of the system to help.

Judge: Defense you may begin your opening.

Defense: Thank you. Your honor *(acknowledging the court)*, counsel *(acknowledging opposing counsel)*, *(Approaches the jury, centering herself on the jury box and then waiting in silence until she has the attention of the entire jury).*

She fought back *(pause)*. Against her husband, against the system, against a world that had done nothing but abandon and abuse her Jessica took the only steps she could take towards safety and freedom - and that is why she is here today *(making eye contact across the jury)*. Members of the jury we will show you through the course of this trial that this is a case about self defense and an abused wife who did the only thing she could do, that anyone could have done. The state has arrayed its overwhelming power against her, but just as she did the day she made her husband stop abusing her, Jessica sits her today ready and

> willing to fight back, and regain her life. She
> asks only that you listen with an open mind.
> Let's talk about the events bringing us here to-
> day....

A superior opening will often contain a line, usually close to the beginning, but not always, capturing the essence of the moral theme, factual
theory, and legal theory. The example above uses the words "She fought
back," identifying that the defendant acted in response to what had happened to her. When delivered properly the jury should want to know why
she fought back. Answering that why question successfully maximizes the
possibility of acquittal in this example.

Counsel must place this grabber or hook where the jury will remember it.
The doctrine of primacy and recency establishes that an audience is more
likely to remember the first and last portions of a presentation. Using this
understanding counsel would be well served to both begin and end with
the hook that focuses the jury on their story in a way that creates a call to
justice. In effect, counsel wants this hook to be an "ear worm" that sticks
with the jury throughout the entirety of the trial, and becomes one of the
first things jury members come back to when deliberating the case. This
type of hook has the additional benefit of giving the jury something worth
focusing on when they are at their peak level of attention.

Placing a thematic statement at the beginning and
end of the opening statement is an organizational
construct often referred to as "bookending." This
provides structure to the opening. Counsel should
use this technique to quickly capture and present
their theme and theory of the case in a memorable
way. The story told between those bookends previews the evidence that will be presented, supporting counsel's position with persuasive power while
also buttressing their credibility.

As the jury listens the story of the case, they should easily perceive how it
is tied directly to the moral theme. The need to right the wrong identified
by the introductory phrase creates an avenue for communication which
moves the jury to at least entertain a version of the facts supporting counsel's case. The more tightly tied the theme is to the story of the case, the
more credible and believable counsel appears to the jury. Opening the door
to consideration and acceptance of the facts as counsel presents them is a
key component for a successful outcome.

2.   Relevant Story

Counsel must choose which story, from a myriad of possibilities, they will tell the jury during opening. This story is not a representation of a core truth about the case, but is rather a construct based upon the applicable law and admissible evidence. There is a choice that is implicit in this process - to tell the best version possible ethically while achieving a resolution in favor of the client. These choices not only encourage, but require careful editing based upon the law. The law works in concert with the facts to create the most persuasive presentation.

Creating the story of the case is not an exercise in creative writing, but rather a logical process informed by counsel's understanding of human nature while also taking into consideration how the jury is likely to react to both the evidence and witnesses. It is guided with the knowledge of the questions that each jury member what answered during the opening —"Why am I here?" and "What do you want me to do about it?" There is an art to this, but it also lends itself to a formulaic series of steps designed to create an interesting presentation. When crafting openings counsel should consider the following storytelling techniques:

- Use present tense verbs
- Tell the story from a defined point of view
- Avoid passive voice
- Structure the story to achieve your goal
- Edit, edit, and then edit again
- Use sensory words
- Use Contrast to highlight important facts
- Use surprise to focus the listener's attention
- Be Concrete
- Let the listener know where they are going (foreshadow)
- Never sacrifice believability for performance

Counsel must identify the core story designed to bring the jury to the moment of decision in a way which opens them up to the evidence which will be presented. The story of the case told in the opening is a promise made by counsel to the jury. A promise as to what the case is about. Promises made in court must be kept, or the consequences for failing to keep them will be paid. In telling the story each word matters.

The use of present tense verbs and sensory language lends itself to natural storytelling with a heightened level of persuasion. Counsel should conceptualize their opening as if they have a go-pro camera following the action of the case. What counsel wants the jury to feel, hear, see, smell, touch or taste in each moment of the story should be carefully considered, and sensory language added to enhance these moments of storytelling opportunity. This way, without ever violating the golden rule by asking the jury to put themselves into the scene directly, a similar effect can be achieved.

Example: the following portion from a state opening tells the story of a young victim sexually abused by her father. Consider carefully the use of words, structure, and tone. Look to see where the hook is placed in this presentation and consider the effectiveness in how the story is arranged.

Judge: State you may begin.

State: Thank you your honor, counsel, members of the jury.

2662 Fergusson Circle is a small townhouse at the end of the street. As we walk down the street we notice the two story townhouses with their red brick first floor and white siding on the second floor. The front yards are filled with children and toys, the backyards with family barbecue grills. It looks, sounds, feels, and even smells like a neighborhood where young parents are busy raising children.

When we get to the end of the street and turn to the right we are standing in front of Sarah's home. It is the townhouse at the end of the row. If we look up we can see Sarah's bedroom. A rainbow sticker is in the corner of the window. Her bedroom is right on the end of the row, in the corner. While we can't see her parent's room, it is right behind Sarah's.

Her home is surrounded by a green chain link fence. The bars across the top of the fence are bent from years of children placing their hands on the top and leaping over. You can see where the grass has been worn away by the movement of small feet.

If we open up the gate to Sarah's yard, we can step inside. The yard is covered with toys. You can almost hear the sound of children's laughter as they play here. In one corner is a small plastic clubhouse where Sarah plays with her brother Tommy. If we open the door the small clubhouse and crawl inside we can look out the front door - directly at Sarah's home. Sometimes her home is a happy place, filled with laughter. Sometimes it is not.

When we crawl out of the clubhouse and walk up to the front door we notice that it has an old screen door. We open it and go inside. Directly to the left of the front door is a kitchen, we can almost smell the cookies that Sarah's mom bakes. The kitchen is a happy place. If we walk through the kitchen we find ourselves in the family room/den. Sarah watches her favorite cartoons her with Tommy and eats dinner at the table in the corner. It is happy place. When we go back through the kitchen to the front door we can look up the stairs to the bedrooms. Sometimes that is a happy place - sometimes it is not.

Walking up the stairs we come to the landing. Directly in front of us is Sarah's grandma's room. She lives with them and that room is a very happy place. We turn left and walk down a short hall, passing the bathroom. On the left hand side is the door to Sarah and Tommy's room - that is a happy place. Looking inside we we see that Tommy's bed has Thomas the Tank

> Engine bedroom sheets, Sarah's bed has my lit-
> tle ponies on it.
>
> When we look to the right we see Mommy and
> Daddy's room. Sometimes their room is a happy
> place, sometimes it is not. Sarah knows it will
> NOT be a happy place if daddy opens the closet
> door and reaches for the strawberry flavored
> "love juice." When Sarah smells the love juice
> she knows it will not be a happy place, not at all.

This section of the opening uses the unseen threat that floats in the back-ground. Everyone listening knows that something bad is coming, they are just wondering how it will come to light. The structure of the opening and word selection by counsel increases the tension and suspense with each passing moment. Based on the instructions of the judge during jury selec-tion, the jury will know they're deciding a criminal case. The seemingly pleasant setting is contrasted with that information in the back of the jury's head, especially when combined with the repeated nature of various loca-tions as "happy places." By the time counsel gets to a description of the love juice the jury is ready to physically respond. Their attention is now focused completely on that bottle of strawberry flavored lubricant. There is no doubt that great attention will be paid when it is opened during her testimony.

3.　Preview the Hard Questions of Fact

During case analysis counsel identify those hard questions of fact upon which the case turns. It is important to have a theory dealing with every hard question of fact in the case. Failure to answer the hard questions, ei-ther by attempting to ignore them, or inadequately explaining them, can destroy the quality of an opening statement, not to mention the strength of the entire case. The answer to the hard question of fact can be addressed through other facts, attacking the credibility of the witnesses who testify as to the hard questions of fact, or by using the law to reduce the impact of the hard questions of fact.

Counsel must identify the hard questions of fact, create a plan for dealing with the hard questions, and then implement the plan. This implementation must occur through out all stages of the trial, flowing from the opening statement, through the examination of witnesses, and into the closing ar-gument. By showing the jury a willingness to discuss these hard questions, counsel increases their credibility with the members of the jury. It displays that they are sufficiently confident in their case that they will not back down from difficult issues. If this is carried throughout the trial, it makes it far more likely that the jury will decide in favor of counsel and their position.

Example: the following portion from a state opening tells the story of a young victim sexually abused by her father. The alleged victim in this case did not report the sexual assault by her father for almost fourteen months. Counsel must deal with the hard question of fact revolving around the amount of time it took for the young victim to come forward. Note the techniques used by counsel to place this issue in context.

State: When we look to the right we see Mommy and Daddy's room. Sometimes their room is a happy place, sometimes it is not. Sarah knows it will NOT be a happy place if daddy opens the closet door and reaches for the strawberry flavored "love juice." When Sarah smells the love juice she knows it will not be a happy place, at all.

    You will learn today that for as long as Sarah lives in the house with her daddy she never tells anyone about the love juice. It is only after she moves away with her mom and grandma. When she goes to New Mexico, almost fourteen months later, that she finally tells her mom about those unhappy times. Her mom will share with us the details of that moment, from this witness stand right here she will describe how her daughter broke down that day.

    Sarah was 5 years old when she first tasted the love juice. Her age, and how she responded, how she was affected is important to this case. We will call Dr. Jones, a specialist in treating victims of sexual abuse. Dr. Jones will share with you why young children do not come forward, sometimes for years, when their abuser is a family member. Dr. Jones will help us understand how the inaction of Sarah should be considered in order properly determine if her father is guilty of sexually assaulting Sarah.

4.   Introduce self, bring jury to the present

During the opening statement counsel must take the time to introduce themselves to the jury, identifying whom they represent. Counsel often begin the opening statement by introducing themselves, this is not always the best approach. It may be the accepted practice in a particular jurisdiction to begin by introducing themselves, but just because it is an accepted practice does not necessarily mean that it should be followed without first thinking about it critically.

Recall that this is not the first time a representative for counsel's side of the case will have spoken with the members of the jury. Whether it was counsel themselves or another member of their team an entire set of interaction has taken place during jury selection. While it is crucial for counsel to cover their positioning in the case during opening and polite to remind the jury of their name, simply introducing themselves as if it is the first time they have spoken to these people can give the impression that counsel was not fully engaged and aware of their actions in that initial conversation. Rather than ignore that interaction, calling back to jury selection during the opening can be a powerful way to remind the jury of the relationship that has already begun.

Sometimes counsel can use the need for an introduction as a break between emotional points in the opening. It allows for a contrast in the story, a break for the jury to gather their attention and then refocus it where it does the most good.

Example:This portion from the state opening telling the story of a young victim sexually abused by her father uses the need to introduce counsel to the jury as a means of reducing the emotional intensity of the opening, and then refocusing it more effectively. Note the techniques used by counsel to create the contrast and change in emotion.

State: Dr. Jones will help us understand how the inaction of Sarah should be considered in order properly determine if her father is guilty of sexually assaulting Sarah. We will connect his testimony to the physical evidence in this case, the bottle of strawberry flavored lubricant.

Members of the jury, once again my name is Javier Centonzio and like we talked about in jury selection I represent the state in this case. The bottle of strawberry flavored "love juice"

described by Sarah is bottle of lubricant purchased by the defendant and kept on the top
shelf of his closet. We will prove to you today
that the defendant used it when he sexually assaulted his daughter.

Sarah will identify that bottle today. I ask only
that you watch her face closely when she opens
it. Watch as she, and you, smell the scent of
strawberries in the room. Her reaction to that
moment will be all that you need to find the defendant guilty of sexually assaulting his daughter - because he is.

5.   Preview Relevant Legal Standard

The judge is required to discuss the standard of proof with the jury during
instructions. This conversation often occurs at the close of the case, long
after counsel might benefit from underlining and reinforcing the standard,
although in some jurisdictions it is also addressed during preliminary matters. It is a best practice to highlight the standard early in the trial process
in the hopes that the jury will view the evidence in light of the applicable
standard - when such focus benefits the client. Attorneys customarily address the standard of proof at some point during opening statements. This
discussion is both legal and procedural, and while it does not directly impact the credibility of evidence or the believability of witnesses, it serves
to orient the jury to the interaction of the law and the facts, laying the
foundation for the argument to follow during closings.

The way in which counsel addresses the standard of proof is situationally
dependent, and driven by a variety of factors, to include, the strength of
opposing counsel's case, the emotional impact of the facts, the perceived
way in which the jury defines the client, and the moral theme identified
during case analysis which will be presented during the trial.

***Example: this portion from the state opening telling the story of a young
victim sexually abused by her father previews the relevant legal standard in
the case and posits that they state will meet their burden.***

> *State:*   Her reaction to that moment will be all that you
> need to find the defendant guilty of sexually as-
> saulting his daughter - because he is.

Members of the jury we the state bear the burden of proof in this case. We must prove, to you a beyond a reasonable doubt, that this grown man *(pointing directly at the defendant)* sexually molested his daughter over a period of eighteen months. We welcome that burden. Beyond a reasonable doubt is a legal standard the court uses to establish how confident you must be in the evidence before you can find the defendant guilty. We will bring you witness testimony, physical evidence, and the expert opinion of a world renowned Psychiatrist who deals with sexually abused children.

Once you have heard the testimony, seen the evidence, and been instructed on the law we will have far exceeded our burden of proof. The facts, evidence, and your own common sense will overwhelm any unreasonable doubt of the defendant's innocence. We will do our job in meeting that burden of proof, and then it will be time for you to do yours - finding him guilty.

Example: this next example, taken from a portion of a defense opening in the same case, showcases how the defense can also focus on the burden of proof to highlight the difficulty in overcoming such a standard. It is often wise for counsel to reference the expected instructions of the court, particularly when the standard reads in a way favorable to the theme and theory of the defense case.

Defense: The government just stood before you and told you that they would meet their burden of proof today. I'd like to talk about that for a moment. *(Walking over to stand before the state's table, pointing at the state's table while looking at the jury)* The law in our state, in our nation, is very clear. In a criminal trial the burden of proof rests at this table throughout the entire trial, and well it should.

We have no legal requirement to prove anything today. The government must prove, beyond and to the exclusion of any reasonable doubt, that my client committed this horrible crime. This burden of proof is the highest in our legal system for a reason. This standard protects society from unfair prosecutions by the unlimited resources of the state. We ask only that you listen to the court when they instruct you on this standard and that you then apply it in light of your own common sense.

To meet this standard the state must explain to you how this could have happened when the family lived together through out the time of the alleged abuse, why no one ever complained, why no police were ever called, and no physical examinations of Sarah were ever conducted during the time of the alleged abuse. They must explain to you, to a beyond a reasonable doubt, why this allegation only came to light after Sarah's mother took the children and moved to New Mexico to live with a man she met in an online chat room.

6.   Connect, Law, Facts, Moral Theme

In the section on trial preparation and analysis this text discusses how the law, facts, and moral theme must connect holistically to support the requested outcome during closing argument. Closing argument is the final destination at trial, the opening statement is the embarkation point, the beginning of the journey so to speak. To begin well is to end well, and proper opening statements connect to the closing argument both directly and obliquely.

During opening statements counsel must tell the jury what happened, how the law impacts what occurred, and then explain why the requested relief is the morally right thing to do. The presentation must focus on "what happened" while previewing "how" the law impacts the story, and "why" the case should be decided in their favor.

Counsel must properly balance the facts, law and morality during the opening statement. During openings the presentation should focus on the

> *What, how and why are the linchpins upon which the case pivots.*

facts, telling the story in a light most beneficial to the client without ever making promises that will not be kept, misstating evidence, or attempting to improperly persuade. The law is previewed but not discussed in depth, and the moral theme of the case is present at both the beginning and end of the opening statement, while at the same time woven into the fabric of the relevant facts shared through the story of the case. One effective method counsel should consider is to ask the jury to pay particularly close attention to witnesses whose testimony constitutes those hard questions of facts that must be answered. By doing so, counsel is in effect signaling to the jury those witnesses that have the most impact on the outcome of the case.

The connection between the facts, law and moral issues within the case are ever present. Balancing the presentation properly, in light of local customs and procedural rules, normally produces an opening statement focused on the relevant facts counsel expects to prove, with sufficient mention of the relevant law to focus the critical listening skills of the jury, surrounded by an emotional, or moral, tone that makes them care about the outcome of the case.

7.   Forecast Prayer for Relief (Say the words)

The prayer for relief is a term used to describe the request by counsel for a specific outcome in the case. It is important that the jury hear the words from the attorney's own mouth during the opening statement. Saying the actual words capturing the requested verdict makes them real within the court room. It is also provides the final answer to the questions we know juries have during opening statements—namely, what counsel wants them to do about what has happened in the case. Properly done the prayer for relief ends the opening statement on an emotional note that reconnects to the theme and theory of the case as it is expressed in the grabber or hook used by counsel.

Example: the following prayer for relief is taken from a state opening focusing on a problem, a process, and a prize. It involves a woman charged with the murder of her husband so that she could collect his life insurance policy.

> State: A problem, a process, and a prize. At the close of this trial we will have proven the defendant's problem - she needed money and lots of it. We will have shown you conclusively that she took out a large life insurance policy on her husband,

far exceeding what was recommended. You will have heard from multiple witnesses, to include the owner of the range she visited with an unknown friend, and the conversations she had with the life insurance agent, Ms. Barry. We will have established her access to the type of weapon used to kill her husband, and provided you with multiple reasons to determine that she either shot him herself or hired someone to do it.

We will review this evidence together. The facts, the applicable law, and the testimony of witnesses. I will then ask you to simply apply the greatest invention of our shared legal system, your own common sense. It will bring you to one unshakable conclusion. On the 6th of June the defendant had a problem, she identified a process, and received her prize - over 500,000 dollars. It will then be up to you to write the last policy on this case, one that finds her guilty of first degree murder - because she is.

Example: the following prayer for relief is taken from a defense opening in criminal case where the focus of the defense's efforts is the failure of the state to prove their case to the beyond a reasonable doubt standard.

Defense: Members of the jury at the close of this trial I will come back to you and together we will look at what has been proven, not proven, or not even mentioned. Together we will discuss the facts, the evidence, and the lack of evidence in light of their burden of proof.

We will see that the fancy speech you just heard was nothing more than a case of the state making promises they couldn't keep. I will then ask you to keep the promise you made to justice during jury selection. I will ask you to set my client free because they failed to prove their case.

E.   Delivering the Opening

Counsel communicates with the jury each and every moment both are present in the courtroom. That being said, some moments are more conducive to effective communication - opening statements are such a moment. Counsel will never have the same degree of focus from the jury as they do in those first few precious moments. Words have not yet been spoken, the canvas is mostly blank, but the time is at hand to take up the brush of words and begin to paint the story of the case.

The colors with which counsel choose to paint are theirs alone. Their palette includes eye contact, body movement, word choice, and delivery. Counsel should both feel and show enthusiasm for their case without the need for histrionics, the preliminaries have been dispensed with and it is time to get down to business, professionally. Cheerleading and pounding tables are not required, but caring and believing strongly are. Care and belief are reflected through the opening statement and carries over into the testimony of witnesses. Most importantly, counsel must craft an opening that not only persuades, but is genuine in its reflection of the care and belief they have for the case. Juries can pick up when counsel does not connect to the story they convey, and will punish any perceived "fakeness" when it comes down to deliberations. Word choice, tone, focus, delivery, all of them matter and must be connected properly to the theme and theory of the case.

Counsel should carefully prepare for the opening. This may include creating note cards, outlines, or even writing the entire presentation before giving it. Each of these methods are designed to marshal the case and to make counsel comfortable, but they are not delivery methods! Opening statements should never be read. Reading a document robs counsel of several incredibly persuasive tools. First, it will pull counsel's eyes away from the jury, sacrificing personal connection for a false sense of security. Second, if counsel is reading from a document, their voice will go down into the podium, muting any use of variance in tone and inflection. Finally, when reading an opening, there is a tendency to use a podium in the courtroom and stand behind it. This puts a physical barrier between counsel and the jury, which may be perceived as counsel needing to hide something from the jury, or, perhaps worse, be seen as the counsel "talking down" to the jury and lecturing them rather than telling the story of the case.

Word choice is important, and counsel should paint an active picture for the jury. Passive voice should be avoided unless necessary to shift responsibility, and the present tense is preferable, particularly during the story portion of the case. Active voice is heightened by the use of sensory language—words dealing with sights, sounds, smells, tastes and feelings. Using such words creates a more vivid picture for the members of the jury, giving them the ability to relate what counsel is describing to their own life experiences. The presentation itself must have a clear beginning, middle, and end, with a structure which pulls the jury into the story, allowing them to follow along and potentially predict what should come next. The narrative style of present tense ensures believability, simplicity, and credibility - it moves the jury towards persuasion.

Counsel must carefully choose the structure of their opening statement. Acceptable formats include chronologies, flashbacks, and parallelism. Whatever structure counsel chooses to use, they must continually check that they are complying with the law of opening statements, the preferences of their local judge and jurisdiction, and they are answering the questions of why the jury is there and what they want the jury to do. The key components of successful storytelling definitely apply. Preparation, preparation, and more preparation will bring comfort. Gerry Spence says "Prepare, prepare, prepare, and win."[3] Command of the trial arena comes from developing the ability to communicate through the spoken word as viewed through knowledge of, and comfort with, the factual and legal issues present in the case. The ultimate goal is to have the jury convinced by the end of opening statements that no one knows the facts and issues of the case as well as counsel does, and that comfort can only be earned through hard work.

1.   Beginning

Counsel should carefully choose the first words of the opening. They will never have the undivided attention of the jury in quite the same way. Proper word choice, physicality and presence can all be used to effectively set the tone for the rest of the case. The proper theme and theory will resonate through out the opening statement, be supported by the testimony of witnesses during direct and cross, then be expounded upon during closing arguments. People make up their minds quickly, and generally focus on the first words out of counsel's mouth - make them count.

The previous example concerning how to begin on opening is illustrative:

Judge: *(Turning to face the jury)* Members of the jury we are now going to hear opening statements from the attorneys in this case. The openings should give you an overview of what the attorneys expect the evidence they will introduce will show. The opening statements themselves are not evidence, but merely counsel's expectation of what the evidence will be. The party bearing the burden of proof normally goes first. State you may proceed with opening statement.

State: Thank you. Your honor *(acknowledging the court)*, counsel *(acknowledging opposing counsel)*, *(Approaches the jury, centering herself on the jury box)*, members of the jury....

Note how counsel acknowledges the court and opposing counsel before beginning. The acknowledgment of the court and opposing counsel reinforces the importance of what is about to take place with the jury - ritual makes the process important, and by showing respect to the process counsel increases their credibility and believability with the jury. By the same token, centering the body on the jury so that everyone is included also matters, sending the message that everyone is important. It also forces counsel to choose a physical position that will allow them to reach each member of the jury while not intruding into their personal space. Location is important and will drive the tone, volume and delivery of the words which are to follow.

When beginning the delivery counsel should be careful to make eye contact, beginning only after every member of the jury is focused on the attorney. While this may take time, it is crucial to not rush this process, as counsel gets one opportunity to have that first moment of connection with the jury in opening statements. As they await that moment of connection, best practice is for counsel to stand with their feet shoulder width apart, firmly planted in their position within in the courtroom. By removing unnecessary movement, counsel is able to start from a literal physical position of strength, which enhances the story they are about to tell. Once the physical connection has been made through the eyes, it is time to begin to speak.

All eyes in the courtroom should be on counsel as they begin. Getting them there, and then keeping the jurors engaged and keeping them that way, is a critical skill. Counsel must connect with the jury. That connection is created with words, movements, and eye contact.

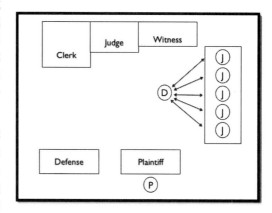

Some attorneys find it difficult to make direct eye contact with jurors and adopt the public speaking approach of "staring at their forehead" in order to avoid eye contact. That ap-proach is a stop gap measure designed to get the lawyer through the dis-comfort of public speaking - it is not a preferred communication tech-nique. While it may work fine for public speaking situations with a large audience, in front of jury it is a poorer choice. Juries, at most, consist of twelve other individuals, and thus it is easier for them to pick up on this crutch technique. Also, difficulty in making eye contact reflects fear—fear of connecting with others. It is a crutch designed to allow counsel to "get through" the opening statement, it sends the wrong message to the jury. Jury members may not view it as discomfort with public speaking, but may interpret it instead as discomfort with counsel's client, the case, or with the jury themselves. Refusal to engage in eye contact is an admission to the jury that counsel is not completely comfortable with the process, which may lead the jury to infer that counsel is not truly behind their case.

More importantly, why should counsel be afraid to look the people who will decide the case in the eye? By the time openings begin, these people are not strangers. They already know a great deal about the jury, having read questionnaires, asked questions, and literally assisted in choosing them. Now is not the time to be afraid to extend to them the gift of trust. Counsel is going to ask the jury to trust them to guide them through the factual legal issues in the case, and in order for that to happen they must display their own willingness to be vulnerable in front of the members of the jury. Counsel should give themselves permission to truly connect to the people on the jury, and that requires eye contact.

Another powerful tool in the advocate's arsenal that often goes underval-ued is silence. Silence at the beginning of the opening can be quite effec-tive. It pulls attention to the advocate, focuses the jury, settling them down into the moment, and reinforces the importance of what is to come. The longer counsel stands silent at the beginning of an opening statement, the greater the tension within the room. It can seem like forever to the attorney, but not to others. When counsel has crafted a particularly emotionally powerful phrase or scene with their language, silence should also be used. By taking that pause, counsel signals to the jury that this fact is something they should allow to weigh on their minds. It places emphasis on it without resorting to overly dramatic theatrics.

Silence is filled with countless possibilities. Counsel should use it to capture the attention of the jury

In the initial stages of the opening, counsel should center themselves on the jury, but not so close as to invade their personal space. Most "trial" experts advise counsel not to touch the railing, and many jurisdictions specifically prohibit counsel from getting too close the jury box, others are more forgiving. Counsel should know the local customs and follow them, unless there is a good tactical or strategic reason not to do so. In those instances where counsel are allowed to get up close and personal with the jury they should be careful to experiment in practice before attempting this technique. One classic indicator that counsel has gotten too close to the jury in their movements is people physically leaning back in their chairs. Where counsel can stand without invading the jury's space will vary widely based on the size of the courtroom, the local preferences of the judge, and counsel's own physical presence.

Counsel must find a comfortable position from which they can survey and connect with the entire jury. If the attorney is too close it makes the jury uncomfortable, and an important persuasion goal is to make this group as comfortable with the advocate as possible.

2.   Using Body Language

Physical presence in the courtroom is part of counsel's persuasive arsenal, and sometimes there is a need to fill the space without using words. This is best accomplished by body language and presence. Presence is another way of saying attitude, body language is physicality. While the concept of body language means different things to different people, we are concerned here with how body language can open communication between the lawyer and her audience. Body language must create a sense of credibility and believability. Counsel should not forget that they are the first, last, and best witness for their case. So body language that indicates one is closed off—such as crossed arms or hands clasped in front of the body—fights against counsel's goal of credibility. If counsel physically closes themselves off from the members of the jury, there is an increased likelihood that the jury will believe counsel is attempting to hide something. The choice of body language is important, because it can either open, or close, avenues of communication.

Once the silence has focused jury attention, counsel should allow their hands to drop to their sides, exposing their body to the members of the jury. Letting their hands drop sends a message to the jury that counsel is open to communication, is not hiding anything, and trusts the jury. While it can make counsel feel exposed, this is actually a powerful communication position. By standing in front of a jury with your hands at your sides; counsel are both vulnerable and powerful at the same time. In the courtroom, making oneself vulnerable to interpretation by the jury often leads to an increase in the power of what is said. By walking out on that limb of vulnerability, counsel enhances the jury's ability to see them as genuine, believable and credible. When counsel stands before the jury, hands at their side with no physical barrier impeding them, all they have to convince the jury of their story is their case, their voice, and their body. When done properly counsel now have no choice but to forge forward with the best impression possible.

After acknowledging the jury through body language it is time to begin, using the types of "hooks," "grabbers," and structures previously discussed. It is a best practice to begin with a statement capturing the essence of the case identified through the factual theory, legal theory, and moral theme. It can be something as simple as a one-word statement like, "Accountability," "Credibility," "Gold-digger," "Rage," or "Greed."

Short pithy statements capturing the essence of what must be said without falling into a cliché is preferable. The classic example in recent history is "If it doesn't fit, you must acquit." Counsel must be careful not to fall into the patterns and methods that juries come to expect from books, television and movies. While strong cultural connectors, rarely do the facts of real life cases align as neatly as those for a planned drama. Counsel's knowledge and preparation of the facts at hand, when done properly, should be reflected in the beginning of the opening statement, and it should come organically out of the hard work already done.

Counsel should allow their hands to move in concert with your words, just as they do in the real world. Planned and scripted hand movements are disingenuous, and should be avoided, much in the same way that haphaz-

ard movements are discouraged. That is not
to say that counsel should not spend time
blocking out some portion of their gestures
and movements, but rather that to do so for
the entirety of the opening leaves the jury
with an impression that this is an act, rather
than counsel speaking to them in the moment. The movement of the hands should
follow and complement the voice, with some

Remember to

VaRy ThE

PaCe

motions choreographed ahead of time to make specific points. If gestures
are to be used, counsel should allow them to flow to the natural extension
of their body. This means fully gesturing with the arms and hands, rather
than limiting movements to the area surrounding the torso. Think of it like
a dancer—the most compelling ones allow their movements to extend
through the end of their limbs. Counsel should make note of this and apply
it to their own body movements in the courtroom.

Like words, movement in the courtroom has persuasive power. Counsel
must understand this, develop the skills necessary, and then use them.

3.   Verbal Keys

Counsel should ensure that their tone matches the case. Outrage is good,
but should be saved for the lying witness or the clear overreaching charge.
The jury should be relatively neutral at this point so counsel should take
care to not scare them over to the other side with histrionics. Persuasion
can occur without arguing when movement, language and delivery come
together.

Overly emotional presentations or theatrics should be avoided. They will
not persuade anyone and call into question counsel's believability as well
as exposing a perceived unfair bias. Just as the jury does not have enough
information for counsel to argue the case to them, they have also not yet
created an emotional connection to the case. Both of these reasons require
counsel to not advocate in an overly dramatic fashion. Counsel should
strive for a conversational tone accurately reflecting the story of the case.
Counsel should think in terms of talking *with* the jury instead of *at* them.
This will allow an appropriate level of emotion to come through for storytelling purposes, without giving the jury the impression that counsel is acting like an advocate rather than simply advocating.

Jurors will summon mental images of people, places, facts, objects, and
locations from the words spoken. Choose carefully, with a full and complete understanding of the possible connotations they may hold for the
jury. While the terms "billiards parlor" and "pool hall" both describe a
place where a game is played, they create very different images. The bil-

liards parlor is filled with well-heeled individuals who drink expensive whiskey and talk about their stock investments. The guys in the pool hall are crouched under a cheap stained-glass florescent lamp, counting the beer stain circles on the pool table railing.

Gripping and persuasive language does not have to be flamboyant, but it should capture an image for the listener. Counsel should not strain to be a poet. Capture the truth simply, using language the jurors will accept, understand, and interpret in a way counsel can both influence and predict. Care should be taken to avoid legal jargon and cop-speak, counsel do not need to remind the jury they are a professional doing their job. Instead the goal is allow them to see you as a fellow human being helping them to discover the truth.

4.   Dangers of Improper Argument

A well-prepared and well-delivered opening is in and of itself persuasive. When the statements made during opening cannot be tied to a fact that a witness will disclose through testimony, then counsel is not making an opening statement—they are arguing. Comments on the credibility, believability, or reliability of the expected evidence are not a forecasting of what the evidence will be, but a comment on its validity.

Once counsel slide down the slippery slope towards argument there is a very real danger of losing the jury. During openings counsel want to reinforce in the minds of the jury that they are present to assist the jury in sorting through some complex issues to find the truth. Arguing during openings reminds the jury that counsel is a lawyer and potentially not to be trusted. Counsel should save argument for closings, when being argumentative is not only expected, but encouraged.

Opening statement is also not the appropriate time to tell the jury the function of an opening. It sounds defensive, juries don't care, and it invites them to ignore the substance of the opening. By beginning with a civics lesson during the opening statement, counsel are simply throat-clearing and buying time because they are not prepared to deliver a cogent theme and theory. It is wasted time and space. That being said, legal concepts should be discussed as appropriate to advance the theme and theory of the case while not wasting the jury's time.

5.   A Call to Action (a Satisfactory Conclusion to the Opening)

As discussed above, juries want to know why they are in court, and what it is counsel expects them to do about the situation that has brought them to court. As counsel comes to the conclusion of their opening, they must ensure that they answer the latter in a fashion that is satisfactory from a story telling perspective and also empowers the jury to reach the verdict that will bring about justice.

Counsel should preview what will happen at the end of trial during closing argument. This gives the jury information about how their experience in court will draw to a close, and also gives counsel a moment to point out a truism of trial work. At the end of the day, the decision making power in every case lies in the hands of the members of the jury. That power is not to be diminished, but rather used as a way to point the jury toward counsel's end goal for the case. By reminding them of that power, counsel is able to have their theme ring out with the words that will be placed on the verdict form, thus tying the two together in the mind of the jury.

F.   Examples

The following examples are taken from a selection of cases. Each takes the lessons of this chapter and applies them through the creative lens of the individual attorney. As you read through them consider the information you have reviewed in this chapter and see if you can identify how, and why, the advocate chose that approach.

Example: Opening in a Robbery Case. The following state and defense openings are taken from a criminal case where a convicted felon, who has been paroled to a halfway house, is accused of robbing a Cash 4 Free check cashing place sometime before lunch on the 8th of December.

Judge:	*(Turning to face the jury)* Members of the jury we are now going to hear opening statements from the attorneys in this case. The openings should give you an overview of what the attorneys expect the evidence they will introduce will show. The opening statements themselves are not evidence, but merely counsel's expectation of what the evidence will be. The party bearing the burden of proof normally goes first. State you may proceed with opening statement.
State:	It's a dark day in a man's life when he sits down and plans to get his hands on easy money. To get his hands on cash he didn't earn. To fill his fists with it any way he can.

When all a man can hear is the call of Easy money all around him... in a passing coat pocket...in that cash register...in that Cash 4 Free. Calling him, begging him, testing him...some men will fail that test, and the darkness that follows consumes them.

My name is Claudette Goyanes and I represent the people of our state today. During this trial, its my job to prove that in December of 20XX-2 the Defendant finally gave in to the whisper of easy money he had been hearing from the local Cash 4 Free. I will bring you evidence and testimony to take you back to December of 20XX-2... to Edward Whalen's darkest day. Let's go there together....

The defendant, Edward Whalen, walked into that darkness the day he walked into the Cash 4 Free with a note, a mask, and a gun. How did he get there?

Back then the defendant woke up each morning alone in his small room, at 5 AM...He'd like to keep sleeping but he's got to be at check-in by 5:30. No exceptions. In a moment he'll make sure his shirt's tucked in. And at check in, he'll follow his answers with "sir" or "ma'am." But right now, he sits in the darkness, listens for a moment...to Easy money whispering to him...from just down the street, around the corner, inside the Cash 4 Free.

While everyone on the outside gets to walk around with their wallets full, easy money mocks him, louder each week, because the halfway house he is living in takes his paycheck from him, and hands him an allowance of $8.50 a day.

Today you'll learn that on December 8th, 20XX-2, He walks into Cash 4 Free, with a mask, a gun, and a threat written on a piece paper to get his hands on that easy money. He goes to Samantha Steven's station, hands her a note, a note that has her name on it, and just in case his message is not completely clear, he lifts his dark sunglasses and looks her dead in the eye.

What does she do? She hands over more than $5000 in cash. The defendant takes the money and runs out of the Cash 4 Free. A few seconds later the sound of a single gun shot echoes across the parking lot. The defendant is gone, but he leaves a calling card, a .22 caliber bullet in Ms. Steven's car's tire. You will learn today that the 22-caliber pistol kept by the defendant's boss at his place of work is missing. Missing for a while now. And you'll see that the bullet left in that tire matches the type of gun-- a Ruger 22--missing from the computer repair shop where he works.

You will also learn that the surveillance camera at the Cash 4 Free took a photo of the robber that day. We ask that you look at the photo, compare it to how the defendant looked before he cut his long flowing hair. We will also show you the money stolen from the Cash 4 Free that was found underneath the dumpster behind the computer repair shop where the defendant worked.

The defendant is being charged with two crimes today, robbery and possession of a firearm while he did it. As the prosecution in this case we have the burden prove that the defendant is guilty of those crimes. That is a burden we welcome and it's one we will meet today.

Although the defendant may have hid his face, cut his hair and covered his head to hide on the day of the robbery, he cannot hide from the evidence we will present here at trial today. He can't cover up the trail of of easy money leading literally to the back door of the place where he works. It may have been whispering in the defendant's ear, but it will be heard loud and clear by all of us in this courtroom today.

That is why, at the close of this trial I will come back to you and ask you to render a verdict based upon the law, the facts, and what your own common sense tells you happened that day. A verdict finding the defendant guilty *(Counsel returns to counsel's table)*.

Judge: Defense you may proceed.

Defense: Thank you. Your honor (acknowledging the court), counsel (acknowledging opposing counsel), (Approaches the jury, centering herself on the jury box), members of the jury....

Defense: It is inconceivable that Edward Whalen could have committed this crime. Inconceivable. And while those words are true, I was not the first one to say them. No, no. Today you will hear that the prosecutor's witness said those very same words when asked about the likelihood that Edward Whalen robbed the Cash 4 Free on December 8, 20XX-2. That's what the witness who knew best said back then. And that's what you will say at the end of this trial. "Edward Whalen, guilty? That's inconceivable."

I want you to meet Mr. Whalen. This is Edward. He spent the past few years living right here in our community. And for many who live here he is their neighborhood mechanic. That's what he does and he's good at it. Thank you, Mr. Whalen.

It is important for you to remember, Members of the Jury, that this is a criminal trial. And today, all day, the burden of proof lies at this table. The prosecutor must prove to you beyond and to the exclusion of every, single reasonable doubt that Edward Whalen did exactly what they have accused him of doing. That burden – and it is called a burden for a very good reason – is like a huge boulder that the prosecutor must roll up a hill. And that hill is the steepest in our legal system.   Beyond a reasonable doubt. They will not get that boulder up that steep hill here today because the evidence simply will not allow it.

Let's talk about the evidence that you will see and hear in this courtroom today. You'll learn today that Mr. Whalen made some mistakes when he was a young man and it was these mistakes that resulted in his getting in trouble with the law. So after paying his debt to society he moved right here to our community and began his fresh start at the halfway house located in Pinellas Park. While at this half-way house you will learn that Mr. Whalen began to take steps to turn his life around. You will learn he was good employee and even got a job at Same Day Computer Repairs, doing exactly what he loved, fixing and rebuilding computers.

So what will you hear today? Today you will be presented with one witness, the state's only witness who saw the crime committed. But first let me start by taking you back, back the morning of December 6, 20XX-2.

Mr. Whalen began his day just like any other day at the morning check-in. It was there he ran into his friend Julian, since they both had the day off they decided to meet up before lunch and play some dice. You will learn that it was during that time that robbery at the Cash 4 Free took place. The state will have to answer a question based upon testimony we expect to hear today, how could Mr. Whalen be in two places at the same time? You will discover today that he couldn't, making it inconceivable for Mr. Whalen to have committed this crime - just as their witness will testify.

While the State will argue that there is plenty of time for Mr. Whalen to have left the halfway house and made it back in time for lunch the evidence you will see and hear in this courtroom today will tell you the opposite. Today you will hear from the State's own witness, Bobby Taylor, the director of the halfway house, that Mr. Whalen was at every check in and every meal on the day of the robbery and in his opinion is was simply inconceivable that Mr. Whalen could have made to all of the check ins and meals and robbed the Cash 4 Free.

So if everything I have told you so far is true why are we here? Well, you will learn we are here as a result of mistaken identity. You see Pinellas Park is a high crime area and Mr. Whalen, well he was an easy target. You will hear no testimony today from anyone else in the Cash 4 Free…no employees, no customers, no security guards, or any other witnesses from Cash 4 Free on the day of the robbery except Samantha Stevens, the teller working that day. A woman who you will learn had money missing from her drawer in the past... a woman who owed money to an angry ex-lover.

But the lack of evidence in this case does not stop there. No. You will learn today that the robber of the Cash 4 Free was suspected of being armed. However, the only testimony you will hear about the gun is from Ms. Stevens, an individual who you will learn today isn't herself so sure the robber even had gun, so how can we be sure? You will not hear that anyone else saw the robber, much less a robber with a gun. Nor will you hear testimony that Mr. Whalen owned a gun or that the gun claimed to be used in this robbery was found with his fingerprints because as you will learn today none of that evidence exists. So you'll see by the end of this trial that while the prosecution is pointing the finger at Mr. Whalen the evidence is pointing away from him.

Members of the jury, at the end of this trial, it will be clear to you that Mr. Whalen did not and could not have committed this crime... because it was just inconceivable for him to do so. You have the power to make sure that Mr. Whalen gets justice. At the close of this trial I will come back to you discuss the case with you. I will then ask for nothing more, and nothing less, than justice. The justice that comes when you follow the law, the facts, and most importantly members of the jury - your own common sense. I will ask you find him not guilty - because he is. Thank you.

Example: Openings in a Sexual Assault CaseThe following state and defense openings are taken from a criminal case where a patient is accusing her doctor of improper sexual advances.

Judge: (*Turning to face the jury*) Members of the jury we are now going to hear opening statements from the attorneys in this case. The openings should give you an overview of what the attorneys expect the evidence they will introduce will show. The opening statements themselves are not evidence, but merely counsel's expectation of what the evidence will be. The party bearing the burden of proof normally goes first. State you may proceed with opening statement.

State: Thank you. Your honor (*acknowledging the court*), counsel (*acknowledging opposing counsel*), (*Approaches the jury, centering herself on the jury box*), members of the jury....

He turned the sign. He turned the handle. And then, He turned the key.

You are going to learn that this Defendant turned away from being Kristen Wallace's doctor, and he turned into being her rapist.

My name is Patricia Johnson. Along with my co-counsel, Jeremy Stevens, we represent the State in the case against Dr. Roger Pearl, who has been charged with the rape and sexual battery of Kristen Wallace.

You are going to learn that Kristen Wallace trusted Dr. Pearl to be her doctor, a good doctor. She went to his office for several visits for a knee injury. But, this time, the visit on May 1, 20XX-3, it wasn't just an ordinary visit to see the good doctor.

There was no examination of the knee.

There was no treatment performed.

The evidence is going to show you that Ms. Anderson, who was usually present at the office visits, left the office that morning. This was the Defendant's only employee- leaving Ms. Wallace and Dr. Pearl alone. And on his way out, the sign on the door was turned to "closed".

All alone, the Defendant took Ms. Wallace into the examination room. He turned the handle and closed the door. It was then when he instructed her to remove her clothing- all of her clothing- so that he could examine her knee. And all the while they were in this examination room, the Defendant turned the key to the door. Locking him inside with Ms. Wallace.

As she laid on the examination table, Dr. Pearl- who you will learn is an overweight man- forced himself on top of her. He forcefully penetrated her.

Hurting her. Leaving behind redness and abrasions.

As soon as she had the chance, Ms. Wallace ran to the door, turned the key to unlock it and ran out of the exam room. You will learn that she went to a clinic that evening to get an examination.

You see, members of the jury, it is our burden as the state to prove to you beyond a reasonable doubt that these events did in fact occur. We must prove to you that Dr. Felix Pearl is guilty of the sexual battery and rape of Kristen Wallace. We will meet this burden through the evidence you will see here today and the testimony you will hear from the witnesses.

Listen closely to the testimony of Kristen Wallace as she recounts the events as they happened on May 1, 2006. It is not easy for her to come here today and tell her story. But, for the many other patients out there, she has made that choice.

And, Detective Murphy, the investigating officer for the State, will also explain to you Ms. Wallace's reactions after the incident occurred.

After you evaluate all of the evidence and testimony, you will see how it was the Defendant who turned the sign on the office door to closed. It was the defendant who closed the door to the examination room. And that the Defendant turned the key and locked that door. I trust that at the end of this trial you will return the only verdict that speaks the truth. A verdict finding Dr. Felix Pearl guilty.

Judge: Defense you may proceed.

Defense: Thank you. Your honor *(acknowledging the court)*, counsel *(acknowledging opposing counsel)*, *(Ap-*

proaches the jury, centering herself on the jury box), members of the jury….

She thinks he's handsome. She calls him by his first name. She even sees him on the weekends. Those were the actions of Kristen Wallace, the alleged victim in this case.

Today, you will learn Ms. Wallace had feelings for Dr. Pearl, that she acted on those feelings, and afterward she regretted it. A classic case of buyer's remorse. On May 1, 20XX-3, Kristen Wallace and Dr. Pearl had consensual sex. *(Pausing for emphasis)* And while it is not a crime, it is the reason we are here today.

Good morning. My name is Megan Martinez. This is my co-counsel, Joseph Clark. Together we represent Dr. Roger Pearl: the man who is here today because he is accused of rape and sexual battery of his patient, Kristen Wallace. It is important to understand that Dr. Pearl is presumed innocent. Not because I say so, or because Mr. Clark says so, but because the law says so. Dr. Pearl remains innocent unless the State proves, beyond and to the exclusion of all reasonable doubt, that he raped and sexually assaulted Kristen Wallace.

But the State will not be able to prove that to you today. Because the evidence and testimony in this case will show you that Dr. Pearl shouldn't be here. Because he did not do what he is accused of doing.

Let me introduce you to the Doctor. [WALK OVER].

This is Dr. Pearl. He's lived right here in Calusa County for most of his life. In 1981, he got his undergrad degree from Columbia University in New York where he found a love for medicine. So went to medical school right here in Sunshine State University. He graduated in 1984. Then went on to Harvard---as a research fellow in the orthopedics lab. And later, Dr. Pearl opened his own practice right here in town—The Pearl Medical Offices— in 1996. He specializes in orthopedics and sports medicine. [Quietly: Thank you, Dr. Pearl].

Let's talk about why we are all here today.

The evidence will show that Kristen Wallace hurts her left knee at work. She hurts it badly enough that she makes an appointment to see a doctor for the injury—Dr. Pearl. The two meet for the first time on April 3, 20XX-3.

Dr. Pearl evaluates her and begins treatments. The evidence will show that over the next month, Kristen Wallace visits Dr. Pearl five times—two of which were Sundays.

After the first couple of visits, they start to feel more…comfortable around each other. They laugh. They flirt. They continuing laughing. Continue flirting. And after a month, it just happens. They have sex in the office.

Let's talk about What happened on May 1, 20XX-3.

On their sixth visit together, Kristen Wallace comes in around lunch time. Just as she gets there, Ryan Anderson, Dr. Pearl's assistant, is leaving for lunch.

Ms. Anderson will take the stand today. She will tell you that on May 1, 20XX-3, she did as she always does every day when she leaves the office for lunch: She takes a sign. She tapes it up. And she locks the office door.

Ryan Anderson will also tell you that comes back from her lunch break and sees Kristen Wallace leaving. She will explain Ms. Wallace's demeanor to you. And she'll tell you that as Ms. Wallace walked—not ran—out the office, she confirmed her next appointment. Just four days later.

What Ms. Wallace does next is interesting.

She goes shopping. For several hours. And some eleven hour later, right around midnight, she visits the Sunshine State University Rape Center. Where she is examined by Sexual Assault Trauma Nurse, Jamie Gerrard. Now the State just told you that Ms. Gerrard's findings include redness, tenderness, and abrasions on Kristen Wallace's external genitalia. You will have an opportunity to see Ms. Gerrard's report today.

Now, we are not going to dispute the findings of redness, tenderness, and abrasions. But we will dispute what those finding mean. As you consider Ms. Gerrard's report, keep in mind what the state told you: Kristen Wallace hasn't been intimate with someone in 10 years. And as you listen to Jamie Gerrard's testimony today. And remember what Ms. Gerrard tells you about her job: that she is a State employee. <u>That it's her job to find evidence of sexual assault.</u>

You will also hear from Sexual Assault Nurse Expert Alex Costaine. Ms. Costaine is a consultant. Sometimes she works for the State. Sometimes for the defense. Ms. Costaine will tell you that it is her job to objectively review evidence presented to her.

Ms. Costaine will agree that there is redness, tenderness, and abrasions. But she will explain to you that there are a number of other explanations for these findings—that some bodies are more fragile than others. Or that some people have aggressive sex. That these findings are a result of consensual sex. Ms. Costaine will tell you she does not agree with Nurse Gerrard's findings. Why? Because Ms. Costaine will this stand and tell you what these findings really mean: that it is impossible to tell if the sex between Kristen Wallace and Dr. Pearl was consensual or non-consensual sexual activity.

We ask you to remember that she think's he's handsome. She calls him by his first name. She even sees him on the weekends. You will learn that those were the actions of a woman in a consensual relationship. The actions of Kristen Wallace.

At the end of this case, my co-counsel, Mr. Clark, is going to stand right here and ask you to consider a few things. He will ask you to consider the all of the evidence, the lack of evidence, and the conflicts in the evidence. And after doing so, we are confident you will render the only verdict that is supported by the evidence and the law: NOT GUILTY.

Example : In the following example defense counsel delivers a defense opening in a wrongful death case allegedly caused by a traffic accident.

Defense:　She pulled out without looking. She sped up without reason. And now, she's cast blame without evidence. My name is Erika Wilson and I represent Overnight Express Shipping Company, and one of their drivers, David Diamond. I'd like for you to meet him. This is David Diamond. He's a truck driver. It's what he does. It's what he's always done. He's been driving trucks, big and small ones, since he was 18 years old. He's got more than 25 years worth of experience on the road.

Now we agree with plaintiff's counsel that both Mrs. Anderson and Mr. Diamond were on the same stretch of Rt. 231 at the same time, on the same day. We also agree that Mrs. Anderson was injured that day after she was struck head-on by a garbage truck driven by a Mr. Johnson. And all of us feel sympathy for Ms. Anderson. It's only natural. But members of the jury, sympathy is not evidence. And this plaintiff must prove her case to you today. She must prove that what happened to her was Mr. Diamond's fault. And she must prove that to you, not with sympathy, or guesses, or maybes, but with evidence. By what's called the greater weight of the evidence . The law calls that a burden, because it is just that. And that burden belongs to this plaintiff, and will stay at this table (hover) throughout today's trial. But today, the evidence will show that she pulled out without look-ing. she sped up without reason. And now she casts blame without evidence. Let's talk about each one of those, and what you'll see and hear in this courtroom today.

You will hear that Mr. Diamond was making a run to Tennessee hauling a load of ash in his 18-wheeler. Another day. Another load. It was his job and he was doing it. You will learn that as he approached Rt. 231, he pulled up to a 4-way stop. And he stopped. [Put up the board and draw the route. He looked both ways. No one was coming so he turned right and began driving north on Rt. 231. As usual, he went through his gears and got to 55 mph– the speed limit. About that time he sees up ahead a white car approaching Rt. 231. He sees that a small woman is driving and as he gets closer and closer he sudden-ly realizes that she does not see him. She doesn't even look his way. She doesn't even…look. Instead she pulls out right in front of him. She just did.

And so after she pulled out without looking, you will learn Mr. Diamond had three options: You'll learn that he could have just driven his truck into the ditch on the right. He could have run right over her OR he could move into the passing lane. Mr. Diamond saw that it was clear enough for him to pass safely, and so he moved into the left lane to pass her. And when he did, for no apparent reason, she stepped on the gas. She accelerated. She sped up with no reason. Why? We don't know. Mr. Diamond will tell you it seemed like she was trying to make it difficult for him to pass. But even though it was now taking much longer to get around her, he couldn't be sure that if he put his brakes on, that she wouldn't do the same. So he continued to pass her.

Just as he reached the south end of this [point] bridge, he saw from his rear view mirror that he was clear – in other words, he was fully past her – and so he went back into his lane.

What about her? What did she do? Well, the evidence will show that after Mr. Diamond passed the plaintiff she swerved into the southbound lane. Why did she do that? We don't know. But for whatever reason – there she was in the southbound lane. And that's where she was when she was hit head on by that other truck I told you about – driven by Mr. Johnson.

That's what happened. This plaintiff drove into the oncoming lane and was hit head on by a different truck driven by a different driver after she drove into his lane. And since that's what happened – and the evidence will show that it is – you're probably wondering why is Overnight Express Shipping and Mr. Diamond here? We're here, Members of the Jury, because the evidence will show that this woman has cast blame without evidence. She blames Mr. Diamond for what happened to her. But pointing a finger of blame – just like sympathy – is not enough, not nearly enough. She must prove that it was Mr. Diamond's fault that she was hit by Mr. Johnson.

But she won't. She will not because she cannot and she cannot because the evidence just won't allow it.

So – what evidence will you see and hear today?

Today you will hear from two experts – one brought to you by Plaintiff and one by us. The Plaintiff's expert is going to take this stand and talk to us in a language that is not easy for everyone to understand. That language? Math, fractions and variables, calculations and equations. Now, some of us may not totally understand all of the logic behind it, but we all know that what comes up after you press the "=" button on a calculator is only valuable if the numbers pressed into that calculator were correct. In other words – "garbage in" . . . and you know what comes out. The evidence will show that the plaintiff's expert put guesses into his calculator and the garbage that came out was just that. Guesses, speculations, maybes: Garbage.

Our expert, Cheryl Dubose, is going to explain in words that we all understand why those guesses are just that: Maybes. Possibilities . Not the kind of evidence that would tip the scales in the Plaintiff's favor to help her prove that Mr. Diamond was the cause of her injuries.

Members of the jury She pulled out without looking, she sped up without reason, and She's cast blame without evidence. That's what you'll hear today. And that's why at the end of this trial I will come back before you and ask you to deliver the only verdict that speaks the truth. A verdict supported by the law, the facts and your own common sense. A verdict finding Overnight Express Shipping and Mr. Diamond not liable for the injuries to Ms. Anderson. Because they're not.

Example : In the following example the defense counsel is delivering an opening statement which combines concepts of reasonable

doubt, failure to investigate properly and a credible alternative suspect.

A hand has both a front and a back. To know it, to understand it, to judge it, you need to see both sides. The state has ONLY shown you one side of their hand, the hand that killed Barbara - let me show you the other.

Phil Williams and Barbara Leigh get into the car together on December 25th and drive up to Indianapolis for some private time. They spend the next five days together. On December 27th they are sitting at a table in a restaurant in Indianapolis when Barbara tells Phil she is leaving him and going back to Kevin Cartwright. Now Phil and Kevin are friends, and Kevin owes Phil money. Phil has been sleeping with Barbara behind Kevin's back for months. And now she is leaving him and going back to Kevin?

Phil is not happy. Women don't dump him. Women do as they are told, or he makes them pay. When his previous girlfriend crossed Phil he beat her so badly he wound up with a felony conviction. Barbara is dumping him? Not going to happen. He gets angry. They fight, in the restaurant. In Indianapolis. In public. Three days later, on December 30th, Phil and Barbara are driving back to Louisville. Phil is going to his apartment, and Barbara thinks that she is going home to Kevin. Phil has other ideas.

They stop at his place first and go inside. Phil takes his hands, the hands that beat his former girlfriend, and wraps them around the throat of his soon to be ex girlfriend. He squeezes, choking Barbara. She struggles, but cannot get free. Gasping for air, her world goes dark, the last thing that she feels are Phil Williams's hands around her throat. Phil then drops her in the bathtub like a slab of meat, cuts of her hand with a knife like a butcher and by his own admission dumps her remains into canyon lake where no one will ever find her. Someone got dumped all right that night, but it wasn't Phil.

That might be the end of it, but Phil has a problem, he's been sleeping with Barbara for a while now, and it's just a matter of time till someone traces her disappearance to him. He knows that he has a record, a history of violence with women and that the cops will be coming. He needs someone else to take the blame. So he takes the only piece of Barbara that isn't laying at the bottom of the lake, her hand. A hand still wearing a ring that Kevin gave her. He throws it into the back of Kevin Cartwright's truck.

Now when he puts that hand in the back of the truck it is out in the open, in a clear plastic bag, with the tailgate down. Someone anonymously calls the police later that day, and the investigation begins. No one knows who made that call, but you may have a suspicion who did by the time this case is done.

You will hear the State's star witness explain in his own words how he strangled and butchered Barbara Leigh in his own home, with his bare hands. He will tell you how "She died pretty quickly." Now we don't know for certain that she was dead when he hacked her hand off. He claims she was. What we do know is that when the state searched his home over two months later her blood was still in his bathtub.

After they arrested him for her murder he cut a deal with state, telling them a story that conveniently relies upon the hand found in the back of

Kevin's truck when pointing the finger at my client.

These are the undisputed facts of the case. That's right Members Of The Jury, the State's star witness is a convicted felon, a liar, and self confessed murderer who is now trying to blame my client for his actions. We'll take a look today at the way in which Phil Williams is trying to pass the blame. You will hear different interpretations of every alleged piece of evidence supposedly connecting my client to this murder.

We ask only that you consider those interpretations in light of the all the circumstances in this case, to include the character of the people who make those claims.

We're here today because Phil Williams wants to implicate Kevin Cartwright for a crime he didn't commit. The state has chosen to believe the stories of this convicted felon, this self confessed murderer - today they are hoping that you do the same. Members Of The Jury they don't just want you to believe this murderer's word, they need you to believe it. Phil Williams is the only witness that you will hear from today who will suggest that Kevin Cartwright had anything to do with the death of Barbara Leigh. That's it.

As you listen to the state's case today we implore to ask those common sense questions that the law empowers you to ask. "Would Phil Williams lie about this?" "Does Phil Williams have an incentive to deceive us?" "Is there any real possibility that Phil Williams's story isn't true?" Listen carefully when we tell you about Phil's deal with the state. Pay attention when we go into Phil's past. It is our position that the evidence will show that the answer to all three of those questions is yes.

At the end of this trial I will come before and discuss the other side of the hand in this case, the other side of Phil Williams. Then I will ask you to deliver a verdict based on the laws of this great state, the facts, and your own common sense. A verdict that say you can't trust a liar...you can't trust a murderer...you can't trust a convicted felon. You can't trust Phil Williams. I will ask you to find our client not guilty.

G. Checklist

The following checklist summarizes the information counsel should consider when developing persuasive opening statements. It should be used as a starting point for developing appropriate openings showcasing the theme and theories developed during case analysis.

I.   Effective Opening Statements:
    a.   Thematic Statement
        i.   Grabber
        ii.   One-Liner
        iii. Hook
    b.   Primacy and Recency
        i.   Bookend the theme front and back
        ii.   Most important information up front
        iii. Weaknesses fronted during the middle
    c.   Tell the Story
        i.   Use structure
        ii.   Present tense verbs
        iii. Appropriate language
    d.   Preview the Law
        i.   Give them a taste
        ii.   Identify how the law is important for this case
        iii. Use the instructions you know will be coming
    e.   Set the Hook for Closing Argument
II.   Basic Legal Principles of Opening Statements
    a.   Judge is in charge
    b.   Do not waste time arguing, tell the story!
    c.   Do not vouch for witness credibility

    d.   No personal opinions

    e.   If evidence is excluded do not mention it

    f.   Do not mention evidence if you have no good faith basis to believe it will be admitted

    g.   Do not violate the "Golden Rule" argument

III.   The Art of Opening Statements

    a.   Structuring

        i.   Cohesive and complementary legal and factual themes

        ii.   Powerful moral theme

        iii.   Thematic statement

        iv.   Bookending

        v.   Focus on the story

        vi.   Preview the Law

        vii.   End on a reminder of what is coming in Closing (thematic bookending)

    b.   Delivering

        i.   First impression

        ii.   Beginning the Opening

            1.   Acknowledge the court

            2.   Assume the position

            3.   Breathe

            4.   Eye contact

            5.   Jury gives you permission to begin

            6.   Start strong!

        iii.   Body Language

            1.   Fill the space quietly

            2.   Command the room

            3.   Start from a still position

            4.   Movement follows the words

            5.   Podium – BAD

            6.   Eye contact – GOOD

        iv.   Verbal Keys

            1.   Present tense verbs

            2.   Clear language

            3.   Concise

            4.   Dynamic language

            5.   Sensory Words

            6.   Positive approach

        7.   Tone

        8.   Modulation

    v.   Dangers of Improper Argument

        1.   Do not stretch the envelope

        2.   Persuasion comes from structure, not argument

        3.   Civics lesson waste time

        4.   No throat clearing

        5.   Do not spend time on your weaknesses

H.   Evidentiary Rules to Consider During Openings

Issues Arising During Opening Statements	Applicable Federal Rule of Evidence
Character of a witness for truthfulness	608
Out of court statements offered for the truth of the matter asserted therein (hearsay)	801–807
Offering evidence of other crimes, wrongs and acts (*see Chapter 10*)	404(b)
Prior convictions of a witness (*see Chapter 10*)	609
Legal relevancy: Is the probative value substantially outweighed by the danger of unfair prejudice?	403
Are the questions logically relevant	401, & 402
Competency of a witness	610
Personal knowledge of the witness	602

Table 1 - Potential Evidentiary Rules Applicable During Opening Statements

I. Conclusion

In this chapter we have discussed the reason for opening statements, reviewed the applicable law, and provided the advocate with a template for how to begin the process of creating effective, persuasive, and successful openings. Counsel should carefully consider the approach we have suggested, but not required. This information is advice, and you should feel free to depart from these basics when the situation warrants it. That being said, norms exist for a reason, and the information contained in this chapter will always produce an opening statement connected to case analysis and closing arguments. Remember, while you cannot win your case during opening, you can definitely lose it.

Chapter 5: Direct Examinations

A. Introduction 167
B. How the Law Impacts Direct...170
C. Structuring the Direct..172
D. Asking Proper Questions..179
E. Creating and Delivering the Direct.....................................189
F. Examples..202
G. Checklist..217
H. Evidentiary Rules to Consider During Direct....................219

A. Introduction

During direct examination counsel have an opportunity to present evidence designed to substantively prove their theory of the case. The first side to conduct direct examination is the party having the burden of proof in the case. In a criminal case it will be the prosecutor, in a civil case it is normally the plaintiff. The party with the burden of proof conducts direct examination first because direct examination is the means by which elements of the charge or claim is normally proven. Direct examination is also where the bulk of any exhibits are admitted into evidence. While evidence may also be presented during cross examination, it is not normally the primary purpose of cross-examination.

The first direct examination in the case usually occurs after opening statements are completed. The court will turn to the side having the burden of proof and ask them if they are ready to call their first witness. This is the beginning of the portion of the trial normally referred to as the case-in-chief, where witnesses are called

> *The jury MUST understand, accept, and remember the testimony on direct examination.*

167

and testimony given.

The majority of the substantive evidence upon which the jury must rely in deciding the case is introduced during direct examination. From counsel's perspective the direct should be a controlled presentation of the relevant evidence conducted in a fashion designed to maximize the believability, credibility, and likability of the testifying witness. It must also be con-

structed around the central idea that the witness is telling the story of the case, with counsel serving as the guide for the members of the jury.

Direct Examination is a witness centered process designed to provide information to the jury supporting counsel's position in the case. The subject matter of the direct is determined by effective case analysis, governed by the rules of evidence and procedure, and presented using effective advocacy skills. When done well a direct examination pulls the jury into the memory of the witness, presenting the testimony in a way that allows the jury to "experience" the events as they are described. Counsel must showcase the witness, placing themselves in the background, while simultaneously moving the story forward based upon the legal and factual case analysis previously conducted.

Formulaic, stilted, direct examinations are relatively easy to create and conduct. Telling the story of the case more effectively requires strong organizational skills, the ability to personally connect to the jury, and an understanding of the substantive legal issues in the case. Competent direct examinations are within the reach of any attorney, truly persuasive ones can only be accomplished through analysis, practice, and witness preparation.

Counsel are more likely to keep the jury focused on the witness during direct examination if they adopt the following techniques:

• Case analysis drives the direct

• Use a logical organization that is succinct but complete

- Use simple language, varying the pace of your voice with tone, body position and movement within the courtroom

- Use exhibits!

- Use correct questioning techniques

- Framing questions to get answers that use sensory language

- When setting the scene use descriptive words, action words

- Remain engaged with the witness throughout the examination

- Listen to the witness - have a guided conversation

These techniques serve as a fundamental backdrop counsel may rely upon when creating effective direct examinations. Think of them as a checklist that will provide the boundaries when developing a direct examination plan, preparing the witness, and presenting the testimony. Counsel should always remember that direct examination involves the management of information - analyzing, arranging, and then presenting.

Counsel use open-ended questions during direct examination to place the facts of their case before the jury. The rules of evidence require open ended questions in most circumstances. Open ended, non leading questions, are a "best practice" approach because they keep the focus on the witness and not the attorney. When done effectively, it as if counsel fades in to the background and asks the questions the jury naturally has as they progress through the examination.

Counsel must carefully manage the flow of information from the witness to the jury, ensuring the believability of the witness is not impeded by the quality of the direct. The goal is to elicit from the witness, in a clear and logical progression, their observations and activities so that the jury understands, accepts, and remembers the testimony. In addition to telling the story of the witness, direct also lays the foundation for the admission of physical and demonstrative evidence. Finally, it admits the relevant evidence counsel will argue during the closing. Counsel can ensure these goals are accomplished through the use of checklists based upon their case analysis.

Direct examination involves the management of information—analyzing, arranging & presenting.

Experienced attorneys agree that the key to success in the courtroom is preparation, preparation, and more preparation—of both the trial lawyer and the witness. It is critical for the witness to be comfortable and confident enough to tell the facts as they occurred, without becoming overly nervous and unsettled to the point where serious mistakes occur. Hopefully counsel have been there before, if not, it is recommended that they first watch others try a case, then serve as second chair in a case before finally trying a case on their own.

B. How the Law Impacts Direct

The law impacting the performance of direct examination can be found in the local rules of court, applicable rules of procedure (either civil or criminal), and the relevant evidentiary rules and case law. While each of these impact the performance of the direct, evidentiary rules are the most important in that regard. Counsel should carefully review each aspect of their direct examination to ensure they are adequately prepared for any and all evidentiary matters that derive from the possible testimony. Additionally, substantive law indirectly impacts the subject matter of the direct. The substantive law impacts what must be proved, and how the jury should conduct itself when considering admitted evidence. It is normally sourced, at least from the jury's perspective, in the instructions given to the jury by the judge. Instructions are the tool the court uses to guide the jury in applying a process to the facts. Counsel must consider the likely instructions by the court and the relevant procedural law when planning, preparing, and conducting direct examination. Each piece of testimony and all exhibits to be possibly elicited from the direct should go to support one or more of the elements of the claims or charges brought by counsel, and their admission must be supported by the Federal Rules of Evidence.

Federal Rule of Evidence (FRE) 611 addresses witnesses. It establishes the manner and scope of witness testimony. The considerations of FRE 611 are a key starting point for counsel in constructing a persuasive, substantive direct examination. Under FRE 611 the judge has a great deal of latitude when it comes to the form of questions posed by counsel. While FRE 611 provides guidelines and empowers the judge to enforce them, they are just that—guidelines. FRE 611(a) clearly establishes that the judge is in control and counsel

Examples of Open-Ended Questions:

- Wide-open questions
- Directive questions
- Open questions
- Probing or testing questions
- Coupling questions

should conduct questioning within the court to assist in ascertaining truth, avoid wasting of time, and to protect witnesses from harassment or undue embarrassment. Counsel who understand the breadth of the judge's authority will be better situated to respond concerning objections in a fashion maximizing their potential success.

Rule 611. Mode and Order of Examining Witnesses and Presenting Evidence

(a) CONTROL BY THE COURT; PURPOSES. The court should exercise reasonable control over the mode and order of examining witnesses and presenting evidence so as to:

(1) make those procedures effective for determining the truth;

(2) avoid wasting time; and

(3) protect witnesses from harassment or undue embarrassment.

(b) SCOPE OF CROSS-EXAMINATION. Cross-examination should not go beyond the subject matter of the direct examination and matters affecting the witness's credibility. The court may allow inquiry into additional matters as if on direct examination.

(c) LEADING QUESTIONS. Leading questions should not be used on direct examination except as necessary to develop the witness's testimony. Ordinarily, the court should allow leading questions:

(1) on cross-examination; and

(2) when a party calls a hostile witness, an adverse party, or a witness identified with an adverse party.

Unless counsel are laying a foundation or discussing preliminary or introductory matters, they are generally not allowed to lead witnesses on direct examination. Counsel must ensure that proper foundation is laid for the witness to give their testimony, as it ties back to the overarching purpose of direct examination. The purpose of direct examination for most witnesses is to use the examination to get evidence supporting counsel's version of the facts from the individuals who have firsthand knowledge of the event with knowledge of the events they are testifying to that is sufficient to satisfy FRE 602, the requirement of personal knowledge. In order to ensure that the information comes from the witness and not the attorney, open or non-leading questions are required. If the information does not come from the witness and their own observations, it is not sufficiently reliable to allow the finder of fact to consider it, and may not be either logically or legally relevant under the Federal Rules of Evidence.

FRE 611 specifically states that cross examination will be conducted by leading questions, and most jurisdictions have inverted that rule to require open-ended questioning during direct examination for the reasons stated here. This has structural implications for direct examination. The questioning techniques used during direct examination should be designed to focus the attention on the witness while minimizing the presence of the lawyer and meeting the requirements of local practice and the rules. The approaches found in this section are based upon this legal standard.

Whenever witnesses testify and the testimony contains disputed facts, the primary issue facing the jury is whom to believe. Most courts provide the jury with a set of instructions designed to assist them in sorting through issues of credibility. Understanding how the judge will inform the jury about credibility issues should assist you in structuring your direct examination. This becomes particularly important when there are facts that are negative to counsel's position in the case where the witness is testifying. While it may be tempting to disguise these facts from the members of the jury, the stronger move is to discuss the problems in the witness' testimony openly, so that when the jury recalls their testimony the witness has a better chance of being seen as forthcoming on any particular issue. The superior attorney uses the information provided in the jury instructions to structure their direct examinations in accordance with the basic principles the judge will use to assist the jury in deciding whom to believe.

C.   Structuring the Direct

1.   Identify Goals of the Direct

When considering how to structure the direct examination counsel should always keep in mind that direct is an educational opportunity. The purpose is to present the facts persuasively, providing the jury with a reason to accept them as the truth. To effectively accomplish this goal counsel must identify which facts to present, and how to to do it. Case analysis is an excellent tool for identifying "what" should be presented, the "how" of the actual presentation is grounded in the facts, but must go beyond the factual basis to be effective. In a very real sense the structure of the direct is built upon the bones of the facts, and the delivery of the direct takes those facts and covers them with language, context, and meaning.

Counsel must begin the process of structuring the direct by reviewing their earlier case analysis. That case analysis, if done properly, will identify what facts must be produced from a particular witness to support the theme and theory of the case. They should start by preparing an outline of topics relevant to their moral theme, legal theory, and factual theory. This outline should then be compared to the individual witnesses. Done properly this process will identify which facts each witness can provide to assist in the three facets of case analysis. The outline should address the anticipated direct, potential cross examination, and the follow on redirect based upon the expected cross.

The outline can also greatly assist counsel in that it shows where the peaks and valleys of a particular witness' testimony lie. By going through and viewing the entirety of possible witness testimony in this fashion, counsel can gain a better sense as to what topics they need to cover not only to prove their case, but to show the jury the witness is giving them as complete a version of the facts as possible, even ones that may not reflect favorably upon counsel's case. While discussing negative facts with a witness may seem counterintuitive, doing so pays big dividends with members of the jury. By being the first to mention these facts, counsel not only enhances the believability of the witness overall, but also their own credibility with the jury. Jury members are more likely to view a direct that deals with negative issues favorably, because it will feel less like the attorney is attempting to disguise facts or hide truths from the jury. Rather, the jury is left with the impression that counsel has presented the most holistic view of the case possible, and counsel's credibility is thus enhanced.

> **Three Steps to Identify Topics on Direct:**
>
> • List all factual theories for the witness with supporting facts
>
> • Decide whether to avoid any factual theories for the witness based upon your case analysis—create a final list of topics addressing the best and worst facts for each witness
>
> • Organize the presentation order for each topic in direct examination

When preparing in this way counsel must review the relevant documentary evidence for each witness. The relevant documentary evidence is both witness and case dependent, but common examples include depositions, prior statements, e-mails, text messages, social media postings, and other relevant documents. Witness interviews may be applicable here as well, but as a general rule counsel should only conduct such interviews after initial case analysis identifies particular areas of interest. This allows counsel to guide the witness to the pertinent points needed for the case, and can go a long way in assuaging fears of being involved in litigation.

The more prepared counsel is to get to the heart of the matter, the more reassurance they provide to the witness. This can cause the witness to feel more at ease with counsel, and often results in the procurement of unsolicited documentary evidence that does far more to enhance counsel's case than a casual witness interview ever could.

2.   Prepare the Witness

Once documents have been reviewed and a direct examination outline completed, counsel should conduct an initial witness interview. The initial witness interview confirms early case analysis and may also identify new issues. It is at this point that counsel should perform a witness specific case analysis, identifying the disputed and undisputed facts this particular witness provides as related to the case. To maximize the success of the direct examination counsel should use an outline of topics, key facts and sources of the facts for the witness when structuring the direct. This outline should also enfold the "peak and valley" portions of the testimony discussed earlier.

Counsel should meet with the witness for preparation sessions after creating the topic and key facts outline. The number of sessions will depend upon the complexity of the issues identified during witness case analysis and the abilities of the witness and attorney. At some point a final witness preparation session is scheduled. During this final session counsel should go over possible testimony at trial to make sure that everyone is comfortable with the substance and process. Remember, the witness will not have the same level of comfort or experience with litigation as counsel. By taking the time to walk them through the process of testifying, counsel sets the witness' mind at ease. Witness' who have been properly prepared are more believable when they testify.

Counsel must ensure the witness understands what is going to happen when they testify. The duty to assist the witness extends beyond the substance of their testimony to the mundane facts of how it happens. To the witness who has never testified explaining how things are going to happen is important. While counsel may frequently appear before the court, the average witness does not often find themselves in the courtroom. By the nature of what happens in court, courtrooms can be very intimidating places, and failure to properly prepare a witness on the formalities of court is to leave them stranded in an unfamiliar and intimidated place. This may very well prevent the witness from testifying effectively, reducing the persuasiveness of their presentation. Counsel should end the session by making certain the witness knows and believes that their primary duty while on the stand is to tell the truth as they remember it, free from the influence of others, to include any attorney involved in the case.

The witness must understand, accept, and internalize the belief that their primary duty is to simply and effectively tell the truth. Witnesses who internalize this belief are more persuasive. They have conversations with the attorney for the benefit of the jury - the ultimate goal for an effective direct examination. This conversation is a guided one, the believability of what the witness says and the manner in which they say it will be greatly enhanced if the attorney has created a careful topic outline based upon a thorough case analysis, especially when the witness is committed to the truth as they remember it.

Focusing the witness on the task at hand also reduces their fear and stress. Counsel should remember that it is a best practice approach to tell the witness that the two of you are going to have a conversation in the courtroom. This is also why time spent preparing the witness is so important—the more frequently counsel is able to spend time with a witness, the more comfortable the witness will be and the more natural conversation between the two will sound. When proper preparation is put in with a witness, all they have to do is listen to the questions and then truthfully answer them.

Example:

The following examples captures a possible conversation between a witness and an attorney during their initial witness preparation session. It is important make the following point with witnesses early in the preparation process, and then again as counsel is wrapping up the session.

> *C:*   Good afternoon. My name is _____. I represent the plaintiff and I need to spend some time talking to you about your upcoming testimony at trial.

> *W:*   Okay.

> *C:*   Is there anything you are particularly worried about today?

W: Well.... I have watched all the trouble my neighbor has had since the accident, and I really want to help her out if I can.

C: Ma'am all you are expected to do is to be truthful. During the trial I will ask you questions and you will answer them. All I ask, all that the system requires, is that you answer truthfully to the best of your ability. If there is something else I need you to talk about I will ask. The only thing that I need you to do is to listen, and then answer honestly. Will you be able to do that?

W: (with relief in her voice) Absolutely. I just don't want to mess it up.

C: Ma'am the truth is our friend, all I need you to do is to share it by answering my questions. Is there anything else we should talk about before we go over your testimony?

By beginning in this fashion counsel has identified the truth as a core component of the expected witness testimony. This removes any game playing allegation from the cross of the witness, and also ensures that the witness understands the expectations. It is a best practice to address this again at the end of the witness preparation session.

Example:

In the following civil case counsel is completing the witness preparation process with a plaintiff witness who is the neighbor of the plaintiff. She will testify in the near future on behalf of her friend.

C: Ma'am. In the near future you may get a phone call from the defendant's counsel. They may wish to talk with you on the phone, or in person. You may remember them from your deposition testimony.

W: Yes. I remember them. Do I have to talk with them when they call?

C: Ma'am you don't have to talk to them but are free to do so if you want to. If you do talk with them I would ask that you do us the courtesy of letting us know that they called you.

W: Okay. If I talk to them what do you want me to tell them?

C: Tell them the truth. If they ask about our conversations you should tell them the truth. That I asked you to be truthful, to listen to my questions and then to answer them honestly. There is no reason in the world to be worried or to be afraid to tell them that.

W: Okay. So I should tell them you told me to tell the truth?

C: Ma'am it is your choice as to what you talk with them about, but I just want to remind you that the only thing I am concerned with is that you are able to testify truthfully and completely. The rest will take care of itself.

W: I promise I will.

When a witness is properly prepared they are more likely to present themselves in the best possible light. Counsel should focus on removing stressors, identifying relevant testimony, and then ensuring the witness will be truthful. Counsel should consider all outside resources available to help their witness feel as comfortable as possible in the courtroom. For example, many courthouses now have programs through which a therapy dog can sit with a child witness during in court testimony to provide comfort and support. The superior advocate makes the most of such programs, as ease in presence will only enhance the witness' ability to tell their story. This not only sets the witness at ease, but also removes the possible cross examination that implies an attempt by counsel to unfairly coach answers.

3.   Organizing

Once counsel identify which topics the witness will cover, they must decide how the topics should be organized for the most effective presentation of the witness and the case.   Maximum persuasion is the desired result, case analysis drives these decisions. Counsel must ensure that the trilogy of factual theory, legal theory, and moral theme are in harmony throughout the witness's direct examination, and that the witness' testimony supports each of these pillars equally. During this process counsel must identify whether or not this witness can answer any of the deciding questions of fact faced by the jury. These deciding questions of fact are those which, if believed by the jury, cause them to decide the case in counsel's favor. If they can, those lines of questioning are best given either right at the beginning of the direct examination or as last set of questions asked by counsel. By using primacy and recency in this fashion, counsel enhances the jury's ability to recall these key facts as related by the witness.

Topic outlines for each witness should contain the parts of the overall case analysis the witness supports. A well-prepared case analysis provides specific topics that can be lifted and reorganized for each witness, supporting the overall case theme and theory.   The ultimate goal for every direct, cross, and redirect examination is to persuade the jury to accept the witness's answers to the deciding questions of fact, as well as the underlying contested fact questions.

When organizing the direct examination counsel must always remember that the jury is hearing this information for the first time. They will not be able to make the leaps of inference and logic that become common place for the attorneys who have worked and lived with the case during the pretrial phase of the litigation. It is not that the jury is incapable of making such leaps, but rather that they have not yet been exposed to sufficient information to make them. Counsel's primary job during direct is to educate the jury so that they can make the logical and legal inferences necessary for their side to prevail.

Counsel begin this organizational process by taking the topics for closing argument and comparing them to what the witness can say. The connection between the direct and closing is not only within counsel's control, it is the core reason for the direct examination. When making this connection counsel should consider both the strengths and weaknesses of their position to properly develop the flow of the direct examination. The discussion found earlier in this text concerning case analysis and preparation is directly applicable during this process. The key is for counsel to make those connections across the discreet portions of the case-in-chief. Attention to this type of detail is the trademark of a superior advocate.

Counsel accomplish these goals by applying an organizational construct to a complex and often chaotic version of reality found within the facts of the case. Structure is also important from a presentation perspective, and it is best for the direct to have a clear beginning, middle, and end. Timelines and chronologies can be effective tools for developing and imposing structure on the presentation. When deciding how to organize counsel should focus on organizational tools that increase the ability of a new listener to understand and recall the testimony. To achieve the highest level of advocacy, the structure must also mirror some of what we expect in normal day to day conversations when covering multiple topics. Keeping the structure of the direct examination in line with such expectations enhances the idea that the witness is merely telling their story while the attorney serves as a substitute for the jury, asking the questions which naturally occur to them. Once the structure has been identified counsel must then develop the specific questioning techniques to accomplish the goals identified when structuring the direct.

D.   Asking Proper Questions

A thorough knowledge and understanding of Basic Questioning Techniques is an *essential skill* for any competent advocate in an adjudicative proceeding—at trial, during arbitration, or otherwise. Every fact received by the jury during a case is delivered through the asking of questions and the answers which follow. The substantive evidence introduced at trial is birthed from the art of asking questions.

Counsel must master the basic questioning techniques available to an attorney if they wish to maximize the effectiveness of their directs and crosses. Questioning is the primary means of presenting information to the fact-finder, the ability to properly formulate and ask questions is a fundamental skill that all attorneys must continually develop and practice. In this section we will identify the fundamental questioning techniques and then suggest ways in which they can be used.

There are three basic questioning techniques for examining a witness: (1) headlines, (2) open or non-leading questions, and (3) closed or leading questions. Each of these techniques are used when questioning witnesses. As a general rule open ended questions are either required or preferred during direct examination. Basic examples of where to start open ended questions are questions that begin with who, what, where, when, why, how, describe, or please explain. Leading questions either not allowed on direct examination or severely limited by the court. Leading questions are the preferred method during cross examination. Like most general rules there are instances where counsel use leading questions on direct and open ended questions on cross, but both of those instances are exceptions to the accepted practice and should only occur based upon specific situations or instances.

Once counsel learn these Basic Questioning Techniques they will be able to use them to achieve the goals of any direct or cross examination. It is a "best practice" to include the appropriate questioning techniques when planning for direct examination, preparing witnesses, and performing the actual direct.

Counsel use these techniques in situations controlled by procedural rules, case law, and others local rules. As we discuss the various portions of a trial where these techniques may be used, we will identify which techniques you should employ and why. Each technique has a specific use, and learning them now will assist an attorney in developing superior direct and cross examinations. Let us begin with how we introduce questions, through headlines.

1.   Headlines
A *headline* is a statement consisting of two parts: an introductory phrase and a topic. They are used to introduce the witness and jury to a particular topic and are designed to serve as signposts that increase the flow and understanding of testimony. There are three main types: (1) basic introductory phrases, (2) transitional introductory phrases, and (3) looping or coupling introductory phrases.

The primary purpose of a headline is to orient both the witness and the fact-finder to the area of the witness's testimony counsel wish to discuss. It creates a feeling of flow and ease to the examination, enhancing the conversational nature and thus showcasing witnesses on direct. When we talk about headlines in cross examination, we talk about them in terms of limiting or controlling the witness. To accomplish this effective headlines should be both succinct and to the point. They serve, in effect, as a conversational guidepost allowing the jury and the witness to know where counsel is going next in the story. Counsel create ineffective headlines when they construct long or complex introductory phrases. Long and complex headlines defeat the primary purpose of orienting the witness and the fact-finder to the specific area or issue. Witnesses being cross examined will use these long and complex headlines to misconstrue the question and respond in a non-responsive fashion or give an outright destructive answer.

Headlines can and should be used in all the various types of witness examination: direct, cross, redirect, impeachment on cross, rehabilitation on redirect, laying foundation for and using exhibits, expert testimony, taking depositions, and even when speaking to the judge, jury, or arbitrator on jury selection, opening statements, and closing arguments. In each of these situations a focus on clearly delineating the subject being discussed increases its persuasive value.

When using headlines in these situations it is a best practice to combine the headline with other basic questioning techniques discussed in this chapter. Those include wide open questions, directive open questions, probing or testing questions, looping questions, coupling questions, and closed or leading questions.

The headline by itself does not provide substantive evidence to the witness, but serves rather as a signpost along the highway of the testimony. Counsel want the fact-finder to travel along, headlines tell them where to go and sometimes why it is necessary to make the trip. It signals to the jury where the witness is going, and keeps them focused and on track, making headlines useful during both direct and cross examination.

Counsel's earlier witness specific case analysis should identify areas that must be covered during the witness's testimony. Each subject identified in the witness specific case analysis needs a series of headlines. At a minimum counsel should have at least one headline for each area of inquiry.

Example:

In this example the witness, Cheryl Hart, is a young lady who works as a bank teller. In the early evening hours of March 21, 20XX-2 she was walking home from work on 39th Street. She lives in the area and has walked home 3-4 days a week along this route for the last four years. The time was approximately 7 p.m. While walking north on 39th Street she sees four young children attempt to cross the busy street. She observes the children make it halfway across the street when they are hit by a south-bound panel van.

Counsel is calling her as a witness for the plaintiff in a civil case the mother of the children has brought against the panel driver. Initially counsel might focus on introducing the witness to the jury, focusing them on the reason for her testimony.

Introducing the Witness:

Q: Please turn and introduce yourself to the jury.

A: Good afternoon, my name is Cheryl Hart.

Q: Why are you here today?

A: I was walking down 39th Street when those poor children were run over. I'm here to tell what I saw that night.

Q: Thank you ma'am, we'll get to that in a moment, but first I would like to talk to you about your background. *This leads into a series of questions designed to explore this headline. The questions might include:*

Where are you from?

What is your profession?

Where do you work?

How long have you worked there?

Moving the conversation forward with more specificity:

Once counsel has identified the reason for the witness' testimony, introduced them to the jury and established their background it is time to provide another headline to move the conversation forward.

Q: I would like to discuss the evening of March 21, 20XX-2. Do you remember that evening? *This headline is designed to focus the witness on the night in question.*

A: Yes, I will never forget it. *The next few questions should develop this subject further. They might include:*

What did you do that day?

When did you leave work?

How did you leave?

Where were you going?

Why did you walk that way?

Focusing on details:

Counsel may have identified during case analysis specific goals for this witness' testimony, to include properly enhancing her credibility. Focusing on the details of the scene are one way to accomplish this. The following headline can be useful when doing so:

> Q: I want to talk about how that part of town looks. *This headline is designed to show the witness's familiarity with the accident scene—to increase her credibility. It should be followed with more narrowly tailored questions designed. To focus the witness. Acceptable approaches might include:*

Are you familiar with that area?

How so?

How many times have you walked on this street?

Please describe 39th Street for the jury.

Once counsel have asked sufficient questions to clearly meet the goal identified in case analysis, in this instance increasing the credibility of this witness' observations, they should use a headline to shift the testimony.

> Q: I want to discuss what you observed while you were walking home on 39th Street that night. *See how this headline lets the witness know that we are getting ready to get into the "meat" of their testimony? It also lets the jury know something important is coming. Follow on questions might include:*

Which direction were you walking?

As you were walking north what did you see?

Where were the children going?

One of the benefits of this approach is that it creates the format of a conversation, and forces counsel to pay attention to the witness's response to their questions. This showcases the witness properly and allows the jury to follow along.

Headlines make certain the witness understands where counsel want to go and assists the jury in understanding what happened and why it is important. Headlines assist the witness in testifying comfortably and persuasively, enhancing the witness's credibility. They also allow counsel to keep the witness on topic and provide a ready means to bring them back to the issues at hand if they begin to stray or wander while testifying.

Another valid technique used in concert with headlines is to number specific portions of the direct examination, using them to assist jurors who are taking notes, providing them with a template that both counsel and the jury can refer back to during closing argument. These numbers come from the witness case analysis and preparation. Consider the following:

Example:

The witness is testifying for the defense in a wrongful death case involving multiple children who were run over by a car. The witness is being called to testify about three substantive issues, (1) what they observed the night of the accident, (2) what they saw when they attempted to help the injured children, (3) how the person in the car the night the children were run over acted. These three items were identified during case analysis and have been built into the witness testimony. Using the numbering technique might work as follows:

C: Mr. Broadsides there are three things I want to discuss with you today. Number 1 - what you saw when the accident happened. Number 2 - What you observed when you tried to help the victims, and Number 3 - how the person driving the car that night acted.

W: *Okay.*

C: Good. Let's start with the first one - What you saw when the accident happened. Where were you on the night of March 21, 20XX-2? *From this point on the direct is developed factually, telling the story of the first topic. When ready to transition counsel would use a new headline.*

C: Thank you Mr. Broadsides. I would like to shift our focus now from what you saw when the accident happened to the second subject on our list of things to talk about - What you observed when you tried to help the victims. Do you understand what I want to talk about now?

W: Yes sir.

C: Okay. After you saw the car run over the largest child who was carrying the younger child, what did you do? *Note how the use of this headline reiterates earlier testimony in the direct that was persuasive, highlighting it as part of the transition.*

Counsel can further refine this technique by using the same headlines in the opening, witness examination and closing argument. Using the Rule of Threes in this fashion greatly increases the chance that the fact-finder will remember both the headlines and the response. This holds true regardless of whether counsel is conducting direct or cross examination. In either instance headlines function to identify the topics to be discussed.

When examining an adverse witness on cross examination or when taking a deposition, headlines help the examining lawyer control the witness. Headlines keep the witness on the examining lawyer's topic, requiring the witness to answer the examining lawyer's question, regardless of the witness's desires. This allows counsel to establish control and limit the scope of a witness's testimony during cross examination.

The caveat here is that headlines also orient the witness being cross examined as to the subject counsel wishes to discuss. In certain instances, depending upon the purpose of the cross examination, it is better to choose to forgo headlines in order to ensure the witness does not have time to formulate a coached or untrue answer.

Headlines serve as road signs for anyone listening to the examination, focusing the inquiry. Using headlines helps the judge and jury take notes, better understand witness testimony, and connect it to counsel's theme and theory.

Focused headlines also assist the judge in ruling on disputed evidentiary issues, creating jury instructions, and writing the judgment when the case is a trial to the bench. Finally, headlines assist the appellate court to better understand the transcript and trial record on appeal.

2.   Open or Non-Leading Questions

An open or non-leading question is one that showcases the witness and not the attorney. It invites a complete answer from the witness on a topic chosen by the lawyer. It does not, however, suggest an answer to the witness. Instead, open questions identify a topic with varying degrees of specificity, allowing the witness to testify fully regarding that topic. It is common for the witness to talk for a longer period of time than the questioner when a proper open ended, or non-leading question is asked.

One way for counsel to identify an open ended question is to listen to the structure of the question and the length of the witness's response. The type of open question chosen depends upon the demeanor and knowledge of the witness, as well as the specificity of the issue the questioner wishes to discuss. Examples of open questions include: (1) wide open questions, (2) directive open questions, (3) probing or testing questions, and (4) coupling questions.

Open questions are designed to get out relevant information about a specific time, place, person, or event that the advocate wishes to discuss in greater detail by allowing the witness to answer with more details. The structure of open questions allows for the possibility of maximum explanation by the witness. Open questions free the witness to answer with greater specificity by throwing open the door for them to answer completely based upon their own knowledge and experience. It should be noted that open questions must be preceded by the appropriate foundation for a witness' knowledge of the topic to be examined under FRE 602.

Counsel use wide open questions on direct examination to identify a particular topic they want the witness to address. Most effective wide open questions are used immediately following a headline that has oriented the witness to the topic the attorney wishes to discuss. Wide open questions normally direct the witness to a specific **time**, **place**, **person,** or **event** identified in an earlier question or headline.

Counsel use directive open questions to narrowly focus the topic the witness should address. Directive open questions are normally coupled with a headline so that the witness and fact-finder understand the scope and direction of the advocate's inquiry. Directive open questions, when coupled with a headline, are an effective and capable means of orienting the witness to a very spe-

Example: Wide Open Questions

- Please describe for us the accident scene you discovered on the 21st of March?

- Please explain where you were going that evening?

- Tell us about what you did?

cific issue while also ensuring the fact-finder and judge understand fully the meaning of the answer. Directive open questions normally appear after wide open questions in an examination. They are often followed by open questions allowing the witness to further explain the specific issue identified with directive open questions.

Example: Directive Open Questions Using a Headline

- I'd like to draw your attention to the package you received that day —what did you do with the package?

- Please direct your attention to the store on the corner of 15th Avenue South and 58th Street—did you or didn't you go into the store?

- Let's now talk about the window of the store—could you see inside the store through the window?

Counsel employ a more specific type of open question to elicit those last few bits of relevant information once the subject has been sufficiently developed by both wide open and directive open questions. These types of open questions are usually referred to as probing or testing questions. While they are narrowly construed, they are still open questions. They lead the witness to a specific fact counsel wants to discuss, and are appropriate under the rules as long as it does not suggest the appropriate answer to the witness. Due to their specificity, these types of questions often serve to highlight something of particular importance to the jury, particularly when they are used in a probing fashion. Counsel should be aware of this, and not structure their direct with too many directive open questions in a row.

These focused questions normally begin with a verb or some other element that either clarifies or explains an issue in the case. Although they do address narrowly defined issues, these types of questions do not suggest the answer. When deciding whether or not an apparent probing or testing question is appropriate under the rules, the court will focus on whether or not there is a specific item addressed in the question that requires further inquiry in order to effectively explain an issue in the case.

After counsel have fully developed their line of inquiry in a way designed to get every last bit of information they then use coupling questions to emphasize particular portions of the testimony they want the jury to remember. A coupling question takes a word or words from the witness's answer and connects or couples the answer from the last question to the current question. Coupling questions underline important facts while also providing flow and continuity to the direct examination. When used properly coupling questions allow both the witness and the jury to understand where the examination is going. This mimics normal speech patterns, creating a sense of believability and credibility concerning the examination.

Example: Coupling Questions

> *Q:* Mr. Witness, I draw your attention to what happened immediately after the gun went off, what did you see the defendant do next?
>
> *A:* I saw the defendant drop the gun to the floor and walk quickly towards the exit of the restaurant.
>
> *Q:* After the defendant let his gun drop to the floor and he began to quickly walk towards the restaurant door, what did you do?

This particular technique should only be used when appropriate. Within those circumstances this type of questioning technique can be very effective in highlighting the important points of the witness's testimony identified during case analysis.

While open ended questions may be used through out the trial, they generally must be used during direct examination of a non-hostile witness. Whenever a witness is called by counsel, and is not subsequently declared adverse by the court, counsel must examine that witness using open ended, non-leading questions. Under the rules of evidence counsel are generally not allowed to ask closed or leading questions of their own witnesses when addressing disputed issues within the case.

This fundamental premise regarding the questioning of witnesses is grounded in the idea that the witness is the person who was involved in the disputed events and knows the facts, not the attorney. Because the witness is the fount of factual knowledge at trial, the focus is on their ability to relate the facts without assistance from counsel. There are certain situations where closed questions are allowed during direct. For example, most jurisdictions will allow closed or leading questions to lay foundations for exhibits or to take care of background information.

While procedural law generally requires the use of open questions during direct examination of witnesses, it does not prohibit counsel from using open questions during other portions of the trial as well. There is a great deal of difference however, between being *allowed* to do something and it being a *good idea* to do it. Counsel should concentrate on using open questions during direct examination. There are sound tactical reasons for adopting this strategy as a general rule.

E.   Creating and Delivering the Direct

The creation and delivery of the direct examination encompasses the earlier discussions within this text concerning case analysis, a clear understanding of the relevant procedural rules, along with a connection to what is often referred to as the art of advocacy. The organizational constructs and suggested approaches contained within this text are designed to remove confusion from the process, allowing counsel to properly focus on the very human connection that is the core of the art of advocacy. In this section we will review those earlier concepts connecting them with specificity to the direct examination process. We will then discuss how the selection of language, tone of voice, and physicality directly impact the art of advocacy when presenting direct examinations.

1.   Factual Theory of the Case

Once counsel properly understands the relevant questioning techniques, and have properly conducted case analysis and witness preparation, it is time to create the actual direct examination. Case analysis must develop a persuasive factual theory and a sound logical legal theory, invoking a persuasive and compelling moral theme. The factual theory explains the undisputed evidence, the disputed evidence, and the opponents evidence, establishing the facts necessary to carry the case for the client.

The factual theory chosen by counsel must carry the burden of common sense. When determining whether or not their factual theory carries the burden of common sense counsel should apply the logical theory often referred to as Occam's razor. In other words, the most likely explanation which is the easiest to understand is normally accepted as being true.

Effective factual theories rely upon the everyday experience and common sense of the jury. The judge will instruct the jurors to use their common sense during deliberations, and counsel should rely upon the common sense lens of experience when developing their factual theory. Once counsel have chosen a factual theory of the case everything they do at trial must support that theory. This is particularly true during direct examination when counsel is charged with providing evidence on the disputed questions of fact.

List All Factual Theories

- Documents authored by the witness
- Documents associated with the witness
- Other exhibits associated with the witness
- Other witnesses
- The witness

---

2. Legal Theory of the Case

The legal theory of the case applies the laws of the facts, allowing the jury to decide the case based on the facts presented by counsel during the trial. Counseling use the law to shape the facts, telling the story which the law allows the jury to hear. The legal theory is of great importance in any particular case, because it establishes the factual "truth" upon which the jury will decide the case. In some instances the legal theory of the case may very well prevent the jury from learning of particular facts that would improperly guide their decision-making.

The legal theory has a sorting function, in that it denies the jury access to certain things that are objectively true but not legally relevant to the case. Counsel must understand the impact a strong legal theory can have on an otherwise compelling set of factual circumstances. When properly used a legal theory empowers the factual theory of the case, serving as the source of energy for the facts in a way designed to create a compelling moral theme.

3.   Moral Theme of the Case

The moral theme of the case is sometimes incorrectly described as the persuasive theory of the case. Persuasion theory is a scientific process used to describe this portion of case analysis, often in an attempt to bring a rational process to an emotional reality. The use of the word persuasion is misleading. While psychologically based concepts of persuasion theory are relevant to the jury's decision making process, they are actually a subset of the way in which jury's address issues.

The jury represents society within the legal process-most of society does not function rationally, but rather emotionally. Persuasion theory is a part of that emotional process, but not the entirety of it. The phrase "moral theory" more accurately encompasses how human beings react to situations, and is a more effective tool for counsel when developing their case for trial.

Since most people do not make decisions in a rational fashion, relying instead upon a set of guidelines working underneath the surface of the rational mind, counsel should use the concept of moral theme when analyzing cases. It is more appropriate to describe the emotional compelling component of case analysis as the moral theme, giving counsel a better conceptual construct around which to build the presentation of evidence.

Counsel can use the moral theme to appropriately create emotional force in the courtroom. A strong and compelling moral theme invokes a sense within the jury of the innate correctness of councils position. The moral theme also serves as the linchpin around which counsel can present their factual theory of the case. This approach allows counsel to answer the why question underneath the surface of the trial, guiding the jury to a solution in the client's favor.

When developing the direct examination of a witness counsel must ask themselves the extent to which this particular direct examination impacts the factual, legal, and moral questions of the case. The factual theory, when combined with the legal theory, provides the jury the tools to right the wrong expressed in the moral theme. An effective direct examination of a witness will contribute to one or more, and hopefully all three, of these areas.

4.   Outlining the Testimony

Direct examination is an organizational process requiring counsel to properly identify for the jury each specific section of the direct. Care must be taken to organize the testimony in a way that creates a conversational tone. This conversational tone extends to the attorney reacting to the witness'

answers as if this is the first time they have heard this information. Therefore, if there is something confusing about the way the witness describes
something, counsel's voice should reflect that confusion as they ask the
next logical clarifying question. This gives an added benefit in that any
members of the jury who were confused by the original answer see that
there is no problem in being so, that more information was simply needed.
The conversational tone of the direct examination comes from both the
structure and the presentation of the witness's testimony.

For each piece of the factual theory addressed by a witness on direct examination counsel should include an introductory portion for that piece of
the factual theory, substantive testimony addressing the factual issue, and a
logical endpoint which transitions to another another issue for this witness.
When doing so counsel must remember that the jury is not familiar with
the facts of the case and direct examination is their first opportunity to
place the promises made to them during opening statements in context.

A structural flow designed to connect the jury to the promises made during
the opening is necessary, requiring an outline process based upon either
topics or chronologies. In many instances the chronological approach is
preferable, with specific attention paid to particular topics during the
chronological approach.

The jury should feel as though they are listening in on a conversation focusing the witness on providing relevant and admissible information in an
interesting and believable manner. Background information questions introduce the witness to the jury and explain the relevancy of their testimony. Counsel should spend sufficient time to ensure that the introduction of
the witness and development of her background contributes to their moral
theme, factual theory, or legal theory without wasting time. There is an art
to this process which should be influenced by the nature of the case, the
court, and the relevant social norms of the jurisdiction where the case is
tried.

Counsel should organize their direct examination into discrete sections of
substantive testimony for each witness. When deciding which, of many
different options exist for presenting the substantive blocks of testimony,
counsel should focus on the importance of developing narrative flow
throughout the direct examination. The discrete substantive blocks chosen
and developed must connect to one another in a logical and persuasive
fashion. Appropriate ways for counsel to develop narrative in the direct

examination include chronologies, the use of cause and effect, and addressing specific topics organized by subject matter.

Each section of the direct examination must be carefully thought out and structured for a specific goal. This includes the introduction and discreet subsections as previously discussed, as well as the final point made during the direct examination. Counsel should end the direct examination on a series of questions focused on either the theme or theory of their case. When planning the end of the direct examination it is important to choose a topic that is not vulnerable to a timely objection by opposing counsel, as well as one that is not subject to an immediate powerful and persuasive attack on cross examination. It is a best practice for the direct examination to end on a point of importance to the jury. Doing so will ensure that the concepts of primacy and recency work in counsel's favor.

5.   Physicality

Physicality encompasses many different aspects of courtroom performance. It includes how the attorney appears physically, the way in which counsel move, tone of voice taken by counsel when asking questions, and their actual locations while conducting direct examination. In a very real sense physicality is a phrase that can be used to capture all nonverbal communications occurring in the courtroom.

Different jurisdictions place different types of limitations on where counsel can be located during direct examination, as well as the degree to which they may move while conducting direct examination. In some jurisdictions all questioning of witnesses must be done while counsel remains seated. Other jurisdictions, most notably United States federal courts, require the attorney to remain at the podium when questioning witnesses. Many state courts, on the other hand, will freely allow counsel to move around the courtroom as long as they do not intrude into the personal space of the jury. It is important for an attorney to know beforehand the accepted local practices concerning movement within the courtroom, and to be prepared to request exceptions to those local practices when the need to represent the client properly might require them. There are unique challenges to each approach outlined above.

Regardless of where the attorney is physically confined in terms of location, there are some portions of physicality that must remain consistent. They attorney's posture must show a balance of respect for the court, but comfort and familiarity with one's surroundings. Counsel should not employ body language that indicates they are closed off from the experience, but rather keep their arms away from the front of their torso to indicate an openness in conversation with the witness.

a.   Tethered to the Podium

In those jurisdictions where counsel are tethered to the podium by the court, careful thought must be given to the way in which other aspects of physicality can be used to increase the persuasive impact of the direct examination. For example, it is possible to remain at the podium while also occupying a location allowing counsel to connect with the witness and the jury. Acceptable techniques including asking the court for permission to move (which should be granted if the request is valid), standing to the side of the podium, or standing in front of it.

This is necessary because the podium represents a physical barrier between the attorney and the witness, creating an inference that the lawyer has something to hide, or is not truly interested in the testimony. Use of the podium will also tempt counsel to focus on their notes, missing an opportunity to connect with the witness.

Counsel can reduce these inferences through a technique as simple as moving to the side of the podium so that they are in the clear view of both the jury and witness, while leaving their notes on the podium. In the event they need to review those notes they can return to them, but they are no longer bound by them.

b.   Required to Remain Seated

In those jurisdictions with counsel are required to remain seated during direct examination a different set of challenges arise from a persuasive perspective. Counsel should keep in mind that the overwhelming concern is one of connection to the witness and acceptance of the witnesses testimony by the jury. Acceptable techniques to maximize this in those jurisdictions requiring counsel to remain seated include careful attention to posture while seated at counsel's table, the degree to which other items on the table draw the jury's attention away from the witness, the use of hand movements, and the use of proper tone during questioning.

c.   Allowed to move around the courtroom

In those jurisdictions where the court allows counsel to move around the courtroom counsel should verify with the court the parameters for such movement. The exchange between counsel and court in those circumstances usually occur during preliminary matters and often begins as follows:

> J: Counsel do you have any preliminary matters to take up with the court before we begin today?

> C: Your honor I wanted to verify that we are allowed to move freely around the courtroom today?

> J: Counsel I let the lawyers in my court move freely with the following restrictions. I do not want you to intrude into the personal space of a member of the jury, and you must ask when approaching witness for the first time. Do you understand my restrictions?

> C: Yes your honor.

 If the court allows counsel to position themselves freely during direct examination care should be taken to choose a location that maximizes the persuasive power of the witness's testimony. One way to increase the focus on the witness is for counsel to place themselves in a location that forces the witness to look at the jury. When deciding where to locate themselves counsel should consider the shape of the courtroom, the ability of the witness to be easily heard by all members of the jury, as well as the subject matter about which the witness will testify.

Many attorneys begin direct examination by standing at the end of the jury box that is the furtherest away away from the witness, forcing the witness to speak loudly enough to be heard by all. The concept of looking at the jury during testimony is something counsel should review with witnesses during preparations, and adopting the position at the end of the box helps reinforce that for the witness. This encourages eye contact between the witness and the jury, while counsel's presence at the end of the jury box implies that the jury and the lawyer have a common goal.

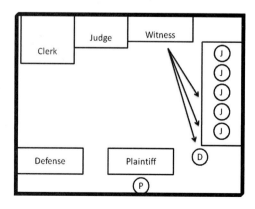

At certain points during the direct counsel may wish to draw focus away from the witness. Counsel can accomplish this by changing their location in the courtroom. The witness will turn and face the attorney, breaking eye contact with the jury. The movement of the attorney will also draw the eyes of the jury to the attorney and away from the witness. Counsel can use this technique to shift focus, break the monotony of a direct examination, or to focus the jury on the words coming from the lawyer.

When deciding when to move, counsel should move with a purpose. The assumption of a new location should be tied to a topic in your direct examination that will benefit from this shift in focus. Over time counsel will develop "comfort zones" — positions from which they prefer to address certain issues within a particular trial. When done appropriately, returning to that spot in the courtroom during your closing argument will bring the jury back to the testimony given at that time. This can greatly increase the jury's memory of the testimony by providing them with a visual clue that ties into the words and demeanor of the witness.

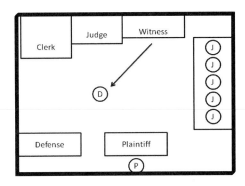

6.   Language

Words are the tools of the trade; counsel must choose them wisely. It is a best practice to use short, plain, concise words when possible. The larger and more complex the word the more likely that its use is tied to an argument the attorney wants to make or an evidentiary objection they are attempting to avoid.

When the goal is persuasion one syllable words work best. "Car" is better than "vehicle," and much better than "motor vehicle." The first suggests a picture to the jury and is the language of everyday life, the second, "Vehicle" and "motor vehicle" are cop-speak that most jurors normally hear on TV. They have no place in a superior advocate's courtroom vocabulary.

Counsel who use language properly increase their credibility. Counsel who rely upon big words and fancy phrases run the risk of placing a barrier between themselves and the jury based upon education. The choice of language should fit the nature of the witness and the desired impact of the direct examination.

It is preferable to use the short, common words of everyday speech, those suggesting mental pictures. These words increase the jury's understanding of the witness's testimony and allow for clearer communication by the witness. The use of sensory language is also key here. When jurors hear language that are tied to their ability to see, hear, taste, touch or smell, they naturally empathize and connect the testimony and question to their own experiences, thus enhancing counsel's overall persuasive capabilities. Action verbs and a commitment to avoiding the passive voice will help counsel avoid sounding like a lawyer.

Some advocates fear using simple words. They are afraid their use will remove persuasion from their voice and keep them from swaying the jury with the strength of their position. Nothing could be further from the truth. Counsel must speak the language of your audience. Failure to use words that help create a mental picture can destroy the meaning of an otherwise generally accepted and clearly understood position.

Along with the use of simple words that create mental pictures, counsel should eliminate unnecessary words, redundancies, and doublespeak. Instead of saying "emergency situation," say "emergency." Have "innovations," not "new innovations." Doublespeak words deceive, distort, misrepresent, and confuse. Juries hate them, and opposing counsel love to point out their qualities.

Counsel should also rid their vocabulary of clichés that have lost power amid the clutter of colloquial speech. Words clutter if they do not contribute to the narrative's persuasiveness, supply a reason for how someone acted, make an important fact more or less likely, impact witness credibility, believability, or reliability, or enhance your moral theme.

Simple questions are best. Consider the following examples:

> Questioner: ***Where*** *were you going that evening?*

> Questioner: ***Who*** *was with you in the car?*

> Questioner: ***When*** *did you get to the bar?*

> Questioner: ***What*** *was the first thing you did when you got to the bar?*

Questioner: *Why did you do that?*

Lawyers fear appearing stupid, often wrapping themselves in officious-sounding words to avoid the appearance of a lack of knowledge. It does not work. Practice can minimize this fear by exposing stupidity before it is shared with others. One way to do this is to employ the best practice of reading questions out loud prior to actually using them in court. The sound of the spoken language is different and counsel ignore those differences at their peril, reading them out loud will reduce the possibility of asking stupid questions, stupid answers are a different issue.

7.   Fundamental Techniques

The following techniques make up a series of issues that counsel should have in mind as they prepare direct examinations. Using them in combination with fundamental questioning skills, case analysis development, and knowledge of procedure will create direct examinations that persuade.

- **Introduce the witness:** Introduce the witness and develop the necessary background to connect the witness with the case. This is the internal introduction that places the witness in context for the jury. It must be sufficiently developed to assist the jury in understanding why they should listen to this witness, but not so developed that it becomes the central portion of the case—unless it just so happens to be the core of the case. There are two dangers here, the first is: the witness is not introduced sufficiently and the jury misses the connection between this witness and the issues at trial. This can normally be rectified, but it is lost time. Every moment that a juror is thinking "Why is this person testifying?," is a moment they are not paying attention. Hence best practice is to simply ask the witness why they are testifying within the initial portion of testimony. The second danger is: the introduction of the witness overwhelms the substance of their testimony. When this happens the response of the jury is often "Why did the attorney think that was important. I liked the witness but what they had to say was just not that important." Either one of these responses does not effectively increase the persuasiveness of the witness testimony.

- **Describe the scene:** This sets the stage for the action to follow. It must create a world that supports the story of the witness. Details matter here. The witness must fully explain the relevant scene, using words that work. Descriptive words are a must here, as are sensory words. Witnesses often wish to testify in a conclusory fashion and lawyers like to ask conclusory questions. Convert subjective witness descriptions into more objective and meaningful ones. If a witness testifies that it was "dark" ask a number of follow-up questions to flush out the details; such as, "Was it too dark to read a newspaper headline?" Advocates set the scene, tell the story, paint pictures with words—be an advocate, not a lawyer.

- **Describe the action:** Elicit visual and sensory images through testimony. An effective direct examination should paint a picture of what occurred. The key here is to use language in a way that creates visuals. This is easier to accomplish when using exhibits and demonstrations.

- **Let the witness tell the story all the way through**. Do not interrupt to clarify minor points. This can break the logical flow of testimony, cause jury confusion, and get the witness off-track. After the witness tells the story completely, go back and cover items that need to be clarified or emphasized. Use exhibits to clarify or emphasize testimony. This allows for repetition and creates believability.

- **Repeat the action:** Have the witness go over key moments or details. Your goal is to have the witness cover important facts three times. You do this by going through the story of the witness's testimony at a general level, returning to the different topics within the testimony has separate lines of inquiry designed to produce more detail, and then reiterating it one last time by using exhibits. This order can be flipped when either the story or the issues support doing so.

- **Present exhibits or demonstrations:** Present photographs, diagrams, and exhibits to explain the witness's testimony. It is important to show the jury relevant photographs and diagrams for the same reason it is important for you to visit the scene—everyone learns from walking in the footsteps of the witness. So does the jury. Conduct demonstrations to amplify key points and teach through repetition. Always explore how exhibits can be used to enhance testimony; they attract the jury's attention, clarify testimony, increase retention, and persuade. When deciding to use an exhibit counsel should consider:

    o **Type:**

        - **Real evidence, both fungible and non-fungible.** Real evidence is evidence that has a historical connection to the crime. Use it. You cannot show them to the jury until relevancy, foundation, and authenticity have been established. After you admit the evidence, request permission to publish it to the jury while the testimony is fresh in their minds.

- **Photographs and videos.** If you do not have real evidence, use photographs or videos to provide demonstrative explanations of witness testimony. Use photographs of real evidence if you cannot produce the real evidence. Consider the following pointers to maximize their impact:

  - Enlarge photos when possible.

  - Mount photos. Large photos can be handled better if mounted on a firm backing. It works even better if you can publish them through a projector and display software. Make certain that the system works, and that the resolution does not distort the evidence.

  - Use succession. Use photos or videos in chronological succession to track events as they occurred. Creating witness testimony that moves from photo to photo in a successive development of testimony can be extremely persuasive to the jury.

  - **Diagrams.** Diagrams help witnesses explain their testimony, especially when showing the layout of building or setting the scene for specific testimony. Diagrams must be easy for the jury to both see and understand. Good diagrams persuade, bad ones confuse and irritate. Consider some of the following techniques when using diagrams:

    - Large lettering.

    - Vary colors.

    - Professional appearance.

    - Clear, simple labels—clearly label all items depicted on the diagram—use sequential letters and numbers.

    - Proper marking—mark the diagram as the witness testifies, or have the witness mark—ensure you point to the item on the diagram being marked and describe the mark for the record.

- Scale—while diagrams are not required to be to scale, you should strive for accuracy—at a minimum, orient the diagram with an arrow depicting which direction is "North."

o **Visual memory.** Photographs, diagrams, and real evidence cause the jury to see the testimony. This boosts retention. Emphasize important testimony with exhibits, but make sure you do not overdo it. Everything is not equally important. Select exhibits based on what you think are the most important facts that support your theory. Focus on quality, not quantity.

o **Relevance.** Avoid exhibits that are merely interesting. Focus on significant details that advance an issue in your case. Particular attention must be given to the ability of the exhibit to "assist" the witness in explaining what happened.

o **Weaknesses.** Consider the counter-attack. Think about whether your opponent can use the exhibit against you.

o **Prepare exhibits.** Examine all exhibits you intend to use well before trial. You do not want them to contain conflicting information. Be keenly aware of all markings, contents, and physical characteristics. If admitted, the jury will have the item during deliberations and examine it without you being present. Mark all exhibits you intend to admit and admit anything you can before trial. This will reduce unnecessary delays and objections. Have copies ready for opposing counsel, the judge, and the jury.

o **Track exhibits.** It is easy to lose track of what has been offered and admitted into evidence. Use a simple chart to keep track and refer to it during conferences with the judge before the jury deliberates.

o **Know the mechanics.** Counsel must be proficient at handling exhibits in the courtroom. Commit exhibit handling "boilerplate" to memory or have a written guide at trial.

- **Use non leading questions.** Avoid complex questions that may confuse the witness. Do not insert unsolicited facts or legal conclusions into your questions, it will reduce your credibility and draw objections that detract from the flow of your case. Flow is key during witness testimony. You do not want to remind the jury that you are a lawyer presenting information to persuade them to do something. They should never see the hand of persuasion.

- **Demonstrations.** When physical activity is relevant, demonstrate it. Demonstrating an event or displaying an injury can greatly enhance your direct examination. If you decide to perform a demonstration—rehearse. Ask the judge for permission to conduct the demonstration and ensure you do not obstruct the jury's view. Describe the demonstration accurately for the record and measure distances ahead of time so that you get it right in the courtroom.

- **Documentary evidence.** Keep it simple. Keep the number of documents to the minimum necessary to prove your case. If you have voluminous records to present, segregate the significant parts and make them separate exhibits. Present the documentary evidence with a live witness who can explain the document and translate any technical or unfamiliar terms for the jury. Consider enlarging key or complex documents and having them either mounted or projected.

This group of techniques builds upon the lessons you learned earlier in this text. You should understand and internalize the belief that each of these techniques focuses on persuasion—as you should, too.

F. Examples

1. **Example: Direct Examination of a fact witness in a wrongful death case.** In the following example the plaintiff's attorney is examining Mr. Dimitri Merinov, a friend of the family who was playing basketball on the court near the scene of the accident. He is testifying in a wrongful death case where a driver allegedly ran over the children why they were crossing the street. At issue in the case is whether the children were crossing the street properly and which car, or cars, struck them.

> *Q:*   Good morning, would you please turn and introduce yourself to the jury?
>
> *A:*   Good morning, my name is Dimitri Merinov.
>
> *Q:*   Why are you here today?

A: I was playing basketball right by where Ms. Washington's kids were killed on the 21ˢᵗ of March.

Q: Thank you Mr. Merinov, we'll cover that night in more detail in just a moment. Where do you live?

A: In the Royal Park Apartment building over by 39th street.

Q: How long have you lived there?

A: Around 4 years now.

Q: Do you know Ms. Washington?

A: Yes. I've known her for around three years now. I also knew her four children.

Q: I'd like to turn your attention to the night of March 21st, where were you that evening?

A: Playing basketball with a few friends of mine

Q: Where were you playing?

A: At the Community Center across the street from my apartment.

Q: Do you recall what time you started playing that evening?

A: My game started at around 6:00 that night, and we played for about an hour.

Q: What did you do once the game was over?

A: I hung around for a few minutes with some of the guys from the game, but not for too long because that's when I heard the accident.

Q: What did you hear?

A: Well like I said I was just talking with some people on the court and all of a sudden there was this loud "boom" from in front of the Community Center.

Q: Could you see what caused the "boom" you heard?

A: Not from the courts, but right when I heard it I grabbed my phone from my bag and ran out towards to road to try to find out what was going on.

Q: What did you see once you ran out to the road?

A: That's when I saw the cars and some of the kids lying in the street.

Q: Did you know the children involved in the accident?

A: Yea, they're my neighbor Monique's kids.

Q: Had you seen them in the area at any point that night?

A: Yea, I had noticed them earlier sitting over in the grass by the courts watching us play.

Q: You said earlier that you could only see some of the children, what did you mean by that?

A: Well when I first ran out I could see three of the kids right away and they looked like they were hurt pretty badly. But there were four of them earlier, and it wasn't until someone started screaming that I saw that the youngest kid was about 150 feet down the road from the others over by the car.

Q: Let's talk about those cars you saw for a moment, do you remember what type they were?

A: Yea I saw a white van that was driving really slowly and then all of a sudden took off, and there was a Toyota further down the street.

Q: Could you tell about how far down the road you saw the Toyota?

A: Yea it was about 150 down the road right where I saw the fourth kid. It was stopped when I first got out there and that's when I pulled out my cell phone to try and get a video of it. I realized that it was probably stalled because all of a sudden I heard the gears grinding and then that car took off too.

Q: Could you tell the direction the cars were facing?

A: They were both heading north, but the van was closer to the courts and the Toyota was further down the road.

Q: Thank you Mr. Merinov, now you mentioned earlier the mother of these children, Ms. Washington, was your neighbor. What type of relationship did the two of you have?

A: We were just really good friends. I went by her house the day after the accident and everything because I could hear her crying and upset when she got home. That's when I found out that two of the boys had died. She just kept blaming herself, but I just don't see how it was her fault.

Thank you, Mr. Merinov. No further questions.

2. **Example: Direct Examination of a fact witness in a murder case.** In this example the state attorney is questioning Mr. Billy Bob Schifflet, the owner of a shooting range the defendant allegedly used in the days leading up to the murder of her husband.

Q: Good afternoon, would you please turn and introduce yourself to the jury?

A: Hello, my name is Bob Schifflet.

Q: What do you do for a living Mr. Schifflet?

A: I own a shooting range, From My Cold Dead Hands.

Q: Where is that located?

A: It is in a small area called Gulfport, right outside of Pelican Bay in Calusa County. I like the area.

Q: What is it about the area do you enjoy?

A: It is a small, unincorporated place where people can do what they like without the government interfering with our business. It's the way we like it here.

Q: Mr. Schifflet I would like to speak with you more about your business, how long have owned From My Cold Dead Hands?

A: Won it in a poker game about five years ago now from some guy who is not around these parts anymore.

Q: Would you explain what you normally require of people who come into your range?

A: Just some things that the federal government makes us follow ever since 9/11 happened.

Q: What it is the federal government makes you do?

A: Before anyone can go down to the range they have to take a safety test, we give them a briefing and check their ID's to make sure they are who they say they are.

Q: Once all of that clears, what happens?

A: That's when they can go downstairs to one of the shooting ranges.

Q: How many ranges are there?

A: Four. It depends on what a person wants to shoot. Range 1 is for rifles and the rest are for pistols.

Q: Are there any additional procedures once they get down to the range?

A: Yea, they've got to sign in before they shoot. We've already checked out their information upstairs, so when they get down there it is an honor system that they put down the right name.

Q: Let's talk about May 25th, 20XX-2, do you remember who came into From my Cold Dead Hands that day?

A: Yes. I remember Chris and Brandi coming in that day.

Q: How do you know them?

A: We went to school together when we were younger. Chris has bought quite a few guns from me over the years and Brandi has come with him a few times.

Q: What type of guns has Chris bought from you?

A: He's bought a few, but I specifically remember a .45 caliber pistol he bought about a year ago.

Q: You mentioned that Brandi had been with him, do you remember when that was?

A: Not particularly, like I said, it was only a few times. The date on that roster you just showed me says she and Chris came in on May 25th.

Thank you, Mr. Schifflet. No further questions. Your witness counsel.

3.   **Example: Direct Examination of a neighbor in a murder case.** In this example the state attorney is questioning Mr. Robert Hightower, the neighbor of the victim, Chris Alexander. Mr. Hightower observed certain activities on the night of the murder and is also able to provide background information about the Alexander family.

Q: Good Morning, Mr. Hightower, please turn and introduce yourself to the jury and tell us why you are here today.

A: Good morning, I'm Bob Hightower. Chris and Brandi Alexander were my neighbors for many years.

Q: Where did you live?

A: We lived across the street from each other in Pelican Bay. I'm still here though, have been for most of my life.

Q: Did you know them well?

A: Not really, I did not talk to either of them much. We had neighbor type troubles, but nothing major. I only really know what was said around town over the years.

Q: What type of neighbor trouble are you talking about?

A: One of her kids hit a baseball through my window. I tried to avoid a confrontation and just get her to pay for the window but she was not having it.

Q: What do you mean by 'she was not having it'?

A: I tried to talk calmly to her about it but she was too busy yelling and screaming to listen. She even told me to stop lecturing her about how she should raise her children. Guess that's why she has such a reputation as a hothead.

Q: You say she had a reputation as a hot head, did you hear anything else about Ms. Alexander?

A: It was common knowledge that her husband was cheating on her.

Q: You heard Mr. Alexander was cheating on her?

A: Yea, Chris. He had his own issues though.

Q: What issues are you talking about?

A: Well, He had some pretty seedy characters come by the house late at night. He was also friends with Ricky, and lets just say those are people I tried to avoid whenever possible. We all know that old saying about the company you keep.

Q: Who is Ricky?

A: He's one of my older brothers. He's one of those who has never cared about the consequences of his actions. Drugs, trouble with the law, you name it he did it. He's in jail finally. It's where he deserves to be. He's been nothing but an embarrassment to the family, especially with my other brother being a police officer.

Q: Thank you, Mr. Hightower. Now I'd like to shift gears with you for a moment and talk about the night of June 8th 20XX −2. Where were you?

A: I was at home in bed that night when I was woken up by the gunshots. Although at the time I did not know what was going on, they were so loud I thought shots were coming from my front yard.

Q: What did you do?

A: I grabbed my gun and ran to the window to see what was going on.

Q: Could you see anything from the window?

A: No, there was nothing in my yard and I remember looking across the street and didn't see anything in the Alexander's yard either. There weren't any house alarms, or any cars leaving so I did not know what was going on. I told my brother and the other officers all of this when they came by the house.

Q: Is this the brother you mentioned earlier?

A: Yes, Eric. He's the commander of the Pelican Bay Police Force and he was on duty that night. He's the best cop in the state. Unlike with Ricky my family and I are very proud of him.

Q: When did your brother and the other officers come by the house?

A: It was about 45 minutes after the shots woke me up. I told them what I knew about the family, and what happened. It's a tragedy, but I'm not surprised at what happened.

Q: Why do you say you aren't surprised?

A: Like I said before everyone knew about Chris and the other women. The word around town was that Brandi was at her breaking point.

Thank you Mr. Hightower, no further questions.

4. **Example: Direct Examination of a police officer.** In this direct examination a state attorney is directing a police officer who was working with an anti-crime unit. The officer observed suspicious drug activity as part of his official duties and is testifying about those events.

Q: Officer Morris, why are you here in court today?

A: Because I saw a drug sale on Cavalier Street.

Q: We will discuss that drug sale in detail in a moment. First I'd like to talk about your job. Where do you work?

A: I'm currently a patrolman with the Pelican Bay City Police Department.

Q: As a patrolman, what are your duties?

A: I work a particular area of Pelican Bay. I walk a beat, and also patrol. I am involved in most of your garden variety law enforcement duties.

Q: What specialized training have you had?

A: I have been trained to work with our Anti-Crime Unit. It is part of our neighborhood anti-crime program. I have had classes in evidence collection, stake out procedures and interrogation.

Q: You mentioned that the Anti-Crime Unit is part of the neighborhood anti-crime program. What does that unit do?

A: I worked in the division that dealt with narcotic surveillance and arrest.

Q: How long have you been part of the neighborhood anticrime unit?

A: Five years.

Q: What special training did you receive while working with the Anti-Crime Unit?

A: I went to a state police narcotics school as well as a County top gun school and just the experience in working on the streets with the Anti-Crime Unit.

Q: Approximately how many arrests have you made?

A: Over a thousand.

Q: I'd like to talk with you about the December 4th, 20XX -3, what was your official assignment then?

A: I was working surveillance with the Anti-Crime Unit.

Q: I want you to remember that morning. Where are you?

A: I am in the area of Cavalier Street, 15 Cavalier Street which is a street right off of Route 29.

Q: Why are you there?

A: We have information that people are selling narcotics in that area. I am going to this area to establish a surveillance point.

Q: What is a surveillance point?

A: It is a location that police officers take to observe potential drug activity. You need to be able to see the area you need to watch and you need to be able to remain unobserved.

Q: Are you able to find a good surveillance point?

A: Yes.

Q: Where?

A: In an abandoned building near 15 Cavalier Street.

Q: If we were at that surveillance point on that day what would we see?

A: It's an abandoned apartment building. Across the street there is a neighborhood grocery store where a lot of drug transactions occur. Usually in the parking lot.

Q: Is the parking lot visible from the surveillance point?

A: Absolutely. That is one of the reasons we chose it.

Q: Tell us about the building the surveillance point is in.

A: It's an abandoned apartment building. No one lives there except for an occasional squatter. Most of the rooms are terribly run down, many of the windows are missing.

Q: Is it occupied?

A: No.

Q: Detective I want to take you back in time to that day. What do you do that morning when you get to the building?

A: We go inside through the back entrance and climb the stairs up to the second floor.

Q: What do you do once you get there?

A: I find a good vantage point where I can observe the parking lot and watch the area with a pair of binoculars.

Q: So, you are set up on the second floor with your binoculars what do you see?

A: I see the parking lot, the traffic going in and out and most of the general foot traffic in the neighborhood.

Q: What are you looking for?

A: Activity that is suspicious.

Q: How do you decide what is suspicious activity?

A: I use the training I've had and my years of experience. You get an itch in the back of your head, a tickling feeling really. There are certain things that people selling drugs do. They have look outs, walk in certain fashion, things like that.

Q: While watching the parking lot do you see anything suspicious?

A: Yes. I see Jamie Roberts. She is standing in the middle of the street in 15 Cavalier Street. Other people are in the area. I see several abandoned cars as well, but there are always a lot of abandoned cars around. I see a gentlemen working on the cars, fixing up the cars, and at one time I see someone -- she was later identified as Cheryl Horton -- walk into the area. She talks for a moment with Jamie Roberts and then they walk across the street into a grocery store and then come back. At one point Jamie Roberts pulls out a packet of heroin from the fifth pocket of her pants and hands it to Cheryl Horton and in return she receives cash.

Q: What is the fifth pocket of the jeans?

A: The small change pocket in the jeans in the front of your pants.

Q: Please show us?

A: The small pocket in the jeans. (Indicating.)

Q: You can see all of this through the binoculars?

A: Yes.

Q: And what exactly do you see?

A: She pulls out a packet of heroin and hands it to Cheryl Horton and in return she receives cash.

Q: What does Jamie Roberts do next?

A: She walks over to a car parked in front of Cavalier Street, 15 Cavalier Street. A person later identified as Ms. Rogers is in the vehicle and Jamie gives her the money she just got from Cheryl.

Q: Okay. What happens next?

A: Ms. Rogers gives Jamie Roberts more packets of heroin and Jamie holds the packets of heroin in her hand. There are four packets.

Q: How can you tell it is four packets?

A: With the binoculars. I can see them clearly in Ms. Robert's hand. She has them in the palm of her hand. She's counting them.

Q: So you see her count four packets?

A: Yes.

Q: Okay. And who gives that to her?

A: Ms. Rogers.

Q: What happens then?

A: She goes back into the area of the street and --and another gentleman comes up - Mr. Dupree, Chris Dupree, and they talk. Ms. Roberts holds out the packets of heroin in her hand and Mr. Dupree picks one of the packets of heroin out and holds it up to the sun, flicking it to see if the package was full, if it was a good package. He keeps the package and gives Ms. Roberts cash.

Q: What does Ms. Roberts do?

A: She goes back to Ms. Rogers and gives her the money. It looks like Mr. Dupree needs change because I see Jamie or Ms. Rogers trying to get into her pocket. She cannot do it so she gets out of the car and gives Ms. Roberts some change. Ms. Roberts walks back to Chris Dupree and gives him the change.

Q: Why does it appear that Ms. Rogers gets out of the car?

A: She is not a small woman and can't seem to get her hand inside her pocket while she is sitting down. She gets out of the car so that she can get her hand into her front pocket.

Q: Do you see the money?

A: Yes.

Q: Where does the money come from?

A: From Ms. Roger's pocket.

Q: Then what happens?

A: She gives it to Ms. Roberts and then Ms. Roberts gives it to Mr. Dupree.

Q: Okay. Now, what -- Ms. Horton, what is she doing while all of this is going on?

A: She is in a parked car in front of Ms. Rogers, and it is an abandoned car and she is sitting in the passenger side of the vehicle snorting the bag of heroin.

Q: You can see her snorting the heroin?

A: Yes.

Q: Okay. And after you see this happen what do you do?

A: I call my lieutenant, Lieutenant Lister, and tell her and other individuals of the Anti-Crime Unit to come into the area. I give them a description of the people involved and where they are on the street.

Q: How do you call the lieutenant?

A: With a handheld radio.

Q: Now, while you are waiting for your back up officers to come in do you see anything else?

A: Well, as she pulls into the area Ms. Roberts is walking back over, she is by Ms. Rogers and Cheryl Horton and she is showing Ms. Horton more packets of heroin, and when the officers come in I see her drop a couple of packets on the ground.

Q: Now, where is Ms. Horton was in a car in front of Ms. Rogers, is that correct?

A: At one point she is in the car in front of Ms. Rogers. Later she gets out of that car and then jumps into the car with Ms. Rogers.

Q: While she was in the car with Ms. Rogers what does Ms. Roberts do?

A: She comes by. She is standing outside the car conversing and showing Ms. Horton more bags of heroin.

Q: Were they doing this when the officers show up?

A: Yes.

Q: What happens?

A: When then lieutenant pulls up Ms. Roberts drops a couple packets of heroin that she has in her hand on to the ground and she is placed under arrest. A later search revealed that she also has another bag in her fifth pocket.

Q: What officer makes that arrest?

A: Fucci.

Q: Okay. Does anyone arrest Ms. Horton.

A: Yes I see them stop her and take the opened package she had purchased. When the officer approaches her she drops it to the ground.

Q: Okay. Okay. Who is arrested?

A: Ms. Roberts, Cheryl Horton and Ms. Rogers.

G.   Checklist

The following checklist summarizes the information counsel should consider when developing persuasive direct examinations. It should be used as a starting point for developing appropriate direct examinations focused on persuading the jury by showcasing the theme and theories of the case developed during case analysis.

I.   Direct Examination Overview:

    a.   It is all about asking questions that the jury wants to know the answer to so that they can decide the issues in the case.

    b.   When we mimic conversational tones during direct examination we create interest and anticipation in the jury.

II.   Seven Steps to Superior Direct Examination:

    a.   Start and end direct preparation with case analysis.

    b.   Organize logically. Be brief, but sufficient.

    c.   Simple language—vary pace with tone, body position, movement.

    d.   Exhibits—use them.

    e.   Use headlines, orientations, transitions, and coupling questions.

    f.   Set the scene though background, descriptive words, action words.

    g.   Listen to your witness—build your next question on their response. Remember to ask the questions you planted in the juror's mind during voir dire and opening statement.

III.   Identifying Topics for Direct Examination:

    a.   List all factual theories for the witness with supporting facts. Potential sources include:

        i.   Documents authored by the witness

        ii.   Documents associated with the witness

        iii. Other exhibits associated with the witness

        iv. Other witnesses

        v.   The witness

    b.   Decide whether to avoid any factual theories for the witness based upon your case analysis—create a final list of topics addressing the best and worst facts for each witness.

    c.   Organize the presentation order for each topic in direct examination. Methods include:

        i.   Time lines or chronologies.

        ii.   Presentation must make logical sense to a first-time listener.

        iii. Organize to maximize persuasion.

IV.   Good Direct Examination Techniques:

    a.   Form of the Question on Direct

        i.   Wide-open questions

        ii.   Directive questions

        iii. Open questions

        iv. Probing or testing questions

        v.   Coupling questions

    b.   Planning and Presenting the Direct Examination

        i.   Chronological examination.

        ii.   The development of cause and effect.

        iii. Topical examination by subject matter.

    c.   Organization

        i.   Headlines

        ii.   Accredit the witness

        iii.   No compound questions

        iv.   Looping

        v.   Limit use of notes

        vi.   Go from general to specific

        vii. Brevity is your friend

        viii. Exhibits are your friend

        ix.   Build direct around key facts

    d. Physicality

        i.   Make eye contact

        ii.   Gesture appropriately

        iii.   Relax

        iv.   Posture

        v.   Listen

        vi.   React to the witness

        vii. Do not talk over the witness

        viii. Body position matters

    e. Language

        i.   Emphasis where needed

        ii.   Paint pictures with words

        iii.   Use normal language

        iv.   Delete filler words

        v.   Conversational tone

        vi.   Let the silence work for you

        vii. Voice inflection persuades

        viii. Less is usually more

H.   Evidentiary Rules to Consider During Direct

Issues Arising During Direct Examination	Applicable Federal Rule of Evidence
Character traits of the victim or accused	404(a), 404(b) & 405
Character of a witness for truthfulness	608

Out-of-court statements offered for the truth of the matter asserted therein (hearsay)	801 – 807
Offering evidence of other crimes, wrongs and & acts (*Chapter 10*)	404(b)
Prior convictions of a witness (*Chapter 10*)	609
Legal relevancy: Is the probative value substantially outweighed by the danger of unfair prejudice?	403
Are the questions logically relevant?	401 &, 402
Competency of a witness	610
Personal knowledge of the witness	602
Questioning witnesses	611 &, 614

Table 1: Potential Evidentiary Rules Applicable During Direct Examination

Chapter 6: Exhibits

A. Introduction 221
B. How the Law Impacts Exhibits................................222
C. Admitting Exhibits...230
D. Laying Foundations 232
E. Persuasive Use of Exhibits......................................242
F. Sample Foundations 243
G. Foundation Checklists 248
H. Evidentiary Rules to Consider 271
I. Conclusion..271

A.   Introduction

This section establishes a process for admitting exhibits based upon the nature of the evidence to be offered. This method relies upon concepts of relevancy, foundation, and authenticity. Counsel should remember that admitting exhibits is primarily a sorting game - proper identification of the type of evidence is the first step to admitting it, followed by its appropriate use in a systemic fashion designed to increase its persuasive impact.

There is something inherently persuasive in an object people can see, feel, and sometimes even smell. These things remove the case from the walls of the courtroom, and instead place the members of the jury viscerally into the story of the case. The credibility of the story will be enhanced by a silent piece of evidence that in reality speaks volumes to the jury. It engages multiple senses, is less inclined to be interpreted as having a bias, and works as a visual focus for the argument counsel will make to the jury during closings.

Counsel use exhibits to persuade. Counsel who identify the correct exhibits through case analysis, admit them during the testimony of witnesses, and then rely upon them during closings are properly using exhibits to increase the credibility of their case. This approach provides information to visual learners through a medium designed to maximize their acceptance of the information packaged within the exhibit. Used properly they reinforce testimony and exist substantively on their own merits, providing a pathway into the courtroom for evidence that cannot enter through other ways.

B.   How the Law Impacts Exhibits

1.   Introduction

The Federal Rules of Evidence control the admission of exhibits at trial. Admissibility is the first step, and the legal concepts which must be mastered to ensure admissibility are also useful in determining how to most effectively persuade with the exhibit once it has been admitted. As a lawyer in the courtroom there are few things are more enjoyable than seeing the opponent's exhibits sitting out of the sight of the jury, unused and unappreciated. This happens because counsel did not understand the law behind exhibits, the foundational elements needed to admit them, and the proper way to use them once admitted.

When confronted with the perceived difficulties attached to the use of exhibits, many advocates simply turn away and leave them at counsel's table. Counsel who adopt the methods discussed in this section will find themselves the master of the exhibit—not their opponent, not the witness, and certainly not the judge.

To properly admit and use exhibits counsel must first be able to place the exhibit into its proper evidentiary category. To lay a proper foundation counsel must begin by determining within which of the three fundamental evidentiary categories the evidence resides. They include:

> (1) testimonial,
>
> (2) demonstrative, and
>
> (3) real.

Real evidence can be further divided into two subcategories: (1) fungible and (2) non-fungible. Properly identifying the nature of the evidence is the first step in determining the foundational requirements for admissibility. The required foundation questions depend on the type of evidence offered and the purpose of the offered evidence. Categorizing the evidence is the single most important step in this process because it feeds into the next step - laying foundations.

Once the proper category is identified counsel must next lay a proper foundation, showing the court that the item is what it claims to be and that the court can rely upon its authenticity and relevancy. Each type of evidence must be properly authenticated and admitted through the testimony of a sponsoring witness. The Federal Rules of Evidence provide general guidance on authentication, and then, by way of illustration, give suggested ways to establish admissibility. This text covers the theory behind laying foundations and then provides specific examples.

2.   Foundations

Foundational requirements are derived from the evidentiary rules addressing each particular type of evidence. The foundation must be "laid" through the questions of the offering counsel and the responses of the witness. An improper foundation will prompt an objection and may prevent the offered evidence from being accepted by the court. Authentication represents a more specific application of the requirement of relevancy. Counsel are responsible for meeting both the relevancy and authenticity requirements for each exhibit referenced, offered, and admitted into evidence. If counsel cannot offer testimony establishing an exhibit is "what its proponent claims," it lacks relevance under FRE 401 and is subject to exclusion as confusing and misleading under FRE 403.

Rule 401. Test for Relevant Evidence

Evidence is relevant if:

(a) it has any tendency to make a fact more or less probable than it would be without the evidence; and

the fact is of consequence in determining the action.

Rule 403. Excluding Relevant Evidence for Prejudice, Confusion, Waste of Time, or Other Reasons

The court may exclude relevant evidence if its probative value is substantially outweighed by a danger of one or more of the following: unfair prejudice, confusing the issues, misleading the jury, undue delay, wasting time, or needlessly presenting cumulative evidence.

Counsel should understand that FRE 104(b) establishes the authority of the court to decide questions of admissibility, laying the ground rules for the process. It is applied in conjunction with the rules establishing the actual test for admissibility, to include FRE 401 and FRE 403.

Rule 104. Preliminary Questions

(a) In General. The court must decide any preliminary question about whether a witness is qualified, a privilege exists, or evidence is admissible. In so deciding, the court is not bound by evidence rules, except those on privilege.

(b) Relevance That Depends on a Fact. When the relevance of evidence depends on whether a fact exists, proof must be introduced sufficient to support a finding that the fact does exist. The court may admit the proposed evidence on the condition that the proof be introduced later.

(c) Conducting a Hearing So That the Jury Cannot Hear It. The court must conduct any hearing on a preliminary question so that the jury cannot hear it if:

(1) the hearing involves the admissibility of a confession;

(2) a defendant in a criminal case is a witness and so requests; or

(3) justice so requires.

(d) Cross-Examining a Defendant in a Criminal Case. By testifying on a preliminary question, a defendant in a criminal case does not become subject to cross-examination on other issues in the case.

(e) Evidence Relevant to Weight and Credibility. This rule does not limit a party's right to introduce before the jury evidence that is relevant to the weight or credibility of other evidence.

Under this rule the judge performs a screening function. When counsel are attempting to authenticate a piece of evidence they must understand that the relevant legal standard is not by a preponderance of evidence but rather an assessment as to whether there is evidence sufficient to support a jury finding of authenticity. If this standard is satisfied, the judge is usually required to admit the exhibit (unless excludable on other grounds), even if the judge has not been personally persuaded of its authenticity.

Opposing counsel is free to admit evidence challenging the authenticated evidence's authenticity. The fact that evidence has been sufficiently authenticated to be admitted does not prevent the opponent from introducing counter-proof challenging its authenticity. Similarly, satisfying the authentication requirement does not mean the jury is bound to accept the matter or give it the significance in the case that the proponent suggests. The jury remains free to reject the matter as not authentic or accept it as authentic while giving it little or no weight.

The type of evidentiary objections that must be overcome are derived from the nature of the evidence counsel is seeking to admit, the foundational questions asked, and the responses received. Finally, sometimes evidence may fall into more than one category. Counsel must properly offer the evidence to ensure that they can use it for their intended purpose. This becomes important during jury deliberations since most jurisdictions do not allow demonstrative evidence back into the jury deliberation room.

Attorneys are required to ask foundational questions to establish the admissibility of evidence. These foundational questions are derived from the common law, evidentiary law, and local court practices. They serve as a short cut for answering challenges to a piece of evidence based upon potential objections. Foundational questions normally deal with issues in best evidence, authenticity, relevancy, personal knowledge, and hearsay. "The requirement of authentication or identification as a condition precedent to admissibility is satisfied by evidence sufficient to support a finding that the matter in question is what its proponent claims."

3.   Authentication

FRE 901 addresses authentication, identifying the general procedure required to authenticate a piece of evidence while also providing illustrative examples. FRE 902 identifies those types of evidence that are self authenticating. The text of FRE 901(a) is as follows:

Rule 901. Authenticating or Identifying Evidence

(a) In General. To satisfy the requirement of authenticating or identifying an item of evidence, the proponent must produce evidence sufficient to support a finding that the item is what the proponent claims it is.

For example, only a witness with personal knowledge of the scene may authenticate a diagram. They must be able to testify that the diagram is a "fair and accurate" depiction of the scene in question. The proponent of the diagram should ensure that the witness also explains labels and other markings present on the diagram before admitting it and using it. By laying a thorough authentication foundation, counsel guards against attacks as to authenticity being raised as potential appellate issues.

> **Easy Guide to Courtroom Objections (BARPH):**
>
> **B** – est Evidence
> **A** – uthentication
> **R** – elevance
> **P** – ersonal Knowledge
> **H** - earsay

Regardless of the type of proffered evidence, it is the judge who determines the sufficiency of the authentication. That issue is a question of fact under Federal Rule of Evidence 104(a). Along with the authentication requirement, the proponent of demonstrative evidence must be prepared to respond to other evidentiary objections raised by opposing counsel that may bar the admissibility of the evidence.

An easy acronym to use when addressing possible evidentiary objections to exhibits is BARPH. Counsel should always lay all foundational elements when dealing with exhibits. These foundational questions can be used to not only authenticate the evidence, but to persuade the jury that the evidence is worthy of consideration.

4.   Voir Dire & Objections

When an exhibit is offered into evidence opposing counsel must decide whether to object. In the initial thought process they should consider how allowing this evidence to be admitted will affect the chosen theme and theory. If it doesn't hurt, counsel should consider letting it in, especially if they have found a way to make it work to their advantage. If it does hurt, opposing counsel may: (1) voir dire on the exhibit, (2) object as to the foundation, or (3) object based upon Best evidence, Authenticity, Relevancy, Personal knowledge, and Hearsay.

Opposing counsel request to voir dire the witness on the exhibit for the purposes of developing an objection to the exhibit's admissibility. This voir dire is a cross-examination of the witness about an exhibit limited in scope to questions addressing only the potential admissibility of the exhibit. Questions concerning the weight that the evidence might be given are outside the scope of the voir dire and should instead be asked during normal cross examination of the witness.

> ***Example: the following example showcases the interplay between counsel, the court, and the witness when conducting voir dire concerning the potential admissibility of a piece of evidence.***

State: The state offers into evidence what has previously been marked as Prosecution Exhibit 1 for Identification as Prosecution Exhibit 1.

Defense: Objection. Your honor may I voir dire for purposes of forming an objection?

Judge: You may, briefly.

Defense: You have never been to the site of the accident?

Witness: No.

Defense: You did not take this photograph (referring to the proffered exhibit)?

Witness: No.

Defense: Your honor we object to the admissibility of this exhibit. The witness does not have the requisite personal knowledge to authenticate the exhibit, or to lay foundations.

Judge: Sustained. Proceed State.

At this point the counsel who was unable to admit the evidence is free to attempt to lay a proper foundation and offer it into evidence again.

Since voir dire on an exhibit occurs during the direct examination of a witness by opposing counsel, judges are careful to restrict the scope of voir dire on exhibits. Counsel should save questions designed to attack the weight of the exhibit for cross examination, where it is not only appropriate, but will do more good persuasively speaking.

A common objection often made during the voir dire is that it is "improper, being outside the scope of the direct." When a judge sustains this objection you can be confident that she perceives that you are asking questions about weight and not admissibility. Another common objection is "Your honor that goes to weight, and not admissibility." That is another way of saying "outside the scope" that is accepted in most jurisdictions.

Example: the following example demonstrates the interplay between counsel and the court when dealing with objections con-

cerning voir dire that is outside the scope permitted when con-
ducting voir dire on the admissibility of an exhibit.

State: The state offers into evidence what has previously been marked as Prosecution Exhibit 1 for Identification as Prosecution Exhibit 1.

Defense: Objection. Your honor may I voir dire for purposes of forming an objection?

Judge: You may, briefly.

Defense: You don't like my client very much, do you?

Witness: No.

Defense: He was dating your daughter?

Witness: Yes.

State: Objection. Outside the scope. This is improper voir dire going to weight and credibility, not admissibility.

Judge: Sustained. Do you have any voir dire on admissibility counsel?

Defense: Nothing further your honor.

State: The state offers into evidence what has previously been marked as Prosecution Exhibit 1 for Identification as Prosecution Exhibit 1.

Judge: Admitted as marked.

Normally, questions asked during voir dire on the exhibit will not be allowed during cross, but creative counsel can easily tie what was earlier an admissibility issue to a greater weight issue later. If counsel chooses to not request voir dire on an exhibit then they must either agree to its admission or object.

When counsel stands and says: "Objection, insufficient foundation," the judge must either rule on the objection, or respond to the objecting counsel by asking how the foundation is insufficient. If the court sustains the objection without an explanation, the proponent of the exhibit may inquire for the reasons for the ruling under the rules of evidence.

Example: In the following example opposing counsel has objected to the foundation of a photograph. Pay attention to how the court rules and counsel's response.

State:	The state offers into evidence what has previously been marked as Prosecution Exhibit 1 for Identification as Prosecution Exhibit 1.
Defense:	Objection. Insufficient foundation.
Judge:	State, response?
State:	I can lay a further foundation.
Judge:	Very well. the objection is sustained.
State:	Mr. Jones, is the photograph of the intersection a fair and accurate representation of the area where the accident occurred?
Witness:	Yes. It looks just like it.
State:	The state offers into evidence what has previously been marked as Prosecution Exhibit 1 for Identification as Prosecution Exhibit 1.

When the objection is other than foundational, the counsel opposing admissibility should stand and say "Objection," and then give a BRIEF statement of the grounds for the objection without testifying with a rambling objection that is really designed to make arguments to the jury. The judge will either rule on the objection or ask the proponent of the exhibit how they respond to opposing counsel's objection. If the court sustains the objection, the proponent is not barred from continuing to attempt to lay an adequate foundation to get the exhibit into evidence.

Example: in this example counsel has objected with a brief explanation as to why it is not admissible, the court responds, and finally opposing counsel takes action.

State: The state offers into evidence what has previously been marked as Prosecution Exhibit 1 for Identification as Prosecution Exhibit 1.

Defense: Objection. Lack of personal knowledge.

Judge: Sustained.

State: Mr. Jones how do you know that this photograph is a fair and accurate representation of the intersection.

Witness: I was there that night and saw the accident at this intersection.

State: The state again offers into evidence what has previously been marked as Prosecution Exhibit 1 for Identification as Prosecution Exhibit 1.

Defense: No objection.

Judge: Admitted as marked.

C. Admitting Exhibits

Admitting Exhibits

1. Introduce the exhibit.

2. Lay the foundation for admission.

3. Authenticate the exhibit.

4. Offer into evidence.

5. Have witness mark the exhibit as needed.

6. Publish the exhibit to the jury.

Counsel must place the exhibit into its proper evidentiary category when determining how to admit it. This is necessary to lay a proper foundation, showing the court that the item is what it claims to be and that they can rely upon its authenticity and relevancy. Properly identifying the nature of the evidence is the first step in determining the foundational requirements for admissibility.

The required foundation questions depend on the type of evidence offered and the purpose of the offered evidence. Categorizing the evidence is the single most important step in this process. Each type of evidence must be properly authenticated and admitted through the testimony of a sponsoring witness.

There are a variety of ways to approach admitting exhibits at trial, most of which are either derived from the customary practices of the particular local jurisdiction or promulgated in the local rules of court. Advocates must also take the time to ascertain the particular local rules that are "unwritten" when preparing exhibits. When in doubt it is appropriate to ask colleagues as to an individual judge's preferences when it comes to the admission of evidence. Enhancing knowledge gained from other attorneys in the office, counsel should also watch other lawyers at work when they have time. When doing so counsel should remember that customs of the court are just that—customs. An advocate should not refrain from approaching the court and requesting they be allowed to use an exhibit in a particular fashion when the law so allows and it provides the best chance for their client.

Admitting Exhibits at Trial:

- Have the exhibit marked by the court reporter
- *Show* exhibit to opposing counsel for inspection and objection
- Ask the judge's *permission* to approach the witness
- *Show* the exhibit to the witness
- Lay *foundation* for the exhibit—Focus on relevancy, authenticity and reliability
- *Offer* exhibit into evidence: "I offer what has been marked as prosecution exhibit 1 for ID into evidence as prosecution exhibit 1."

There are no surprises when it comes to exhibits so there is no valid reason for counsel to attempt "exhibit by ambush." They should be shown to the court and opposing counsel early and often. Counsel should address any concerns about an exhibit's relevancy and authenticity early in the process and then use them during the trial.

Advocates following the recommended steps for dealing with exhibits at trial will ensure that the exhibit is not only admitted, but used in a persuasive fashion. By learning these steps and adopting them into their litigation practice, counsel automates a portion of the trial experience, allowing greater focus to be given to the individual moments of trial. These fundamental steps serve as the guideline for properly handling the exhibit in a manner removing potential objections, ensuring that proper foundations are laid; allowing the jury to focus on the viability of the exhibit.

Counsel should use this checklist, paying particular attention to step five. The foundation for each piece of evidence is unique to the nature of the evidence, with some commonalities based upon the category of the evidence.

D.   Laying Foundations

The following questions serve as a general template that will ensure that counsel meet the foundational requirement for various types of exhibits. Each jurisdiction may modify or rearrange these foundational questions, but they serve as a competent and thorough basis from which to begin. Note the specific differences for each type of exhibit. The foundational requirements vary because the evidentiary rules necessary to authenticate the evidence and establish its relevancy are influenced by the physical nature of the offered exhibit.

Step 3 is specific to the item being offered into evidence. Its foundation is tied to its nature. When in doubt ask: What it is, How do they know what it is, Where did they last see it, Is it in the same, or substantially same condition - these are great starting points.

Foundational requirements are derived from the evidentiary rules addressing each particular type of evidence. It is often a combination of authentication as defined in FRE 901 and 902, in conjunction with the specific evidentiary rule addressing that type of evidence. The foundation must be "laid" through the questions of the offering counsel and the responses of the witness. An improper foundation will prompt an objection and may prevent the offered evidence from being accepted by the court. The type of evidentiary objections that must be overcome are derived from the nature of the evidence counsel is seeking to admit, the foundational questions asked, and the responses received.

"The requirement of authentication or identification as a condition precedent to admissibility is satisfied by evidence sufficient to support a finding that the matter in question is what its proponent claims." FRE 901 addresses authentication. For example, only a witness with personal knowledge of the scene may authenticate a diagram. They must be able to testify that the diagram is a "fair and accurate" depiction of the scene in question. The proponent of the diagram should ensure that the witness also explains labels and other markings present on the diagram prior to admitting it and using it.

Finally, sometimes evidence may fall into more than one category. Counsel must properly offer the evidence to ensure that they can use it for their intended purpose. This becomes important during jury deliberations since most jurisdictions do not allow demonstrative evidence back into the jury deliberation room.

Regardless of the type of proffered evidence it is the judge who determines the sufficiency of the authentication. That issue is a question of fact under Federal Rule of Evidence 104(a). Counsel should lay all foundational elements when dealing with exhibits. These foundational questions can be used to not only authenticate the evidence, but to persuade the jury that the evidence is worthy of consideration.

1.   Admitting Diagrams

Let us use our earlier example of a diagram to discuss how you would admit it. After going through the initial steps of asking to approach the witness and showing opposing counsel the diagram prior to that approach, it is time for counsel to allow the witness to interact with the diagram. First the diagram must be shown to the sponsoring witness, giving them the opportunity to examine it. Next you should ask the witness if the diagram is a "fair and accurate" depiction of the scene at the time of the action in the case. Unless exact distances are crucial the diagram need not be to scale, although this is a common objection that you will have to deal with if you have not created a diagram that is to scale. The lack of scale may be established on either direct or cross-examination. If the diagram is drawn to scale, it should be noted on the record and the scale clearly shown on the diagram. Additionally, if the diagram contains any labels or keys, the witness should explain the nature of these labels and keys prior to the admission of the diagram.

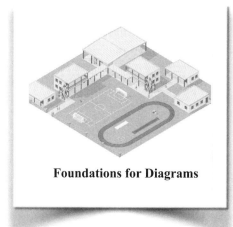

Foundations for Diagrams

> ### Foundation Elements for Diagrams
>
> - The diagram depicts a certain area or object;
>
> - The witness is familiar with that area or object;
>
> - The witness explains the basis for his knowledge of the area or object;
>
> - The witness affirms the accuracy of the diagram.

Once counsel have established that the diagram is relevant and authentic, they turn to the court and offer it into evidence. They must then use it in the testimony of the witness and publish it to the jury. Publication may be accomplished in a variety of ways, to include providing copies to the jury, blowing the exhibit up so that everyone may see it or placing it in a location where the jury is able to reference as the witness testifies. There is room for creative advocacy during publication. For example, if counsel in a violent crime manages to admit a photograph of the victim, one publishing technique is for counsel to hold the exhibit in their hands, and walk down the line of the jury box. This gives counsel a moment with the members of the jury, and silently adds to the importance of the given exhibit. Advocates should make certain that the jury can see the exhibit, that the witness has access to it and that the judge can see it. Opposing counsel should request permission of the judge to move around the courtroom so that they may also observe the use of the diagram.

Example: In the following excerpt counsel is laying a foundation to admit a diagram. In many jurisdictions plaintiff exhibits are marked with numbers and defense exhibits are marked with letters. Counsel should check local customs before having their exhibits pre-marked.

Plaintiff: Officer Morris I would like to talk with you about the accident scene. Do you remember how it looked on the night of March 21st?

Witness: Absolutely.

Plaintiff: *(approaching opposing counsel with an exhibit in hand)* I am showing opposing counsel what has been previously marked as plaintiff's exhibit 1 for I.D for inspection and objection. May I approach the witness?

Judge: You may.

Plaintiff: *(Showing the exhibit to the witness)* I am showing you what has been previously marked as PE 1 for ID. Do you recognize it? *(Establishing personal knowledge)*

Witness: Yes.

Plaintiff: What is it? *(Identification)*

Witness: This is a diagram of the area where the accident occurred on the 21st of March.

Plaintiff: What is in the diagram? *(establishing the content of the diagram - relevancy)*

Witness: It shows the street, the community center, basketball courts, housing area and woods.

Plaintiff: Are you familiar with this area? *(establishing personal knowledge)*

Witness: Yes.

Plaintiff: How are you familiar with the area depicted by this diagram?

Witness: I was the responding officer the night Ms. Washington's children were struck by Ms. Hartwell's car.

Plaintiff: Is the diagram reasonably accurate? *(Establishing accuracy of the diagram)*

Witness: Yes. It shows the area as I remember it that night.

Plaintiff: Is the diagram drawn to scale? *(It is not required to be drawn to scale to be admissible)*

Witness: No.

Plaintiff: Despite the fact that it is not drawn to scale, would this exhibit assist you in your testimony?

Witness: Yes. *(Retrieve the exhibit from the witness and offer to admit it into evidence)*

Plaintiff: Your Honor, I offer into evidence what has been previously marked as PE-1 for ID as PE-1.

2. Admitting Photographs

A photograph is authenticated by a witness who attests that the photograph accurately and fairly depicts the scene in question. There is no need to address the mechanics of exposing or developing the film or the working condition of the camera. Also, it is important to note that a photograph does not need to be authenticated by the photographer, but must be authenticated by a witness with personal knowledge of the scene depicted in the photograph.

Example: In the following excerpt counsel is laying a foundation to admit a photo from the accident scene. Photographs can be real or demonstrative evidence, depending upon how the foundation is laid. In this example the foundation is for a photo that is real evidence.

<dl>
<dt>Plaintiff:</dt>
<dd>Officer Morris I would like to talk with you about how you investigated the accident scene. What was one of the first things you did?</dd>

<dt>Witness:</dt>
<dd>I got out our accident camera and began to take photos of the accident scene.</dd>

<dt>Plaintiff:</dt>
<dd>(approaching opposing counsel with an exhibit in hand) I am showing opposing counsel what has been previously marked as plaintiff's exhibit 2 for I.D for inspection and objection. May I approach the witness?</dd>

<dt>Judge:</dt>
<dd>You may.</dd>

<dt>Plaintiff:</dt>
<dd>(Showing the exhibit to the witness) I am showing you what has been previously marked as PE 1 for ID. Do you recognize it? (Establishing personal knowledge)</dd>
</dl>

Foundation - Photographs

Witness: Yes.

Plaintiff: What is it? *(Identification)*

Witness: This is a picture of the accident scene I took on the 21st of March. *(It is not necessary for the witness to have taken the photo, but merely that they have sufficient personal knowledge to compare the photo to their memory of the scene).*

Plaintiff: "Is this photograph a fair and accurate representation of the accident scene on the night of March 21st?

Witness: Yes. It does not show the bodies of the children but it does show one of the cars.

Plaintiff: *(Retrieve the exhibit from the witness and offer to admit it into evidence)* Your Honor, I offer into evidence what has been previously marked as PE-2 for ID as PE-2.

3.   Admitting Non-fungible Evidence

Non-fungible evidence is evidence having a unique characteristic allowing it to be identified by individuals having personal knowledge of that unique characteristic. The nature of the unique characteristic is not identified by the rules of evidence, but in practice it is a relatively common sense rule. The person who initially takes custody of the evidence has the opportunity to observe the evidence carefully. They look for indications of uniqueness. Such indications might include a serial number on a weapon, a nick in a particular location on the blade of a knife, the nature of a scratch or disfiguring mark on the piece of evidence.

Additionally, relatively common items can be given unique characteristics by the individual taking them into custody. The classic example of this is when the police officer places her initials on the butt of a weapon seized at the crime scene. Conversely, fungible evidence is evidence that does not have a unique characteristic rendering it readily identifiable. Fungible evidence requires additional foundational steps before it can be admitted, usually involving some type of chain-of-custody. Examples of non-fungible evidence include a gun with a serial number or other unique items seized for their evidentiary value.

> ***Example: In the following excerpt counsel is laying a foundation to admit a pistol allegedly used to commit a murder. The actual pistol seized, or a photo of it, can be admitted as substantive evidence. Photographs can be real or demonstrative evidence, depending upon how the foundation is laid. In this example the foundation is for a photo that is real evidence.***

State: Officer Baxter-White I would like to talk with you about any weapons you discovered during your investigation?

Witness: Okay.

State: *(Approaching opposing counsel with an exhibit in hand)* I am showing opposing counsel what has been previously marked as prosecution exhibit 2 for I.D for inspection and objection. May I approach the witness?

Judge: You may.

State: *(Showing the exhibit to the witness)* I am showing you what has been previously marked as PE 2 for ID. Do you recognize it? *(Establishing personal knowledge)*

Witness: Yes.

State: What is it? *(Identification)*

Witness: This is the .45 calibre pistol I found in the car of Ms. Alexander.

State: How do you recognize it?

Witness: I wrote down the serial number. I also recognize the three notches in the barrel. They are quite distinctive.

State: Is it in substantially the same condition as the last time you saw it?

Witness: Yes.

Plaintiff: *(Retrieve the exhibit from the witness and offer to admit it into evidence)* Your Honor, I offer into evidence what has been previously marked as PE-2 for ID as PE-2.

Sometimes a non-fungible piece of evidence also contains fungible evidence. Consider the scenario of a bloody knife seized at the crime scene. The knife will have some unique characteristic that will allow the police officer testifying at trial to properly identify it—the blood does not. If the police intend to test the blood for DNA identification they must safeguard that blood from the moment it is taken into custody. That process is normally referred to as establishing the chain of custody. It is important to note, however, that gaps in the chain of custody do not guarantee that the evidence will fail the authentication test. Rather, it becomes a question of how large a gap exists within the change. The smaller the gap, the more likely the judge is to rule that this becomes a question of weight not admissibility.

Certain procedures, normally captured in the documents accompanying the tested fungible evidence, must be followed to ensure that the fungible blood is what it purports to be—blood taken from the knife found at the scene of the crime. Before the court would allow a witness to testify as to the nature of that blood the judge must be satisfied that the blood has not been adulterated either intentionally or unintentionally. That concern does not exist as to the knife because it has unique characteristics making it an identifiable non-fungible piece of evidence—you can mark it in a manner that lets you ensure it is controlled. But, while you cannot mark the blood in order to ensure it remains in the state that it was when collected, but you can create both procedures that safeguard the fungible evidence and documents that verify those procedures.

Because the blood does not have unique characteristics a court will be concerned with the chain-of-custody documents that establish that the blood has not been tampered with. The offering party must lay the foundation for the chain-of-custody documents first, admitting them subject to a relevancy connection to the case.

4.   Admitting Fungible Evidence

Fungible evidence has the potential to be easily modified, adulterated, or replaced by people having access to it. In order to guarantee its relevance and authenticity, fungible evidence must be carefully guarded to prevent contamination or destruction. As part of the process in laying the foundation for the admissibility of fungible evidence the offering party must first establish that the fungible evidence has been properly safeguarded against potential contamination. Chain-of-custody procedures accomplish this purpose. To admit fungible evidence, the chain-of-custody documents relating to the evidence must be offered and admitted before the fungible evidence itself can be offered and admitted.

Establishing a proper chain-of-custody for fungible evidence is a condition precedent to its admissibility. This is a precise and important skill that a competent trial attorney must master. Improperly authenticated evidence may result in crucial evidence being excluded that could deal a fatal blow to your case. While this skill is important, it is relatively easy to master. All that is required is attention to the local rules of court, an understanding

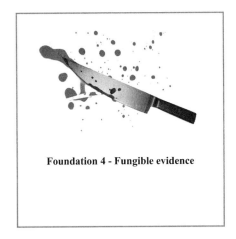

Foundation 4 - Fungible evidence

of how the rules of evidence impact foundational questions, and a commitment to preparation that includes taking examples of foundational requirements for your intended exhibits into court with you and having them readily available if you run into difficulties.

Example: In the following example a prosecutor is laying the foundation to admit the chain of custody document accompanying the substance tested by the state crime lab.

State: Your Honor, I am showing opposing counsel what has previously been marked as PE-1 for I.D. for inspection and objection.

May I have permission to approach the witness?

Judge: You may.

State: I am showing the witness what has been previously marked as PE-1 for ID. Do you recognize this?

Witness: Yes.

State: What is it?

Witness: It is the document that we receive with exhibits sent to the crime lab for testing.

State: Does the crime lab have a filing or records system for these documents?

Witness: Absolutely.

State: Are you personally familiar with that system?

Witness: Yes. I use those documents in my day to day work when testing samples. I also have access the filing system where they are stored.

State: Did you remove this document from a file in that system?

Witness: I did. I took it out of our completed testing file in the laboratory.

State: Is this document a proper file entry in that system?

Witness: Yes.

State: How do you know that this record is a proper file entry?

Witness: I recognize our control number on the document which I used to retrieve it from our file system. I also signed this particular document.

State: *(Retrieve the exhibit from the witness and offer to admit it into evidence).* Your Honor, I offer into evidence what has been previously marked as PE-1 for ID as PE-1.

Once counsel establishes the authenticity of a business record they must next establish that the contents of the chain-of-custody document are admissible as an exception to the hearsay rule, usually under the business records exception found in FRE 803(6). After laying the foundations for the fungible evidence and the chain-of-custody documents counsel can then move to admit both into evidence. When laying the foundation in court counsel can choose to lay the fungible foundation first, or the hearsay exception first. That choice is normally dependent upon the witnesses needed to lay an appropriate foundation.

E. Persuasive Use of Exhibits

Although foundations for exhibits are relatively easy to establish, the effective use of diagrams and other exhibits as persuasive tools depends upon how well counsel prepare for, and practice, their use. Jurors live in the video age and slick presentations are now expected on cell phones, let alone by attorneys in court. Advocates should strive to meet or exceed expectations in order to increase the effectiveness of their exhibits. Tablets, laptops and presentation programs have made this easier than it has ever been - perhaps easier to do, but not necessarily easier to do effectively.

A shabby diagram may well be interpreted as an indication that the case or investigation is also less than average, especially if opposing counsel has chosen the high-tech route. A powerful diagram will continue selling the case long after the witness has left the stand. Diagrams should appear in opening statements, be used by witnesses during testimony, and referred to during closing arguments. In jurisdictions that allow demonstrative evidence into the jury room, exhibits will continue to speak until the case is decided, long after counsel's final closing exhortations have faded from the courtroom and the minds of the jurors.

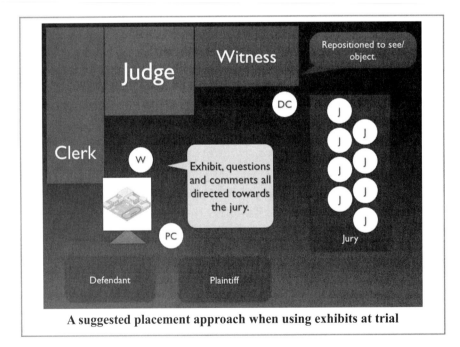

A suggested placement approach when using exhibits at trial

Regardless of the type of exhibit, the actual presentation and use must be fluid and focused. This requires a commitment to practicing with the exhibit, both alone and with the witness that will authenticate it. Counsel should know, for example, how to set up easels used for enlargements efficiently and effectively. The more practice counsel is with the tools used to present their exhibits, the smoother the presentation appears, and the greater the persuasive power of the exhibit. Different courtrooms are going to require different types of demonstrative evidence to be truly effective. Counsel should take the time to learn what delivery systems will be available in court, and then decide which ones will be most effective.

Once they have chosen a delivery system that works best for a particular location, counsel should create exhibits, practice, modify, and then practice some more until both they and the witness are comfortable in the type, manner, and effectiveness of the presentation. When doing so counsel should ensure that everyone is positioned so that the jury and the judge can see the exhibit and counsel is able to use it effectively.

One collateral benefit of diagrams and other demonstrative evidence is they permit counsel to have the witness testify more than once about issues related to the diagram. First, the witness tells the story during direct examination without the assistance of a diagram or other demonstrative aid. Next, counsel lays the foundation for the exhibit while being careful to explain through foundational questions how the use of the exhibit further develops the witness's testimony. During this second step the witness will necessarily relate elements of their previous testimony a second time while laying the foundation for the exhibit and explaining its relevance. Finally, the witness testifies in greater detail, relying upon and using the exhibit to explain what happened. It is possible that this approach may engender a cumulative objection, but proper organization of the questions as outlined above should overcome and prevent such objections.

Counsel should always inform the judge when they intend to use demonstrative evidence and be sure to give her an opportunity, along with opposing counsel, to view the demonstrative aids they intend to use. Judges hate surprises. Counsel should never hide demonstrative aids or exhibits until the last minute in a futile attempt to surprise the opposing side; the surprise may be their own when the judge sustains the objection and does not allow counsel to use them.

F.   Sample Foundations

The following two examples demonstrate laying proper foundations for exhibits as discussed infra. Note the degree of control and direction the advocate has over their witness even though this is direct examination. Counsel is able to sprinkle a certain number of leading questions during direct examination when they are laying a foundation for the admissibility of an exhibit. When used artfully these leading questions reinforce control, establish pace and let the witness know with little to no uncertainty the direction the attorney wishes to take.

1.   Diagram Foundation

State: Mr. Witness, WHERE did the robbery occur?

Witness: At the ATM machine located in the grocery store parking lot across from the Mini-Mall on State Street.

State: Please look at the diagram located on the easel to your left, marked Prosecution Exhibit 1 for identification. Do you recognize it?

Witness: Yes.

State: WHAT is it?

Witness: It is a diagram of the area around the ATM machine where I was robbed.

State: HOW do you recognize it?

Witness: I've lived in this neighborhood for fifteen years and have done most of my ATM banking through that machine for the last eight years. I am very familiar with that area.

State: HOW often do you use this ATM?

Witness: I used it about three times a week for the last eight years before the robbery. Since the robbery I haven't been able to go back to that spot.

State: Is this diagram a fair and accurate representation of the area around the ATM?

Witness: Yes, it looks good to me.

This completes the foundation of an unmarked diagram. If the diagram has been pre-marked by counsel, it is now necessary to have the witness explain the labels that have been superimposed on various objects on the diagram. That explanation could go as follows:

> *State:*   Mr. Witness, HOW did you get to the ATM on the night of the robbery?
>
> *Witness:*   I drove my car there.
>
> *State:*   WHERE did you park your car when you got there?
>
> *Witness:*   In the grocery store parking lot on State Street, about 40 feet from the ATM Machine.
>
> *State:*   Is the position of your parked car shown on this diagram, P.E. 1 for ID?
>
> *Witness:*   Yes, it is shown as a car with the word "Car" next to it on the diagram.
>
> *State:*   HOW is the ATM machine marked on the diagram?
>
> *Witness:*   There is a picture of a building with the letters "ATM" next to it.
>
> *State:*   You testified earlier that it was dark outside when you arrived at the ATM. Was the area around the ATM also dark?
>
> *Witness:*   No. It was lit fairly well by the streetlight located about fifteen feet from the ATM.
>
> *State:*   Please point out the location of the street lamp for the jury.
>
> *Witness:*   Okay. There is a picture of a street lamp which is labeled "Light" on the diagram.
>
> *State:*   Mr. Witness, what happened after you arrived at the ATM?

Witness: Well, my friend stayed in the car and I went to the machine to withdraw some cash. As I was entering my PIN number, a man in a ski mask came around the side of the machine and pointed a gun at me. He said that he would kill me if I didn't give him all my money.

State: [To the Judge] Your honor, request permission to have the witness approach the diagram.

Judge: Go ahead.

State: Using the blue marker, please place an "X" where you were standing when the masked man approached you.

Witness: All right.

State: The witness marked P.E. 1 for ID, as directed. Now using the red marker, draw an arrow to indicate the approach used by the gunman before he robbed you.

Witness: Right here.

State: [To the Judge] The witness marked P.E. 1 for ID with a red arrow as directed.

Counsel may offer the diagram into evidence at this time or any time before passing the witness. The diagram may not be further marked after it is admitted. Opposing counsel may ask that the judge instruct the jury that the diagram is not to scale.

2. Photograph Foundation

State: Mr. Witness, where do you work?

Witness: I work at the grocery store on State Street across from the Mini-Mall.

State: [To the Judge] I am showing opposing counsel what has previously been marked as Prosecution

Exhibit-1 for Identification. *(Show it to opposing counsel.)* Your Honor, may I approach the witness? *[Most jurisdictions require counsel to do this when initially approaching each witness, but you usually only need to ask once per witness.]*

Judge: You may approach the witness counsel.

State: I now hand you P.E.-2 for Identification. What is it?

Witness: It is a picture of the ATM Machine located in our grocery store parking lot.

State: How do you recognize it?

Witness: I have worked at that store as the assistant manager in charge of the night shift for the last twelve years. I was there when it was installed and have used it many times. I took this picture of the machine at the request of the store owner about 6 months ago. We were worried about the safety of our customers when they used it.

Prosecution Exhibit 2 for ID

State: From what angle was this photograph taken?

Witness: The picture is slightly left of center from the front of the ATM machine where customers use it.

State: Does this photo fairly and accurately depict the ATM Machine as it appeared six months ago?

Witness: Absolutely.

> *State:*   Your Honor, I offer P.E.-1 for Identification into evidence as P.E.-1.

These two examples are excellent starting points for developing techniques when laying foundations for admitting exhibits. Counsel should review the foundational requirements that may be unique to the particular jurisdiction when preparing for trial. It is appropriate to place scripts within the trial notebook allowing counsel to quickly and efficiently ask the appropriate foundational questions when it comes to that point in your direct examination. I have included foundational checklists at the end of this chapter to assist in this endeavor.

Proper use of exhibits is a fundamental skill for both cross and direct examination. Applying the skills discussed in this section, in concert with earlier discussions about direct and cross examination, will empower counsel to competently deal with a tremendous component of persuasion at trial—visuals. It also serves as the third component in the basic understanding of witness testimony.

G. Foundation Checklists

Here are sample foundations for common evidentiary offerings. Counsel should adapt these as necessary when preparing to lay the foundation for an evidentiary offering, or to ensure the opposing counsel has fully laid the foundation for their evidence. Each example contains the minimum required information about the evidence the attorney needs to elicit from the witness to authenticate that evidence or, in the case of the witness, to validate their competency to testify. The sample questions are intentionally written to be vague. When preparing their own foundations counsel should make their questions as specific as necessary to ensure each element is thoroughly met.

1. Diagrams

1. **Mark the exhibit (ideally, this is done before the trial starts...).**

2. **Show opposing counsel the exhibit:**

   "Your Honor, I am now showing opposing counsel what has been previously been marked as PE-1 for I.D. for their inspection and objection."

3. **Ask the judge for permission to approach the witness with the exhibit:**

"Your Honor, may I have permission to approach the witness?"

4. **Show the exhibit to the witness:**

"Your Honor, I am showing the witness what has been previously marked as PE-1 for ID."

5. **Lay the foundation for the evidence, establish what it is:**

"Do you recognize this?"

"What is it?"

Establish what the diagram depicts, the certain area or object in the diagram:

"What is in the diagram?

Establish that the witness is familiar with that area or object:

"Are you familiar with it?"

Establish the witness's basis for their knowledge of the area or object:

"How is it that you are familiar with it?"

Have the witness affirm the accuracy of the diagram:

"Is the diagram reasonably accurate?"

"Is the diagram drawn to scale?"

6. **Retrieve the exhibit from the witness and offer to admit it into evidence:**

"Your Honor, I offer into evidence what has been previously marked as PE-1 for ID as PE-1."

2. **Photographs**

1. **Mark the exhibit (ideally, this is done before the trial starts...).**

2. **Show opposing counsel the exhibit:**

"Your Honor, I am now showing opposing counsel what has been previously been marked as PE-1 for I.D. for their inspection and objection."

3. **Ask the judge for permission to approach the witness with the exhibit:**

"Your Honor, may I have permission to approach the witness?"

4. Show the exhibit to the witness:

"Your Honor, I am showing the witness what has been previously marked as PE-1 for ID."

5. Lay the Foundation, establish what it is:

"Do you recognize this?"

"What is it?"

Establish that the witness is familiar with the object or scene:

"Are you familiar with it?"

Have the witness explain the basis for his familiarity with the object or scene:

"How is it that you are familiar with it?"

Establish that the witness recognizes the object or scene in the photograph:

"How is it that you recognize this?

Verify that, to the witness, the photograph is a "fair & accurate" or "true" or "correct" depiction of the object or scene at the relevant time:

"Is this photograph a fair and accurate representation of the [object or scene] at the [relevant time]?"

~or~

"Is this photograph a true representation of the [object or scene] at the [relevant time]?"

~or~

"Is this photograph an accurate representation of the [object or scene] at the [relevant time]?"

6. Retrieve the exhibit from the witness and offer to admit it into evidence:

"Your Honor, I offer into evidence what has been previously marked as PE-1 for ID as PE-1."

3.   Fungible Evidence

1. Mark the exhibit (ideally, this is done before the trial starts...).

2. Show opposing counsel the exhibit:

"Your Honor, I am now showing opposing counsel what has been previously been marked as PE-1 for I.D. for their inspection and objection."

3. **Ask the judge for permission to approach the witness with the exhibit:**

"Your Honor, may I have permission to approach the witness?"

4. **Show the exhibit to the witness:**

"Your Honor, I am showing the witness what has been previously marked as PE-1 for ID."

5. **Lay the Foundation, establish what it is:**

"Do you recognize this?"

"What is it?"

Establish that the witness is familiar with the item:

"And you are familiar with this particular [item]?"

Establish that the witness acquired this familiarity by obtaining the item:

"How did you come to be familiar with this particular [item]?"

Establish that the witness uniquely marked the item of evidence to enable him to identify it later:

"Did you mark the [item] in anyway?"

"Why did you do this?"

Establish that the witness properly safeguarded the item to prevent it from being lost or altered:

"What did you do with the [item] after you [acquired] it?"

"Why did you do that?"

Establish that the witness ultimately disposed of the item:

"When you were finished collecting and marking the [item], what did you do with it?"

Establish that, to the best of his knowledge, Witness can positively identify the item as that which he previously had:

"Can you positively identity this [item] as the one you collected and marked on [the relevant date and time]?"

Establish that the item is in the same condition as it was when he had the item previously:

Is the [item] in substantially the same condition as when you had it last?"

6. **Retrieve the exhibit from the witness and offer to admit it into evidence:**

"Your Honor, I offer into evidence what has been previously marked as PE-1 for ID as PE-1."

4. **Non-fungible Evidence**

1. **Mark the exhibit (ideally, this is done before the trial starts...).**

2. **Show opposing counsel the exhibit:**

"Your Honor, I am now showing opposing counsel what has been previously been marked as PE-1 for I.D. for their inspection and objection."

3. **Ask the judge for permission to approach the witness with the exhibit:**

"Your Honor, may I have permission to approach the witness?"

4. **Show the exhibit to the witness:**

"Your Honor, I am showing the witness what has been previously marked as PE-1 for ID."

5. **Lay the foundation:**

Establish what it is:

"Do you recognize this?"

"What is it?"

Establish that the object has a unique characteristic:

"Does it have any unique characteristics?"

Establish that the witness observed the characteristic on a previous occasion:

*"Was this [*unique characteristic*] present on the [*item*] before?*

Establish that the witness identifies the exhibit as the object:

"Do you recognize this [item] as the [item] from the [incident] on [relevant date]?"

Establish that the witness rests the identification on his present recognition of the characteristic:

"And you know this is that [item] because you recognize here the [unique characteristic] on the [item]"

Establish that to the best of the witness' knowledge, the exhibit is in the same condition as it was when the witness initially saw or received the object:

"Is the [item] in substantially the same condition as it was when you initially [saw or received] it?"

6. **Retrieve the exhibit from the witness and offer to admit it into evidence:**

"Your Honor, I offer into evidence what has been previously marked as PE-1 for ID as PE-1."

5. Chain of Custody Documents

1. **Mark the exhibit (ideally, this is done before the trial starts...).**

2. **Show opposing counsel the exhibit:**

"Your Honor, I am now showing opposing counsel what has been previously been marked as PE-1 for I.D. for their inspection and objection."

3. **Ask the judge for permission to approach the witness with the exhibit:**

"Your Honor, may I have permission to approach the witness?"

4. **Show the exhibit to the witness:**

"Your Honor, I am showing the witness what has been previously marked as PE-1 for ID."

5. **Lay the foundation, establish what it is:**

"Do you recognize this?"

"What is it?"

Establish that the witness has personal knowledge of the business' filing or records system:

*"Does the [*entity or organization in question*] have a [*filing or records system*]?"*

"And you are personally familiar with their [filing or records system]?"

Establish that the witness removed the record (CoCD) in question from a certain file:

"Did you remove this [CoCD] from a file in that system?"

"And from what file in that system did you remove it?"

Establish that the record (CoCD) in question was a proper file entry:

"Was this [CoCD] a proper file entry in the system?"

Establish that the Witness recognizes the exhibit as the record (CoCD) he removed from the file:

"Do you recognize this [CoCD] as the record you removed from the file?"

Witness specifies the basis on which he recognized the exhibit:

"How do you recognize this [CoCD] as the record you removed from the file?"

6. **Retrieve the exhibit from the witness and offer to admit it into evidence:**

"Your Honor, I offer into evidence what has been previously marked as PE-1 for ID as PE-1."

6. Chain of Custody Documents (Hearsay)

1. **Mark the exhibit (ideally, this is done before the trial starts...).**

2. **Show opposing counsel the exhibit:**

"Your Honor, I am now showing opposing counsel what has been previously been marked as PE-1 for I.D. for their inspection and objection."

3. **Ask the judge for permission to approach the witness with the exhibit:**

"Your Honor, may I have permission to approach the witness?"

4. **Show the exhibit to the witness:**

"Your Honor, I am showing the witness what has been previously marked as PE-1 for ID."

5. **Lay the foundation, establish what it is:**

"Do you recognize this?"

"What is it?"

The CoCD was prepared by a person having a relationship with the agency preparing the CoCD:

"Who prepared this [CoCD]"?

"Does [name] have a relationship with [the agency preparing the CoCD]?"

The person had a duty to record the information on the CoCD:

"Whose responsibility was it to complete this [CoCD]?"

"So, it was [name]'s duty to fill in the [CoCD]?"

The person had personal knowledge of the facts or events recorded in the CoCD:

"From where did [name] get the information they used to fill in the [CoCD]?"

The CoCD was prepared contemporaneously with the events:

"When did [name] complete the [CoCD]?"

"And this was at the same time as [the event in question]?"

It was a routine practice of the business to prepare CoCD:

"When are the [CoCD]s normally completed?"

"And this was the routine practice of [the agency preparing the CoCD]?"

The CoCD was reduced to written form:

"After the [CoCD] is completed, what happens to it next?"

"So, this is when it is [reduced to written form]?"

The CoCD was made in the regular course of business:

"And this particular [CoCD] was completed in the normal or regular course of business of [the agency preparing the CoCD]?"

6. **Retrieve the exhibit from the witness and offer to admit it into evidence:**

"Your Honor, I offer into evidence what has been previously marked as PE-1 for ID as PE-1."

7.   Child Witnesses

Depending on the jurisdiction, children below a certain age may be presumed incompetent. This rebuttable presumption may be overcome if the side offering the child as a witness can demonstrate the child possesses the requisite abilities to testify: the capacity to observe, remember, relate, and a recognition of the need to tell the truth.

In other jurisdictions there is no presumption of incompetence and it is simply a question of fact decided by the trial judge whether the child witness possesses the requisite abilities. In either jurisdiction, the side offering the witness should lay an adequate foundation for those abilities.

1. **Call the witness. If opposing counsel objects to the child as an incompetent witness, offer to voir dire the child.**

2. **Lay the foundation by showing the four capacities, show the child has the capacity to observe:**

    "How well do you see?"

    "Do you wear glasses?"

    "How well do you hear?"

    Show the child has the capacity to remember:

    "How old are you?"

    "When is your birthday?"

    "What is your address?"

    Show the child has the capacity to relate:

    "What school do you go to?"

    "What grade are you in?"

    "What classes do you have?"

    "What do you learn in [topic] class?

    Show the child has a recognition of a duty to tell the truth:

    "What does it mean to tell the truth?"

    "Why should you tell the truth?"

    "What happens when you don't tell the truth?"

3. **Offer the witness as competent:**

    "Your Honor, I have no further questions about his competency. The child's answers demonstrate the capacities

to observe, remember, and relate, and his recognition of a
duty to tell the truth."

8.   Spouse Witnesses

The spouse as a witness is problematic depending on the jurisdiction. The
common-law view is that if the marriage exists when the spouse is called,
the accused has the power to prevent the spouse from testifying. The majority trend, adopted by the U.S. Supreme Court in *Trammel v. U.S.*, is the
spouse witness holds the power to choose to testify at their discretion and
the accused may not object. Other jurisdictions provide that both the accused and the spouse witness may invoke privilege independently and prevent the testimony. Finally, some jurisdictions do not hold any spousal
privilege and treat spouses like any other witness. Ensure you research the
requirements in your jurisdiction before proceeding.

Two exceptions may apply to disqualifying a spouse witness: the injured
spouse doctrine, and pre-marital facts. If the spouse is the victim of the
accused's charged offense, the accused cannot invoke the privilege to prevent the victim from testifying. In some jurisdictions, if the facts to which
the spouse will testify occurred before the marriage, the jurisdiction may
bar the accused from preventing the testimony.

1. **Call the witness. Opposing counsel may object to the
   spouse as incompetent and seek to voir dire.**

2. **The opposing party will seek to show the witness has
   married the accused and the marriage still exists.**

   Show the witness married the accused:

   "Mr. Gordon, isn't it true that on July, 14, 1984, you married
   the accused, Margaret Gordon?"

   "Isn't it also true that Margaret Gordon is the accused in this
   case?"

   Show the witness is still married to the accused:

   "Mr. Gordon, isn't it true that there have been no divorce
   proceedings since the marriage?"

   "And, further, that there haven't been any annulment
   proceedings since the marriage?"

3. **The proponent of the witness will need to show the
   witness is the victim of the accused, or that the facts to be
   presented preceded the marriage.**

   Show the witness is the victim of the accused:

"Mr. Gordon, I see you are missing your left arm. Is the person who cut off your arm in the courtroom today?"

Show the facts about which the spouse witness is to testify occurred before the marriage:

"Mr. Gordon, when did Mrs. Gordon cut off your arm?"

"And this was before your wedding to Mrs. Gordon on July 14, 1984?"

9. Lay Witness with Personal Knowledge

Common-law and the Federal Rules require that non-expert witnesses have first-hand knowledge of the facts or events about which they will testify. Although the bar set by FRE 104(b) is rather low, the side offering the witness may want to far exceed the minimal showing needed. The jury's consideration of what the witness testifies to is often tempered by how convinced the jury was that the witness actually observed the facts or events in the testimony. Persuasively showing the personal knowledge of the witness is key to the fact-finder's acceptance of the testimony as offered.

1. **Call the witness.**

2. **Lay the foundation for the competency of the witness to testify by showing the witness was in a location to perceive the event, that they did perceive the event, and that they remember the perceived event.**

   Show the witness was in such a position as to be able to perceive the event (normally, observation is by sight, but any sense may have been used):

   "Mr. Gordon, you testified that at 7:00 p.m. on the night of June 22, 2008, you were standing on the corner of 5th Avenue and Main Street. Could you see the entire intersection from where you were standing?"

   "What direction were you facing?"

   "Was there any other traffic present other than the two vehicles that were involved in the collision?"

   Show the witness did perceive the event in question:

   "Did you see the collision?"

   "What did you see?"

   "Could you hear anything?"

Show the witness remembers what they perceived (why they remember it so well, how it is significant to them):

"Mr. Gordon, how well do you remember seeing the collision?"

"Why do you remember the collision so well?"

10. Lay Opinions

Two types of lay opinions commonly accepted in courts are the collective fact opinion and the skilled lay observer opinion. The collective fact opinion is based on the concept that lay persons commonly and reliably draw inferences from perceived facts and form an opinion on subjects such as height, distance, speed, color and identity by virtue of common human experience. They are then allowed to testify about these "collectively" as a lay opinion.

1. **Call the witness.**

2. **Lay the foundation for the opinion of the lay witness by showing the witness was in a location to observe, that they did observe, that they observed enough to form a reliable opinion, and that the witness can state the opinion.**

   Show the witness was in a position to observe the event about which they formed an opinion:

   "Mr. Gordon, where were you standing at the intersection of 5th Avenue and Main Street?"

   "What direction were you facing?"

   Show the witness did observe the event about which they formed an opinion:

   "And from this position, Mr. Gordon, what could you see?"

   Show the witness observed enough of the event to form a reliable opinion:

   "How long were you able to see the truck as it approached the intersection?"

   Have the witness state their opinion:

   "Do you have an opinion of the truck's speed?"

   "In your opinion, what was the speed of the truck as it approached the intersection?"

The other type of lay opinion is the skilled lay observer opinion and includes lay opinions about someone's handwriting style, the sound of that person's voice, or that person's sanity. All of these opinions require intimate familiarity with the particular subject by the witness through their repeated exposure and observation.

1. **Call the witness.**

2. **Lay the foundation for the skilled lay opinion by showing the witness is familiar with the subject, the subject's voice, or the subject's handwriting through repeated prior opportunities for observation.**

   Show the witness is familiar with the subject:

   "Mr. Gordon, how long have you known Ned Miller?"

   "How did you come to meet Mr. Miller?"

   "In the time Mr. Miller has been your neighbor, have you had occasion to spend time with him?"

   "Are you familiar with the sound of Mr. Miller's voice?"

   "Have you ever heard Mr. Miller speak?"

   "How often have you spoken with Mr. Miller?"

   "Under what circumstances have you heard Mr. Miller speak?"

   "How well do you know Mr. Miller's handwriting style?"

   "How did you become familiar with Mr. Miller's handwriting?"

11. Expert Opinion

The Federal Rules allow an expert to testify when the trier of fact requires assistance in understanding "scientific, technical, or other specialized knowledge … to determine a fact in issue." While the standard in the Federal rules is simply that the expert just possess more knowledge than the trier of fact, in *Daubert v. Merrell Dow Pharmaceuticals, Inc.*, the U.S. Supreme Court held that the trial judge must ensure the expert's testimony "rests on a reliable foundation and is relevant to the task at hand."

The burden is on the side presenting the witness to show the witness is an expert. Reliable foundations for an expert's knowledge may include presenting information on:

- Academic degrees earned by the witness in their field
- Specialized training in their field
- Professional licenses held by the witness in their field

- Length of time spent by the witness in their field.

- Publications by the witness in their field.

- Membership in professional organizations in the field.

- Honors or prizes presented to the witness.

- Previous experience as an expert witness on this topic.

Some or all of these areas may be touched on when laying the foundation for the expert, depending on the specific nature of their expertise and the needs of the case. Case analysis will identify these needs.

Call the witness. Show the witness has specialized knowledge:

"Mr. Gordon, please introduce yourself to the jury."

"Where did you go to school?"

"Do you have a degree?"

"What is your degree in?"

Show the witness has specialized training:

"Do you have any technical training?"

"Where did you receive this training?"

"When did you complete this training?

Show the witness has specialized experience:

"After your technical training, did you work in this field?"

"How long have you been the operations safety officer for the Calusa County Nuclear Power Plant?"

"What are your duties as the operations safety officer at the Calusa County Nuclear Power Plant?"

"Your honor, I tender Mr. Gordon to this court as an expert in nuclear power plant operations."

These are sample questions; design your foundation questions with the specific expert witness and subject matter in mind.

12. Bias

The bias a witness holds is a potential means of impeachment. There are no particular requirements for laying a foundation for bias evidence; the side seeking to show bias may prove any fact or event that logically shows the bias.

1. **Call the witness.**

2. **Lay the foundation by proving an event that indicates bias.**

   Show when and where the event occurred:

   "Mr. Gordon, isn't it true that at 7:00 p.m. on the night of June 22, 2008, you were present at O'Neil's Irish Pub?"

   Show who was present at the event:

   "Mr. Gordon, isn't it also true that the defendants, Nicholas Cox and James Thaler, were both there with you at O'Neil's Irish Pub that night?"

   Show what occurred at the event:

   "And, Mr. Gordon, finally, isn't it true that you, and Nick, and James, were all drinking beer at O'Neil's Irish Pub that night?"

Note: it is probably not necessary to get the witness to concede their bias. It is unlikely the witness would actually admit to it, and trying to force it may make counsel appear argumentative. It is often better to simply prove the fact or event showing bias and then later invite the jury to make the inference during closing arguments.

13. Habit

Habit evidence may be used as circumstantial proof of conduct. Unlike character evidence, which is usually only admissible if the accused first raises the issue, habit evidence may be admitted by either side. The elements of the foundation for habit evidence are:

- The witness is familiar with the person or business.

- The witness has been with the person or business for a substantial length of time.

- The witness has an opinion about a specific behavioral pattern of the person or business.

- The witness has observed the conformity of the person or business with the specific behavioral pattern on numerous occasions.

Some jurisdictions may additionally require that there be either no eyewitnesses to the specific conduct involved in the case, or that the specific conduct be corroborated by an eyewitness that described the conduct as consistent with the habit.

Call the witness. Show the witness is familiar with the person or business:

"Mr. Gordon, are you familiar with the UtoteEm in Calusa County?"

"How is it you are familiar with the UtoteEm?"

Show the witness has been with the person or business for a substantial length of time:

"How long have you been shopping at the UtoteEm?"

"How often do you shop at the UtoteEm?"

Show the witness has an opinion about a specific behavioral pattern of the person or business:

"When shopping at the UtoteEm did you ever observe the attendant use the cash register?"

"How did the attendant use the cash register when you shopped at the UtoteEm?"

"How consistently did the attendant use the cash register when you shopped at the UtoteEm?"

The witness has observed the conformity of the person or business with the specific behavioral pattern on numerous occasions

"How often did you see the attendant use the cash register at the UtoteEm?"

"Have you ever seen the attendant at the UtoteEm fail to use the cash register?"

"Have you ever seen the attendant at the UtoteEm use the cash register in any other way?"

Don't seek to have the witness actually state their opinion; that would be improper. Instead, similar to bias evidence, during closing arguments argue in favor of the inference you want the jury to make.

14. Reputation

In most jurisdictions, the character of the accused does not become an issue unless the accused presents character evidence, that is, something more than simply testifying on their own behalf. Character evidence presented by the prosecution is normally only allowed in rebuttal.

Call the witness. Show the witness is a member of the same community as the accused (home, work, or social):

"Mr. Gordon, who is Marlin Fischer?"

"How do you know Marlin Fischer?"

"Where does Mr. Fischer live?"

"Where do you live, Mr.Gordon?"

"And how close do you live to Mr. Fischer?"

Show the witness has been a member of that community for a substantial period:

"Mr. Gordon, how long have you lived in your current residence?"

"How long has Mr. Fischer lived next door to you?"

"How long have you known Marlin Fischer?"

Show the accused has a reputation in that community, either a general reputation or a reputation for a specific character trait:

"Mr. Gordon, does Mr. Fischer have a particular reputation in your neighborhood?"

Show the witness knows the reputation:

"Do you know that reputation?"

Have the witness state the reputation:

"What is that reputation?"

15.   Prior Bad Acts Resulting in Conviction

Proof that a witness other than the accused has suffered a past conviction can be a telling blow during impeachment and the Federal Rules allow these facts to be admitted under certain circumstances, especially if one of the elements of the crime of conviction involved dishonesty or false statements. While all courts allow this method of impeachment, they differ on what offenses may be used.   Ensure you check your jurisdiction's standards as you plan your cross examination.

Begin cross examining the witness. Show the witness is the person who suffered the prior conviction:

"Isn't it true, Mr. Gordon, that you are the same Bufford Gordon who was once convicted of a felony?"

Show the conviction is for a crime the jurisdiction considers impeaching:

"Isn't it a fact, Mr. Gordon, that felony was smuggling prescription drugs?"

Show the conviction was entered in a particular jurisdiction:

"Isn't it correct that you were convicted of that crime in Calusa County?"

Show the conviction was entered in a particular year:

"And isn't it also correct that you were convicted of that crime in 2005?"

Show the witness received a particular sentence:

"And, Mr. Gordon, isn't it also a fact that as a result of that conviction, you were sentenced to 10 years in prison for smuggling?"

If you are using a copy of the judgment, there is an additional element to the foundation:

Show the copy of the judgment is authentic:

"Your Honor, may this be marked as D.E. 1 for I.D.?

"Please let the record show I am showing what has been marked as D.E. 1 for I.D. to opposing counsel."

"I now offer D.E. 1 for I.D. into evidence as D.E. 1., a copy of the judgment including a properly executed attesting certificate, making this exhibit self-authenticating under Rule 902."

16.   Prior Bad Acts Not Resulting in Conviction

Most jurisdictions allow impeaching a witness on cross examination with proof the witness has committed untruthful acts. However, there is a risk: because extrinsic evidence of the untruthful act may not be admitted, opposing counsel must accept whatever answer the witness gives.

Begin cross examining the witness.

Show when the witness committed the untruthful act:

"Mr. Gordon, isn't it a fact that in 1998 you filed a false tax return?"

Show where the witness committed the untruthful act:

"Mr. Gordon, isn't it also true that you submitted this false tax return to the IRS from Calusa County?"

Show the nature of the act reflects against the character of the witness for truthfulness:

"Mr. Gordon, in this tax return, you claimed that your wife requires 24-hour care. That wasn't true, was it?"

"You also claimed, Mr. Gordon, in this 1998 return, that your 10-year-old son had been wounded in Vietnam. This wasn't true, was it?"

"And, Mr. Gordon, when you tried to claim nine children as dependents, including one who was a member of the clergy, you were not telling the truth, were you?"

17. Other Crimes, Wrongs or Bad Acts

The Federal Rules allow the prosecution to introduce evidence of other crimes or of uncharged misconduct, not to show the accused is a law-breaking immoral person, but to show other things, such as motive, intent, opportunity, knowledge, etc.[7] If the evidence of the uncharged act is logically relevant to a fact in issue other than character, it may be admitted. The trier of fact will decide whether the logical relevance of the evidence outweighs its prejudicial nature.

Call the witness (assume the defendant has been charged with possession of stolen goods).

Show where the other criminal act or uncharged misconduct occurred:

"Mr. Gordon, please tell the jury where you were when you first encountered the defendant, Snake Berman."

Show when the other criminal act or uncharged misconduct occurred:

"And, Mr. Gordon, when was it that you first came into contact with Mr. Berman?"

Show the nature of the other criminal act or uncharged misconduct:

"Mr. Gordon, please describe to the jury what happened when the defendant entered your home."

"Mr. Gordon, when Mr. Berman left your house, was he carrying anything?"

Show the accused committed the other criminal act or uncharged misconduct:

"How well did you see Mr. Berman when he left carrying your television?"

"How close were you to Mr. Berman when he took your television?"

"Is Snake Berman in this court room right now?"

Show the relevance of the other criminal act or uncharged misconduct to the charged offense:

"Mr. Gordon, did Mr. Berman have permission to take your TV set?"

"Did you give anyone permission to take your television?"

"Did you report the theft to the police?"

"After you reported your television as stolen, did you get a police report number?"

The defense will have the right to seek a limiting instruction, under FRE 105, where the judge will inform the jury they may not use this evidence as general character evidence but only use it to decide the existence of the fact the evidence was admitted to prove (the accused's motive, intent, opportunity, knowledge, etc).

18.   Character Trait of Untruthfulness

Extrinsic evidence, usually a second witness, may be used to impeach the credibility of a witness. This is usually in the form of a second witness, who testifies to the trait in the witness being impeached.

Call the second witness. Show the second witness is a member of the same community (home or social) as the witness being impeached:

"Mr. Gordon, who is Marlin Fischer?"

"How do you know Marlin Fischer?"

Show the second witness has been a member of that community for a substantial period of time:

"How long have you been a next-door neighbor of Marlin Fischer?"

"How long have you lived in Calusa County?"

"How long have you attended the same church with Marlin Fischer?"

Show the witness being impeached has a reputation for untruthfulness in the community:

"Mr. Gordon, does Marlin Fischer have a reputation for truthfulness or untruthfulness in Calusa County?"

Show the second witness knows of the reputation for untruthfulness of the witness being impeached:

"What is that reputation?"

"Given Mr. Fischer's reputation, would you believe him under oath?"

Note: some jurisdictions allow the second witness to add that, considering the reputation of the witness being impeached, the second witness would not believe him or her under oath.

19. Character Trait for Truthfulness

Proving the character trait of truthfulness in a witness is necessary after the opposing side has attempted to impeach the witness and rehabilitation is necessary. Typically after the second witness impeaches the first witness, the court will allow the proponent of the impeached witness to call a third witness, to testify to the reputation for truthfulness of the impeached witness. The elements of the foundation are the same as the Character Trait for Untruthfulness just discussed.

Call the third witness. Show the third witness is a member of the same community (home or social) as the witness being impeached:

"Reverend Miller, who is Marlin Fischer?"

"How do you know Mr. Fischer?"

Show the third witness has been a member of that community for a substantial period of time:

"How long has Marlin Fischer been a member of your church?"

Show the witness being impeached has a reputation for truthfulness in the community:

"Reverend Miller, does Marlin Fischer have a reputation for truthfulness or untruthfulness in Calusa County?"

Show the third witness knows of the reputation for truthfulness of the witness being impeached:

"What is that reputation?"

"Given Mr. Fischer's reputation, Reverend Miller, would you believe him under oath?"

20. Prior Inconsistent Statement

Another means of impeaching the credibility of a witness is to show they made prior statements that are inconsistent with their current testimony. The fact of these inconsistencies calls into question the ability of the witness to recall and relate what was observed.

> **Begin to cross-examine the witness. Get the witness to commit to the testimony given during direct examination:**
>
> "Mr. Hightower, you just testified that Mr. Gordon was not at your Planet Calusa County restaurant the night of the incident, correct?"
>
> **Show the witness made an earlier statement at a certain place (if the earlier statement was in writing, where it was written is not essential):**
>
> "Mr. Hightower, isn't it true that after the incident you were present during a meeting at the Calusa County Town Hall to discuss what had happened?"
>
> **Show the witness made an earlier statement at a certain time:**
>
> "Mr. Hightower, that meeting at Town Hall was at 11:00 p.m., immediately after the incident occurred?"
>
> **Show that certain persons were present when the witness made the earlier statement:**
>
> "Mr. Hightower, weren't Doctor Jones and Mayor Stevens both present with you at this meeting?
>
> **Show the earlier statement made by the witness was of a certain tenor:**
>
> "In that meeting with Doctor Jones and Mayor Stevens, didn't you say that Mr. Gordon was present and participating in the all-you-can-eat buffet, and you were concerned about your losses?"
>
> **Show the earlier statement made by the witness is more likely reliable than the present testimony:**
>
> "Isn't it a fact, Mr. Hightower, in that point of time, that conversation was closer to the incident than your testimony today?"
>
> "Isn't it a fact your memory was fresher then?"

Note: it may be preferable to not force the final concession from the witness. Merely elicit the facts of the statement's timing and then argue the relative reliability of the earlier statement compared to the testimony during your closing arguments. Indeed, the judge may find these final questions are objectionably argumentative.

21.   Prior Consistent Statement

Similar to recovering from an impeachment for untruthfulness, when a witness has been impeached for making prior inconsistent statements, it may be necessary to rehabilitate them by showing past statements that are consistent with their testimony. For procedural reasons, many jurisdictions impose a requirement that the prior consistent statement precede the prior inconsistent statement or that the prior consistent statement have been made before the witness had any motive to lie.

> 1. **Call the witness. Show where the prior consistent statement was made:**
>
> "Mr. Hightower, after the incident at your Planet Calusa County restaurant, did you speak to anyone there?"
>
> **Show when the prior consistent statement was made:**
>
> "And this interview took place immediately after the incident?"
>
> **Show who was present when the prior consistent statement was made:**
>
> "Was anyone with Brad Bradley during the interview?"
>
> **Show the tenor of the prior consistent statement:**
>
> "During that interview, did you tell Mr. Bradley who was present in the restaurant?"
>
> "During that interview, what did you say to Mr. Bradley about Mr. Gordon?"
>
> **If a temporal requirement must be met, show the prior consistent statement preceded (1) the prior inconsistent statement or (2) any motive on the part of the witness to lie:**
>
> "Was this interview with Brad Bradley before or after the meeting at the Town Hall with Doctor Jones and Mayor Stevens?"
>
> "Was this interview with Brad Bradley before or after you had been contacted by attorneys regarding this legal action?"

Typically the judge will be asked to give the jury a limiting instruction, that although the jurors could consider the testimony for credibility purposes, they should not treat the prior statement as proof "Mr. Gordon" was (or was not) present during the incident.

H. Evidentiary Rules to Consider

Issues Arising Dealing with Exhibits	Applicable Federal Rule of Evidence
Authentication and identification rules	901–902
Best evidence rules	1001–1004
Business records	803(6)
Contents of writings, recordings and photographs	1001–1008
Documents and instruments	901–902
Public records	803(8)
Real and demonstrative evidence	901

Table 1: Potential Evidentiary Rules Applicable to Exhibits

I. Conclusion

In this chapter we have discussed the connection between FRE 401, 403 and 104. We have also developed foundational questions for all of the major types of evidence most commonly offered at trial. Counsel should remember that a focus on the nature of the evidence leads directly to the type of foundational questions that must be asked to establish authentication and relevancy. Begin by determining whether the evidence is testimonial, demonstrative, or real.

If counsel determine that the evidence offered is real evidence then they must also decide if the evidence is fungible or non-fungible. Properly identifying the nature of the evidence is the most important step in determining foundational requirements for admissibility. The required foundation questions depend on the type of evidence offered and the purpose of the offered evidence. Counsel who adopt this approach are well on their way to being able to deal with admitting any type of evidence on the fly - it is a sorting game.

-Notes-

Chapter 7: Cross Examination

A. Introduction 273
B. How the Law Impacts Cross...274
C. Structuring the Cross 277
D. Asking Proper Questions 285
E. Creating and Delivering the Cross 289
F. Impeaching Witnesses 303
G. Dealing with Difficult Witnesses...304
H. Examples 307
I. Checklist..312
J. Evidence Rules to Consider During Cross..............................314
K. Conclusion 315

A. Introduction

Cross examination, like any other advocacy skill, is subject to the rules of evidence, local rules of practice, and substantive law. Attorneys following the approach suggested in this text will be capable of competently cross examining witnesses immediately. This text deconstructs the process of cross examination, removing mystery and replacing it with a systemic approach guaranteed to produce results. It builds upon the earlier discussion concerning case analysis and preparation, and is, in many respects, the mirror image of the process required to create effective direct examinations.

This text focuses on the purpose, preparation, and process required to effectively cross examine witnesses. It discusses what is required to do so, explains how to do it, and then provides the rationale for adopting a specific approach. Many of the ideas discussed in this text were developed by Mr. Terry MacCarthy, the father of modern cross examination. His lectures and demonstrations on the science of cross examination, often referred to as "the look good" cross, are the number one resource for anyone desiring to develop true mastery in this area. Teachers of cross examination owe a great deal to his seminal work in this field.

Much of what has historically been written about cross examination covers it in mystery, asserting it is the "most difficult" skill learned by a trial lawyer, and even suggesting that a large number of trials must be completed before an attorney can competently cross examine a witness. While there is some difficulty in mastering the emotional component of cross examination, a proper analytical approach to the process allows the attorney to manage those emotional moments, focusing the human component based upon a logical approach designed to harness the persuasive power of the moment.

Contrary to conventional wisdom, cross examination is a skill easily learned and readily applied in most situations, as long as the attorney conducting cross can maintain their emotional equilibrium during what is to some degrees an inherently confrontational process. Counsel must remember that they are merely questioning the witness on the facts of the case, and maintain equilibrium in the face of an emotionally reactive witness. In effect, when counsel encounters the unreasonable the witness who flies into histrionics in response to simple questions, they are best served by remaining as reasonable as possible. This cool headed approach enhances their believability and credibility with the jury, and can often head off argumentative or badgering objections. This can be accomplished by adopting an approach guided by a common sense approach grounded in superior case analysis. Counsel must develop and apply a working logical construct when preparing and conducting cross examination. Taking this approach ensues the attorney has all of the tools necessary to conduct effective, efficient and persuasive cross examinations. What is required is preparation, attention to detail and a commitment to approaching cross examination through the lens of counsel's theme and theory of the case.

B. How the Law Impacts Cross

Federal Rule of Evidence (FRE) 611 addresses witnesses, establishing the manner and scope of witness testimony, to include cross examination. While the form of cross examination is governed by FRE 611, other evidentiary rules impact counsel's ability to refresh memory, attack the foundations of a witness's testimony, admit character evidence, address prior criminal activity of a witness, or to impeach witnesses during cross examination. These are examples of common law and evidentiary rules based theories of impeachment. They are specific forms of cross examination, but each is sufficiently important that it needs to be presented and discussed separately and this text will address them in a subsequent section..

Rule 611. Mode and Order of Examining Witnesses and Presenting Evidence

(a) Control by the Court; Purposes. The court should exercise reasonable control over the mode and order of examining witnesses and presenting evidence so as to:

(1) make those procedures effective for determining the truth;

(2) avoid wasting time; and

(3) protect witnesses from harassment or undue embarrassment.

(b) Scope of Cross-Examination. Cross-examination should not go beyond the subject matter of the direct examination and matters affecting the witness's credibility. The court may allow inquiry into additional matters as if on direct examination.

(c) Leading Questions. Leading questions should not be used on direct examination except as necessary to develop the witness's testimony. Ordinarily, the court should allow leading questions:

(1) on cross-examination; and

(2) when a party calls a hostile witness, an adverse party, or a witness identified with an adverse party.

Under both the Federal Civil and Criminal Rules of Procedure in court testimony is the preferred means of testimony unless otherwise specified by statute in criminal cases or at the discretion of the court, for good cause shown, in civil cases. Counsel addressing the possibility of out-of-court testimony in a criminal case would do well to consider those cases that have attempted to work around the confrontation clause, understanding that most litigation in this area has revolved around sexual assault and child victims. In normal circumstances the confrontation clause bars most, if not all, contemporaneous transmissions of testimony in a criminal case.

This preference for in court testimony directly impacts cross examination. Counsel must consider their location in the courtroom, the different tones of voice they employ, and their physical reactions to the witness. The ad-

---

RULE 26. TAKING TESTIMONY

In every trial the testimony of witnesses must be taken in open court, unless otherwise provided by a statute or by rules adopted under 28 U.S.C. §§ 2072-2077.

RULE 43. TAKING TESTIMONY

(a) In Open Court. At trial, the witnesses' testimony must be taken in open court unless a federal statute, the Federal Rules of Evidence, these rules, or other rules adopted by the Supreme Court provide otherwise. For good cause in compelling circumstances and with appropriate safeguards, the court may permit testimony in open court by contemporaneous transmission from a different location.

versarial system understands that the jury measures credibility on substance, appearance, and delivery. Counsel should consider the impact of these issues when preparing and conducting cross examination. Counsel must remember that whenever witnesses testify concerning disputed facts one of the primary questions that the jury will ask is whom do they believe? This is the essence of cross examination, and the goal is for counsel to be the most believable person in the room and the conclusion of the examination.

The court instructs the jury on issues of witness credibility, to include impeachment. Such instructions are particularly important to counsel when structuring sections of their closing arguments designed to persuasively address how a jury should consider the testimony of a witness subjected to a well-developed and delivered cross examination.

Most courts provide the jury with a set of instructions designed to assist them in sorting through issues of credibility and impeachment. These instructions are particularly important when dealing with a witness that has been subjected to a well-developed cross examination. Issues of impeachment and credibility often go hand-in-hand in these situations. Consider the following credibility instruction and how it might impact the planning and delivery of your cross examination, as well as the comments concerning credibility that you might make during closing arguments.

This example from a set of civil jury pattern instructions used in

Three Primary Goals of Cross:

- establish facts building to a theme and theory

- control the witness, and

- establish facts impacting witness credibility

3.4 Credibility of Witnesses

When I say you must consider all the evidence, I don't mean that you must accept all the evidence as true or accurate. You should decide whether you believe what each witness had to say, and how important that testimony was. In making that decision you may believe or disbelieve any witness, in whole or in part. The number of witnesses testifying concerning a particular point doesn't necessarily matter.

To decide whether you believe any witness I suggest that you ask yourself a few questions:

Did the witness impress you as one who was telling the truth?

Did the witness have any particular reason not to tell the truth?

Did the witness have a personal interest in the outcome of the case?

Did the witness seem to have a good memory?

Did the witness have the opportunity and ability to accurately observe
the things he or she testified about?

Did the witness appear to understand the questions clearly and answer them directly?

Did the witness's testimony differ from other testimony or other evidence?

the 11th circuit showcases how substantive evidentiary doctrine concerning cross examination and impeachment is expressed in jury instructions.

The credibility of witnesses is a key issue during trial. Much of the use of cross examination revolves around assisting the jury in determining witness credibility. Competent counsel will use the information provided in the jury instructions on credibility to focus cross examination on exposing those issues the court will identify as impacting credibility.

C.   Structuring the Cross

1.   Identify Goals of the Cross

When considering how to structure the cross examination counsel should always keep in mind the three primary goals: (1) establish facts building to a theme and theory, (2) control the witness, and (3) establish facts bolstering the credibility of counsel's witnesses, and/or diminishing the credibility of opposing counsel's witnesses. The goal is to present facts persuasively when they support your case, attack the basis of facts which support your opponent's case, and find ways to reduce the credibility of the opposing counsel's weaknesses.

When presenting facts designed to persuasively support counsel's case the focus is on a non-confrontational cross examination style when possible that is designed to get the facts out. If the facts supporting counsel's case are not in controversy the cross examining attorney should consider placing that section of the cross examination early in cross, allowing for the development of such information before the witness is no longer inclined to impartially answer questions.

a.   Admitting Facts the Witness Agrees To

Counsel identifies these non-controversial facts through case analysis, and then uses the specific questioning techniques of cross examination to admit them when questioning the witness. Case analysis is an excellent tool for identifying "what" should be presented, the "how" of the actual presentation is grounded in the facts the witness must admit to, even if it is on cross examination. These facts are normally captured in the case file in a form that allows the cross examiner to "control" the witness, forcing them to admit the fact in question.

> ***Example: during direct examination the witness was asked about an accident they observed on the 21ˢᵗ of March when two children were hit by a speeding driver. The direct testimony focused on what the witness observed about the car driven by the defendant in this civil case, a blue Toyota. The witness did not testify about any other vehicles that might have been present at the time of the accident, but has mentioned other vehicles that were also present in other statements. The defense attorney seeks to introduce facts concerning other vehicles during cross.***

Plaintiff: No further questions your honor.

Judge: Defense?

Defense: Good afternoon Mr. Broadsides.

Witness: Good afternoon.

Defense: I would like to talk to you about the automobiles you saw that night.

Witness: Okay.

Defense: You testified on direct that you saw a blue Toyota?

Witness: Yes. It hit the children.

Defense: Let's talk about that. You were playing basketball when the accident happened?

Witness: Yes.

Defense: You did not see the accident?

Witness: No, but I heard it.

Defense: Exactly. You heard the accident?

Witness: Yes.

Defense: You ran towards the street?

Witness: Yes.

Defense: When you ran towards the accident you saw a white van?

Witness: Yes.

Defense: The white van was traveling south?

Witness: Yes.

Defense: The accident scene was immediately north of the white van when you saw the van?

Witness: Yes. I guess so.

Defense: But you did not see the white van hit anyone?

Witness: No. The blue Toyota hit those children.

Defense: Mr. Broadsides you cannot tell us that you ever saw the Toyota hit those children.

Witness: Well no, not if you put it like that.

Defense: So the white van was on that street when the accident happened?

Witness: Yes.

b. Admitting Facts the Witness Does Not Agree To

The way in which these facts are addressed during cross examination depends upon the goal of the examiner and the source of the information. Counsel must not only identify the earlier source of the valid information, they must also know the relevant evidentiary standards to admit those earlier statements. Sometimes the witness changes their earlier statements, testifying in a different fashion on the witness stand at trial. Counsel must have identified the previous statements of the witness, the relevant facts within those statements, and selected methods to admit those facts during cross in a situation where the witness is not willing to admit the earlier information.

> ***Example: A defense counsel is crossing a witness for the plaintiff in a civil case. In this particular instance the defense needs to show that the car causing the accident was a Toyota, and not the Ford driven by their client. The witness has just testified that the they observed a blue Toyota cause the accident. The defense counsel has reviewed the file and realizes that the witness said a Ford caused the accident when speaking to the cops, and that the witness also said a Ford caused the accident during her deposition testimony.***

Plaintiff: No further questions your honor.

Judge: Defense?

Defense: Good afternoon Mr. Brantley.

Witness: Good afternoon.

Defense: You just testified on direct examination that the blue Toyota caused the accident?

Witness: Yes.

Defense: Do you remember telling the police at the accident scene that a Ford caused the accident?

Witness: Yes. But I was mistaken then. *(Sighing)* It was a traumatic experience.

Defense: Exactly. But you also testified at a deposition?

Witness: *(Warily)* Yes.

Defense: At the deposition you testified, under oath, that the car causing the accident was a Ford?

Witness: I'm not sure.

Defense: Well let's look into this in more detail. *(Defense counsel would now shift to an impeachment with a prior inconsistent statement)*

c.   Admitting Facts Attacking Witness Credibility

Counsel use case analysis to identify facts that call into question the credibility of the witness. These facts are case and witness specific, and serve as the basis for various cross examination questions. Generally speaking, when impeaching on the basis of credibility, counsel create a series of questions based upon the type of cross examination credibility point they are trying to make. This series of questions are designed to suggest an answer before the question is actually asked.

Earlier during case analysis counsel prepared an outline of topics relevant to their moral theme, legal theory, and factual theory. This outline should then be compared to the individual witness to determine any potential credibility based cross examination approaches. Part of this process requires counsel to review the relevant documentary evidence for each witness. The documentary evidence is both witness and case dependent, but common examples include depositions, prior statements, social media postings, and other relevant documents.

Example: A witness has just testified on direct examination in a criminal case, stating that he saw the defendant attack the victim in an alley outside of Murphy's bar in the early morning hours. Defense counsel is cross examining the witness to reduce their credibility. Case analysis has focused their cross examina-

tion on how much alcohol the witness consumed that night and the environment in the alley in order to attack the ability of the witness to properly observe the events on the night in question.

State:	No further questions your honor.
Judge:	Defense?
Defense:	Good morning Mr. Pearlman.
Witness:	Good morning.
Defense:	I would like to talk to you about Murphy's Bar.
Witness:	Okay.
Defense:	You visited Murphy's bar every Friday and Saturday.
Witness:	Yes. For the last 4 years.
Defense:	You would call yourself a regular?
Witness:	Yes. I like the food and people.
Defense:	And the beer?
Witness:	(Smiling) Well that too.
Defense:	Exactly. You drank beer that night?
Witness:	Yes.
Defense:	You started drinking around 9?
Witness:	Yes.
Defense:	You ran a tab that evening?
Witness:	Yes.

Defense: You tab shows that you paid for more than 12 beers?

Witness: Yes. But some of those were for friends.

Defense: True. You testified previously at deposition that you bought three beers for your date?

Witness: Yes. I guess so.

Defense: But you drank the other nine?

Witness: Yes, but that isn't that much beer.

Defense: Okay, but you did drink those nine beers in a forty-five minute span?

Witness: Yes, but I did get up to go the bathroom.

Defense: But you missed the door to the bathroom and stumbled into the alley?

Witness: Well I wouldn't say stumbled, but I was out in the alley.

Defense: That is when you saw the fight?

Witness: Yes.

Defense: Let's talk about what you were actually doing during that time....*(Now the defense would shift focus to a new line of inquiry, having established the intoxicated state of the witness)*

2.   Organizing

Once counsel identify which topics should be covered during cross examination they must decide the order of the questions. A well-prepared case analysis provides specific topics that can be lifted and reorganized for each witness, supporting the overall case theme and theory. The ultimate goal for every cross examination is to persuade the jury to accept the witness's answers to the deciding questions of fact, the underlying contested fact questions, and the credibility questions specific to each particular witness.

When organizing the cross examination counsel must remember that the jury has just heard the witness testify in a specific fashion, usually chronologically. If counsel approaches cross examination using the same structure from the direct they will be questioning using a structure with which the witness and the jury is already familiar. The witness will be comfortable with this structure, and the jury, if it hears the same approach again, will be more likely to find the testimony on direct more credible. Counsel who cross chronologically are ceding both control and organization to the opposing side - not an ideal persuasive approach. Counsel's primary job during cross is to test the credibility of the witness, not to reiterate the facts already presented during direct.

Counsel begin this organizational process by taking the topics for closing argument and comparing them what the witness said on direct. The connection between the direct and

Reasons to Cross:

- Provides facts supporting your case

- Exposes facts or bias that weakens your opponent's case

- Bolsters or establishes the credibility of your own witnesses

closing is not within counsel's control, but the subjects chosen for cross examination are. They should be based on a case analysis that considers the expected direct examination, and then posits how cross examination can be used to reduce the facts presented during direct and to call into question the witness's credibility, reliability, and believability. When making this connection counsel should consider both the strengths and weaknesses of their position based upon the testimony of other witnesses at trial.

Of all the skills in trial advocacy, cross examination is all the skill that requires the most fluidity in terms of organization. All too often, witnesses do not want to follow down counsel's narrowly tailored path of questions, and instead insist on attempt to either reemphasize the points of the direct or steer the line of questioning down another avenue. Counsel must learn the topics of potential cross examination well enough to make the adjustments needed in the moment of trial. If the witness wants to talk about a topic that counsel has already planned a line of cross for later in examination, counsel should not hesitate to go there with the witness. While it may feel like ceding control, in reality it gives counsel the opportunity to show off how well prepared they are to the members of the jury. Think about it logically for a moment—instead of being thrown by the witness' attempts to derail the cross, counsel makes an in the moment adjustment to the new topic, and then further establishes control through their mastery of the subject. This type of advocacy establishes that counsel is control no matter what the witness tries to do, and they can adjust the flow of their questions as needed in the moment.

When deciding how to organize counsel should focus on organizational tools increasing the ability of the attorney to transform the jury's use and opinion of the witness, adopting them when possible, reducing their credibility when relevant or asking no questions at all - when their case analysis indicates that cross examination will not increase the possibility of victory. Sometimes the best cross examination is no cross examination at all.

D.   Asking Proper Questions

Evidentiary and procedural rules, as well as local customs, required leading questions during cross examination, except in those instances where the relationship between counsel and witness is not adversarial, or when the attorney adopts the witness in order to address an area so clearly outside the scope of direct examination that the court would not otherwise allow the line of questioning.

Closed or leading questions are designed to identify the witness's knowledge of the facts or to challenge the credibility of the witness. The structure of the closed question ensures the witness can only respond with one possible truthful answer, an answer, crucially, that is always already known by the attorney asking the question. Techniques available to formulate closed or leading questions include: (1) telling the witness instead of asking, (2) using taglines to force agreement by the witness, and (3) asking one-fact questions. These statements require agreement or disagreement from the witness, nothing more.

Two "styles" of phraseology are normally used when performing cross examination. The first is a leading question with a "tag" on the end of it. An example would be "You own a baseball bat, *don't you?*" The "tag" is "don't you?" and takes many forms (e.g., "*didn't you?*", "*isn't it true?*", etc.). The other style is to drop the tag entirely. A leading question can still be asked with identical language without the tag.[9] When you do this properly, there is a much greater emphasis on voice inflection. For example, "You own a baseball bat." Make this declarative sentence a leading question by placing the inflection on the word "bat."

Because leading questions are not truly inquisitive, voice inflection makes the critical difference. This is especially true with non-tag, leading questions. Thus, the question "You own a baseball bat" can be leading or non-leading. If the inflection drops when saying "bat," it is leading. As discussed above, the falling inflection of the questioner does not reflect doubt

With Taglines	Without Taglines
You got out of the car, didn't you?	You got out of your car.
You closed the car door, correct?	You closed the car door.
Isn't it true that you walked across the sidewalk?	You walked across the sidewalk.

or true inquisitiveness. If, however, inflection rises on the word "bat," it demonstrates the questioner is uncertain or at least inviting an explanation. A good cross-examination question marries proper form with tailored inflection. This skill comes with practice and is both fundamental and crucial.

When counsel make statements on cross examination that requires agreement or disagreement by the witness, it establishes a high degree of control and accuracy. The absence of taglines allows counsel to state the issue as though it is a fact that merely requires agreement or disagreement. In effect, counsel gets to inform the jury as to the facts from which the witness cannot get away.

When asking questions on cross examination counsel must make certain that the witness answers in way that clearly makes the record. Sometimes a witness will respond with words that are not understandable or through some sort of gesture that indicates an answer. Indeterminate words and physical gestures cannot be accurately captured by the court reporter and should be corrected on the spot by the attorney:

> *Example: In the following example the state is cross examining an alibi witness for the defendant who was actually in the county jail at the time of the alleged alibi.*

Defense: No further questions your honor.

Judge: State?

State: Good morning.

Witness: Morning.

State: I would like to talk about July 4th, 20XX-1.

Witness: Okay.

State: You had a barbecue that day?

Witness: Yes. We do that every year.

State: There was beer?

Witness: *(Witness nods head yes, smiles)*

State: Mr. Hearns, I noticed that you smiled and nodded your head yes in response to my question. Your testimony is being transcribed, and we need you to speak your answers clearly so that the court reporter can get it down correctly. Let me ask you again - There was beer at the barbecue?

Witness: *(Smiling and nodding head)* mhmmm.

State: Sir I notice again that you were smiling and that you made a noise in response to my question that sounded like "mhmmm," was that a yes?

Witness: Yes.

State: Thank you. Please answer the questions with full words so that the court reporter can record it. Will you do that?

Witness: Yes.

State: Good. Let's continue*(from here on the focus of the cross examination can shift back to the substance of the questions).*

When confronted with a witness like this who is non-responsive counsel must take the time to slow down, properly make the record, advise the witness how to answer correctly, and then listen to make sure they follow the instructions given. This can be frustrating, but is crucial - if it is not in the record clearly counsel cannot be sure that the jury heard it, but they can be sure it will not be available in the event an appeal becomes necessary.

Counsel must make certain that the witness's response is in words and not through some sort of gesture. The record of trial will not include head movement or grunts that may or may not indicate agreement or disagreement with your stated position. When witnesses try to avoid answering through noncommittal sounds or body movements counsel must inform them that it is important that they speak clearly for the benefit of the court reporter and then make sure they do.

Each of these questioning techniques requires agreement or disagreement by the witness, but they do have differences in use and impact. First, the voice rises when using a tagline. The rising inflection indicates that counsel have some doubts as to the veracity of their position. It may invite the witness to challenge their position or imply to the jury that counsel are really not sure if the question they are asking is correct. Second, the use of taglines can become an annoying habit. At a certain point, if counsel consistently uses the same tagline over and over, the words will lose any value they might have originally had for the jury. Meaningless language is the enemy of counsel at all time, but particularly during cross examination. Concise, pointed questions are the best practice, and tagline often cause issues in this coming to fruition. The choice of whether or not to use taglines is one of style and demeanor. Counsel should experiment with both and then choose one that works best in a given set of circumstances.

Counsel often forget to ask one-fact questions, choosing instead to either ask argumentative questions that are complex, giving the witness the ability to pick and choose which portion or portions of the question to answer. This often occurs as a result of counsel being unsure that the jury is following the logic of successive one fact questions. However, one fact questions allows the attorney to control the witness and focus the inquiry so that it is understood by the jury. It becomes very difficult for a witness to prevaricate when only one factual issue is posed in the question.When done effectively, several one-fact questions in succession get the witness on a roll, and the jury can sense the ultimate point that the witness cannot evade. One-fact questions are the building blocks that allow counsel to make their ultimate conclusion to the jury during closing argument when the witness is not there to argue about it.

Closed and leading questions are normally used during cross examination of adverse witnesses, when laying a foundation for the admissibility of evidence through any witness, or when the witness's demeanor or nature requires closed or leading questions in order to assist the fact-finder in getting to the testimony of the witness. This usually occurs when the witness has diminished communication ability due to their age or status as a victim of a violent crime. Always keep in mind that these closed/leading questions are used to control witnesses, showcase the attorney, and to lay foundations for the admissibility of evidence. The focus for leading questions is on counsel, not the witness. Closed questions allow the attorney to probe for logical weaknesses or fallacies in the witness's testimony, while also providing a vehicle to test the credibility of the witness through the crucible of cross examination.

The third tool to ensure questions will be closed or leading is to only ask one fact per question. Counsel should think of one-fact questions as building blocks that allow them to effectively argue to the jury during closing argument, when the witness is not there to argue about it. Attorneys use one-fact questions to control witnesses. It becomes very difficult for a witness to prevaricate when only one factual issue is posed in the question.

Counsel should think of one-fact questions as the means to place the witness in a box. Imagine the witness is a butterfly and her leading one-fact questions are pins counsel uses to hold the butterfly down. The examination is done when the butterfly cannot move. This is an excellent image to keep in mind as counsel focus on one-fact leading questions that drive to a conclusion the witness must accept.

E. Creating and Delivering the Cross

1. Creating the Cross

During case analysis counsel listed the good and bad facts with the location of the documentation supporting the facts in question. This data should be captured in a form allowing for its retrieval, creating a matrix counsel can use to easily and quickly retrieve the evidence supporting each identified fact when necessary during cross examination. *It is a best practice for* counsel to take the time to properly analyze the legal issues and facts supporting them in light of their case theme and theory they are guaranteeing an effective cross examination.

Once counsel have compared the identified "hard questions of fact for the jury" with their list of good and bad facts for the witness they should choose the best points and worst points for each hard question of fact. Counsel must then organize each of these clusters of good and bad facts into different sections of the cross examination. Counsel must cross reference these facts with the legal theory, factual theory, and moral theme developed during case analysis.

Counsel should look to see if any of these potential good or bad facts contradict their theme and theory, are of minimal persuasive value, or are too dangerous to use during cross examination. Counsel should always keep in mind the first rule of trial advocacy—do nothing that is not in accordance with their case theme and theory. If the best facts for the witnesses support their theme and theory and do not contradict their version of the facts then counsel should use them to create potential topic headlines for the cross examination.

After identifying the topic headlines for the cross, counsel must employ advocacy techniques maximizing the persuasive impact of the answers to the questions asked. When the cross is focused on drawing out facts supporting their case analysis the following techniques are effective:

> (1) cluster together all of the facts that enhance and support the topic,

> (2) lay out the facts one question at a time leading up to their final point, and

> (3) identify similar facts based upon knowledge of human nature supporting their final topic.

Counsel should then finish their inquiry by asking questions addressing similar facts before making their final point.

Each of these techniques is designed to create tension by building suspense and sparking the interest of the jury, while suggesting the answer everyone expects is coming. There is nothing wrong with that expectation. If the case analysis was sufficient to the task, the story that told in opening statement and developed through the testimony of witnesses on direct examination has already laid a trail of bread crumbs leading to this moment in the cross examination of the witness. When counsel approach cross in this fashion, they must take care to ensure they have the available resources to impeach the witness if they stray from the good or bad facts previously identified through case analysis. ***This point is crucial. If the witness challenges counsel during cross, and the law allows counsel to respond to that challenge—they must, decisively.*** Failure to do so empowers the witness, weakens counsel's theme and theory of the case, and calls into question the credibility of the advocate in the eyes of the fact finder.

Hard questions of fact are those questions upon which the case turns. Sometimes there is nothing to be gained from addressing a hard question of fact with a particular witness. In those instances counsel should avoid addressing hard questions of fact during cross, and save those issues for witnesses that will be more helpful. Cross is a guerrilla operation—counsel should have the goal to get in, get the information they need, and get out while minimizing the negative impact the witness may have on their case. Now is not the time to try and battle with witnesses who are not inclined to be helpful to counsel's position. The law of direct, cross, and redirect will not allow opposing counsel to use it again on redirect if it is not addressed during cross. If it is not beneficial to counsel's case it is bad enough that the jury heard it once, they must not make the mistake of going over the information for a second time on cross, thereby allowing opposing counsel to address it yet a third time during redirect.

> **Starting the Cross:**
>
> *Begin your cross exam with non-threatening or uncontroverted fact questions that support your theme and theory to keep the same momentum as on direct.*

When counsel decide to cross on hard questions of fact, or on a difficult issue identified as a "worst point" during case analysis, they must first make certain that the reward is worth the risk. If the fact in question will not be addressed during closing argument, then counsel should not consider crossing on it, even when they can explain it or put it in context. This is because, due to the difficult issue posed combined with a potentially uncooperative adverse witness, there is a danger that counsel can lose the point of the questions in the argument that must be had to get it answered. This may cause the members of the jury to lose track of counsel's story of the case. In essence, going after the difficult issue on cross often leads to counsel snatching defeat from the jaws of victory.

If counsel decides to go after one of these worst points on cross the best approach is to identify a cluster of questions that either minimize, place in context, or explain the worst fact. This places the worst point in the best light possible as it relates to counsel's theme and theory of the case. To increase the persuasive nature of this type of cross examination counsel should break down the questions as simply as possible into one-fact increments. This controls the witness and leads the jury to counsel's position. It is imperative that the attorney have the supporting points to control the witness if they attempt to wander during the one-fact build up.

After identifying the facts to address during cross counsel must next organize the topics to cover in cross examination. The arrangement of topics must be both effective and persuasive. Each topic either relates to a point in counsel's favor or diminishes the opponent's position. The order of presentation is dictated, initially, by the impact counsel expect the witness will have on the jury. Counsel must be prepared, however, to rearrange the topics on a moments notice to adjust to the flow of the trial and deal with a difficult witness, as discussed above.

In those instances where the witness has facts helpful to counsel's case it is generally best to get those out of the witness first, before it becomes necessary to challenge or control the witness on more problematic issues. Once counsel asserts control of the witness in a forceful questioning it becomes difficult, if not impossible, to go back and get testimony that is helpful to the case.

A smooth cross examination can flow from the direct into the cross in a non-confrontational manner—forcing the witness to agree with facts that help the case. Cross does not have to be "cross" to be effective. Put another way, there is no reason to treat the witness with anything other than civility and respect - unless their actions give you permission to do so. Counsel should not be the bad guy until the witness asks for it through their behavior.

Remember the primary goals during cross examination are to: (1) control the witness, (2) establish facts that bolster your theme and theory, and (3) establish facts that build up the credibility of counsel's witnesses and diminish the credibility of your opponent's witnesses, including the witness being cross examined.

One of the best ways to accomplish these goals is to begin the cross examination with a series of non-threatening questions. Set a professional and businesslike tone with short, leading questions. Keep it to one fact per question. This gets the witness in a rhythm. They become used to answering "yes", "no", or some other short answer. This subconsciously conditions the witness to answer your questions without conflict. Make that first topic an easy one and it will give witness control. This is a great place in the cross examination to identify those uncontroverted facts that this witness must admit to that support the case. This methods works like a series of steps, with each individual question leading to the next, like steps on a staircase leading to the landing where the the final questions is asked, and answered.

> *Example: the plaintiff is cross examining a defense witness to establish what they observed at the accident scene:*

Plaintiff: No further questions your honor.

Judge: Defense?

Defense: I would like to talk about what you observed on the 21st of March around 7 PM.

Witness: Okay.

Defense: You were outside?

Witness: Yes.

Defense: At the barbecue?

Witness: Yes.

Defense: You got there at 2?

Witness: Yes.

Defense: Stayed there?

Witness: Yes.

Defense: All day?

Witness: Yes.

Defense: I want to talk to you about what you were doing around 7 PM that day *(Having established a questioning rhythm using non-confrontational questions counsel now prepares to shift to a more controversial area of the cross).*

After establishing control of the witness counsel should move to the next topic based upon their case analysis, being careful to ***not rehash the direct examination by chronologically covering the same testimony the jury just heard***. If counsel violate this the jury will hear it three times, once on direct, once on cross and then again on redirect. Any doubts they may have had about the veracity of the witness's version of events will be wiped away by this reverse use of the rule of threes. This is a common mistake made by most advocates. If the witness has practiced the direct so that they were fully prepared, why in the world would counsel think that asking them about it a second time would produce a result appreciably different from the direct? It will not, and counsel will look ineffective while the client's cause suffers.

Counsel should use the doctrine of primacy and recency to place their strongest points where the jury will be sure to notice them. This doctrine, when used in conjunction with a cross examination that is organized around substantive sections, each with a purpose and a connection to other sections, is very effective in producing witness control and a persuasive presentation of the case. As a general approach weaker points addressed during the cross examination should be strengthened by sandwiching them between strong points.

When crossing effectively on these weak points, counsel should use the same words in their questions that are found in the previous statements of the witness. This narrowly defines the inquiry, and prevents the witness from running for cover or explaining away the issue. This is particularly important when attempting to cross on a "weak point" that has the potential to hurt counsel's case. The key to conducting this type of cross effectively is adequate preparation.

> ***Example: the defense is cross examining a plaintiff witness to reduce the impact of the in court identification of their client as the person driving the car at the time of the accident.***

Plaintiff:	Is the person who was driving the Blue Toyota that night present in the courtroom today?
Witness:	Yes.
Plaintiff:	Please point to her and identify her based upon an item of clothing she is wearing.
Witness:	Certainly. *(pointing at the defendant)* She is sitting over there is a blue outfit with a yellow scarf.
Plaintiff:	Let the record reflect that the witness has identified the defendant. No further questions your honor.
Judge:	So noted. Defense?

Defense: Mr. Broadsides you saw the driver of the Honda?

Witness: Yes.

Defense: You ran up to the side of the Honda?

Witness: Yes.

Defense: Began beating on the window?

Witness: Yes.

Defense: The person inside freaked out?

Witness: Yes.

Defense: They drove off?

Witness: Yes. Almost ran my foot over.

Defense: The person who almost ran your foot over, they looked like a woman?

Witness: Yes.

Defense: You then ran up to the Toyota?

Witness: Yes.

Defense: You gave a statement to the police after this happened about the driver of the Toyota?

Witness: Yes.

Defense: In that statement you said that *(looking at the police statement)* It peeled out before I had a chance to see who was driving it. Those were your words?

Witness: Yes.

Defense: Did I read them correctly?

Witness: Yes.

Using the witness's precise words is a way to establish control and credibility. It puts the witness between a rock and a hard place—they either admit that counsel is correct or appear to prevaricate just because they do not want to admit the truth of what they said earlier. Either way, it's a win.

2.   Delivering the Cross

While every cross examination is unique, there are certain fundamental precepts that counsel should always consider when preparing cross examinations. Some of these are part of the historical development of our collective advocacy consciousness and are grounded in two seminal works— The Art of Cross Examination written by Francis L. Wellman[1] and a lecture given by one of the best CLE presenters that has ever taught—Professor Irving Younger.[2] The more relevant and useful ideas can be found in Terry MacCarthy's work, as well as the text by Larry Posner and Roger Dodd.[3] Wellman's book is an excellent read for historical reasons, but is otherwise of little practical use. There are, however, certain eternal questions about how to cross examine that all attorneys should consider. They include:

a.   What Should I Cross On?

Trying to cross a witness on every fact reduces the impact of the cross and runs the danger of boring the fact-finder. When counsel limit the issues addressed with a particular witness to the important information germane to that witness they tell a better story. This is good as a general rule, but sometimes you can cluster important points with more than one witness, teaching through repetition. Terry MacCarthy points out that when the only thing you have is a large number of small issues, then the sheer number of points you are making on cross examination is best supported by a long and detailed inquiry into each small inconsistency.   Terry refers to this in his famous impeachment "fishing lecture" as catching a mess of small fish.[4]

---

[1] Francis Wellman was an excellent lawyer at the turn of the 19th to the 20th century. His book is a must-read for individuals interested in the historical development of cross examination as a teachable skill. It does not, however, teach someone how to conduct cross examination. It is a wonderful historical work that has little practical use as a teaching text.

[2] These tapes are available through the National Institute for Trial Advocacy.

[3] *See* LARRY POSNER AND ROGER DODD, *CROSS-EXAMINATION: SCIENCE AND TECHNIQUES*, Lexis.

[4] *See* MacCarthy's lecture on impeachment at www.youtube.com/TRIALADVOCACY

When trying to decide how much detail to enter into with each witness counsel should use the rule of threes, parallelism and the theory of primacy and recency when deciding what to ask, what not to ask, and when to ask it with each witness. Effective and ongoing case analysis is the best solution to the question "What should I cross on?"

b.   Primacy and Recency

People tend to remember the first thing presented and the last thing presented.   Counsel who use this to their advantage make their strongest points at the beginning and end of the cross, sandwiching the less important or controversial issues of fact in the middle of the presentation where they can get credit for addressing them but the potential damage that might happen if the inquiry goes badly is much less.

Attorneys using this approach begin and end the cross of the witness with a point strongly supporting their theory of the case. It must also be a hook that the witness cannot remove themselves from with sufficient wriggling. Counsel should begin and end cross examination with an unassailable point on an island of safety. When making these choices they should consider whether the need to initially establish control through questioning on uncontroverted facts is sufficiently important to put up front in the cross, even if it is not the most important point from a case theory perspective.

c.   Avoid the Ultimate Question

The idea of avoiding the ultimate question can be traced back, at least in the modern era, to Professor Younger's lectures on cross. His thought process was that cross examination is an art that is just too difficult and the dangers of asking the ultimate question were not worth the potential damage. He often argued that more than one attorney snatched defeat from the jaws of victory by ruining a successful cross-exam when they erroneously believed that the witness would admit the critical and ultimate fact at issue. He would tell the stories focusing on how the witness would skewer the advocate with the answer that destroyed the inference made during the cross examination.

Now it is true that the witness may be able to do that. It is also true that counsel can prevent them from doing that during cross examination by not asking the ultimate question. As a general rule it is a very good basic technique to not push the envelope. Like every good basic rule there is an exception and a problem with it—in this case it is called redirect. When counsel don't deal with the ultimate question head on they have just laid out the scope and purpose of the redirect. The redirect often begins like this:

Counsel: Mr. Witness, on cross examination the defense
              counsel asked you a series of questions about X,
              but he didn't ask you why X happened. Would
              you like an opportunity to explain X, placing it
              in context?

Witness: Absolutely.

Counsel: Why did X happen?

Witness: Blah, blah, blah, blah, blah.

By the time the witness is through on redirect much of the damage of the cross examination has been repaired, if the jury even remembers what the point might have been to begin with.

d.   Single-Fact Questions

Questions should be short, single-fact, and leading. Lead the witness, and the jury, to a desired response. Do not allow the witness to give expansive narratives. There is seldom a place for "How" or "Why" or "Tell the court" lines of questioning. When counsel ask that question they are effectively turning over control to the witness. If counsel have hurt them or insulted them during the cross they are waiting for the chance to get even; don't give it to them.

e.   Vary Questioning Techniques

As discussed previously, counsel can judiciously use taglines to direct the questioning, but prefacing every question with "isn't it true?" or ending every question with "wouldn't you agree?" can be very distracting. When used sparingly, taglines may help maintain control of the witness, the flow of cross examination and the topics discussed. The key word here is "sparingly." On balance, taglines are a crutch and one only uses a crutch when one needs to use it. In court that should rarely be the case.

f.   Understand Potential Answers

Normally counsel should not ask questions to which they do not know the answer. Doing so places them in a position where they are at the mercy of a witness that has been called by the opposing side and is normally not inclined to assist. On rare occasions it may be necessary to ask the question for which counsel do not know the answer. If the worst possible answer to the question leaves counsel in a position that is not any worse than their current one then take the plunge. The proper methodology is to limit those instances, and proceed carefully when counsel must go fishing for information.

g.   Dealing with a Non-responsive Witness

The non-responsive witness[5] can be the worst nightmare for the unprepared cross-examiner. They refuse to answer questions and fight to get their own version of events before the jury. Often they descend into verbose narratives that are at best tangentially related to counsel's query. There are as many different techniques for handling the unresponsive witness as there are styles of lawyering. Counsel should choose the technique that works for them based upon the circumstances, their personal style, and the people involved. The adopted approach must be controlled, professional, and focused. If counsel do not descend into a table-pounding and sarcasm-laden approach they can use attitude to assert control, but it must be the right attitude.

Counsel can project attitude without being rude through the use of tone of voice, inflection, and cadence. Sometimes counsel need only slow down to assert control. The non-responsive witness is interrupting the presentation in a non helpful fashion. Counsel must respond in a way that gets them to stop, but does not muddy the waters of the presentation. Staying engaged is one way to accomplish this.

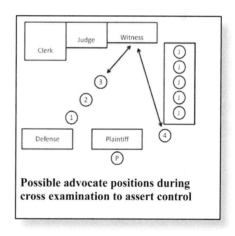

Possible advocate positions during cross examination to assert control

Counsel have a tendency to disengage with non-responsive witnesses. They look down, sigh, stare up to the heavens in disgust, or roll their eyes. These techniques are not effective. Counsel should keep eye contact and focus on the witness. They should take the time to look them in the eye and consider carefully what the witness just said. Sometimes the silence is enough to bring them back in line. Looking them in the eye is an acknowledgement of their presence in the courtroom, delivered sometimes with a bit of puzzlement over their choice of answers.. Eye contact is a good way to stay engaged. Body position is also an important technique counsel can use to show focused attention on the witness.

Physical movements when dealing with the non-responsive witness are crucial. Counsel cannot allow nervous energy to pull them around the courtroom like a dog on a leash. They must remain still while posing the question and waiting for a response. Movement between questions is per-

---

[5] Posner and Dodd refer to this witness alternatively as either nonresponsive or "runaway."

missible in most jurisdictions, as long as it is movement with a purpose. This diagram shows in visual detail how moving closer to the witness between questions can be effective. The point here is to make the movements match the questions. Physicality supports the verbal, enhancing retention and focusing the witness.

h.   Listen Actively

During cross counsel must listen to the witness carefully. The non-responsive witness often offers up a "gem" in their non-responsive answer. It can lead to one of the other identified series of questions or it might create an additional line of impeachment. At other times the answer may be so much hot air, signifying nothing. If counsel are not actively listening to the witness they will not be able to take the best next step in dealing with their answer.

This is difficult because a lot is going on. There are additional questions to consider, language to formulate, judges to deal with, and all this while watching out for opposing counsel. None of this matters as much has hearing correctly what has just been said. Counsel must listen actively to properly control the witness.

One way to ensure active listening is to not move when the witness is answering. Counsel should train themselves to be still, receiving information without distraction. It is a polite technique that has the added benefit of intimidating the witness, sometimes all the way to compliance. Remember as a child when parents, teachers, or others in authority focused completely on what you were saying and how you were saying it? We have probably all felt the cold hand of someone listening closely to what we were saying when we were perhaps less truthful that we should have been. If you close your eyes you can almost recall that sense of impending disaster hidden in the stillness and focus of that authority figure. Using this technique allows the witness to feel the impending doom that waits if they are not truthful.

i.   General Control Techniques

The following techniques make up a series of issues that counsel should consider when developing control techniques for witnesses during cross examination. Some reiterate examples in the proceeding section, others either build on what we have previously discussed or present new ideas. Counsel should consider the ways they might employ them to accomplish cross examination goals.

- **Repeat the question three times:** When a witness refuses to respond to a fairly-asked question counsel can underline this fact and achieve control by repeating the question. There is no need to become aggressive or overly-cyn-ical in tone. Take a deep breath, slow down, and repeat the question while maintaining eye contact with the witness. By the third asking of the question most witnesses will respond appropriately. This presumes, of course, that counsel have employed the fundamental questioning tech-niques previously discussed.

- **Use an honorific:** Every witness has a formal name or title. It might be Sir, Ma'am, Professor, Doctor or their full name. Use of these titles in a professional tone signals to the witness, the jury, and the judge, that counsel isd se-rious about the question just asked. We learned from childhood that the use of our full name was a precursor to a difficult learning experience. Witnesses remember those childhood lessons and counsel can use that fact to focus the witness on the need to answer properly.

- **Go to an undisputable fact:** When the witness refuses to answer affirmatively on an issue that is not disputed coun-sel must underline that fact for the jury. Break the question into its component part, forcing an answer. Counsel can even ask the question in a negative if the jurisdiction al-lows for negative impeachment.

- **"My question to you was . . . . ":** This lead-in placed before the restatement of the question focuses the witness and the audience on the fact that counsel knows the wit-ness was non-responsive and they are not going to allow them to continue with that behavior. Alternatively, coun-sel can also use a phrase such as **"Perhaps you did not understand..."** then repeat the question again.

- **"Was that a yes?":** Sometimes the witness will run on, never quite answering the question. Listen carefully to their soliloquy. Somewhere within the story that they tell resides an affirmation of the question asked. Focus on that affirmative response and then move on.

- **By Process of Elimination:** This technique works well on specific facts. Consider a situation where you need the witness to identify the specific brand of soft drink con-sumed by the plaintiff They initially refuse to agree with you. You could use this technique to create compliance. Eventually the witness agrees just to move it along, they do not want to be seen has an obstructive presence and this line of questioning points out how obstructionist they are being.

Q: Ms. Davis drank a Pepsi?

A: Well it was a soft drink, or carbonated beverage.

Q: She drank a Coke?

A: No…

Q: She drank a Dr. Pepper?

A: No.

Q: Ms. Davis drank a root beer?

A: No.

Q: She drank a generic cola?

A: No

Q: She drank a Pepsi, didn't she?

A: Yes.

- **Use a blackboard or whiteboard.** The person in our past who wrote on the blackboard was usually a teacher. We tend to believe those who write on blackboards. If the witness is refusing to answer a question, and that question has been formulated properly, write it down on the board while they are being non-responsive. Read it to them. They will answer, and everyone will know that they have been difficult. Often the judge will chime in with a "let's just move this along" comment that underlines the non-responsiveness of the witness. Teachers write on the blackboard and most of us still trust teachers.

F.   Impeaching Witnesses

The fundamental purpose of impeachment is to discredit the witness as a reliable source of information. Counsel must use all of the skills developed for cross examination, including case analysis, goal questions and physicality when performing effective impeachments.

As soon as a witness testifies, their credibility becomes an issue. Successful attorneys are able to articulate how a particular fact or set of facts tend to impeach the credibility of a witness and satisfy the logical relevancy requirements of the Federal Rules of Evidence. Probative impeachment evidence is both logically and legally relevant, but may be excluded by the judge based on FRE 403 if its probative value is substantially outweighed by the danger of unfair prejudice, confusion of the issues, waste of time or due to its cumulative nature.

Determining If You Should Impeach a Witness:

- Has the witness's testimony factually supported your case?
- Will the impeachment destroy the witness's entire credibility or only undermine their truthfulness on the impeached points?
- Can I effectively impeach?
- Will the jury see the impeachment as significant or only a lawyer trick?
- How does the witness present: basically truthful or basically untruthful?

A properly planned impeachment is an effective exclamation point to a strong cross examination. Sometimes the opportunity to impeach comes as a surprise and counsel must develop it on the fly. When that happens the experience is akin to a high wire act where the attorney must place themselves "in the moment" to achieve maximum effect. Careful study and development of the skills identified in the section on impeachment will allow counsel to take advantage of the moment when the opportunity presents itself. For now counsel should remember that witness credibility has three facets at trial—bolstering, impeachment, and rehabilitation. We will discuss each of these in great detail during the specific section on impeachment by focusing on the specific evidentiary rules and common law doctrine behind those methods of impeachment.

G. Dealing with Difficult Witnesses

During cross examination counsel will have a variety of opportunities to deal with difficult witnesses. It is important for counsel to develop some fundamental approaches to use when confronting witnesses who do not play nice. The challenge is to assert control without bullying or abusing the witness. While the natural inclination might be to descend into a confrontational approach, it is rarely effective. Proper organization and delivery of these suggested approaches, along with a great deal of patience, is required.

1. The Polite Approach

This first approach is polite focusing on the ability of counsel to ask a good question the witness understands. It is designed to assert control by being reasonable and polite. It requires careful listening, patience, and then restatement of the earlier question. Consider the following:

> **Example: A witness is refusing to answer a simple question about her location on the night of the incident.**

State:	You were in the bar at 8 PM on the 5th of May?
Witness:	I've always enjoyed Cinc de Mayo parties. We have so much fun. I get to spend time with all of my friends, laugh a lot, enjoy food and sometimes even have a margarita. It is so much fun! But I wasn't drunk that night.
State:	(listen politely to the non-responsive answer) I'm sorry, perhaps I was not sufficiently clear in my question. You were in the bar on the 5th of May at 8 PM.
Witness:	I went to a lot of places that night. We went dancing, I saw the fireworks, we stopped by my mom's house, and then we went out to celebrate.
State:	I appreciate you felt the need to share all of that information to us, but it doesn't answer my question. Let's try this a different way.

State:	You were called as a witness in this case?
Witness:	Yes.
State:	Called by the defense counsel?
Witness:	Yes.
State:	You answered the questions they asked you?
Witness:	Yes.
State:	To the best of your ability?
Witness:	Yes.
State:	You understand that it is your responsibility to answer question?
Witness:	Yes.
State:	Truthfully?
Witness:	Yes.
State:	To the best of your ability?
Witness:	Yes.
State:	Good. Let's try this again....

2.   The Polite but Firm Response

This second approach is polite, but firm, focusing on the perceived inability of the witness to understand the cross examination question. It is designed to assert control by being both reasonable and focused. It requires careful listening, patience, hand movements, headline use, and then restatement of the earlier question. Consider the following:

Example: A witness is refusing to answer a simple question about her location on the night of the incident.

State:	You were in the bar at 8 PM on the 5th of May?

Witness: I've always enjoyed Cinc de Mayo parties. We have so much fun. I get to spend time with all of my friends, laugh a lot, enjoy food and sometimes even have a margarita. It is so much fun! But I wasn't drunk that night.

State: *(listen politely to the non-responsive answer)* Perhaps you did not understand my question. My question to you was "You were in the bar at 8 PM on the 5th of May?"

Witness: I went to a lot of places that night. We went dancing, I saw the fireworks, we stopped by my mom's house,....

State: *(Hold up hand during the non-responsive answer, listen politely, once they stop talking)* Thank you, but that was not my question. Let's try this a third time. My question to you was, "You were in the bar at 8 PM on the 5th of May?"

Witness: Yes.

Occasionally the witness will continue to be non-responsive, and will not answer the question properly, even after it has been placed as before. At that point counsel should raise their hand again when the witness is being non-responsive, if they do not stop talking counsel should drop their hand, go back to counsel's table and look through their notes. Once the witness stops talking counsel should count to three, close their notes, look up and say:

State: Thank you, but that was not my question. Let's try this again. Please listen carefully. My question to you was, "You were in the bar at 8 PM on the 5th of May?"

Witness: Yes.

Sometimes the witness will continue to be non-responsive even after counsel has made it crystal clear as describe above. If these control techniques have not worked it is now appropriate to get the court involved.

State: *(Turn and face the judge)* Your honor move to strike the witness's testimony as non-responsive *(Wait for the court's response).*

Judge: Your motion is granted. The jury is instructed to disregard the witness's non-responsive answers. *(To the witness)* I am instructing you to properly answer counsel's questions. Do you understand?

Witness: Yes.

Judge: Counsel you may inquire.

H.   Examples

Example: plaintiff's attorney is cross examining the father of the defendant, Bill Hartwell. Mr. Hartwell's daughter, Rebecca, is being sued for wrongful death and defamation by Ms. Washington. This section of the cross examination focuses on the actions of Mr. Hartwell on the night of the accident.

Plaintiff: Mr. Hartwell, you say your daughter was upset the night of the accident?

Witness: Yes.

Plaintiff: She was balled up on the floor crying?

Witness: Yes. Weeping uncontrollably.

Plaintiff: She tried to get her keys to go back to the scene?

Witness: Yes.

Plaintiff: You stopped her?

Witness: Yes.

Plaintiff: Told her not to go back?

Witness: Yes.

Plaintiff: Because you wanted to keep her safe?

Witness: Of course. She is my little girl, always has been, always will be.

Plaintiff: Exactly. So after you talked to Rebecca you went out to the driveway and checked on her car?

Witness: Yes. It was a mess.

Plaintiff: You pulled the car into your garage?

Witness: Yes.

Plaintiff: The front and side of the car was covered in a lot of blood?

Witness: You could say that.

Plaintiff: Well actually you said that previously during your deposition testimony.

Witness: Yes I did.

Plaintiff: So you saw a lot of blood, and other stuff?

Witness: Yes.

Plaintiff: You grabbed some items to clean the car?

Witness: Yes.

Plaintiff: paper towels,

Witness: *Yes.*

Plaintiff: the hose,

Witness: Yes.

Plaintiff: A can of Lysol,

Witness: Yes.

Plaintiff: You took these items and cleaned off the blood?

Witness: Yes.

Plaintiff: You cleaned off the "other stuff" as you describe it?

Witness: Yes.

Plaintiff: You then took that stuff and put it in a bag?

Witness: Yes.

Plaintiff: You took it out to the curb?

Witness: Yes.

Plaintiff: Where they pick up the trash?

Witness: Yes.

Plaintiff: The trash as picked up on Friday?

Witness: Yes.

Plaintiff: You called the cops on Monday?

Witness: Yes.

Plaintiff: After the trash was picked up?

Witness: Yes.

Plaintiff: After you called your lawyer?

Witness: Yes.

Example: The following cross examination focuses on the actions of the plaintiff who has brought a suit alleging that the

defendant wrongfully caused the death of her children. This portion of the direct focuses on the plaintiff's actions on the night in question.

Defense: Good morning, Ms. Washington. Now I know this is difficult for you and I am very sorry for your loss, but I do have some questions I need to ask you. Let's begin with what you were doing on the afternoon of March 21st.

Witness: Okay.

Defense: You did not want the children to go to the park that evening?

Witness: Not really. I was tired and it had been a long week.

Defense: But your son, Jordan, he convinced you to let them go?

Witness: Yes, Jordan was responsible and they deserved a chance to get out.

Defense: Even against your better judgment?

Witness: Well I thought they would be okay.

Defense: You know the road along your house is dangerous?

Witness: Yes, but we had crossed it many times.

Defense: You   walked them to the park that evening because the road is dangerous?

Witness: Yes, I wanted my babies to be safe.

Defense: You told them you would be back to pick them up?

Witness: Yes.

Defense: You told the children to wait for you in the park?

Witness: Yes.

Defense: Because you are always nervous about the traffic on that road?

Witness: Yes, and the fact that the street lights were always out.

Defense: That's why you were going to pick them up that evening?

Witness: Yes, and I was on my way too, just didn't get there in time.

Defense: You did not stay with the kids in the park?

Witness: No I did not.

Defense: You decided to leave them there alone - without you?

Witness: Yes.

Defense: Even though you worried about them going in the first place?

Witness: Yes.

Defense: Now Ms. Washington, you weren't the only person who has ever worried about your children?

Witness: I don't understand what you mean.

Defense: In fact, you had trouble with the department of children and families before?

Witness: Yes.

Defense: But regardless, You were going to pick them up   on the night of 21 March before it got dark?

Witness: Yes.

Defense: But the children, they did not wait for you that night?

Witness: No they didn't, I will always regret it.

Defense: They had to walk home alone?

Witness: They weren't supposed to do that.

Defense: But they did.

Witness: Oh yes, I wish I could go back and change things.

I.   Checklist

The following checklist summarizes the information counsel should consider when developing persuasive cross examinations. It should be used as a starting point for developing appropriate cross examinations focused on persuading the jury by showcasing the theme and theories of the case developed during case analysis, with an eye towards establishing, reducing, or destroying witness credibility - as appropriate.

I.   Seven Steps to Superior Cross Examinations:

   a. Start and end preparation with case analysis.

   b. Every section has a clearly defined purpose tied to theme, theory or credibility.

   c. CONTROL THE WITNESS.

   d. Details give control.

   e. Organize the cross to accomplish your goals—not your opponent's.

   f. Impeachment must matter.

   g. Use the witness's own words.

II.   Primary Goals of Cross Examination:

    a. Control the witness.

    b. Establish facts that bolster your theme and theory.

    c. Establish facts that build up the credibility of your witnesses and diminish the credibility of your opponent's witnesses.

III. Maximize the Persuasive Impact of Answers on Cross:

    a. Cluster together all of the facts that enhance and support the topic.

    b. Lay out the facts one question at a time leading up to your final point.

    c. Identify similar facts based upon your knowledge of human nature and then using them to make your final point.

IV. Why Cross?

    a. To elicit facts supporting your legal theory, factual theory or moral theme.

    b. To expose facts or bias that weakens your opponent's legal theory, factual theory or moral theme.

    c. To establish the credibility of your own witnesses or attack the credibility of opposing witnesses (when required by your legal theory, factual theory or moral theme).

V. Fundamental Precepts of Cross:

    a. It is a commando raid, not an invasion.

    b. Use primacy and recency.

    c. Avoid the ultimate question.

    d. One fact questions.

    e. Vary questioning techniques.

    f. Do not play with fire.

    g. Develop control techniques.

VI. Cross Examination Sequencing:

    a. Do not use chronological order in confrontational cross examinations.

    b. Avoid chronological order in informational cross examinations.

    c. Lay your theme early and often.

    d. Close cross examination with a theme vignette.

    e. When attacking credibility, attack in the first vignette.

    f. Show bias, interest, or motive early in the cross examination.

g. End with a power vignette.

h. Develop risky areas only after establishing control of the witness through safe vignettes.

i. Never lead or end with a risky vignette.

j. If you have more than one impeachment vignette, use the cleanest first.

k. Disperse impeachment vignettes throughout the cross examination.

l. When expecting a 'no' answer to one goal question, precede that chapter with a sure 'yes' answer.

m. Bundle vignettes that need to be done together in order to complete a coherent picture of a single event.

n. Prepared vignettes countering the power of the opponent's case are best performed in the middle of cross examination.

J.   Evidence Rules to Consider During Cross

Issue Arising During Cross Examination	Applicable Federal Rule of Evidence
Character traits of the victim or accused	404(a), 404(b), 405
Character of a witness for truthfulness	608
Out of court statements offered for the truth of the matter asserted therein (hearsay)	801 - 807
Offering evidence of other crimes, wrongs & acts (*see Chapter 10*)	404(b)
Prior convictions of a witness (*see Chapter 10*)	609
Legal relevancy - Is the probative value substantially outweighed by the danger of unfair prejudice et al	403
Are the questions logically relevant	401, 402
Competency of a witness	610
Personal knowledge of the witness	602
Questioning witnesses	611, 614

Table 1: Potential Evidentiary Rules Applicable During Cross Examination

K. Conclusion

Now that we have laid the groundwork for a thorough understanding of how cross examinations are built, it is time to expand your understanding by considering some additional resources. An excellent place to start would be by reviewing the presentations and examples found at www.youtube.com/TRIALADVOCACY.

Once you have mastered the fundamental tenets of direct and cross examination, you should next develop additional skills that are specific to certain situations in either direct or cross. The cross examination trail blazed by Terrance MacCarthy, Irving Younger, and Roger Dodd will serve you well as you continue to mature as a trial lawyer.

-Notes-

Chapter 8: Impeachment

A. Introduction 317
B. How the Law Impacts Impeachment 320
C. Prior Untruthful Acts 322
D. Prior Convictions 325
E. Prior Inconsistent Statements 331
F. Bias and Motive 339
G. Defects in Capacity 344
H. Impeachment by Omission 351
I. Impeachment by Contradiction 357
J. Checklist 358
K. Evidentiary Rules to Consider During Impeachment 360
L. Conclusion 361

A.   Introduction

One of the three goals during cross examination is to establish facts that build up the credibility of witnesses and decrease the credibility of the opponent's witness. Impeachment is the tool lawyers use to accomplish this latter goal, it is the procedural format that allows lawyers to call people liars in open court. The fundamental purpose of impeachment is to discredit the witness as a reliable source of information. Lawyers must use all the skills developed for cross examination, including case analysis, goal questions, and physicality.

This section builds upon the skills of case analysis, basic questioning techniques, and cross examination previously discussed. It is the next step a lawyer takes in developing a thorough set of cross examination skills. Counsel should think of it as a subset of cross examination driven by the rules of evidence and their own common sense. Mastering the law behind these methods of impeachment, the human element is always present when confronting someone about a lie, and the theories of contradiction and omission allowed for at common law will ensure counsel are prepared to deal with a witness when they misstate the truth. Remember, most, if not

> *Impeachment is a subset of cross examination driven by the rules of evidence and their own common sense*

all, witnesses make that mistake to some degree during direct examination. There are some common legal and practical considerations counsel must address before choosing which type of impeachment to employ.

A complete understanding and mastery of the relevant facts is the first step. Counsel must have prepared sufficiently, and a continuing case analysis is the best means available to a lawyer to guarantee sufficient knowledge to ensure success. It is essential that counsel consistently review their case analysis and the underpinning facts to gain complete mastery over their case. That level of fluency is required to employ impeachment techniques effectively, meaningfully, and judiciously. If counsel is not that familiar with the facts of their case, there can be no way they can make the judgment call at trial on if impeaching on a fact is worth it or not. There are seven primary means of impeachment. Each has a slightly different legal basis, and the manner in which counsel accomplish each type of impeachment is tied to the reason they are legally allowed to impeach the witness.

When a witness testifies, his credibility becomes an issue. Because credibility is intrinsically tied to testifying it is always logically relevant. The limitations of the Federal Rules of Evidence on impeachment establish the degree to which the credibility of a witness is legally relevant, in other words it establishes the extent to which counsel can cross examine on issues of witness credibility. Lawyers must be able to articulate how a particular fact or set of facts tends to impeach the credibility of a witness and satisfy the logical relevancy requirements of the Federal Rules of Evidence.

Rule 607. Who May Impeach a Witness

Any party, including the party that called the witness, may attack the witness's credibility.

After a witness has been impeached the proponent may attempt to rehabilitate his credibility by giving him the opportunity to explain or deny an apparent inconsistency, prior bad act, or prior untruthfulness. Impeachment is not limited to opposing counsel. Under FRE 607 "the credibility of a witness may be attacked by any party, including the party calling the witness." Counsel should remember that witness credibility has three facets at trial—bolstering, impeachment, and rehabilitation.

For reasons of judicial economy, certain matters offered for impeachment of a witness may not be proven by extrinsic evidence because they raise questions that are too collateral to the issues in the trial. If courts allowed this sort of inquiry, examinations would consist of mini-trials within trials. This is referred to as the Collateral Fact Rule. If a matter is deemed collateral, the court will only permit inquiry on cross examination.

> **Goals During Cross Examination:**
>
> * Control the witness
> * Establish facts that build to a theme and theory
> * Establish facts that build up the credibility of your witnesses and diminish the credibility of your opponent's witnesses

Prior untruthful acts of the witness are generally considered collateral, whereas prior convictions and proof of bias are rarely collateral. When an issue is collateral, extrinsic proof cannot be offered to establish the veracity of the impeachment. Some forms of impeachment may be proven by extrinsic evidence while others only permit inquiry on cross examination. Regardless of which impeachment technique is used, counsel must have a good faith belief that the impeaching facts are true.

The impeachment techniques contemplated here are designed to create tension by building suspense and sparking the interest of the jury, while suggesting the answer that everyone expects. There is nothing wrong with that expectation during impeachment—provided counsel can deliver on it. Counsel must make certain they have the available resources to impeach the witness when they stray from the good or bad facts identified through case analysis. This means clearly identifying witness statements, and being familiar enough with those statements to get to the location of prior inconsistent statements, for example, as quickly as possible. This point is crucial. If the witness challenges you and the law allows you to respond to that challenge—you must. Failure to properly control empowers the witness, weakens the theme and theory of the case, and calls into question counsel's credibility as a lawyer in the eyes of the fact-finder.

While an effective impeachment depends upon accurate knowledge of the law, good technique, and projection of the right attitude, impeachment is not the end in and of itself. Counsel must analyze not only whether impeachment of a particular witness will help their case, but how it will help the case. A clear theory of the case and the opponent's case is critical before counsel can adequately determine whether an impeachment is warranted and will be effective. If the potential impeachment does not go to a material issue in the case, but is instead an issue of semantics or different word choice on a narrative fact, the impeachment is less powerful and not

> *You know that the impeachment is going well when you hear a soft "yes" from the jury box at the moment of confrontation.*

likely to be worth the fight impeachment entails with adverse witnesses. Counsel should always strive for clarity and simplicity because clarity and simplicity will assist the jury in understanding and using the impeachment for its proper evidentiary purpose.

If the witness testified in a way that exposes them to impeachment, counsel should consider whether clarification or refreshing their recollection will accomplish the same purpose that a full-blown impeachment would produce. If the witness has hurt counsel's case and they decide to impeach them, counsel should first consider which tone and style of impeachment will be most effective. If the witness is cocky, partisan, or simply lying, then a hard-hitting, aggressive tone may be appropriate. If the witness seems sincere, then a gentler approach may be warranted. Counsel must make this decision quickly, relying upon their impressions of the witness's recent direct testimony and their early interactions with the witness.

B.   How the Law Impacts Impeachment

FRE 611 addresses witnesses and establishes the manner and scope of witness testimony during cross examination. While FRE 611 governs the form of cross examination questions, many other evidentiary rules also impact counsel's ability to impeach witnesses. Attorneys must understand

---

Seven Primary Means of Impeachment:

- *Prior untruthful act*: FRE 608(b)
- *Prior conviction*: FRE 609
- *Prior inconsistent statement*: FRE 613
- *Bias, prejudice, or motive*: Common Law
- *Defects in capacity to observe, recall or relate*: Common Law
- *Impeachment by contradiction*: Common Law, FRE 401, 402, 403
- *Impeachment by omission*: Common Law FRE 401, 402, 403

---

the legal doctrine behind the rules governing impeachment, and should begin their inquiry by developing a deeper basis of knowledge concerning prior untruthful acts under FRE 608(b), prior convictions under FRE 609, and prior inconsistent statements under FRE 613.

Rule 611. Mode and Order of Examining Witnesses and Presenting Evidence

(a) Control by the Court; Purposes. The court should exercise reasonable control over the mode and order of examining witnesses and presenting evidence so as to:

(1) make those procedures effective for determining the truth;

(2) avoid wasting time; and

(3) protect witnesses from harassment or undue embarrassment.

(b) Scope of Cross-Examination. Cross-examination should not go beyond the subject matter of the direct examination and matters affecting the witness's credibility. The court may allow inquiry into additional matters as if on direct examination.

(c) Leading Questions. Leading questions should not be used on direct examination except as necessary to develop the witness's testimony. Ordinarily, the court should allow leading questions:

(1) on cross-examination; and

(2) when a party calls a hostile witness, an adverse party, or a witness identified with an adverse party.

Beyond the evidentiary rules, counsel must also master the common law concerning bias, motive, and defects in capacity to observe, recall, or relate information. While an in-depth study of these evidentiary rules is beyond the capacity of this text, in the following pages when each type of impeachment is discussed, the rule and the fundamental questioning steps counsel must take to establish a valid impeachment under that particular legal basis will be provided.

Using the text will make counsel competent, but it will not make them superior when it comes to impeachment. Impeachment is a legally relevant activity at trial because the rules of evidence and the common law make it so. The law of evidence allows counsel to specifically point out certain defects in the testimony of witnesses. Counsel should consider the evidentiary rules mentioned above and sprinkled throughout this chapter as examples of the legal relevance standard that must exist before the court will allow them to impeach. When dealing with cases in their own jurisdiction, counsel must make equal efforts to master the local evidentiary rules as they do to master the facts of the case. A combination of both is the only way to use impeachment techniques to their most damaging effects.

C. Prior Untruthful Acts

FRE 608(b) permits counsel to impeach a witness by cross-examining her concerning certain prior bad acts. Only those prior acts, which are probative of the witness's character for truthfulness, may be used to impeach under this rule. Impeachment by prior untruthful acts is limited to cross examination. When counsel impeach for this purpose extrinsic evidence is not allowed. If the witness denies or minimizes the deceptive nature of the act for which they are attempting to impeach her, counsel cannot use extrinsic evidence to refute her answer, or to establish the untruthful nature of the witness's prior act. They are, in a very real sense, stuck with her answer.

Rule 608. A Witness's Character for Truthfulness or Untruthfulness

(a) Reputation or Opinion Evidence. A witness's credibility may be attacked or supported by testimony about the witness's reputation for having a character for truthfulness or untruthfulness, or by testimony in the form of an opinion about that character. But evidence of truthful character is admissible only after the witness's character for truthfulness has been attacked.

(b) Specific Instances of Conduct. Except for a criminal conviction under Rule 609, extrinsic evidence is not admissible to prove specific instances of a witness's conduct in order to attack or support the witness's character for truthfulness. But the court may, on cross-examination, allow them to be inquired into if they are probative of the character for truthfulness or untruthfulness of:

(1) the witness; or

(2) another witness whose character the witness being cross-examined has testified about.

By testifying on another matter, a witness does not waive any privilege against self-incrimination for testimony that relates only to the witness's character for truthfulness.

Although extrinsic evidence is not admissible to prove the prior untruthful act, counsel may be required to disclose the basis for believing that the act occurred. The inability to articulate a good faith basis for an inquiry under FRE 608(b) may result in a mistrial or other judicial sanction. Additionally, the judge may forbid inquiry into prior untruthful acts if they violate the requirements of FRE 403. The most common objections raised when lawyers attempt to impeach a witness with prior untruthful bad acts deal with the fact that the impeachment is either unduly prejudicial or a waste of time. Judges pay particular attention to this issue when the individual being impeached is the defendant.

There are several ways to approach the prior untruthful act. If counsel know the witness will admit the prior act, it may be possible to impeach with a few direct, dramatic questions. More commonly, counsel will need to pursue a more oblique approach, committing the witness to specific facts surrounding the prior incident before confronting her with the specific untruthful act. If counsel demonstrate to the witness their knowledge of the prior act through detailed, succinct, leading questions, she will be reluctant to deny their account. This calls back to why thorough case analysis is so important to success at trial. It is only through complete mastery o f the facts of the case that counsel can build the needed tension in the cross examination. Too much detail and counsel risks the jury getting lost in unneeded portions of the story, too little and counsel risks the witness feeling as if they have room to weasel out of admitting the prior untruthful act. Counsel can make any attempts at weaseling especially difficult for the witness if in their questions they refer to witnesses who could corroborate the allegations. The witness doesn't understand that counsel are barred from presenting extrinsic proof of the prior untruthful act. The subtle handling of documents during cross examination may also lead the witness to believe that counsel possess documentary proof of the prior act which is admissible.

Rule 403. Excluding Relevant Evidence for Prejudice, Confusion, Waste of Time, or Other Reasons

The court may exclude relevant evidence if its probative value is substantially outweighed by a danger of one or more of the following: unfair prejudice, confusing the issues, misleading the jury, undue delay, wasting time, or needlessly presenting cumulative evidence.

Since counsel are not permitted to present extrinsic evidence of the prior bad act, if the witness denies any such act during questioning, counsel are stuck with the witness's denial. Counsel may, however, test the witness's commitment to that denial. An initial denial may need clarification to ensure that counsel is referring to the same event as the witness. Counsel will do well to remember that a main point of cross examinations is to probe the credibility of a witness' version of events, and often that requires detailed, probing lines of questioning. If counsel persist after a denial, they may draw an "asked and answered" objection from opposing counsel.

They must be able to explain to the judge that are simply attempting to refresh the witness as to the surrounding facts or clarifying the incident to which they are referring.

Special care is warranted when using prior bad acts to impeach the accused in a criminal case. It is in this situation that constitutional protections are at their highest, and counsel must make all efforts to show that fact the respect it is due. Counsel should alert the judge and opposing counsel as to the intent to impeach the accused with such information. This is appropriate given the requirements of both FRE 103 and FRE 104. This gives opposing counsel an opportunity to object to such impeachment prior to cross examination. The judge will appreciate the opportunity to weigh the matter in advance outside the presence of the jury. Since the judge is the gatekeeper in determining whether counsel will be allowed to ask these questions it makes perfect sense to not try and hide the ball.

> ***Example: in the following case counsel is attempting to impeach a witness about their prior untruthful acts.***

Q: Isn't it true that you once lied to your insurance company by filing an incorrect claim about an allegedly stolen car stereo?

A: I don't know what you are talking about.

Q: GEICO refused to renew your car insurance recently, isn't that correct?

A: They canceled it because I had too many points on my license.

Q: You filed a claim with GEICO based on the alleged theft of your car stereo, right?

A: Right.

Q: At the time you filed the claim your policy was still in effect?

A: Yes.

Q: GEICO refused to pay your claim?

A: Yeah, they refused.

Q: Your car stereo was never stolen?

A: No.

Q: Isn't it true that you filed a false claim for your car stereo with GEICO?

A: No.

Q: It's true isn't it that GEICO canceled your policy right after you claimed your stereo was stolen?

A: No.

Q: We can at least agree that GEICO canceled your policy after you filed your stolen stereo claim?

A: Yes. But that was not the reason they cancelled it.

At this point counsel have probably gone as far as they can go with this impeachment. The law will not allow them to go further, but if the jury has been following, they should get the clear impression that this witness is not truthful.

D. Prior Convictions

The admissibility of prior untruthful acts is normally decided during a motion in limine. Resolution of issues of admissibility under FRE 609 often requires judicial balancing. Both the proponent and the opponent of the witness should consider a motion in limine to obtain a ruling prior to trial so that they can make tactical decisions regarding the examination of the witness based upon potential impeachment. On the other hand, counsel may consider waiting for the other side to raise the issue of the prior conviction if they believe it to be clearly admissible. In some jurisdictions discovery rules may re-quire disclosure of this information even if they do not seek a ruling through a motion in limine. The impeaching party can choose the form of impeachment. Options include eliciting the fact of the conviction on cross examination, admitting into evidence an authenticated record of the conviction, or by testimony of someone present when the witness was convicted.

Rule 609. Impeachment by Evidence of a Criminal Conviction

(a) In General. The following rules apply to attacking a witness's character for truthfulness by evidence of a criminal conviction:

(1) for a crime that, in the convicting jurisdiction, was punishable by death or by imprisonment for more than one year, the evidence:

(A) must be admitted, subject to Rule 403, in a civil case or in a criminal case in which the witness is not a defendant; and

(B) must be admitted in a criminal case in which the witness is a defendant, if the probative value of the evidence outweighs its prejudicial effect to that defendant; and

(2) for any crime regardless of the punishment, the evidence must be admitted if the court can readily determine that establishing the elements of the crime required proving--or the witness's admitting--a dishonest act or false statement.

(b) Limit on Using the Evidence After 10 Years. This subdivision (b) applies if more than 10 years have passed since the witness's conviction or release from confinement for it, whichever is later. Evidence of the conviction is admissible only if:

(1) its probative value, supported by specific facts and circumstances, substantially outweighs its prejudicial effect; and

(2) the proponent gives an adverse party reasonable written notice of the intent to use it so that the party has a fair opportunity to contest its use.

(c) Effect of a Pardon, Annulment, or Certificate of Rehabilitation. Evidence of a conviction is not admissible if:

(1) the conviction has been the subject of a pardon, annulment, certificate of rehabilitation, or other equivalent procedure based on a finding that the person has been rehabilitated, and the person has not been convicted of a later crime punishable by death or by imprisonment for more than one year; or

(2) the conviction has been the subject of a pardon, annulment, or other equivalent procedure based on a finding of innocence.

(d) Juvenile Adjudications. Evidence of a juvenile adjudication is admissible under this rule only if:

(1) it is offered in a criminal case;

(2) the adjudication was of a witness other than the defendant;

(3) an adult's conviction for that offense would be admissible to attack the adult's credibility; and

(4) admitting the evidence is necessary to fairly determine guilt or innocence.

(e) Pendency of an Appeal. A conviction that satisfies this rule is admissible even if an appeal is pending. Evidence of the pendency is also admissible.

This rule permits counsel to use either cross examination or extrinsic evidence to prove the prior conviction. When the witness admits the facts pertaining to the conviction on cross examination, however, the judge may exclude further evidence on the grounds that it is cumulative. While there is more than one way to prove a prior conviction, cross examination of the witness about the conviction is the preferred method. There is more power in directly confronting the witness with this information, and having their reaction to that information be on full display to the jury, than there is in simply entering a conviction report that provides little emotional impact. This does not mean the conviction report is devoid of value. To the contrary, if the witness denies, mischaracterizes, or minimizes the nature of the conviction, then the impeachment value of the record is magnified. Counsel must always be prepared to do it both ways. When preparing for possible impeachment with a conviction they should remember that a properly certified record of conviction is a self-authenticating document and needs no sponsoring witness. If opposing counsel objects to the record of conviction on hearsay grounds, the proponent should cite to FRE 803(8); that should be sufficient to overcome a hearsay objection.

It is important to note that most courts do not permit counsel to explore the details of the prior conviction. Getting in the conviction itself is enough for impeachment, but the details do not come in, i.e. they cannot ask what led her to commit the crime of the past conviction, etc. Some courts do permit proof of the sentence imposed, and counsel should be aware that the record of previous conviction usually indicates the sentence imposed. If the record is admissible, then counsel should cross examine about the sentence imposed because that should also be admissible. It is a best practice to first determine how far the judge will permit counsel to go. This is easily accomplished by speaking with other members of the local bar, or by talking directly to the judge and asking them during the pretrial hearing.

Determining If You Should Impeach a Witness:

* Has the witness's testimony factually supported your case?
* Will the chosen method of impeachment destroy the witness's entire credibility or only undermine their truthfulness on the impeached points?
* Can I effectively impeach?
* Will the jury see the impeachment as significant or only a lawyer trick?
* How does the witness present—basically truthful or basically untruthful?

When sorting out which convictions may be used to impeach a witness under FRE 609, it is helpful to sort the convictions into either crimes of dishonesty and false statement (usually referred to as crimen falsi crimes) and all other crimes. Crimen falsi crimes are admissible to impeach any witness, including the accused, regardless of the punishment authorized or imposed.

Convictions for other crimes depend upon whether the crime was punishable by death or confinement in excess of one year. If so, impeachment by conviction may be admissible subject to the discretion of the court. The law of the jurisdiction in which the conviction was obtained governs the determination of maximum punishment. Maximum punishment is determined based upon the statutory possibility, not the actual punishment received. For instance, a conviction for robbery that carried a maximum sentence of five years would be a qualifying conviction, even if the court only sentenced the accused to less than one year confinement.

The "other crimes" category of convictions is subject to judicial balancing under FRE 403 for all witnesses other than the accused when determining admissibility. When the accused is the witness then his conviction is admissible for impeachment purposes only if the judge determines that the probative value outweighs the prejudicial effect to the accused.

For convictions other than crimen falsi crimes there is a 10-year window. If the conviction was obtained or the sentence of confinement, to include any probation, was completed more than 10 years ago it is not admissible for impeachment purposes. However, the judge can still admit such evidence if the proponent of the evidence gives written notice and the judge determines that the probative value of the evidence substantially outweighs the prejudicial effect in accordance with the FRE 609 balancing test.

Counsel should note that this test differs from the normal FRE 403 balancing test, with a preference for excluding the evidence under this standard. They should keep in mind that pendency of an appeal will not render such convictions inadmissible, but pardon, annulment, or certificate of rehabilitation may bar use of such evidence. It is also important to note that evidence of juvenile adjudications is generally not admissible.

> *Example: the following witness has had an uncomfortable acquaintance with the truth over the last few years. Counsel has multiple opportunities to impeach based upon the witness's previous convictions.*

> *Q:* Mr. Bones, isn't it true that you were convicted in state court nine years ago?

> *A:* Yes.

> *Q:* That court convicted you for filing a false claim with the state unemployment agency?

> *A:* Yes, sir.

> *Q:* And you were convicted of making a false claim for lying on several forms filed with the state?

> *A:* Yes.

> *Q:* Thank you. Let's move on and discuss your other issues. Are you the same Mr. Bones who was previously convicted in federal court in December 20XX?

> *A:* Well, I don't know if it was a federal court.

> *Q:* Isn't it a fact that you were convicted of conspiracy to destroy the original manuscript of the Declaration of Independence in 20XX?

> *A:* It should have never been signed!

Q: Please answer the question. Were you convicted of conspiracy to destroy the Declaration of Independence?

A: No, I was not.

Q: Isn't it a fact that you were sentenced to five years confinement for conspiracy to destroy the Declaration of Independence?

A: Uh, no, it was only two years.

Q: So, you now admit that you were convicted of that crime?

A: Well, yes, but it wasn't a "federal" court I wasn't sentenced to five years in jail.

Q: Your honor, the state moves to admit P.E.-10 for ID into evidence as P.E.-10.

J: Defense?

D: We object to this exhibit on the grounds of hearsay and lack of authentication.

J: State?

Q: Your honor P.E.-10 for ID is a self-authenticating document under FRE 902(4) and also falls within the hearsay exception under FRE 803(8).

J: The objection is overruled. P.E.-10 for ID will be admitted as P.E.-10. You may proceed.

Q: I am handing the witness P.E.-10. Mr. Bones, this is an official record of your conviction. Please take a moment to read block "5e" of that record of conviction. Tell the court what block f states as the sentence you were given for the conspiracy to destroy the Declaration of Independence.

> *A:*   It says that I was sentenced to five years confinement.

> *Q:*   Thank you. Nothing further.

E. Prior Inconsistent Statements

FRE 613 governs the use of the prior inconsistent statements (PIS) for impeachment purposes. When impeaching under this rule counsel can use the inconsistency established through the impeachment to argue witness credibility in closing argument. They may not use the impeachment to suggest an alternative factual position – unless the witness adopts their position or an additional evidentiary rule allows for the admittance of the out-of-court statements that form the basis of the impeachment.

Rule 613. Witness's Prior Statement

(a) Showing or Disclosing the Statement During Examination. When examining a witness about the witness's prior statement, a party need not show it or disclose its contents to the witness. But the party must, on request, show it or disclose its contents to an adverse party's attorney.

(b) Extrinsic Evidence of a Prior Inconsistent Statement. Extrinsic evidence of a witness's prior inconsistent statement is admissible only if the witness is given an opportunity to explain or deny the statement and an adverse party is given an opportunity to examine the witness about it, or if justice so requires. This subdivision (b) does not apply to an opposing party's statement under Rule 801(d)(2).

The form of the PIS can be varied. Possible options include written statements, transcripts of prior testimony, oral statements made by the witness, omissions of a material nature from a prior statement, and assertive or communicative conduct. The focus of the inquiry is whether counsel has a good faith basis to believe that the statement was made by the witness.If they do then it is potentially impeachment material.

Before FRE 613 was adopted a common law requirement existed that counsel had to give the witness an opportunity to see the prior written statement before they could cross examine them on its contents. While FRE 613 disposed of this requirement, some state jurisdictions still expect it. Counsel should check the local rules before impeaching without first

Using the "3 C's:"

- Commit to the in-court testimony
- Credit the earlier statement
- Confront with the inconsistency

showing the written statement to the witness. In any event, counsel must disclose the written statement to opposing counsel upon their request. Most competent counsel routinely request disclosure of all impeachment materials during discovery. When impeachment occurs under the auspices of FRE 613 it is admitted for the limited purpose of showing a lack of credibility. If the impeaching counsel wishes to argue that evidence substantively then it must also either be adopted as fact by the witness or be otherwise admissible under an appropriate hearsay rule. Should opposing counsel argue impeachment evidence substantively, counsel must be prepared to call them on it zealously on the record.

The PIS may be admitted as extrinsic evidence only if (1) the witness denies making the prior statement or denies that it is inconsistent, (2) the inconsistency goes to a non-collateral matter, and (3) the statement is otherwise admissible under the hearsay rules. If the witness acknowledges the prior statement, then it is not allowed into evidence because it has been adopted by the witness. If counsel is able to introduce the prior statement the witness must be given the opportunity to explain or deny the statement.

When a PIS is used, the judge shall give a limiting instruction to the jury upon request by the opposing party. The PIS is not substantive evidence and cannot be relied upon to prove an element of the offense or a defense. The statement, if admitted, will be accompanied by a limiting instruction from the judge stating it can be considered only on the issue of the witness's credibility. A PIS offered solely to impeach the witness under FRE 613 is hearsay and not admissible for the truth of the matter contained therein. However, a PIS is not hearsay if the declarant and the witness are the same and the prior statement was made under oath and subject to cross examination. A PIS is also not hearsay if it is a party-opponent admission.

When conducting PIS impeachment on cross examination, lawyers use the three-step process commonly referred to as the "3 C's." The order of the three steps may vary depending on the witness, but in most situations they (1) commit the witness to their in-court testimony, (2) credit the earlier statement of the witness, and (3) confront the witness with the inconsistency. The degree to which each step in the "3 C's" is emphasized depends upon the strength of the available information. It may be counsel can spend a great deal of time crediting the earlier statement because of the circumstances under which it was made. Other times the difference between the prior statement and the current in-court testimony is so great that counsel spend a good deal of time working on the confrontation. Points of emphasis also depend on counsel's personal style, as well as how material the impeachment is to the issues of the case. If counsel is impeaching on a central issue of the case, it is best practice to spend time emphasizing the

> **You May Admit a Prior Inconsistent Statement if:**
>
> - The witness denies making the prior statement or denies that it is inconsistent
> - The inconsistency goes to a non-collateral matter, and
> - The statement is otherwise admissible

impeachment so that the jury is clear on the weight of the lie. Counsel choose which to emphasize based on their case's strength and the reason for the impeachment.

Witness impeaches himself. Lawyers may highlight the relevant portion of the witness's statement, mark the document as an exhibit for identification (always coordinate with the court reporter when marking an exhibit in advance), and present the document to the witness. The witness will then identify the document and confirm that it is his statement. Counsel may confront the witness with the conflicting language by having the witness read aloud the portion that counsel selected. Counsel may also have the witness read the preceding question (if the statement is in question-and-answer format) and then his own answer to that question. Be sure to control the witness during this maneuver. Focus the witness to do exactly what you want with clear, succinct and direct words. As a result, this is a technique best used with witnesses who have been relatively cooperative during cross examination. If a witness is more inclined to be confrontational with counsel, they are advised to use one of the other methods of impeachment.

> *Example: counsel is impeaching the witness concerning her ability to see a weapon in the waistband of their client. The witness has just testified on direct examination that she "clearly saw the handle of a pistol" tucked into the front of the defendant's waistband. She previously hand wrote a statement to police where she stated that "I did not see any weapon."*

>> *Defense:* You just said on direct examination that you clearly saw the handle of a pistol tucked into my client's waistband. Have I said your word correctly.

Witness: Yes that is what I said and what I saw.

Defense: Ma'am do you remember talking to police the night of the bar fight?

Witness; Yes.

Defense: You gave them a statement that night?

Witness: I guess so. I did write down what I saw that night.

Defense: In your own handwriting?

Witness: Yes.

Defense: Voluntarily?

Witness: Yes.

Defense: When you wrote that statement you had just witnessed the bar fight?

Witness: Yes.

Defense: Showing opposing counsel what has been marked as Defense Exhibit A for Identification. May I approach the witness?

Judge: You may approach.

Defense: Ma'am I am handed you what has been marked as Defense Exhibit Alpha for Identification, a copy of your handwritten statement to police. Do you agree it is your statement?

Witness: Yes.

Defense: Those are your initials at the top of each page?

Witness: Yes.

Defense: That is your signature on the last page?

Witness: Yes.

Defense: Ma'am please read the highlighted portions of your own handwritten statement out loud.

Witness: *(Reading)* I did not see any weapon.

Defense: Thank you. May I have the exhibit back please?

Lawyer impeaches the witness. Lawyers may simply have the witness confirm the existence of the prior statement, reinforce its credibility, and verify the conflicting testimony by quoting it to the witness. This approach removes the necessity of fumbling with the document, since it does not need to be handed to the witness. Based upon the facts in our previous example the inquiry would go like this:

Defense: You just said on direct examination that you clearly saw the handle of a pistol tucked into my client's waistband. Have I said your word correctly.

Witness: Yes that is what I said and what I saw.

Defense: You talked to the police the night of the fight?

Witness; Yes.

Defense: You gave them a statement that night?

Witness: I did.

Defense: A voluntary handwritten statement?

Witness: Yes.

Defense: Showing opposing counsel what has been marked as Defense Exhibit A for Identification for inspection or objection.

Defense: Ma'am I am going to read a portion of your handwritten statement, please listen as I read it. "I never saw a weapon." Did I read your words correctly?

Witness: Yes.

Defense: You wrote these words immediately after the fight?

Witness: Yes.

Defense: You signed it?

Witness: Yes.

Defense: You were truthful to the police?

Witness: I tried to be.

Defense: I see. Let's move on.....

Graphic aid impeaches the witness. Lawyers may wish to convert the documentary statement into a clear graphical aid and then project the document onto a screen. This way the jurors themselves can see the words that damn the witness. Consider how that might work with the same set of facts.

Defense: You just said on direct examination that you clearly saw the handle of a pistol tucked into my client's waistband. Have I said your word correctly.

Witness: Yes that is what I said and what I saw.

Defense: You talked to the police the night of the fight?

Witness;   Yes.

Defense: You gave them a statement that night?

Witness: I did.

Defense: A voluntary handwritten statement?

Witness: Yes.

Defense: Showing opposing counsel what has been marked as Defense Exhibit A for Identification for inspection or objection.

Defense: (To the court) Your honor I ask that we be allowed to publish Defense Exhibit A for ID as demonstrative aid for purposes of impeachment?

Judge: How do you wish to publish?

Defense: We would prefer to use a document camera.

Judge: Objection?

State: As long it is for impeachment purposes only no objection.

Judge: Defense you may publish.

Defense: (Placing the letter on the document camera and displaying it so that all in the courtroom can see it) Ma'am is this your handwritten statement?

Witness: Yes.

Defense: You wrote these words immediately after the fight?

Witness: Yes.

Defense: You signed it?

Witness: Yes.

Defense: Ma'am do you see the highlighted portion of your letter on the display?

Witness: I do.

Defense: Please read the highlighted portion out loud.

Witness: (sighing) I never saw a weapon.

Defense: (Removing the exhibit from the document camera) Thank you. No further questions.

Statement impeaches the witness. When the witness denies making the statement, and the statement does not relate to a collateral matter, counsel may, after the witness has departed, present another witness who over-heard the witness's out-of-court statement or who took the written state-ment from the witness. In such a case, the statement may be admitted for the limited purpose of showing that it was made, unless the statement is admissible as substantive evidence (see FRE 801).

The important facts lawyers should rely upon while validating the prior statement vary, depending on the form of the statement. If the prior state-ment was a sworn statement, then it is important to elicit the fact that the witness had the opportunity to review the statement, initialed each page, took an oath, and signed his name.

PIS Using the 3 C's:

Commit the witness to what she said on direct: *"You told us on direct examination that you saw the accused with a knife, correct?"*

Credit the witness's prior statement and its accuracy: *"You made a statement about this case on July 4th last year?*

Things were fresh in your mind when you made that statement?

You swore to tell the truth before you gave that answer?

You signed the statement?

Initialed the top of each page?

Initialed the bottom of each page?

Made corrections?

When you gave that statement you had never been interviewed by a prosecutor?

When you gave that statement you had not had the opportunity to discuss what happened that night with others who were there?

You have had that opportunity since you gave that statement?"

Confront the witness with the prior statement: *"You said in your July statement, and I quote, 'The accused was not carrying any weapon that I could see.' Those were your words?"*

When should a lawyer impeach? A good rule of thumb is to impeach only on significant inconsistencies. Juries understand that there will be minor variations in detail each time a human tells a story. Repeated attempts to call the witness a liar on the basis of these variations will be perceived as overreaching, rather than effective impeachment of the witness's credibili-ty. Lawyers should make certain there is a true factual inconsistency rather than a mere semantic difference. Recall that the jury has not spent as much time with the details of the facts as counsel has—if the inconsistency is not something that can be clearly, and concisely communicated to them, it is not worth the impeachment. Care should also be taken to ensure that the ability to prove the prior inconsistent statement exists when the rules will allow for the admission of extrinsic evidence to prove the inconsistency. Any evidence used to do so must meet other evidentiary requirements.

F.   Bias and Motive

Bias, prejudice, or any motive to misrepresent may be shown to impeach the witness either by the witness or by evidence otherwise adduced. Such evidence is relevant because it may show that the witness is not an impartial observer or witness of the truth. As long as the impeaching counsel can articulate a theory of why the witness may be predisposed to favor the other side, the evidence should  be admissible. Common law allows this under the theory of bias, prejudice or motive. Each of these issues is not collateral to the testimony of the witness, even when the witness in question is not the victim.

The foundation that must be laid for bias, motive, or prejudice is case-specific and does not require any specific foundational elements. Lawyers can prove bias, prejudice, or motive to lie by direct or circumstantial evidence. To impeach the witness, counsel must persuade the fact-finder that the witness has some reason to perceive or recall events in a skewed manner, or to abandon his oath and become a partisan for one side.

Evidence of bias is not limited only to cross examination of the witness. While the best evidence often may be concessions from the witness himself, supplemental proof may be necessary to give it full impact. Counsel will ordinarily be given wide latitude in proving facts that establish bias. Even if the witness admits his bias, or facts from which bias may be inferred, the judge may permit extrinsic evidence of the same facts, unless such evidence is cumulative. For example, if the witness acknowledges his friendship with the accused, the judge may still allow other witnesses to drive the fact home with specific examples of acts of friendship.

When deciding whether to impeach with bias or motive to lie, lawyers must remember that they cannot use it if they do not have it. Assumptions and stereotypes will not suffice. Successful bias impeachment is developed through thorough pretrial investigation and case analysis. Interview every witness, talk to neighbors and social contacts. Ask your investigators to assist with this effort, even though it goes beyond element-based evidence gathering. In the current era, spending time reviewing witness social media accounts provides ample opportunity to discover areas of bias that may not have been as readily apparent to lawyers of previous years. Counsel need to know as much as possible to prepare for effective impeachments in this area. They should begin this process by asking themselves why the witness is saying something that other evidence contradicts. People are untruthful for a reason, even when they are not aware of it themselves.

Fruitful Areas of Possible Bias:

Lay witnesses: Family relationships, grudges, prior conflicts, romantic interests, friends, racism, common memberships, superior-subordinate relationships, officer-enlisted relationships, threats and coercion, peer pressure

Experts: Defense or prosecution orientation, hourly rate, depth of expertise, academic or real-world experience

Police: Pressure to obtain convictions, fear of disclosing departure from regulations

Suspects: Promise of clemency, threat of adverse action, immunity, avoiding suspicion

Accused: Desire to avoid conviction and punishment

Impeaching witnesses about issues that are obvious to everyone in the courtroom is wasted time. We all know that mothers love their sons. What benefit is received by impeaching a mother about her familial love when she has testified? It may have been pointed out to the jury, but does it matter? Without evidence to the contrary there is little if any reason to belabor the obvious. It is better to subtly establish facts from which bias can be inferred, rather than confronting the witness directly.Establish the predicate facts that add up to bias, prejudice or motive to lie, but "do the math" for the jury during closing argument. However, sometimes the relationship creating the bias can be developed in a very persuasive fashion.

Example: consider the following bias impeachment questions for a jailhouse snitch that has cut a deal with the government:

> *Defense:* You just testified against my client, Johnny.
>
> *Witness:* Yes.
>
> *Defense:* How long have you been in prison now?

Witness: Four years.

Defense: How long is your sentence?

Witness: 16 years.

Defense: So you have 12 years left to do?

Witness: Yes.

Defense: You have family?

Witness: Yes.

Defense: You have children?

Witness: Yes.

Defense: You miss them?

Witness: Of course.

Defense: You have pictures of them in your cell?

Witness: Yes.

Defense: What time of year do you miss them most?

Witness: Holidays.

Defense: They miss you?

Witness: Yes, we are close despite everything.

Defense: Is there anything more important to you than your kids?

Witness: No.

Defense: Wouldn't you like to hold them in your arms again as a free man?

Witness: I will.

Defense: True, but that won't happen until you get out?

Witness: We'll see.

Defense: You might get out sooner now?

Witness: I do not know.

Defense: Maybe after you've testified against Johnny?

Witness: Not for me to say.

Defense: It must have been very hard for you to do this. Family is a powerful motivator, isn't it?

You can hear the sorrow in the voice of the impeaching attorney. The regret at the situation in which the snitch finds himself and the implicit argument that anyone in such a situation must be biased in favor of finding and providing information that would shorten the amount of time before they could hold their children again.

On the other hand if the attorney chooses to just ask the bias question and is foolish enough to ask the witness to sum it up they will, but the lawyer will not like their math. Witnesses usually respond with a dramatic reaffirmation of their oath or a statement of their heartfelt pain in admitting mistakes for the good of the "truth." Control is the better approach.

> ***Example: in the following example a character and fact witness for the defendant in an assault and battery criminal case is impeached based upon bias and prejudice.***

Q: Mr. Jones, you and the defendant, Mr. Smith, work on the same line in the cardboard factory?

A: Yes.

Q: You are both quality control inspectors on the end of the line?

A: Yes.

Q: What is your current position on the line?

A: I am the assistant quality control manager.

Q: You are the assistant quality control manager. Who is the quality control manager?

A: Mr. Smith.

Q: How long have you been his assistant?

A: About eight years.

Q: You got the job when Mr. Smith recommended you for it?

A: Yes.

Q: Who writes your quarterly employee reports?

A: Mr. Smith does.

Q: You work with him on a daily basis?

A: Yes.

Q: You and the defendant are a good quality control team?

A: Best in the plant.

Q: You and the defendant spend time together after work?

A: Sure, all the time.

Q: You go to movies together?

A: Sometimes.

Q: You go to ball games together?

A: We've been to a few.

Q: You are both on the company softball team?

A: Yes.

Q: You guys practice year round, don't you?

A: Yes.

Q: In fact you are the team's star catcher?

A: Yes.

Q: And the defendant is your pitcher?

A: He's the best.

Q: You get along well with Mr. Smith, don't you?

A: What do you mean?

Q: You are good friends?

A: Yes.

Q: He's one of your best friends, isn't he?

A: I guess so.

Q: And you certainly don't want him to go to jail, do you?

A: No.

Q: You don't believe he should be tried, do you?

A: No.

Q: You weren't in the bowling alley the night Mr. Smith hit Mr. Johnson with a spare bowling pin?

A: No.

Q: All you know about the incident has been told to you by Mr. Smith?

A: I guess so.

G.   Defects in Capacity

While there is not a specific federal rule of evidence that addresses the ability of counsel to impeach a witness based upon defects in observation, such defects are not collateral and inquiry is generally permissible. When lawyers prepare the cross examination of a witness who will provide testimony about a visual observation they must consider both the internal and the external factors that may affect the accuracy of such testimony. Internal factors are those physical and mental aspects of the witness that may have impacted their ability to fully and accurately observe, recall, or relate the questioned events.

How to Respond to Objections

When Crossing on Defects in Capacity:

- "A witness may not testify to a matter unless evidence is introduced sufficient to support a finding that the witness has personal knowledge of the matter." *See* FRE 602.
- "The credibility of a witness may be attacked by any party, including the party calling the witness." *See* FRE 607.
- "Leading questions are permitted on cross-examination." *See* FRE 611(c).

External factors are factors that exist outside of the witness but that had an impact on the ability of the witness to observe the questioned events. The lawyer calling the witness will normally try to emphasize the positive internal and external factors supporting the credibility of the witness's observations. They may also try to remove the sting of negative factors by fronting them on direct. When impeaching, lawyers should try to demonstrate as many unreliable factors as possible and arrange them in a way that impacts the overall credibility of the witness's testimony.

The most obvious example of internal physiological factors is poor eyesight, usually combined with a failure to wear prescription eye wear. Other visual factors include color blindness, physical disabilities, age, and night vision. Sometimes a witness has prior training that increases their ability to adequately recall and relate incidents they have observed. The classic example is an experienced police officer or other trained observers. Internal psychological factors include perception, memory and the witness's ability to communicate.

Perception is effected by a variety of factors, such as distorted focus on certain elements of the scene to the exclusion of others. Examples of this type of distorted focus include a preoccupation with the weapon in an assault rather than the facial features of the assailant. Personal expectations, such as bias, stereotypes, interpretations and assumptions also affect the perceptual process. This has led courts to develop model instructions to jurors to assist them in weighing the credibility of eyewitness identifications.

External or environmental factors include such things as exposure time, line of sight, obstructions, lighting, weather, speed of movement, and distance. The traumatic nature of the event observed is also an important external factor that may have an impact on the witness's ability to observe or remember. Lawyers weave external and internal factors together, pointing out to the jury those issues that call into question the validity of the testimony of the witness. This is an artful way of saying that the witness believes what they are telling you, but you should not. When done properly impeachment as to defects in capacity allow counsel to persuade the jury to not believe a witness without ever needing to call the witness a liar. They are instead merely mistaken. This is an easier position to take and a more realistic bar to reach for during this type of cross examination.

4.14 Eyewitness Identification

In any criminal case, the government must prove beyond a reasonable doubt that the defendant was the perpetrator of the crime[s] alleged. You have heard testimony of eyewitness identification. In deciding how much weight to give to this testimony, you may take into account the various factors mentioned in these instructions concerning credibility of witnesses. In addition to those factors, in evaluating eyewitness identification testimony, you may also take into account:

1. the capacity and opportunity of the eyewitness to observe the offender based upon the length of time for observation and the conditions at the time of observation;

2. whether the identification was the product of the eyewitness's own recollection or was the result of subsequent influence or suggestiveness;

3. any inconsistent identifications made by the eyewitness;

4. whether the witness had known or observed the offender at earlier times; and

5. the totality of circumstances surrounding the eyewitness's identification.

Example of Eyewitness Identification Instructions – Model Crim. Jury Instr. 9th Circ. 4.14 (2003).

Because these types of impeachment need not be as confrontational as when an attorney directly challenges the truthfulness of a witness, lawyers should carefully consider the tone they choose to adopt while examining the witness. It is not necessary to adopt a hostile or sarcastic tone when cross examining a witness who is called to testify as to a visual observation. A friendly tone may produce better results in most cases. Even if the witness has given testimony that is adverse to counsel's cause, the goal of such cross examination is simply to elicit facts that affect the witness's ability to observe, interpret, and recall relevant facts accurately, not to beat them up on the stand.

Witnesses are naturally reluctant to concede the inaccuracy of their observations and recollections, especially after they have testified on direct. Lawyers should avoid the temptation to ask a question that directly challenge the accuracy of the witness by reciting the factors bearing on accuracy and then challenging the witness to agree that his original report or testimony was wrong. Besides being argumentative, such ultimate questions usually produce unsatisfactory responses. When confronted with a direct challenge, most witnesses forcefully reassert the certainty of their observations and memory. As a general rule the reliability argument should be saved for summation.

When preparing for impeachment concerning defects in capacity, counsel should take the time to carefully scrutinize the witness's prior statements. They should examine the record for statements by the witness that show a greater certainty about their observations at trial than immediately after the event when they observed it. The intervening preparation for trial can often inadvertently (or purposefully) focus the memory of the witness in a fashion not consistent with their initial unadulterated observations. These inconsistencies may not be sharp enough to clearly qualify as prior inconsistent statements, but they do tend to show that the witness has lost their objectivity over time. When necessary counsel may impeach on this issue, again without ever calling the witness a liar, but showing the jury why their current testimony is just not as useful as what they said earlier.

Example: a group of students in a high school classroom are listening to a lecture. Another person comes into the room and stands quietly for around 15 seconds. They then scream "I can't take it anymore," throwing a pile of papers at the feet of the teacher. They then run out of the room. A witness from the class has been called to testify about this incident on direct examination. The witness stated that they observed the unknown person and identified them as a white male, approximately 5 feet 6 inches tall and weighing around 130 pounds. The witness also stated on direct that the person's hair was blond and their eyes were green.

Q.   You were seated in the classroom when the unidentified person came into the room?

A.   Yes.

Q.   There were forty-three other students in the class?

A.   If don't know. I didn't count them.

Q.   You were there in class to listen to the lecture?

A.   Yes.

Q.   Someone came into class?

A.   I believe so.

Q.   Through an entrance located about 30 feet to the right of the podium?

A.   Yes.

Q.   You were seated in the back?

A.   Yes.

Q.   There were 16 rows of students between you and the person?

A.   Yes.

Q.   How tall are you?

A.   Five feet, three inches.

Q.   You had your laptop?

A.   Yes.

Q.   That laptop is an Apple with a 19 inch screen?

A.   Yes.

Q.   You were typing?

A.   Yes, but I was paying attention.

Q.   So the screen was up?

A.   Yes.

Q.   The screen was between you and the teacher?

A.   Yes.

Q.   She was lecturing and you were typing what you heard?

A.   Correct.

Q.   You want to do well in class?

A.   Yes.

Q.   This was important to you? It might affect your grade?

A.   I guess so.

Q.   You were focused on the teacher when the person entered the room?

A.   Yes, but I did notice him.

Q.   You did not recognize him?

A.   No.

Q.   You noticed nothing remarkable about his clothing?

A.   Nope.

Q.   You didn't look closely when they first came in?

A.   Well, I noticed him walk in the room.

Q.   He looked like a regular student, right?

A.   Right. I figured he might be late for class.

Q.   He did not say anything when he walked in the room?

A.   Not then, no.

Q.   Your attention was focused on the lecture?

A.   Yes.

Q.   You were surprised when the person yelled and threw some papers on the floor?

A.   We all were.

Q.   After he yelled he immediately turned and left the room?

A.   Yes, it happened pretty fast.

Q.   They went out the same way they came in?

A.   Yes.

Q.   Everybody in the class was looking and whispering when this happened?

A.   Yeah.

Q.   You didn't stand up to get a look at him, did you?

A.   No.

Q.   Some of those standing blocked your view?

A.   I suppose.

Q.   You couldn't see the person as he left the room?

A.   Well, I saw him when he threw the papers.

Q.   You could not see him the whole time?

A.   No.

Q.   You did look at the teacher to see what she would do?

A.   Yes.

Q.   When was your last eye examination?

A.   I think it was about two years ago.

Q.   When you had your last eye examination, the doctor prescribed new glasses?

A.   Yes.

Q.   The doctor said your eyesight had become worse and you needed a new prescription?

A.   They were only slightly worse.

Q.   But the doctor gave you a new prescription?

A.   Yes.

Q.   You have had multiple eye examinations over the years?

A.   Yes.

Q.   Each time your prescription has changed?

A.   Yes.

Q.   It has been two years since your last eye exam?

A.   Yes.

H.   Impeachment by Omission

One of the most difficult types of impeachment to accomplish is impeachment by omission or "negative impeachment." The other six forms of impeachment are fundamentally different in that there is another source of information that serves as the basis for the impeachment. When dealing with a situation where impeachment by omission is necessary the witness has just said something important to the case that has never been mentioned before. It is often a piece of information that may very well be case dispositive. It is also the type of fact that if the witness is being truthful, would have reasonably been disclosed at an earlier point in the process. Some jurisdictions frown upon negative impeachment as an accepted form of inquiry. Counsel must review not only the local norms and practices, but find a way to construct an argument to allow impeachment by omission if strictly necessary.

Impeachment by Omission:

- Fact stated for the 1st time during testimony at trial
- Issue is material to the case
- The witness stating the fact either made a prior statement or had the opportunity to make a statement

---

While not identified by a specific evidentiary rule, impeachment by omission falls under relevancy. When the fact is non-collateral in nature opposing counsel can test the validity of the evidence, to include admitting extrinsic evidence to establish that fact in question had not been previously provided when an opportunity to do so presented itself.

The seminal decision a lawyer must make when deciding whether to impeach by omission revolves around the nature of the omission. Impeachment by omission only works if you can set up the impeachment by pointing out the overwhelming importance of the newly disclosed fact. It has to be the type of information that the witnesses would not have kept to themselves prior to trial. Usually this means that the substance of the statement is an answer to a question that any normal person asking about the case would ask prior to trial. Another good indicator is if it is a fact so strong for the witness' side of the case that its existence could have a large impact on the jury's findings in the case. If the omission is not central to the case then the game is usually not worth the candle.

To effectively conduct impeachment by omission the setup of the impeachment is crucial. It is similar in nature to the process that a lawyer uses to credit the validity of an earlier statement when impeaching with a PIS. The foundation for the earlier statement is crucial. When impeaching by omission no earlier statement exists contradicting the in court testimony. Regardless, multiple opportunities do exist to disclose the fact in question before trial. This is the key point that must be brought out in the impeachment by omission. The wind-up is critical. If not done properly the entire process falls flat. This type of impeachment can be difficult to accomplish, but when done properly the results are devastating.

Example: in the following example of an impeachment by omission the witness has just stated on direct examination that she heard the deceased identify his attacker, the accused, while talking to him on the cell phone immediately before he was shot. This came out during testimony on direct examination. The witness has never stated this fact before. She was previously interviewed by two different detectives, testified at the grand jury hearing and has been interviewed by both the state prosecutor and the criminal defense attorney. After picking his jaw up from the floor the defense attorney proceeds as follows:

Q: Mrs. Jones, you just told us on direct examination that you heard Mr. Smith identify his shooter, the defendant, immediately before he was shot?

A: Yes.

Q: You were on the phone with Mr. Smith at the time?

A: Yes.

Q: You could hear him?

A: Yes.

Q: He identified his attacker?

A: Yes.

Q: You then heard the gunshots?

A: The line went dead?

Q: You did not call 911?

A: No.

Q: You did speak with the police eventually?

A: Yes.

Q: They called you?

A: Yes.

Q: They told you they got your number from the deceased's phone?

A: Yes.

Q: They asked to interview you?

A: Yes.

Q: They came to your home?

A: Yes.

Q: You met with the police?

A: Yes.

Q: You met with them twice?

A: Yes.

Q: You answered their questions?

A: Yes.

Q: You wanted to help?

A: Yes.

Q: They told you they got your number from the deceased's phone?

A: Yes.

Q: They asked to interview you?

A: Yes.

Q: They came to your home?

A: Yes.

Q: You met with the police?

A: Yes.

Q: You met with them twice?

A: Yes.

Q: You answered their questions?

A: Yes.

Q: You wanted to help?

A: Yes.

Q: You were truthful?

A: Yes.

Q: They talked with you several hours each time?

A: Yes.

Q: You gave a statement each time?

A: Yes. Well I signed a statement, they typed it.

Q: The cops typed it?

A: Yes.

Q: But you reviewed it?

A: Yes.

Q: You initialed the top of each page?

A: Yes.

Q: The bottom of each page?

A: Yes.

Q: You signed it?

A: Yes.

Q: Promised it was truthful?

A: Yes.

Q: Complete?

A: Yes.

Q: Fair?

A: Yes.

Q: Accurate?

A: Yes.

Q: You never told them you heard the deceased identify the accused as the shooter?

A: I told them but they didn't write it down.

Q: This was a murder investigation?

A: Yes.

Q: You identified the killer?

A: Yes.

Q: It is your testimony now that you told the investigating officer in a homicide case who the killer was but they never wrote it down in your statement?

A: Yes.

Q: When you reviewed the statement you didn't add it?

A: No. I missed it.

Q: You missed it. Is that why you didn't tell the grand jury about it?

A: I was nervous that day and forgot. The state's attorney never asked either.

Q: You never told me when I interviewed you?

A: Yes I did.

Q: Just like you told the police officer?

A: Yes.

Q: Told them both times?

A: Yes.

This is probably as much as a lawyer could do with this particular witness. The idea that she never told anyone this terribly important fact is not credible. The next step would be to call the detectives who took the sworn statements and use them to verify what the witness said, the manner in which the statement was taken, and the investigative steps taken as a result of those interviews. When done there is little, if any chance, that the jury believes this witness. It should be clear now that the devil is in the details. When done properly not only is the witness's credibility irreparably damaged, but closing argument just got a boost as well.

I.   Impeachment by Contradiction

This form of impeachment exists at common law. It occurs when a witness makes an in-court statement that differs from either their out-of-court statements or out-of-court actions. When this occurs, and the issue is one that is not collateral, extrinsic evidence is allowed to prove the contradiction. This type of impeachment is not effective when the lawyer has not done a thorough and continuing case analysis. They cannot stand up and effectively impeach on an issue by contradiction when you have not identified those key disputed questions of fact in light of your case theme and theory.

Impeachment by contradiction calls into question the specific in court statement and casts doubt on all aspects of the witness's testimony. Counsel cannot use impeachment by contradiction when the issue is collateral. Case analysis and preparation ensure that counsel have identified a non-collateral issue for impeachment by contradiction. The trap for this type of impeachment is set on cross examination. Counsel use cross to force contradiction. Either the witness agrees with their version of the fact in controversy or counsel impeaches them with the information that contradicts them. This approach supports the closing argument identified during case analysis and can be devastating when done effective.

J.　Checklist

I.　Primary Goals of Cross Examination:

    a.　Control the witness.

    b.　Establish facts that bolster your theme and theory.

    c.　Establish facts that build up the credibility of your witnesses and diminish the credibility of your opponent's witnesses.

II.　Seven Primary Impeachment Methods:

    a.　Prior untruthful act:　FRE 608(b).

    b.　Prior conviction:　FRE 609.

    c.　Prior inconsistent statement:　FRE 613.

    d.　Bias, prejudice, or motive:　common law.

    e.　Defects in Capacity to Observe, Recall or Relate:　common law.

    f.　Impeachment by Contradiction: common law, FRE 401, 402, 403.

    g.　Impeachment by Omission: common law FRE 401, 402, 403.

III.　Dealing with Witness Credibility:

    a.　Bolstering.

    b.　Impeachment.

    c.　Rehabilitation.

IV.　Should you Impeach:

    a.　Has the witness's testimony factually supported your case?

    b.　Will the chosen method of impeachment destroy the witness's entire credibility or only undermine their truthfulness on the impeached points?

    c.　Can I effectively impeach?

    d.　Will the jury see the impeachment as significant or only a trick?

    e. How does the witness present—basically truthful or basically untruthful?

V. Impeachment with Prior Convictions:

    a. Cross examining the witness with the conviction.

    b. Entering the authenticated record of the conviction.

    c. Testimony by someone present when witness was convicted.

VI. Impeachment with Prior Inconsistent Statements, the 3 C's:

    a. Commit.

    b. Credit.

    c. Confront.

VII. Impeachment By Omission:

    a. Fact stated for the 1st time at trial.

    b. Issue is material to the case.

    c. The witness stating the fact either made a prior statement or had the opportunity to make a statement.

VIII. Impeachment By Contradiction:

    a. Statement in court, and either:

        i. Out of court statement contradicts.

        ii. Out of court actions contradicts.

    b. Issue is material to the case.

    c. Allowed to cross and offer extrinsic evidence through cross or other witnesses.

IX. Maximize the Persuasive Impact of Answers on Cross:

    a. Cluster together all of the facts that enhance and support the impeachment.

    b. Lay out the facts one question at a time leading to your final point.

    c. Identify similar facts based upon your knowledge of human nature and then using them to make your final point.

X. Fundamental Precepts of Cross:

    a. It is a commando raid, not an invasion.

    b. Use primacy and recency.

    c. Avoid the ultimate question.

    d. One-fact questions.

    e. Vary questioning techniques.

f.   Do not play with fire.

g.   Develop control techniques.

XI.   Cross Examination Sequencing:

a.   Do not use chronological order in confrontational cross examinations.

b.   Avoid chronological order in informational cross examinations.

c.   Lay your theme early and often.

d.   Close cross examination with a theme vignette.

e.   When attacking credibility, attack in the first vignette.

f.   Show bias, interest, or motive early in the cross examination.

g.   End with a power vignette.

h.   Develop risky areas only after establishing control of the witness through safe vignettes.

i.   Never lead or end with a risky vignette.

j.   If you have multiple impeachment vignettes, use the cleanest first.

k.   Disperse impeachment vignettes throughout the cross examination.

K.   Evidentiary Rules to Consider During Impeachment

Issue Arising During Impeachment	Applicable Federal Rule of Evidence
Character traits of the victim or accused	404(a), 404(b), 405
Character of a witness for truthfulness	608
Out of court statements offered for the truth of the matter asserted therein (hearsay)	801–807
Offering evidence of other crimes, wrongs & acts (Chapter 10)	404(b)
Prior convictions of a witness	609
Legal relevancy—is the probative value substantially outweighed by the danger of unfair prejudice, et al	403
Logical relevance of the questions	401, 402
Competency of a witness	610

Personal knowledge of the witness	602
Questioning witnesses	611, 614

Table 1 - Potential Evidentiary Rules Applicable During Impeachment

L. Conclusion

This chapter fleshed out our understanding of cross examination so that we can now effectively deal with a witness that is either lying or mistaken. It addressed a crucial set of advocacy skills that occupy a space where case analysis, common sense, and the rules of evidence intertwine to put the "teeth" into cross examination. This skill set is the first step to truly mastering the advanced cross examination techniques where trials are won or lost.

-Notes-

Chapter 9: Advanced Direct & Cross

A. Developing Superior Direct Examinations 363
B. Refreshing Memory 372
C. Past Recollection Recorded 376
D. Developing Superior Cross Examinations..............................379
E. Planning Advanced Direct & Cross Examination....................388
F. Advanced Direct Examination Checklist.................................395
G. Advanced Cross Examination Checklist..................................398
H. Conclusion...400

A. Developing Superior Direct Examinations

1. Start with the Fundamentals

As we begin to look at creating persuasive advanced direct examinations, we must start with the firm foundation discussed in Chapter 5. There, you learned the fundamentals of direct examination. You should remember that advocates use open-ended questions during direct examination except when dealing with foundational issues or when otherwise allowed to lead by the court. Use these fundamentals to assist you in focusing the direct examination on showcasing the witness. We showcase witnesses to increase their believability.

While a deft touch is required to manage the flow of information from the witness to the jury without impeding its believability, the organization of the presentation is a key focus of an advanced approach to direct examination. You must carefully consider the final point that you wish to make with the direct, as well as

---

Advanced Direct Examinations:

- Prepare using case analysis
- Organize logically
  - Brief
  - But sufficient
- Use simple language, use
  - Tone
  - Body position
  - Movement
- Use exhibits
- Use guideline phrases
  - Headlines
  - Orientations
  - Transitions
  - Coupling questions
- Set the scene, use
  - Background
  - Descriptive words
  - Action words
- Build on the witness's answers

---

those intermediate points that increase the persuasive impact of the witness. A careful arrangement of the witness's story is a key component in the difference between a workmanlike direct examination and one that sings.

The checklist you develop for each witness serves admirably as the bones of an advanced direct examination, but it is only the first step in developing superior directs. The manner in which you present it will further emphasize, or reduce, the importance of certain parts. Never forget that direct examination is an educational opportunity. You are teaching the members of the jury a set of facts in the most persuasive fashion possible. Determining the focus of the presentation is the crux of the matter.

Your initial case analysis drives the structure and substance of each direct examination, including the subsequent witness case analysis you must perform for each witness called. You build your directs upon the bones of those facts and issues already identified. Tools that you can use to further develop advanced direct examinations include the concepts of time, location, and structure. Let us begin by discussing time.

2. Time

You should always consider the element of time in the direct examination. Life occurs at a steady pace, but all of us know that storytelling does not accurately reflect the mundane elements of life. When we read a book or watch a television show we can see that time is compressed in some places, edited out in others and expanded during those times of importance. Advanced direct examinations use a sophisticated understanding of time to drive the length, organization and specificity of questions.

We can break the witness's testimony down into small component parts by carefully choosing the scope and focus of our questions. Accepted techniques include beginning with a broad overview, focusing on a small piece, bouncing back out to a general point with a headline and then returning to specificity—when it complements and supports the focus of our case analysis. This should sound familiar to you. It is a concept reflecting the building blocks present in our discussion of questioning techniques. It is yet another reason why you must properly develop them. They allow you to play with time to highlight, or lessen, the impact of witness testimony during direct examination.

3. Location

Location and point of view are two additional tools you have on direct examination to tell the story of the witness. These two concepts are complementary to one another, but distinct. Location comes into play when setting the scene for action that is to follow, establishing the validity of the witness's ability to observe, recall, or relate, and creating a moral argument about the activity of the witness based upon the physical circumstances confronting the witness. The discussions in this book concerning the use of natural language, clear/concise words, and witness preparation, as well as the use of exhibits, are all designed empower you to properly identify and use the locations in the stories of your witnesses to increase the validity of the stories they are sharing with the jury.

> *"When you rehearse a play 60% of your time is spent practicing entrances. If they work the rest of the play has a chance."*
>
> \JOSHUA KARTON

Point of view is related to location, but different in that it also has the ability to explain differences between witness testimonies. It allows you to explain how two witnesses can both testify truthfully, but be inconsistent on key issues. Oftentimes, the inconsistencies are a result of the witness's point of view and their limited understanding of what they observe. This bleeds into our earlier discussion of impeachment as it related to the ability to observe, recall, and relate. It allows you to show how two witnesses can believe themselves truthful yet their testimony is in fact contradictory. This is often caused by their incomplete ability to either understand what they have seen or to share it with others. Point of view allows you to explain inconsistencies—or establish them—depending upon *your* point of view, so to speak.

4. Structure

Do not forget that the jury is hearing the witness's story for the first time. They will not be able to make the leaps of inference and logic you have trained yourself to make through extensive exposure to the witness and the case as a whole. They will get it, but only if the story is properly told. Do not commit the unpardonable advocacy sin of assuming the jury is stupid. They may lack knowledge; educate them and you will reap the benefits. In order to properly develop the right mind set to creating structure, you must be receptive to the information surrounding you. A commitment to learning, to absorbing everything that is relevant is a crucial component in this process.

When trying to determine what topics will accomplish this ultimate goal, remember that just as all roads lead to Rome, all actions at trial lead to your closing argument. You must understand the connection between your witness's testimony and your closing argument. If you see how one leads into the other, you can make intelligent decisions about structure and presentation of witness testimony. Remember, you address both your weaknesses and your strengths during a superior direct examination.

> *"Be a sponge, not a spear."*
>
> MARK CALDWELL

You must consider the connection between your "grabber" in the opening statement and witness testimony. How will this phrase be built into the witness testimony? Will it come from the witness or will it be a part of your questions—or both? A grabber that is not used during witness testimony is like a great movie preview that misleads you about the actual film. In the end, it leaves the audience wanting something else and vaguely upset about the misleading tack taken by the advocate. Do not make this mistake—use the tools of organization we discussed previously to increase the jury's understanding of the witness's testimony.

You must plan each witness's testimony: background, substantive testimony, and an ending. The fact-finder should feel as though they are listening in on a conversation that focuses the witness on providing relevant and admissible information in an interesting and believable manner; one that also supports your theme and theory. Background information questions introduce the witness to the jury and explain the relevancy of their testimony. Spend sufficient time to ensure that the introduction of the witness and development of her background contribute to your moral theme, factual theory, or legal theory without wasting time.

> **Grabber Test:**
>
> *"If they accept this much, can I win the case with it?"*
>
> JOSHUA KARTON

Each discrete section of substantive testimony uses these advanced techniques to establish those facts supporting your case theme and theory. You must present substantive blocks tied to these goals. Opportunities for blocks of narrative exist within each section and should be used in an advanced direct examination. The goal is to produce a series of stories which are complete in and of themselves but which also contribute to the overall story of the witness. Well-built advanced directs seamlessly accomplish this goal without seeming complex. When properly developed, complexity breeds simplicity in presentation, which makes it easier for the jury to follow along.

The advice about making your direct examination end on a question that focuses the jury on your theme or theory is crucial, however you do not want your last question subject to suppression by a timely objection. The direct cannot end with a whimper; it must resonate in the mind of the jury. If done properly, it echoes in the courtroom after the witness has left.

The last point that you must consider when developing advanced directs is not only how they work internally, but also how they connect to one another in the overall scheme of your case-in-chief. You can start with the idea that primacy and recency suggests that you begin with a strong witness, put weak witnesses in the middle, and end with a strong witness. You should consider this advice as a starting point, but only a starting point. Stories develop over time, and some witnesses are just not interesting. A judicious use of witnesses that pop, interspersed with witnesses that are necessary but mundane, works well.

The overall flow of information from one witness to another should reflect your chosen organizational construct for the case. Sometimes, this is topical, sometimes it is a mosaic, and other times it is a chronology. It can also be story-driven. It might even work based upon the "grabber" in the case. When the structure of individual witnesses reflects the structure of the story of the case you create internal consistency that increases believability. You must order witnesses in the most persuasive way.

Many times a chronological order comporting with your theory of the case is very effective because it is easy to follow. Remember, humans will always attempt to place into context what they hear. If you don't give them a context, they will create one, and it will probably *not* be one that accrues to the benefit of your client. The chronological approach is always good but it may not be the best. If you have one or two particularly powerful witnesses, consider primacy and recency. If you have a witness that will evoke sympathy for your case, consider using them first. ("If they believe my expert, I'll win" versus "If they want me to win, they'll believe my expert"). The order of witnesses and exhibits should support your theme and theory. It should follow the story you developed in your opening statement, and flow into the arguments you intend to make in closing.

5. Advanced Direct Examination Techniques

The following techniques make up a series of issues that you should have in mind as you prepare your direct examination. Using them in combination with your fundamental questioning skills, case analysis development, and knowledge of procedure will create direct examinations that persuade. Consider the following:

- **Introduce the witness:**   Introduce the witness and develop the necessary background to connect the witness with the case. This is the internal introduction that places the witness in context for the jury. It must be sufficiently developed to assist the jury in understanding why they should listen to this witness, but not so developed that it becomes the central portion of the case—unless it just so happens to be the core of the case. There are two dangers here. The first is the witness is not introduced sufficiently and the jury misses the connection between this witness and the issues at trial. This can normally be rectified, but it is lost time. Every moment that a juror is thinking "Why is this person testifying?," is a moment they are not paying attention. The second danger is the introduction of the witness overwhelms the substance of their testimony. When this happens the response of the jury is often "Why did the attorney think that was important? I liked the witness but what they had to say was just not that important." Either one of these responses does not effectively increase the persuasiveness of the witness testimony.

- **Describe the scene:** This sets the stage for the action to follow. It must create a world that supports the story of the witness. Details matter here.   The witness must fully explain the relevant scene, using words that work. Descriptive words are a **must** here. Witnesses often wish to testify in a conclusory fashion and lawyers like to ask conclusory questions. Convert subjective witness descriptions into more objective and meaningful ones. If a witness testifies that it was "dark," ask a number of follow-up questions to flush out the details, such as, "Was it too dark to read a newspaper headline?" Advocates set the scene, tell the story, and paint pictures with words. Be an advocate, not a lawyer.

- **Describe the action:**   Elicit visual and sensory images through testimony. An effective direct examination should paint a picture of what occurred. The key here is to use language in a way that creates visuals. This is easier to accomplish when using exhibits and demonstrations.

- **Let the witness tell the story all the way through**. Do not interrupt to clarify minor points. This can break the logical flow of testimony, cause jury confusion, and get the witness off-track. After the witness tells the story completely, go back and cover items that need to be clarified or emphasized. Use exhibits to clarify or emphasize testimony. This allows for repetition and creates believability.

- **Repeat the action:** Have the witness go over key moments or details. Your goal is to have the witness cover important facts three times. You do this by going through the story of the witness's testimony at a general level, returning to the different topics within the testimony has separate lines of inquiry designed to produce more detail, and then reiterating it one last time by using exhibits. This order can be flipped when either the story or the issues support doing so.

- **Present exhibits or demonstrations:** Present photographs, diagrams, and exhibits to explain the witness's testimony. It is important to show the jury relevant photographs and diagrams for the same reason it is important for you to visit the scene—you learn from walking in the footsteps of the witness. So does the jury. Conduct demonstrations to amplify key points and teach through repetition. Always explore how exhibits can be used to enhance testimony; they attract the jury's attention, clarify testimony, increase retention, and persuade. When deciding to use an exhibit you should consider:

  - **Type:**

    - **Real evidence, both fungible and non-fungible.** Real evidence is evidence that has a historical connection to the crime. Use it. You cannot show them to the jury until relevancy, foundation, and authenticity have been established. After you admit the evidence, request permission to publish it to the jury while the testimony is fresh in their minds.

    - **Photographs and videos.** If you do not have real evidence, use photographs or videos to provide demonstrative explanations of witness testimony. Use photographs of real evidence if you cannot produce the real evidence. Consider the following pointers to maximize their impact:

      - Enlarge photos when possible.

      - Mount photos. Large photos can be handled better if mounted on a firm backing. It works even better if you can publish them through a projector and display software. Make certain that the system works, and that the resolution does not distort the evidence.

- Use succession. Use photos or videos in chronological succession to track events as they occurred. Creating witness testimony that moves from photo to photo in a successive development of testimony can be extremely persuasive to the jury.

- **Diagrams.** Diagrams help witnesses explain their testimony, especially when showing the layout of building or setting the scene for specific testimony. Diagrams must be easy for the jury to both see and understand. Good diagrams persuade, bad ones confuse and irritate.

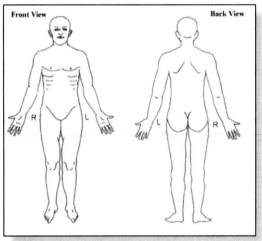

Consider some of the following techniques when using diagrams:

- Large lettering.

- Vary colors.

- Professional appearance.

- Clear, simple labels—clearly label all items depicted on the diagram—use sequential letters and numbers.

- Proper marking—mark the diagram as the witness testifies, or have the witness mark—ensure you point to the item on the diagram being marked and describe the mark for the record.

- Scale—while diagrams are not required to be to scale, you should strive for accuracy—at a minimum, orient the diagram with an arrow depicting which direction is "North."

o **Visual memory.** Photographs, diagrams, and real evidence cause the jury to see the testimony. This boosts retention. Emphasize important testimony with exhibits, but make sure you do not overdo it. Everything is not equally important. Select exhibits based on what you think are the most important facts that support your theory. Focus on quality, not quantity.

o **Relevance.** Avoid exhibits that are merely interesting. Focus on significant details that advance an issue in your case. Particular attention must be given to the ability of the exhibit to "assist" the witness in explaining what happened.

o **Weaknesses.** Consider the counter-attack. Think about whether your opponent can use the exhibit against you.

o **Prepare exhibits.** Examine all exhibits you intend to use well before trial. You do not want them to contain conflicting information. Be keenly aware of all markings, contents, and physical characteristics. If admitted, the jury will have the item during deliberations and examine it without you being present. Mark all exhibits you intend to admit and admit anything you can before trial. This will reduce unnecessary delays and objections. Have copies ready for opposing counsel, the judge, and the jury.

o **Track exhibits.** It is easy to lose track of what has been offered and admitted into evidence. Use a simple chart to keep track and refer to it during conferences with the judge before the jury deliberates.

o **Know the mechanics.** You must be proficient at handling exhibits in the courtroom. Commit exhibit handling "boilerplate" to memory or have a written guide at trial.

• **Use non leading questions.** Avoid complex questions that may confuse the witness. Do not insert unsolicited facts or legal conclusions into your questions, it will reduce your credibility and draw objections that detract from the flow of your case. Flow is key during witness testimony. You do not want to remind the jury that you are a lawyer presenting information to persuade them to do something. They should never see the hand of persuasion.

• **Demonstrations.** When physical activity is relevant, demonstrate it. Demonstrating an event or displaying an injury can greatly enhance your direct examination. If you decide to perform a demon-stration—rehearse. Ask the judge for permission to conduct the demonstration and ensure you do not obstruct the jury's view. Describe the demonstration accurately for the record and measure distances ahead of time so that you get it right in the courtroom.

- **Documentary evidence.** Keep it simple. Keep the number of documents to the minimum necessary to prove your case. If you have voluminous records to present, segregate the significant parts and make them separate exhibits. Present the documentary evidence with a live witness who can explain the document and translate any technical or unfamiliar terms for the jury. Consider enlarging key or complex documents and having them either mounted or projected.

This group of techniques builds upon the lessons you learned earlier in this text. You should understand and internalize the belief that each of these techniques focuses on persuasion—as you should, too.

B. Refreshing Memory

For the advocate, the courtroom is home. They know it, understand it, and have spent countless hours in practice and study with the goal of being able to stand and deliver in the well of the courtroom when the time is right. For witnesses at trial, they feel like they are in a strange and different land and approach the courtroom experience from a different place. Unless they are professional witnesses, such as law enforcement personnel or experts, they do not have much experience with testifying. Their concepts of what to expect have been driven by books, movies, and television. As a result, a lot of stress is associated with testifying, even when the witness intends to tell the truth.

That stress and worry leads to mistakes. Such mistakes include forgetting information or misstating information. The forgetful witness is a common feature of trial practice. Witnesses are not necessarily lying when they cannot remember an issue; they just cannot recall what it is the advocate is desperately trying to get them to say. This often leads to additional stress, making it even more difficult to remember what happened. Fortunately, the Federal Rules of Evidence recognize this very human response and provide a template for dealing with the effects of allowing recollections to be refreshed.[1]

---

[1] *See* Fed. R. Evid. 612.

When faced with a witness who cannot recall a particular fact, advocates can try to refresh her memory by referring to a writing, a document, or other aid. This is commonly known as "refreshing recollection." The goal is to simply assist the witness in remembering what they already know by using a document or other object to "jog" their memory and remind them of the facts. There are few, if any, limitations on the means advocates can use to refresh a witness's recollection. Some common aids include letters, objects, documents, magazines, newspaper clippings, income tax returns, smells, police reports, notes, photographs, prior testimony, and tape recordings.

While the limitations on the type of item that can be used are relatively small, it is important that advocates procedurally follow the steps laid out when refreshing recollection. The primary concern is to make certain that, after the witness's memory is refreshed, they testify based upon what they remember and not what is in the document. To that end, certain foundational steps must be used by the advocate when refreshing the witness's recollection.

Foundation for Refreshing Recollection:

Witness states she cannot recall a fact or event;

Witness states that a particular writing or other aid could help jog her memory;

Witness is given the writing to read silently to herself;

Witness returns the writing to counsel;

Witness states that the writing has refreshed her memory; and

Witness testifies to the fact or event, without further aid of the writing.

In actual practice, refreshing recollection is usually accomplished as follows:

Q. Agent Edwards, what was the address of the house where you first encountered the accused on the date of his apprehension?

A. *I can't remember. I know it was in Niles Township, but I can't remember anything more specific.*

Q. Is there anything you could review which would help you remember?

A. *Yes. I made a report shortly after the apprehension.*

Q.   Agent Edwards, I'm handing you what has been marked as
     Prosecution Exhibit 5 for Identification, a copy of which I
     am handing to the defense. What is it?

A.   It's a copy of the report I made regarding this case.

Q.   Please read it over silently to yourself. (pause)

Q.   I have retrieved Prosecution Exhibit 5 for Identification
     from the witness. Agent Edwards, does that refresh your
     memory?

A.   Yes.

Q.   What is the address of the house where you first en-
     countered the accused on the day of his apprehension?

A.   It was 1551 Ferndale Boulevard.

When done properly, refreshing recollection is a seamless process that allows the advocate to remind the witness of what they already know without making a big deal out of it. It is not a disaster that the witness cannot
remember, but merely a normal
human reaction to a stressful
situation.

The advocate who cannot calmly handle refreshing recollection
runs the risk of creating an impression in the jury's mind that
the witness is trying to "pull a
fast one" or is less credible because of the need to refresh recollection. This is a skill that is
easily mastered if you practice
it.   With that precept in mind,

> **Suggested Keywords to Prompt the
> Witness for Refreshing Memory:**
>
> • Do you recall anything else?
>
> • Would anything help you to refresh
>   your recollection?
>
> • Is there anything that would assist
>   you in prompting your memory of
>   what happened that day?
>
> • What would help remind you of
>   those facts?

you must explain the elements of the foundation for recorded recollection
to your witness before trial and rehearse with them so that both of you are
comfortable with the process. Make sure they know that there is nothing
wrong with failing to remember and reading a piece of paper on the stand
to refresh their memory.

You should decide which cue words you will use to prompt the witness. A
suggested approach is: "Do you recall anything else?" "Not that I remember." "Would anything help you to refresh your recollection?"   "Yes."
"What is that?" Practice those specific phrases with your witnesses during
preparation. Do not be afraid to use this technique. It is in no way sneaky
or under-handed.   Instead, it is a legitimate advocacy tool and especially
appropriate for witnesses testifying about technical data, easy-to-forget

matters such as dates, license plates, serial numbers and scientific data, as well as for the young or nervous witness.

The only danger areas in refreshing recollection from an objections perspective occur when advocates fail to follow procedures. Be exact about the procedure. Withdraw the document so the witness testifies from memory (albeit her refreshed memory) and not from the piece of paper. Distinguish the use of a document to refresh memory from use of the document as a substitute for testimony, which will require an exception to the hearsay rules.

When you are refreshing memory, the testimony, not the document, is the evidence. However, you still mark the document as an exhibit and it becomes part of the record although it is not admitted into evidence. You must show a copy of the document you use to refresh the witness's memory to opposing counsel. More importantly, opposing counsel can introduce into evidence the portions your witness relies upon. You must ensure that it does not contain embarrassing or unhelpful information to your case. Do not try to be sneaky and use an excerpt from a document if the full document will harm your case. Although the full document is potentially admissible, you should be careful to mask the document so that irrelevant or

---

Seven Principles of Past Recollections:

- Witnesses will forget essential facts.
- Memorize the foundational elements for refreshing memory and past recollection recorded or know where to find those foundations when your memory fails.
- Memory can be refreshed by any document.
- Past recollection recorded must be a document made or adopted by the witness when the matter is fresh in the witness's memory.
- Documents used merely to refresh memory are not admitted into evidence.
- Documents qualifying as past recollection recorded may be admitted, but are only read to the fact-finder unless offered by the adverse party.
- Plan, prepare, and practice with each witness.

---

privileged information cannot be read Have a masked copy and an original ready for inspection.

When you are on the opposing side, always take the time to read the entire document. Be sure to object if refreshing the witness's memory sounds unduly suggestive or prompts the witness in a way you think the jury ought to know. If you are given the opportunity to be present during an out-of-court witness refreshment, do not decline and go to lunch. You never know what you might learn. Finally, remember that even though the writing is read into evidence, it is not taken back with the jury members into deliberations unless offered by the adverse party.

C. Past Recollection Recorded

Sometimes, despite your best efforts to refresh recollection, you are un-successful. When that happens, the witness cannot independently remember a particular fact about which he has been called to testify. If a written record of the earlier fact or event exists, the writing may qualify as an exception to the hearsay rule and be introduced into evidence as past recollection recorded. The jury can then consider it substantively.[2]

In order to admit evidence pursuant to FRE 803(5), the advocate must lay a proper foundation to show that the witness cannot remember, but earlier in time could remember and that a record of that memory was made. The following elements establish the foundation for introducing evidence of a

> **FRE 803(5) Recorded recollection.**—A memorandum or record concerning a matter about which a witness once had knowledge but now has insufficient recollection to enable the witness to testify fully and accurately, shown to have been made or adopted by the witness when the matter was fresh in the witness' memory and to reflect that knowledge correctly. If admitted, the memorandum or record may be read into evidence but may not itself be received as an exhibit unless offered by an adverse party.

past-recorded fact as an exception to the hearsay rule for a witness's present recall of that fact.

Here is an example of a foundation by defense counsel:

Q. Mr. Simpson, did you see the automobile as it sped away?

A. *I was on the ground, but I looked up and saw the license plate.*

Q. What was the tag number?

---

[2] See Fed. R. Evid. 803(5).

A. *I don't recall. I know it was a Missouri tag, but I can't remember the numbers.*

Q. Is there anything that would help you to recall?

A. *Yes, I thought the number would be important so I scribbled it down a few minutes later when I found some paper.*

NOTE: At this point, you would lay the same foundation you would to refresh recollection under FRE 612.

Q. I'm handing you what's been marked as Defense Exhibit D for Identification, a copy of which I have provided the government. What is it?

A. *It's the note I made of the license number.*

Q. Please take a moment to read it over.(pause)

Q. I'm retrieving Defense Exhibit D for Identification from the witness. Now, Mr. Simpson, please tell the jury the number of the license plate

A. *Sir, I know it's going to sound strange, but I still can't remember.*

Q. Mr. Simpson, think again about Defense Exhibit D for Identification.   When did you write this note?

A. *About 10 minutes after the car sped away with the guys who stole my wallet.*

Q. Are you sure it is accurate?

A. *Yes. I kept repeating the license number to myself until I had a pencil and paper.*

Q. I'm handing you again Defense Exhibit D for Identification. Your honor, I ask the court's permission for Mr. Simpson to testify from past recollection recorded using Defense Exhibit D for Identification.

J. Objection?

P. None.

J. *The witness may testify.*

Q. Tell the jury the numbers on the license plate.

A. *It was a Missouri plate with the number TGV 8765.*

Q. Your honor, the defense offers Defense Exhibit D for I.D. into evidence as Defense Exhibit D and asks that it be published to the jury.

P. The government objects your honor. The evidence is the witness's testimony, not the actual exhibit.

J. Agreed. The exhibit will not be published.

Unlike refreshing memory, in past recollection recorded you are offering an out-of-court statement (the contents of the contemporaneous writing) as evidence for the truth of its contents. This creates a hearsay issue that is not present when the memory is merely refreshed. The focus of analysis is on the ultimate source of the information. If it comes from the witness's memory, then there is no hearsay issue, although there may very well be potential cross examination concerning defects in capacity.

If the source of the information is an out-of-court statement, there is a hearsay issue and the statement must fall into a hearsay exception. The

---

Foundation for Past Recollection Recorded:

* *Witness cannot remember a fact or event on the stand;*
* *Witness had firsthand knowledge at one time;*
* *That knowledge is reflected in a memorandum or record made at or near the time the fact or event occurred, made or adopted by the witness;*
* *Record was accurate and complete when made;*
* *Record is in same condition now as when made; and*
* *Witness still cannot completely and accurately recall the fact or event even after reviewing the record.*

---

hearsay statement is admissible under past recollection recorded because it carries sufficient circumstantial guarantees of trustworthiness that are derived from the fact that the statement was made at or near the time of the incident. It is important to note that the witness on the stand does not necessarily need to have been the one who made the writing. As long as the witness adopted the written document, it suffices for purposes of FRE 803(5). The test is whether or not the witness adopted the record, if the record was made at or near the time of the event, and the witness testifies. If the test is satisfied, the record accurately reflects the facts.

When dealing with these issues it always looks better to the jury if your witness can testify from present memory. If the witness cannot remember, first try to refresh their memory. If the witness still cannot remember, then

lay the foundation for past recollection recorded. When you refresh memory, keep in mind that,
although the witness may read
from the document, the evidence
is testimonial – the oral statement
of the witness – not documentary.
The writing itself should not be
admitted into evidence unless of-

> Control is not rude, it is focused
> and analytical questioning while
> remaining professional and hu-
> man when asking them.
>
> *Kindness kills – the witness.*

fered by the opposing counsel. On the other hand, if you have to use past
recollection recorded, the document is the evidence, not the testimony of
the witness.

D.   Developing Superior Cross Examinations

1. Getting Beyond the Fundamentals

In Chapter 7, you learned the fundamental techniques of cross examination, techniques that are part and parcel of successfully interrogating witnesses. You developed core competencies, including basing cross examination on the theme and theory of your case, organizing cross examination
for maximum logical persuasive impact, and using the proper form of
questions and techniques to ensure witness control.

You must approach cross examination with the idea that the advocate
chooses the time, the place, and the manner of confrontation. It is also a
given that most witnesses will not give you "push back" on uncontroverted
facts during cross examination. In other situations, however, the cooperat-
ing witness on cross examination is
an uncommon occurrence. At some
point in every cross examination,
you are going to have to deal with
witness behavior that challenges
your authority. If you have not prepared for that occurrence, you may
very well respond in a way that undermines the goals that you have set
for cross examination. In the words
of Steve Prazenka: "If you learn it
right, you'll do it right the rest of
your life.   If you learn it wrong,
you'll do it wrong and spend the
rest of your life trying to learn to do

**Maximize the Persuasive Impact
of Answers on Cross:**

- Cluster together all of the facts
  that enhance and support the
  topic

- Lay out the facts one question at
  a time leading up to your final
  point

- Identify similar facts based upon
  your knowledge of human nature
  and then using them to make
  your final point

it right."[3]

This section is designed to help you learn it right. It considers the most common problems arising during cross examination, proposing solutions for you to practice and implement when the time is right. One of the reasons advanced cross examination can become difficult has to do with the reaction of the advocate to the situation they find themselves in when the witness balks. By its very nature, cross examination addresses an adverse witness. The advocate identifies certain goals to achieve during cross examination and the witnesses usually focus on making certain that their story does not change. The witness is worried about being made to look foolish or, even worse, untruthful. This causes the witness to become difficult in a variety of ways. At the same time, the advocate is worried they will not be able to control the witness. Control does not mean being cross, it means being focused and analytical in choosing questions while remaining professional and human when asking them.

Determining If You Should Impeach a Witness:

* Has the witness's testimony factually supported your case?
* Will the impeachment destroy the witness's entire credibility or only undermine their truthfulness on the impeached points?
* Can I effectively impeach?
* Will the jury see the impeachment as significant or only a lawyer trick?
* How does the witness present: basically truthful or basically untruthful?

The advocate is waiting for that moment when the witness goes south and says the thing that should not be said. The advocate does not want to allow that to happen because it cuts against the entire purpose of the cross examination. So you have two entities filled with emotion in a situation that may very well lead to direct confrontation. Both may in fact be seeking control of the presentation. It is ripe for disaster. The experienced advocate and the experienced witness, whether expert or otherwise, know this. Add to this the likelihood that miscommunication between the witness and the lawyer may very well be the stressor that makes the tenor of the cross examination change. While that is not the primary focus of ad-

---

[3] Steve Prazenka was a platoon sergeant and he trained Colonel David Hackworth, who was one of the most decorated American soldiers of the last century. RANDOLPH T. HOLHUT, COL. DAVID HACKWORTH: A MAN WHO TRULY SUPPORTED OUR TROOPS, May 24, 2005. http://cirrocsworld.blogspot.com/2005/05/col-david-hackworth.html (accessed on Apr. 14, 2010).

vanced cross examination, the section will discuss some strategies for dealing with such situations.

You need to employ advanced cross examination techniques at your most vulnerable point from a cross examination perspective. That vulnerability may come from the expertise of the witness, the degree of preparation that the advocate has engaged in prior to cross examination, and the attitude of the witness. Sometimes a witness can be prepared to be difficult and sometimes the witness is difficult regardless of your preparation. In most situations, the difficulty comes from the fear of an unknown situation that by its very nature engenders an adverse reaction by the advocate at a moment when the advocate is most vulnerable. If you have prepared properly to deal with it before they occur, you can avoid the pitfalls they represent.

Consider the following: You have been working on a case for months; the preparation is complete. Questions have been drafted, and your theme and theory of the case is clearly identified. You gave a wonderful opening statement. The main witness for the opposing side testifies on direct and you stand to cross examine them. After your first question, something totally unexpected flows out of their mouth. Something you have never heard before, something quite frankly so unbelievable you don't even know where to begin. Your hands began to sweat. Your eyes tightened slightly. You feel that primal urge to reach across the courtroom grab the

witness and rip their tongue from their mouth.

You must resist this urge. Now is the time to proceed in a way that empowers you and does not turn the cross examination into a wrestling match with a pig. Remember the old adage, when you wrestle with a pig you both get dirty and only the pig enjoys it. The witness has just turned himself into a big mud-covered pig in the middle of the courtroom. While the advocate cannot let the witness wiggle away, the cross examination must be accomplished in a manner that gets the pig under control while at the same time keeping the lawyer clean. The goal is to wrestle the pig, putting them back in their place while keeping the mud exactly where it belongs, on the witness's face and not the advocate's.

2. Advanced Cross Examination Techniques

The following techniques will assist you in wrestling the pig. They are a series of issues that you should always have in mind as you prepare cross examinations. Using them in combination with your fundamental questioning skills, case analysis development, and knowledge of procedure will create cross examinations that persuade. Difficult witnesses during cross examination fall into several different categories. They include: (1) nonresponsive witnesses, (2) the runaway witness, (3) the forgetful witness, (4) the authoritative witness, and (5) the expert witness. Each of these can present difficult challenges to the advocate performing the cross examination. Fortunately, there are strategies that you can learn from a skills perspective that enable you to deal with each situation on the stand. These techniques build upon the fundamental concepts of cross examination we learned in Chapter 6.

a. Handling Witnesses

The nonresponsive witness[4] can be the worst potential nightmare of the unprepared cross-examiner. They refuse to answer questions and fight to get their own version of events before the jury. Often they descend into verbose narratives that are at best tangentially related to the advocate's query. They sometimes have a tendency to not respond to the proffered question at all. There are as many different techniques for handling the unresponsive witness as there are styles of lawyering. These are based in part on the personalities involved. You should choose the technique that works for you. When doing so, consider the circumstances, your own personal style, and the people involved. The idea behind this approach is that you do not have to be cross to effectively cross the nonresponsive witness. You must be controlled, professional, and focused. If you do not descend into a table-pounding and sarcasm-laden advocate, you can use attitude to assert control. Attitude is extremely important, but it must be the right attitude. Never forget that you ultimately have power over the witness, subject only to the objections of opposing counsel, actions by the court, and your own ethos. You can project attitude without being rude through the use of tone of voice, inflection, and cadence. Sometimes, you only need to slow down to assert control. Think of the nonresponsive witness as someone who is interrupting your presentation in a non-helpful fashion. You must respond to this person in a way that gets them to stop, but does not muddy the waters of your presentation. Let us consider some specific techniques.

---

4 Posner and Dodd refer to this witness alternatively as either nonresponsive or "runaway."

i. Stay Engaged

There is a real tendency to disengage with a witness that is nonresponsive. We might look down, sigh, stare up to the heavens in disgust, or roll our eyes. None of these help. Keep eye contact. Focus on the witness. Look them in the eye and consider carefully what they have just said. Sometimes, the silence is enough to bring them back in line. You are not attempting to threaten them; you are merely promising to follow through with your assigned task. It can be easy for them, it can be cordial, or it can be hard. This is not an attempt to stare them down the way you would a mad dog. It is instead an acknowledgement of their presence in the courtroom, delivered sometimes with a bit of puzzlement over their choice of answers. Looking them in the eye is crucial when there is a pending question. In between questions, you can look at notes or whatever else you need to refer to in preparing the next question. When asking the question, however, as well as when receiving the answer, you must be focused on the witness. Eye contact is a good way to stay engaged. Body position is also an important technique you can use to show focused attention on the witness.

Your physical movements when dealing with the nonresponsive witness are crucial. You cannot allow nervous energy to pull you around the courtroom like a dog on a leash. Remain still while posing your question and waiting for the answer. You can move between questions. We have discussed previously the impact that something as simple as taking a step toward the witness can have in asserting control. This diagram shows in visual detail how moving closer to the witness between questions can be effective. The point here is to make the movements match the questions. Physicality supports the verbal, enhancing retention and focusing the witness. Let us talk about listening to the answers the witness gives you.

You must listen to the witness carefully. The nonresponsive witness often offers up a "gem" in their nonresponsive answer. It can lead to one of your other identified series of questions or it might create an additional line of impeachment. At other times the answer may be so much hot air, signifying nothing. If you are not actively listening to the witness, you will not be able to take the best next step in dealing with their answer. This can be hard to do because you have a lot going on. There are additional questions to consider, language to formulate, judges to deal with, and all this while watching out for opposing counsel. None of this matters as much has hearing correctly what has just been said. You must listen actively to properly control the witness.

One way to ensure that you actively listen is to not move when the witness is answering. Train yourself to be still, receiving information without distraction. It is a polite technique that has the added benefit of intimidating the witness, sometimes all the way to compliance. Remember as a child when your parents, teachers, or others in authority focused completely on what you were saying and how you were saying it? We have probably all felt the cold hand of someone listening closely to what we were saying when we were perhaps less truthful that we should have been. If you close your eyes, you can almost recall that sense of impending disaster hidden in the stillness and focus of that authority figure. Using this technique allows the witness to feel the impending doom that waits if they are not truthful.

ii. Questions Should Control

One of the most important things that you can do to assert control is to return to the fundamental questioning techniques you have already developed. Short, one-fact questions do not allow room for the witness to fairly give a nonresponsive answer. If the question is properly constructed the following techniques will normally bring the witness back into the fold:

> Q: You saw the defendant leave the bar?
> A: *Well it was smoky in there, the music was playing and I'd been drinking a bit. Bill is a friendly guy and I really like him a lot. He would never hurt a fly, I can't ever believe he got in a fight in the parking lot and knifed someone.*

The advocate must repeat the question, slowing the pace slightly to ensure that the witness understands. This lets the witness, the judge, and the jury know that the question is a fair one and the witness should answer.

> Q: You saw the defendant leave the bar?
> A: *Like I said, he's a great guy and it was very crowded in there.*

The advocate must repeat the question a second time, maintaining the slow pacing of words, but not so slow as to be insulting. It is also permissible to take a step forward, or to at least lean towards the witness in anticipation of their answer. Sometimes, it also works to place an honorific before the question, pause, and then repeat the question a third time.

> Q: Sir. You saw the defendant leave the bar?
> A: *Yes.*

This technique works well with rational witnesses. Children in particular are used to having the same question posed to them multiple times. They are comfortable answering when confronted with this technique. Lay witnesses often realize that they are not being polite in answering your question and they comply once they get it. The witness who does not get it and continues to fight after you have asked the question three times is now withdrawing money from their credibility bank with the jury. If they still will not answer the question, you can focus the jury on that fact.

> Q: Sir. My question to you was—You saw the defendant leave the bar? Do you understand the question?
> A: *Yes.*
>
> Q: Please answer it then. Let me ask you again. You saw the defendant leave the bar?
> A: *Yes.*

> Another approach is to seek agreement from the witness, changing the question slightly.

> Q: Sir. We can agree that you saw the defendant leave the bar?
> A: *Yes.*

Another approach is to comment lightly on the witness's nonresponsive conduct and then refocus them on the question.

> Q: You saw the defendant leave the bar?
> A: *Well it was smoky in there, the music was playing and I'd been drinking a bit. Bill is a friendly guy and I really like him a lot. He would never hurt a fly, I can't ever believe he got in a fight in the parking lot and knifed someone.*
>
> Q: I understand that you and the defendant are friends and this is hard for you. My question to you was—You saw the defendant leave the bar? Please answer.
> A: *Well I don't know if you would call us "friends."*
>
> Q: You saw the defendant leave the bar?
> A: *Yes.*

On other occasions, it may be appropriate to ask the question in the negative, forcing them to choose between giving an untruthful answer and responding to your question. This works best if you have the ability to impeach if they respond affirmatively to the negative question.

Q: You saw the defendant leave the bar?

A: *Well it was a long night and I was talking to friends.*

Q: You did not see the defendant leave the bar? (Of course, you have a statement to impeach with here).

A: *Wait. I'm not saying that.*

Q: So, you saw the defendant leave the bar?

A: *Yes.* (The tone of the witness may actually be aggravated at this point, but that just underlines their nonresponsive behavior in refusing to answer initially).

One of these techniques will work. After you have gotten the answer that you wanted, reward the witness by moving on. Do not give up the moral high ground you have so recently acquired by abusing the witness for his non-responsiveness. You have made your point so it is time to move on. The jury and the judge will appreciate your professionalism and you have trained the witness to understand that you will not accept nonresponsive answers.

b. General Control Techniques

The following techniques make up a series of issues that you should have in mind as you develop control techniques for witnesses during cross examination. Some reiterate examples in the proceeding section, others either build on what we have previously discussed or present new ideas. As you study them, consider the ways that you might employ them to accomplish your cross examination goals.

- **Repeat the question three times:** When a witness refuses to respond to a fairly-asked question, you can underline this fact and achieve control by repeating the question. You do not need to become aggressive or overly-cynical in tone. Take a deep breath, slow down, and repeat the question while maintaining eye contact with the witness. By the third asking of the question, most witnesses will respond appropriately. This presumes, of course, that you have employed the fundamental questioning techniques previously discussed.

- **Use an honorific:** Every witness has a formal name or title. It might be Sir, Ma'am, Professor, Doctor, or their full name. Use of these titles in a professional tone signals to the witness, the jury, and the judge that you are serious about the question you have just asked. We learned from childhood that the use of our full name was a precursor to a difficult learning experience. Witnesses remember those childhood lessons and you can use that fact to focus the witness on the need to answer you properly.

- **Go to an undisputable fact:** When the witness refuses to answer affirmatively on an issue that is not disputed, you must underline that fact for the jury. Break the question into its component part, forcing an answer. You can even ask the question in a negative when you have the ability to impeach if they change their statement.

- **"My question to you was . . . . ":** This lead-in placed before the restatement of the question focuses the witness and the audience on the fact that you know the witness was nonresponsive and you are not going to allow them to continue with that behavior. Alternatively, you can also use a phrase such as **"Perhaps you did not understand..."** then you repeat the question again.

- **"Was that a yes?":** Sometimes the witness will run on, never quite answering the question. Listen carefully to their soliloquy. Somewhere within the story that they tell resides an affirmation of the question that you have asked. Focus on that affirmative response and then move on.

- **By Process of Elimination:** This technique works well on specific facts. Consider a situation where you need the witness to identify the specific brand of soft drink consumed by the plaintiff. They initially refuse to agree with you. You could use this technique to create compliance. Eventually the witness agrees with you just to move it along, they do not want to be seen has an obstructive presence and this line of questioning points out how obstructionist they are being.

Q: Ms. Davis drank a Pepsi?
A: Well it was a soft drink, or carbonated beverage.

Q: She drank a Coke?
A: No...

Q: She drank a Dr. Pepper?
A: No.

Q: Ms. Davis drank a root beer?
A: No.

Q: She drank a generic cola?
A: No

Q: She drank a Pepsi, didn't she?

A: Yes.

- **Use a blackboard or whiteboard.** The person in our past who wrote on the blackboard was usually a teacher. We tend to believe those who write on blackboards. If your witness is refusing to answer a question, and that question has been formulated properly, then write it down on the board while they are being nonresponsive. Read it to them. They will answer, and everyone will know that they have been difficult. Often the judge will chime in with a "let's just move this along" comment that underlines the non-responsiveness of the witness. Teachers write on the blackboard and most of us still trust teachers.

Let us move on now to putting all of this together in creating our witness testimony plans for advanced direct and cross examinations. This knowledge should rest in the back of your mind and be ready for use when the situation warrants. In order to be free to properly use such information, you must be sufficiently organized, with the appropriate materials before you for reference while the witness is testifying. Let us move on now to developing in-court checklists for direct and cross examination.

E.   Planning Advanced Direct & Cross Examination

Many advocacy texts provide you with multiple examples of in-court experiences. They are often presented as either notional or actual transcripts. Authors have historically presented them in this fashion so that they can model correct behavior or point out poor technique. I have used both methods here when teaching the fundamentals. Observing one way of doing something is effective in teaching you the basics of developing that particular skill. It is time to go further. In this section, we will actually prepare a witness testimony plan that we will then use in presenting the direct, and performing the cross.

> **Witness Testimony Plans:**
> - Verbatim questions and expected answers
> - Bullet topic outlines
> - Required answers

You need to move beyond the basics in your quest to develop persuasive witness testimony. A core component of this search revolves around the way in which you prepare to conduct your witness examinations. There are three primary ways to prepare witness testimony plans: (1) verbatim questions and expected answers, (2) bullet topic outlines, and (3) required answers. Many texts suggest that after you have completed your case analysis, you next create an outline of topics and subtopics, and then build specific questions and expected answers, placing them in your final trial notebook. This is an adequate approach, but not a preferable one.

When you use this technique, you have a defined response that you have "scripted" for the witness. When you do not get that response, you are off-script. When an advocate who expects the examination to go a certain way does not get that type of performance, they experience cognitive dissonance; the story is not right and they respond in a negative fashion. You have to worry about memorizing all of the questions correctly, and the witness has to worry about memorizing all of the answers correctly. It can work, but requires a great deal of practice and it is prone to a stilted performance.

Conversely, a less defined direct examination plan is actually more effective. If you own the ability to employ the fundamental skills as needed, you are set free to respond in the moment. It does require great detail in planning, but the planning is modular. By the time you get to the testimony, you are able to perform the examination using a set of bullet points that cover the areas identified through case analysis. You use the topic list to remind you of the questions that you want to ask to get the answer that you need.

Consider the following exhibits from one of the case files contained in the teacher's manual. After reviewing the information, we will prepare a direct examination plan for the witness, Mr. Hansen.

Excerpts from *State v. Saunders*:

Introduction to the Case:

Alex Saunders is charged with assault with a dangerous weapon in violation of State statute § 128.01, and one charge of possession of an unregistered firearm in violation of State statute § 92.01. At an earlier session Mr. Saunders was arraigned, pled not guilty and requested a jury trial. There were no pretrial motions. He refused to testify at the grand jury. The court is scheduled to reconvene on March 3, 20XX with opening statements.

On July 2, 20XX-2, Mr. Saunders and Pat O'Brien were at The Rattler Room, a local night club, to hear a local bluegrass band, Johnny Sod and the Busters. Around 11:00 p.m., a scuffle broke out. Witnesses allege they heard O'Brien screaming at Saunders, "Tim Tebow was the greatest college quarterback to ever play the game!" Saunders shouted back, "No, Peyton Manning was!" "Tebow!" "Manning!" "Tebow!" "Manning!" The two eventually took it outside, where the posturing continued. About

15 minutes later, Sergeant Christopher Cross, an off-duty police officer, arrived. Cross assessed the situation and decided to apprehend Saunders.

Witnesses:

(1) <u>Sergeant Christopher Cross</u>. Cop on the scene. He seized a pistol from Saunders and two bullets from an unidentified onlooker. He will testify that no weapon of any sort was found on O'Brien, although he was not searched until after midnight. He conducted a search of local files to see if Saunders had registered any weapons with the city. He can also authenticate the diagram of the club.

(2) <u>Pat O'Brien</u>. He will testify that the accused pointed a weapon at him. He can also authenticate a diagram of the club. He will deny possessing any type of a weapon. O'Brien has a prior conviction for armed robbery nine years and six months prior to the date of trial.

(3) <u>Mr. Alex Saunders</u>. He may claim self defense. He received a misdemeanor conviction for failing to pay just debts in 20XX-9. He was involved in a previous bar brawl on July 18, 20XX-3.

(4) <u>Mr. Jurczy Shores</u>. He is Saunders's current supervisor at the paper plant. He can testify about Saunders's character for peacefulness and general character as an all-around good guy.

(5) <u>Vic/Victoria Hansen</u>. He/she is an eyewitness to the events of July 2nd.

Witness Statement - Sergeant Christopher Cross:

He is a 29 year old patrolman and a four year veteran of the police department. Before joining the police, he was a bounty hunter from Kingman, Arizona. Cross was off-duty the night of July 2d and just happened to be driving by The Rattler Room, a drinking establishment, on the way to Donuts Haven when he heard what sounded like a ruckus coming from the club. He saw two guys, who were later identified as Alex Saunders and Pat O'Brien, being restrained by an unruly mob. He couldn't hear what was being said, but he did see some sort of shiny object in Saunders's belt. He called for back-up, peeled up on the sidewalk, exited his metallic gray-in-color vehicle, ordered everyone to freeze, and immediately took O'Brien and Saunders into custody.

He heard Saunders blurt out: "Yeah, this was my piece but I've only had it a few days. I only pulled it out because I had no choice. Yah gotta believe me, I was just protecting myself. I know there was a weapon. Check his pockets, I tell ya." Cross ordered Saunders to calm down and pulled out his trusty standard issue rights advisement card. However, much to Cross's chagrin, Saunders refused to answer any questions. He eventually "patted" O'Brien down, about an hour later, as Saunders had requested. No weapon or shiny object was recovered. He can identify the weapon seized from Saunders, which was unloaded, because he etched the initials "CC" on the butt. The weapon has been in the police evidence room since July 2d.

He was given two rounds of ammunition at the scene by an obviously ex-cited and emotionally distraught eyewitness, who told him he just picked up the rounds from the ground after Saunders unloaded his gun. Cross seized the ammunition, marked it with his initials, noted that it matched the caliber of Saunders's weapon, and stored the ammunition in the police evidence room. He is familiar with State Statute § 92.01, requiring all per-sons to register all firearms within 72-hours of purchase. He conducted a diligent and thorough search of the weapons registration files two weeks ago and did not find any registration for the weapon seized from the ac-cused. He also conducted a functions check of the pistol two days ago and it is operational. Finally, last week, Cross drove by the address that Mr. Saunders gave and verified it was his address. He saw Saunders get out of a car and walk into the home.

Witness Statement – Vic/Victoria Hansen:

Hansen is 28 years old, married with two children, and is an advertising sales representative for the newspaper. Hansen told his/her spouse that he/she had to work late the night of July 2nd on some paperwork. This was not so. Hansen was at The Rattler Room when Saunders and O'Brien be-gan arguing. In fact, Hansen had been there since 10 p.m. celebrating the dramatic play of the Chicago Cubs, hoisting at least two pitchers (of beer) in their honor. Hansen's memory and vision may be a bit fuzzy. Hansen does recall a spirited debate between Saunders and O'Brien about who was the best college quarterback of all time. Hansen remembers thinking 'how stupid, everyone knows it was Doug Flutie.' O'Brien appeared to be the aggressor, getting in Saunders's face and expectorating something fierce.

When drinking, Hansen loves a good fight just as much as the next drunk, and followed the pack when the fracas moved outdoors. The area had three street lights, one of which was out. The lighting was sufficient to get a pretty good look at what was going on. Hansen estimates that O'Brien was 6'4" and weighed 225 pounds, and Saunders is 5'8" and weighed 120 lbs. Hansen saw Saunders with a weapon; at least, Hansen saw Saunders take it out after O'Brien began approaching.

---

1. Direct Examination Plan – Vic/Victoria Hansen

Once you review the case file and performed case analysis, you need to create a witness presentation plan for Mr./Ms. Hansen. Let us assume that you are the defense counsel in this case and you need to prepare a direct examination template for Hansen. By the time you proceed to trial this list would be sufficient to present the witness (with attendant exhibits). You could proceed as follows:

I.   Introduce
    a.   Name.
    b.   Address.
    c.   Family.
    d.   Work

II.   Headline—night of July 2, 20XX-2
    a.   Doing?
    b.   Where?
    c.   Why?

III.   Rattler Room (Defense Exhibit A – photo)
    a.   Location.
    b.   Description.
    c.   Arrived?

IV.   Why was Hansen there?
    a.   Relax.
    b.   Cubs.
    c.   Lied to spouse.
        i.   Why?
        ii.   Lying today?
        iii. Hard to testify.
        iv.   Had to tell spouse?

V.   First saw O'Brien
    a.   Description.
    b.   Doing.
    c.   Location.

VI.   First Saw Saunders
    a.   Description.

     b.   Doing.

     c.   Interaction with O'Brien.

VII.   Take it outside

     a.   Where they went?

     b.   Why?

     c.   Describe.

VIII.   Diagram (Defense Exhibit B—diagram of parking lot)

     a.   Foundation.

     b.   Step down.

     c.   Return to seat.

IX.   Fight in parking lot

     a.   What O'Brien:

        i.   Said?

        ii.   Did?

     b.   What Saunders:

        i.   Said?

        ii.   Did?

X.   What Hansen did:

     a.   When Sergeant Cross appeared?

     b.   Did not see person approach Sergeant Cross.

     c.   Size of crowd?

     d.   Actions of police?

The beauty of this type of construct at trial is that you identify the topics that you wish to discuss and the conversation on direct flows from one issue to the next. You have to listen to your witness's response to frame your next question. This allows you to focus on the witness and increase persuasiveness, preventing you from doing it by the numbers.

It also has the advantage of maximizing your flexibility. You can modify your presentation based upon the witness and the court, while also ensuring that all of the topics you need to cover are, in fact, covered.

---

2. Cross Examination Plan – Vic/Victoria Hansen

Once you review the case file and performed case analysis, you need to create a witness presentation plan for Mr./Ms. Hansen. Let us assume that you are the prosecution and the defense has given you notice of their intent to call Hansen. By the time you proceed to trial, this list would be sufficient to cross the witness. You could proceed as follows:

I.   HL—alone in the bar
    a.   No spouse.
    b.   Not at work.
    c.   Told spouse working.
    d.   Out drinking.
    e.   Celebrating Cubs victory.
    f.   Two pitchers of beer.

II.   Rattler Room
    a.   Crowded.
    b.   Focused on Cubs.
    c.   Focused on TV.
    d.   Focused on relaxing.
    e.   Focused on drinking.

III.   Crowd in parking lot
    a.   Lots of people.
    b.   Drinking.
    c.   Yelling.
    d.   Excited by fight.
    e.   Didn't know everyone.
    f.   Didn't see everyone.

IV.   Rattler Room parking lot.
    a.   Lack of lights.
    b.   Crowded.
    c.   Drinking.

V.   What Hansen did
    a.   Alone at the bar.
    b.   Lied to husband.
    c.   Drinking for hours.
    d.   Saw Saunders with weapon.
    e.   Did not see O'Brien with a weapon.
    f.   Memory is fuzzy.

The beauty of this type of construct at trial is that you identify the topics that you wish to discuss and the conversation on cross flows from one issue to the next. These are topics and you can rearrange them at will. You would also identify the run of questions that you need to be able to produce when faced with objections.

This approach creates flexible witness plans that empower the advocate to do what needs to be done in that moment without fear. Additional comments on the list might include likely objections and places in the record where the witness provided statements and substantive facts that you know the witness must agree with.

F.   Advanced Direct Examination Checklist

The following checklist summarizes the information presented throughout this book on direct examination. You should use it as the next step in developing advanced direct examination techniques. This checklist is not "Holy Writ" and is merely the soil in which you should plant the seeds of your own creativity.

I.   Good Direct Examination Techniques:

    a.   Form of the Question

        i.   Wide open questions.

        ii.   Directive questions.

        iii.   Open questions.

        iv.   Probing or testing questions.

        v.   Coupling questions.

    b.   Planning and Presenting

        i.   Chronological examination.

        ii.   The development of cause and effect.

        iii.   Topical examination by subject matter.

    c.   Organization

        i.   Headlines.

        ii.   Accredit the witness.

        iii.   No compound questions.

        iv.   Looping.

        v.   Limit use of notes.

        vi.   Go from general to specific.

        vii.   Brevity is your friend.

        viii.   Exhibits are your friend.

        ix.   Build direct around key facts.

    d. Physicality

        i.   Make eye contact.

        ii.   Gesture appropriately.

        iii.   Relax.

        iv.   Posture.

        v.   Listen.

        vi.   React to the witness.

        vii.   Do not talk over the witness.

        viii.   Body position matters.

    e. Language

        i.   Emphasis where needed.

        ii.   Paint Pictures with words.

        iii.   Use normal language.

        iv.   Delete filler words.

        v.   Conversational tone.

        vi.   Let the silence work for you.

        vii.   Voice inflection persuades.

        viii.   Less is usually more.

II.   It is all about asking questions that the jury wants to know the answer to so that they can decide the issues in the case.

    a. Mimic conversational tones to create interest and anticipation.

    b. Lessons from direct examination.

i.   Conversational.

ii.   Headlines.

iii.   Eye contact.

iv.   Looping.

v.   Emphasis where appropriate.

vi.   Paint pictures with words.

vii.   Use English.

viii.   Delete filler words.

ix.   Limit the use of notes.

x.   Organize.

xi.   Relax.

xii.   Let the silence work for you.

xiii.   Posture.

xiv.   Gesture appropriately.

xv.   Do not talk over the witness.

xvi.   No compound questions.

xvii.   Listen.

xviii. Less = more.

xix.   React to the witness.

xx.   Go from the general to the specific.

xxi.   Brevity is your friend.

xxii.   Exhibits should work for you, not against you.

xxiii. Build your direct around your key facts.

xxiv.   Body position matters.

xxv.   Voice inflection persuades.

xxvi.   Accredit the witness.

xxvii. Listen and follow up.

G. Advanced Cross Examination Checklist

The following checklist summarizes the information presented throughout this book on cross examination. You should use it as the next step in developing advanced cross examination techniques. This checklist is not "Holy Writ" and is merely the soil in which you should plant the seeds of your own creativity.

I.   Seven Steps to Superior Cross Examinations:

    a. Start and end preparation with case analysis.

    b. Every section has a clearly defined purpose tied to theme, theory or credibility.

    c. CONTROL THE WITNESS.

    d. Details give control.

    e. Organize the cross to accomplish your goals—not your opponent's.

    f. Impeachment must matter.

    g. Use the witness's own words.

II.   Primary Goals of Cross Examination:

    a. Control the witness;

    b. Establish facts that bolster your theme and theory;

    c. Establish facts that build up the credibility of your witnesses and diminish the credibility of your opponent's witnesses.

III.   Maximize the Persuasive Impact of Answers on Cross:

    a. Cluster together all of the facts that enhance and support the topic.

    b. Lay out the facts one question at a time leading up to your final point.

    c. Identify similar facts based upon your knowledge of human nature and then using them to make your final point.

IV.   Why Cross?

    a. To elicit facts supporting your legal theory, factual theory or moral theme.

b. To expose facts or bias that weakens your opponent's legal theory, factual theory or moral theme.

c. To establish the credibility of your own witnesses or attack the credibility of opposing witnesses (when required by your legal theory, factual theory or moral theme).

V.   Fundamental Precepts of Cross:

a. It is a commando raid, not an invasion.

b. Use primacy and recency.

c. Avoid the ultimate question.

d. One fact questions.

e. Vary questioning techniques.

f. Do not play with fire.

g. Develop control techniques.

VI.   Cross Examination Sequencing:

a. Do not use chronological order in confrontational cross examinations.

b. Avoid chronological order in informational cross examinations.

c. Lay your theme early and often.

d. Close cross examination with a theme vignette.

e. When attacking credibility, attack in the first vignette.

f. Show bias, interest, or motive early in the cross examination.

g. End with a power vignette.

h. Develop risky areas only after establishing control of the witness through safe vignettes.

i. Never lead or end with a risky vignette.

j. If you have more than one impeachment vignette, use the cleanest first.

k. Disperse impeachment vignettes throughout the cross examination.

l. When expecting a 'no' answer to one goal question, precede that chapter with a sure 'yes' answer.

m. Bundle vignettes that need to be done together in order to complete a coherent picture of a single event.

n. Prepared vignettes countering the power of the opponent's case are best performed in the middle of cross examination.

VII. Relating Impeachment to Cross:

a. Build credibility into your witness plan.

b. Cross walk impeachment with your overall cross examination plan.

c. Impeach when it fits the theory of your case, sometimes it just makes sense to let it go.

H. Conclusion

This discussion about advanced direct and cross examination builds on the fundamental tenets you learned previously. You should realize that in large part it is an issue of organization, tone, and structure. When you understand your primary goal, as derived from a proper case analysis, and see the way in which all of the witness testimony falls into place for the larger story, you are on your way to creating a case-in-chief that consistently delivers your message to the jury. Let us move on now and discuss the care, feeding, and presentation of expert witness testimony.

Chapter 10: Expert Witnesses

A. Introduction 401
B. How the Law Impacts Experts...............................403
C. Selecting and Preparing Experts 410
D. Structuring Direct Expert Testimony.......................416
E. How to Cross Examine Experts 434
F. Checklist...440
G. Evidence Rules to Consider.................................442

A.   Introduction

Expert witnesses occupy a special place at trial. They are one of the few witnesses allowed to testify without any personal knowledge, and their opinions can speak to the ultimate issues in the case. In effect, they are specialized witnesses charged with instructing the jury on areas within the case that require more specialized knowledge than a lay person could provide. Judges treat them differently under the rules, and their testimony carries more weight with juries. In a world where technology is king, experts reign supreme. Counsel must approach the presentation of expert witness testimony, and the cross examination of opposing experts, with care. The goals are twofold: meet the evidentiary requirements for admissibility and persuade the jury to rely upon the expert's opinion.

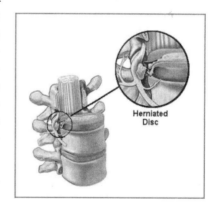

Herniated Disc

When accepted by the court the testimony of the expert is often dispositive.

Counsel should consider the expert witness to be very much like a genie in a lamp—within their world they have phenomenal cosmic power, but their living space is small. In other words, an expert witness has a wide range of possible testimony, but only as it goes to their specific, narrowly tailored area of expertise. Displaying the expert to maximum effect is the goal of direct examination, controlling and differentiating expert testimony is often the goal of cross. Unlike normal lay witnesses, an expert's purpose is to assist the jury in understanding evidence or in determining a fact at issue in the case. They are able to accomplish these twin goals because they possess scientific, technical, or other specialized knowledge that gives them the ability to make sense of complex and counter intuitive subjects. They are there to teach the members of the jury on complex issues, and it is counsel's job to serve as the guide through these difficult subjects.

> **Rule 702. Testimony by Expert Witnesses**
>
> A witness who is qualified as an expert by knowledge, skill, experience, training, or education may testify in the form of an opinion or otherwise if:
>
> **(a)** the expert's scientific, technical, or other specialized knowledge will help the trier of fact to understand the evidence or to determine a fact in issue;
>
> **(b)** the testimony is based on sufficient facts or data;
>
> **(c)** the testimony is the product of reliable principles and methods; and
>
> **(d)** the expert has reliably applied the principles and methods to the facts of the case.

Establishing the source of an expert's expertise, the first step in admitting their opinions, involves qualifying the expert witness by laying a foundation meeting the requirements of FRE 702. There are two threshold questions that must be established: (1) does the witness possess sufficient scientific, specialized or technical knowledge, and (2) will the expert's knowledge assist the trier of fact in determining a complex or counter intuitive issue in the case? If both of these questions can be answered affirmatively through the testimony of the witness then they may be accepted by court and allowed to testify.

B. How the Law Impacts Experts

The selection, preparation, and presentation of expert witnesses is heavily governed by the applicable evidentiary rules. The rules can best be addressed as a series of questions that counsel should ask themselves as they go through the process of deciding how experts should best be employed in a particular case.

Deciding how and when to employ experts is a tactical and strategic decision that has factual, theoretical, and legal implications for the case. One of the first decisions counsel must make is how to categorize the expert. If the expert is a member of the defense team and is brought on to assist counsel in understanding the case, they are covered by attorney-client privilege and their comments to counsel, reports they produce and their conversations with the client are not discoverable by the opposing side. Once counsel decide to make them a witness however, the attorney-client privilege dissipates, subject to any relevant rules of procedure.

Counsel who do not properly understand the status of experts as they relate to the case can inadvertently disclose information. Alternatively it could also result in a well qualified expert not being allowed to testify because they have had access to information counsel wishes to lawfully keep from the opposing side. If this issue is thought out ahead of time during case analysis, it can, to a certain extent be ameliorated through careful planning. Counsel should frequently check in on what the goal of the expert they are bringing in is—are they using the expert so that they themselves can better understand and prepare for the issues of the case, or is the intent of this expert to allow the jury to better understand the issues? If it is the former, than counsel will have to consider the need for finding an additional witness to testify at trial. If it is the latter, counsel will be far better able to safeguard those sensitive issues they do not wish the other side to

---

Rule 104. Preliminary Questions

(a) In General. The court must decide any preliminary question about whether a witness is qualified, a privilege exists, or evidence is admissible. In so deciding, the court is not bound by evidence rules, except those on privilege.

---

have during discovery. Accordingly, counsel must be extremely familiar with local rules and procedures concerning expert witnesses, and take said rules and procedures into account during every stage of case analysis and trial preparation.

Once counsel decides to call an expert witness they must review the standard for admissibility applied by the court to experts. FRE 104(a) establishes that the trial judge decides preliminary questions concerning the relevance, propriety and necessity of expert testimony, the qualification of expert witnesses, and the admissibility of his or her testimony.

In addition to the overarching guidance for the court found in FRE 104(a), the Federal Rules of Evidence provide trial judges with six factors to consider when determining whether or not counsel should be allowed to call an expert witness. Those include (1) the qualifications of the proffered expert witness, (2) is the subject matter of the testimony "proper", (3) does the proffered expert witness testimony have a proper basis, (4) is the experts' testimony relevant, (5) are the methods used by the expert in arriving at their opinion reliable, (6) is the probative value of the expert's opinion and the information upon which it is based outweighed by the substantial danger of prejudice, and (7) can the expert testify as to the ultimate issue in the case?

These seven factors are found in the Federal Rules of Evidence and the accompanying commentary. Counsel should plan the presentation of their expert witness testimony around these rules. Most suggested approaches for expert witness presentations are based in part on a clear understanding of the impact evidentiary rules have on admitting such evidence. The relevant issues are:

- **Qualified Expert**. To give expert testimony, a witness must qualify as an expert by virtue of his or her "knowledge, skill, experience, training, or education." *See* FRE 702.

- **Proper Subject Matter**. Expert testimony is appropriate if it would be "helpful" to the trier of fact. It is essential especially if the trier of fact could not otherwise be expected to understand the issues and rationally resolve them. *See* FRE 702.

- **Proper Basis**. The expert's opinion may be based on admissible evidence "perceived by or made known to the expert at or before the hearing" or inadmissible hearsay if it is "of a type reasonably relied upon by experts in the particular field in forming opinions or inferences upon the subject. . . ." The expert's opinion must have an adequate factual basis and cannot be simply a bare opinion. *See* FRE 702 and 703.

- **Relevant**. Expert testimony must be relevant. *See* FRE 402.

- **Reliable**. The expert's methodology and conclusions must be reliable. *See* FRE 702.

- **Probative Value.** The probative value of the expert's opinion, and the information comprising the basis of the opinion, must not be substantially outweighed any unfair prejudice that could result from the expert's testimony. *See* FRE 403.

- **Ultimate Issue.** In order to determine if the expert can testify as to the ultimate issue counsel must consider FRE 702 and FRE 704 in concert. Read together, and expert can testify as to the ultimate issue in a case if such testimony will be helpful to the jury. Opinions that infer the intent or state of mind of a party are generally not helpful to the jury, particularly when the issue is the state of mind of the defendant in a criminal case. In those instances experts can provide factual information that assists the jury in coming to a conclusion, but they may not state their own conclusions because they would not be "helpful."

1. Qualification to Form an Opinion

During trial counsel can establish the knowledge, training, and education foundation for an expert witness based upon the standard found in FRE 702. Specifically, counsel must show that:

Rule 702. Testimony by Expert Witnesses

A witness who is qualified as an expert by knowledge, skill, experience, training, or education may testify in the form of an opinion or otherwise if:

This information is normally found in the curriculum vitae of the expert and is fertile grounds for foundational questions during the direct examination. Counsel should use the curriculum vitae, publications, and accomplishments of the expert to lay this foundation. It is also important that counsel spend time discussing those things laid out in an expert's curriculum vitae with the expert. Not only will counsel gain a deeper understanding of the expert, their abilities, and their subjects of expertise, but there is an even greater potential benefit. Often counsel may discover that in the details of things broadly discussed in the curriculum vitae are things that strengthen the validity and credibility of the expert's opinion on the particular issues of the case.

Qualifications are normally presented by counsel during the direct examination of the expert while laying the foundation for the acceptance of an expert by the court. The qualification bar is not high, as long as the expert has the requisite qualifications under the rule. Experts will vary in this regard, but once they are acceptable any inquiry afterwards goes to weight and not admissibility.

Examples of fertile areas used to establish the qualifications of an expert witness include degrees attained from educational institutions, other specialized training in the field, licenses for practice in their field, practical experience (if applicable) for a long period of time, teaching experience in the field, the witness's publications, membership in professional organizations, honors or prizes received, and previous expert testimony. The potential qualification of the expert are therefore case specific and experience specific.

2.   Proper Subject Matter ("Will assist the fact-finder")

The current standard is whether the testimony assists the trier of fact, not whether it embraces an "ultimate issue" so as to usurp the jury's function. At the same time, ultimate-issue opinion testimony is not automatically admissible, opinions still must be relevant and helpful as determined through Rules 401-403 and 702.

Rule 702. Testimony by Expert Witnesses

(a) the expert's scientific, technical, or other specialized knowledge will help the trier of fact to understand the evidence or to determine a fact in issue;

Often counsel attempt to use the expert to short circuit the independent judgement of the jury. The goal should be for the expert's testimony to assist the finder of fact in their decision making process, not to supplant it. Experts should not opine that a certain witness's rendition of events is believable or not. The court is supremely skeptical about whether any witness could be qualified to opine as to the credibility of another. **An expert may not become a "human lie detector."**

Questions like whether the expert believes the victim was raped, or whether the victim is telling the truth when she claimed to have been raped (i.e. was the witness truthful?) are impermissible. However, the expert *may* opine that a victim's testimony or history is consistent with what the expert's examination found, and whether the behavior at issue is *typical* of victims of such crimes. When presenting the scope of the expert's opinion counsel should focus on symptoms and supporting facts, not conclusions concerning veracity.

3.   Basis for the Expert's Testimony

The language of the rule is broad enough to allow three types of bases: facts personally observed by the expert; facts posed in a hypothetical question; and hearsay reports from third parties. **Expert testimony must be**

based on the facts of the case, but not necessarily the first-hand observations of the expert.

Rule 702. Testimony by Expert Witnesses

(b) the testimony is based on sufficient facts or data;

(c) the testimony is the product of reliable principles and methods; and

(d) the expert has reliably applied the principles and methods to the facts of the case.

For instance, the fact that an expert did not interview or counsel the victim would not render the expert unqualified to arrive at an opinion concerning rape trauma syndrome. In this scenario, the defense objected to the social worker's opinion that the victim was exhibiting symptoms consistent with rape trauma accommodation syndrome and suffered from PTSD on the basis that the opinion was based solely on observing the victim in court, reading reports of others and assuming facts as alleged by the victim were true. However, such an objection goes to the weight to be given an expert opinion, not its admissibility. Counsel should focus on the quality and relevancy of the information as it relates to the expert opinion.

Rule 703. Bases of an Expert's Opinion Testimony

An expert may base an opinion on facts or data in the case that the expert has been made aware of or personally observed. If experts in the particular field would reasonably rely on those kinds of facts or data in forming an opinion on the subject, they need not be admissible for the opinion to be admitted. But if the facts or data would otherwise be inadmissible, the proponent of the opinion may disclose them to the jury only if their probative value in helping the jury evaluate the opinion substantially outweighs their prejudicial effect.

If the expert opinion is based on personal observations, then the foundational elements must include: (1) where and when the expert witness observed the fact, (2) who was present, (3) how the expert witness observed the fact, and (4) a description of the observed fact. These facts may not even necessarily be found within the record of the court. Facts presented out-of-court (non-record facts), are allowed if they are "of a type reasonably relied upon by experts in the particular field" (this is allowed even if inadmissible because it is not being offered for its truth but the expert's testimony based on that evidence).

It is also permissible for expert opinions to be based on hearsay reports by third parties. "The rationale in favor of admissibility of expert testimony based on hearsay is that the expert is fully capable of judging for himself what is, or is not, a reliable basis for his opinion. This relates directly to one of the functions of the expert witness, namely to lend his special expertise to the issue before him."[1]

Beware: there is a potential problem of smuggling in otherwise inadmissible evidence. When attempting to determine whether or not the underlying hearsay statements may themselves be admissible during direct examination counsel should compare *Hutchinson v. Groskin*, 927 F.2d 722 (2d Cir. 1991) where the testimony that expert's opinion was "consistent with" prognoses of three non-testifying physicians, not disclosed during discovery, conveyed hearsay testimony to the jury, with *Primavera v. Celotex Corp.*, 608 A.2d 515 (Pa. Super. Ct. 1992) where the court sustained the expert's reliance on hearsay reports since they were the kind of data ordinarily used by practitioners, and because the expert *used* the reports to arrive at and explain his opinion, not as a "mere conduit or transmitter" of the hearsay.

4.   Relevance

Expert testimony, like any other testimony, must be relevant to an issue at trial in order to be admissible.[2] In *Daubert,* the Supreme Court held that nothing in the Federal Rules indicates that "general acceptance" is a precondition to admission of scientific evidence Instead, the rules assign the task to the judge to ensure that expert testimony rests on a reliable basis and is relevant. The judge assesses the principles and methodologies of such evidence pursuant to FRE 104(a).

The general relevancy requirements outlined in FRE 401 and 402 are met relatively easily, the more complex analysis for experts revolves around the application of FRE 702, 703 and 704. These rules are best viewed through the gatekeeping function assigned to the court when it conducts a reliability assessment. In a very real sense the reliability assessment func-

---

[1] United States v. Sims, 514 F.2d 147, 149 (9th Cir).

[2] *Daubert v. Merrell Dow Pharmaceuticals, Inc.* 509 U.S. 579 (1993) and FRE 401 and 402 establish the baseline requirements for admissible expert testimony.

tions as an additional relevancy check on the admissibility of expert testimony.

Rule 402. General Admissibility of Relevant Evidence

Relevant evidence is admissible unless any of the following provides otherwise:

• the United States Constitution;

• a federal statute;

• these rules; or

• other rules prescribed by the Supreme Court.

Irrelevant evidence is not admissible.

---

5.   Reliability

The role of the judge as a "gatekeeper" allows the court to a determine whether the evidence counsel offers through expert testimony is based upon a methodology that is "scientific," and therefore reliable. The judgment is made before the evidence is admitted, and entails "a preliminary assessment of whether the reasoning or methodology is scientifically

---

Rule 704. Opinion on an Ultimate Issue

(a) In General--Not Automatically Objectionable. An opinion is not objectionable just because it embraces an ultimate issue.

(b) Exception. In a criminal case, an expert witness must not state an opinion about whether the defendant did or did not have a mental state or condition that constitutes an element of the crime charged or of a defense. Those matters are for the trier of fact alone.

---

valid." The trial court is given broad discretion in admitting expert testimony; rulings are tested only for abuse of discretion.[3] The Supreme Court discussed a nonexclusive list of factors to consider in admitting scientific evidence, including as a separate consideration the test from *Frye v. United States*, 293 F. 1013 (D.C. Cir. 1923). It is important to note that after

---

[3] General Electric Co. v. Joiner, 522 U.S. 136 (1997).

Daubert, "helpfulness" alone will not guarantee admission of evidence because it does not guarantee "reliability." The Supreme Court resolved whether the judge's gatekeeping function and the *Daubert* factors apply to non-scientific evidence.

Daubert Factors:

1. Whether the theory or technique can be and has been tested;

2. Whether the theory or technique has been subjected to peer review and publication;

3. Whether the known or potential rate of error is acceptable;

4. Whether the theory or technique enjoys widespread acceptance.

In *Kumho Tire v. Carmichael*, 526 U.S. 137 (1999), the Court held that the trial judge's gatekeeping responsibility applies to *all types* of expert evidence. The Court also held that, to the extent the *Daubert* factors apply, they can be used to evaluate the reliability of this evidence. Finally, the Court ruled that factors other than those announced in *Daubert* can also be used to evaluate the reliability of non-scientific expert evidence.

C. Selecting and Preparing Experts

Counsel must consider previous discussions about case analysis, persuasion theory, direct examination and cross examination as the backdrop when determining the potential use of expert witnesses at trial. When doing so, it is useful to consider the potential benefits, and detriments, when using expert witnesses. This process requires counsel to consider the nature of the jury, the particularities of their chosen expert, and how the jury may perceive the expert's testimony.

1. Goal of the Expert Testimony

Counsel must proceed carefully when choosing an expert witness. The rules of evidence show a preference for education and experience that separates the expert from the common person. These professionals, by nature, have assumed a position in society that places them apart. Put differently, the very thing that produces their expertise can cut against their ability to communicate the expertise to the rest of us. Counsel must assess their experts not only on the level of their education and accomplishments, but, more importantly, their ability to communicate that expertise.

A great deal of the communication burden must be born by counsel, and not the expert. The attorney calling the expert has the ability shape the questions, both individually and systemically. Questions that focus the expert, simplify the issues without altering them, and then put the expert in a position to share effectively are preferable. It is also best practice for the attorney to adopt an attitude in direct questioning of a person who the expert must educate on each and every thing in the direct. By doing so, counsel serves as a stand in for the members of the jury, and, through example, shows them that learning from the expert is the point of the testimony. The goal is for the jury to like the expert, trust the expert, and then rely upon what they learned from their testimony. In the best case scenario the jury adopts the expert and then uses their "shared expertise" to resolve the complex issues in the case.

Unfortunately intelligent people often get lost in the weeds of their expertise, descending into a discussion that is either boring or arrogant. When experts do this, their words lose meaning and they begin to sound similar to the adults in Charlie Brown cartoons. It is counsel's job to prevent this from happening. Jurors are concerned about the way in which the expert views them, the possibility of not understanding what the expert is talking about, and the very real chance that they will be bored by an impenetrable and not understandable presentation. The concepts discussed previously in case analysis, witness preparation and presentation are key tools that counsel must use to overcome the perceptions of the jury, showcase their expert for the benefit of all concerned, and to ensure the jury can clearly follow the logic behind the expert's opinion.

2.   Dealing with Jury Expectations

Jury's understand that experts are paid, usually by the side that calls them, and they have some of the same concerns about bias that they have for counsel. They are looking for someone that will help them deal with the issues of the case. Counsel must overcome these bias concerns, and should consider them when choosing experts and preparing their testimony. The overall goal is that the jury believes that the expert is not there for one side or the other, but is instead there to share their expertise with them. Jury members do not expect people to work for free, and if the payment the expert receives is explained adequately in connection with the case that bias issue is likely to have less of an impact on the jury. The autonomy and impartiality of the expert witness is a key component in getting the jury to overcome their bias.

> *Juries trust experts that are likable, impartial, and understandable.*

Many experts either teach, or desire to share, their expertise. There is a natural persuasive relationship between teachers and students. Almost every member of our society that serves on a jury has experienced the benefits of a teacher student relationship. The teacher occupies a position of trust in our society, and counsel can use this dynamic to overcome the suspicions of bias against their expert. Experts who can simplify, identify key concepts, use the blackboard, whiteboard, or other delivery system to share their expertise are preferred. Experts should be excited about their area of expertise, and particularly to educate others on their expertise. This enthusiasm in combination with a willingness to demonstrate their expertise in easily creates a persuasive moment that brings the jury to the side of the expert - but it must appear genuine and not contrived.

Juries tend to trust the experts that are likable, impartial, and understandable. The way in which experts are prepared and presented can influence, to the degree that the expert's individual personality allows it, all three of these categories. In a battle of the experts juries often choose the one they like and trust - as long as their credentials meet the requirements to truly be identified as an expert. Counsel should keep these factors in mind during expert witness selection, preparation, and presentation.

3.   Selecting Experts

Much has been written about the possible considerations that counsel must address when selecting experts. Different sections of the bar have a list of "approved" or "suggested" experts, and some experts are professionals, who do it for a living. There are conferences on expert witnesses where they learn how to sell their expertise. This can be both a benefit to counsel and a detriment. It is a best practice to consider experts that others have used, but not to rely upon them as the first choice. Litigation strategy should be driven by counsel's case analysis, not local customs of use. That being said, it is always helpful to know whom other trial lawyers have used, how it went, and what they would do next time. However, counsel must ensure that the recommendations of the bar appropriately fits with the case analysis they have done in the instant case. Counsel should be careful when using recommendations of the local bar, particularly if those recommendations go to people who repeatedly testify as experts. Full time experts often have a weakness that is easily exposed by a competent cross examination.

Sometimes counsel will not have a choice as to which expert is used, particularly in those cases where testimony is being presented dealing with scientific testing performed by a specific laboratory. In those situations the expert will usually come from the lab where the work was done. Regardless, the same rules of communication, credibility and likability remain. In truth, the more complicated and esoteric the witness' area of expertise, the more important counsel's role in smoothing the communication connection becomes.

Part of the selection process should include either a face to face or telephonic interview between counsel and the potential expert witness. During this interview counsel should be testing expertise, credibility and communication skills. If the expert cannot "sell" counsel on their abilities it is unlikely they will be able to communicate with the jury sufficiently to carry the day. While many experts never make it to trial, often because their reports or deposition testimony establish their bona fides to the point that opposing counsel settle, the ultimate goal of how they will present a trial remains a key consideration for counsel when selecting them. Counsel should always, in effect, practice like they play. If counsel selects and prepares experts from the very beginning as if the case were guaranteed to go to trial, they 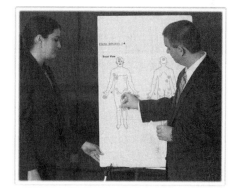 can best prepare for the most persuasive presentation of their expert at all stages of litigation. A successful interview, or interviews, normally ends in a request to use the services of the expert, followed by a contract or letter which defines the scope of the relationship and the work to be performed.

Once the expert has been selected they are usually provided access to the underlying materials relevant to their expertise. Once the expert reviews this material, taking care to request any additional information upon which they would also normally rely, a preliminary expert report or analysis is provided to the attorney. If that report is not sufficient to resolve the case the expert must be prepared to testify, both at deposition or trial. Many of the preparation techniques discussed here are applicable when experts are testifying at trial or during deposition, but the ability of counsel to control the questioning of opposing counsel during cross is much greater at trial.

For our purposes here we will presume that the expert was prepared for deposition previously, and will focus our discussions about expert preparation on the trial process.

4. Preparing Experts

Expert witnesses are both like, and unlike, fact witnesses. Many will have had previous experience testifying in court, but not all of them. They are well educated for the most part, but education does not always equate to likability. Credibility can normally be established, unless they are "professional hacks," but likability can be a challenge. Once the initial report of the expert has been provided it is time for counsel to begin trial preparation.

This involves working with the expert to identify appropriate areas for direct examination, potential areas for expected cross examination, and assessing the ability of the expert to communicate effectively. Time is almost aways a consideration during this preparation phase and counsel must take the time, and make the expert take the time, to properly prepare. Counsel can use the fact that many experts enjoy educating others on their areas of expertise to their advantage in gaining adequate preparation time. Time

> **Preparation Identifies:**
> - Poor word choices
> - Need for Analogies
> - "expert speak"

spent with an expert in a particular field will influence the structure of direct examination, the choice of appropriate demonstrative aids and possible demonstrations at trial. All of these have the potential to greatly increase the credibility of the expert and the jury's interest level during their testimony.

The problem is one of volume and selection. The expert almost always has more information than the jury truly needs to decide the case. Preparation includes selecting which portions of the witness's expertise should be highlighted, and which portions should be touched briefly, if at all. This is a judgement call that is ultimately made by counsel, but is best made by counsel with input from the expert witness. Counsel should take time in the preparation phase to emphasize to the expert that they are on the same team, working toward the goal of greater understanding for the jury. By doing so, they loop the expert in to a common goal, and once again emphasize the importance of making their testimony understandable to the average listener.

Working with the expert witness during the preparation phase will assist counsel in identifying the communication techniques that will best work to showcase this expert. Attention must be paid to vocabulary. Word choice is important when dealing with experts, and counsel should be aware of the potential harm that "expert speak" can have on the ability of the jury to understand the witness.

Counsel can use their position as the presenter of the evidence to ask those questions about word choice in a fashion that brings the expert down to an understandable level while highlighting their expertise yet remaining understandable. This is a key component of successful expert witness preparation. Time spent with the expert will also identify those areas of the witness's expertise that lend themselves to "expert speak." Those areas must be translated into "jury speak" so that everyone can understand. This is an opportunity for counsel to step in and serve as a facilitator and translators. Time spent with an expert during the preparation phase allows counsel to identify potential places where the expert may slip into words, language or concepts the jury cannot understand.

> *Example: counsel have called an expert in DNA analysis to explain the results of DNA testing. The expert is attempting to explain how the testing works and is talking at a level that is difficult to understand. Note how the attorney deals with this.*

     State:　　Doctor I want to discuss how DNA works. What exactly is DNA?

     Witness:　DNA is a nucleic acid carrying the genetic information in the cell which is capable of self-replication and synthesis of RNA. DNA consists of two long chains of nucleotides twisted into a double helix and joined by hydrogen bonds between the complementary bases adenine and thymine or cytosine and guanine. The sequence of nucleotides determines individual hereditary characteristics.

     State:　　I'm sorry doctor, I went to law school because science wore me out in college. Let's break that down. Please explain for us how DNA helps experts in your field.

     Witness:　Sure. DNA is like a chemical identification tag which allows scientists to match DNA samples to their potential sources.

> *State:*   I would like to talk with you about how that works....

In addition to identifying those areas where counsel can focus on translating for the expert, preparation also provides an opportunity to identify those exhibits within the file which should be used with the expert, while allowing the attorney to make certain that proper foundations for the exhibit can be laid with by the witness. Counsel should review the exhibits to see if there is a chance for the expert to show off their knowledge for the members of the jury by stepping off the stand and giving them a mini-lesson on its contents.

After counsel have sufficiently prepared the witness so that the jury can understand them and that evidence can be admitted, they must also spend sufficient time with the witness to practice the direct examination. During these dry runs counsel should focus on finding the questions and organization that will showcase the expert effectively, maximizing their believability, impartiality and likability. During these sessions it is often a best practice to have other members of the litigation team watch - paralegals are particularly adept at identifying traits that need to be corrected. Experienced counsel within the firm or organization can also provide feedback that is crucial in developing a better presentation. Part of the preparation for the direct examination should include potential areas for cross examination. Counsel can learn a great deal by watching their expert being cross examined by another attorney who understands how to cross. It is also essential that counsel explains this process to their chosen expert. Even if the expert has testified in other cases, this may be the first time they encounter someone with counsel's preparation strategy. By educating the expert on how their trial preparations are structured, counsel gives the expert a degree of comfort and the opportunity to reciprocate that teaching when it comes to their area of expertise. Time spent in preparation also has another added benefit, it helps to decide on questions of structure for the actual direct examination.

D.   Structuring Direct Expert Testimony

We have previously discussed how the evidentiary standards impact the qualification and admissibility of expert testimony. They also provide a structure for the outline of direct. When presenting an expert witness counsel must: (1) tell the jury why the expert is here, (2) establish conclusively the foundations for the expertise of the expert, (3) tender the expert as an expert in the specific area identified to the jury and for which the foundation is laid, (4) ask the expert to provide the major opinions needed,

(5) explore the specific basis for these opinions (usually research or learned treatises in the field of expertise), (6) diffuse weaknesses, and then, (7) restate the main opinion. Following these seven steps will competently prepare and present expert testimony that is tied to the case theme and theories.

Counsel must spend significant time educating themselves on the way in which the expert's testimony will assist the jury in understanding the issues in controversy. The greater the amount of knowledge counsel gains on this foundational topic, the easier it becomes to have the expert qualified. That assistance begins with qualifying the expert witness. The first step in accomplishing this is to fully understand how the qualification process works and the steps to take to lay appropriate foundations for the admissibility of the expert's testimony. When counsel qualifies a witness they should focus on:

1. Why they expert is testifying

2. Establishing the foundations for the expertise

3. Tendering the witness as an expert (when the jurisdiction allows)

Mastery of these processes require an understanding and working use of the lessons discussed previously. All of these same advocacy principles apply when dealing with expert witnesses, they are merely impacted to a greater degree by the applicable legal standards, and by the need to ensure that the expert's testimony is easily and readily understandable by the members of the jury. Counsel must master the legal issues surrounding the admissibility of expert testimony while connecting it to the the substantive knowledge necessary to present and test the validity of the expert's conclusions.

1. Why is the expert testifying

Counsel must combine advocacy principles, legal principles, and substantive knowledge when dealing with expert witnesses. The core legal principles regulating expert testimony fall into three primary categories: (1) will the expert be allowed to testify, (2) what is permissible testimony, and (3) how broad is the scope of cross examination of the expert witness. Qualifying an expert witness is the first step an advocate masters to ensure the court will allow the expert to testify as an expert. The witness must first be qualified by reason of knowledge, skill, experience, training, or education in a field of specialized knowledge.

2. Qualifications

To qualify a witness as an expert counsel calls that witness to the stand and elicits testimony about his or her credentials. In some cases opposing counsel will stipulate to the expertise of the witness in an attempt to prevent the jury from hearing the witness' qualifications. It is not a best practice to agree to a stipulation of expertise, unless you are at a bench trial where the court is already aware of your expert's expertise. Persuasively it is much more effective to allow the jury to hear the impressive credentials of the witness instead of a cold, dispassionate, and unemotional instruction from the judge that "the witness is qualified as an expert.

In those situations where the judge "encourages" counsel to stipulate, an acceptable alternative is to have a copy of the witness's résumé or curriculum vitae admitted as an exhibit for the jury to read during deliberations, or to ask for the most favorable instruction concerning the witness's expertise.

Example: counsel is qualifying an expert from the crime lab. The expert performed ballistics testing on ammunition and rounds at the request of law enforcement. Counsel is attempting to qualify the expert so they can opine on whether or not the weapon owned by the defendant fired the bullets that killed the victim.

State:	Investigator Price, please identify yourself to the jury.
Witness:	My name is Investigator Ray Price, I work at the United States Army Criminal Investigative laboratory.
Q:	Is that the Army equivalent of NCIS or the FBI?
A:	Yes. Without the good looking actors.
State:	*(chuckles)* Why are you here today?
Witness:	I conducted testing on evidence in this case.
State:	We will get to your specific work involving this case in a moment. First I would like the jury to understand your qualifications. How long have you been in law enforcement?
Witness:	I spent my first 20 years as an agent investigating crimes in a regional office. I have been working at

USACIL as an analyst for the last 15 years. So I guess that's 35 years total.

State: That's a long time. What are your primary duties at USACIL?

Witness: I have spent the last 10 years in the firearms division. My particular expertise is in ballistics data for handguns.

State: What does your job at USACIL require?

Witness: I identify weapons, reconstruct shooting scenes, test weapons, conduct ballistic tests and gunshot residue testing, to include splatter identification.

State: Over the course of your 35 year career how many ballistic tests have you conducted?

Witness: I've lost count. At lNorth several hundred.

State: What specialized training have you received in ballistics testing?

Witness: I attended the FBI lab in Quantico, Virginia as a student many years ago. I have gone back for yearly updates. For the last 5 years I have been honored to serve as one of their senior ballistics instructors teaching new agents how to conduct ballistic testing.

State: Have you testified about ballistics testing in court?

Witness: Yes.

State: How many times?

Witness: Approximately 59 times.

State: Were you accepted as an expert in ballistics by the court on those 59 occasions?

Witness: Yes.

3.   Tendering the Witness

After establishing the credentials of the expert counsel must officially tender them to the court and have them accepted in order for them to be able to provide expert level testimony. When tendering the witness, the expert should be offered with sufficient specificity to clearly identify their area of expertise. Counsel should not, for example, qualify the witness as an expert in "child abuse or chemistry" but in the area in which the case needs help, such as child abuse accommodation by reporting victims, or biochemical drug testing of urine samples. The devil is in the details. When counsel is as accurate as possible as to the nature of the witness' expertise, it gives structure to the direct, and limits opposing counsel's ability to use void dire of the expert to argue that counsel is trying to unnecessarily expand the expert's opinion to matters on which they are not qualified. Let's return to our USACIL witness example whom counsel counsel is now tendering:

> *State:*   Your honor I offer Investigator Price has an expert in ballistic testing for handguns.
>
> *Judge:*   Objection?
>
> *Defense:* No objection.
>
> *Judge:*   Investigator Price is accepted by the court as an expert in ballistic testing for handguns. You may enquire.

Some jurisdictions do not allow for tendering, but instead prefer for counsel to continue with direct examination once the qualifying foundation for the expertise has been laid. In those jurisdictions the thought is that the court acknowledging the witness as an expert gives an additional imprimatur of legitimacy to the testimony. The federal courts routinely allow for, and in fact expect, the witness to be tendered as an expert. In the example above counsel chose not to challenge the credentials and qualifications of the expert witness. Alternatively counsel may choose to challenge those credentials. In those instances where opposing counsel wish to challenge the witness's qualifications as an expert the court will normally allow voir dire for that limited purpose.

> *State:*   Your honor I offer Investigator Price has an expert in ballistic testing for handguns.
>
> *Judge:*   Objection?

> *Defense:*   Your honor may I voir dire for the purposes of forming an objection?

> *Judge:*   Briefly counsel. Please limit your inquiry to qualifications.

4.   Voir Dire for Purposes of Forming an Objection

Preparation is the key for effective voir dire when attacking the credentials of an expert or when attempting to limit the scope of an expert's court-accepted expertise. When preparing to voir dire in this situation, counsel should address each of the following issues long before the witness actually takes the stand. First they need to know the subject area of the expert, in as detailed a manner as possible. They should begin by interviewing the witnesses and talking to their own experts in the area. Counsel cannot effectively voir dire an expert witness if they don't understand the subject matter. This makes sense as a practical matter, for if counsel does not sufficiently educate themselves as to the area of a witness' expertise, they can never find the details that might otherwise limit the scope of the expert's opinion. Counsel should review all documentation within the file, including that received through discovery. Next they should connect their case analysis to the expertise of the witness, thereby developing an understanding of how the evidence ties into the testimony of the expert, and how well that probable testimony falls in line with the experts lauded expertise.

Counsel must carefully identify the basis of the proffered expert's testimony. Did he actually perform any tests or is he merely commenting on the work of others? Is there any indication that the expert started their work on the case with an opinion prior to reviewing any of the facts and exhibits of the case? That type of work often raises quality control issues. Has he interviewed everyone involved? Did he spend sufficient time familiarizing himself with the case? Is he basing his theories or opinion solely on government-provided evidence or has he conducted his own tests? Is he aware of the defense's alternative theory; if not, why not? Is he a "professional" expert? The answer to these questions will provide fruitful grounds to challenge either the qualifications of the witness or the validity of their testimony. Continuing with the USACIL witness discussed previously the defense attorney is attempting to challenge the qualifications of the witness while also preparing the subsequent cross examination.

> *Defense:*   Investigator Price you conduct ballistic tests as part of your duties at USACIL.

> *Witness:*   Yes.

Defense: You did not conduct any tests in preparation for testifying today?

Witness: Correct.

Defense: You reviewed tests that another lab conducted?

Witness: Yes.

Defense: You were not present for those tests?

Witness: No I was not.

Defense: You would have performed some of those tests differently?

Witness: Yes, but that doesn't mean their results were not valid.

Defense: You reviewed work you did not do?

Witness: Yes.

Defense: You cannot tell us conclusively that proper testing procedures were followed based upon your own direct observation?

Witness: No I cannot.

Defense: Your honor we object to this witness, he has no personal knowledge and is merely serving has a mouthpiece for what would otherwise be inadmissible hearsay.

Judge: Response?

State: Your honor we have laid a proper foundation for this witness's expertise under FRE 702. Personal knowledge is not required for expert witness testimony.

Judge: Defense?

Defense: Your honor while we concede that personal knowledge is not a requirement for expert witnesses, in this instance the state is using this witness to pass through hearsay that is not otherwise admissible.

Judge: A point I am sure you will bring out on cross examination. The witness is accepted as an expert. State you may inquire.

Counsel may strategically decide not to voir dire the expert, or even attack their testimony When to let it go is an important decision. Consider the following example. Sometimes there is no reason to challenge the expert. If he doesn't hurt the case, is not involved in the theory or is so qualified that counsel aren't going to get anywhere then it is often best not to object, allowing the witness to slide into expert status. If counsel choose to voir dire an expert that is qualified the end result is often to merely assist opposing counsel in verifying the expertise of their chosen witness. Consider the following exchange concerning an expert in animal pathology.

Example: the following is the presentation of an expert witness, a veterinarian, by the plaintiff's attorney, to testify in a tort case regarding intentional neglect of a horse:

Judge: Call your first witness.

Plaintiff: Thank you, Your Honor. The Plaintiff will call Dr. Frank Fortuna.

Judge: [To Dr. Fortuna] Come forward and the court reporter will swear you in.

CR: Raise your right hand. Do you solemnly swear that the testimony you are about to give in the cause now pending is the truth, so you help you God?

Witness: I do.

Judge: Please watch your step, be seated and spell your last name for the court reporter.

Witness: My last name is Fortuna, F-O-R-T-U-N-A.

Judge: You may inquire counsel.

Plaintiff: Doctor Fortuna. Please state your full name and occupation for the record.

Witness: Frank Fortuna, and I'm a Professor at State University and a Diagnostic Pathologist at the SU Center for Population and Animal Health.

Plaintiff: Do your duties include performing pathological examinations on horses?

Witness: Yes.

Plaintiff: How long have you been doing this?

Witness: For almost 12 years now.

Plaintiff: Approximately how many pathological examinations have you performed on horses during that period of time?

Witness: At lNorth probably 250.

Plaintiff: Why do you conduct these examinations?

Witness: Usually it is to determine the cause of death or to look for infectious diseases that might affect the population.

Plaintiff: Doctor, in March of 20XX-5, did you perform a pathological examination on a horse sent in by the County Animal Control Agency?

Witness: Yes, I did.

Plaintiff: Your Honor, we offer Dr. Frank Fortuna as an Expert in the field of pathology.

Judge: Any objection?

Defense: I'd like to voir dire, Your Honor. I don't believe that expertise has been established.

Judge: *(in a slightly disgusted tone)* Very well counsel. You may voir dire for purposes of forming an objection.

Defense: Doctor, do you have a curriculum vitae here with you today?

Witness: No, I don't.

Defense: Do you have one in your file back at your office?

Witness: Yes, I do.

Defense: But you did not bring it with you today?

Witness: No one asked. I can send someone to go and get it if you like.

Defense: And what is your educational—what is your degree?

Witness: I have a doctorate in Veterinary Medicine from State University. I have nine years of clinical practice. I did a residency in anatomic pathology at SU and I have a Ph.D. in comparative pathology from Vine Covered University.

Defense: Have you been published in any kind of scholarly journals or written any books Anything of that nature?

Witness: Yes.

Defense: How many articles have you written, specifically?

Witness: Approximately 10 are currently published.

Defense: For veterinary-type journals or ...?

Witness: Veterinary journals.

Defense: And how long have you been doing pathological evaluations?

Witness: As a Board Certified Pathologist, since 2002.

Defense: You're Board Certified as a Pathologist?

Witness: As a Veterinary Pathologist.

Defense: Okay. So you've been with SU since September 5th of 20XX-7. Is that correct?

Witness: Correct.

Defense: How many pathology evaluations have you done at State University since September of 20XX-7?

Witness: In the area of necropsies, I've probably done in the vicinity of 50 a month since then. That would be, what, 450.

Defense: And you're talking about all sorts of animals?

Witness: All sorts of animals. That's correct.

Defense: Your Honor, I have no other questions of Dr. Fortuna at this moment.

Plaintiff: We renew our motion, Your Honor and ask that the court recognize Dr. Fortuna as an expert in the field of pathology.

Judge: I am going to grant the motion based on the background criteria of the witness for purposes of preliminary examination. You may continue.

Plaintiff: Thank you.

Any doubts the jury may have had about the qualifications of this expert witness have been obliterated by the voir dire that covered all of the additional foundational elements of expertise not covered when the witness was tendered. This is exactly what a defense attorney opposing an expert's qualifications should not do.

Sometimes opposing counsel will try to stretch the bounds of the witness's expertise. It is extremely embarrassing to miss this point and have the court recognize the expert for an area that counsel were not expecting. Do not let this happen. Limit – limit – limit (!) the testimony to established areas of knowledge and pertinence. Let us return to the veterinarian example and see voir dire approached in a different fashion, focusing on the scope of the expertise.

Plaintiff: Doctor, in March of 20XX-5, did you perform a pathological examination on a horse sent in by the County Animal Control Agency?

Witness: Yes, I did.

Plaintiff: Your Honor, we offer Dr. Frank Fortuna as an Expert in the field of pathology.

Judge: Any objection?

Defense: I'd like to briefly voir dire, Your Honor.

Judge: *(in a slightly disgusted tone)* Very well counsel.

Defense: Doctor you are a board certified veterinary pathologist?

Witness: Yes.

Defense: That pathology certification does not extend to human beings?

Witness: No.

Defense: Your honor we object to Dr. Fortuna being accepted by this court as an expert in pathology, but have no objection to his expertise in veterinary pathology.

Judge: Plaintiff?

Plaintiff: We modify our motion and ask that the court recognize Dr. Fortuna as an expert in the field of veterinary pathology.

Judge: Your modified motion is granted. You may inquire.

Plaintiff: Thank you.

In the above example defense counsel has been able to clearly define the limitations of the witness's expertise. Proper preparation will allow counsel to effectively use the voir dire process to break up the rhythm of the opponent's case, confuse the basis of the expert's opinion, and limit the expert's opinion while putting forth an alternative theory for their client. Preparation is the key to effective voir dire and cross examination of any witness, particularly one that is an expert. Once the expert has been tendered and accepted by the court, in those jurisdictions which allow it, the next step is to provide the major opinion.

5. Provide the Major Opinions

After the court accepts the witness as an expert counsel should focus on previewing the major opinion. This is the crux of the opinion that identifies the expert's conclusions. Think of it as the bottom line up front. By asking the question early in the direct examination of the expert, the jury now has context to understand the processes the expert went through and can piece the rational of the expert's opinion together with the information presented. Counsel then follow it up with an in depth discussion of how the opinion was realized. In the following example counsel continues to develop the testimony of investigator Price, focusing on the major opinion:

State: Investigator Price, as an expert in ballistics, have you formed an opinion concerning the slugs that were retrieved from the decedent's corpse?

Witness: Yes.

State: What is that opinion?

Witness: The slugs in question were fired by a .357 magnum revolver belonging to the accused in this case.

State: To what degree of certainty can you state this opinion?

Witness: I have no doubt concerning the weapon which fired the rounds retrieved from the victim's body.

> *State:* Investigator Price I'd like to talk with you now about the basis for your opinion. How did you come to this conclusion?

Sometimes counsel may be concerned about an attack on their witness because they have been paid. Depending upon the nature of the expert witness, it may be appropriate to draw the sting of that expected attack during the direct. Counsel should consider doing this after the major opinion has been given, but before the basis for the opinion is discussed in detail. Remember, jury members are not going to expect people to work for free. If counsel is careful to present the information as just a factual part of the expert's job, it can lessen the effect of any attempts to cross on the bias that money might provide. Consider the following exchange based upon our earlier example with the testimony of Dr. Fortuna.

> *Plaintiff:* Your Honor we ask that the court recognize Dr. Fortuna as an expert in the field of pathology.

> *Judge:* I am going to grant the motion based on the background criteria of the witness for purposes of preliminary examination. You may continue.

> *Plaintiff:* Thank you. Dr. Fortuna, as and expert in pathology have you formed an opinion as to the cause of death of the racehorse *Victory*?

> *Witness:* Yes I have.

> *Plaintiff:* What is that opinion?

> *Witness:* *Victory* was fed tainted food by containing a bacteria deadly for horses.

> *Plaintiff:* Before we discuss the basis of your opinion I would like to talk to you about your work here as an expert. Are you being compensated for you time?

> *Witness:* I am. My hourly rate is 200.00 dollars.

> *Plaintiff:* How many hours have you worked on this case?

Witness: Including my testimony today it is around 11 hours at this point.

Plainitff: Dr. Fortuna how often do you testify as an expert in these types of cases?

Witness: Not often, maybe two or three times a year.

Plaintiff: Do you testify only for the plaintiff?

Witness: No, I've testified for both plaintiffs and defendants.

Plaintiff: Is working as an expert your primary job?

Witness: No. By profession I am a professor, researcher and teacher at the university.

Plaintiff: Thank you Doctor, let's turn to how you arrived at your opinion in this case. You said that *Victory* was fed tainted food. How did you come to that conclusion?

This approach has drawn the sting of potential issues on cross examination, established the credibility and impartiality of the witness and the focused the jury back on the reason for the witness' opinion. The next step is to move on and develop the basis of that major opinion in depth.

6.   Basis for the Major Opinions

The next step would be to further explore the evidence, procedures and results from the testing either reviewed or conducted by the expert witness. During this section of the direct examination the expert witness shines. This is their time and counsel should make certain that the jury is getting a show. The expert should teach, engage and explain. Getting the witness of the stand to interact with exhibits is crucial so that the jury can learn both from the experts words and the visual aids the exhibits represent. Counsel should plan to use exhibits, diagrams and charts as identified during the witness preparation sessions.

Word choice and analogies are particularly important in this section of the direct examination. Counsel should listen carefully, and whenever there is doubt about the ability of the jury to understand what has just been said counsel should take the time to bring it back to a level where the jury gets it. By taking it upon themselves to ask for further explanation, counsel will make the jury feel more at ease in being taught the subject by the expert.

Example: counsel have called an expert in accident reconstruction to explain the forces involved in a car accident.

Defense: Professor I want to discuss with you how you arrived at your mathematical conclusions in this case.

Witness: Absolutely. We identified multiple variables on a sliding scale and then assigned them a probability quotient relative to the complexity of the physical forces involved. We considered them contextually, accounting for spatial differences.

Defense: Professor I'd like to break that process down so that I can understand it. What exactly were the multiple variables involved?

Witness: Oh. Well the variables included the size of the vehicles, their weight, the directions in which they were traveling before impact and their state and location after impact.

Defense: I see. So you input data based upon the cars and what the drivers said happened?

Witness: Exactly. We then modified that data to account for other variables which were present but not known to the witnesses.

Defense: I see, let's talk about those....

Counsel should particularly be on the watch for word choice during this section. It is always appropriate to ask the witness to explain a term in a more basic fashion. It is not necessary that counsel truly do not understand the term. The purpose of doing this is to make the jury get it without having the expert talk down to them. As discussed in the direct examination chapter, when done at the highest level a direct examination should feel like counsel is asking the questions that the jury naturally considers in their minds. This especially includes clarification questions when dealing with expert witnesses. Counsel must be on heightened awareness when directing an expert witness—by watching the faces of the members of the jury during questioning, counsel can ensure that sufficient clarifications on confusing issues are handled with ease. Put succinctly: if the jury looks lost or confused, counsel must fix that issue with further questioning. Counsel should also take care to break up this portion of the direct with exhibits that are relevant to the witness's testimony. This is the moment in the direct where counsel bring in the supporting documentations, research, tests, treatises, and the like, supporting the relevant opinions of the expert.

7.   Diffusing Weaknesses

Advocates should use the techniques of primacy and recency when dealing with the weaknesses of an expert's opinion. Counsel want to honestly disclose any shortcomings in the opinion, but are not required to highlight them is such a fashion that they negatively impact on the relevant portions of the opinion that assist. Counsel should admit those weaknesses, but sandwich them between strengths so they get credit for being straightforward while minimizing the damage. They should differentiate when necessary, but not spend too much time on the defensive—that is what redirect is for.

> *Example: counsel is diffusing weaknesses in the basis of an expert's opinion concerning ballistics testing.*

Plaintiff:	Investigator Price do you conduct ballistic tests as part of your duties at USACIL?
Witness:	Yes.
Defense:	Did you conduct any tests in preparation for testifying today?
Witness:	No I didn't.
Defense:	Really. I'm not sure I understand. If you did not conduct the tests how can you testify today?
Witness:	While I did not do the tests, I am perfectly capable of reviewing them based upon the appropriate standards.
Defense:	Have you done that here?
Witness:	I have.

Defense: How familiar are you with the applicable standard of work?

Witness: I have applied it for the last 35 years, and in the last 10 years I have been on the subcommittee that produces the training manual.

Defense: Based upon your review of those tests and the applicable standards have you been able to develop an opinion in this case.

Witness: Absolutely.

Defense: And what is that opinion?

By taking the time to diffuse the weakness concerning a lack of personal knowledge in the case counsel has protected their witness against the pending cross examination and established grounds for how to argue the validity of their results in closing.

8.   Restating the Major Opinion

The final wind up of the direct examination of the expert brings you back to the opinion that was first given, but with a more developed statement of that opinion, connecting it to the basis previously mentioned. Consider the following example based upon the earlier testimony of Dr. Fortuna.

Plaintiff: Dr. Fortuna we have just discussed the nature of the bacteria found in the food fed to *Victory.* We have also spent a great deal of time talking about the specifics of what you discovered during the autopsy and subsequent pathological tests. How did these activities influence your opinion in this case?

Witness: The lack of disease in the autopsy results, the status of the swollen digestive tract, and the specific presence of the deadly bacteria in the food found   within *Victory's stomach* establishes conclusively that he was fed tainted food containing a bacteria deadly for horses.

Plaintiff: What effect did that food have.

Witness: I can testify to a medical certainty that the tainted food caused the death of the racehorse *Victory*.

Plaintiff: Nothing further your honor. Thank you Doctor Fortunata I believe defense counsel may have some questions for you.

This restatement of the major opinion by tying it to the basis of the opinion testimony allows for admissible repetition, providing an emotional end to the expert's testimony that is persuasive. In cross examination opposing counsel will be forced to deal with the challenge presented by this approach.

E.   How to Cross Examine Experts

While the actual cross examination relies upon the same structures, techniques and methodologies discussed earlier in the section on cross examination, effective cross examination of expert witnesses requires additional preparation on the part of counsel. The need for additional preparation that is expert specific comes from the unique nature of expert witnesses. The ability of an expert to testify as to the ultimate issues in the case, along with their ability to rely upon third party information, creates specific challenges when preparing cross. Counsel must create cross examination runs addressing the expert as a normal witness with all of the potential impeachment possibilities inherent whenever anyone testifies, while also developing specific cross examination approaches focusing on the expert opinion.

> ***Example: plaintiff attorney is crossing a defense expert who has testified on direct examination that the doctor being sued followed the standard of care. The attorney begins by establishing a standard that doctors should conform to when deciding whether to conduct surgery:***

Plaintiff: Dr. Richards you agree that doctors should know it's safe to perform surgery on a patient before they perform surgery?

Witness: They should know their patients medical history.

Plaintiff: Health problems?

Witness: Yes.

Plaintiff: Medications the patient was taking?

Witness: Of course.

Plaintiff: It's important for doctors to get a full medical history?

Witness: Well that depends.

Plaintiff: Do you remember testifying in a deposition about the need for doctor's to get a full medical history before treating a patient?

Witness: I do.

Plaintiff: So you agree that if possible a doctor should get a full medical history before treating a patient?

Witness: Sure.

Plaintiff: In fact you think its responsible practice to do so, don't you?

The plaintiff attorney now moves to a different headline, or set of issues, focusing the next portion of the cross on how a doctor can determine if a patient is a good candidate for surgery?

Plaintiff: Let's talk about ways a doctor can find out if their patient is a good candidate for surgery. One way would be to get a medical clearance from the patients primary physician?

Witness: That would be a good idea, but it is not required by the standards of care.

Plaintiff: We will get to that in a minute. You were Ms. North's primary doctor?

Witness: Yes I was, sweet person.

Plaintiff: For 10 years maybe longer?

Witness: Yes.

Plaintiff: You knew her medical history?

Witness: Yes.

Plaintiff: You knew about her health problems?

Witness: Yes, and her struggles to control them.

Plaintiff: Her high blood pressure?

Witness: Yes. We tried to get that down.

Plaintiff: Her high cholesterol?

Witness: Yes. That too.

Plaintiff: You knew what kind of medication she was on?

Witness: Yes. In fact I prescribed it.

Plaintiff: Exactly. Now Dr Reynolds never called you about Ms. North?

Witness: No he did not.

Plaintiff: He never called you for a medical clearance?

Witness: No, but he wasn't required to do that.

Plaintiff: But it would have been a best practice to do so?

Witness: Yes.

Plaintiff: No one from Dr. Reynolds's office called you about her?

Witness: No.

Plaintiff: And you would remember if Dr. Reynolds called you?

Witness: Yes.

Plaintiff: You would remember because of how well known Dr. Reynolds is?

Witness: Yes. He is the best at that surgery in the nation.

Plaintiff: And if Dr. Reynolds did call you, you would have told him Ms. North was not a good candidate for plastic surgery?

Witness: Well yes, but probably not exactly that way.

Plaintiff: You would have told him no-just like you told Ms. North?

Witness: Yes I suppose so.

Having established a failure on the part of the surgeon to communicate with Ms. North's primary care physician the attorney now moves to another way to determine if a person is a good candidate for surgery:

Plaintiff: Let's talk about another way that a doctor can check to see if a patient is a good candidate for surgery?

Witness: If you like.

Plaintiff: There are tests doctors can do?

Witness: Yes.

Plaintiff: Objective tests?

Witness: Yes, if they are properly administered.

Plaintiff: Tests that can be done to see if the patient is high risk?

Witness: Yes.

Plaintiff: Tests that are available to all doctors and should be done if the patient is a high risk?

Witness: Yes.

Now that the plaintiff has defined the circumstances properly they segue into a line of questioning designed to focus the expert on a hypothetical question based on the facts developed during the previous portions of the cross examination.

Plaintiff: Doctor, hypothetically speaking, would you agree that a patient with Ms. Reynolds medical history, to include obesity, high blood pressure and high cholesterol, was at a high risk for complications or possible death if operated on in the manner described during direct examination.

Witness: Yes. I would agree that the risk would be high, but sometimes you have to take those risks when the situation require it.

Plaintiff: That's why you thought it was dangerous for her to get the surgery?

Witness: Yes.

Plaintiff: You thought she would have a heart attack?

Witness: Yes, possibly.

Plaintiff: And that's why you could not give her a medical clearance to do the surgery?

Witness: Yes, that's correct.

Now that the hypothetical question has been answered the attorney ties up any potential avenues for rehabilitation on redirect. Here they are focusing on the need to discuss potential surgery with the patient before proceeding with the surgery.

Plaintiff: Lets talk about another way a doctor can see if their patient is a good candidate for surgery. By talking to the patient?

Witness: Of course.

Plaintiff   You knew Ms. North medical history?

Witness: Yes.

Plaintiff: You asked about her medical history?

Witness: Yes.

Plaintiff: You had that conversation with her?

Witness: Yes.

Plaintiff: In your office?

Witness: Yes, as usual.

Finally the attorney moves to a series of summary questions drawing upon the earlier cross but restating the points for use in closing. The restatement of the questions allows for the development of additional questions that are not cumulative.

Plaintiff: You can't say she had that same conversation with Dr. Reynolds?

Witness: No, I can't, but I would be surprised if she did not.

Plaintiff: You can't say that doctor Reynolds asked Ms. North about her medical history?

Witness: No I can't say that, but again I can't imagine that he didn't.

Plaintiff: All you can say is that if Dr. Reynolds called you- you would have told him Ms. North is not a good candidate for plastic surgery because of her heart problems?

Witness: Yes, that is exactly what I would have said.

When focusing on expertise specific cross examination questions, counsel should turn to their expert first. This expert may be a consultant who is part of the team and does not testify (and is covered by attorney client work product and privilege), or they may be a testifying expert. If they are also going to testify their conversations with counsel may be discoverable. In either instance though, counsel's expert is the first place they should turn when developing an understanding of the quality and basis of the opposing side's expert witness. Counsel should also do whatever outside research is necessary for them to understand the basis of the opposing expert's opinion. Again, if counsel does not understand what the expert is talking about, they cannot possibly construct a cross examination that cuts to the heart of the issues. Once counsel understands the issues in play they should write them down as a list. This list forms the structure for additional expert witness case analysis. The next step is to turn to resources that are normally relied upon by experts when addressing the controverted issues in the case.

The sources experts rely upon when forming their opinions include legal treatises, journals and trade publications. Reviewing these materials will educate counsel on potential substantive bases for cross examination designed to challenge either the nature of the expert's conclusions or the methodologies relied upon by the expert in making their decisions. Both are potential grounds for cross, but counsel should only approach and develop them in concert with their own expert's advice and expert identified supporting materials. These materials must be properly identified and managed so they are available for use during impeachment under FRE 803(18). The next step is to review any publications written by the testifying expert. When reviewing the previous writings of the expert counsel should look for opinions, methodologies or assertions that are contrary to the expected testimony at trial, or the experts preliminary report.

If the expert has previously testified as an expert they may very well be in the database of various organizations. A review of the available databases may provide counsel with copies of prior testimony in cases with similar issues. It may also identify previous litigants who may have deal with this expert in the past. An email or phone call to a counsel who has previously dealt with an expert can produce potential lines of inquiry based upon actual experience.

Experts are often paid for their testimony and a bias inquiry will always have some merit in situation. Other experts are associated with a particular cause or side in the litigation or in the public arena that cannot help but color their opinions. There are many resources available to assist counsel in sorting out issues of bias. Do not forget them: they are safe island in the dangerous seas of expert witness cross examination.

F. Checklist

The following checklist summarizes the information counsel should consider when developing persuasive expert witness testimony. It should be used as a starting point for developing appropriate examinations focused on persuading the jury by showcasing the theme and theories of the case.

I.   Presenting Expert Witness Testimony:

        a.   Tell the jury why the expert is here.

        b.   Establish foundation for expertise.

        c.   Tender the witness.

        d.   Provide the major opinion.

        e.   Explore the basis for the major opinion.

        f.   Discuss weaknesses.

        g.   Restate the major opinion.

II.   Cross examining the expert:

        a.   Control the witness.

        b.   Establish facts that bolster your Theme and Theory.

        c.   Establish facts that build up the credibility of your witnesses and diminish the credibility of your opponent's witnesses.

        d.   Stay on the Island unless prepared.

        e.   Cluster together all of the facts that enhance and support the topic.

        f.   Lay out the facts one question at a time leading up to your final point.

        g.   Identify similar facts based upon your knowledge of human nature and then using them to make your final point.

        h.   Do not forget that experts are people too—look for bias, motive

III.   Cross Examination Sequencing:

        a.   Do not use chronological order in confrontational cross examinations.

        b.   Avoid chronological order in informational cross examinations.

        c.   Lay your theme early and often.

        d.   Close cross examination with a theme goal question.

        e.   When attacking credibility, attack in the beginning.

        f.   Show bias, interest, or motive early in the cross examination.

        g.   End with a power goal question that is unassailable.

        h.   Develop risky areas only after establishing control of the witness through safe goal questions.

        i.   Never lead or end with a risky line of questions.

j.   If you have more than one impeachment, use the cleanest first.

k.   Disperse impeachment throughout the cross examination.

l.   When expecting a 'no' answer to one goal question, precede that chapter with a sure 'yes' answer.

m.   Bundle goal questions that need to be done together in order to complete a coherent picture of a single event.

n.   Prepared questions countering the power of the opponent's case are best performed in the middle of cross examination.

G.   Evidence Rules to Consider

Issues Arising During Direct of Experts	Applicable Federal Rules of Evidence
Expert testimony	701–705
Character of a witness for truthfulness	608
Out-of-court statements offered for the truth of the matter asserted therein (hearsay)	801–807
Legal relevancy - is the probative value substantially outweighed by the danger of unfair prejudice, et al.	403
Are the questions logically relevant?	401, 402
Competency of a witness	610
Personal knowledge of the witness. (See FRE 701 - 705 for expert witness exception to this requirement).	602
Questioning witnesses.	611, 614

Table 1 - Potential Evidentiary Rules Applicable During Direct Examination of Experts

Chapter 11: Closing Argument

A. Introduction 443
B. What the Jury Sees and Thinks..445
C. How the Law Impacts Closing..446
D. Creating the Closing..448
E. Delivering the Closing 462
F. Rebuttal...466
G. Examples 470
H. Checklists...504
I. Evidentiary Rules to Consider During Closings 506

A.   Introduction

Counsel weave the legal and factual theories of the case together into their closing argument, guided by the moral theory they have chosen as the "emotional engine" of the case. The legal and factual theories are nothing more than the application of the relevant law to the specific facts of the case. Each fact, exhibit, and piece of testimony are strands in the tapestry counsel must weave to convince the jury of their case. At the close of the case in chief the facts are now identified, both those that are disputed and undisputed. Closings must address the hard questions of fact that are part of the disputed facts of the case in a persuasive manner. Now is the time for counsel to embrace these hard questions, and explain to the jury why their side has the best answers for each and every one. Persuasion is created when the attorney addresses the hard questions of fact using law and morality in a way that rings true in the individual and collec-

> **Best Practices:**
> - Candid & Reasonable
> - Confident
> - Personal Connection
> - Structure
> - Address applicable legal standard
> - Appeal to Common Sense
> - Use of exhibits

tive minds of the jury. All other things being equal the side with the best explanation for those hard questions of fact wins the case.

The law and facts form the basis for the legal or procedural reasons counsel win. These two theories are how the jury is empowered to decide the case in counsel's favor. The moral theme, on the other hand, is the emotional reason counsel *should* win. It is why the jury wants to decide the case in counsel's favor. Attorneys must weave these three facets together when creating superior closing arguments. This is not a magic act, a play, or a movie. Counsel have just guided the jury on a long journey, throughout each stage of the case. It may have been dangerous, it may have been boring, but it must have been important, and counsel must have been genuine throughout each piece of trial. Closing argument reminds the jury why the journey of the trial was important, and explains what the journey signifies in a way the jury can accept, understand as true, and take action upon. Counsel who main their likability, believability, and credibility in each stage of the trial will find a jury ready to listen and agree with their arguments.

Closing must fairly and clearly outline the issues and provide an acceptable solution. In earlier discussions on primacy and recency, this text outlined the steps as a triplicate of 1) tell them what you are going to tell them; 2) tell them; 3) tell them what you just told them. Closing arguments are where counsel completes the triplicate, walking the jury through how each moment of the trial mattered as proof of the elements under the law. It is when counsel solves any questions that remain in the mind of the jury. This is the essence of a powerful argument, a call to action providing a solution the jury can adopt as their belief that it is the right thing to do - once this occurs the jury will act consistently with the belief, with the final verdict becomes an expression of that consistency.

> **Worst Practices:**
> - Misstate law or evidence
> - Argue facts not in evidence
> - State personal belief
> - Personally vouch for witnesses
> - Comment on the exercise of a fundamental right
> - Make personal attacks on opposing counsel
> - Argue issues not in dispute

Closing arguments must contain the words empowering the jury to decide the case in counsel's favor. It melds the facts and the law of the case, casting them in a moral light. That moral light must shine for the members of the jury as the only acceptable solution for the case. A good closing argument demands that the jury do nothing other than what is asked. If counsel properly identified the legal issues, factual issues, and picked the right theme and theory, the closing argument comes as an organic expression of what has been shown to be true during the trial.

To be successful the jury must accept the closing as a credible expression of the facts and law admitted to the jury and ruled upon by the court. This is why counsel must do their utmost to maintain their likability, believability, and credibility in front of the members of the jury at all times, while basing all things in the facts and law. Choosing a closing argument that is not grounded in the facts and law is dangerous. Counsel may sound like an extremely persuasive and competent attorney, but it simply will not matter. Counsel's argument must be in line with all the jury has seen and heard throughout the trial, or the most eloquently crafted word-smithing will fall flat. The jury will be left cold in the end, and will turn to the side of the attorney whose argument makes the most sense, both rationally and emotionally.

There are certain organizational techniques that counsel should employ, but they will ultimately not be successful if counsel has not developed an internal understanding of the true source of their position and how the argument must flow from that source. As with all other trial skills, the strength of the closing is rooted in counsel doing a thorough case analysis that they continually review to be as fluent as possible in their case. To do otherwise is to risk the jury discovering counsel is not genuine and should therefor be ignored. Counsel must not make this mistake. It is in the center of the case that counsel will find their superior closing argument. Once the center has been discovered, organizational structures help present the argument, but they can never become the argument.

B.   What the Jury Sees and Thinks

The entire weight of a trial—the testimony, the exhibits, the legal arguments, rests upon counsel's shoulders when they begin to close. This is the moment the entire trial has been building towards—when facts are interwoven with exhibits, testimony and law to bring about justice for a cause of action. The eyes of the client or the needs of the people represented are focused on the words of the closing. The jury is looking for guidance, clarity and fairness, hoping to find justice through the words of counsel. The court hopes for an appropriately delivered version of the case, grounded in law, supported by the facts, and argued in a way that explains to the jury using analogies, inferences, and appeals to common sense. They want to be entertained, but need to be guided - superior closings do both.

During the trial the jury has been paying attention to the lawyers and the witnesses. Juries understand that lawyers represent clients, and that their presentations are slanted towards one side. Jury members look to see if counsel are fair, they are trying to decide whom they can trust on the hard questions of fact. The credibility of counsel is of paramount importance. Fairness in dealing with witnesses, the court, and opposing counsel increases the perceived fairness of the attorney, accruing to their benefit.

This makes for a strong utilitarian argument in favor of professionalism. When counsel conduct themselves externally in a fashion designed to appear fair they are perceived as fair, often benefiting on those questions of fact that are arguable as a result of their perceived nature by the jury. Reality follows perception in such instances, where the appearance of professionalism leads to professional conduct. In the close cases the jury's belief in the fairness of counsel can serve as the fulcrum around which the lever of counsel's rhetoric works - during the closing argument.

At this the point the jury hopes for guidance, clarity and justice. If counsel have properly analyzed and prepared the case the majority of what they planned to talk about is present in the courtroom. Now is the time to pull from the testimony the facts needed and juxtapose them with what the law requires or allows. Properly done the jury hears counsel argue during closings for what they previewed during opening statements and provided as evidence during the testimony of witnesses. To focus on this artistic moment of success counsel must have laid the proper foundations through out the case, and must show their awareness of those moments by citing back to them as clearly as possible.

C.   How the Law Impacts Closing

Most jurisdictions define the procedural requirements for closing argument in rules of procedure or local practice. In most courts counsel having the burden to proof argue first, followed by the defense counsel. Rebuttal argument is then allowed by counsel who has the burden, unless not permitted by statute or rule. The procedural rules also address permissible contents for argument, to include reasonable comments on the evidence in the case, drawing reasonable inferences from the evidence, arguing the credibility of witnesses and positing how the evidence should be viewed by the

Counsel Must Address:

- Elements of Each Claim
- Elements of Each Defense
- Elements of Each Counter Claim

jury. As a general rule objections during closings are rarely sustained, unless they involve arguing facts not in evidence, grievously mischaracterizing the evidence, or extremely inflammatory arguments or images.

The substantive law impacts the case and must be addressed during closings. The cause of action in a civil case, or the indictment or information in a criminal case, established the elements that must be proven by the moving party during the trial. We have addressed how to handle those elements during case analysis, and counsel should have admitted evidence meeting the standard of proof for every legal element. During the closing counsel must come back to those legal elements and explain to the jury how they have not only met their burden of proof, but how any counterclaims or affirmative defenses have not been proven, or depending upon who has the burden (for examples in many criminal jurisdictions raising an affirmative defense creates a burden on the government to disprove it) establish that the affirmative defense is not valid. Proof alone, however, is not enough. If counsel cannot present their proof in a fashion that is understandable and tied to the moral theme they have established, they will have an incredibly difficult time convincing the jury.

This area of the trial may become confusing for the jury. While the court will instruct the jury on the law, counsel should use the same instructions to form the basis of the portion of their closing which addresses the elements and the burden of proof. The jury will hear counsel speaking in the same language as the judge about these legal issues, increasing the perception that counsel is both credible and impartial. They become the framework through which counsel presents the facts, evidence, and testimony to persuasively lead the jury to the correct verdict. Using instructions, particularly for the side having the burden of proof, can assist the jury in understanding the argument and organizing their own thoughts for the deliberation room. It is a moment where counsel can take the overwhelming amount of information that has been presented during trial and show the purpose behind each moment to the members of the jury. Counsel should encourage juries to take notes during this portion of the argument if it is permitted, and refer to the instructions either through the use of published demonstratives, copies given to the jury by the court, or both.

Most trial and appellate legal issues regarding closing arguments revolve around problems dealing with the effects of impermissible argument. A review of the case law dealing with what constitutes impermissible argument will provide counsel with some broad legal principles advocates can rely upon in setting the limits as to what is appropriate argument in most jurisdictions. Counsel who find themselves in a position where they wish to push the boundaries of permissible argument would do well to take the time to review the case law in their jurisdiction regarding these suggested legal principles, and then adopt as a best practice walking up to the line, but not over it.

The development of the case law concerning closing arguments has generally taken two paths. The first path is an analysis of whether or not the conduct of the attorney making the argument was ethical. The courts often refer to rules of professional conduct and the American Bar Association guidelines for prosecution and defense conduct concerning closing arguments when trying to make this decision. Once a determination has been made as to whether or not the attorney violated ethical norms (at this point the lawyer in question often has a bar related issue), the next question is whether or not that violation resulted in the loss of a substantial right of a party, usually the accused. If so then relief may be provided by the court.

When an improper argument is made by opposing counsel there are several potential ways to deal with it. The available remedies are to a certain extent dependent upon the nature of the improper argument. In those instances where the argument is both improper and unfairly prejudicial the court should stop the argument sua sponte if opposing counsel does not object. In those cases where the improper argument is either less obvious or less prejudicial the court will normally look to opposing counsel to object, and if they do not it is normally treated as a waiver issue at the appellate level.

While failure to object is often considered waiver of the issue, some forms of improper argument are plain error even when counsel does not object. For error to be plain the objectionable argument must be obvious and substantial, having possibly had an unfair prejudicial impact. Remedies for improper argument include curative instructions, the court requiring counsel to retract the improper portion of the argument, or, in those circumstances where the prejudice cannot be repaired - declaring a mistrial.

D.   Creating the Closing

1.   Case Analysis

The seeds for successful closing arguments were planted during case analysis, watered by the words of the opening statement, and then carefully tended during direct examination while also being weeded during cross.

In the closings the seeds of case analysis bear fruit - persuading and connecting with the jury.

During case analysis counsel should have focused on identifying what they needed to say and how they wanted to say it through the testimony of witnesses. They next developed theories and themes designed to bring the jury to the point where they would accept, believe and then internalize their vision of the case. These themes were then crafted into each and every direct and cross examination. The ultimate goal of this process was to find the story within the case that would ring true with the jury so that the jury members would adopt that version of events during the final arguments in the deliberation room.

The closing argument, or summation as it is called in some jurisdictions, exists separately from the earlier case analysis and preparation, but is nonetheless the emotional and logical child of that earlier work. The goal is to empower the jury to argue for counsel in the deliberation room where all true final arguments are made. The work of counsel that was done up front pays off during closing arguments in that counsel know what they need to talk about: the question is how.

Counsel must explain to the jury what happened, how the law addresses it, and why they should decide the case a certain way. This what, how and why approach is connected to case analysis, and mirrors the decision making process of people. The closing must address each of these components separately, and then bring them together in an efficient and persuasive fashion. The "what" is found in the facts, the "how" is explained by the law, and the "why" is the moral reason the jury wants to use to decide the case. Counsel must consciously identify all three elements during case analysis and then bring them back together closings. Each of the three must work seamlessly with one another. If the what, how, and why do not flow with one another, it is an indication that counsel's case analysis was not on the mark and must be adjusted to ensure success.

Closing argument is the destination of the trial. It is imperative that counsel identify the closing argument's legal theories, factual theories and moral themes during case analysis. This must be done at the start of the case, and the revisited through out the process to ensure the message is both understandable and supported by the work being done. It must also be continuously revisited as counsel prepare for trial. They should use the expected closing argument as a sanity check on the case. When counsel find themselves straying from the original destination of a planned closing created during case analysis they must ask why?

If they cannot answer the "why" question it indicates a strong probability that either the case analysis was incorrect, facts were not properly identified or admitted, or the moral ground has shifted. When this occurs the probability of losing increases. Most cases are lost through a lack of organization and cohesive presentation. The dangers of losing focus are particularly high when the closing argument shifts based upon the presentation during the case. Counsel must continually revisit their understanding of the case, and make sure they keep their eyes on the target of the most persuasive case analysis possible.

Before delivering the closing counsel must go back and review the evidence admitted at trial. Every trial lawyer has a methodology for managing the exhibits and testimony admitted. Now is the time to review the evidence that can fairly be argued. Once counsel review what has been admitted they must compare it to what they expected would be admitted. Has evidence been excluded which formed a part of their proposed closings? Has other evidence been admitted that helped a portion of the case? How were witnesses perceived? What, if any, impeachments occurred over the course of the trial? These questions should assist counsel in finding the argument that must be made now, as opposed to the argument they hoped to make when the case was first analyzed.

When counsel can effectively answer these questions they are prepared to begin crafting a closing argument. When doing so it is helpful to use accepted rhetorical devices such as the rule of threes, parallelism, analogies and alliteration.

2.   Structure

a.   Theme

Closing argument should use primacy and recency by beginning with a high impact point. The jurors are tired from sitting through a contested trial and are seeking clarity. Counsel should begin with a point that matters, one which grabs the interest of the jury and pulls them into the presentation. This high impact approach should include the moral theme of the case and is often built upon the actual statements of a party or witness, a piece of physical evidence, or a theme chosen by counsel that reflects alliteration, trilogies, or parallelism. It is in a very real sense the hook of the case. This is the theme that is built into the openings, and then repeated in each and every direct and cross. This hook becomes the fulcrum around which the closing turns, and counsel will often return to it as a refrain through out the closing. One famous example of this is Johnnie Cochran's "If it doesn't fit, you must acquit" line which he used to great effect when dealing with several different issues in State v. Simpson.

Here are three small examples from Mr. Cochran's hook taken from a portion of his closing argument in the Simpson case. Counsel should note how he initially sets up the issue, and then drives it home with each subsequent use.

> And so as we look then at the time line and the importance of this time line, I want you to remember these words. Like the defining moment in this trial, the day Mr. Darden asked Mr. Simpson to try on those gloves and the gloves didn't fit, remember these words; *if it doesn't fit, you must acquit.....*
>
> ....[T]hey don't have any mountain or ocean of evidence. It's not so because they say so. That's just rhetoric. We this afternoon are talking about the facts. And so it doesn't make any sense. It just doesn't fit. *If it doesn't fit, you must acquit....*
>
> ....[I]'m still Johnnie Cochran with a knit cap. And if you looked at O.J. Simpson over there--and he has a rather large head--O.J. Simpson in a knit cap from two blocks away is still O.J. Simpson. It's no disguise. It's no disguise. It makes no sense. It doesn't fit. *If it doesn't fit, you must acquit.*

Another example of a hook can be found in the following example taken from a criminal case. In this case the defendant is accused of assaulting a US Marshall with a vehicle.

> Defense: *They believed he was there because they needed him to be there* - but believing something does not make it so.
>
> We are here today because Mr. Grimes wanted to believe that Samantha Jones would come back to him and to make that happen he needed George Johnson to be in that parking lot. Marshall Dilliard wants to believe that George Johnson was in that car, he needs George Johnson to be in that car, because he couldn't find him, becoming so desperate that eventually he arrests an off duty deputy

sheriff. He believes George was there because he needs George Johnson to be there.

At the beginning of this trial I told you that this was a case of mistaken identity....

In the following selection a civil defense lawyer is shifting blame onto other parties and the plaintiff in a wrongful death case revolving around a traffic accident.

Defense: May it please the court. Counsel. Members of the Jury. At the beginning of this trial, my co-counsel, told you that this case was about **a Renal Van that was in the wrong place . . . a semi-truck driver who made the wrong choice . . . and that these lawyers were going to come in this courtroom and blame the wrong person.** And now that you have seen all the evidence and heard all the testimony you now know she was exactly right. These lawyers just expected to come in here, point a finger, pick up a check and go home. But that's not enough, not nearly enough..............

The hook should capture the jury's attention, ring true as something counsel has used throughout their trial to their persuasive benefit, and challenge their perceptions. By its very existence, the hook must argue continually, long after closing arguments have concluded. It is the phrase that counsel wants on repeat in the jury's mind as they begin their deliberations. Counsel want that initial impact to resonate in the jury deliberation room where the true final arguments are made.

b.   Burden

After counsel have appropriately identify the theme of the case, they must next address the burden of proof. Burden of proof is a term of art which captures the legal standard that must be met to win the case. The burden of proof is different depending upon both the nature of the case, whether civil or criminal, and the impact of any potential defenses that may have been raised during the case. It is the responsibility of the court to instruct the jury on the relevant burden of proof. That being said, such instructions can be found by counsel in the relevant case law and pattern instructions for the jurisdiction in which the trial is held. It is important for counsel to review those pattern instructions on burdens of proof and incorporate them into their closing argument where appropriate. This prevents the jury from feeling as if counsel is trying to hide things from them, and gives counsel yet another opportunity to educate them on what are likely unfamiliar topics. There is persuasive value in echoing the legal standards the court will instruct on when making arguments during closings

Consider the following examples from the pattern instructions in 11th Circuit's Pattern Civil Jury Instructions:

1.1 General Preliminary Instructions, Burden of Proof

[Name of plaintiff] has the burden of proving [his/her/its] case by what the law calls a A preponderance of the evidence. That means [name of plaintiff] must prove that, in light of all the evidence, what [he/she/it] claims is more likely true than not. So, if you could put the evidence favoring [name of plaintiff] and the evidence favoring [name of defendant] on opposite sides of balancing scales, [name of plaintiff] needs to make the scales tip to [his/her/its] side. If [name of plaintiff] fails to meet this burden, you must find in favor of [name of defendant].

To decide whether any fact has been proved by a preponderance of the evidence, you may - unless I instruct you otherwise - consider the testimony of all witnesses, regardless of who called them, and all exhibits that the court allowed, regardless of who produced them. After considering all the evidence, if you decide a claim or fact is more likely true than not, then the claim or fact has been proved by a preponderance of the evidence.

[Optional: On certain issues, called Affirmative defenses, [name of defendant] has the burden of proving the elements of a defense by a preponderance of the evidence. I will instruct you on the facts [name of defendant] must prove for any affirmative defense. After considering all the evidence, if you decide that [name of defendant] has successfully proven that the required facts are more likely true than not, the affirmative [his/her/its] claims.]

1.2 Burden of Proof Clear and Convincing Evidence

Sometimes a party has the burden of proving a claim or defense by clear and convincing evidence. This is a higher standard of proof than proof by a preponderance of the evidence. It means the evidence must persuade you that the claim or defense is highly probable or reasonably certain. The court will tell you when to apply this standard.

The attorney should choose where to place their discussion about the burden of proof within the closing based upon an analysis of what they most need to highlight from a legal standard perspective. Generally speaking it is helpful for the jury to address the standard of proof before covering the different elements that must be proven. When the standard of proof is identified first, it can then serve as a benchmark which counsel can use to discuss the value of the evidence presented at trial.

In the following example taken from a civil case, counsel uses the discussion of the burden of proof to set up the argument on the evidence submitted during the trial.

> Defense: ....But that's not enough, not nearly enough. And why? Because the Judge will tell you in a few minutes that the burden of proof today is still at this table-with the Plaintiff. You see it's not enough for them to just say Robert McGee caused this accident-they had to prove it. This plaintiff had to prove her case by the greater weight of the evidence - by the entire force and effect of all the evidence in this case. That's the law.

In this example the defense attorney is addressing the government's burden of proof, using language taken from the relevant instruction in the jurisdiction where the case is being tried.

> *Defense:*   Today it was the government's burden, and their burden alone, to prove to you each element of the crimes charged against George Johnson. Not only was it their burden to prove those elements, but they had to prove them beyond a reasonable doubt. What you'll hear the judge tell you today is that proof beyond a reasonable doubt would leave you firmly convinced that the defendant is guilty. And today the government has failed to do that. They have failed to satisfy the burden placed upon them by our legal system and because they failed, you must acquit George Johnson.

In this final example counsel is addressing a specific clear an convincing standard in a civil case based upon a specific statutory requirement.

> *Defense:*   Members of the jury, as you consider the appropriate place for baby Jamie, I want you to remember the law, and be guided by it. The law of our state tells us that when deciding this question of what is in the best interest of a child, we must

presume that a child under the age of nine, is always better off with their biological mother. In
other words, unless the Plaintiff's provide evidence that clearly and convincingly shows that
Jamie Jr. would be better off with the them, the
law mandates that it is with his mother where his
interests are best served. It is with his mother
where he will grow and develop into the best
young man he can be. It is with his mother where
he will be best situated to learn, and laugh, and
love.

c.   Elements

 Once the theme has been reiterated and the burden of proof addressed, it
is time to discuss the elements of the charge, any affirmative defenses that
have been raised, or other relevant standards. This is the section of the
closing argument where counsel must address the evidence that has been
admitted and the credibility of that evidence, to explain why the jury
should or should not use that evidence to prove or disprove the alleged
crime or cause of action. In short, this is where counsel connects the dots
as to why the facts, exhibits and testimony proves they win the case. There
is a delicate balancing act here. It is important for counsel to concede those
facts not in controversy while also clearly identifying and arguing about
the controverted facts. This is the time to answer the hard questions of fact
in a way empowering the jury to decide the case in their favor.

This section of the closing argument is always case specific, and does not
lend itself well to a formulaic approach. Counsel should use exhibits or
copies of the relevant elements when necessary, but the order or structure
of the argument is driven by the evidence admitted. Scripting out a full
closing argument is a recipe for disaster, as much of what comes in
throughout the course of the trial is situationally dependent on many variables, which counsel cannot predict with complete accuracy. There is not a
single best approach here, it is instead a best practice for counsel to focus
on those persuasive techniques discussed earlier, adapting them to the
specifics of their case. This is where the art of accuracy truly comes into
play. Stories, analogies, parables, appeals to common sense, are all acceptable ways to bring the jury to a decision about whether or not the standard
of proof has been met as to each element of the crime or cause of action.
Counsel should take the time to organize the structure and find the story
that moves the jury to interpret the evidence in the way the attorney wishes.

The following example showcases an element by element approach to the discussion of the indictment by a defense lawyer in a criminal case:

Defense: Mr. Johnson is charged with assault on a federal officer with a dangerous weapon. I want to go through the elements of this crime one last time with you. I want to show you exactly how the Government has failed to meet their burden.

[PULL UP CHARGE AND DISPLAY]

The indictment is an assault charge. You'll notice that every element of this charge requires the Defendant, and only the Defendant, as the culprit. But during this entire trial, we have given you countless reasons why George Johnson was not the man in that blue Ford. More importantly, the Government has failed to prove that George Johnson was in that car. Why? Because they haven't proven that the Defendant was there. And because of that, they haven't proven that he assaulted Marshal James. They haven't shown you evidence that suggests he was in that car. And they can't even prove that the driver of that vehicle, whoever he may be, operated that vehicle in a dangerous or deadly manner.

So, how do we know George Johnson wasn't there? Today you heard the Government present their case. You heard the testimony of Adam Grimes. He told you that he was the one calling the Marshal's service and providing all of those tips. But he never told the Marshal's service that he dated Samantha Jones. Why didn't he tell them? You know exactly why. He didn't tell them because he was trying to win Samantha Jones back. You heard him tell you all today that his relationship with her ended the second George Johnson entered her life. He went from being her lover to being her co-worker. He needed to get George Johnson out of the picture, so he began telling the Marshals service that George Johnson was still in her life. Every day he would sneak across the hallway from his office and look out the window into the parking lot. You can picture him peeling back the curtain and staring longingly into that parking waiting for someone—ANYONE—to show up with Samantha.

So how does he describe this suspect that he saw? Medium build with brown hair. Think of how many people fit that description. Think of how desperate Adam Grimes was to find George Johnson. Think of how desperate Adam Grimes was to be back in Samantha Jones's life. In fact, we know how desperate he was. He provided 15 total tips in a three month period to Marshal Dilliard. But the Marshal never once found George Johnson in that parking lot…ever. He got so frustrated with the countless bad tips, that he insisted Adam Grimes reveal his identity. But even then, Marshal Dilliard was never able to put George Johnson in that parking lot.

Marshal Dilliard took the stand and told us all about that today. He was the star of the show—the man with all of the information. There's no denying that he has years of experience, but this time he was sloppy. After searching countless hours for George Johnson, Marshal Dilliard began shooting from the hip. You heard him today. He went through all of Johnson's records and never found him. He searched his home of record and no one was there. He went to Samantha's neighborhood and questions the neighbors. After two visits, speaking with uninterested third parties, he still was unable to find anyone who saw George Johnson. He even went inside Samantha's home and looked around and even then he admitted that there was no sign of Johnson. So, in an act of desperation, he begins taking tips from a man he's never met before. In his haste, he never even bothers to ask Adam Grimes about his relationship to Samantha or George. Had he, he would have found out that Grimes was a jealous lover. Instead

of performing his job thoroughly, he began rushing to bring Johnson in. He spent countless hours
sitting across from the Big Lots parking lot, waiting for Johnson to show up.

In the example directly above the defense counsel has placed the elements
checklist for the indictment in front of the jury, and then made a series of
arguments attacking each element - while the jury can see it. This is a superior persuasive technique and an appropriate use of both instructions and
demonstratives during closing argument.

d.   Address the Opposition

During closing argument counsel must also take the time to address the
opposing side's argument. This is an opportunity to frame the debate in a
way that places opposing counsel on the defensive, forcing them to argue
about facts that are better for your case as opposed to theirs. There are
several different ways to accomplish this objective, to include the use of
selected rhetorical questions that you asked the jury to have opposing
counsel answer, or the use of questions Council realizes it cannot be answered, and in some circumstances creating a list of things that are important to the case which do not support the core of opposing counsel's case.
The structure used by an attorney when addressing the opposing side's
case during closing argument should be driven by the available evidence
and any witness credibility issues that have arisen at trial.

Let's continue with an example from the same closing used
above. In the following example the defense counsel is now attacking the credibility of the government's identification evidence.

> *Defense:*   And that's when he got desperate. Today, the
> Marshal had to admit there were various occasions
> where he thought he had his guy. On April 8, Mar-
> shal Dilliard approached a man sitting in the Big
> Lots parking lot, asked him to stand up and put his
> hands high in the air. It was only then, after he
> was face to face with this man, that he determined
> it was not George Johnson. Three days later, Mar-
> shal Dilliard makes the same mistake again. This
> time, he goes so far as to make an actual arrest.
> And who did he arrest? Not George Johnson, but a
> local Deputy Sheriff, Victor Hansen. This is the
> same Deputy Sheriff who has worked previously
> directly with Marshal Dilliard. This U.S. Marshal

went through the process of putting this man in handcuffs before he ever figured out that it wasn't George Johnson. MOJ, your common sense tells you that if Marshal Dilliard mistakenly thought a deputy sheriff was the man he was looking for, he had absolutely NO IDEA what George Johnson looked like.

Which leads me to the events on April 24—only 5 days after the debacle with the deputy sheriff. Grimes called in, for the fifteenth time, swearing up and down that Johnson would be in that parking lot. That's when Dilliard asked Marshal James to help. From this viewpoint **[PULL UP EX. 12]**, both Marshals say they positively identify George Johnson sitting in the driver's seat of Samantha Jones's blue Ford. These two Marshals, who had never even seen a picture of Johnson before, positively identify this man with a medium build and brown hair sitting in the car. So from this distance, they were somehow 100% positive that behind that absurdly dark tinted window[1] was George Johnson. To this day, Marshal Dilliard is still 100% sure it was Johnson. Even after he snuck up behind the car on the passenger's side. Even after he watched the car drive away as he was on his back. And even after he tried to chase the vehicle down after it was already gone.

It is for these reasons, members of the jury, that you know there is no way the Defendant was in that parking lot. Certainly not beyond a reasonable doubt. Because to suggest that these elements have been satisfied would be speculation and that is not the standard. And because all three of these elements must be met beyond a reasonable doubt, there is no way George Johnson can be found guilty.

In the following examples in a civil case for wrongful death the defense counsel is now addressing the core of the plaintiff's case designed to attack her client. Note how the attorney combines the discussion of the opposing side's evidence with an attack on the credibility of the source of that evidence.

Defense: Now at the start of this trial my co counsel also told you that there will be someone that points the finger of blame at Mr. McGee. And not only would you know who-you know why. And now you do. Trooper Head. He sat on this stand today, pointed a finger and said-Robert did it. But, what's interesting is not how he did it, but why. And now you know why he blamed Robert McGee for this accident. It's no secret that Trooper Head is not Robert's biggest fan. He made that pretty clear today, but what he also made clear is how far he would go to make sure that Robert would be blamed for Vivian's death. Because he made it clear from the time that Valentine's Day when Trooper Head sat outside Vivian Rizzo's house, in the dark, watching her. And his eyes were just not on her that night-they were on the guy that Vivian was going on a date with. The guy that she choose over Trooper Head. The guy that she wanted to be with-not him. And that guy was Robert McGee.

Now, the judge will also instruct you when you are weighing witnesses testimony you can weight it anyway you want. In other words, you can choose who to believe and who not to believe. And when you are doing that I want you to think back to when Trooper Head told you today about how he lied to his supervisor, and then he lied to him again. About where he was the night he was supposed to be setting a speed trap. Because instead of setting a speed trap in the right place...he was in the wrong place...stalking a 17 year old girl. And why? Because he was jealous. He was jealous that Vivian chose Robert McGee over him. And his jealously cost him a restraining order from his supervisor forcing him to stay away from Vivian Rizzo. And, when he got to the accident scene that day, he saw three things. He saw Vivian Rizzo, Robert McGee and a chance.

e.   Prayer for Relief and Summation

During the prayer for relief and summation the attorney reminds the jury of what has been proven. This is different from the element by element analysis discussed earlier, and focuses instead squarely on the ultimate decision the jury must make. Now is the time for counsel to use the jury verdict form which will be provided by the court to the foreman of the jury when deliberations begin. It is often quite helpful from a persuasive standpoint to enlarge the verdict form and actually walk the jury through the form. As counsel addresses each element of the form, each line, each decision that the jury must make, it is an opportunity to highlight how counsel has proven the issue., and to model the action that the jury should take. This modeling includes marking the form as appropriate. Now is the time for counsel to bring the jury to what is specifically needed and asked for. In these final moments, counsel empowers the jury in their decision making capacity, and recognizes the grave importance of their mandate. It is not the time for hysterics or table pounding, but instead of reasonable analysis colored by appropriate emotion.

The final part of the closing argument is a plea for justice. It wraps up the case in a thematic construct, appealing to the common sense of the jury, their sense of justice, empowering them to do what they know to be right and what the law allows. It is often useful for counsel to mirror the language used at the beginning of the closing argument again at the end of the closing argument. Doing so uses concepts of privacy and recency, working like the music at the end of the movie to let the audience know it's time to clap. It is important for counsel to end the closing argument at a place that emotionally, logically, and legally makes sense. Counsel must call back to everything that has occurred, and remind the jury that with all that has been set before them, the only logical, common sense decision is to find in counsel's favor. It is this moment that hopefully rings in the ears of the jury as they begin to deliberate.

> In this example of a prayer for relief in a civil case the defense attorney is bringing the jury back to the core of her case, an connecting it to what she wants them to do.

> > *Defense:*   Now this is my last chance to talk to you. Opposing counsel gets another chance, because they have a burden to prove something, and that's fine. But, if she wants you to blame Mr. McGee – and we wouldn't be here if she didn't, would we?

> – then she needs to look you in the eye and say
> that even if those other two vehicles had continued
> legally down Rt. 431, that Robert McGee's actions
> would have caused Ms. Rizzo's death anyway.
>
> And when she can't say that – and we all know
> that she cannot – then you will know for sure that
> your answer on line #1 needs to be – can only be,
> "NO." Mr. McGee did not cause Ms. Rizzo's
> death. And that's what your verdict needs to say.

In this prayer for relief the defense counsel in the criminal case
used in the above examples is now focusing the jury back on the
theme and theory of his case as defined by his hook.

> *Defense:*   Now this is my last chance to address you all. The
> government gets the last word and that's alright. It
> is what it is. But it doesn't matter what they say
> anymore. Despite their efforts to convince you
> otherwise, you all know that George Johnson did
> not commit these crimes. You all know now that
> they saw what they needed to see and did what
> they wanted to do. A simple case of misinforma-
> tion and misidentification. We are counting on you
> to not let that turn into a miscarriage of justice.
> That is why I ask you to return the only verdict
> supported by the evidence, the facts and the law.
> That's a verdict finding George Johnson not guilty
> - because he isn't.

E.   Delivering the Closing

1.   Themes

Themes are as varied as the people, places and situations they capture and
represent. Theme provides the moral force bringing the case to life. A
good theme not only gets the jury on counsel's side, it creates a feeling of
comfort within them about deciding things a particular way. If counsel
cannot find a theme within the case that will resonate with the jury, they
should try to determine what sense of injustice exists. Is there a wrong
that has been committed against the client that will get the jury to decide
the case for the client? Examples of such themes include the government
rushing to judgment because the client is a member of a minority, the in-

nocent person wronged by circumstance, and the ubiquitous "some other dude did it" defense. Other examples pit the little person agains a soulless corporation. The storylines are as varied and complex as the tales of humanity that surround us each day. Whatever theme that counsel choses, it must be one they believe in without any reservation. The jury will pick up on any lack of genuine belief, and if the hook the case is centered around does not ring true to them counsel cannot be successful in their arguments.

2.   Argue

Counsel must ARGUE! Now is the time to tell the jurors why they must decide in the client's favor. Inferences must be made based upon what is before the jury. The word "because" should be used often to tie the facts to the law, and convince the jury of the righteousness of counsel's cause. Counsel use their knowledge of the case, as presented at trial, to connect through logical inferences disparate portions of the closing. The issues must be placed in context during closings so that the jurors will draw the appropriate inferences from the evidence, the law and their own personal knowledge. Counsel can use different emotional approaches here, depending upon their own personalities and the relevant issues. Acceptable approaches include sarcasm, historical context, common sense observations of life, and humor. The key is that the approach must be genuine to who counsel is as a person, or else counsel risks losing the jury's faith.

The important point is that now is the time for counsel to connect what is known with what is not known in light of the experiences and knowledge of the jury. They must rely upon their common sense and understanding of human nature to sort through all of the trial testimony. Counsel should use this to fashion a closing argument echoing their own experiences. It gives the argument's interpretation credibility, and creates synergy in favor of the positions taken by counsel during closing. Now is not the time to rehash the evidence, but to explain what it means.

Counsel should not be afraid to show enthusiasm for the case - but it must be genuine. This does not necessarily mean cheerleading or table pounding like a caricature of a bad TV lawyer, but it does mean caring—or seeming to care—strongly about the case and the position taken. Enthusiasm can be reflected in a number of ways, most obviously in inflection and word choice, but also by command of the courtroom, presentation of a case, and unapologetic advocacy for the client. If counsel does not care enough about this case to get excited and energized, how can they expect the jury to care? The words that counsel chooses, and the arguments that they place before the jury, must be grounded in counsel truly believing in the cause for which they advocate.

During the opening statement a member of the litigation team should have taken careful notes about the promises made by opposing counsel. If they have not kept those promises then during closing argument counsel should hold the other side's opening against them. Listen carefully during the opponent's opening and remind the jury, in closing, of the promises they made in the opening and then did not keep. When those promises show an attempt to hide the ball or manipulate the process, counsel should drive that home and use it to attack the credibility of opposing counsel's case (but not necessarily the credibility of opposing counsel themselves). Sometimes counsel can win merely by the other side losing.

Now is the time to use the exhibits that were admitted during the testimony of witnesses. Each exhibit represents a particular moment in the trial, a factual issue that is important, or an emotional moment during the testimony correlating directly to the credibility of the witness. It is important to think both creatively and logically about how and where to use the exhibits that have been made. When doing so counsel should focus on the persuasive value the exhibits have to the closing argument. Too many exhibits can confuse the issue, too few exhibits are a persuasive opportunity lost. Counsel must take the time to practice with the exhibits and any enlargements made with them so they do not get lost in trying to shuffle through them for the first time during trial. Counsel should make the decision about which exhibits to use based upon their analysis of the case and the responses of the jury during the trial itself. This is a decision point that can only be properly realized by paying attention throughout the trial.

It is inappropriate for counsel to argue that the jury should or should not do something based upon counsel's own personal belief. This is improper argument, and should draw an objection from the opposing side. This is not to say that counsel cannot argue for the importance or relevancy of a piece of evidence, but rather that whether or not counsel personally believes the evidence is important to relevant does not matter. What the evidence demands, what common sense supports, what a basic understanding of human nature requires, that is where counsel should spend their time arguing. These are the persuasive points that move juries to decide the case in Council favor – not the personal belief of the attorneys involved.

Many attorneys like to spend time during closing argument talking about the civic responsibility of the jury. While such information might be interesting to some, civics lessons have a tendency to make the person delivering them seem either defensive or condescending. Neither of these emotional responses is what an attorney wants a jury to feel. A real danger exists that the audience can be lost when the attorney waste time discussing things that are not relevant to the case. It invites the jury to ignore the argument which follows. The court will inform the jury of the nature and structure of closing argument, and it is not the attorney's job to do this.- Counsel would better spend their time discussing other legal concepts that are relevant to the case, such as the burden of proof. The jury appreciates a well planned, lucid explanation of the law, when it is relevant to their job.When structuring the argument counsel must spend the majority of their time addressing the strengths of their case, not their weaknesses. Opposing counsel may attempt through the use of rhetorical questions or other devices to draw the attorney into a discussion about the opposing side's case during their own portion of the closing argument. This is a temptation to be avoided. The other side will spend a great deal of time attacking the weaknesses of their opponent's case. Counsel should focus their efforts on the strong portions of their case initially, dealing with weaknesses only when necessary to appear fair and credible in the eyes of the jury.

The obvious weaknesses of the case—perhaps compromises made by a victim, lab errors, and admissions by the client—need to be addressed, but counsel should do so with a plan. This is an opportunity to establish candor and credibility with the jury and suggests a sense of balance. It is a best practice persuasively to couple the admission with a compensating fact that diminishes the damage and gives the jury an "out" or better context in which to place the weakness so that it has less of an impact on counsel's case. Just as primacy and recency work for the strongest points, common sense should tells the advocate to sandwich weaker points in the middle of their argument.

The court will normally give counsel liberal rein to argue inferences from the evidence and matters outside of the evidence that are part of generally accepted knowledge. Counsel must be careful, however, only to rely on evidence that has been properly admitted for an appropriate purpose. Care must be taken to ensure that evidence that is admitted by the court with a limiting instruction is not used to argue a point for which it has not been allowed. To do so is to not only lose credibility with the jury, but also with opposing counsel and the judge, who counsel is likely to see again during their legal career. One example of this would be to take evidence of a prior inconsistent statement, admitted for the limited purpose of attacking a witness's credibility, and then arguing the facts within that statement to prove an element or to disprove an element of an offense or cause of action. The extra burden on defense counsel is to abide by the ethical rule that forbids calling the attention of the jury to the absence of evidence when in fact that evidence was suppressed.

F.   Rebuttal

Rebuttal arguments are the province of plaintiff attorneys and prosecutors. When done correctly they serve to strike devastating blows to the defense case. To be effective they must be focused and lethal, reiterating those key issues that will carry the day. Done well it is the final nail in the defense coffin. Done poorly it can so confuse the issues that the jury must struggle through the maze of defense tactics without clear guidance.

Advocates often overlook this portion of effective trial advocacy because there is an element of afterthought to making such arguments. Counsel should focus upon it, it is the final argument the jury hears before deliberations.

The rebuttal argument gives the prosecution or plaintiff an opportunity to regain the momentum, to reestablish focus on the key issues in the case, and to refute the defense's arguments on key issues. A purely reactive point-by-point response to defense arguments cannot accomplish this mission. The rebuttal must refute the defense arguments on key issues and forcefully reassert the theory of guilt or culpability. The leading causes of weak and ineffective rebuttal arguments are inadequate preparation and ineffective organization of the argument. Counsel can use the following structure to consistently fashion rebuttal arguments that are on point, effective and devastating to the defense case.

1.   Beginning

Start by preparing the rebuttal as an integral part of the case. It is often said that the preparation of a case should begin with an outline of the closing argument. The government or plaintiff gets to argue first and last. The benefits of primacy and recency should be fully exploited by careful planning. The initial closing and then the rebuttal must work together to maximize the persuasive presentation of the case. The primary mission of the rebuttal is to restore commitment to the theories and theme that were clearly constructed in the first closing. Counsel should remember that it is a restoration project, not new construction. The structures of the two arguments must be carefully coordinated to contribute to the same persuasive goal.

2.   Common Mistakes

Counsel usually makes one of the following mistakes when fashioning and delivering a rebuttal argument. The first is attempting to fully analyze and neutralize the defense arguments presented during their closing. While it is tempting to immunize the jury against defense arguments, too much attention on the defense case will distort the focus of the closing. Focus instead on counsel's affirmative burden, only occasionally warning about the defense tactics to come. This allows counsel to set up rebuttal points in accordance with their warnings. Those warnings must be tied to case analysis and the key elements upon which the evidence will most likely turn.

Counsel should save their full refutation on those issues for rebuttal, if the defense attempts to address them. Use this tactic to shape the argument of the defense. If they do not rise to the challenge, then counsel can draw the jury's attention to their failure to adequately address the damning evidence facing their client.

3.   Sandbagging

Another temptation is to sandbag the defense by saving everything for rebuttal. This tactic surrenders the advantage of primacy and may also run afoul of the scope limitations on rebuttal argument. Rebuttal is generally limited to matters that are raised by the defense argument. If the defense ignores the issues counsel are saving for rebuttal they may very well be precluded from arguing them during rebuttal. Defense counsel could also counter the sandbagging tactic by offering argument only on some of the charged offenses or by waiving argument entirely. Therefore sandbagging surrenders primacy and the shaping of the final argument to the defense and is not a good idea!

4.   Control the Agenda

Counsel must control the agenda during closing arguments. The initial closing must establish the key issues, so that the rebuttal begins by reminding the jury that resolving those issues will determine the verdict. Counsel must organize rebuttal around these issues if they want it to be effective. They should resist the temptation to engage in a point-by-point response to the defense argument. That allows the defense to control the agenda and makes the rebuttal quickly deteriorate into an uncoordinated attack. The picture of counsel wildly flailing away at the defense argument is not pretty.

A better method is to identify the three main issues in the case and to construct an outline for rebuttal based on those issues. Counsel should anticipate and "war game" arguments on those main points. If they are prepared, counsel can then listen and refine the rebuttal during the defense argument. If the defense fails to address one of the issues selected for rebuttal, counsel can explain to the jury why that omission is so glaring. Having analyzed the key issues in the case, counsel can prepare an outline of rebuttal arguments before trial. Use the following template to control the agenda:

• **Introduction**. Regain the momentum for your side during the opening seconds of the rebuttal argument. Identify the crucial shortcomings in the defense argument or turn the defense theme against them. Develop an arsenal of responses for standard defense themes and use them to fashion a one-line rebuttal introduction.

- **Restate your theme**. A strong initial closing puts counsel in the best position for rebuttal. Having already made the case, they can confidently begin the rebuttal argument by recapping the most compelling evidence of guilt. If the defense has stressed the reasonable doubt standard, acknowledge the government's burden of proof and confidently embrace it. This restores the proper focus on what counsel perceive as the real issue or issues in the case and sets up the outline for rebuttal.

- **Key Point Rebuttal**. Having set the stage by restoring focus on the crucial issues, counsel is now ready to proceed with the negative aspect of the rebuttal—refuting selected arguments of the defense. The three-step process of restate, refute, and recap should be used to address each key point that you selected for rebuttal.

Counsel cannot effectively refute an argument without clearly restating it. Any attempt to make a straw man out of the defense argument will undermine credibility with the jury and will draw an objection from an attentive defense counsel. Refuting the defense argument is the heart of negative rebuttal. Refutation takes a variety of forms, but it all boils down to this: refute the fact or refute the inferences drawn from the facts. No matter which tactic counsel use they must always appeal to common sense and explain why their theory offers a better alternative. The quality of this part of the argument will dramatically increase if advocates devote time during case preparation to anticipating defense arguments and thinking through avenues of rebuttal.

Counsel should end by recapping the theory of your case. After each defense argument is identified and refuted, explain how that conclusion affects the big picture and why it makes your theory the only certain conclusion. At the end of their rebuttal counsel must appeal for the verdict they want from the jury. The final appeal for a verdict is the final word before instructions. Counsel should use it to make a final appeal to the jury or judge. This appeal combines the plea for justice, the restatement of the theme, and a summary of the reasons that compel a verdict in their favor. This portion of the argument should be committed to memory and delivered with appropriate enthusiasm.

A defense attorney's issues concerning rebuttal argument deal primarily with how to devise strategies that reduce the impact of rebuttal argument. A strong and effective tactic for defense counsel is to use their closing as a tool. Hone in on promises not fulfilled by plaintiff's counsel. Implore the jury to listen for the "answers to unanswered questions by the plaintiff" or "ask them why" statements. Giving the jury a number of issues to think about while the plaintiff is putting on their rebuttal automatically puts plaintiff's counsel in a precarious situation. Do they take the bait and answer your questions? Or do they stay on message and ignore the issues as a whole? Either way counsel have planted those seeds in the juror's minds and they will remember them while deliberating. In addition, engaging the jury this way, in an active role, instead of strictly a spectator role, can be immensely effective.

Counsel should focus on key issues from their argument. This is rebuttal. Counsel is the filter for what is important and what is not. Bring the jury back to the strength of the case, while highlighting the weakness of theirs. Do not allow the arguments of defense counsel to sidetrack the rebuttal. The worst mistake counsel can make is to address, point by point, the defense's position. It can breathe life into what was otherwise a "dead Frankenstein monster." Every piece of the rebuttal should turn the jury back, like an inexorable tide, to the strength, right and justice of counsel's argument.

Remember, not only is counsel a witness for their case, so is their worktable, papers, and the way counsel use the evidence. The ability to have at your fingertips each and every item is expected of competent counsel, and devastating when coupled with a strong rebuttal. Organize, organize and then organize again. In the heat of rebuttal it is devastating to the defense to use their evidence, or counsel's own, to destroy their point. It is devastating for counsel's case though, if they reach for the evidence, and cannot find it there, or are unable to adequately use it because they just cannot get it together.

Finally counsel should not forget that less is more. Trust the jury. They have heard the evidence and want to get their job done. Do not insult their intelligence by holding them captive. While counsel may love the sound of their own voice, the jurors will love the silence of the deliberation room even more. Lead them to the right conclusion. Do not drag them to it and then rub their faces in it for an extended period of time. That approach will not accomplish anything, and risks losing some measure of the respect they normally accord professionals. It is a best practice to not waive rebuttal. While there may be the rare case where waiving rebuttal is conceivable, waiver often reflects either undue confidence or a lack of understanding of the dynamics of a trial. Both can be interpreted in a negative fashion by the jury. When counsel have the chance to have the last word they should do so.

G.   Examples

1.   Defense Criminal Assault Closing

The following defense closing was delivered in a criminal case for parole violation and assault on a U.S. Marshall.

> *Defense:*   They believed he was there because they needed him to be there - but believing something does not make it so.
>
> We are here today because Mr. Grimes wanted to believe that Samantha Jones would come back to him and to make that happen he needed George Johnson to be in that parking lot. Marshall Dilliard wants to believe that George Johnson was in that car, he needs George Johnson to be in that car, because he couldn't find him, becoming so desperate that eventually he arrests an off duty deputy sheriff. He believes George was there because he needs George Johnson to be there.
>
> MOJ, at the beginning of this trial I told you that this was a case of mistaken identity. On April 24, 20XX-1 at approximately 4 PM in the afternoon, US Marshal's Dilliard and James attempted to execute an arrest warrant in the parking lot of the West End Big Lots. By now, you all know that those two Marshals believed George Johnson was the person sitting in Samantha Jones's blue Ford Escape that day. But now, you also know that there is no way George Johnson was in that parking lot on April 24, and there is no way he fled the scene in a flurry, dragging Marshal James along. Why? Because this was a case of misidentification and misinformation.
>
> Today it was the government's burden, and their burden alone, to prove to you each element of the crimes charged against George Johnson. Not only was it their burden to prove those elements, but they had to prove them beyond a reasonable doubt. What you'll hear the judge tell you today is that proof beyond a reasonable doubt would leave

you firmly convinced that the defendant is guilty. And today the government has failed to do that. They have failed to satisfy the burden placed upon them by our legal system and because they failed, you must acquit George Johnson.

Mr. Johnson is charged with assault on a federal officer with a dangerous weapon. I want to go through the elements of this crime one last time with you. I want to show you exactly how the Government has failed to meet their burden.

[PULL UP CHARGE]

The indictment is an assault charge. You'll notice that every element of this charge requires the Defendant, and only the Defendant, as the culprit. But during this entire trial, we have given you countless reasons why George Johnson was not the man in that blue Ford. More importantly, the Government has failed to prove that George Johnson was in that car. Why? Because they haven't proven that the Defendant was there. And because of that, they haven't proven that he assaulted Marshal James. They haven't shown you evidence that suggests he was in that car. And MOJ, they can't even prove that the driver of that vehicle, whoever he may be, operated that vehicle in a dangerous or deadly manner.

So, how do we know George Johnson wasn't there? Today you heard the Government present their case. You heard the testimony of Adam Grimes. He told you that he was the one calling the Marshal's service and providing all of those tips. But he never told the Marshal's service that he dated Samantha Jones. Why didn't he tell them? You know exactly why, MOJ. He didn't tell them because he was trying to win Samantha Jones back. You heard him tell you all today that his relationship with her ended the second George Johnson entered her life. He went from being her lover to being her co-worker. He needed to get

George Johnson out of the picture, so he began telling the Marshals service that George Johnson was still in her life. Every day he would sneak across the hallway from his office and look out the window into the parking lot. You can picture him peeling back the curtain and staring longingly into that parking waiting for someone—ANYONE—to show up with Samantha.

So how does he describe this suspect that he saw? Medium build with brown hair. Think of how many people fit that description. Think of how desperate Adam Grimes was to find George John-son. Think of how desperate Adam Grimes was to be back in Samantha Jones's life. In fact, we know how desperate he was. He provided 15 total tips in a three month period to Marshal Dilliard. But the Marshal never once found George Johnson in that parking lot...ever. He got so frustrated with the countless bad tips, that he insisted Adam Grimes reveal his identity. But even then, Marshal Dilliard was never able to put George Johnson in that park-ing lot.

Marshal Dilliard took the stand and told us all about that today. He was the star of the show—the man with all of the information. There's no deny-ing that he has years of experience, but this time he was sloppy. After searching countless hours for George Johnson, Marshal Dilliard began shooting from the hip. You heard him today. He went through all of Johnson's records and never found him. He searched his home of record and no one was there. He went to Samantha's neighborhood and questions the neighbors. After two visits, speaking with uninterested third parties, he still was unable to find anyone who saw George John-son. He even went inside Samantha's home and looked around and even then he admitted that there was no sign of Johnson. So, in an act of des-peration, he begins taking tips from a man he's never met before. In his haste, he never even bothers to ask Adam Grimes about his relationship to Samantha or George. Had he, he would have found out that Grimes was a jealous lover. Instead of performing his job thoroughly, he began rushing to bring Johnson in. He spent countless hours sitting across from the Big Lots parking lot, waiting for Johnson to show up.

And that's when he got desperate. Today, the Marshal had to admit there were various occasions where he thought he had his guy. On April 8, Marshal Dilliard approached a man sitting in the Big Lots parking lot, asked him to stand up and put his hands high in the air. It was only then, after he was face to face with this man, that he determined it was not George Johnson. Three days later, Marshal Dilliard makes the same mistake again. This time, he goes so far as to make an actual arrest. And who did he arrest? Not George Johnson, but a local Deputy Sheriff, Victor Hansen. This is the same Deputy Sheriff who has worked previously directly with Marshal Dilliard. This U.S. Marshal went through the process of putting this man in handcuffs before he ever figured out that it wasn't George Johnson. MOJ, your common sense tells you that if Marshal Dilliard mistakenly thought a deputy sheriff was the man he was looking for, he had absolutely NO IDEA what George Johnson looked like.

Which leads me to the events on April 24—only 5 days after the debacle with the deputy sheriff. Grimes called in, for the fifteenth time, swearing up and down that Johnson would be in that parking lot. That's when Dilliard asked Marshal James to help. From this viewpoint [PULL UP EX. 12], both Marshals say they positively identify George Johnson sitting in the driver's seat of Samantha Jones's blue Ford. These two Marshals, who had never even seen a picture of Johnson before, positively identify this man with a medium build and brown hair sitting in the car. So from this distance, they were somehow 100% positive that behind that absurdly dark tinted window[2] was George Johnson. To this day, Marshal Dilliard is still 100% sure it was Johnson. Even after he snuck up behind the car on the passenger's side. Even after he watched the car drive away as he was on his back. And even after he tried to chase the vehicle down after it was already gone.

It is for these reasons, MOJ, that you know there is no way the Defendant was in that parking lot. Certainly not beyond a reasonable doubt. Because to suggest that these elements have been satisfied would be speculation and that is not the standard. And because all three of these elements must be met beyond a reasonable doubt, there is no way George Johnson can be found guilty.

But MOJ, not only did the government not find George Johnson guilty beyond a reasonable doubt, they didn't even find the driver of that vehicle guilty. You heard Samantha Jones tell you today that her brother Chris had access to those keys, so we know that someone else certainly could have been driving that car. On top of that, Paula Baquette took the stand and told you what the scene looked like. She was walking to lunch, minding her own business when she saw two people, dressed in all black, sneaking across the road. From her viewpoint, she thought they were carjackers. Imagine how scared the driver of that blue Ford was. He sees two people sneaking up and when one of them reaches in the car to steal the keys, he does the only thing he can to save himself, he puts the car in reverse and gets out of that parking lot as soon as possible. Everyone agrees that Marshal James yelled something at the driver, but in all of that commotion, we can't be certain that the driver heard what she said. Even if he did, the way these two Marshals were approaching his car, he probably thought they were willing to take his car at all costs. So this third element can't be satisfied, because to qualify as a dangerous weapon, it must be used in a way that would make it deadly, i.e., intentionally trying to ram someone with it—not fleeing for his life. Which is why no matter who you believe was driving this car, the government has failed to satisfy these elements beyond a reasonable doubt.

Now this is my last chance to address you all. The government gets the last word and that's alright. It is what it is. But it doesn't matter what they say anymore. Despite their efforts to convince you otherwise, you all know that George Johnson did not commit these crimes. You all know now that they saw what they needed to see and did what they wanted to do. A simple case of misinformation and misidentification. We are counting on you to not let that turn into a miscarriage of justice. That is why I ask you to return the only verdict supported by the evidence, the facts and the law. That's a verdict finding George Johnson not guilty - because he isn't.

2.   Defense Closing in a Civil Wrongful Death Case

Defense: May it please the court. Counsel. Members of the Jury. At the beginning of this trial, my co-counsel, told you that this case was about a Renal Van that was in the wrong place . . . a semi-truck driver who made the wrong choice . . . and that these lawyers were going to come in this courtroom and blame the wrong person. And now that you have seen all the evidence and heard all the testimony you now know she was exactly right. These lawyers just expected to come in here, point a finger, pick up a check and go home. But that's not enough, not nearly enough. And why? Because the Judge will tell you in a few minutes that the burden of proof today is still at this table-with the Plaintiff. You see it's not enough for them to just say Robert McGee caused this accident-they had to prove it. This plaintiff had to prove her case by the greater weight of the evidence - by the entire force and effect of all the evidence in this case. That's the law.

So then why are we here?   Well – because the plaintiff has tried to blame the wrong person-Robert McGee-for her daughter's death.   And you know what, that's understandable.   Her daughter is gone and it's only natural to look for someone to blame when a child dies. When anyone dies.   But this courtroom, in fact all courtrooms in this country, were not built for the purpose of providing sympathy.   They were built for the purpose of finding the truth and the truth is, members of the jury, if that Rental Van was in the right place, and that semi truck made the right choices that day... we wouldn't be here...and Vivian Rizzo might be alive.

In any event, the plaintiff has brought us here and now you know that she just did not prove her case and she did not because she could not.   And she could not because the evidence would not allow it. And the evidence wouldn't allow it because while these Plaintiff lawyers were so busy pointing their fingers at the wrong person, the evidence was pointing in the opposite direction...Away from Robert McGee... and right on to the Rental Van and Semi truck.

Now today you heard about how this accident started-with the Rental Van.   The Rental Van that was overturned on the interstate.   Now your common sense tells you that a Rental Van should not-should not- just be overturned on the interstate. And if your common sense isn't enough-Trace Parker, an expert in the field of human factors and traffic engineering told you for ANY reason; it should not have been there.   Now members of the jury were not saying that Rental Van was purposely put in the road.   But that doesn't change the fact that people should not lose control of their vehicle when they're driving it.   And most importantly, it doesn't change the fact that it was in the wrong place.

But it doesn't stop there-oh no- because the Rental Van wasn't the only vehicle in the wrong place. But to make matters worse Billy's –the Semi truck driver—made a series of wrong choices that day. His first wrong choice started when he decided to not to pull his semi truck off to the shoulder of the road.   What did he do instead? He stopped his Semi truck in the right hand lane.   Now, your common sense tells you that it was-it is- a mistake to park a semi truck on a highway.   Then he makes his 2nd wrong choice- he chooses not to put out any warning flares, no cones no nothing to warn drivers that his semi truck was stopped in the right hand lane of traffic.   I mean when you heard that you had to be asking yourself.   "WHAT?   He didn't want to take the time to warn other drivers that his huge semi truck was parked in the middle of an interstate."   Members of the jury opposing counsel may call that something-but we all know the one thing it really means: negligence.

And because of his wrong choices, Robert McGee was left with no room for error. No room at all. Trace Parker explained to you that when Mr. McGee did not see ANY warning signals, there was nothing to cause him to understand that any-thing was wrong. but the truth is something was wrong-dead wrong- but Mr. Parker explained to you by the time Robert-or anyone-any driver- was able to figure out the truck was in fact parked, it was too late. There was no room to stop.   We all know that choices have consequences, and Vivian Rizzo's life was a consequence of the wrong choices that Billy made that day.

Now at the start of this trial my co counsel also told you that there will be someone that points the finger of blame at Mr. McGee. And not only would you know who-you know why. And now you do. Trooper Head. He sat on this stand today, pointed a finger and said-Robert did it.　　But, what's interesting is not how he did it, but why. And now you know why he blamed Robert McGee for this accident. It's no secret that Trooper Head is not Robert's biggest fan. He made that pretty clear today, but what he also made clear is how far he would go to make sure that Robert would be blamed for Vivian's death. Because he made it clear from the time that Valentine's Day when Trooper Head sat outside Vivian Rizzo's house, in the dark, watching her.　And his eyes were just not on her that night-they were on the guy that Vivian was going on a date with. The guy that she choose over Trooper Head. The guy that she wanted to be with-not him. And that guy was Robert McGee.

Now, the judge will also instruct you when you are weighing witnesses testimony you can weight it anyway you want.　In other words, you can choose who to believe and who not to believe. And when you are doing that I want you to think back to when Trooper Head told you today about how he lied to his supervisor, and then he lied to him again. About where he was the night he was supposed to be setting a speed trap.　Because instead of setting a speed trap in the right place…he was in the wrong place…stalking a 17 year old girl. And why? Because he was jealous. He was jealous that Vivian chose Robert McGee over him. And his jealously cost him a restraining order from his supervisor forcing him to stay away from Vivian Rizzo. And, when he got to the accident scene that day, he saw three things. He saw Vivian Rizzo, Robert McGee and a chance.

His chance to point the finger at Robert McGee. That's when his finger pointing started. But the one thing that Trooper Head didn't have when he was pointing the finger was the evidence to back it up.　All he had was the memory of him sitting, waiting in the dark watching Vivian go out with Robert.　And to him-that jealously- was enough to point the finger. But it's not enough, not today, not in this courtroom. Because even though these lawyers and trooper Head are choosing to ignore the evidence in front of them, you—as the jury— can't. Because the evidence points to the Rental Van that was in the wrong place and the Semi truck driver who made the wrong choices.

But the truth is, Members of the Jury, all of us wish this didn't happen. Vivian Rizzo's death is truly sad. That is not an issue. The only issues for you to decide are on this Verdict Form:

"Did the negligence, if any, of the parties below proximately cause the death of Vivian Rizzo? "

The one term on that line that may not be totally familiar to all of you would be "proximately cause." In a few minutes Judge ------ will read you the definition in legalese, but in essence it means that "without or 'but for' a particular event, the accident in question would not have happened." That jury instruction also allows that there could be more than one of these who "prox- imately caused" this accident – in other words contributed to the death of Ms. Rizzo.

So – let's apply that test to each of these. AND let's do them in the order that they stopped that day over on Rt. 431.

Daniel Hunter. It's true that there are several things we don't know as to exactly why she turned that U-Haul over on that road. But this we do know: She was the driver, and drivers should maintain control of their vehicles. No question about it. So – did anyone here today suggest that "but for" Ms. Hunter's Rental Van being in the middle of this lane, Ms. Rizzo would have died anyway? Of course not. That means that what she did was a proximate cause of this accident. A "yes" goes on this line.

Billy Barnett. Here's what we know for sure about what he did and failed to do. He chose to park – stop right in the middle of that lane and put out no flairs, cones or flags to alert drivers coming behind him. In fact no one saw anything whatsoever that he did to alert drivers of his choices. Was that a mistake? Of course it was and his choices were yet another **cause** of Ms. Rizzo's death. Another "yes."

Robert McGee. Here we are. With the one – the ONLY one the plaintiff is pointing the finger of blame at here today. You must have wondered. You must be wondering now. What?? Does this plaintiff really expect you to believe that if neither of those vehicles were on Rt. 431 that day, that Ms. Rizzo would have died within feet of the Speedway overpass anyway? Is that what they're saying? Actually . . . it is, isn't it? That's why they brought Officer Park-in-the-dark-and-lie-about-it Head to the stand. Right. It is all Mr. McGee's fault those two vehicles were parked in the middle of that interstate.

Now this is my last chance to talk to you. Opposing counsel gets another chance. It is what it is. But, if she wants you to blame Mr. McGee – and we wouldn't be here if she didn't, would we? – then she needs to look you in the eye and say that even if those other two vehicles had continued legally down Rt. 431, that Robert McGee's actions would have caused Ms. Rizzo's death anyway.

And when she can't say that – and we all know that she cannot – then you will know for sure that your answer on line #1 needs to be – can only be, "NO." Mr. McGee did not cause Ms. Rizzo's death. And that's what your verdict needs to say.

3. Defense Closing in a Murder Case

Defense: At the beginning of this trial my co-counsel told you that the state didn't read every chapter in this book, and that is why the wrong man, Pat Morris, is sitting here today. But after hearing the State's story, I'm just going to tell you what your common sense tells you – the State didn't even read a full chapter. They took a paragraph out of a chapter, a sentence out of a paragraph and a word out of a sentence. That's not a complete story, and it CERTAINLY is not beyond a reasonable doubt.

Let's review – they didn't bring you a weapon, they guessed. They didn't bring you forensic evidence, they assumed. And they didn't bring you Amanda's killer. They got it wrong. So let's read those chapters, the ones the State missed, skipped & just plain ignored.

The State missed the first Chapter, The Untouchable Man, Jamie Johnson. The State came before you today and told you that Mr. Morris killed Amanda Lynd. But notice how every means, motive and opportunity Mr. Morris had, Jamie Johnson ALSO had. For instance, the State told you it must have been Mr. Morris, because he knew about the ticket. Well, so did Jamie Johnson. Remember – you heard testimony today about how Amanda found out she won the lottery and went to the Johnson law office. Then, she came out of that meeting and told Thomas Kaye that her lawyer wanted a 50/50 split of her winnings. Members Of The Jury, make no mistake about it – the ONLY lawyer in that firm is JAMIE Johnson, the same Jamie Johnson who refused to give Amanda her ticket back, and told her it was in a safe place. Next, the State told you it must have been Mr. Morris, because he had no alibi. Well, again, neither did Jamie Johnson. Members Of The Jury, why would someone, KNOWING their wife was in another State, call her on their house phone unless they were trying to create an alibi??? Try as he might to create an alibi, the fact is that NO ONE can tell you where Jamie Johnson was the night Amanda Lynd was attacked. The State said it must have been Mr. Morris, because he had access to the billy club that they guess killed Amanda. Once again, you guessed it, so did Jamie Johnson. He was forced to admit today that he held it in his hands on the night Ms. Lynd was attacked.

Members Of The Jury, you heard that Jamie Johnson was the kind of man who easily could be, and probably should be, sitting in the defendant's chair instead of on the witness stand. But he's not, and you know why. He became untouchable the second the State gave him immunity. Immunity without interview, inquiry or investigation into Jamie Johnson. REALLY?

Because the State missed the chapter on Jamie Johnson, they skipped the Chapter on the Amazing Disappearing Ex-Con Ex-Husband, Matt Jones. Had the State actually read that chapter, they would have learned that Matt Jones is a felon, that Matt Jones married Amanda for money, and that Amanda ended their sham marriage, divorced Matt Jones the day before she was assaulted. And you heard how Matt Jones treated Amanda during their marriage – like his own personal piggy bank. 5K to get married. 1K to get divorced. Members Of The Jury, what do YOU think Matt Jones could have done if Amanda had 52K and when he shook that piggy bank nothing dropped out, not a cent?

But, everything you know about Matt Jones comes from other people, and you know why – Because the State did not , could not, or would not find him. We know he was in town around the time of Amanda's assault to pick up his $1K, but we DON'T know that he wasn't in the alley that night because the State didn't interview, inquire or even investigate him. Same as Jamie Johnson.

What's more appalling than the chapters the State missed and skipped, though, is that they just plain ignored the chapter on The Roommate of the Year, Marsha Mathews, a chapter they had in their hands, in their very own OFFICE, the whole time.

Now, if there is one thing we know about Marsha Mathews, it is that she HATES Mr. Morris. This time, it wasn't Brutus doing the stabbing – it was Mathews. She has complained about Mr. Morris to everyone with ears. Members Of The Jury, you have to really ask yourselves what it says about Marsha Mathews that no one takes her seriously at all. And you know why they don't. Because you know that when you look out a dirty window, everything looks cloudy. Her view of the world, of Mr. Morris, is completely skewed by her hatred of him. We're not saying that Ms. Mathews is a liar, just that she is seeing what she wants to see, clouded by the extreme bias she has against Mr. Morris. That is the only conceivable way that her memory of the attack is miraculously better 2 months after the attack when she finally tells the Grand Jury, for the first time ever, all this important information. She never saw what she claims to have seen, and that's apparent from the absence of detail in her initial story, the changes in her story, and her creation of new facts.

Speaking of unclear views, let's discuss what the reality of Ms. Mathews's line of sight was the night of the attack. Thomas Kaye told you that he saw someone in Pat Morris's room immediately after the attack. Now it is undisputed, uncontested, undeniable that Mr. Morris was not home then. So that leaves only one other person with access to Mr. Morris's apartment, his bedroom, his drawer, is Marsha Mathews. And looking down from his room, you know there is no way she could have seen what she claims she saw. Amanda was attacked by the back door to the law office, in the alley. Look at this view – Ms. Mathews literally would have had to be able to see through the Bakery, through bricks, mortar – she would have had to have XRAY vision. That's impossible.

And even if we take Ms. Mathews at her word, which we now know is significantly less than credible, and she was at her own window, Members Of The Jury – look at this picture. You can't see anything. It's too dark in that alley between the two buildings. And this picture is of the DAYTIME – imagine how dark that alley is at 1:35 in the morning, streetlights out – PITCH BLACK.

Members Of The Jury, as the defense, we did not have to prove anything to you. That was the State's burden – started right here, stayed right here the entire trial. We didn't have to prove what the murder weapon was. The State guesses it's a billy club, but they can't prove it. They can't even FIND it. We didn't have to prove that Mr. Morris never saw, never held that lottery ticket, even though the State had it the whole time. They could have fingerprinted it, but they didn't bother. But one thing we know for sure – the State's star witness, Marsha Mathews's, fingerprints are all over that ticket, from when she bought it for Ms. Lynd, and when she planted it in Mr. Morris's drawer. And we didn't have to prove to you that someone else was the killer, even though we brought you Matt Jones, who the State didn't investigate, and Jamie Johnson, who had the same means, motive and opportunity.

Members Of The Jury, that was all the State's burden to prove. They had to prove that beyond and to the exclusion of any reasonable doubt, the highest burden in our entire legal system. They didn't even come close. If not for us, you would not even know half of this story because the State either didn't want to tell you, or they never knew it themselves. Either way, that's not justice for Amanda Lynd, it's not fair to my client, and it's not beyond a reasonable doubt.

In a moment you'll go back to the jury room to deliberate. The story is not done yet. The last page is blank and it is for you, Members Of The Jury, to fill in. And after considering all of the chapters that the State missed, skipped, and just plain ignored, you will write the last words. I'm confident that you will return with the only ending to this story that is supported by the law, the facts, and your own common sense – and that last page will read "Pat Morris, NOT GUILTY. The End."

4. Defense closing in a termination of parental rights case

Defense: May it please the court, counsel, members of the Jury,

Just two short months ago, Charlotte Brooks welcomed into this world two beautiful boys, Joseph and Jamie – twins. At that moment when she heard the cries of their tiny little voices, and the doctor wrapped them in those tiny blankets and handed them to Charlotte for her to hold, she made up her mind. She knew then that she couldn't go through with the agreement; she wasn't willing to give them up, wasn't willing to part with them, wasn't willing to let them go, and as their mother she-had-that-right.

As you've heard today, just a few hours after they were born, Charlotte Brooks learned that one of those boys was born with a heart condition. He had hydroplasty left heart syndrome, an illness that could be treated, but only with a treatment that she couldn't afford, and so she had a choice - Allow Joseph to be adopted by the Plaintiffs who had the financial means to help him, or allow Joseph to be taken by God.

And in that difficult situation, Charlotte made the only choice that any mother in her shoes would have made, the only choice that would save her son.....she let him go. And, because she did - because she did that selfless act - the Plaintiffs are now here asking you to take her other son, to take her son that for the last two months has been nurtured, cared-for , and loved by his mother – by Charlotte. Members of the Jury, the Plaintiff's don't-have-that-right.

They sit here in court today, trying to convince you that it is in the best interest of that young child to take him away from his own mother? We know better than that. And, we don't need experts to tell us that, our common sense tells us.

Even so, members of the jury, we did hear from experts today, and they confirmed what we already knew. Dr. Bones, a doctor immensely qualified in child development told us unequivocally, (look at notes) "it is in Jamie Jr.'s best interest to be raised by Charlotte" – those are his words. She can love him, and nurture him, and raise him better than the Plaintiffs. Not because they're bad people, but because she is Jamie's mother, because there's already a special bond between the two of them, because being with his biological mother is more important in Jamie's development than being with his twin that will grow up radically different because of his illness.

We heard today from Dr. Duchane. A doctor that explicitly refuted the Plaintiff's claims that Charlotte would not be the best mother for baby Jamie. His told us that the claim by the Plaintiffs that Charlotte's pain would hamper her ability to be a good mother is "wholly unsupported by the medicine or the science." He said that he actually "thinks it is absurd" to make such a claim, and that "there is no evidence whatsoever that would indicate that Ms. Brooks cannot care for her child." Again, those are the doctor's words, not mine.

But, more than the experts, the Howard's themselves told us what they thought of Charlotte Brooks. George Howard, sat on this stand and told us that when they met Charlotte she was "perfect." (begin to raise voice/increase pace) 11 months ago, they trusted her enough to have her bare the burden of carrying what they thought would be their own child, and today they sit here trying to convince us - trying to convince you – that somehow all of that has changed?

Members of the jury, none of that has changed. Charlotte Brooks is still perfect... the perfect person to raise her beautiful baby boys. Unfortunately, she won't be able to raise Joseph, we know that, she made that decision because it was what was best for Joseph, but she can raise Jamie Jr., and she should, because it is in his best interest for her to do so.

Members of the jury, as you consider the appropriate place for baby Jamie, I want you to remember the law, and be guided by it. The law of our state tells us that when deciding this question of what is in the best interest of a child, we must presume that a child under the age of 1, is always better off with their biological mother. In other words, unless the Plaintiff's provide evidence that clearly and convincingly shows that Jamie Jr. would be better off with the them, the law mandates that it is with his mother where his interests are best served. It is with his mother where he will grow and develop into the best young man he can be. It is with his mother where he will be best situated to learn, and laugh, and love.

Members of the jury, as we finish up this trial, I want you to think of baby Jamie. You see, often we can get caught up in lawyerly language, and passion, and emotion...but, what's at stake here today is so much more important. We're not here because of some business deal gone awry, or some broken contract, or because someone committed a crime.....(quiet) we're here today to decide how little Jamie Jr. will live the rest of his life. We here to determine, only two months into his young life, what will be best for the many years to follow. We're here to help define how a young child will grow into a young man....Will he be pulled away from his mother, who has spent the last 11 months with him, or will he placed into the arms of the woman who spent 9 months nourishing him, and bringing him into life, and the last two months holding him, feeding him, bonding with him?

Members of the jury, I'm asking each you to listen to your hearts. Find that Jamie Jr. should remain with his mother. You'll be asked one question on this verdict form. That question is this "Does clear and convincing evidence establish that awarding [the Plaintiffs] custody of the baby boy is in the child's best interest." Members of the jury, the answer to that question is "No." Baby Jamie deserves to be raised by his mother. Return a verdict that says Charlotte Brooks, Jamie's mother, is the best person to nurture him, to raise him, and to love him. (make eye contact with one person) I'm confident that you will.

5.   Portion of Defense Closing ((State v. Simpson)(delivered by Johnnie Cochran))

Defense: The Defendant, Mr. Orenthal James Simpson, is now afforded an opportunity to argue the case, if you will, but I'm not going to argue with you, ladies and gentlemen. What I'm going to do is to try and discuss the reasonable inferences which I feel can be drawn from this evidence.

Ultimately, it's what you determine to be the facts is what's going to be important, and all of us can live with that. You are empowered to do justice. You are empowered to ensure that this great system of ours works. Listen for a moment, will you, please. One of my favorite people in history is the great Frederick Douglas. He said shortly after the slaves were freed, quote, "In a composite nation like ours as before the law, there should be no rich, no poor, no high, no low, no white, no black, but common country, common citizenship, equal rights and a common destiny." This marvelous statement was made more than 100 years ago. It's an ideal worth striving for and one that we still strive for. We haven't reached this goal yet, but certainly in this great country of ours, we're trying. With a jury such as this, we hope we can do that in this particular case.

I'd like to comment and to compliment Miss Clark and Mr. Darden on what I thought were fine arguments yesterday. I don't agree with much of what they said, but I listened intently, as I hope you'll do with me. And together, hopefully these discussions are going to be helpful to you in trying to arrive at a decision in this case where you don't compromise, where you don't do violence to your conscious (sic), but you do the right thing. And you are the ones who are empowered to determine what is the right thing. Let me ask each of you a question. Have you ever in your life been falsely accused of something? Have you ever been falsely accused? Ever had to sit there and take it and watch the proceedings and wait and wait and wait, all the while knowing that you didn't do it? All you could do during such a process is to really maintain your dignity; isn't that correct? Knowing that you were innocent, but maintaining your dignity and remembering always that all you're left with after a crisis is your conduct during. So that's another reason why we are proud to represent this man who's maintained his innocence and who has conducted himself with dignity throughout these proceedings. Now, last night, as I thought about the arguments of my colleagues, two words came to mind. And I want to--I asked my wife this morning to get the dictionary out and look up two words. The two words were "Speculative" and "Cynical." Let me see if I can get those words that she got for me.

And I want you to tell me what does it mean to speculate, what does it mean to be cynical, as I thought about my colleagues' arguments and their approach to this case and their view of this case. "Cynical" is described as contemptuously distrustful of human nature and motives, gloomy distrustful view of life. And to speculate--to speculate, to engage in conjecture and to surmise or--is to take to be the truth on the basis of insufficient evidence. I mention those two definitions to you because I felt that much of what we heard yesterday and again this morning was mere speculation.

People see things that are totally cynical. Maybe that's their view of the world. Not everybody shares that view. Now, in this case--and this is a homicide case and a very, very, very serious case. And of course, it's important for us to understand that. It is a sad fact that in American society, a large number of people are murdered each year. Violence unfortunately has become a way of life in America. And so when this sort of tragedy does in fact happen, it becomes the business of the police to step up and step in and to take charge of the matter. A good efficient, competent, noncorrupt police department will carefully set about the business of investigating homicides. They won't rush to judgment. They won't be bound by an obsession to win at all costs. They will set about trying to apprehend the killer or killers and trying to protect the innocent from suspicion.

In this case, the victims' families had an absolute right to demand exactly just that in this case. But it was clear unfortunately that in this case, there was another agenda. From the very first orders issued by the LAPD so-called brass, they were more concerned with their own images, the publicity that might be generated from this case than they were in doing professional police work. That's why this case has become such a hallmark and that's why Mr. Simpson is the one on trial. But your verdict in this case will go far beyond the walls of Department 103 because your verdict talks about justice in America and it talks about the police and whether they're above the law and it looks at the police perhaps as though they haven't been looked at very recently. Remember, I told you this is not for the naive, the faint of heart or the timid. So it seems to us that the evidence shows that professional police work took a back-seat right at the beginning. Untrained officers trampled--remember, I used the word in opening statement--they traipsed through the evidence.

Because of their bungling, they ignored the obvious clues. They didn't pick up paper at the scene with prints on it. Because of their vanity, they very soon pretended to solve this crime and we think implicated an innocent man, and they never, they never ever looked for anyone else. We think if they had done their job as we have done, Mr. Simpson would have been eliminated early on.

Now, at the outset, let's talk about this time line for the Defense. I said earlier that Mr. Darden did a good job in his argument, but one thing he tended to trip over and stumble over was when he started to talk about our case. He doesn't know our case like we know our case. It was interesting, wasn't it, because first he stood up and started talking about the time line being at 10:15. Then he said, well, they didn't prove anything, but, "Golly, well, it may have been as late as 10:30." That's interesting, isn't it? Never heard that before.

And so as we look then at the time line and the importance of this time line, I want you to remember these words. Like the defining moment in this trial, the day Mr. Darden asked Mr. Simpson to try on those gloves and the gloves didn't fit, remember these words; if it doesn't fit, you must acquit. And we are going to be talking about that throughout. So to summarize, if you take the witnesses that we presented who stand unimpeached, unimpeached, and if you are left with dogs starting to bark at 10:35 or 10:40, 10:40 let's say--and we know from the most qualified individuals, Henry Lee and Michael Baden, this was a struggle that took from five to 15 minutes. It's already

10:55. And remember, the thumps were at 10:40 or 10:45--O.J. Simpson could not be guilty. He is then entitled to an acquittal.

And when you are back there deliberating on this case, you're never going to be ever able to reconcile this time line and the fact there's no blood back there and O.J. Simpson would run into an air conditioner on his own property and then under her scenario, he still has the knife and the clothes. But what does she tell you yesterday? Well, he still has the knife and he's in these bloody clothes and presumably in bloody shoes, and what does he do? He goes in the house. Now, thank heaven, Judge Ito took us on a jury view. You've seen this house. You've seen this carpet. If he went in that house with bloody shoes, with bloody clothes, with his bloody hands as they say, where's the blood on the doorknob, where's the blood on the light switch, where's the blood on the banister, where's the blood on the carpet? That's like almost white carpet going up those stairs. Where is all that blood trail they've been banting about in this mountain of evidence? You will see it's little more than a river or a stream. They don't have any mountain or ocean of evidence. It's not so because they say so. That's just rhetoric. We this afternoon are talking about the facts. And so it doesn't make any sense. It just doesn't fit. If it doesn't fit, you must acquit.

And so she (Ms. Clark) talks about O.J. being very, very recognizable. She talks about O.J. Simpson getting dressed up to go commit these murders. Just before we break for our break, I was thinking--I was thinking last night about this case and their theory and how it didn't make any sense and how it didn't fit and how something is wrong. It occurred to me how they were going to come here, stand up here and tell you how O.J. Simpson was going to disguise himself. He was going to put on a knit cap and some dark clothes, and he was going to get in his white Bronco, this recognizable person, and go over and kill his wife. That's what they want you to believe. That's how silly their argument is. And I said to myself, maybe I can demonstrate this graphically. Let me show you something. This is a knit cap. Let me put this knit cap on (Indicating). You have seen me for a year. If I put this knit cap on, who am I? I'm still Johnnie Cochran with a knit cap. And if you looked at O.J. Simpson over there--and he has a rather large head--O.J. Simpson in a knit cap from two blocks away is still O.J. Simpson. It's no disguise. It's no disguise. It makes no sense. It doesn't fit. If it doesn't fit, you must acquit.

Consider everything that Mr. Simpson would have had to have done in a very short time under their timeline. He would have had to drive over to Bundy, as they described in this little limited time frame where there is not enough time, kill two athletic people in a struggle that takes five to fifteen minutes, walk slowly from the scene, return to the scene, supposedly looking for a missing hat and glove and poking around, go back to this alley a second time, drive more than five minutes to Rockingham where nobody hears him or sees him, either stop along the way to hide these bloody clothes and knives, et cetera, or take them in the house with you where they are still hoisted by their own petard because there is no blood, there is no trace, there is no nothing. So that is why the Prosecution has had to try and push back their timeline. Even to today they are still pushing it back because it doesn't make any sense. It doesn't fit.

As I started to say before, perhaps the single most defining moment in this trial is the day they thought they would conduct this experiment on these gloves. They had this big build-up with Mr. Rubin who had been out of the business for five, six, seven, eight years, he had been in marketing even when he was there, but they were going to try to demonstrate to you that these were the killer's gloves and these gloves would fit Mr. Simpson. You don't need any photographs to understand this. I suppose that vision is indelibly imprinted in each and every one of your minds of how Mr. Simpson walked over here and stood before you and you saw four simple words, "The gloves didn't fit." And all their strategy started changing after that. Rubin was called back here more than all their witnesses, four times altogether. Rubin testified more than the investigating officers in this case, because their case from that day forward was slipping away from them and they knew it and they could never ever recapture it. We may all live to be a hundred years old, and I hope we do, but you will always remember those gloves, when Darden asked him to try them on, didn't fit.....

[S]o we heard last night and we are treated to this morning some very, very interesting observations by my learned colleague, Mr. Darden.

Now, this is interesting because Mr. Darden started off by saying, well, you know, we are going to put together this other piece, it is not really one of the elements of the crime of murder, motive, but we are going to talk to you about motive now. We are going to tell you and convince you about the motive in this case, and then he spent a long time trying to do that. As I say, he did a fine job and addressed the facts and conjured up a lot of emotion. You notice how at the end he kind of petered out of steam there, and I'm sure he got tired and he petered out because this fuse he kept talking about kept going out. It never blew up, never exploded. There was no triggering mechanism. There is nothing to lead to that. It was a nice analogy, almost like that baby analogy, the baby justice and the house of fire. You don't have to go through the house of fire. You have to keep yourself on the prize, the house of justice, a city called Justice, and that is what this is leading to, so this is what it is all about. The court--Mr. Darden looks up there, says, well, gee, judge, whatever limited purpose, but let's talk about the limited purpose for which all of his argument was about. When you talk about this evidence of other crimes, such evidence was received--excuse me, sir--and may be considered by you only for the limited purpose of determining if it tends to show the characteristic method or plan or scheme about identity or motive.

For the limited purpose for which you may consider such evidence, you must weigh it in the same manner as you do all other evidence in the case. You are not permitted to consider such evidence for any other purpose. So this isn't about character assassination of O.J. Simpson, as you might think at first blush. This is about Mr. Darden trying to conjure up a motive for you. And at the outset let me say that no, none, not one little bit of domestic violence is tolerable between a man and a woman. O.J. Simpson is not proud of that 1989 incident. He is not proud of it. But you know what? He paid his debt to that and it went to court. He went through that program. And the one good thing, and no matter how long Darden talked, from 1989 to now there was never any physical violence between O.J. Simpson and Nicole Brown Simpson.

It is wonderful that we live in the age of videotape because it tells you about who O.J. Simpson. Cindy Garvey tells you how O.J. Simpson was. He was this mean dark brooding person at this concert, that he was going to kill his ex-wife because he didn't like his seats. Because he didn't like his seats or because he didn't invite her to dinner. That is how silly what they are talking about in this case as he tries to play out this drama. But let me show you, rather than talk--a picture is worth a thousand words, so let me show you this video. You watch this video for a moment and we will talk about it. This is for Chris Darden. (At 4:19 P.M. a videotape was played.)

You will recognize some of the people in this videotape after awhile. Mr. Simpson kissing Denise Brown, Miss Juditha Brown, Mr. Louis Brown. Talking to a friend. That is his son Justin who he kisses, smiling and happily waving. Mr. Brown is happy. Laughing and falling down and laughing again, bending over laughing. You see that. You see that with your own eyes. You will have that back in this jury room. How does that comport with this tortured, twisted reasoning that he was angry in some kind of a jealous rage? Did he look like he was a jealous rage to you? Your eyes aren't lying to you when you see that. Thank heaven we have videotape. I didn't tell you about that in opening statement. Do you think that is pretty compelling? Thank heaven we have that. And we know in this city how important video-tapes can be when people don't want to believe things even when they see on it videotapes and you saw that yourself.

And even after that video, like any proud papa, you know what O.J. Simpson did? Took a picture, a photograph with his daughter. Let's look at this photograph for a minute, if you want to see how he looks while he is in this murderous rage, while this fuse is going on that Darden talks about. Where is the fuse now, Mr. Darden? Where is the fuse? Look at that look on his face liked (sic) any proud papa. He is proud of that little girl and who wouldn't be proud of her.

Then we know that at nine o'clock he talked to Christian Reichardt, his friend Dr. Christian Re-ichardt, and you saw Chris Reichardt come in here and talk to you. I thought he made a very, very, very good witness from the standpoint of what he had to say. He told you that O.J. Simpson sound-ed even happier than usual. He was more jovial, he got his life back together and he was moving on. Isn't that interesting? Isn't that an interesting way of looking at circumstantial evidence. Let me show you how we differ in this case. A doctor witness comes in and says O.J. Simpson is jovial at nine o'clock on June 12th. Pretty good evidence, wouldn't you say? I think you would love to have that. Anybody would in a case where you are supposedly in a murderous rage. Instead of Chris Darden standing here and saying, well, that is pretty tough evidence for us to overcome, he says O.J. Simpson was happy because he was going to kill his wife.

Now, if you believe that, I suppose I might as well sit down now and I am probably wasting my time. I don't think any of you believe that. That is preposterous. It flies in the face of everything that is reasonable. You have these two reasonable hypotheses, his isn't reasonable, but assume it is reasonable, you would have to adopt this, that he is jovial, he is happy. They make a date for that next Wednesday and O.J. Simpson returns from back east. You remember that. That is the testimony. Mr. Darden tries to make a big thing of the fact, well, gee, you know, golly, was he depressed about the fact that they had broken up or they had finally broke up? He said, yeah, he had been down. He never said he was depressed. Said he was down or upset and who wouldn't be.

Remember the last questions I asked. If you had just ended a 17-year relationship and it was over, you would feel down for a short period of time until you got your life on track. You wouldn't go kill your ex-wife, the mother of your children. O.J. Simpson didn't try to kill or didn't kill Nicole Brown Simpson when they got a divorce, when they went through whatever they went through when Faye Resnick moved in.

In this case in opening statement I showed you Bob Shapiro's foresight and wisdom. He had these photographs taken I think on June 15th. Instead of praising this lawyer who was interested in the truth, the Prosecution says, well, they went to Dr. Huisenga. That wasn't really his doctor. Isn't that preposterous. Dr. Huisenga, by all accounts, is a qualified doctor. He was the Raiders team doctor. I suppose he is supposes qualified. This is Mr. O.J. Simpson's body as it appeared on June 15th. Wouldn't you expect to see a lot of bruises and marks on that body? You see his back. Some of these aren't very flattering, but this is not about flattery; this is about his life.

Now, on his hands--there is some slight abrasions on his hands, but nothing consistent with a fight like this. You know it. I know it. We all know it. We will talk more about this, this so-called fish-hook cut and where he got that. It will become very clear when we talk about demeanor where that came from. Miss Clark wants to try and confuse that, but that is very, very clear. So with regard to Mr. Simpson's physical condition, I don't want to just tell you to take my word, stand here and say, oh, yeah, he was in great shape on that day or he looked good or whatever. Fortunately we had photographs again, we had graphic evidence of this man's body. This man had not been in a life and death struggle for five to fifteen minutes.

And just before we take the dinner break, let's talk briefly about these witnesses from the family and what they had to say. The first. We first called Arnelle Simpson, and you saw Arnelle on the stand. Arnelle Simpson, the Defendant's daughter, born the day he won the Heisman trophy.

And she told you how her father reacted when he got the news that his ex-wife had been killed. She told you. She had never before heard her father sound like that, how upset he was, how he lost control of himself, how distraught he was. You heard and you saw her on that stand. That is why we called her, so you would have better understanding, because we knew, I knew there would come a day that Marcia Clark would stand here and say, well, you know, he wouldn't react like he does when somebody gets this information, just like he did yesterday, because what Miss Clark forgot was I examined Detective Phillips. And you look back through your notes. The first thing that O.J. Simpson said to Detective Phillips was, "What do you mean she has been killed?" And then he kept repeating himself and repeating himself, and Phillips, to his credit, said he became very, very upset, kept repeating himself, and Phillips gave the phone to Arnelle Simpson.

So they can make--she can again theorize, fantasize all she wants. Well, he didn't ask, well, it was a car accident? Have you ever had some bad news given to you? There is no book that you go to. The only book you should go to is the bible or your God, whomever you believe in to help get you through it. There is nothing that says how you would handle yourself in those times. These Prosecutors don't understand that. They would stand here and tell you that that is preposterous. This man was upset. And you are going to see at everything he did from that moment that he found out that his ex-wife had been killed was consistent only with innocence absolutely that day. And so Arnelle Simpson helps us in that regard.

Now, when you want to think about the depths to which people will go to try to win, when you want to talk about an obsession to win, I'm going to give you an example. There was a witness in this case named Thano Peratis. This is a man who's their man who took O.J. Simpson's blood. This is a man who had a subpoena, at one point said he could have come down here and testify. They didn't call him. By the time we wanted to call him, he's unavailable because of his heart problem, remember? So what we did is, we read you his grand jury testimony I believe and we played for you his preliminary hearing testimony. And in that testimony, it's very, very consistent. He's been a nurse for a number of years. You saw him. He works for the city of Los Angeles. He says that when he took this blood from O.J. Simpson on June 13th, he took between 7.9 and 8.1 cc's of blood. That's what he said. That's real simple, isn't it? We knew that. He's sworn to tell the truth under oath both places, the grand jury and preliminary hearing. Pretty clear, isn't it? Pretty clear. You remember in my opening statement, I told you, you know, something's wrong here, something's sinister here, something's wrong, because if we take all their figures and assume they took 8 cc's of blood, there's 6.5 cc's accounted for, there is 1.5 cc's missing of this blood. There's some missing blood in this case. Where is it?

It took all four detectives, all four LAPD experienced detectives to leave the bodies. They had to notify the Coroner. They didn't have a criminalist to go over to notify O.J. Simpson. Who's fooling who here? This is preposterous. They're lying, trying to get over that wall to get in that house. You don't believe so? You're talking about saving lives. Remember what Arnelle said. First of all, they all make this big mistake. They forget and they say, "Well, when we leave from the back, we go right in that back door of the house there, go right in the back door." But they forgot. Arnelle Simpson comes in here and testifies you can't go in the back door because remember, Kato had put on the alarm. You had to go around the house to the front. Arnelle had to open the keypad to let them in, remember? You think who knows better? You'd think she knows better or they know better? She had to let them in. So they're worried about dead bodies and people being in that house and saving lives? Who goes in first? Arnelle Simpson goes in first. These big, brave police officers, and the young lady just walks in there first. They don't go upstairs looking. They just want to be inside that house and make her leave to give Fuhrman a chance to start what he's doing, strolling around the premises and doing what he's doing there.

Then we come, before we end the day, to Detective Mark Fuhrman. This man is an unspeakable disgrace. He's been unmasked for the whole world for what he is, and that's hopefully positive.

And they put him on the stand and you saw it. You saw it. It was sickening. And then my colleague, Lee Bailey, who can't be with us today, but God bless him, wherever he is, did his cross-examination of this individual and he asked some interesting questions. Some of you probably wondered, "I wonder why he's asking that." He asked this man whether or not he ever met Kathleen Bell. Of course, he lied about that.

Then Bailey says: "Have you used that word, referring to the `n' word, in the past 10 years? "Not that I recall, no. "You mean, if you call someone a Nigger, you had forgotten it?

"I'm not sure I can answer the question the way it's phrased, sir." And they go on. He says, "Well--" And then pins him down. "I want you to assume that perhaps at some time since 1985 or `86, you addressed a member of the African American race as a Nigger. Is it possible that you have forgotten that act on your part? "Answer: No, it is not possible. "Are you, therefore, saying that you have not used that word in the past 10 years, Detective Fuhrman? "Answer: Yes. That is what I'm saying. "Question: And you say under oath that you have not addressed any black person as a Nigger or spoken about black people as niggers in the past 10 years, Detective Fuhrman? "That's what I'm saying, sir. "So that anyone who comes to this court and quotes you as using that word in dealing with African Americans would be a liar; would they not, Detective Fuhrman? "Yes, they would".

Let's remember this man. This is the man who was off this case shortly after 2:00 o'clock in the morning right after he got on it. This is the man who didn't want to be off this case. This is the man, when they're ringing the doorbell at Ashford, who goes for a walk. And he describes how he's strolling. Let me quote him for you. Here's what he says:

"I was just strolling along looking at the house. Maybe I could see some movement inside. I was just walking while the other three detectives were down there." And that's when he walks down and he's the one who says the Bronco was parked askew and he sees some spot on the door. He makes all of the discoveries. He's got to be the big man because he's had it in for O.J. because of his views since '85. This is the man, he's the guy who climbs over the fence. He's the guy who goes in and talks to Kato Kaelin while the other detectives are talking to the family. He's the guy who's shining a light in Kato Kaelin's eyes. He's the guy looking at shoes and looking for suspects. He's the guy who's doing these things. He's the guy who says, "I don't tell anybody about the thumps on the wall." He's the guy who's off this case who's supposedly there to help this man, our client, O.J. Simpson, who then goes out all by himself, all by himself.

Now, he's worried about bodies or suspects or whatever. He doesn't even take out his gun. He goes around the side of the house, and lo and behold, he claims he finds this glove and he says the glove is still moist and sticky. Now, under their theory, at 10:40, 10:45, that glove is dropped. How many hours is that? It's now after 6:00 o'clock. So what is that? Seven and a half hours. The testimony about drying time around here, no dew point that night. Why would it be moist and sticky unless he brought it over there and planted it there to try to make this case? And there is a Caucasian hair on that glove. This man cannot be trusted. He is sinful to the Prosecution, and for them to say he's not important is untrue and you will not fall for it, because as guardians of justice here, we can't let it happen.

Why did they then all try to cover for this man Fuhrman? Why would this man who is not only Los Angeles' worst nightmare, but America's worst nightmare, why would they all turn their heads and try to cover for them? Why would you do that if you are sworn to uphold the law? There is something about corruption. There is something about a rotten apple that will ultimately infect the entire barrel, because if the others don't have the courage that we have asked you to have in this case, people sit sadly by.

We live in a society where many people are apathetic, they don't want to get involved, and that is why all of us, to a person, in this courtroom, have thanked you from the bottom of our hearts. Because you know what? You haven't been apathetic. You are the ones who made a commitment, a commitment toward justice, and it is a painful commitment, but you've got to see it through. Your commitment, your courage, is much greater than these police officers. This man could have been off the force long ago if they had done their job, but they didn't do their job. People looked the other way. People didn't have the courage. One of the things that has made this country so great is people's willingness to stand up and say that is wrong. I'm not going to be part of it. I'm not going to be part of the cover-up. That is what I'm asking you to do. Stop this cover-up. Stop this cover-up. If you don't stop it, then who? Do you think the police department is going to stop it? Do you think the D.A.'s office is going to stop it? Do you think we can stop it by ourselves? It has to be stopped by you.

But the capper was finding those tapes, something that you could hear. Lest there be any doubt in anybody's mind, Laura McKinny came in here, and I can imagine the frustration of the Prosecutors, they've had the glove demonstration, they have seen all these other things go wrong and now they got to face these tapes.

We owe a debt of gratitude to this lady that ultimately and finally she came forward. And she tells us that this man over the time of these interviews uses the "N" word 42 times is what she says. And so-called Fuhrman tapes. And you of course had an opportunity to listen to this man and espouse this evil, this personification of evil. And so I'm going to ask Mr. Harris to play exhibit 1368 one more time. It was a transcript. This was not on tape. The tape had been erased where he said, "We have no niggers where I grew up." These are two of 42, if you recall. Then this was his actual voice. (At 10:00 A.M., Defense exhibit 1368, a videotape, was played.)

This is the word text for what he then says on the tape. Now, you heard that voice. No question whose voice that is. Mr. Darden concedes whose voice that is. They don't do anything. Talking about women. Doesn't like them any better than he likes African Americans. They don't go out and initiate contact with some six foot five inch Nigger who has been in prison pumping weights. This is how he sees this world. That is this man's cynical view of the world. This is this man who is out there protecting and serving. That is Mark Fuhrman.

H. Checklists

The following checklist summarizes the information counsel should consider when developing persuasive closing arguments. It should be used as a starting point for developing appropriate closings focused on persuading the jury by showcasing the theme and theories of the case developed during case analysis.

I.   Use the Rule of Threes

    a.   Tell them what you are going to tell them.

    b.   Tell them.

    c. Tell them what you told them and why it means you win.

II.   Remember the Three Primary Steps of Case Analysis:

    a. Identify and analyze the legal issues.

    b. Identify and analyze the factual issues.

    c. Develop a moral theme and legal theory.

III.   Use the Seven Steps to Superior Closing Arguments:

    a. Case Analysis, first, last, always (opening).

    b. Grabber, one-liner, hook (moral).

    c. Argue! Use the law and evidence to create inferences supporting your theme and theory.

        i. Answer the questions in the jury's mind.

        ii. Beware the burden of boredom.

    d. Uses appropriate rhetorical devices.

        i. Primacy & recency.

        ii. Rule of threes.

        iii. Parallelism.

        iv. Analogies & inferences.

        v. Engage multiple senses.

    e. Meet the burden of common sense (facts).

    f. Instructions are your friend (law).

    g. Tell the jury what you want them to do (what the evidence demands).

IV.   The Do's of Closing Argument:

    a. Be confident in arguing your position.

    b. Maintain eye contact, but not so much to make jurors uncomfortable.

    c. Structure your argument—don't simply re-hash the facts.

    d. Draw on the jury's common sense.

    e. Use visual aids or physical evidence from the trial.

    f. Address the standard of proof.

    g. (Prosecution) Use rebuttal argument to hammer home your strongest points, how you refuted the defense's contentions, and remain positive in your case!

V.   The Don'ts of Closing Argument:

   a.   Misstate the evidence or the law.

   b.   Argue facts not in evidence.

   c.   State your personal belief in the justice of your cause.

   d.   Personally vouch for the credibility of a witness.

   e.   Comment on the accused's exercise of a fundamental right (prosecution).

   f.   Make personal attacks on opposing counsel.

VI. Legal Principles for a Proper Closing Argument:

   a.   You are confined to the record. If evidence is not admitted you cannot argue it.

   b.   The trial court has supervisory authority over the scope and direction of closing argument, but should give deference to counsel unless the law is misstated.

   c.   Prosecutors cannot argue merely to inflame or arouse passions. The courts will consider whether a substantial right of the accused was violated when reviewing this issue.

   d.   Advocates cannot intentionally misstate evidence or attempt to lead the jury to draw improper inferences from admitted evidence.

   e.   Personal beliefs and opinions of counsel are forbidden.

   f.   Reasonable inferences are permissible and expected.

   g.   It is improper to refer to evidence which was either successfully objected to as to admissibility, stricken from the record, or otherwise excluded.

I.   Evidentiary Rules to Consider During Closings

Issues Arising During Closing Arguments	Applicable Federal Rules of Evidence
Properly address evidence admitted with a limiting instruction	105(b)
Out-of-court statements offered for the truth of the matter asserted therein (hearsay)	801–807

Properly arguing evidence of other crimes, wrongs & acts (Chapter 10)	404(b)
Legal relevancy—is the probative value substantially outweighed by the danger of unfair prejudice, et al	403
Are the questions logically relevant	401, 402

Table 1 - Potential Evidentiary Rules Applicable During Closing Arguments

-Notes-

Chapter 12: Motions and Objections

A. Motions...509
B. How the Law Impacts Motions...............................512
C. Drafting the Motion 514
D. Arguing the Motion...520
E. Checklist - Writing Motions..................................525
F. Checklist - Motion Hearings..................................526
G. Objections...527
H. How the Law Impacts Objections...........................528
I. Planning Objections 529
J. Making the Objection 534
K. Offers of Proof..534
L. Objections as to Form 536
M. Objections as to Substance...................................539

A.   Motions

Attorneys use motions practice to identify the law that will apply and the evidence that will be admitted during the trial The legal decisions by the judge have a tremendous impact on the manner in which counsel will either defend or prosecute any case.   Much as counsel use instructions to mold closing argument, motions are used to set the stage for the development of the final legal theory, factual theory and moral theme. Pre-trial, they are used to clarify these issues and obtain a ruling before the jury is ever seated. This is advantageous to counsel because juries do not like when legal arguments stop the flow of a trial, and often feel like they are being unnecessarily excluded from interesting topics within a case. They are also used during the trial to deny opposing counsel the opportunity to use evidence identified as inadmissible or to force counsel to live with an interpretation of the law that does not support their theme and theory.

Since motions serve as the gate through which disputed evidence or potentially applicable law must pass in order to be used at trial, a complete and thorough understanding of how to approach motions practice is important. Counsel must understand it from not only a case analysis perspective, but from a common sense "this-is-what-I-do-and-this-is-when-I-do-it" perspective.

Our earlier case analysis discussion identified the relationship between motions and the various sections of the trial process. Counsel must know the legal issues and the facts, both disputed undisputed, impacting the judge's decision as to those legal issues. Some of these legal issues will not be controversial, and counsel should be able to readily forecast the admissibility or inadmissibility of some types of evidence based upon settled law. However, in other areas the legal issue you have identified is either one of first impression, or more commonly, one whose application is greatly influenced by factual determinations.

> *Example: counsel is analyzing a criminal case for potential search and seizure violations of the 4th amendment. Using case analysis as a methodology should result in the following approach:*

Written Motion	Offer Evidence During Motion Hearing	Argument During the Motion
Identify facts – uncontroverted and controverted	Police Officer – call, examine based upon departmental procedures and failure to follow, show no warrant, show bias against defendant.	Legal Theory – deny state evidence of crime seized in home
Identify applicable law		Factual theory – police did not follow departmental procedures used to ensure compliance with Constitution
Argue law to facts	Defendant – call for limited purpose of showing right was expressed.	
Offer to produce evidence		
Request relief	Witness 1 – call to show police ignored refusal to consent to search	Moral Theme – we cannot reward state for violating constitutional rights

There is nothing particularly earth-shattering in the example above. It merely identifies the legal theory, organizes the facts needed to support the legal theory and then previews the motions hearing in writing to the court. The Rule of Threes adequately organizes and presents this information in a fashion helpful to the judge. It is also helpful to the advocate because it provides a template for organizing, analyzing and presenting a motion.

The same thought process applies regardless of the legal issue. Certain fundamental tasks must always be accomplished to guarantee success in motions practice.

Once counsel have identified these fundamental tasks they merely need to develop the skills that will allow them to be successful in these tasks. That is a question of preparation, not knowledge. One of the first steps to be fully prepared for motions practice is to develop the written advocacy tools to properly frame issues so that the actual hearing maximizes the opportunity to persuade the judge to rule in counsel's favor.

Successful Motions Practice:

• Know the local rules for filing deadlines, both according to the legal issue when appropriate and according to time

• Draft sound legal motions in writing when required—use law, facts and inference to your advantage

• Identify the source of your evidence for the motions hearing and have it available in an appropriate form to admit before the judge—do not forget the effect of FRE 104, or its state equivalent

• Do not forget to balance your law, facts and moral theme, even when dealing with motions—there is always a reason for the legal protection—remind the judge of that necessity when necessary

• Know whom you are trying to persuade—the judge

• Do not argue with opposing counsel, argue to the judge

• Know when a ruling is preserved on appeal and when you must raise it again during the case-in-chief—understand the tactical and strategic reasons behind any decision to raise such issues at trial

---

Many of the skills applicable to appellate motion practice are transferable to pretrial motions practice, with some differences. The first difference is an overarching one that cannot be overstated - at this point in the litigation the ultimate outcome of the case, potential strategies, and tactical considerations exist in a much more fluid state. Pretrial motions fundamentally shape the legal and factual issues applicable at trial, they have the potential to be transformative. The nature of appellate advocacy requires that it be constrained to the record, while pretrial motions assist in creating that record. Some specific differences include:

• Number of judges involved
• Importance of the issues
• Impact of a ruling
• Source of facts

- Length of the written product
- Impact of local rules on form and substance
- Nature of the record
- Stage of the litigation
- Relative degree of formality

Counsel must develop an understanding of the similarities and differences between motions practice and appellate advocacy to maximize their approach to each. Counsel must remember that in the trial phase of litigation, these motions may be in areas where the law is undecided, and therefore counsel has greater leeway for creativity and emphasis than in appellate practice. Attorneys should approach motions practice in a more creative fashion given their greater ability to discovery both factual and legal issues at this stage in the litigation process.

B.　How the Law Impacts Motions

Motions practice begins and ends with a complete understanding of the Relevant Rules of Procedure, Local Rules of Court and any standing orders of the judge hearing the motion. The Federal Rules of Civil Procedure and their state equivalents define the basic procedures applicable during civil litigation, while the Federal Rules of Criminal Procedure and their state equivalents define the rules for criminal litigation. States have used these Federal Rules as a model for state procedure rules. A few states adopted the Federal Rules of Civil Procedure in their entirety, others have adapted federal rules when creating their state practice rules. These rules govern the type of motions counsel can bring, the grounds for such motions, how they are addressed in court, to include issues of timing and notice.

These court rules regulate the practices and procedures before the tribunal. The court has latitude when creating these rules, but they must remain consistent with the other laws and rules of procedure. They are designed to identify, with specificity, exactly how a motion may be brought. These local rules cover the areas of the form and format of legal memoranda, declarations, exhibits, notice requirements, stipulations, and motion hearing procedures.

Most judges, both state and federal, issue standing orders or procedures governing matters not covered in either the rules of procedure or the local rules of court. These might include timelines identifying the dates for particular motions, continuances, and procedures for discovery motions within their court. Such standing order are an excellent glance into the preferences of an individual jurist and counsel should take the time to collectively consider these standing orders for their insight into the courts judicial philosophy. In addition to the local rules and standing orders many court systems also have certain customs and courtesies that operate as unwritten rules, establishing some baseline procedures that may be unwritten, but nonetheless followed within the jurisdiction.

Counsel should be aware that more courts are requiring parties to meet and confer before filing formal motions. When addressing motions to compel; some federal judges require the parties to meet and confer in person, followed by a submission of a join letter to the court specifying disagreements. Practically speaking, motions are now routinely served and filed electronically, some jurisdictions even require electronic service and filing.

Some motions lend themselves more readily to written as opposed to oral arguments; others are more persuasively presented in person. The FRCP allow for written motions in all instances, but not necessarily oral argument. Most jurisdictions allowing for oral argument have a tendency to restrict it to certain issues that have been deemed by custom or local rule to lend themselves to an oral hearing. That same court may very well not allow oral argument as to other issues. Counsel must consult the local rules and make themselves aware of local custom prior to filing motions. In those instances where counsel need to make oral argument and the court is not so inclined options are still available, to include filing a specific request to the court explaining why oral argument should be scheduled in this instance.

In some jurisdictions the court will issue a preliminary decision based on the written submissions and provide that decision to the attorneys electronically, usually by telephone or email. At that point either counsel has the ability to request oral argument for the purpose of changing the court's mind.

In each of the situations described above the attorneys involved must conduct a cost benefit analysis when deciding whether or not to request oral argument. This analysis should consider the time, expense and effort involved. Usually it cuts in favor of oral argument, particularly when the movant bears the burden of persuasion. Sometimes though the nature of the motion may be sufficiently straightforward that no additional benefit would be derived from oral argument. In those cases not only will a written motion suffice, but the court will appreciate the ability of counsel to properly address the issues in the most effective and efficient way possible.

C.   Drafting the Motion

Preparing an effective brief requires careful blending of law, facts, and persuasion theory (moral theme). This approach requires a particular style of writing, one that avoids a monotone voice while remaining both clear and concise. Acceptable techniques to accomplish this include:

- Different length and form of sentences.
- Varying length and format of paragraphs.
- Beginning opening paragraph sentences with different phrasings.
- Use transitional words, phrases, and sentences.

In addition to concerns about the "voice" of the motion, counsel have available to them a plethora of drafting approaches that increase the persuasive power of written motions and oral arguments. They include:

- Be specific and concrete
- Use simple sentences
- Edit longer sentences, breaking them into simpler structures when possible
- Use simple and common words
- Positive statements
- Avoid legalese
- Selectively use foreign language words and phrases only as necessary
- Primarily use active voice
- Use passive voice occasionally and for variety
- Make verb tenses match across sentences
- Follow the conventions of grammar
- Parentheses are not your friend
- Eliminate unnecessary words
- Employ parallelism across paragraphs were appropriate
- Clarity strengthens argument, ambiguity weakens it
- Use gender-neutral terminology
- Modify dangling participles
- Ignore all of these rules when necessary to communicate effectively

Counsel should remember that fundamentals of grammar, language and punctuation, when properly employed, increase the persuasive power of their arguments.

1.   Balance the Law, Facts and Moral Theory

Balancing the relevant law, facts, and moral theme of your motion will create a presentation that persuades the judge to either grant or deny the motion. Attorneys must understand and approach the combination of law, facts and morality from a persuasion perspective. Every motion calls out for a central and unifying theme. This theme becomes the hook around which the discussion of the law and facts rotate. This quickly becomes problematic during motions practice, often because the complexity of the legal issues overwhelm the factual story. A careful reminder of the very real factual issues, to include the immediate impact of the court's decision, can go a long ways towards cutting through the clutter of complex issues to their real world impact.

While themes vary from case to case, counsel should consider using the primary issue within the motion, or reason for the motion. That core concept benefits from careful repetition and insertion through out the motion. The phrase, or series of words, used to highlight those issues needs to capture the essence of moral question behind the issue while also emphasizing whether or not the motions should be granted or denied. The words themselves are case dependent, the thought process behind selecting them is universal.

The issues themselves in motions practice tend to be more legal as opposed to factual. Counsel should consider the elements of the legal issues and craft their argument around the issues thematically to push the court towards the resolution sought by the client. It is important, when seeking the best argument, to reflect accurately the applicable legal standards. Word smithing is nice, themes are interesting, but counsel must be careful not to pick a theme that modifies a legal standard.

Counsel should consider the relative complexity of their motion when deciding on their thematic approach. A complex series of legal arguments married to a simplistic (but not simple) resonates effectively as a persuasive tool. The theme in that instance becomes the unifying concept spanning the various complex legal issues.

2.   Understanding the Legal Standard

Understanding motions requires that counsel become adept at identifying the legal issues normally present, both substantively and procedurally. The majority of pretrial motions will deal with the application of a particular legal standard to a particular set of facts. Most of these motions rely in large part upon a proper identification of the legal issues. These legal arguments fall into several different categories, to include:

- A case of first impression
- Applying established legal precedent
- Adapting precedent from another jurisdiction
- Application of precedent from another area of the law in the same jurisdiction
- Need to follow legislative history

- Application of recognized rules of statutory construction
- Agency ruling would support a specific decision
- Judicial discretion is the controlling standard

Many of these legal issues are often intertwined with factual arguments. In these situations a movant is requesting relief from the court based upon a certain set of facts. Examples include:

- facts match the facts of similar cases where similar or identical relief was granted
- facts can be distinguished from previous cases where relief was denied
- Statistical data/analysis supports the movant's requested relief

The way in which the motion organizes the applicable legal standards is important. Supporting cases, statutes, rules, regulations, constitutional provisions, secondary authorities, and other persuasive legal sources must be precisely and professionally organized. The court will be moved by the quality of the legal sources cited, as well as the manner in which the legal standards impact the factual issues.

The core of the legal argument put forth in the motion should be built around the legal authorities with the greatest precedential value. Appellate court decisions within the same jurisdiction have the highest precedential value and will be both applicable and persuasive. Federal district judges are most persuaded, all else being equal, by the opinions of their circuit. Some judicial decisions from outside the jurisdiction of the motion court may be persuasive, but not necessarily controlling precedent. The degree of such persuasion can be determined by:

- The status of the court
- Similarities between the issues
- Age of the precedent
- Basis of the precedent
- Location of the court
- Reputation of the judge
- Nature of the case (first impression, leading, unusual, moderate)
- Philosophy of the court and judge

If the motion involves the identical law, rules, or procedures adopted in another jurisdiction, then how those courts interpreted and applied the law to the facts will hold a great deal of sway. Older decisions may be influential when dealing with common law matters. Newer decisions may be more influential in a case addressing more modern issues. Precedent from other jurisdictions can be persuasive if the reasoning of the courts matches similar public policy or other concerns in the jurisdiction of the motion.

When discussing the law counsel should focus on the grammatical and organizational structure of the legal argument to increase its persuasive power. Common mistakes that counsel make include inaccurate descriptions, vague explanations and incomplete statements of the law. Additional issues include failure to embrace the twin guideposts of clarity and brevity and descending instead into rambling dissertations, needlessly explaining issues already addressed in the written motion, using quotes so long that they are not applicable, and inserting citations within the motion as opposed to in a table of authorities.

3.   Organize the Facts

Facts can be divided into multiple categories, those giving rise to the litigation, those giving rise to the specific motion, those not yet discovered or developed, and those deemed non relevant by the parties. The facts most relevant to the court will depend upon the nature of the motion before the court. Facts should be broken down during case analysis into three categories for purpose of their application to a specific legal issue:

- Disputed
- Stipulated and admitted
- Undisputed

Facts can be presented in one of two primary fashions, as a statement of fact at the beginning of a written brief or oral argument, or intermittently explained in the body of the brief as necessary to place the law in context. Counsel should determine which structure baed upon the type of facts and their importance to the motion. When the facts are simple, a concise explanation at the beginning is sufficient. When confronted with more complex facts, an outline of the basic facts might suffice at the beginning of the motion, followed by more detailed explanations within the motion where most appropriate. When the motion revolves primarily around a legal issue then their explanation within the motion may very well be minimal.

The movant initially explains the factual basis of the motion to the judge. In some situations, normally where there are disputed issues of fact, the opposing party may also need to address the facts. Both sides should take care not to inaccurately provide distorted, incomplete or otherwise defective versions of the facts. The provided facts, regardless of their form, should be objective, accurate and descriptive. They should be delivered with brevity and clarity.

4.   Apply the Law to the Facts

The type of motion determines whether the law or the facts are most important for the court. Effective arguments will mix factual and legal issues, selecting useful facts based upon their relationship with, and impact upon, the controlling legal standard. The effectiveness of a particular legal precedent often depends upon the relationship between the facts supporting that precedential application. In both the written brief and oral argument counsel must provide a reasoned analysis of the law and facts. In support of these arguments counsel should also consider:

- The impact of emotion and concepts of equity
- Language
- Rhetorical questions
- Candor
- Weaknesses of the opposition
- Personalize the argument
- Other considerations
- Economic factors
- Pragmatic concerns

Counsel should consider how the principles of classic rhetoric inform current motions practice when analyzing facts contextually. While drafting arguments addressing the intertwined impact of the law and the facts care should be taken to follow certain fundamental precepts of legal drafting, to include:

- Brevity is best
- Start with your requested relief
- Use Primacy and Recency
- Address your weakness points in the middle of your arguments
- Check citations and verify their validity
- Avoid string citations
- Include facts and quotes from significant cases. Explain their context
- Be candid, never mislead the court

5.   Focus on the Judge

Practically speaking the judge has enormous substantive and procedural discretion. Counsel must take the time to research the judge, as well as the law. It is important to understand the court's predilections and any unusual procedural preferences for both the form of motions, as well as the substance of their arguments. When researching a particular judge counsel should take the time to identify case specific knowledge, flexibility on the law or procedure, and any potential biases. Counsel would be well advised to make use of the new decision tools that can be found on legal research sites like Westlaw. Through proper use of these analytical tools, counsel can see which arguments have been successful in their jurisdiction, and which judges are more likely to dismiss out of hand. This may sound like forum shopping, and to a certain extent it may be, but it is also accepted practice and an ethical approach. More importantly, failing to perform analysis on these issues may be fatal to the client's case.

When conducting research on a particular member of the judiciary, counsel should begin by asking their colleagues. In all likelihood other members of the firm will have appeared before this judge, and they should be more than willing to share any relevant information about the court's preferences. Additionally, judicial profiles can be found on web sites and print resources. Court web sites have biographies and court opinions written by their judges. Bar associations are another resource for judicial profiles. Finally, the best source for learning how a particular judge likes to handle motions is the judge themselves. Counsel should take the time to observe a motion session conducted by the court. Once counsel understand the judge that will hear the motion, it is time to draft a motion, and prepare an oral argument, based upon that information.

How the judge decides a motion depends upon how counsel present their positions through written briefs and oral arguments. Attorneys must plan this presentation in advance to maximize its persuasive impact on the judge. Complete and thorough planning of the motion, based upon ongoing case analysis, increases the persuasive impact of the motion. In drafting the motion, counsel must also consider rules of court, the preferences of the judge, and local customs. Even with all of this, the attorney must also make additional tactical decisions about the specific points to be made, and the order in which to make them.

Attorneys use written and oral motions to convince the court that a series of factual and legal contentions require the court grant their request. The facts and law are arranged in an order to make the court believe a series of issues leading it to grant the movant's request. Each point is supported by some combination of facts and the law, arranged in a fashion that logically leads the court to one conclusion. This cannot be accomplished when the logical inferences and arguments are tangentially related to the key question before the court. In order to effectively persuade the judge counsel must reduce or remove these tangential facts and inferences from their persuasive presentation, whether it is written, oral, or both. This decision of what to remove, or take away, is as important as the decisions about what to include. In deciding which issues to remove, and the order of presentation for the remaining points, counsel should ask themselves the following questions:

- Which point is the strongest one for their issue?
- Which point is the most important one for their issue?
- Which point should be made first?

When seeking to answer these questions counsel should imagine how each of these points will impact the judge, and then create a structure to maximize their strong points and minimize their weak ones. The most important point for the motion is usually identified through case analysis properly focusing on the relevant law and facts. The key factor within the relevant law or facts supporting the decision can be used to identify the potential most important fact for a particular motion. Often this will also be the strongest point of the presentation. In those instances the motion has a strong probability of success when properly argued.

Occasionally the most important point is not your strongest point, in those instances more "creative" factual arrangements may be necessary. Counsel would be well advised in those situations to carefully arrange their points to maximize persuasive value. Accepted methods include beginning with a fact that captures the attention of the audience, next creating a belief that the merits of counsel's position cut in favor of the requested relief, and then using a framework to connect each salient point into a persuasive argument.

Once maximum persuasive impact has been achieved the remaining points should be arranged in either a chronological or logical order, depending upon the structure of the argument. Generally speaking most counsel will formulate their arguments using either inductive or deductive reasoning. Inductive goes from the specific to the general, while deductive takes the argument from the general to the specific. Both are effective, and the choice of structure depends upon the nature and strength of counsel's strongest and most important point. When formulating their arguments counsel should use primacy and recency to bookend the beginning and the end of the presentation with their strongest point supporting their requested relief.

D. Arguing the Motion

1. Introduction

Prior to the motions hearing, mark the written motions and responses as required by the local court rules. During the hearing the judge will state that the purpose of this particular session is to litigate motions. The judge will then identify any appellate exhibits previously provided or offered to the court. If she does not do this counsel should respectfully remind her which exhibits have been admitted. The judge may next inquire into who has the burden and what the standard of proof is for this particular issue. After identifying the burden the judge is normally ready to hear the motion. Most judges give both sides an opportunity to briefly state their position before the presentation of evidence. Normally the moving party has the burden and presents its evidence first. The opposing party then presents its evidence, if any. Afterwards rebuttal and surrebuttal evidence, if any, is presented. The advocates then argue their positions to the judge. The judge deliberates on the motion and makes a ruling, either orally or in writing. This sequence may vary from judge to judge and such variance has no effect on the validity of the ultimate ruling. Remember also that a judge is typically more proactive and inquisitive during motions practice than in open court session before a jury. You should be prepared for the judge to attempt to focus counsel on the pertinent issues and be unhappy with wasted time.

Although the argument must be tailored for motions practice, the basic concepts of persuading the judge to rule in counsel's favor apply. Typically, a good motions argument will initially state counsel's position, move to the facts, present the law, apply the law to the facts and, finally, restate the position on the requested relief. Knowing the judge and the local rules will provide greater insight on the general scheme for the motion argument.

2.   How the Law Impacts the Motion Argument

FRE 104 establishes the authority of the judge to decide questions of admissibility in a motions hearing. This rule gives the judge authority to make decisions during motions without regards to the limitations on admissibility that the other federal rules of evidence might place upon the offered evidence. The only limitation on what evidence the judge may consider is found in the rule on privileges. The courts have determined that we will not destroy the privilege protections when deciding motions.

The rule also allows for the conditional admissibility of evidence even though counsel has not yet established that it will be relevant. Conditional relevancy exists so that the court can control the flow of the trial and keep cases moving forward in a timely manner. It also reflects the modernization of trial process as part of the federal rules of evidence. Finally, the rule allows the accused to testify for the limited purpose of addressing the subject of the motion without otherwise waiving his right to silence in a criminal case.

While FRE 104 authorizes the trial judge to decide preliminary issues of admissibility, the impact of that authority and the limitations upon its exercise are discussed in FRE 103. FRE 103 establishes that once the judge rules conclusively on an issue raised during a motions hearing that issue is preserved on appeal for the losing side. Prior to this recent change to the Federal Rules of Evidence the losing party was required to object when the evidence addressed during the pretrial motion was actually admitted at trial.

The change obviates the need for counsel to object a second time when the evidence is offered in the presence of the jury. Advocates should check to determine whether or not the rules of evidence in their jurisdiction have adopted a similar standard. If not, the motions hearing does not end the issue when it comes to objecting. In order to ensure that the issue is preserved on appeal the losing advocate must make the record and object again when the evidence is proffered in open court.

This change to FRE 103 settled an issue that had created much confusion within the practice. Advocates often use pre-trial motions to address inflammatory evidence that they hope to exclude. If they lose, they do not want to underline that fact from a persuasive perspective when the jury is receiving the evidence. Some jurisdictions required that before the change to FRE 103. Those advocates practicing in state court should check and see if your jurisdiction follows the new FRE 103, the old FRE 103, or some local variant thereof.

If the pretrial motion is the best way to get a handle on issues that will affect the way you plan for trial, then the degree of persuasion that you bring to the pretrial motion is every bit as important as the persuasive techniques you use when communicating with the jury. While the ability to organize information and to tie the issue to your legal theory, factual theory, and moral theme are always important, the primary difference during motions practice is the focused nature of the particular issue you are addressing and the audience you must convince. A motion is an application to the judge for particular relief based upon your understanding of the facts of your case, and how the law applies to those facts.

Both sides should consider getting advanced rulings on the admissibility of their own evidence if admissibility is in doubt. Consider challenging the admissibility of your opponent's evidence in advance. Knowing whether key pieces of evidence are admissible will impact your theory of the case. A motion in limine asks the judge to rule on an evidentiary matter outside the hearing of the jury either before trial or during a recess. Check local court rules concerning motions in limine; some jurisdictions require advanced notice. Although often associated more with defense motion practice, motions in limine are available for both parties. Most jurisdictions allow motions to be oral or, at the discretion of the judge, in writing. An effective motion states the grounds upon which it is made and sets forth the ruling or relief sought. You should employ all of the techniques discussed elsewhere regarding eye contact, voice modulation, and the use of exhibits, but the key persuasive techniques you choose to use must reflect your knowledge of the audience—a judge.

3.   Power of the Court

Judges have discretion to decide pretrial motions when made, or may chose to defer a decision until the issue or evidence arises during the trial. That deferral is normally not allowed if a party's right to review or appeal would be adversely affected. Where factual issues are involved in determining a motion, the judge is normally required to state the essential findings of fact on the record in most jurisdictions. If a motion is denied, you have the ability to have the judge reconsider a past ruling upon request, or sua sponte, at any time prior to the end of trial. Judges are concerned with judicial economy—moving the case along in a fair but efficient fashion. They do not waste time and do not want you to waste their time either. A fifteen minute soliloquy on the wonders of the right to privacy under the United States Constitution will not be appreciated. Relevant and applicable case law, hopefully with precedential value, will be.

It is important that counsel understand the procedures involved with motions practice in order to maximize their ability to persuade the judge. Judges look for the fair, honest, and reliable advocate. Honesty is a by-product of both attitude and preparation. One is of limited value to the court without the other. The honest, but bumbling advocate is of no use to a judge ruling on a pre-trial motion. f they doubt counsel's competency with the law they will not rule in their favor, even if they like them. The judge is concerned with protecting the record and not being overturned on appeal. They view everything counsel tell them through the lens of the appellate process. When counsel understand this they can arrange facts, law, and the presentation to make the judge comfortable with the idea that the "safest" path to a non-appealable decision is by deciding the motion in counsel's favor.

A competent advocate must be familiar with the procedures to complete his or her preparation for trial. The bulk of motion practice procedure is set forth in the local rules of court, and your familiarity with those rules and compliance with their procedures will be perceived by the trial judge as evidence of your competency. Sources of procedural guidance include regional or appellate court rules, as well as those specific ones published by your respective judge. The Rules of Professional Responsibility governing attorneys engaging in motions practice are inextricably intertwined with procedural rules. While oral motions are allowed, written motions are often more persuasive, articulate, and organized. To maximize persuasion and preserve issues on appeal written motions should be the rule rather than the exception whenever possible. The writing process forces the advocate to carefully craft their rendition of the facts and the law to increase persuasion and the chances of a favorable ruling on the motion.

4.   Identify the Audience

When the time comes to actually argue the motion, be prepared. The moving party normally states the relief sought to the judge to begin the motion hearing. The opposing advocate is allowed to briefly respond and then the party that has the burden of proof admits evidence to support their position. The other counsel will then have an opportunity to proffer additional evidence, after which the judge will normally allow both sides to argue. Sometimes the judge will also allow the party that brought the motion, usually a criminal defense attorney, to make a rebuttal argument. Afterwards a ruling is entered and the case proceeds to the next issue.

During this process the judge is your audience, not the opposing counsel. Remain silent when the other side is speaking. Give the same degree of respect to the other advocate that you would want when it is your turn to speak. Advocates interrupt each other when they are trying to prevent the opposing counsel from making a point that hurts their position. Do not fall into this habit. Wait for the judge to speak, speak when it is your turn, and respond when allowed to do so. All arguments are made directly to the judge, never to opposing counsel. Nothing is gained by getting into an argument with the other advocate. You have a referee and an umpire there —use her. By acknowledging the power and authority of the judge through the respectful nature of your conduct you increase your believability and reliability. These are key factors that the judge will consider when deciding which advocate to trust.

The advice in the preceding paragraph is predicated on the idea of a judge that is attempting to discharge their duties in accordance with the judicial code of conduct. If that is not the case, then the ability to persuade falls into a different category. In those rare instances you may find yourself with the might of both the opposing side and the bench arrayed against you. The record is your friend when this occurs. The more behaviors and actions of the opposing counsel or judge that are unfair, and which you place on the record, the better your chance is of winning on appeal.

Note that the audience you are attempting to persuade has changed now. If the trial judge is not being fair then your audience becomes the appellate court. This may make for an unpleasant trial experience, but advocates understand the necessity of properly identifying their audience as they choose the manner in which they will proceed. That advice holds true in motions practice just as it does elsewhere in the trial process.

E.   Checklist - Writing Motions

The following checklist summarizes the information counsel should consider when drafting motions. It should be used as a starting point for developing appropriate motions driven by case analysis.

I.   Identify the objective(s) of the motion

II.   Write with the objective in mind. Focus on:
    a.   Clarity
    b.   Brevity
    c.   Structure

III.   Creating the right persuasive "voice" for the motion. Make sure you:
    a.   Focus on the objective
        i.   Put your issue up front in the motion brief
        ii.   Write Clearly, Directly, and Succinctly
        iii.   Avoid Doctrine without context - use story to make the legal argument relevant
        iv.   Avoid unnecessary
            a)   cliche's
            b)   repetition
            c)   bluntness
    b.   Clearly identify the specific relief requested
    c.   Include supporting materials establishing your version of the facts and law, such as:
        i.   Affidavits
        ii.   Discovery Responses
        iii.   Disclosures
        iv.   Documents
        v.   Depositions
        vi.   Copies of Statutes, rules, or regulations
        vii. Copies of applicable cases
    d.   Comply Procedurally with:
        i.   Federal Rules of Civil Procedure
        ii.   Local Rules of the Court
        iii.   Standing Orders of the Court

        iv. Local customs
   e. Review motions to ensure that:
        i. The structure is appropriate
        ii. The meaning is clear
        iii. The impact is persuasive
        iv. The writing style is understandable
        v. Grammatical mistakes have been corrected
        vi. Typographical errors eliminated
        vii. The brief is spell-checked
        viii. Citations have been cite checked

F. Checklist - Motion Hearings

The following checklist summarizes the information counsel should consider when arguing motions. It should be used as a starting point for developing appropriate motion arguments driven by case analysis.

I. Before arguing
   a. Know your Objective
   b. Outline the structure of your argument
   c. Plan based upon allotted time
   d. Rank order your arguments
   e. Create a list of talking points prior to argument so that you do not "read" your oral argument to the court

II. While arguing
   a. Observe Proper Decorum
        i. Acknowledge Court and Counsel
        ii. Proper body language
        iii. Tone of voice
        iv. General Decorum
        v. Eye contact
        vi. Composure
        vii. Professionalism at all times
   b. Concentrate on most compelling argument initially
   c. Respond to questions appropriately
        i. Answer
        ii. Turn the question back into your argument where appropriate
        iii. Read the bench and respond accordingly
        iv. Remember that it is also a conversation

     v. Treat questions as an opportunity to persuade

     vi. Listen critically:

        a) Identify friendly questions & use them

        b) Recognize trick questions & avoid their intended effect

        c) Build your answers in response to the flow of questions, learn to identify when less is more

   7. Use questions to sense out potential judicial misunderstandings or misinterpretations of the issues in the case, to include:

       a) relevant facts

          (1) legal issues

          (2) counsel's arguments

          (3) legal and factual theory of the case

 d. End well

     i. Plan a specific closing series of lines to your argument beforehand

     ii. Segue to those arguments appropriately

     iii. Connect questions asked into your wrap up

     iv. State the relief requested clearly, and why it should be granted

G. Objections

Counsel must develop an understanding of evidentiary law that is sufficiently detailed to allow for immediate responses during the course of a trial. These responses border on the instinctual, in that experienced counsel find themselves objecting to anticipated violations of evidentiary law based upon either the situation or language indicating an incipient objectionable question or answer. To develop the ability to object in a proper and timely fashion counsel must learn the key phrases and situations which foreshadow a potential violation of an evidentiary rule, along with the moments during the trial where they are most likely to occur.

Most new attorneys list objections as one of the areas of trial practice with which they are least comfortable. This discomfort comes from the fast-paced nature of objections during the trial and the lack of connectivity between evidentiary law and trial skills when the attorney first learned evidence and trial advocacy. Fortunately, both of these issues can be overcome through practice and study.

H.   How the Law Impacts Objections

The first step along the path to mastering objections is to identify objectionable questions and evidence in the context of the moment in trial where they are going to arise.   This process begins during case analysis and continues throughout the trial. Counsel should review all prior statements of the noticed witness, identify the potential fungible and non-fungible evidence that the witness may be used to admit and review carefully any interview notes. This review process should focus on potential evidentiary issues that may occur.   Counsel should note those issues, forecast how opposing counsel may object, and then identify their potential response to counsel's objection.

Once counsel master case analysis by witness, for potential objectionable issues, it becomes a simple matter to then decide whether a question is objectionable, and if so is it to counsel's benefit to object. Case analysis assists counsel in determining when they want to fight over an objectionable piece of evidence or testimony and when letting it go will help their case. Counsel should always evaluate the situation before deciding whether or not to object.

The question is a simple one - is the evidence is probably going to come in anyway? For example, if the objection is strictly to a lack of proper foundation, they objection may merely allow opposing counsel to fix the problem, making additional advocacy points while doing so. If that is the case why object?   Counsel may wind up keying jury members to the importance of evidence upon which they would rather they not focus.

Making and meeting objections is a key skill for trial attorneys. To properly exercise these skills they must not only understand the rules of evidence, but also have a system that allows them to recall needed information amidst the heat of trial.   This is a reactionary advocacy skill in most situations, in that counsel are responding to the actions of opposing counsel. This can be comforting for newer counsel, because it allows for planning. It is a skill that develops through practice.

Counsel should keep a list of common objections and the corresponding rules of evidence in their trial notebook. One such possible list is included as an appendix to this book, and has been made available by Professor Emeritus Bill Eleazer. His company, Elex Publishers, creates jurisdiction specific materials and I recommend them to you.

Practice with the rules is another step toward competency in the area of trial advocacy. You should not despair; making good objections is a skill you can develop. Given that most evidentiary rulings by the court are reviewed at the appellate level under an abuse of discretion standard, this is an important skill to have so you may win this battle at trial.

I.   Planning Objections

Objections are both strategic and tactical. A thorough case analysis and preparation of direct and cross examinations will alert counsel to possible objections from opposing counsel, as well as arm them with objections to make when opposing counsel is examining a witness. These objections are planned in depth and fall into the strategic category. Others arise in the heat of the moment and more fairly can be said to fall into the tactical category of objections. Sometimes something will simply not sound right and counsel will be on their feet objecting while still formulating the specific basis for your objection.

One aspect of objecting that counsel may consider is whether an objection will cause the opponent to lose momentum or get flustered. While it is improper to make an objection solely to disrupt the opponent, it is proper to object whenever counsel have a good faith basis. Caution is warranted, because   tactical objections may work against counsel by making them appear overly contentious to the jury. It may also annoy the judge, rarely a wise advocacy decision.

The mechanics of making an objection depend upon the local jurisdiction and the preferences of the trial judge. Some judges will require counsel to state the basis and the applicable rule of evidence. Others only need to hear the word "objection," and they will start to interrogate opposing counsel. Be aware, especially as defense counsel, that appellate courts will often find waiver of an issue if the objection is not sufficiently specific. This may sometimes require a citation to relevant case law. Some judges will try to get counsel to agree or simply will listen to evidentiary arguments and never actually rule. Attorneys must be prepared to force the issue of a final ruling when that happens. Waiver occurs in some jurisdictions if the objection is not renewed each time the disputed evidence or testimony is offered. Conversely, counsel can request that the judge note their continuing objection to evidence of the same type. When in doubt—object!

Counsel must always consider what was just said in court and how it was said. Reasons it might be objectionable include: (1) how the question was phrased (leading, argumentative, vague, ambiguous, compound); (2) what counsel was asking the witness (answered a question that you already asked, gave a conclusion or opinion that is improper, answered with hearsay, gave a narrative response, disclosed privileged information); or perhaps (3) counsel has gotten ahead of themselves (assuming a fact not in evidence, incomplete or improper foundation, bolstering a witness before credibility is attacked).

Once an objection is made counsel should first key in to the judge's response. She may overrule the objection outright. If she invites a response, counsel should state their position succinctly. If the problem is a matter of phrasing or an attempt to enter evidence before the foundation was complete, counsel should ask for leave to rephrase the question or to complete the foundation. If counsel does not understand the objection, but the point they were attempting to make was critical, they ask the judge for clarification before responding.

Whenever opposing counsel violates the rules of evidence as to either the form of the question or the nature of the evidence they are attempting to admit, counsel must decide whether or not to object. They should consider whether the theme and theory identified through case analysis will be aided by the potential objection. It is also appropriate to use objections to assist counsel in preventing their opponent from furthering their theme and theory. If either of these two predicate possibilities exist then it may be appropriate to object. If the potential objectionable question or answer does not hurt the case, counsel may consider passing on raising an objection.

Counsel should structure their objections for maximum persuasive impact. The court is the target of the objection, so counsel should consider how the objections appear from the court's perspective. The devil is in the details. Counsel must consider the potential evidence from all possible objectionable grounds.

Example: a letter written by the alleged victim in a homicide case is being offered into evidence. The defense counsel who is trying to keep this evidence out has a variety of objections potentially available. The order in which she chooses to raise these objections is crucial. Consider the following attempt to exclude the evidence:

State: Ma'am I hand you what has been marked as PE-1 for ID. Do you recognize it?

Witness: Yes.

State: What is it?

Witness: It is a letter written by my dear sweet murdered daughter. She was talking about her sorry husband in it.

Defense: *[To the Judge]* Objection, this violates 403. May I be heard?

Judge: Briefly counsel.

Defense: Your honor this note has a high probability of unfairly prejudicing my client. Any probative value is substantially outweighed by the danger of unfair prejudice.

Judge: Overruled. You may proceed, State.

State: *I offer PE-1 for ID into evidence as PE-1.*

Judge: *Admitted as marked.*

Consider what would have happened if the young defense counsel had planned her objections to create a greater degree of concern about the ultimate substantial danger of unfair prejudice. In order to accomplish this she needs to stack and arrange her objections so that she gets the judge's attention. It might go like this:

State: Ma'am I hand you what has been marked as PE-1 for ID. Do you recognize it?

Witness: Yes.

State: What is it?

Witness: It is a letter written by my dear sweet murdered daughter. She was talking about her sorry husband in it.

Defense: *[To the Judge]* Objection, may I be heard?

Judge: Briefly counsel. Basis?

Defense: Your honor counsel has not laid a proper foundation.

Judge: Overruled. You may proceed, State.

Defense: Objection, best evidence rule.

Judge: Explain.

Defense: Your honor this letter is a copy of an original that is not available for comparison.

Judge: I'm going to overrule that objection as well. You may proceed, State.

Defense: Objection - authentication. May I be heard?

Judge: All right counsel.

Defense: Your honor the state has not properly authenticated this letter to show that it was in fact written by the alleged victim. We would request they do so before you admit it.

Judge: Okay. Lay a foundation, State.

State: *[State lays a foundation]* I offer...

Defense: Objection, authentication and hearsay.

Judge: Counsel, I am overruling the authentication objection. State, how do you respond to the hearsay objection?

State: Your honor it is a dying declaration.

Defense: Your honor, how can a letter be a dying declaration? The state has not laid sufficient foundation to support that hearsay exception.

Judge: I disagree, counsel. Objection as to hearsay is overruled.

Defense: Objection, impermissible character evidence.

Judge: Counsel this getting old. How is this letter impermissible character evidence?

Defense: It relates alleged prior misconduct by my client that the jury could improperly consider.

Judge: How do you respond, State?

State: Your honor, we offer it under the 404(b) exception and request a limiting instruction to the jury as to its permissible use under 105.

Judge: Based upon that offer I overrule the objection.

Defense: Your honor, may I be heard?

Judge: Extremely briefly counsel.

Defense: Your honor, we have established concerns with admitting this letter that include foundation, authentication, hearsay and impermissible character evidence. Although you have overruled each of these objections their cumulative effect is to point out quite clearly the substantial danger of unfair prejudice to my client if this letter is admitted. We request you exclude it under 403.

Judge: *[rubbing his eyes]*   Counsel, I'll consider your objection over lunch. We are in recess.

The defense counsel in this second example may very well lose the 403 objection, but they have made an excellent record. They have also raised so many concerns that the judge may decide to exclude this piece of evidence. This technique is useful when counsel want to send the signal to the judge that this particular issue is important and worthy of careful consideration. This approach will only work if saved for the right moment. If counsel throw every objection available out indiscriminately then the judge will eventually tune you out.

Another danger exists if the judge either prefers or requires that counsel state every relevant objection to a piece of evidence when raising an objection about that evidence. Advocates must know the local court's preference on this issue. While the preference of the judge is not dispositive on whether or not they raise all issues at one time, it may be that counsel need to do so to get the judge's attention. When that is the case counsel should still stack their objections, but they just make a complete stack at one time.

J.   Making the Objection

When making objections counsel should stand and say "objection" and then briefly state the basis. Objections are addressed to the court, not to opposing counsel. The judge will either rule on the objection outright or ask opposing counsel to respond. It is important to listen carefully both to what opposing counsel says and the judge's response. If opposing counsel cannot give the judge a valid basis to overrule the objection then counsel should remain silent, unless the judge requests additional information. If the court requests additional information, counsel would do well to recall the format for argument they learned in their legal research and writing class, namely: Issue, Rule, Analysis, and Conclusion. When modified for objections, this format looks like: Grounds for Objection, Rule the Objection Stems From, Analysis of the Facts under that rule, request for the objection to be sustained. If it appears that the court is inclined to overrule an objection made against them, then counsel may make an offer of proof as to why the objections should be sustained. Alternatively, an offer of proof may also be made when laying the basis for why the objection should be overruled.

Counsel must plan for potential objections in depth on those important, if not dispositive, legal and factual issues identified during case analysis. This is accomplished by: (1) identifying potentially objectionable issues through case analysis; (2) researching the basis and strength of potential objections (with favorable case law identified and prepared); (3) analyzing potential responses by opposing counsel; and then (4) preparing a counter-response.

K.   Offers of Proof

Counsel use offers of proof to make the record when opposing counsel's objection has successfully excluded evidence from the trial. Offers of proof have two primary purposes. The first is to fully inform the court about the evidence that is being excluded in the hopes that they will reconsider their ruling based upon the additional information. The second purpose is to make the record for the appellate court. If an offer of proof is not made when the trial judge excludes evidence, that issue may be considered waived by the appellate court. FRE 103 contemplates an offer of proof whenever the context of the issues are not apparent from the record of trial.

> **Rule 103. Rulings on Evidence**
>
> **(a) Preserving a Claim of Error.** A party may claim error in a ruling to admit or exclude evidence only if the error affects a substantial right of the party and:
>
> **(1)** if the ruling admits evidence, a party, on the record:
>
> **(A)** timely objects or moves to strike; and
>
> **(B)** states the specific ground, unless it was apparent from the context; or
>
> **(2)** if the ruling excludes evidence, a party informs the court of its substance by an offer of proof, unless the substance was apparent from the context.
>
> **(b) Not Needing to Renew an Objection or Offer of Proof.** Once the court rules definitively on the record-- either before or at trial--a party need not renew an objection or offer of proof to preserve a claim of error for appeal.
>
> **(c) Court's Statement About the Ruling; Directing an Offer of Proof.** The court may make any statement about the character or form of the evidence, the objection made, and the ruling. The court may direct that an offer of proof be made in question-and-answer form.
>
> **(d) Preventing the Jury from Hearing Inadmissible Evidence.** To the extent practicable, the court must conduct a jury trial so that inadmissible evidence is not suggested to the jury by any means.
>
> **(e) Taking Notice of Plain Error.** A court may take notice of a plain error affecting a substantial right, even if the claim of error was not properly preserved.

It is a best practice for counsel to make offers of proof whenever evidence is excluded. The offer of proof should be made outside the presence of the jury, and be presented in a fashion grounded in the applicable evidentiary issue. It is important that the court hear the reasons why the sustained objection should have been overruled so they can decide whether or not to change the ruling. The greater the amount of detail counsel can put in to their offer of proof, the better. This is especially true if it concerns an issue where the ruling results in the exclusion of both testimony and potential exhibits. It is also important to make a clear record for the appellate courts using the offer of proof.

Example: the court sustained an objection as to hearsay. Counsel then makes an offer of proof establishing the relevant Hearsay Exception.

State: Objection, hearsay.

Judge: Sustained.

Defense: Your honor I wish to make an offer of proof. If allowed to answer the question the witness would testify as follows:

> *Question:* What did you hear the lady say?
>
> *Answer:*   She told me she saw the accident as it happened, the red truck caused it.

Defense: Your honor the witness's answer meets the requirements of 803(1) Present Sense Impression and the evidence should be admitted.

Judge: I agree. The earlier objection is overruled. You may inquire.

The nature and substance of the offer of proof is case dependent. Counsel must identify potential evidentiary issues during case analysis, prepare their evidentiary arguments for admissibility, and then present those arguments, to include offers of proof, at at time that is best for their client.

L.   Objections as to Form

Attorneys identify objections to form based upon "feel." They listen for questions that are either not properly formed or are not sufficiently focused based upon the rules of evidence and norms of practice in their jurisdiction. Objections as to form are grounded in poor questioning techniques. Counsel should consider the requirements of FRE 611 as a starting point when identifying objections as to the form of questions.

1.   Ambiguous, Confusing or Unintelligible Question (FRE 611(a))

> *Objection:* The question is ambiguous, confusing, or unintelligible.

Response: I will rephrase.

Explanation: A question is ambiguous if it may be interpreted in several ways, or if it is so vague or unclear that it may confuse the jury, judge, or the witness.

2.　Argumentative Question (FRE 611(a))

Objection: The question is argumentative.

Response: Rephrase the question.

Explanation: A question is argumentative if it is an attempt to make an argument to the jury, to summarize, draw inferences from, or comment on the evidence, or to ask the witness to testify as to his own credibility. A question can also be argumentative if it is unduly hostile or sarcastic.

3.　Asked and Answered or Unduly Repetitious (FRE 403, 611(a))

Objection: The witness has already answered the question.

Response: The witness has not yet answered this particular question.

Explanation: Repetitious questions are unlikely to elicit additional evidence of probative value.

4.　Assumes Facts Not in Evidence (FRE 601, 611(a))

Objection: Assumes facts not in evidence.

Responses:(1) The existence of this fact may be inferred from evidence which has been admitted;

(2) if permitted to answer the fact will be in evidence; or

(3) the fact will be proved during the testimony of Witness X. We will "tie it up" later.

Explanation: A question that assumes facts not yet in evidence effectively allows counsel to testify as to those facts without personal knowledge.

5.   Multifarious; Compound Question (FRE 611(a))

Objection: Compound Question.

Response: I will rephrase the question.

Explanation: A question combining more than one inquiry is likely to be confusing and misleading to both the witness and the factfinder.

6.   Harassing the Witness (FRE 403, 611(a)(3))

Objection: Harassing the witness.

Response: I will rephrase the question.

Explanation: A question that is asked to harass or embarrass a witness, for example, a question that unnecessarily delves into a witness's personal life, is impermissible.

7.   Leading Question (FRE 611(c))

Objection: Leading.

Responses: (1) The question is not a leading question simply because it elicits a yes or no answer. It is generally to elicit preliminary or background information from a witness through leading questions,

(2) the witness is an adverse party, or the witness is hostile,

(3) leading questions are allowed of one's own witnesses on cross examination if the witness is called by the adverse party, or

(4) I'll rephrase the question.

Explanation: A leading question is one that suggests to the witness the answer desired by the examiner. Leading questions are generally impermissible on direct examination.

8.   Calls for Narrative Answer (FRE 403, 611(a))

Objection: I object.   The question calls for narrative testimony and deprives us of an Objection: Calls for a narrative. Counsel is trying to admit inadmissible evidence.

Response: I will rephrase the question.

Explanation: Narrative, unspecific, or long "rambling" answers are not per se objectionable, but are likely to contain hearsay or other inadmissible evidence to which counsel is deprived of an opportunity to object.

9. Mischaracterizes or Misquotes the Witness or Prior Evidence (FRE 611(a))

Objection: I object. The question mischaracterizes, misstates, or misquotes the prior testimony...

Response: I'll rephrase the question.

Explanation: Questions that misquote previous testimony or evidence are likely to mislead or confuse the jury.

M. Objections as to Substance

"Objections to Substance" attack the admissibility of the testimony elicited. These objections are based upon specific evidentiary rules. These objections are both rule and case specific, and counsel should refer to the evidentiary case law in the jurisdiction where the trial is held for specific potential objectionable questions. The following examples of objection as to substance are based upon the Federal Rules of Evidence and relevant case law.

1. Lack of Authentication (FRE 901, 902)

Objection: I object. The evidence has not been properly authenticated.

Response: The item is sufficiently authenticated by ___ (a method listed in Rule 901(b)).

Examples of sufficient authentication include:

- Testimony of a witness with knowledge.

- Non-expert opinion on the genuineness of handwriting.

- Comparison by trier-of-fact or expert witness to authenticated specimens.

- Distinctive characteristics of the item offered.
- Voice identification by opinion based upon hearing the voice under circumstances connecting it with the alleged speaker.
- Public records or reports.
- The item is self-authenticating under FRE 902.

Examples of self-authenticating evidence under FRE 902 include:

- Domestic public documents under seal.
- Domestic public documents not under seal if officer certifies that the signature is genuine.
- Foreign public documents.
- Certified copies or public records.
- Official publications.
- Newspapers and periodicals.
- Acknowledged or notarized documents.
- Commercial paper and related documents.

Explanation: Authentication is not satisfied if insufficient evidence has been offered to support a finding that the matter in question is what its proponent claims is it.

2.   Best Evidence Not Offered (FRE 1001, 1002, 1003, 1004)

> *Objection:* I object. The evidence is not the best evidence.

> *Response:* The evidence qualifies as an original, or as a duplicate.

Explanation: The best evidence rule requires the original writing, recording, or photograph to prove the content of the writing, recording, or photograph. FRE 1001 defines original and duplicate. An "original" is the writing or recording itself, any counterpart intended to have the same effect, the negative or print therefrom if the evidence is a photograph, and any printout or other output shown to accurately reflect the data of an original that is stored in a computer.

A "duplicate" is a counterpart produced by the same impression as the original, or from the same matrix, or by means of photography, including enlargements and miniatures, or by mechanical or electronic re-recording, or by chemical reproduction, or by other equivalent techniques." Duplicates are admissible to the same extent as originals.

> *Response:* The rule is inapplicable because the proponent is not seeking to prove the content of the item.

> *Response:* The original is not obtainable and secondary evidence is therefore admissible.

Explanation: Secondary evidence is admissible if the original has been lost or destroyed except for when the loss or destruction was done in bad faith by the proponent. Other examples for when secondary evidence is admissible from FRE 1004 include: (1) the original is unobtainable by any available judicial process or procedure, (2) the original is under the control of the opponent and the opponent does not produce the original when put on notice that it will be subject of proof at a hearing, (3) the item is offered for a collateral purpose.

3.   Improper Use of Character Evidence (FRE 404, 405, 608)

> *Objection:* I object. The question calls for inadmissible character evidence.

> *Response:* The person's character trait is "in issue."

Explanation: A person's character is "in issue" when it is an element of a charge, claim, or defense. For example, in a claim of negligent entrustment, the trait of incompetence of the person to whom the defendant entrusted the dangerous instrumentality to is an element of the claim and is "in issue." Proof of character may then be made by opinion or reputation testimony, or by evidence of specific instances of conduct. Character evidence is generally inadmissible to show that a person acted in conformity with that character on a particular occasion. Character evidence may be proved only by reputation or opinion testimony, not by specific acts, except where a trait of the person's character is "in issue," or for the purpose of impeachment or rehabilitation on cross examination.

> *Objection:* I object. Evidence of specific acts is impermissible to prove character.

> *Response:* The character evidence is offered for the purpose of impeachment or rehabilitation on cross-examination and is therefore admissible under FRE 608.

Explanation: A witness that has testified as to the character of a person may be asked on cross examination about specific acts of that person in the form of "have you heard?" or "do you know?" questions to test the factual basis of their testimony on direct examination. A witness may always be asked on cross examination about specific instances of his or her own conduct that are probative of untruthfulness. Counsel must have a good faith basis for making the inquiry (FRE 608).

> *Objection:* I object. The question calls for inadmissible character evidence.

> *Response:* The person's character trait is "in issue" because it is an element of a charge, claim, or defense.

Explanation: The specific act is offered to prove something other than character. Evidence of other crimes, wrongs, or acts may be admissible to prove motive, opportunity, intent, preparation, plan, knowledge, identity, or absence of mistake or accident (FRE 404(b)).

3. Bolstering the Credibility of a Witness (FRE 607, 608, 801(d)(1)(B))

> *Objection:* I object. Counsel is bolstering the witness.

> *Response:* The witness's credibility has been attacked and this evidence is proper rehabilitation.

Explanation: FRE 608(a) permits evidence of a witness's character for truthfulness only after the witness's character for truthfulness has been attacked. Bolstering refers to a proponent's attempt to offer otherwise inadmissible character evidence solely to enhance his witness's credibility when the witness has not yet been impeached.

4. Impeachment on a Collateral Matter (FRE 403, 608)

> *Objection:* I object. Extrinsic evidence of specific instances is inadmissible to impeach a witness on collateral matters.

Responses: (1) The extrinsic evidence is independently relevant to a substantive issue in the case,

(2) the evidence is offered to prove bias, which is not a collateral matter, or

(3) evidence of specific acts of a witness are admissible when offered to prove something other than a witness's untrustworthy character.

Explanation: This objection arises most commonly when a party seeks to impeach a witness by introducing extrinsic evidence that contradicts an answer given by the witness.

4.   Conclusion of Law or Ultimate Issue (FRE 701, 702, 704)

Objection: I object. The witness is testifying to an ultimate issue.

Response: The expert or lay witness has knowledge or expertise of the matter, and the evidence is helpful. An adequate foundation has been laid.

Explanation: Testimony phrased in conclusory terms is less helpful than testimony that provides information to the jury so that it may draw its own conclusions. Conclusions of law are generally inadmissible. Lay or expert witness testimony must be based on the lay witness's perception or must be within the scope of the expertise of an expert witness, and must be helpful to the fact finder. Opinions on an ultimate issue are generally admissible (FRE 704).

5.   Cross Examination beyond the Scope of Direct (FRE 611(b))

Objection: I object. The question asked goes beyond the scope of the matters raised on direct.

Response: The question is permissible because the subject matter of direct includes all inferences and implications arising from direct.

Explanation: Cross examination that raises subjects not raised on direct is generally inadmissible.

6.   Cumulative (FRE 403)

Objection: I object. The evidence is cumulative.

Response: A party has a right to present a persuasive case and the cumulative evidence concept should not interfere with that right.

Explanation: If the evidence is needlessly cumulative or repetitious, it may be excluded.

7.   Hearsay (FRE 801, 802, 803, 804)

Objection: I object. The question calls for hearsay.

Responses: (1) The-statement is not hearsay because it is not offered to prove the truth of the matter asserted,

(2) the statement is not hearsay under the rules…

(3) I am offering it for a non-hearsay purpose, or

(4) the statement is hearsay, but is specifically exempted by the rules...

Explanation: Hearsay is inadmissible unless it falls within an established exception. Key exceptions, as listed in FRE 801, 803 and 804, include:

- Prior statements by witness
- Admissions by party-opponent offered against party-opponent
- Present sense impressions
- Excited utterances
- Statement of the declarant's then existing state of mind
- Statements for the purpose of medical diagnosis or treatment
- Recorded recollections
- Records of regularly conducted activity
- Public records and reports
- Learned treatises
- Former testimony of unavailable declarant

- Statement under belief of impending death where the declarant is unavailable

- Statement against interest of an unavailable declarant

8.   Impermissible Hypothetical Question (FRE 705)

> *Objection:* I object. Counsel is posing a hypothetical question that contains facts not in evidence.

> *Response:* A hypothetical question need not refer to all of the relevant facts in evidence. The witness is an expert witness, and an expert may base an opinion on facts that are not admitted into evidence, as long as they are the type reasonably relied upon by experts in forming opinions on the subject.

Explanation: A hypothetical question is inadmissible if it contains facts that are not already in evidence, that will not be introduced before the close of evidence, or that are not reasonably drawn from such facts. .

9.   Witness is Incompetent or Lacks Personal Knowledge (FRE 601 through 606)

> *Objection:* I object.   The witness is incompetent or lacks sufficient capacity to testify, or no showing has been made that the witness has personal knowledge about this matter.

> *Responses:* (1) Rule 601 abolishes objections to a witness's competence,

> (2) The witness is competent under state law,

> (3) A personal assertion by the witness is sufficient to show personal knowledge,

> (4) I will ask additional questions sufficient to lay the foundation to establish personal knowledge.

Explanation: All persons are presumed competent to testify except as otherwise provided in the rules. However, incompetence of a witness may be the basis for an objection in two situations: where state law supplies the rule of decision with respect to an element of a claim or defense, and the witness is incompetent under state law; or where insufficient evidence has been introduced to support a finding that the witness has personal knowledge of the matter.

10.   Misleading (FRE 403)

Objection: I object. The evidence will mislead the jury. Or, if a bench trial: I object, the evidence is misleading.

Response: The probative value of the evidence outweighs the danger of misleading the jury or the court.

Explanation: The danger of misleading the jury usually refers to the possibility that the jury will attach undue weight to the evidence. If the probative value of the evidence is substantially outweighed by the danger of misleading the jury, the evidence may be excluded.

11.   Prejudicial Effect Outweighs Probative Value (FRE 403)

Objection: I object. The probative value of this evidence is outweighed by the danger of unfair prejudice.

Response: All probative evidence is prejudicial. The rule does not afford protection from evidence that is merely detrimental to a party's case. In this instance the probative value of the evidence outweighs the danger of unfair prejudice.

Explanation: Evidence is unfairly prejudicial if it suggests a decision on an improper basis, most commonly an emotional basis. If the probative value of the evidence is substantially outweighed by the danger of unfair prejudice, the evidence may be excluded.

12.   Confusion of the Issues (FRE 403)

Objection: I object. The evidence will confuse the issues.

Response: The probative value of the evidence outweighs the risk of confusion.

Explanation: Evidence is confusing if it tends to distract the jury from the proper issues of the trial. If the probative value of evidence is outweighed by the danger of confusion, it may be excluded.

13.   Privilege (FRE 501)

> *Objection:* I object. The question calls for privileged information.

> *Response:* The privilege asserted is not one created by constitution, court, or state rule, or one recognized by common law. The communication at issue is not privileged.

Explanation: Privileged information based on the attorney-client privilege, doctor patient privilege, spousal privilege, and other privileges recognized by Common or statutory law is inadmissible. Privilege law is generally governed by the principles of common law as interpreted by the United States courts, but in civil actions, state privilege law applies with respect to an element of a claim or defense as to which state substantive law governs.

14.   Speculation (FRE 602, 701, 702)

> *Objection:* I object.   The question calls for the witness to speculate.

> *Response:* I will rephrase the question to establish the witness's personal knowledge or basis for the witness's statement.

Explanation: A question which asks a witness to speculate as to what occurred or what caused an event may conflict with the requirement that a witness have personal knowledge of a matter testified to, or in the case of an expert witness, may be an impermissible attempt to elicit an opinion beyond the scope of the witness's expertise.

-Notes-

Chapter 13: Post Trial Matters

A. Introduction 549
B. Post Trial Matters - Pretrial.....................................550
C. Post Trial Matters – Trial 554
D. Preserving the Record – Post Trial 559
E. Creating the Record Checklist 559

A.   Introduction

Concern over potential post trial matters should exist at every stage of the dispute resolution process. Appellate attorneys develop their case from the work of the trial attorney. If it is not in the record it did not happen - even if it did. Since so many issues revolve around actually trying a case that most attorneys find it too difficult to also consider the appellate issues involved while preparing for trial. This is a shortsighted approach. Proper preparation of the case involves all aspects of litigation—pretrial, trial and post trial. Counsel should properly consider each level when diligently and competently representing a client. This section considers potential appellate issues during each stage of the adversarial process. It serves as a beginning point in counsel's development as a competent trial attorney who wins the victory at trial but who can also protect that victory in the appellate courts.

B.   Post Trial Matters - Pretrial

1.   Motions for Summary Judgment

Counsel use summary judgments as a tool used to remove issues from the case. In a best case scenario it works so well that the entire cause of action is dispensed with by the court. When the entire case is dismissed based upon a motion for summary judgment then the only appellate issue that might exist would be an appeal from the granting of the summary judgment. The court granting summary judgment is a best case scenario for defense attorneys in civil trials, preparing the ground for that possibility during pretrial

Summary judgments are a procedural device available to advocates under Federal Rule of Civil Procedure 56. It allows the court to dispose of a case during civil litigation without a trial. The court grants summary motions when there is not a dispute as to the material facts of the case, and the moving party is entitled to a judgment as a matter of law. The fact in dispute should be central to the case. Disputed facts on irrelevant issues or minor factual discrepancies will not defeat the motion. All parties to the civil litigation can make a motion for summary judgment and both parties often seek it during civil litigation. Even when the litigants do not ask for a summary judgment, the court itself has the ability to grant a summary

---

Rule 56. Summary Judgment

(a) By a Claiming Party. A party claiming relief may move, with or without supporting affidavits, for summary judgment on all or part of the claim. The motion may be filed at any time after:

   (1) 20 days have passed from commencement of the action; or

   (2) the opposing party serves a motion for summary judgment.

(b) By a Defending Party. A party against whom relief is sought may move at any time, with or without supporting affidavit, for summary judgment on all or part of the claim.

(c) Serving the Motions; Proceedings. The motion must be served at least 10 days before the day set for the hearing. An opposing party may serve opposing affidavits before the hearing day. The judgment sought should be rendered if the pleadings, the discovery and disclosure materials on file, and any affidavits show that there is no genuine issue as to any material fact and that the movant is entitled to judgment as a matter of law.

(d) Case Not Fully Adjudicated on the Motion.

(1) Establishing Facts. If summary judgment is not rendered on the whole action, the court should, to the extent practicable, determine what material facts are not genuinely at issue. The court should so determine by examining the pleadings and evidence before it and by interrogating the attorneys. It should then issue an order specifying what facts – including items of damages or other relief – are not genuinely at issue. The facts so specified must be treated as established in the action.

(2) Establishing Liability. An interlocutory summary judgment may be rendered on liability alone, even if there is a genuine issue on the amount of damages.

(e) Affidavits; Further Testimony.

(1) In General. A supporting or opposing affidavit must be made on personal knowledge set out facts that would be admissible in evidence, and show that the affiant is competent to testify on the matters stated. If a paper or part of a paper is referred to in an affidavit, a sworn or certified copy must be attached to or served with the affidavit. The court may permit an affidavit to be supplemented or opposed by depositions, answers to interrogatories, or additional affidavits.

(2) Opposing Party's Obligation to Respond. When a motion for summary judgment is properly made and supported an opposing party may not rely merely on allegations or denials in its own pleading; rather, its response must – by affidavits or as otherwise provided in this rule – set out specific facts showing a genuine issue for trial. If the opposing party does not so respond, summary judgment should, if appropriate, be entered against that party.

(f) When Affidavits are Unavailable. If a party opposing the motion shows by affidavit that, for specified reasons, it cannot present facts essential to justify its opposition, the court may:

(1) deny the motion;

(2) order a continuance to enable affidavits to be obtained depositions to be taken, or other discovery to be undertaken; or

(3) issue any other just order.

(g) Affidavit Submitted in Bad Faith. If satisfied that an affidavit under this rule is submitted in bad faith or solely for delay, the court must order the submitting party to pay the other party the reasonable expenses, including attorney's fees, it incurred as a result. An offending party or attorney may also be held in contempt.

judgment sua sponte.[1]

When making a motion for summary judgment attorneys are allowed, even encouraged if not actually required, to provide supporting evidence. This evidence is needed by the court to assist in deciding whether or not disputed questions of fact exist. The forms of supporting evidence may include affidavits, interrogatories, depositions and admissions. Normally the court requires that evidence admitted in support of the motion be otherwise admissible at trial. The court normally holds arguments when deciding motions for summary judgment, but it may in certain instances decide them based solely on the parties' briefs and supporting documentation.

Summary judgments allow litigants to either avoid unnecessary trials or simplify the contested issues. This occurs when a summary judgment is granted dispensing with certain issues or claims within the larger case. The classic example of this occurs in a personal injury case where liability is established through summary judgment and the trial then proceeds to consider only the issue of damages.

Trial attorneys who lose motions for summary judgment should raise the issue again with a motion for a directed verdict after opposing counsel has presented their case. If the advocate wins a motion for summary judgment in part they must watch carefully to ensure that the dismissed issue does not make it into the trial. If opposing counsel attempts to raise an issue that has been dismissed you should object, reminding the court that this issue has previously been litigated and decided.

2.   Motions in Limine

FRE 103 governs motions in limine.[2] By filing a motion in limine counsel is asking the court to either allow or exclude evidence at trial. Motions in limine are used during pretrial to set the stage for trial by identifying what issues will be allowed by the court and assists the attorney in determining which legal theory should be employed, as well as providing some idea of what evidence will be considered relevant. The idea behind such motions is that certain subjects should not be heard by the jury, normally because their probative value is outweighed by the substantial danger of unfair prejudice, confusion of the issues, or waste of time.[3]

---

[1] On the court's own will or motion. To act on one's own volition.

[2] The translation for the Latin limine means "at the threshold." It refers to the fact that these are motions made and decided by the court at the moment when the trial is about to begin.

[3] *See* FRE 403 in Appendix III.

Rule 103. Rulings on Evidence

(a) Preserving a Claim of Error. A party may claim error in a ruling to admit or exclude evidence only if the error affects a substantial right of the party and:

(1) if the ruling admits evidence, a party, on the record:

(A) timely objects or moves to strike; and

(B) states the specific ground, unless it was apparent from the context; or

(2) if the ruling excludes evidence, a party informs the court of its substance by an offer of proof, unless the substance was apparent from the context.

(b) Not Needing to Renew an Objection or Offer of Proof. Once the court rules definitively on the record--either before or at trial--a party need not renew an objection or offer of proof to preserve a claim of error for appeal.

(c) Court's Statement About the Ruling; Directing an Offer of Proof. The court may make any statement about the character or form of the evidence, the objection made, and the ruling. The court may direct that an offer of proof be made in question-and-answer form.

(d) Preventing the Jury from Hearing Inadmissible Evidence. To the extent practicable, the court must conduct a jury trial so that inadmissible evidence is not suggested to the jury by any means.

(e) Taking Notice of Plain Error. A court may take notice of a plain error affecting a substantial right, even if the claim of error was not properly preserved.

Motions in limine are important because attorneys use them to shape the story at trial. They normally deal with evidence that impacts greatly the chosen theme and theory of the case. Counsel must ensure the trial judge rules dispositively on the motion before trial; if she does not they will be left with an unknown issue sitting squarely in the middle of trial preparation. If granted, during trial counsel should monitor the case, just as they do with partial pretrial summary judgments that are granted, to ensure the excluded evidence is not admitted. If it is admitted, the proper objection is to request a mistrial.

On the other hand, if counsel lose a motion in limine they should raise the objection again at the first moment in the trial when the opposing counsel attempts to offer the evidence you sought to exclude. This is necessary to ensure that the trial judge has one final opportunity to modify its ruling. Such objections should refer to any additional information now before the court that supports your position. Finally, advocates who lost the motion should also look for opportunities to admit the evidence anyway. This normally happens when the opposing counsel opens the door to the excluded evidence, making it admissible on new grounds.

C.   Post Trial Matters – Trial

1.   Making the Record

There are several different potential appellate issues an attorney must be concerned with during trial. The first includes the record of trial itself. If it is not in the record it simply does not exist, and, if it does not exist, it cannot be used on appeal. Counsel must make certain that everything makes it into the record. Many events occur at trial are not properly recorded. Examples include sidebars, chamber conferences, depositions that were read at trial, videos that are played, jury instruction conferences, and any other discussion about legal issues made outside the presence of the jury.

One way to ensure that all of these issues are properly documented for the appellate record is to make certain that every single exhibit corresponding to the issue is properly marked. In some jurisdictions these documents are marked as appellate exhibits. If counsel do not practice in a jurisdiction that uses appellate exhibits, then they must make certain that their exhibits are properly identified and marked when using them during discussion of evidentiary or legal issues outside the presence of the jury. Just because a document is not admitted does not mean that it cannot be used at the appellate level. The test is whether or not the judge saw the document and relied upon it under the rules of evidence in making her ruling.

Another area where potential appellate issues often occur concerns the rulings on motions and objections. Some judges have a tendency to engage counsel in a conversation about an evidentiary or legal issue, seeking to draw the advocate into a position of agreement with the court. Counsel must remember that the judge's main desire is to ensure that the record is clean. Now, to the judge, that means no appellate issues are present that will affect the finality of the trial verdict. It should be immediately obvious to an advocate that they have a slightly different desire. Counsel must listen carefully to the judge's rulings and the conversations that occur regarding evidentiary and legal issues. They should respectfully but forcefully ensure that the judge honors their request for finality in regards to such motions and objections. Without finality there is no appellate issue.

2.   Jury Selection

Throughout jury selection counsel will make both challenges for cause and peremptory challenges. Sometimes the judge grants those requests and sometimes the judge does not grant those requests. In order to ensure any objection counsel made to the rulings are captured for the appellate process, they must renew all objections to any jury members prior to the jury actually being sworn. There is a process that counsel should use, step-by-step, to ensure the denial of a cause for challenges is preserved. They begin by moving to strike the juror in question. Counsel are also required to have exhausted all of their peremptory challenges. Counsel should also request additional peremptory challenges from the court, identifying the specific juror whom they would strike with the additional peremptory if it is granted.

When dealing with peremptory challenges counsel should also be prepared to respond to a Batson challenge.[4] For purposes of this text, from an advocacy perspective counsel must have a neutral explanation for the reason that they are challenging a potential juror. On the other hand, if counsel believe that opposing counsel is improperly using a peremptory challenge they must make the record. They do so by identifying that the juror in question is a member of a distinct group subject to discrimination. Once counsel have made that showing the burden then shifts to the proponent of the peremptory challenge to establish why their challenge is neutral in nature.

Advocates often get lost in the press of time when dealing with jury selection. There are a lot of different things happening when choosing a jury. Counsel are focused on your theme and theory, the beliefs and attitudes of the potential jurors, and how all of these factors relate to the evidentiary rulings on your pretrial motions. Take care during this vulnerable time to not lose sight of the potential appellate issue existing when jurors have been improperly challenged, or when the court has not allowed them to challenge as the law allows.

3.   Evidentiary Issues

In this text we have looked at many of the evidentiary issues that arise at trial. We have learned the primary modes of impeachment, the proper forms of questioning on both direct and cross examination, how to make

---

[4] The challenge stems from the *Batson v. Kentucky* decision discussed previously, where a prosecutor's peremptory challenge, without stating a valid cause for doing so, may not be used to exclude jurors based solely on race. In Florida, this is often referred to as a *Slappy* challenge, from *State v. Slappy*, 522 So.2d 18 (Fla. 1988), where the Florida Supreme Court held the prosecutor's explanation for use of peremptory challenges to exclude four blacks from the panel was insufficient to rebut an inference of discrimination.

an opening statement and closing argument, and the process of selecting juries. We have previously discussed objections and motions practice. Let us look now at objections from the standpoint of making the appellate record, and not just from an advocacy perspective.

The first point counsel should consider is that an objection is not part of the record if it is not made. Standing on their feet and shouting objection is at least a good beginning. Counsel want to make objections as specific as possible. They should be prompt in making the objection so that the judge can address the issue in time. Sometimes counsel will not be able to get the court to rule before the objectionable material has made its way into the courtroom. That does not mean that the objection has been waived. Counsel can still preserve that objection if they state the grounds and move to have the testimony in question stricken from the record. This is what is often referred to as "move to strike."

Sometimes the judge will rule for opposing counsel. There are still additional steps counsel can take to highlight to the court the importance of the legal issue identified, and to blaze a trail for the appellate counsel to follow to this issue. One step counsel should take includes requesting an appropriate limiting instruction. A limiting instruction is designed to ensure that the jury only considers the evidence for is proper legal purpose. We have discussed limiting instructions previously, and I agree with many advocates who find limiting instructions often serve to merely highlight the information that you do not want the jury to consider. While that may be true, it also serves to further define the proper use of the evidence. A proper limiting instruction places limitations on the opposing attorney who wishes to use that evidence as part of their argument and their case. A clear limiting instruction from the court must be followed and that is the way that counsel can often catch someone who violates the proper use of the evidence, at least at the appellate level.

Another way to handle an objection that has been overruled is to ask the court for a standing objection as to that particular line of inquiry. While this is an acceptable way to deal with objectionable questions, counsel must make certain that the line of inquiry does not change, thereby creating a need to renew the objection or to make some other objection as the context of the evidence changes. If counsel are not certain, they should object again At the close of a particular witness's testimony where counsel have made a standing objection and it is their opinion that all of the witness's testimony was objectionable, they should move to strike the witness's entire testimony. This is like taking a bright yellow highlighter and underlining and scoring a certain portion of the record of trial for the appellate court. There is nothing wrong with doing it, but it pays to be right when doing so.

One of the questions that young attorneys often ask is "when do I object and request a mistrial be granted?" As a general rule mistrials are normally granted when the evidence is both truly egregious and prejudicial. This is a relatively rare circumstance, but it does happen. Counsel do not want to be the attorney who acts like a Jack-in-the-Box, leaping up screaming for a mistrial at each and every opportunity. Remember the story of the little boy who cried wolf: if you find everything egregious, then in the eyes of the court nothing identified will be considered egregious. One way to handle this issue is to ask the court, once counsel have made a request that a mistrial be granted, to reserve ruling on the request for mistrial until after the verdict. If counsel take this step, they should make certain to renew your request for mistrial once the verdict has been completed.

Professionalism is an important part of the demeanor of an advocate at trial. Advocates show judges the respect that both their position and circumstances give them. It is absolutely proper to do so, but that does not mean that counsel should concede objections that are valid. When respond ing to an objection by stating "withdrawn," "I'll rephrase," or "I'll move on," they have just waived a potential appellate issue. There is nothing wrong with doing that, but it must be done intelligently and knowingly in light of the theme and theory of the case.

4.   Proffers

One of the techniques counsel should develop is to make proper proffers of proof when the judge rules against them on a motion. A proffer identifies for the court evidence which they believe would have been admitted but for the judge's ruling. It should be as specific as possible but broad enough to cast a wide net for appellate counsel. When making a proffer, counsel should include exhibits, statements of witnesses, and any other evidence supporting the proffer and placing into context the invalid ruling of the trial court. This is an opportunity to show the court that the trial judge made a mistake. It is also a last-ditch chance to change the trial judge's mind. In order for a proffer to be effective it must be complete.

Sometimes counsel are dealing with a proffer from an opposing counsel. Listen carefully to what they offer. If there is something in their proffer that gives you pause, and a witness in relation to that proffer later testifies, a fruitful area of cross examination might be to develop testimony that shows why the evidence was properly excluded. Counsel should also listen to determine what the proffer specifically addresses, and make any objections to that proffer in the same vein. Whenever counsel hear an attorney in court make a proffer of evidence, they should realize that they are speaking directly to the appellate court. These are signal flares that counsel should use to make certain that the case is not going in the wrong direction from an evidentiary perspective.

5.   Openings and Closings

Many attorneys are afraid to object to opposing counsel's opening statement or closing argument. There is almost an unwritten rule of fairness in this refusal to object. The idea goes something like this, "if I don't object to their opening or closing, then they won't object to mine." This approach to opening and closing might make the trial goes smoother, it may ensure that opposing counsel buys you a beer the next time you're together in Murphy's Bar, but it will not properly represent the client or make the appellate record.

When advocates fail to object during opening statements and closing arguments, they have waived almost any potential grounds for relief about improper argument. Listen to the closing: if it is so prejudicial as to preclude a fair trial for the client counsel must object. After objecting they should immediately ask for a curative instruction from the court.

Counsel should also request that the court sua sponte identify and sustain any additional objectionable material from opposing counsel. Finally, they should consider asking for a mistrial when the improper argument calls for it. Advocates should consider opening statements and closing arguments just like they would consider any other portion of the trial when it comes to raising an objection. Look to the theme and theory of the case, the theme and theory of opposing counsel's case, and the proper application of the law when deciding whether or not to object.

6.   Jury Instructions

We have referred to jury instructions on multiple occasions within this book. These instructions are both tools of advocacy and expressions of the rule of law. Most jurisdictions have a set of pattern instructions that serve as guidelines for the court. Counsel should realize that the pattern jury instructions in your jurisdiction are just that: patterns. They are suggestions from the panel that drafted those pattern jury instructions, and are meant to provide a common sense plain meaning tool a judge can use to fashion an appropriate instruction to the jury. The focus is on the word "fashion." The judge is not the only person in the courtroom who has the ability to fashion an appropriate instruction. As an advocate counsel have a duty to properly offer instructions that they believe are warranted based upon the facts and the law of this particular case. Proffered instructions should be fair and not so one-sided as to give the court pause.

When dealing with drafted instructions, proposed instructions, and pattern instructions, you must get clear rulings on the record showing your objections and the ultimate ruling of the court. From an appellate perspective, it does no good to draft a credible competent instruction, propose it to the court, and then not make certain that the judge properly rules on the use of that instruction at trial. The objections to instructions must be clear and concise. Make the record with the basis of their objections and identify the source of that basis. Often counsel can go to either the law or the facts as a good beginning point when objecting to specific instructions.

Most jurisdictions have some form of conference about instructions. Some are on the record and some are not. They must ensure at the ending of any conference on jury instructions that counsel renew your objections to any particular instruction. They should also get the judge to identify on the record that counsel do not have to continually raise an objection of those instructions when the jury is being instructed. Finally, counsel should pay careful attention when the court actually reads the instructions to the jury in case the judge deviates from her ruling in the conference. If counsel does not object, they may very well have waived the issue.

D.   Preserving the Record – Post Trial

Sometimes, despite counsel's best efforts, they actually lose at trial. Coundrl should develop the habit of identifying, as a matter of course, potential post trial matters that can be raised as a motion to the court before the case is passed on to the appellate level. Sometimes these issues are clearly identifiable to the trial lawyer and sometimes they are not. It is well worth the time to consult with an appellate lawyer about potential post-trial motions that may be raised. It is a last gasp chance to modify the record of trial before it goes forward on appeal.

Certain issues are allowed as a matter of law in the post-trial motions process and others are not; it is counsel's job to know which is which and why. The other issue that sometimes presents itself during post-trial is jury misconduct. This subject is well beyond the boundaries of this text and many books have been written on dealing with the jury after the verdict has been read. I commend them but will not discuss them here.

E.   Creating the Record Checklist

The following checklist summarizes the information counsel should consider when developing proper post trial issues. It should serve as a starting

point in developing additional checklists and procedures designed to identify and protect appellate issues prior to their becoming issues.

I.   Pre-trial
      a.   Motions for summary judgment:
           i.   Granted in part, denied in part.
           ii.   Keep track.
           iii.   Motion for directed verdict where appropriate.
      b.   Motions in limine:
           i.   Exclude or include.
           ii.   Object if admitted.
           iii.   Motion for mistrial warranted.
II.   Trial
      a.   Record and Rulings:
           i.   Make the record.
           ii.   Be precise.
           iii.   Ensure the judge rules.
      b.   Jury Selection:
           i.   Make the record.
           ii.   Peremptory.
           iii.   For cause (*Batson* or *Slappy*).
      c.   Evidentiary Issues:
           i.   Object specifically.
           ii.   Request limiting instructions.
           iii.   Standing objections where appropriate.
           iv.   Move to strike.
           v.   Mistrial.
      d.   Proffers:
           i.   Develop thoroughly.
           ii.   Attach supporting documentation.
           iii.   "but for" language.
           iv.   Listen when opponent proffers.
      e.   Openings and Closings:
           i.   Waived if not objected to.
           ii.   No 'gentleman's agreement' here.
           iii.   Egregious and unfairly prejudicial.
           iv.   Request mistrial.
      f.   Jury Instructions:

       i.   Patterns are just patterns.

      ii.   Propose your own.

     iii.   Draft based on case law and facts.

     iv.   Be fair in drafting.

III.   Post-Trial

    a.   Some motions can still be made.

    b.   Last chance to perfect the record.

    c.   Consult appellate counsel when warranted.

-Notes-

Chapter 14: Federal Rules of Evidence

Rule 101. Scope; Definitions 564
Rule 102. Purpose 565
Rule 103. Rulings on Evidence 565
Rule 104. Preliminary Questions 566
Rule 105. Limiting Evidence That Is Not Admissible Against Other Parties or for Other Purposes 566
Rule 106. Remainder of or Related Writings or Recorded Statements 566
Rule 201. Judicial Notice of Adjudicative Facts 567
Rule 301. Presumptions in Civil Cases Generally 567
Rule 302. Applying State Law to Presumptions in Civil Cases 568
Rule 401. Test for Relevant Evidence 568
Rule 402. General Admissibility of Relevant Evidence 568
Rule 403. Excluding Relevant Evidence for Prejudice, Confusion, Waste of Time, or Other Reasons 568
Rule 404. Character Evidence; Crimes or Other Acts 568
Rule 405. Methods of Proving Character 569
Rule 406. Habit; Routine Practice 570
Rule 407. Subsequent Remedial Measures 570
Rule 408. Compromise Offers and Negotiations 570
Rule 409. Offers to Pay Medical and Similar Expenses 571
Rule 410. Pleas, Plea Discussions, and Related Statements 571
Rule 411. Liability Insurance 571
Rule 412. Sex-Offense Cases: The Victim's Sexual Behavior or Predisposition 572
Rule 413. Similar Crimes in Sexual-Assault Cases 573
Rule 414. Similar Crimes in Child-Molestation Cases 574
Rule 415. Similar Acts in Civil Cases Involving Sexual Assault or Child Molestation 574
Rule 501. Privilege in General 575
Rule 502. Attorney-Client Privilege and Work Product; Limitations on Waiver 575
Rules 503 to 600. Reserved for future legislation 576
Rule 601. Competency to Testify in General 577
Rule 602. Need for Personal Knowledge 577
Rule 603. Oath or Affirmation to Testify Truthfully 577
Rule 604. Interpreter 577
Rule 605. Judge's Competency as a Witness 577
Rule 606. Juror's Competency as a Witness 577
Rule 607. Who May Impeach a Witness 578

Rule 608. A Witness's Character for Truthfulness or Untruthfulness............578
Rule 609. Impeachment by Evidence of a Criminal Conviction....................579
Rule 610. Religious Beliefs or Opinions..580
Rule 611. Mode and Order of Examining Witnesses and Presenting
Evidence..580
Rule 612. Writing Used to Refresh a Witness's Memory..............................580
Rule 613. Witness's Prior Statement 581
Rule 614. Court's Calling or Examining a Witness..581
Rule 615. Excluding Witnesses 582
Rule 701. Opinion Testimony by Lay Witnesses..582
Rule 702. Testimony by Expert Witnesses 582
Rule 703. Bases of an Expert's Opinion Testimony 583
Rule 704. Opinion on an Ultimate Issue...583
Rule 705. Disclosing the Facts or Data Underlying an Expert's Opinion 583
Rule 706. Court-Appointed Expert Witnesses...583
Rule 801. Definitions....: Exclusions from Hearsay 584
Rule 802. The Rule Against Hearsay...585
Rule 803. Exceptions to the Rule Against Hearsay--Regardless of Whether the
Declarant Is Available as a Witness 586
Rule 804. Exceptions to the Rule Against Hearsay--When the Declarant Is
Unavailable as a Witness 590
Rule 805. Hearsay Within Hearsay..591
Rule 806. Attacking and Supporting the Declarant's Credibility 591
Rule 807. Residual Exception 592
Rule 901. Authenticating or Identifying Evidence 592
Rule 902. Evidence That Is Self-Authenticating 594
Rule 903. Subscribing Witness's Testimony 596
Rule 1001. Definitions That Apply to This Article..596
Rule 1007. Testimony or Statement of a Party to Prove Content...................596
Rule 1008. Functions of the Court and Jury 596
Rule 1101. Applicability of the Rules..597
Rule 1102. Amendments...598
Rule 1103. Title 598

FEDERAL RULES OF EVIDENCE

Effective July 1, 1975, as amended to December 1, 2012

ARTICLE I. GENERAL PROVISIONS

Rule 101. Scope; Definitions

(a) Scope. These rules apply to proceedings in United States courts. The specific courts and proceedings to which the rules apply, along with exceptions, are set out in Rule 1101.

(b) Definitions. In these rules:

(1) "civil case" means a civil action or proceeding;

(2) "criminal case" includes a criminal proceeding;

(3) "public office" includes a public agency;

(4) "record" includes a memorandum, report, or data compilation;

(5) a "rule prescribed by the Supreme Court" means a rule adopted by the Supreme Court under statutory authority; and

(6) a reference to any kind of written material or any other medium includes electronically stored information.

Rule 102. Purpose

These rules should be construed so as to administer every proceeding fairly, eliminate unjustifiable expense and delay, and promote the development of evidence law, to the end of ascertaining the truth and securing a just determination.

Rule 103. Rulings on Evidence

(a) Preserving a Claim of Error. A party may claim error in a ruling to admit or exclude evidence only if the error affects a substantial right of the party and:

(1) if the ruling admits evidence, a party, on the record:

(A) timely objects or moves to strike; and

(B) states the specific ground, unless it was apparent from the context; or

(2) if the ruling excludes evidence, a party informs the court of its substance by an offer of proof, unless the substance was apparent from the context.

(b) Not Needing to Renew an Objection or Offer of Proof. Once the court rules definitively on the record--either before or at trial--a party need not renew an objection or offer of proof to preserve a claim of error for appeal.

(c) Court's Statement About the Ruling; Directing an Offer of Proof. The court may make any statement about the character or form of the evidence, the objection made, and the ruling. The court may direct that an offer of proof be made in question-and-answer form.

(d) Preventing the Jury from Hearing Inadmissible Evidence. To the extent practicable, the court must conduct a jury trial so that inadmissible evidence is not suggested to the jury by any means.

(e) Taking Notice of Plain Error. A court may take notice of a plain error affecting a substantial right, even if the claim of error was not properly preserved.

Rule 104. Preliminary Questions

(a) In General. The court must decide any preliminary question about whether a witness is qualified, a privilege exists, or evidence is admissible. In so deciding, the court is not bound by evidence rules, except those on privilege.

(b) Relevance That Depends on a Fact. When the relevance of evidence depends on whether a fact exists, proof must be introduced sufficient to support a finding that the fact does exist. The court may admit the proposed evidence on the condition that the proof be introduced later.

(c) Conducting a Hearing So That the Jury Cannot Hear It. The court must conduct any hearing on a preliminary question so that the jury cannot hear it if:

(1) the hearing involves the admissibility of a confession;

(2) a defendant in a criminal case is a witness and so requests; or

(3) justice so requires.

(d) Cross-Examining a Defendant in a Criminal Case. By testifying on a preliminary question, a defendant in a criminal case does not become subject to cross-examination on other issues in the case.

(e) Evidence Relevant to Weight and Credibility. This rule does not limit a party's right to introduce before the jury evidence that is relevant to the weight or credibility of other evidence.

Rule 105. Limiting Evidence That Is Not Admissible Against Other Parties or for Other Purposes

If the court admits evidence that is admissible against a party or for a purpose--but not against another party or for another purpose--the court, on timely request, must restrict the evidence to its proper scope and instruct the jury accordingly.

Rule 106. Remainder of or Related Writings or Recorded Statements

If a party introduces all or part of a writing or recorded statement, an adverse party may require the introduction, at that time, of any other part--or any other writing or recorded statement--that in fairness ought to be considered at the same time.

ARTICLE II. JUDICIAL NOTICE

Rule 201. Judicial Notice of Adjudicative Facts

(a) Scope. This rule governs judicial notice of an adjudicative fact only, not a legislative fact.

(b) Kinds of Facts That May Be Judicially Noticed. The court may judicially notice a fact that is not subject to reasonable dispute because it:

(1) is generally known within the trial court's territorial jurisdiction; or

(2) can be accurately and readily determined from sources whose accuracy cannot reasonably be questioned.

(c) Taking Notice. The court:

(1) may take judicial notice on its own; or

(2) must take judicial notice if a party requests it and the court is supplied with the necessary information.

(d) Timing. The court may take judicial notice at any stage of the proceeding.

(e) Opportunity to Be Heard. On timely request, a party is entitled to be heard on the propriety of taking judicial notice and the nature of the fact to be noticed. If the court takes judicial notice before notifying a party, the party, on request, is still entitled to be heard.

(f) Instructing the Jury. In a civil case, the court must instruct the jury to accept the noticed fact as conclusive. In a criminal case, the court must instruct the jury that it may or may not accept the noticed fact as conclusive.

ARTICLE III. PRESUMPTIONS IN CIVIL CASES

Rule 301. Presumptions in Civil Cases Generally

In a civil case, unless a federal statute or these rules provide otherwise, the party against whom a presumption is directed has the burden of producing evidence to rebut the presumption. But this rule does not shift the burden of persuasion, which remains on the party who had it originally.

Rule 302. Applying State Law to Presumptions in Civil Cases

In a civil case, state law governs the effect of a presumption regarding a claim or defense for which state law supplies the rule of decision.

ARTICLE IV. RELEVANCE AND ITS LIMITS

Rule 401. Test for Relevant Evidence

Evidence is relevant if:

(a) it has any tendency to make a fact more or less probable than it would be without the evidence; and

(b) the fact is of consequence in determining the action.

Rule 402. General Admissibility of Relevant Evidence

Relevant evidence is admissible unless any of the following provides otherwise:

• the United States Constitution;

• a federal statute;

• these rules; or

• other rules prescribed by the Supreme Court.

Irrelevant evidence is not admissible.

Rule 403. Excluding Relevant Evidence for Prejudice, Confusion, Waste of Time, or Other Reasons

The court may exclude relevant evidence if its probative value is substantially outweighed by a danger of one or more of the following: unfair prejudice, confusing the issues, misleading the jury, undue delay, wasting time, or needlessly presenting cumulative evidence.

Rule 404. Character Evidence; Crimes or Other Acts

(a) Character Evidence.

(1) Prohibited Uses. Evidence of a person's character or character trait is not admissible to prove that on a particular occasion the person acted in accordance with the character or trait.

(2) Exceptions for a Defendant or Victim in a Criminal Case. The following exceptions apply in a criminal case:

(A) a defendant may offer evidence of the defendant's pertinent trait, and if the evidence is admitted, the prosecutor may offer evidence to rebut it;

(B) subject to the limitations in Rule 412, a defendant may offer evidence of an alleged victim's pertinent trait, and if the evidence is admitted, the prosecutor may:

(i) offer evidence to rebut it; and

(ii) offer evidence of the defendant's same trait; and

(C) in a homicide case, the prosecutor may offer evidence of the alleged victim's trait of peacefulness to rebut evidence that the victim was the first aggressor.

(3) Exceptions for a Witness. Evidence of a witness's character may be admitted under Rules 607, 608, and 609.

(b) Crimes, Wrongs, or Other Acts.

(1) Prohibited Uses. Evidence of a crime, wrong, or other act is not admissible to prove a person's character in order to show that on a particular occasion the person acted in accordance with the character.

(2) Permitted Uses; Notice in a Criminal Case. This evidence may be admissible for another purpose, such as proving motive, opportunity, intent, preparation, plan, knowledge, identity, absence of mistake, or lack of accident. On request by a defendant in a criminal case, the prosecutor must:

(A) provide reasonable notice of the general nature of any such evidence that the prosecutor intends to offer at trial; and

(B) do so before trial--or during trial if the court, for good cause, excuses lack of pretrial notice.

Rule 405. Methods of Proving Character

(a) By Reputation or Opinion. When evidence of a person's character or character trait is admissible, it may be proved by testimony about the person's reputation or by testimony in the form of an opinion. On cross- examination of the character witness, the court may allow an inquiry into relevant specific instances of the person's conduct.

(b) By Specific Instances of Conduct. When a person's character or character trait is an essential element of a charge, claim, or defense, the character or trait may also be proved by relevant specific instances of the person's conduct.

Rule 406. Habit; Routine Practice

Evidence of a person's habit or an organization's routine practice may be admitted to prove that on a particular occasion the person or organization acted in accordance with the habit or routine practice. The court may admit this evidence regardless of whether it is corroborated or whether there was an eyewitness.

Rule 407. Subsequent Remedial Measures

When measures are taken that would have made an earlier injury or harm less likely to occur, evidence of the subsequent measures is not admissible to prove:

• negligence;

• culpable conduct;

• a defect in a product or its design; or

• a need for a warning or instruction.

But the court may admit this evidence for another purpose, such as impeachment or--if disputed--proving ownership, control, or the feasibility of precautionary measures.

Rule 408. Compromise Offers and Negotiations

(a) Prohibited Uses. Evidence of the following is not admissible--on behalf of any party--either to prove or disprove the validity or amount of a disputed claim or to impeach by a prior inconsistent statement or a contradiction:

(1) furnishing, promising, or offering--or accepting, promising to accept, or offering to accept--a valuable consideration in compromising or attempting to compromise the claim; and

(2) conduct or a statement made during compromise negotiations about the claim--except when offered in a criminal case and when the

negotiations related to a claim by a public office in the exercise of its regulatory, investigative, or enforcement authority.

(b) Exceptions. The court may admit this evidence for another purpose, such as proving a witness's bias or prejudice, negating a contention of undue delay, or proving an effort to obstruct a criminal investigation or prosecution.

Rule 409. Offers to Pay Medical and Similar Expenses

Evidence of furnishing, promising to pay, or offering to pay medical, hospital, or similar expenses resulting from an injury is not admissible to prove liability for the injury.

Rule 410. Pleas, Plea Discussions, and Related Statements

(a) Prohibited Uses. In a civil or criminal case, evidence of the following is not admissible against the defendant who made the plea or participated in the plea discussions:

(1) a guilty plea that was later withdrawn;

(2) a nolo contendere plea;

(3) a statement made during a proceeding on either of those pleas under Federal Rule of Criminal Procedure 11 or a comparable state procedure; or

(4) a statement made during plea discussions with an attorney for the prosecuting authority if the discussions did not result in a guilty plea or they resulted in a later-withdrawn guilty plea.

(b) Exceptions. The court may admit a statement described in Rule 410(a)(3) or (4):

(1) in any proceeding in which another statement made during the same plea or plea discussions has been introduced, if in fairness the statements ought to be considered together; or

(2) in a criminal proceeding for perjury or false statement, if the defendant made the statement under oath, on the record, and with counsel present.

Rule 411. Liability Insurance

Evidence that a person was or was not insured against liability is not admissible to prove whether the person acted negligently or otherwise wrongfully. But the court may admit this evidence for another purpose, such as proving a witness's bias or prejudice or proving agency, owner-ship, or control.

Rule 412. Sex-Offense Cases: The Victim's Sexual Behavior or Predisposition

(a) Prohibited Uses. The following evidence is not admissible in a civil or criminal proceeding involving alleged sexual misconduct:

(1) evidence offered to prove that a victim engaged in other sexual behavior; or

(2) evidence offered to prove a victim's sexual predisposition.

(b) Exceptions.

(1) Criminal Cases. The court may admit the following evidence in a criminal case:

(A) evidence of specific instances of a victim's sexual behavior, if offered to prove that someone other than the defendant was the source of semen, injury, or other physical evidence;

(B) evidence of specific instances of a victim's sexual behavior with respect to the person accused of the sexual misconduct, if offered by the defendant to prove consent or if offered by the prosecutor; and

(C) evidence whose exclusion would violate the defendant's constitutional rights.

(2) Civil Cases. In a civil case, the court may admit evidence offered to prove a victim's sexual behavior or sexual predisposition if its probative value substantially outweighs the danger of harm to any victim and of unfair prejudice to any party. The court may admit evidence of a victim's reputation only if the victim has placed it in controversy.

(c) Procedure to Determine Admissibility.

(1) Motion. If a party intends to offer evidence under Rule 412(b), the party must:

(A) file a motion that specifically describes the evidence and states the purpose for which it is to be offered;

(B) do so at least 14 days before trial unless the court, for good cause, sets a different time;

(C) serve the motion on all parties; and

(D) notify the victim or, when appropriate, the victim's guardian or representative.

(2) Hearing. Before admitting evidence under this rule, the court must conduct an in camera hearing and give the victim and parties a right to attend and be heard. Unless the court orders otherwise, the motion, related materials, and the record of the hearing must be and remain sealed.

(d) Definition of "Victim." In this rule, "victim" includes an alleged victim.

Rule 413. Similar Crimes in Sexual-Assault Cases

(a) Permitted Uses. In a criminal case in which a defendant is accused of a sexual assault, the court may admit evidence that the defendant committed any other sexual assault. The evidence may be considered on any matter to which it is relevant.

(b) Disclosure to the Defendant. If the prosecutor intends to offer this evidence, the prosecutor must disclose it to the defendant, including witnesses' statements or a summary of the expected testimony. The prosecutor must do so at least 15 days before trial or at a later time that the court allows for good cause.

(c) Effect on Other Rules. This rule does not limit the admission or consideration of evidence under any other rule.

(d) Definition of "Sexual Assault." In this rule and Rule 415, " sexual assault" means a crime under federal law or under state law (as " state" is defined in 18 U.S.C. § 513) involving:

(1) any conduct prohibited by 18 U.S.C. chapter 109A;

(2) contact, without consent, between any part of the defendant's body--or an object--and another person's genitals or anus;

(3) contact, without consent, between the defendant's genitals or anus and any part of another person's body;

(4) deriving sexual pleasure or gratification from inflicting death, bodily injury, or physical pain on another person; or

(5) an attempt or conspiracy to engage in conduct described in subparagraphs (1)-(4).

Rule 414. Similar Crimes in Child-Molestation Cases

(a) Permitted Uses. In a criminal case in which a defendant is accused of child molestation, the court may admit evidence that the defendant committed any other child molestation. The evidence may be considered on any matter to which it is relevant.

(b) Disclosure to the Defendant. If the prosecutor intends to offer this evidence, the prosecutor must disclose it to the defendant, including witnesses' statements or a summary of the expected testimony. The prosecutor must do so at least 15 days before trial or at a later time that the court allows for good cause.

(c) Effect on Other Rules. This rule does not limit the admission or consideration of evidence under any other rule.

(d) Definition of "Child" and "Child Molestation." In this rule and Rule 415:

(1) "child" means a person below the age of 14; and

(2) "child molestation" means a crime under federal law or under state law (as "state" is defined in 18 U.S.C. § 513) involving:

(A) any conduct prohibited by 18 U.S.C. chapter 109A and committed with a child;

(B) any conduct prohibited by 18 U.S.C. chapter 110;

(C) contact between any part of the defendant's body--or an object-- and a child's genitals or anus;

(D) contact between the defendant's genitals or anus and any part of a child's body;

(E) deriving sexual pleasure or gratification from inflicting death, bodily injury, or physical pain on a child; or

(F) an attempt or conspiracy to engage in conduct described in subparagraphs (A)-(E).

Rule 415. Similar Acts in Civil Cases Involving Sexual Assault or Child Molestation

(a) Permitted Uses. In a civil case involving a claim for relief based on a party's alleged sexual assault or child molestation, the court may admit evidence that the party committed any other sexual assault or child molestation. The evidence may be considered as provided in Rules 413 and 414.

(b) Disclosure to the Opponent. If a party intends to offer this evidence, the party must disclose it to the party against whom it will be offered, including witnesses' statements or a summary of the expected testimony. The party must do so at least 15 days before trial or at a later time that the court allows for good cause.

(c) Effect on Other Rules. This rule does not limit the admission or consideration of evidence under any other rule.

ARTICLE V. PRIVILEGES

Rule 501. Privilege in General

The common law--as interpreted by United States courts in the light of reason and experience--governs a claim of privilege unless any of the following provides otherwise:

• the United States Constitution;

• a federal statute; or

• rules prescribed by the Supreme Court.

But in a civil case, state law governs privilege regarding a claim or defense for which state law supplies the rule of decision.

Rule 502. Attorney-Client Privilege and Work Product; Limitations on Waiver

The following provisions apply, in the circumstances set out, to disclosure of a communication or information covered by the attorney-client privilege or work-product protection.

(a) Disclosure Made in a Federal Proceeding or to a Federal Office or Agency; Scope of a Waiver. When the disclosure is made in a federal proceeding or to a federal office or agency and waives the attorney-client privilege or work-product protection, the waiver extends to an undisclosed communication or information in a federal or state proceeding only if:

(1) the waiver is intentional;

(2) the disclosed and undisclosed communications or information concern the same subject matter; and

(3) they ought in fairness to be considered together.

(b) Inadvertent Disclosure. When made in a federal proceeding or to a federal office or agency, the disclosure does not operate as a waiver in a federal or state proceeding if:

(1) the disclosure is inadvertent;

(2) the holder of the privilege or protection took reasonable steps to prevent disclosure; and

(3) the holder promptly took reasonable steps to rectify the error, including (if applicable) following Federal Rule of Civil Procedure 26(b)(5)(B).

(c) Disclosure Made in a State Proceeding. When the disclosure is made in a state proceeding and is not the subject of a state-court order concerning waiver, the disclosure does not operate as a waiver in a federal proceeding if the disclosure:

(1) would not be a waiver under this rule if it had been made in a federal proceeding; or

(2) is not a waiver under the law of the state where the disclosure occurred.

(d) Controlling Effect of a Court Order. A federal court may order that the privilege or protection is not waived by disclosure connected with the litigation pending before the court--in which event the disclosure is also not a waiver in any other federal or state proceeding.

(e) Controlling Effect of a Party Agreement. An agreement on the effect of disclosure in a federal proceeding is binding only on the parties to the agreement, unless it is incorporated into a court order.

(f) Controlling Effect of This Rule. Notwithstanding Rules 101 and 1101, this rule applies to state proceedings and to federal court-annexed and federal court-mandated arbitration proceedings, in the circumstances set out in the rule. And notwithstanding Rule 501, this rule applies even if state law provides the rule of decision.

(g) Definitions. In this rule:

(1) "attorney-client privilege" means the protection that applicable law provides for confidential attorney-client communications; and

(2) "work-product protection" means the protection that applicable law provides for tangible material (or its intangible equivalent) prepared in anticipation of litigation or for trial.

Rules 503 to 600. Reserved for future legislation

ARTICLE VI. WITNESSES

Rule 601. Competency to Testify in General

Every person is competent to be a witness unless these rules provide otherwise. But in a civil case, state law governs the witness's competency regarding a claim or defense for which state law supplies the rule of decision.

Rule 602. Need for Personal Knowledge

A witness may testify to a matter only if evidence is introduced sufficient to support a finding that the witness has personal knowledge of the matter. Evidence to prove personal knowledge may consist of the witness' s own testimony. This rule does not apply to a witness's expert testimony under Rule 703.

Rule 603. Oath or Affirmation to Testify Truthfully

Before testifying, a witness must give an oath or affirmation to testify truthfully. It must be in a form designed to impress that duty on the witness's conscience.

Rule 604. Interpreter

An interpreter must be qualified and must give an oath or affirmation to make a true translation.

Rule 605. Judge's Competency as a Witness

The presiding judge may not testify as a witness at the trial. A party need not object to preserve the issue.

Rule 606. Juror's Competency as a Witness

(a) At the Trial. A juror may not testify as a witness before the other jurors at the trial. If a juror is called to testify, the court must give a party an opportunity to object outside the jury's presence.

(b) During an Inquiry Into the Validity of a Verdict or Indictment.

(1) Prohibited Testimony or Other Evidence. During an inquiry into the validity of a verdict or indictment, a juror may not testify about any statement made or incident that occurred during the jury's delibera-

tions; the effect of anything on that juror's or another juror's vote; or any juror's mental processes concerning the verdict or indictment. The court may not receive a juror's affidavit or evidence of a juror's statement on these matters.

(2) Exceptions. A juror may testify about whether:

(A) extraneous prejudicial information was improperly brought to the jury's attention;

(B) an outside influence was improperly brought to bear on any juror; or

(C) a mistake was made in entering the verdict on the verdict form.

Rule 607. Who May Impeach a Witness

Any party, including the party that called the witness, may attack the witness's credibility.

Rule 608. A Witness's Character for Truthfulness or Untruthfulness

(a) Reputation or Opinion Evidence. A witness's credibility may be attacked or supported by testimony about the witness's reputation for having a character for truthfulness or untruthfulness, or by testimony in the form of an opinion about that character. But evidence of truthful character is admissible only after the witness's character for truthfulness has been attacked.

(b) Specific Instances of Conduct. Except for a criminal conviction under Rule 609, extrinsic evidence is not admissible to prove specific instances of a witness's conduct in order to attack or support the witness's character for truthfulness. But the court may, on cross-examination, allow them to be inquired into if they are probative of the character for truthfulness or untruthfulness of:

(1) the witness; or

(2) another witness whose character the witness being cross-examined has testified about.

By testifying on another matter, a witness does not waive any privilege against self-incrimination for testimony that relates only to the witness's character for truthfulness.

Rule 609. Impeachment by Evidence of a Criminal Conviction

(a) In General. The following rules apply to attacking a witness's character for truthfulness by evidence of a criminal conviction:

(1) for a crime that, in the convicting jurisdiction, was punishable by death or by imprisonment for more than one year, the evidence:

(A) must be admitted, subject to Rule 403, in a civil case or in a criminal case in which the witness is not a defendant; and

(B) must be admitted in a criminal case in which the witness is a defendant, if the probative value of the evidence outweighs its prejudicial effect to that defendant; and

(2) for any crime regardless of the punishment, the evidence must be admitted if the court can readily determine that establishing the elements of the crime required proving--or the witness's admitting--a dishonest act or false statement.

(b) Limit on Using the Evidence After 10 Years. This subdivision (b) applies if more than 10 years have passed since the witness's conviction or release from confinement for it, whichever is later. Evidence of the conviction is admissible only if:

(1) its probative value, supported by specific facts and circumstances, substantially outweighs its prejudicial effect; and

(2) the proponent gives an adverse party reasonable written notice of the intent to use it so that the party has a fair opportunity to contest its use.

(c) Effect of a Pardon, Annulment, or Certificate of Rehabilitation. Evidence of a conviction is not admissible if:

(1) the conviction has been the subject of a pardon, annulment, certificate of rehabilitation, or other equivalent procedure based on a finding that the person has been rehabilitated, and the person has not been convicted of a later crime punishable by death or by imprisonment for more than one year; or

(2) the conviction has been the subject of a pardon, annulment, or other equivalent procedure based on a finding of innocence.

(d) Juvenile Adjudications. Evidence of a juvenile adjudication is admissible under this rule only if:

(1) it is offered in a criminal case;

(2) the adjudication was of a witness other than the defendant;

(3) an adult's conviction for that offense would be admissible to attack the adult's credibility; and

(4) admitting the evidence is necessary to fairly determine guilt or innocence.

(e) Pendency of an Appeal. A conviction that satisfies this rule is admissible even if an appeal is pending. Evidence of the pendency is also admissible.

Rule 610. Religious Beliefs or Opinions

Evidence of a witness's religious beliefs or opinions is not admissible to attack or support the witness's credibility.

Rule 611. Mode and Order of Examining Witnesses and Presenting Evidence

(a) Control by the Court; Purposes. The court should exercise reasonable control over the mode and order of examining witnesses and presenting evidence so as to:

(1) make those procedures effective for determining the truth;

(2) avoid wasting time; and

(3) protect witnesses from harassment or undue embarrassment.

(b) Scope of Cross-Examination. Cross-examination should not go beyond the subject matter of the direct examination and matters affecting the witness's credibility. The court may allow inquiry into additional matters as if on direct examination.

(c) Leading Questions. Leading questions should not be used on direct examination except as necessary to develop the witness's testimony. Ordinarily, the court should allow leading questions:

(1) on cross-examination; and

(2) when a party calls a hostile witness, an adverse party, or a witness identified with an adverse party.

Rule 612. Writing Used to Refresh a Witness's Memory

(a) Scope. This rule gives an adverse party certain options when a witness uses a writing to refresh memory:

(1) while testifying; or

(2) before testifying, if the court decides that justice requires the party to have those options.

(b) Adverse Party's Options; Deleting Unrelated Matter. Unless 18 U.S.C. § 3500 provides otherwise in a criminal case, an adverse party is entitled to have the writing produced at the hearing, to inspect it, to cross-examine the witness about it, and to introduce in evidence any portion that relates to the witness's testimony. If the producing party claims that the writing includes unrelated matter, the court must examine the writing in camera, delete any unrelated portion, and order that the rest be delivered to the adverse party. Any portion deleted over objection must be preserved for the record.

(c) Failure to Produce or Deliver the Writing. If a writing is not produced or is not delivered as ordered, the court may issue any appropriate order. But if the prosecution does not comply in a criminal case, the court must strike the witness's testimony or--if justice so requires--declare a mistrial.

Rule 613. Witness's Prior Statement

(a) Showing or Disclosing the Statement During Examination. When examining a witness about the witness's prior statement, a party need not show it or disclose its contents to the witness. But the party must, on request, show it or disclose its contents to an adverse party's attorney.

(b) Extrinsic Evidence of a Prior Inconsistent Statement. Extrinsic evidence of a witness's prior inconsistent statement is admissible only if the witness is given an opportunity to explain or deny the statement and an adverse party is given an opportunity to examine the witness about it, or if justice so requires. This subdivision (b) does not apply to an opposing party's statement under Rule 801(d)(2).

Rule 614. Court's Calling or Examining a Witness

(a) Calling. The court may call a witness on its own or at a party's request. Each party is entitled to cross-examine the witness.

(b) Examining. The court may examine a witness regardless of who calls the witness.

(c) Objections. A party may object to the court's calling or examining a witness either at that time or at the next opportunity when the jury is not present.

Rule 615. Excluding Witnesses

At a party's request, the court must order witnesses excluded so that they cannot hear other witnesses' testimony. Or the court may do so on its own. But this rule does not authorize excluding:

(a) a party who is a natural person;

(b) an officer or employee of a party that is not a natural person, after being designated as the party's representative by its attorney;

(c) a person whose presence a party shows to be essential to presenting the party's claim or defense; or

(d) a person authorized by statute to be present.

ARTICLE VII. OPINIONS AND EXPERT TESTIMONY

Rule 701. Opinion Testimony by Lay Witnesses

If a witness is not testifying as an expert, testimony in the form of an opinion is limited to one that is:

(a) rationally based on the witness's perception;

(b) helpful to clearly understanding the witness's testimony or to determining a fact in issue; and

(c) not based on scientific, technical, or other specialized knowledge within the scope of Rule 702.

Rule 702. Testimony by Expert Witnesses

A witness who is qualified as an expert by knowledge, skill, experience, training, or education may testify in the form of an opinion or otherwise if:

(a) the expert's scientific, technical, or other specialized knowledge will help the trier of fact to understand the evidence or to determine a fact in issue;

(b) the testimony is based on sufficient facts or data;

(c) the testimony is the product of reliable principles and methods; and

(d) the expert has reliably applied the principles and methods to the facts of the case.

Rule 703. Bases of an Expert's Opinion Testimony

An expert may base an opinion on facts or data in the case that the expert has been made aware of or personally observed. If experts in the particular field would reasonably rely on those kinds of facts or data in forming an opinion on the subject, they need not be admissible for the opinion to be admitted. But if the facts or data would otherwise be inadmissible, the proponent of the opinion may disclose them to the jury only if their probative value in helping the jury evaluate the opinion substantially outweighs their prejudicial effect.

Rule 704. Opinion on an Ultimate Issue

(a) In General--Not Automatically Objectionable. An opinion is not objectionable just because it embraces an ultimate issue.

(b) Exception. In a criminal case, an expert witness must not state an opinion about whether the defendant did or did not have a mental state or condition that constitutes an element of the crime charged or of a defense. Those matters are for the trier of fact alone.

Rule 705. Disclosing the Facts or Data Underlying an Expert's Opinion

Unless the court orders otherwise, an expert may state an opinion--and give the reasons for it--without first testifying to the underlying facts or data. But the expert may be required to disclose those facts or data on cross- examination.

Rule 706. Court-Appointed Expert Witnesses

(a) Appointment Process. On a party's motion or on its own, the court may order the parties to show cause why expert witnesses should not be appointed and may ask the parties to submit nominations. The court may appoint any expert that the parties agree on and any of its own choosing. But the court may only appoint someone who consents to act.

(b) Expert's Role. The court must inform the expert of the expert's duties. The court may do so in writing and have a copy filed with the clerk or may do so orally at a conference in which the parties have an opportunity to participate. The expert:

(1) must advise the parties of any findings the expert makes;

(2) may be deposed by any party;

(3) may be called to testify by the court or any party; and

 (4) may be cross-examined by any party, including the party that called the expert.

(c) Compensation. The expert is entitled to a reasonable compensation, as set by the court. The compensation is payable as follows:

(1) in a criminal case or in a civil case involving just compensation under the Fifth Amendment, from any funds that are provided by law; and

(2) in any other civil case, by the parties in the proportion and at the time that the court directs--and the compensation is then charged like other costs.

(d) Disclosing the Appointment to the Jury. The court may authorize disclosure to the jury that the court appointed the expert.

(e) Parties' Choice of Their Own Experts. This rule does not limit a party in calling its own experts.

ARTICLE VIII. HEARSAY

Rule 801. Definitions....: Exclusions from Hearsay

(a) Statement. "Statement" means a person's oral assertion, written assertion, or nonverbal conduct, if the person intended it as an assertion.

(b) Declarant. "Declarant" means the person who made the statement.

(c) Hearsay. "Hearsay" means a statement that:

(1) the declarant does not make while testifying at the current trial or hearing; and

(2) a party offers in evidence to prove the truth of the matter asserted in the statement.

(d) Statements That Are Not Hearsay. A statement that meets the following conditions is not hearsay:

(1) A Declarant-Witness's Prior Statement. The declarant testifies and is subject to cross-examination about a prior statement, and the statement:

(A) is inconsistent with the declarant's testimony and was given under penalty of perjury at a trial, hearing, or other proceeding or in a deposition;

(B) is consistent with the declarant's testimony and is offered to rebut an express or implied charge that the declarant recently fabricated it or acted from a recent improper influence or motive in so testifying; or

(C) identifies a person as someone the declarant perceived earlier.

(2) An Opposing Party's Statement. The statement is offered against an opposing party and:

(A) was made by the party in an individual or representative capacity;

(B) is one the party manifested that it adopted or believed to be true;

(C) was made by a person whom the party authorized to make a statement on the subject;

(D) was made by the party's agent or employee on a matter within the scope of that relationship and while it existed; or

(E) was made by the party's coconspirator during and in furtherance of the conspiracy.

The statement must be considered but does not by itself establish the declarant's authority under (C); the existence or scope of the relationship under (D); or the existence of the conspiracy or participation in it under (E).

Rule 802. The Rule Against Hearsay

Hearsay is not admissible unless any of the following provides otherwise:

• a federal statute;

• these rules; or

• other rules prescribed by the Supreme Court.

Rule 803. Exceptions to the Rule Against Hearsay--Regardless of Whether the Declarant Is Available as a Witness

The following are not excluded by the rule against hearsay, regardless of whether the declarant is available as a witness:

(1) Present Sense Impression. A statement describing or explaining an event or condition, made while or immediately after the declarant perceived it.

(2) Excited Utterance. A statement relating to a startling event or condition, made while the declarant was under the stress of excitement that it caused.

(3) Then-Existing Mental, Emotional, or Physical Condition. A statement of the declarant's then-existing state of mind (such as motive, intent, or plan) or emotional, sensory, or physical condition (such as mental feeling, pain, or bodily health), but not including a statement of memory or belief to prove the fact remembered or believed unless it relates to the validity or terms of the declarant's will.

(4) Statement Made for Medical Diagnosis or Treatment. A statement that:

(A) is made for--and is reasonably pertinent to--medical diagnosis or treatment; and

(B) describes medical history; past or present symptoms or sensations; their inception; or their general cause.

(5) Recorded Recollection. A record that:

(A) is on a matter the witness once knew about but now cannot recall well enough to testify fully and accurately;

(B) was made or adopted by the witness when the matter was fresh in the witness's memory; and

(C) accurately reflects the witness's knowledge.

If admitted, the record may be read into evidence but may be received as an exhibit only if offered by an adverse party.

(6) Records of a Regularly Conducted Activity. A record of an act, event, condition, opinion, or diagnosis if:

(A) the record was made at or near the time by--or from information transmitted by--someone with knowledge;

(B) the record was kept in the course of a regularly conducted activity of a business, organization, occupation, or calling, whether or not for profit;

(C) making the record was a regular practice of that activity;

(D) all these conditions are shown by the testimony of the custodian or another qualified witness, or by a certification that complies with Rule 902(11) or (12) or with a statute permitting certification; and

(E) neither the source of information nor the method or circumstances of preparation indicate a lack of trustworthiness.

(7) Absence of a Record of a Regularly Conducted Activity. Evidence that a matter is not included in a record described in paragraph (6) if:

(A) the evidence is admitted to prove that the matter did not occur or exist;

(B) a record was regularly kept for a matter of that kind; and

(C) neither the possible source of the information nor other circumstances indicate a lack of trustworthiness.

(8) Public Records. A record or statement of a public office if:

(A) it sets out:

(i) the office's activities;

(ii) a matter observed while under a legal duty to report, but not including, in a criminal case, a matter observed by law-enforcement personnel; or

(iii) in a civil case or against the government in a criminal case, factual findings from a legally authorized investigation; and

(B) neither the source of information nor other circumstances indicate a lack of trustworthiness.

(9) Public Records of Vital Statistics. A record of a birth, death, or marriage, if reported to a public office in accordance with a legal duty.

(10) Absence of a Public Record. Testimony--or a certification under Rule 902--that a diligent search failed to disclose a public record or statement if the testimony or certification is admitted to prove that:

(A) the record or statement does not exist; or

(B) a matter did not occur or exist, if a public office regularly kept a record or statement for a matter of that kind.

(11) Records of Religious Organizations Concerning Personal or Family History. A statement of birth, legitimacy, ancestry, marriage, divorce, death, relationship by blood or marriage, or similar facts of personal or family history, contained in a regularly kept record of a religious organization.

(12) Certificates of Marriage, Baptism, and Similar Ceremonies. A statement of fact contained in a certificate:

(A) made by a person who is authorized by a religious organization or by law to perform the act certified;

(B) attesting that the person performed a marriage or similar ceremony or administered a sacrament; and

(C) purporting to have been issued at the time of the act or within a reasonable time after it.

(13) Family Records. A statement of fact about personal or family history contained in a family record, such as a Bible, genealogy, chart, engraving on a ring, inscription on a portrait, or engraving on an urn or burial marker.

(14) Records of Documents That Affect an Interest in Property. The record of a document that purports to establish or affect an interest in property if:

(A) the record is admitted to prove the content of the original recorded document, along with its signing and its delivery by each person who purports to have signed it;

(B) the record is kept in a public office; and

(C) a statute authorizes recording documents of that kind in that office.

(15) Statements in Documents That Affect an Interest in Property. A statement contained in a document that purports to establish or affect an interest in property if the matter stated was relevant to the document's purpose--unless later dealings with the property are inconsistent with the truth of the statement or the purport of the document.

(16) Statements in Ancient Documents. A statement in a document that is at least 20 years old and whose authenticity is established.

(17) Market Reports and Similar Commercial Publications. Market quotations, lists, directories, or other compilations that are generally relied on by the public or by persons in particular occupations.

(18) Statements in Learned Treatises, Periodicals, or Pamphlets. A statement contained in a treatise, periodical, or pamphlet if:

(A) the statement is called to the attention of an expert witness on cross-examination or relied on by the expert on direct examination; and

(B) the publication is established as a reliable authority by the expert's admission or testimony, by another expert's testimony, or by judicial notice.

If admitted, the statement may be read into evidence but not received as an exhibit.

(19) Reputation Concerning Personal or Family History. A reputation among a person's family by blood, adoption, or marriage--or among a person's associates or in the community--concerning the person's birth, adoption, legitimacy, ancestry, marriage, divorce, death, relationship by blood, adoption, or marriage, or similar facts of personal or family history.

(20) Reputation Concerning Boundaries or General History. A reputation in a community--arising before the controversy--concerning boundaries of land in the community or customs that affect the land, or concerning general historical events important to that community, state, or nation.

(21) Reputation Concerning Character. A reputation among a person's associates or in the community concerning the person's character.

(22) Judgment of a Previous Conviction. Evidence of a final judgment of conviction if:

(A) the judgment was entered after a trial or guilty plea, but not a nolo contendere plea;

(B) the conviction was for a crime punishable by death or by imprisonment for more than a year;

(C) the evidence is admitted to prove any fact essential to the judgment; and

(D) when offered by the prosecutor in a criminal case for a purpose other than impeachment, the judgment was against the defendant.

The pendency of an appeal may be shown but does not affect admissibility.

(23) Judgments Involving Personal, Family, or General History, or a Boundary. A judgment that is admitted to prove a matter of personal, family, or general history, or boundaries, if the matter:

(A) was essential to the judgment; and

(B) could be proved by evidence of reputation.

(24) [Other Exceptions.] [Transferred to Rule 807.]

Rule 804. Exceptions to the Rule Against Hearsay--When the Declarant Is Unavailable as a Witness

(a) Criteria for Being Unavailable. A declarant is considered to be unavailable as a witness if the declarant:

(1) is exempted from testifying about the subject matter of the declarant's statement because the court rules that a privilege applies;

(2) refuses to testify about the subject matter despite a court order to do so;

(3) testifies to not remembering the subject matter;

(4) cannot be present or testify at the trial or hearing because of death or a then-existing infirmity, physical illness, or mental illness; or

(5) is absent from the trial or hearing and the statement's proponent has not been able, by process or other reasonable means, to procure:

(A) the declarant's attendance, in the case of a hearsay exception under Rule 804(b)(1) or (6); or

(B) the declarant's attendance or testimony, in the case of a hearsay exception under Rule 804(b)(2), (3), or (4).

But this subdivision (a) does not apply if the statement's proponent procured or wrongfully caused the declarant's unavailability as a witness in order to prevent the declarant from attending or testifying.

(b) The Exceptions. The following are not excluded by the rule against hearsay if the declarant is unavailable as a witness:

(1) Former Testimony. Testimony that:

(A) was given as a witness at a trial, hearing, or lawful deposition, whether given during the current proceeding or a different one; and

(B) is now offered against a party who had--or, in a civil case, whose predecessor in interest had--an opportunity and similar motive to develop it by direct, cross-, or redirect examination.

(2) Statement Under the Belief of Imminent Death. In a prosecution for homicide or in a civil case, a statement that the declarant, while believing the declarant's death to be imminent, made about its cause or circumstances.

(3) Statement Against Interest. A statement that:

(A) a reasonable person in the declarant's position would have made only if the person believed it to be true because, when made, it was so contrary to the declarant's proprietary or pecuniary interest or had so great a tendency to invalidate the declarant's claim against someone else or to expose the declarant to civil or criminal liability; and

(B) is supported by corroborating circumstances that clearly indicate its trustworthiness, if it is offered in a criminal case as one that tends to expose the declarant to criminal liability.

(4) Statement of Personal or Family History. A statement about:

(A) the declarant's own birth, adoption, legitimacy, ancestry, marriage, divorce, relationship by blood, adoption, or marriage, or similar facts of personal or family history, even though the declarant had no way of acquiring personal knowledge about that fact; or

(B) another person concerning any of these facts, as well as death, if the declarant was related to the person by blood, adoption, or marriage or was so intimately associated with the person's family that the declarant's information is likely to be accurate.

(5) [Other Exceptions.] [Transferred to Rule 807.]

(6) Statement Offered Against a Party That Wrongfully Caused the Declarant's Unavailability. A statement offered against a party that wrongfully caused--or acquiesced in wrongfully causing--the declarant's unavailability as a witness, and did so intending that result.

Rule 805. Hearsay Within Hearsay

Hearsay within hearsay is not excluded by the rule against hearsay if each part of the combined statements conforms with an exception to the rule.

Rule 806. Attacking and Supporting the Declarant's Credibility

When a hearsay statement--or a statement described in Rule 801(d)(2) (C), (D), or (E)--has been admitted in evidence, the declarant's credibility may be attacked, and then supported, by any evidence that would be admissible for those purposes if the declarant had testified as a witness. The court may admit evidence of the declarant's inconsistent statement or conduct, regardless of when it occurred or whether the declarant had an opportunity to explain or deny it. If the party against whom the statement was admitted calls the declarant as a witness, the party may examine the declarant on the statement as if on cross-examination.

Rule 807. Residual Exception

(a) In General. Under the following circumstances, a hearsay statement is not excluded by the rule against hearsay even if the statement is not specifically covered by a hearsay exception in Rule 803 or 804:

(1) the statement has equivalent circumstantial guarantees of trustworthiness;

(2) it is offered as evidence of a material fact;

(3) it is more probative on the point for which it is offered than any other evidence that the proponent can obtain through reasonable efforts; and

(4) admitting it will best serve the purposes of these rules and the interests of justice.

(b) Notice. The statement is admissible only if, before the trial or hearing, the proponent gives an adverse party reasonable notice of the intent to offer the statement and its particulars, including the declarant's name and address, so that the party has a fair opportunity to meet it.

ARTICLE IX. AUTHENTICATION AND IDENTIFICATION

Rule 901. Authenticating or Identifying Evidence

(a) In General. To satisfy the requirement of authenticating or identifying an item of evidence, the proponent must produce evidence sufficient to support a finding that the item is what the proponent claims it is.

(b) Examples. The following are examples only--not a complete list--of evidence that satisfies the requirement:

(1) Testimony of a Witness with Knowledge. Testimony that an item is what it is claimed to be.

(2) Nonexpert Opinion About Handwriting. A nonexpert's opinion that handwriting is genuine, based on a familiarity with it that was not acquired for the current litigation.

(3) Comparison by an Expert Witness or the Trier of Fact. A comparison with an authenticated specimen by an expert witness or the trier of fact.

(4) Distinctive Characteristics and the Like. The appearance, contents, substance, internal patterns, or other distinctive characteristics of the item, taken together with all the circumstances.

(5) Opinion About a Voice. An opinion identifying a person's voice--whether heard firsthand or through mechanical or electronic transmission or recording--based on hearing the voice at any time under circumstances that connect it with the alleged speaker.

(6) Evidence About a Telephone Conversation. For a telephone conversation, evidence that a call was made to the number assigned at the time to:

(A) a particular person, if circumstances, including self- identification, show that the person answering was the one called; or

(B) a particular business, if the call was made to a business and the call related to business reasonably transacted over the telephone.

(7) Evidence About Public Records. Evidence that:

(A) a document was recorded or filed in a public office as authorized by law; or

(B) a purported public record or statement is from the office where items of this kind are kept.

(8) Evidence About Ancient Documents or Data Compilations. For a document or data compilation, evidence that it:

(A) is in a condition that creates no suspicion about its authenticity;

(B) was in a place where, if authentic, it would likely be; and

(C) is at least 20 years old when offered.

(9) Evidence About a Process or System. Evidence describing a process or system and showing that it produces an accurate result.

(10) Methods Provided by a Statute or Rule. Any method of authentication or identification allowed by a federal statute or a rule prescribed by the Supreme Court.

Rule 902. Evidence That Is Self-Authenticating

The following items of evidence are self-authenticating; they require no extrinsic evidence of authenticity in order to be admitted:

(1) Domestic Public Documents That Are Sealed and Signed. A document that bears:

(A) a seal purporting to be that of the United States; any state, district, commonwealth, territory, or insular possession of the United States; the former Panama Canal Zone; the Trust Territory of the Pacific Islands; a political subdivision of any of these entities; or a department, agency, or officer of any entity named above; and

(B) a signature purporting to be an execution or attestation.

(2) Domestic Public Documents That Are Not Sealed but Are Signed and Certified. A document that bears no seal if:

(A) it bears the signature of an officer or employee of an entity named in Rule 902(1)(A); and

(B) another public officer who has a seal and official duties within that same entity certifies under seal--or its equivalent--that the signer has the official capacity and that the signature is genuine.

(3) Foreign Public Documents. A document that purports to be signed or attested by a person who is authorized by a foreign country's law to do so. The document must be accompanied by a final certification that certifies the genuineness of the signature and official position of the signer or attester--or of any foreign official whose certificate of genuineness relates to the signature or attestation or is in a chain of certificates of genuineness relating to the signature or attestation. The certification may be made by a secretary of a United States embassy or legation; by a consul general, vice consul, or consular agent of the United States; or by a diplomatic or consular official of the foreign country assigned or accredited to the United States. If all parties have been given a reasonable opportunity to investigate the document's authenticity and accuracy, the court may, for good cause, either:

(A) order that it be treated as presumptively authentic without final certification; or

(B) allow it to be evidenced by an attested summary with or without final certification.

(4) Certified Copies of Public Records. A copy of an official record--or a copy of a document that was recorded or filed in a public office as authorized by law--if the copy is certified as correct by:

(A) the custodian or another person authorized to make the certification; or

(B) a certificate that complies with Rule 902(1), (2), or (3), a federal statute, or a rule prescribed by the Supreme Court.

(5) Official Publications. A book, pamphlet, or other publication purporting to be issued by a public authority.

(6) Newspapers and Periodicals. Printed material purporting to be a newspaper or periodical.

(7) Trade Inscriptions and the Like. An inscription, sign, tag, or label purporting to have been affixed in the course of business and indicating origin, ownership, or control.

(8) Acknowledged Documents. A document accompanied by a certificate of acknowledgment that is lawfully executed by a notary public or another officer who is authorized to take acknowledgments.

(9) Commercial Paper and Related Documents. Commercial paper, a signature on it, and related documents, to the extent allowed by general commercial law.

(10) Presumptions Under a Federal Statute. A signature, document, or anything else that a federal statute declares to be presumptively or prima facie genuine or authentic.

(11) Certified Domestic Records of a Regularly Conducted Activity. The original or a copy of a domestic record that meets the requirements of Rule 803(6)(A)-(C), as shown by a certification of the custodian or another qualified person that complies with a federal statute or a rule prescribed by the Supreme Court. Before the trial or hearing, the proponent must give an adverse party reasonable written notice of the intent to offer the record--and must make the record and certification available for inspection--so that the party has a fair opportunity to challenge them.

(12) Certified Foreign Records of a Regularly Conducted Activity. In a civil case, the original or a copy of a foreign record that meets the requirements of Rule 902(11), modified as follows: the certification, rather than complying with a federal statute or Supreme Court rule, must be signed in a manner that, if falsely made, would subject the maker to a criminal penalty in the country where the certification is signed. The proponent must also meet the notice requirements of Rule 902(11).

Rule 903. Subscribing Witness's Testimony

A subscribing witness's testimony is necessary to authenticate a writing only if required by the law of the jurisdiction that governs its validity.

ARTICLE X. CONTENTS OF WRITINGS, RECORDINGS, AND PHOTOGRAPHS

Rule 1001. Definitions That Apply to This Article

In this article:

(a) A "writing" consists of letters, words, numbers, or their equivalent set down in any form.

(b) A "recording" consists of letters, words, numbers, or their equivalent recorded in any manner.

(c) A "photograph" means a photographic image or its equivalent stored in any form.

(d) An "original" of a writing or recording means the writing or recording itself or any counterpart intended to have the same effect by the person who executed or issued it. For electronically stored information, "original" means any printout--or other output readable by sight--if it accurately reflects the information. An "original" of a photograph includes the negative or a print from it.

(e) A "duplicate" means a counterpart produced by a mechanical, photographic, chemical, electronic, or other equivalent process or technique that accurately reproduces the original.

Rule 1007. Testimony or Statement of a Party to Prove Content

The proponent may prove the content of a writing, recording, or photograph by the testimony, deposition, or written statement of the party against whom the evidence is offered. The proponent need not account for the original.

Rule 1008. Functions of the Court and Jury

Ordinarily, the court determines whether the proponent has fulfilled the factual conditions for admitting other evidence of the content of a writing, recording, or photograph under Rule 1004 or 1005. But in a jury trial, the jury determines--in accordance with Rule 104(b)--any issue about whether:

(a) an asserted writing, recording, or photograph ever existed;

(b) another one produced at the trial or hearing is the original; or

(c) other evidence of content accurately reflects the content.

ARTICLE XI. MISCELLANEOUS RULES

Rule 1101. Applicability of the Rules

(a) To Courts and Judges. These rules apply to proceedings before:

• United States district courts;

• United States bankruptcy and magistrate judges;

• United States courts of appeals;

 • the United States Court of Federal Claims; and

• the district courts of Guam, the Virgin Islands, and the Northern Mariana Islands.

(b) To Cases and Proceedings. These rules apply in:

• civil cases and proceedings, including bankruptcy, admiralty, and maritime cases;

• criminal cases and proceedings; and

• contempt proceedings, except those in which the court may act summarily.

(c) Rules on Privilege. The rules on privilege apply to all stages of a case or proceeding.

(d) Exceptions. These rules--except for those on privilege--do not apply to the following:

(1) the court's determination, under Rule 104(a), on a preliminary question of fact governing admissibility;

(2) grand-jury proceedings; and

(3) miscellaneous proceedings such as:

• extradition or rendition;

• issuing an arrest warrant, criminal summons, or search warrant;

• a preliminary examination in a criminal case;

• sentencing;

• granting or revoking probation or supervised release; and

• considering whether to release on bail or otherwise.

(e) Other Statutes and Rules. A federal statute or a rule prescribed by the Supreme Court may provide for admitting or excluding evidence independently from these rules.

Rule 1102. Amendments

These rules may be amended as provided in 28 U.S.C. § 2072.

Rule 1103. Title

These rules may be cited as the Federal Rules of Evidence.

Chapter 15: Common Objections

The following list of common objections is provided in alphabetical order. You should use this list to assist you in identifying the source of objections raised by others when you are not familiar with the rule that forms the basis for the objection. These materials come from the excellent work of Professor Bill Eleazer and are used here with his permission.

AMBIGUOUS: Confusing question in that it is capable of being understood in more than one sense. FRE 611(a).

ARGUMENTATIVE: (a) Counsel's question is really argument to the jury in the guise of a question. Example: counsel summarizes facts, states conclusion, and demands witness agree with conclusion. (b) Excessive quibbling with witness. FRE 611(a).

ASKED AND ANSWERED: Unfair to allow counsel to emphasize evidence through repetition. An especially useful objection during re-direct examination; greater leeway on cross-exam, however, to test recollection. FRE 611(a).

ASSUMES A FACT NOT IN EVIDENCE: A fact not testified to is contained within the question. FRE 103(c) and 611(a).

AUTHENTICATION LACKING: Proof must be offered that the exhibit is in fact what it is claimed to be. FRE 901(a).

BEST EVIDENCE RULE: If rule applies, original document must be offered or its absence accounted for. If contents of document are to be proved, rule usually applies. FRE 1002. *See also* 1003 and 1004.

BEYOND SCOPE (of direct, cross, etc.): Question unrelated to examination immediately preceding, or to credibility. Questioner should be required to call witness as own. FRE 611(b).

BOLSTERING: Improper to bolster the credibility of a witness before credibility is attacked. FRE 608(a).

COMPOUND: More than one question contained in the question asked by counsel. FRE 611(a).

CONCLUSION: Except for expert, witness must testify to facts within personal knowledge; conclusions are for the jury and counsel during closing argument. FRE 602 and 701.

CONFUSING: Unfamiliar words, disjointed phrases, or question confuses the evidence. FRE 611(a).

COUNSEL TESTIFYING: Counsel is making a statement instead of asking a question. FRE 603.

CUMULATIVE: The trial judge has discretion to control repetitive evidence. Repeated presentation of the same evidence by more exhibits or more witnesses is unfair, unnecessary and wastes time. FRE 102 and 611(a).

FOUNDATION LACKING: No proper foundation for testimony or exhibit. Ex: Offer of "recorded recollection" without showing memory failure; similar to objection for lack of authentication or personal knowledge. FRE 602 and 901(a).

HEARSAY: (answer) - Question did not call for hearsay, but witness gave it anyway. Move to strike and ask judge to instruct that response be disregarded. FRE 802.

HEARSAY: (question) - Answer would elicit hearsay, and no exception has been shown. FRE 802.

IMPEACHMENT BY PROPER MEANS: Methods of impeachment are limited and specific. FRE 607-610.

IMPROPER: When you are sure the question is improper, but cannot think of the correct basis for an objection, try, "Objection, Your Honor, improper question." The judge may know the proper basis and sustain your objection, and if judge asks for your specific basis, you have gained time to think of it. To be used very infrequently. FRE 103(c) and 611.

IMPROPER CHARACTERIZATION: The question or the response has characterized a person or conduct with unwarranted suggestive, argumentative, or impertinent language. Example: "He looked like a crook." FRE 404, 405, and 611(a).

INCOMPETENT WITNESS: Lack of qualification, such as oath or mental capacity. Also applies if the judge or juror is called as a witness. FRE 104(a), 603, 605, and 606.

IRRELEVANT: Would not tend to make any fact that is of consequence more probable or less probable. FRE 402.

LEADING: Form of question tends to suggest answer. Note: this is permitted, of course, on cross-examination. FRE 611(c).

MISQUOTING WITNESS (or MISSTATING EVIDENCE): Counsel's question misstates prior testimony of witness. Similar to objection based on assuming fact not in evidence. FRE 103(c).

NARRATIVE: Question is so broad or covers such a large time period it would allow witness to ramble and possibly present hearsay or irrelevant evidence. The judge has broad discretion in this matter. FRE 103(c) and 611(a). OPINION: Lay opinion or inference that is beyond the scope permitted by FRE 701; personal knowledge lacking; or expert witness has not been qualified as such. FRE 602, 701, and 702.

PREJUDICE OUTWEIGHS PROBATIVE VALUE: Out of the jurors' hearing, argue that "the probative value of the evidence is substantially outweighed by its prejudicial effect." May apply to exhibits as well as testimony. Note: Don't let the jurors hear you say that the evidence is prejudicial. They may be impressed. FRE 403.

PRIVILEGED: Answer would violate valid privilege (lawyer-client, husband-wife, clergyman, etc.) FRE 501.

SPECULATION AND CONJECTURE: Question requires witness who lacks personal knowledge to guess. FRE 602.

UNRESPONSIVE: Answer includes testimony not called for by the question. Especially applicable to voluntary response by hostile witness. NOTE: an objection based <u>solely</u> on this ground is generally deemed appropriate only if made by the examining attorney; thus opposing counsel should state some additional basis for the objection. FRE 103(c) and 611(a).

Chapter 16: MacCarthy's Rules of Trial Advocacy

The following list of Rules of Trial Advocacy are graciously provided by Terry MacCarthy, author of "MacCarthy on Cross Examination" and "MacCarthy on Impeachment." Terry is a great personal and professional friend, a true national treasure.

You should use this list to assist you in navigating the shoals and deep waters of trial advocacy. More wisdom has rarely been found in fewer words!

MacCarthy's Rules of Trial Advocacy

for: Leah, Donal, Jude, Deidre, Dori, Catherine, Terrence and Patrick

1. The most important and necessary quality for a trial lawyer is the ability to communicate.

2. Although there have been many excellent evidence teachers, many of their colleagues have been detrimental to trial advocacy.

3. Always have three things. "I have said it trice: What I tell you three times is true." Lewis Carroll: "The Hurting of the Snark".

4. You never get a second chance to make a first impression.

5. If the jury dislikes you, it is time to fold your tent.

6. Maintaining your credibility is essential.

7. Everything you do or say during trial is important.

8. Prepare your case backwards, starting with the jury instructions.

9. In <u>voir dire</u> it is less your picking the jury, than it is the jury picking the lawyer.

10. Body language is essential to effective communications.

11. Speak in the courtroom the way you would speak in a bar. You speak in a bar to practice speaking in a courtroom.

12. Salutations should be the exception and not the rule.

13. Trial advocacy lends itself to a varieties of approaches, but make sure the one you choose works.

14. Using rhetorical forms of speech will improve your ability to communicate.

15. Trial advocacy break out sessions should concentrate on technique, how to do what you are doing, not the facts.

16. As the salesman or preacher your job is to persuade.

17. Your character (ethos) is critical - stress fair play and some self-deprecation.

18. Rhetorical questions, but not on cross, are most helpful; they elevate your prose and your presentation.

19. Always us an analogy in closing: see specifically R. Eugene Pincham's "sugar story".

20. The chiastic alliteration is exceptionally powerful.

21. You must "point with pride and view with alarm".

22. When the enemy is in the process of destroying itself, do not interfere.

23. The importance of eye contact and smile.

24. Should you start (primacy) with the weather?

25. Adjectives, as distinct from verbs, are wonderful on direct examination.

26. Do not use intensifiers - i.e. "very", "so", "really".

27. Do not use fillers - i.e. "and", "like", "ah".

28. A trial lawyer can learn much from acts, but should not be one.

29. Tell stories - at all costs avoid law school briefs.

30. Your stories should paint pictures.

31. Say to yourself "once upon a time" to get your stories started.

32. Appeal initially to emotions - a granular reaction.

33. Your jury may forget the message but will never forget you.

34. Articulate.

35. Voice modulation.

36. Movement <u>only</u> with a purpose.

37. If possible use the "present tense".

38. Active rather than passive verbs.

39. Primacy - start on a high note.

40. Recency - end on a high note.

41. No legalese (see rule 11).

42. No powerless words - hedges, qualifies.

43. Carefully select the right word - and use it.

44. Fin ways to identify with the jurors.

45. Milk the good.

46. Repetition (looping) helps.

47. Using a rising inflection demands an answer.

48. Never get in the cage with the expert.

49. "One fact per question" makes no sense on cross.

50. Do not "publish" an exhibit until you have finished, and then do not use the term "publish".

51. Do not agree that the witness is an "expert", but merely that he can give opinions.

52. Look for "puffing" if not "mendacity" in an experts qualifications and curriculum vita.

53. Criminal defense and plaintiff lawyers are not well served by "gatekeepers".

54. The "Learned Treatise" is a great tool to impeach an expert.

55. Usually the theory of the case is less important than the themes.

56. The transition is a wonderful tool to use in Direct and Cross-Examination: it is extremely helpful on direct and essential on cross.

57. A blackboard is better than a "powerpoint".

58. Argument in Opening Statements is both wrong and of questionable value.

59. The trial judge is usually without the necessary information to rule on an "argumentative objection" during Opening Statement.

60. Simply mentioning a "white bear" does not paint the picture or do the job.

61. Label all persons and important things.

62. Pause at the beginning and end of all presentations.

63. Never move to "strike" something - it can and will not be done.

64. Cross examination is not an "Art" but rather a science.

65. If the witness is telling the story on cross examination you have goofed.

66. Control during cross is a good thing but not necessarily the only or even the best thing.

67. Cross that involves arguing, bickering, and quibbling is terrible.

68. Today's trial lawyers are much more skilled than their predecessors.

69. Cross and Direct are the most difficult to do.

70. Wellman "The Art of Cross Examination" is not a good source to learn how to cross examine.

71. Try as you may, you will seldom, if ever, do a Perry Mason cross where the witness "confesses" on the stand.

72. On cross never let the witness "slip your punch".

73. Punish, in a mild way, the witness who denies you control on cross.

74. The "Looping Tool" is both proper and most helpful.

75. With few exceptions questions have no place in cross - this is not the time for the discovery channel or to find out what the case is all about. (What was Barney Quill to you?)

76. The "no questions" exception could apply if want to make someone "short" or "tall" of if you want something "close" or "far" away.

77. The "traditional leading question" need not and should not be used in cross.

78. Your story on cross should be presented with short statements.

79. On cross get the witness into the "yes" mode and you can do wonderful things.

80. Many witnesses will say something that is wrong, stupid or deceptive, something the jury will recognize as such. You use "plausibility" cross to "milk" this.

81. Your source material on cross, in addition to what the witness said on direct and possible impeachment, will consist of the witness statements, verisimilitude and plausibility.

82. On cross dominate the witness, but do so without appearing domineering.

83. If you screw-up leave and go to a safe haven.

84. Impeachment is not limited to matters of credibility.

85. Trial lawyers and judges know less about impeachment than any other aspect of the trial.

86. There are at least 16 and not merely 5 ways to impeach a witness.

87. Impeachment with inconsistent statements is the most used and most important method of impeachment.

88. Most trial lawyers know little about how to impeach with an inconsistent statement.

89. There are times, when it is not collateral, when you should <u>not</u> "recommit", an impeaching statement.

90. You must extol the original impeaching statement.

91. You must close possible escape hatches when impeaching with an inconsistent statement.

92. Notwithstanding the Federal Rules of Evidence, show the witness the impeachment statement.

93. Anytime the Federal Rules of Evidence say you do not have to do it the old way, continue to do it the old way.

94. Who reads the inconsistent statement - you or the witness?

95. Do both - have the witness read the statement and you also read Use the "looping tool") the statement.

96. Inconsistent statements may or may not be collateral.

97. Motivation impeachment is never collateral.

98. Truthfulness impeachment is always collateral.

99. When something good happens on direct, or mare particularly on cross, "Milk it".

100. Avoid adjectives on cross, i.e. "large" clock.

101. Ethics is not only important, but exceptionally difficult.

102. Lord Carson's cross examination of Oscar Wilde was not very good.

103. Use motions in limine.

104. When defending a criminal case submit "theory of the case" instructions.

105. When defending a criminal case always consider the use of character testimony.

106. If selecting a "pertinent" character trait, never use "law abiding".

107. If a defendant testifies "Truthfulness" character trait has little downside.

108. The other sides' witnesses "tell their version" or their "story"; your witnesses "testify".

109. It is usually easier to get forgiveness than permission.

110. The commandment to not ask the "one question too many" makes no sense.

111. The commandment to not "repeat the direct" usually makes sense - but not always. What if the witness said something good on direct?

112. On cross examination it is better (with one exception when "tweaking") not to call the witness by name or to mention an honorific.

113. In opening statement you do not suggest the evidence will show: rather you will prove whatever it is.

114. When faced with an evidentiary objection, look at the judge and with your head nodding up an down, start with "as your honor well knows", hopefully followed by a legal citation.

115. Do not assume a burden you do not have.

116. When faced with "facts beyond change", do not fight them.

117. Be yourself, as Oscar Wilde observed, "everybody else it taken".

118. You do the "bragging" for your expert witness.

119. If the defendant will testify, you tell his story in opening statement.

120. Avoid the stupid direct examination questions: "state your full name for the record and spell your last name for the court reporter:; "directing your attention.... what, if anything,unusual occurred?", "did there come a time...."

121. Primacy helps direct "Why are you here to testify"?

122. When you get something good in cross or direct "loop it" by repeating it (three times) and writing it on the blackboard.

123. Maintaining control during cross examination is important, but if the witness looks bad in denying your control, you will gain more than maintaining control.

124. do not walk and talk at the same time.

125. Anger and arrogance are desirable in their witnesses, but not in yours.

126. A theory of the case is important and usually easy to figure out; your story line will come from the themes in your case, both good and bad.

127. Get rid of salutations in opening statement - start with primacy.

128. never waive an opening statement.

129. The lectern is for putting things on, not standing behind.

130. Do not hold a writing instrument (unless you are using it on a blackboard) in your hand while talking.

131. In a criminal case the prosecutor has to convince 12 jurors. The defense only needs to "confuse" one.

132. Three things happen after a jury trial. Two of them favor the defendant.

133. When you find yourself in a deep hole - quit digging.

Chapter 17: Common Foundations

Adapt these common foundations as necessary when preparing to lay the foundation for an evidentiary offering, or to ensure the opposing counsel has fully laid the foundation for their evidence.[1] I have arranged these questions to reflect the comments found in the evidentiary rules based upon the lessons discussed in our text.

Each section contains the minimum required information about the evidence the attorney needs to elicit from the witness to authenticate that evidence or, in the case of the witness, to validate their competency to testify. When preparing your own foundations, make your questions as specific as necessary to ensure each element is thoroughly met.

Chapter 17: Common Foundations..611
A.   DIAGRAM..612
B.   PHOTOGRAPH 612
C.   FUNGIBLE EVIDENCE 614
D.   NON-FUNGIBLE EVIDENCE 615
E.   CHAIN-OF-CUSTODY DOCUMENT (CoCD).....................616
F.   CHAIN-OF-CUSTODY DOCUMENT (CoCD) (Hearsay)........617
G.   CHILD WITNESS...618
H.   SPOUSE WITNESS 619
I.   LAY WITNESS WITH PERSONAL KNOWLEDGE.................620
J.   LAY OPINIONS...621
K.   EXPERT OPINION 622
L.   BIAS 624
M.   HABIT..624
N.   REPUTATION..625
O.   PRIOR BAD ACTS RESULTING IN CONVICTION...............626
P.   PRIOR BAD ACTS NOT RESULTING IN CONVICTION.......627
Q.   OTHER CRIMES/UNCHARGED MISCONDUCT 628
R.   CHARACTER TRAIT OF UNTRUTHFULNESS.....................629
S.   CHARACTER TRAIT OF TRUTHFULNESS..........................630

---

[1] Some portions of this section were adapted from the seminal text on this topic: EDWARD J. IMWINKELREID, *EVIDENTIARY FOUNDATIONS* (7th ed., LexisNexis 2008). In addition to sample foundations, Professor Imwinkelreid also provides limiting instructions and closing arguments for certain kinds of evidence to assist students in understanding what can be said about evidence *after* a foundation has been laid.

T.   PRIOR INCONSISTENT STATEMENT 630
U.   PRIOR CONSISTENT STATEMENT 631

A.   DIAGRAM

1.   Mark the exhibit (ideally, this is done before the trial starts...).

2.   Show opposing counsel the exhibit:

> *"Your Honor, I am now showing opposing counsel what has been previously been marked as PE-1 for I.D. for their inspection and objection."*

3.   Ask the judge for permission to approach the witness with the exhibit:

> *"Your Honor, may I have permission to approach the witness?"*

4.   Show the exhibit to the witness:

> *"Your Honor, I am showing the witness what has been previously marked as PE-1 for ID."*

5.   Lay the foundation for the evidence:

- Establish what it is:

> *"Do you recognize this?"*

> *"What is it?"*

- Establish what the diagram depicts, the certain area or object in the diagram:

> *"What is in the diagram?*

- Establish that the witness is familiar with that area or object:

> *"Are you familiar with it?"*

- Establish the witness's basis for their knowledge of the area or object:

> *"How is it that you are familiar with it?"*

- Have the witness affirm the accuracy of the diagram:

> *"Is the diagram reasonably accurate?"*

> *"Is the diagram drawn to scale?"*

6.   Retrieve the exhibit from the witness and offer to admit it into evidence:

> *"Your Honor, I offer into evidence what has been previously marked as PE-1 for ID as PE-1."*

B.   PHOTOGRAPH

1.   Mark the exhibit (ideally, this is done before the trial starts...).

2.   Show opposing counsel the exhibit:

> *"Your Honor, I am now showing opposing counsel what has been previously been marked as PE-1 for I.D. for their inspection and objection."*

3.   Ask the judge for permission to approach the witness with the exhibit:

> *"Your Honor, may I have permission to approach the witness?"*

4.   Show the exhibit to the witness:

> *"Your Honor, I am showing the witness what has been previously marked as PE-1 for ID."*

5.   Lay the Foundation.

   • Establish what it is:

> *"Do you recognize this?"*

> *"What is it?"*

   • Establish that the witness is familiar with the object or scene:

> *"Are you familiar with it?"*

   • Have the witness explain the basis for his familiarity with the object or scene:

> *"How is it that you are familiar with it?"*

   • Establish that the witness recognizes the object or scene in the photograph:

> *"How is it that you recognize this?*

   • Verify that, to the witness, the photograph is a "<u>fair & accurate</u>" or "<u>true</u>" or "<u>correct</u>" depiction of the object or scene at the relevant time:

> *"Is this photograph a fair and accurate representation of the [*object or scene*] at the [relevant time*]?"*

~or~

> *"Is this photograph a true representation of the [*object or scene*] at the [relevant time*]?"*

~or~

> *"Is this photograph an accurate representation of the [*object or scene*] at the [relevant time*]?"*

6.   Retrieve the exhibit from the witness and offer to admit it into evidence:

> *"Your Honor, I offer into evidence what has been previously marked as PE-1 for ID as PE-1."*

C.   FUNGIBLE EVIDENCE

1. Mark the exhibit (ideally, this is done before the trial starts...).

2. Show opposing counsel the exhibit:

    "Your Honor, I am now showing opposing counsel what has been previously been marked as PE-1 for I.D. for their inspection and objection."

3. Ask the judge for permission to approach the witness with the exhibit:

    "Your Honor, may I have permission to approach the witness?"

4. Show the exhibit to the witness:

    "Your Honor, I am showing the witness what has been previously marked as PE-1 for ID."

5. Lay the Foundation:

    * Establish what it is:

        "Do you recognize this?"

        "What is it?"

    * Establish that the witness is familiar with the item:

        "And you are familiar with this particular [item]?"

    * Establish that the witness acquired this familiarity by obtaining the item:

        "How did you come to be familiar with this particular [item]?"

    * Establish that the witness uniquely marked the item of evidence to enable him to identify it later:

        "Did you mark the [item] in anyway?"

        "Why did you do this?"

    * Establish that the witness properly safeguarded the item to prevent it from being lost or altered:

        "What did you do with the [item] after you [acquired] it?"

        "Why did you do that?"

    * Establish that the witness ultimately disposed of the item:

        "When you were finished collecting and marking the [item], what did you do with it?"

    * Establish that, to the best of his knowledge, Witness can positively identify the item as that which he previously had:

        "Can you positively identity this [item] as the one you collected and marked on [the relevant date and time]?"

- Establish that the item is in the same condition as it was when he had the item previously:

   Is the [item] in substantially the same condition as when you had it last?"

6. Retrieve the exhibit from the witness and offer to admit it into evidence:

   "Your Honor, I offer into evidence what has been previously marked as PE-1 for ID as PE-1."

D.   NON-FUNGIBLE EVIDENCE

1. Mark the exhibit (ideally, this is done before the trial starts...).

2. Show opposing counsel the exhibit:

   "Your Honor, I am now showing opposing counsel what has been previously been marked as PE-1 for I.D. for their inspection and objection."

3. Ask the judge for permission to approach the witness with the exhibit:

   "Your Honor, may I have permission to approach the witness?"

4. Show the exhibit to the witness:

   "Your Honor, I am showing the witness what has been previously marked as PE-1 for ID."

5. Lay the foundation:

   - Establish what it is:

      "Do you recognize this?"

      "What is it?"

   - Establish that the object has a unique characteristic:

      "Does it have any unique characteristics?"

   - Establish that the witness observed the characteristic on a previous occasion:

      "Was this [unique characteristic] present on the [item] before?

   - Establish that the witness identifies the exhibit as the object:

      "Do you recognize this [item] as the [item] from the [incident] on [relevant date]?"

   - Establish that the witness rests the identification on his present recognition of the characteristic:

      "And you know this is that [item] because you recognize here the [unique characteristic] on the [item]

- Establish that to the best of the witness' knowledge, the exhibit is in the same condition as it was when the witness initially saw or received the object:

    Is the [item] in substantially the same condition as it was when you initially [saw or received] it?

6. Retrieve the exhibit from the witness and offer to admit it into evidence:

    "Your Honor, I offer into evidence what has been previously marked as PE-1 for ID as PE-1."

E.   CHAIN-OF-CUSTODY DOCUMENT (CoCD)

1. Mark the exhibit (ideally, this is done before the trial starts...).

2. Show opposing counsel the exhibit:

    "Your Honor, I am now showing opposing counsel what has been previously been marked as PE-1 for I.D. for their inspection and objection."

3. Ask the judge for permission to approach the witness with the exhibit:

    "Your Honor, may I have permission to approach the witness?"

4. Show the exhibit to the witness:

    "Your Honor, I am showing the witness what has been previously marked as PE-1 for ID."

5. Lay the foundation:

    - Establish what it is:

        "Do you recognize this?"

        "What is it?"

    - Establish that the witness has personal knowledge of the business' filing or records system:

        "Does the [entity or organization in question] have a [filing or records system]?"

        "And you are personally familiar with their [filing or records system]?"

    - Establish that the witness removed the record (CoCD) in question from a certain file:

        "Did you remove this [CoCD] from a file in that system?"

        "And from what file in that system did you remove it?"

    - Establish that the record (CoCD) in question was a proper file entry:

        "Was this [CoCD] a proper file entry in the system?"

- Establish that the Witness recognizes the exhibit as the record (CoCD) he removed from the file:

     "Do you recognize this [CoCD] as the record you removed from the file?"

- Witness specifies the basis on which he recognized the exhibit:

     "How do you recognize this [CoCD] as the record you removed from the file?"

6.   Retrieve the exhibit from the witness and offer to admit it into evidence:

     "Your Honor, I offer into evidence what has been previously marked as PE-1 for ID as PE-1."

F.   CHAIN-OF-CUSTODY DOCUMENT (CoCD) (Hearsay)

1.   Mark the exhibit (ideally, this is done before the trial starts...).

2.   Show opposing counsel the exhibit:

     "Your Honor, I am now showing opposing counsel what has been previously been marked as PE-1 for I.D. for their inspection and objection."

3.   Ask the judge for permission to approach the witness with the exhibit:

     "Your Honor, may I have permission to approach the witness?"

4.   Show the exhibit to the witness:

     "Your Honor, I am showing the witness what has been previously marked as PE-1 for ID."

5.   Lay the foundation:

- Establish what it is:

     "Do you recognize this?"

     "What is it?"

- The CoCD was prepared by a person having a relationship with the agency preparing the CoCD:

     "Who prepared this [CoCD]"?

     "Does [name] have a relationship with [the agency preparing the CoCD]?"

- The person had a duty to record the information on the CoCD:

     "Whose responsibility was it to complete this [CoCD]?"

     "So, it was [name]'s duty to fill in the [CoCD]?"

- The person had personal knowledge of the facts or events recorded in the CoCD:

> *From where did [name] get the information they used to fill in the [CoCD]?"*

- The CoCD was prepared contemporaneously with the events:

  > *"When did [name] complete the [CoCD]?"*

  > *"And this was at the same time as [the event in question]?"*

- It was a routine practice of the business to prepare CoCD:

  > *"When are the [CoCD]s normally completed?"*

  > *"And this was the routine practice of [the agency preparing the CoCD]?"*

- The CoCD was reduced to written form:

  > *"After the [CoCD] is completed, what happens to it next?"*

  > *"So, this is when it is [reduced to written form]?"*

- The CoCD was made in the regular course of business:

  > *"And this particular [CoCD] was completed in the normal or regular course of business of [the agency preparing the CoCD]?"*

6. Retrieve the exhibit from the witness and offer to admit it into evidence:

   > *"Your Honor, I offer into evidence what has been previously marked as PE-1 for ID as PE-1."*

G.   CHILD WITNESS

Depending on the jurisdiction, children below a certain age may be presumed incompetent. This rebuttable presumption may be overcome if the side offering the child as a witness can demonstrate the child possesses the requisite abilities to testify: the capacity to observe, remember, relate, and a recognition of the need to tell the truth.

In other jurisdictions there is no presumption of incompetence and it is simply a question of fact decided by the trial judge whether the child witness possesses the requisite abilities. In either jurisdiction, the side offering the witness should lay an adequate foundation for those abilities.

1. Call the witness. If opposing counsel objects to the child as an incompetent witness, offer to voir dire the child.

2. Lay the foundation by showing the four capacities:

   - Show the child has the capacity to observe:

     > *"How well do you see?"*

     > *"Do you wear glasses?"*

"How well do you hear?"

- Show the child has the capacity to remember:

  "How old are you?"

  "When is your birthday?"

  "What is your address?"

- Show the child has the capacity to relate:

  "What school do you go to?"

  "What grade are you in?"

  "What classes do you have?"

  "What do you learn in [topic] class?

- Show the child has a recognition of a duty to tell the truth:

  "What does it mean to tell the truth?"

  "Why should you tell the truth?"

  "What happens when you don't tell the truth?"

3.　　Offer the witness as competent:

　　　"Your Honor, I have no further questions about his competency. The child's answers demonstrate the capacities to observe, remember, and relate, and his recognition of a duty to tell the truth."

H.　　SPOUSE WITNESS

　　　The spouse as a witness is problematic depending on the jurisdiction. The common-law view is that if the marriage exists when the spouse is called, the accused has the power to prevent the spouse from testifying. The majority trend, adopted by the U.S. Supreme Court in *Trammel v. U.S.,*[2] is the spouse witness holds the power to choose to testify at their discretion and the accused may not object. Other jurisdictions provide that both the accused and the spouse witness may invoke privilege independently and prevent the testimony. Finally, some jurisdictions do not hold any spousal privilege and treat spouses like any other witness. Ensure you research the requirements in your jurisdiction before proceeding.

　　　Two exceptions may apply to disqualifying a spouse witness: the injured spouse doctrine, and pre-marital facts. If the spouse is the victim of the accused's charged offense, the accused cannot invoke the privilege to prevent the victim from testifying. In some jurisdictions, if the facts to which the spouse will testify occurred before the marriage, the jurisdiction may bar the accused from preventing the testimony.

---

[2] 445 U.S. 40 (1980).

1. Call the witness. Opposing counsel may object to the spouse as incompetent and seek to voir dire.

2. The opposing party will seek to show the witness has married the accused and the marriage still exists.

    • Show the witness married the accused:

        "Mr. Gordon, isn't it true that on July, 14, 1984, you married the accused, Margaret Gordon?"

        "Isn't it also true that Margaret Gordon is the accused in this case?"

    • Show the witness is still married to the accused:

        "Mr. Gordon, isn't it true that there have been no divorce proceedings since the marriage?"

        "And, further, that there haven't been any annulment proceedings since the marriage?"

3. The proponent of the witness will need to show the witness is the victim of the accused, or that the facts to be presented preceded the marriage.

    • Show the witness is the victim of the accused:

        "Mr. Gordon, I see you are missing your left arm. Is the person who cut off your arm in the courtroom today?"

    • Show the facts about which the spouse witness is to testify occurred before the marriage:

        "Mr. Gordon, when did Mrs. Gordon cut off your arm?"

        "And this was before your wedding to Mrs. Gordon on July 14, 1984?"

I.   LAY WITNESS WITH PERSONAL KNOWLEDGE

Common-law and the Federal Rules require that non-expert witnesses have first-hand knowledge of the facts or events about which they will testify. Although the bar set by FRE 104(b) is rather low, the side offering the witness may want to far exceed the minimal showing needed. The jury's consideration of what the witness testifies to is often tempered by how convinced the jury was that the witness actually observed the facts or events in the testimony. Persuasively showing the personal knowledge of the witness is key to the fact-finder's acceptance of the testimony as offered.

1. Call the witness.

2. Lay the foundation for the competency of the witness to testify by showing the witness was in a location to perceive the event, that they did perceive the event, and that they remember the perceived event.

    • Show the witness was in such a position as to be able to perceive the event (normally, observation is by sight, but any sense may have been used):

> *"Mr. Gordon, you testified that at 7:00 p.m. on the night of June 22, 2008, you were standing on the corner of 5th Avenue and Main Street. Could you see the entire intersection from where you were standing?"*

> *"What direction were you facing?"*

> *"Was there any other traffic present other than the two vehicles that were involved in the collision?"*

- Show the witness did perceive the event in question:

> *"Did you see the collision?"*

> *"What did you see?"*

> *"Could you hear anything?"*

- Show the witness remembers what they perceived (why they remember it so well, how it is significant to them):

> *"Mr. Gordon, how well do you remember seeing the collision?"*

> *"Why do you remember the collision so well?"*

J.   LAY OPINIONS

Two types of lay opinions commonly accepted in courts are the collective fact opinion and the skilled lay observer opinion. The collective fact opinion, also known as a shorthand rendition opinion, is based on the concept that lay persons commonly and reliably draw inferences from perceived facts and form an opinion on subjects such as height, distance, speed, color and identity by virtue of common human experience.

1. Call the witness.

2. Lay the foundation for the opinion of the lay witness by showing the witness was in a location to observe, that they did observe, that they observed enough to form a reliable opinion, and that the witness can state the opinion.

- Show the witness was in a position to observe the event about which they formed an opinion:

> *"Mr. Gordon, where were you standing at the intersection of 5th Avenue and Main Street?"*

> *"What direction were you facing?"*

- Show the witness did observe the event about which they formed an opinion:

> *"And from this position, Mr. Gordon, what could you see?"*

- Show the witness observed enough of the event to form a reliable opinion:

  "How long were you able to see the truck as it approached the intersection?"

- Have the witness state their opinion:

  "Do you have an opinion of the truck's speed?"

  "In your opinion, what was the speed of the truck as it approached the intersection?"

The other type of lay opinion is the skilled lay observer opinion and includes lay opinions about someone's handwriting style, the sound of that person's, or that person's sanity. All of these opinions require intimate familiarity with the particular subject by the witness through their repeated exposure and observation.

1. Call the witness.

2. Lay the foundation for the skilled lay opinion by showing the witness is familiar with the subject, the subject's voice, or the subject's handwriting through repeated prior opportunities for observation.

    - Show the witness is familiar with the subject:

      "Mr. Gordon, how long have you known Ned Miller?"

      "How did you come to meet Mr. Miller?"

      "In the time Mr. Miller has been your neighbor, have you had occasion to spend time with him?"

      "Are you familiar with the sound of Mr. Miller's voice?"

      "Have you ever heard Mr. Miller speak?"

      "How often have you spoken with Mr. Miller?"

      "Under what circumstances have you heard Mr. Miller speak?"

      "How well do you know Mr. Miller's handwriting style?"

      "How did you become familiar with Mr. Miller's handwriting?"

K.   EXPERT OPINION

The Federal Rules allow an expert to testify when the trier of fact requires assistance in understanding "scientific, technical, or other specialized knowledge ... to determine a fact in issue."[3] While the standard in the Federal rules is simply that the expert just possess more knowledge than the trier of fact, in *Daubert v. Merrell Dow Pharmaceuticals, Inc.*, the U.S. Supreme Court held that the trial judge must ensure the expert's testimony "rests on a

---

3 FRE 702.

reliable foundation and is relevant to the task at hand."[4]

The burden is on the side presenting the witness to show the witness is an expert. Reliable foundations for an expert's knowledge may include presenting information on:

- Academic degrees earned by the witness in their field
- Specialized training in their field
- Professional licenses held by the witness in their field
- Length of time spent by the witness in their field.
- Publications by the witness in their field.
- Membership in professional organizations in the field.
- Honors or prizes presented to the witness.
- Previous experience as an expert witness on this topic.

Some or all of these areas may be touched on when laying the foundation for your expert, depending on the specific nature of their expertise and the needs of your case. Your case analysis will identify these needs.

1.   Call the witness.

- Show the witness has specialized knowledge:

    "Mr. Gordon, please introduce yourself to the jury."

    "Where did you go to school?"

    "Do you have a degree?"

    "What is your degree in?"

- Show the witness has specialized training:

    "Do you have any technical training?"

    "Where did you receive this training?"

    "When did you complete this training?

- Show the witness has specialized experience:

    "After your technical training, did you work in this field?"

    "How long have you been the operations safety officer for the Calusa County Nuclear Power Plant?"

    "What are your duties as the operations safety officer at the Calusa County Nuclear Power Plant?"

    "Your honor, I tender Mr. Gordon to this court as an expert in nuclear power plant operations."

---

[4] 509 U.S. 579, 597 (1993).

These are sample questions; design your foundation questions with the specific expert witness and subject matter in mind.

L.   BIAS

The bias a witness holds is a potential means of impeachment. There are no particular requirements for laying a foundation for bias evidence; the side seeking to show bias may prove any fact or event that logically shows the bias.

1.   Call the witness.

2.   Lay the foundation by proving an event that indicates bias.

*   Show when and where the event occurred:

    "Mr. Gordon, isn't it true that at 7:00 p.m. on the night of June 22, 2008, you were present at O'Neil's Irish Pub?"

*   Show who was present at the event:

    "Mr. Gordon, isn't it also true that the defendants, Nicholas Cox and James Thaler, were both there with you at O'Neil's Irish Pub that night?"

*   Show what occurred at the event:

    "And, Mr. Gordon, finally, isn't it true that you, and Nick, and James, were all drinking beer at O'Neil's Irish Pub that night?"

Note: it is probably not necessary to get the witness to concede their bias. It is unlikely the witness would actually admit to it, and trying to force it may make counsel appear argumentative. It is often better to simply prove the fact or event showing bias and then later invite the jury to make the inference during closing arguments.

M.   HABIT

Habit evidence may be used as circumstantial proof of conduct. Unlike character evidence, which is usually only admissible if the accused first raises the issue, habit evidence may be admitted by either side. The elements of the foundation for habit evidence are:

*   The witness is familiar with the person or business.

*   The witness has been with the person or business for a substantial length of time.

*   The witness has an opinion about a specific behavioral pattern of the person or business.

*   The witness has observed the conformity of the person or business with the specific behavioral pattern on numerous occasions.

Some jurisdictions may additionally require that there be either no eyewitnesses to the specific conduct involved in the case, or that the specific conduct be corroborated by an eyewitness that described the conduct as consistent with the habit.

1.   Call the witness.

• Show the witness is familiar with the person or business:

   "Mr. Gordon, are you familiar with the UtoteEm in Calusa County?"

   "How is it you are familiar with the UtoteEm?"

• Show the witness has been with the person or business for a substantial length of time:

   "How long have you been shopping at the UtoteEm?"

   "How often do you shop at the UtoteEm?"

• Show the witness has an opinion about a specific behavioral pattern of the person or business:

   "When shopping at the UtoteEm did you ever observe the attendant use the cash register?"

   "How did the attendant use the cash register when you shopped at the UtoteEm?"

   "How consistently did the attendant use the cash register when you shopped at the UtoteEm?"

• The witness has observed the conformity of the person or business with the specific behavioral pattern on numerous occasions

   "How often did you see the attendant use the cash register at the UtoteEm?"

   "Have you ever seen the attendant at the UtoteEm fail to use the cash register?"

   "Have you ever seen the attendant at the UtoteEm use the cash register in any other way?"

Don't seek to have the witness actually state their opinion; that would be improper. Instead, similar to bias evidence, during closing arguments argue in favor of the inference you want the jury to make.

N.   REPUTATION

In most jurisdictions, the character of the accused does not become an issue unless the accused presents character evidence, that is, something more than simply testifying on their own behalf. Character evidence presented by the prosecution is normally only allowed in rebuttal.

1.   Call the witness.

- Show the witness is a member of the same community as the accused (home, work, or social):

  "Mr. Gordon, who is Marlin Fischer?"

  "How do you know Marlin Fischer?"

  "Where does Mr. Fischer live?"

  "Where do you live, Mr. Gordon?"

  "And how close do you live to Mr. Fischer?"

- Show the witness has been a member of that community for a substantial period:

  "Mr. Gordon, how long have you lived in your current residence?"

  "How long has Mr. Fischer lived next door to you?"

  "How long have you known Marlin Fischer?"

- Show the accused has a reputation in that community, either a general reputation or a reputation for a specific character trait:

  "Mr. Gordon, does Mr. Fischer have a particular reputation in your neighborhood?"

- Show the witness knows the reputation:

  "Do you know that reputation?"

- Have the witness state the reputation:

  "What is that reputation?"

O. PRIOR BAD ACTS RESULTING IN CONVICTION

Proof that a witness other than the accused has suffered a past conviction can be a telling blow during impeachment and the Federal Rules allow these facts to be admitted under certain circumstances, especially if one of the elements of the crime of conviction involved dishonesty or false statements.[5] While all courts allow this method of impeachment, they differ on what offenses may be used. Ensure you check your jurisdiction's standards as you plan your cross examination.

1. Begin cross examining the witness.

- Show the witness is the person who suffered the prior conviction:

  "Isn't it true, Mr. Gordon, that you are the same Bufford Gordon who was once convicted of a felony?"

- Show the conviction is for a crime the jurisdiction considers impeaching:

---

5 FRE 609(a).

"Isn't it a fact, Mr. Gordon, that felony was smuggling prescription drugs?"

• Show the conviction was entered in a particular jurisdiction:

"Isn't it correct that you were convicted of that crime in Calusa County?"

• Show the conviction was entered in a particular year:

"And isn't it also correct that you were convicted of that crime in 2005?"

• Show the witness received a particular sentence:

"And, Mr. Gordon, isn't it also a fact that as a result of that conviction, you were sentenced to 10 years in prison for smuggling?"

If you are using a copy of the judgment, there is an additional element to the foundation:

• Show the copy of the judgment is authentic:

"Your Honor, may this be marked as D.E. 1 for I.D.?

"Please let the record show I am showing what has been marked as D.E. 1 for I.D. to opposing counsel."

"I now offer D.E. 1 for I.D. into evidence as D.E. 1., a copy of the judgment including a properly executed attesting certificate, making this exhibit self-authenticating under Rule 902."

P. PRIOR BAD ACTS *NOT* RESULTING IN CONVICTION

Most jurisdictions allow impeaching a witness on cross examination with proof the witness has committed untruthful acts. However, there is a risk: because extrinsic evidence of the untruthful act may not be admitted,[6] opposing counsel must accept whatever answer the witness gives.

1. Begin cross examining the witness.

• Show when the witness committed the untruthful act:

"Mr. Gordon, isn't it a fact that in 1998 you filed a false tax return?"

• Show where the witness committed the untruthful act:

"Mr. Gordon, isn't it also true that you submitted this false tax return to the IRS from Calusa County?"

• Show the nature of the act reflects against the character of the witness for truthfulness:

---

[6] FRE 608(b)(1), a remnant of the common-law collateral fact rule which limits the impeaching counsel to intrinsic impeachment when the issue relates only to the credibility of the witness.

"Mr. Gordon, in this tax return, you claimed that your wife requires 24-hour care. That wasn't true, was it?"

"You also claimed, Mr. Gordon, in this 1998 return, that your 10-year-old son had been wounded in Vietnam. This wasn't true, was it?"

"And, Mr. Gordon, when you tried to claim nine children as dependents, including one who was a member of the clergy, you were not telling the truth, were you?"

Q.   OTHER CRIMES/UNCHARGED MISCONDUCT

The Federal Rules allow the prosecution to introduce evidence of other crimes or of uncharged misconduct, not to show the accused is a law-breaking immoral person, but to show other things, such as motive, intent, opportunity, knowledge, etc.[7] If the evidence of the uncharged act is logically relevant to a fact in issue other than character, it may be admitted. The trier of fact will decide whether the logical relevance of the evidence outweighs its prejudicial nature.

1. Call the witness (assume the defendant has been charged with possession of stolen goods).

   - Show where the other criminal act or uncharged misconduct occurred:

     "Mr. Gordon, please tell the jury where you were when you first encountered the defendant, Snake Berman."

   - Show when the other criminal act or uncharged misconduct occurred:

     And, Mr. Gordon, when was it that you first came into contact with Mr. Berman?"

   - Show the nature of the other criminal act or uncharged misconduct:

     "Mr. Gordon, please describe to the jury what happened when the defendant entered your home."

     "Mr. Gordon, when Mr. Berman left your house, was he carrying anything?"

   - Show the accused committed the other criminal act or uncharged misconduct:

     "How well did you see Mr. Berman when he left carrying your television?"

     "How close were you to Mr. Berman when he took your television?"

     "Is Snake Berman in this court room right now?"

   - Show the relevance of the other criminal act or uncharged misconduct

---

[7] FRE 404(b).

to the charged offense:

> *"Mr. Gordon, did Mr. Berman have permission to take your TV set?"*

> *"Did you give anyone permission to take your television?"*

> *"Did you report the theft to the police?"*

> *"After you reported your television as stolen, did you get a police report number?"*

The defense will have the right to seek a limiting instruction, under FRE 105, where the judge will inform the jury they may not use this evidence as general character evidence but only use it to decide the existence of the fact the evidence was admitted to prove (the accused's motive, intent, opportunity, knowledge, etc).

R.   CHARACTER TRAIT OF UNTRUTHFULNESS

Extrinsic evidence, usually a second witness, may be used to impeach the credibility of a witness. This is usually in the form of a second witness, who testifies to the trait in the witness being impeached.

1. Call the second witness.

   - Show the second witness is a member of the same community (home or social) as the witness being impeached:

     > *"Mr. Gordon, who is Marlin Fischer?"*

     > *"How do you know Marlin Fischer?"*

   - Show the second witness has been a member of that community for a substantial period of time:

     > *"How long have you been a next-door neighbor of Marlin Fischer?"*

     > *"How long have you lived in Calusa County?"*

     > *"How long have you attended the same church with Marlin Fischer?"*

   - Show the witness being impeached has a reputation for untruthfulness in the community:

     > *"Mr. Gordon, does Marlin Fischer have a reputation for truthfulness or untruthfulness in Calusa County?"*

   - Show the second witness knows of the reputation for untruthfulness of the witness being impeached:

     > *"What is that reputation?"*

     > *"Given Mr. Fischer's reputation, would you believe him under oath?"*

Note: some jurisdictions allow the second witness to add that, considering the reputation of the witness being impeached, the second witness would not believe him or her under oath.

S.   CHARACTER TRAIT OF TRUTHFULNESS

Proving the character trait of truthfulness in a witness is necessary after the opposing side has attempted to impeach the witness and rehabilitation is necessary. Typically after the second witness impeaches the first witness, the court will allow the proponent of the impeached witness to call a third witness, to testify to the reputation for truthfulness of the impeached witness.

The elements of the foundation are the same as the Character Trait for Untruthfulness (above).

1.   Call the third witness.

- Show the third witness is a member of the same community (home or social) as the witness being impeached:

    "Reverend Miller, who is Marlin Fischer?"

    "How do you know Mr. Fischer?"

- Show the third witness has been a member of that community for a substantial period of time:

    "How long has Marlin Fischer been a member of your church?"

- Show the witness being impeached has a reputation for truthfulness in the community:

    "Reverend Miller, does Marlin Fischer have a reputation for truthfulness or untruthfulness in Calusa County?"

- Show the third witness knows of the reputation for truthfulness of the witness being impeached:

    "What is that reputation?"

    "Given Mr. Fischer's reputation, Reverend Miller, would you believe him under oath?"

T.   PRIOR INCONSISTENT STATEMENT

Another means of impeaching the credibility of a witness is to show they made prior statements that are inconsistent with their current testimony. The fact of these inconsistencies calls into question the ability of the witness to recall and relate what was observed.

1.   Begin to cross-examine the witness.

- Get the witness to commit to the testimony given during direct examination:

    "Mr. Hightower, you just testified that Mr. Gordon was not at your Planet Calusa County restaurant the night of the incident, correct?"

- Show the witness made an earlier statement at a certain place (if the earlier statement was in writing, where it was written is not essential):

    "Mr. Hightower, isn't it true that after the incident you were present during a meeting at the Calusa County Town Hall to discuss what had happened?"

- Show the witness made an earlier statement at a certain time:

    And, Mr. Hightower, that meeting at Town Hall was at 11:00 p.m., immediately after the incident occurred?"

- Show that certain persons were present when the witness made the earlier statement:

    Mr. Hightower, weren't Doctor Jones and Mayor Stevens both present with you at this meeting?

- Show the earlier statement made by the witness was of a certain tenor:

    "In that meeting with Doctor Jones and Mayor Stevens, didn't you say that Mr. Gordon was present and participating in the all-you-can-eat buffet, and you were concerned about your losses?"

- Show the earlier statement made by the witness is more likely reliable than the present testimony:

    "Isn't it a fact, Mr. Hightower, in that point of time, that conversation was closer to the incident than your testimony today?"

    "Isn't it a fact your memory was fresher then?"

Note: it may be preferable to not force the final concession from the witness. Merely elicit the facts of the statement's timing and then argue the relative reliability of the earlier statement compared to the testimony during your closing arguments. Indeed, the judge may find these final questions are objectionably argumentative.

U.   PRIOR CONSISTENT STATEMENT

Similar to recovering from an impeachment for untruthfulness, when a witness has been impeached for making prior inconsistent statements, it may be necessary to rehabilitate them by showing past statements that are consistent with their testimony. For procedural reasons, many jurisdictions impose a requirement that the prior consistent statement precede the prior inconsistent statement or that the prior consistent statement have been made before the witness had any motive to lie.

1.   Call the witness.

- Show where the prior consistent statement was made:

    "Mr. Hightower, after the incident at your Planet Calusa County restaurant, did you speak to anyone there?"

- Show when the prior consistent statement was made:

  "And this interview took place immediately after the incident?"

- Show who was present when the prior consistent statement was made:

  "Was anyone with Brad Bradley during the interview?"

- Show the tenor of the prior consistent statement:

  "During that interview, did you tell Mr. Bradley who was present in the restaurant?"

  "During that interview, what did you say to Mr. Bradley about Mr. Gordon?"

- If a temporal requirement must be met, show the prior consistent statement preceded (1) the prior inconsistent statement or (2) any motive on the part of the witness to lie:

  "Was this interview with Brad Bradley before or after the meeting at the Town Hall with Doctor Jones and Mayor Stevens?"

  "Was this interview with Brad Bradley before or after you had been contacted by attorneys regarding this legal action?"

Typically the judge will be asked to give the jury a limiting instruction, that although the jurors could consider the testimony for credibility purposes, they should not treat the prior statement as proof "Mr. Gordon" was (or was not) present during the incident.

Chapter 18: EXCERPTS FROM THE DELAWARE RULES OF PROFESSIONAL CONDUCT

Preamble: A lawyer's responsibilities. 634
Rule 1.0. Terminology 639
Rule 1.1. Competence..640
Rule 1.2. Scope of representation...................................640
Rule 1.3. Diligence 641
Rule 1.4. Communication...641
Rule 1.6. Confidentiality of information 642
Rule 1.7. Conflict of interest: Current clients...............647
Rule 1.8. Conflict of interest: 648
Rule 1.9. Duties to former clients.................................649
Rule 1.10. Imputation of conflicts of interest: General rule.........650
Rule 1.11. Special conflicts of interest..........................651
Rule 1.12. Former judge, arbitrator, mediator 652
Rule 1.13. Organization as client...................................653
Rule 1.14. Client with diminished capacity...................654
Rule 1.16. Declining or terminating representation 655
Rule 1.18. Duties to prospective client..........................657
Rule 2.1. Advisor 658
Rule 2.4. Lawyer serving as third-party neutral 658
Rule 3.1. Meritorious claims and contentions 658
Rule 3.2. Expediting litigation......................................658
Rule 3.3. Candor toward the tribunal 659
Rule 3.4. Fairness to opposing party and counsel 663
Rule 3.5. Impartiality and decorum of the tribunal 665
Rule 3.6. Trial publicity..666
Rule 3.8. Special responsibilities of a prosecutor..........671
Rule 4.3. Dealing with unrepresented person................673
Rule 4.4. Respect for rights of third persons 674
Rule 5.1. Responsibilities of Supervisors......................675
Rule 5.3. Responsibilities regarding non-lawyer assistants 675
Rule 5.4. Professional independence of a lawyer...........676
Rule 6.2. Accepting appointments.................................677
Rule 8.1. Bar admission and disciplinary matters 678
Rule 8.2. Judicial and legal officials.............................678
Rule 8.3. Reporting professional misconduct................678
Rule 8.4. Misconduct..679

The following excerpts from the Delaware Rules of Professional Conduct have been heavily edited for brevity and applicability to the specific rules applicable to trial work. The included rules and comments should be helpful to advocates when studying how the rules of professional conduct interact with the trial process. In some instances the comments for rules have been removed. In other sections both the rules and their comments were omitted in their entirety for the sake of brevity and clarity. These rules are a beginning reference point and a refresher of text for those issues identified and discussed in the previous chapters. Before relying upon a final interpretation of the rule in question you should take the time to refer to the rules of professional responsibility for your jurisdiction.

The Delaware rules were based almost entirely upon the Model Rules of Professional Conduct promulgated and approved by the American Bar Association, and as public law are in the public domain.

THE DELAWARE LAWYERS' RULES OF PROFESSIONAL CONDUCT

(Effective July 1, 2003)

Preamble: A lawyer's responsibilities.

[1] A lawyer, as a member of the legal profession, is a representative of clients, an officer of the legal system and a public citizen having special responsibility for the quality of justice.

[2] As a representative of clients, a lawyer performs various functions. As advisor, a lawyer provides a client with an informed understanding of the client's legal rights and obligations and explains their practical implications. As advocate, a lawyer zealously asserts the client's position under the rules of the adversary system. As negotiator, a lawyer seeks a result advantageous to the client but consistent with requirements of honest dealings with others. As an evaluator, a lawyer acts by examining a client's legal affairs and reporting about them to the client or to others.

[3] In addition to these representational functions, a lawyer may serve as a third-party neutral, a nonrepresentational role helping the parties to resolve a dispute or other matter. Some of these Rules apply directly to lawyers who are or have served as third-party neutrals. See, e.g., Rules 1.12 and 2.4. In addition, there are Rules that apply to lawyers who are not active in the practice of law or to practicing lawyers even when they are acting in a nonprofessional capacity. For example, a lawyer who commits fraud in the conduct of a

business is subject to discipline for engaging in conduct involving dishonesty, fraud, deceit or misrepresentation. See Rule 8.4.

[4] In all professional functions a lawyer should be competent, prompt and diligent. A lawyer should maintain communication with a client concerning the representation. A lawyer should keep in confidence information relating to representation of a client except so far as disclosure is required or permitted by the Rules of Professional Conduct or other law.

[5] A lawyer's conduct should conform to the requirements of the law, both in professional service to clients and in the lawyer's business and personal affairs. A lawyer should use the law's procedures only for legitimate purposes and not to harass or intimidate others. A lawyer should demonstrate respect for the legal system and for those who serve it, including judges, other lawyers and public officials. While it is a lawyer's duty, when necessary, to challenge the rectitude of official action, it is also a lawyer's duty to uphold legal process.

[6] As a public citizen, a lawyer should seek improvement of the law, access to the legal system, the administration of justice and the quality of service rendered by the legal profession. As a member of a learned profession, a lawyer should cultivate knowledge of the law beyond its use for clients, employ that knowledge in reform of the law and work to strengthen legal education. In addition, a lawyer should further the public's understanding of and confidence in the rule of law and the justice system because legal institutions in a constitutional democracy depend on popular participation and support to maintain their authority. A lawyer should be mindful of deficiencies in the administration of justice and of the fact that the poor, and sometimes persons who are not poor, cannot afford adequate legal assistance. Therefore, all lawyers should devote professional time and resources and use civic influence to ensure equal access to our system of justice for all those who because of economic or social barriers cannot afford or secure adequate legal counsel. A lawyer should aid the legal profession in pursuing these objectives and should help the bar regulate itself in the public interest.

[7] Many of a lawyer's professional responsibilities are prescribed in the Rules of Professional Conduct, as well as substantive and procedural law. However, a lawyer is also guided by personal conscience and the approbation of professional peers. A lawyer should strive to attain the highest level of skill, to improve the law and the legal profession and to exemplify the legal profession's ideals of public service.

[8] A lawyer's responsibilities as a representative of clients, an officer of the legal system and a public citizen are usually harmonious. Thus, when an op-

posing party is well represented, a lawyer can be a zealous advocate on behalf of a client and at the same time assume that justice is being done. So also, a lawyer can be sure that preserving client confidences ordinarily serves the public interest because people are more likely to seek legal advice, and thereby heed their legal obligations, when they know their communications will be private.

[9] In the nature of law practice, however, conflicting responsibilities are encountered. Virtually all difficult ethical problems arise from conflict between a lawyer's responsibilities to clients, to the legal system and to the lawyer's own interest in remaining an ethical person while earning a satisfactory living. The Rules of Professional conduct often prescribe terms for resolving such conflicts. Within the framework of these Rules, however, many difficult issues of professional discretion can arise. Such issues must be resolved through the exercise of sensitive professional and moral judgment guided by the basic principles underlying the Rules. These principles include the lawyer's obligation zealously to protect and pursue a client's legitimate interests, within the bounds of the law, while maintaining a professional, courteous and civil attitude toward all persons involved in the legal system.

[10] The legal profession is largely self-governing. Although other professions also have been granted powers of self-government, the legal profession is unique in this respect because of the close relationship between the profession and the processes of government and law enforcement. This connection is manifested in the fact that ultimate authority over the legal profession is vested largely in the courts.

[11] To the extent that lawyers meet the obligations of their professional calling, the occasion for government regulation is obviated. Self-regulation also helps maintain the legal profession's independence from government domination. An independent legal profession is an important force in preserving government under law, for abuse of legal authority is more readily challenged by a profession whose members are not dependent on government for the right to practice.

[12] The legal profession's relative autonomy carries with it special responsibilities of self-government. The profession has a responsibility to assure that its regulations are conceived in the public interest and not in furtherance of parochial or self interested concerns of the bar. Every lawyer is responsible for observance of the Rules of Professional Conduct. A lawyer should also aid in securing their observance by other lawyers. Neglect of these responsibilities compromises the independence of the profession and the public interest which it serves.

[13] Lawyers play a vital role in the preservation of society. The fulfillment of this role requires an understanding by lawyers of their relationship to our legal system. The Rules of Professional Conduct, when properly applied, serve to define that relationship.

SCOPE

[14] The Rules of Professional Conduct are rules of reason. They should be interpreted with reference to the purposes of legal representation and of the law itself. Some of the Rules are imperatives, cast in the terms "shall" or "shall not." These define proper conduct for purposes of professional discipline. Others, generally cast in the term "may," are permissive and define areas under the Rules in which the lawyer has discretion to exercise professional judgment. No disciplinary action should be taken when the lawyer chooses not to act or acts within the bounds of such discretion. Other Rules define the nature of relationships between the lawyer and others. The Rules are thus partly obligatory and disciplinary and partly constitutive and descriptive in that they define a lawyer's professional role. Many of the Comments use the term "should." Comments do not add obligations to the Rules but provide guidance for practicing in compliance with the Rules.

[15] The Rules presuppose a larger legal context shaping the lawyer's role. That context includes court rules and statutes relating to matters of licensure, laws defining specific obligations of lawyers and substantive and procedural law in general. The Comments are sometimes used to alert lawyers to their responsibilities under such other law.

[16] Compliance with the Rules, as with all law in an open society, depends primarily upon understanding and voluntary compliance, secondarily upon reenforcement by peer and public opinion and finally, when necessary, upon enforcement through disciplinary proceedings. The Rules do not, however, exhaust the moral and ethical considerations that should inform a lawyer, for no worthwhile human activity can be completely defined by legal rules. The Rules simply provide a framework for the ethical practice of law.

[17] Furthermore, for purposes of determining the lawyer's authority and responsibility, principles of substantive law external to these Rules determine whether a client-lawyer relationship exists. Most of the duties flowing from the client-lawyer relationship attach only after the client has requested the lawyer to render legal services and the lawyer has agreed to do so. But there are some duties, such as that of confidentiality under Rule 1.6, that attach when the lawyer agrees to consider whether a client-lawyer relationship shall

be established. See Rule 1.18. Whether a client-lawyer relationship exists for any specific purpose can depend on the circumstances and may be a question of fact.

[18] Under various legal provisions, including constitutional, statutory and common law, the responsibilities of government lawyers may include authority concerning legal matters that ordinarily reposes in the client in private client-lawyer relationships. For example, a lawyer for a government agency may have authority on behalf of the government to decide upon settlement or whether to appeal from an adverse judgment. Such authority in various respects is generally vested in the attorney general and the state's attorney in state government, and their federal counterparts, and the same may be true of other government law officers. Also, lawyers under the supervision of these officers may be authorized to represent several government agencies in intragovernmental legal controversies in circumstances where a private lawyer could not represent multiple private clients. These Rules do not abrogate any such authority.

[19] Failure to comply with an obligation or prohibition imposed by a Rule is a basis for invoking the disciplinary process. The Rules presuppose that disciplinary assessment of a lawyer's conduct will be made on the basis of the facts and circumstances as they existed at the time of the conduct in question and in recognition of the fact that a lawyer often has to act upon uncertain or incomplete evidence of the situation. Moreover, the Rules presuppose that whether or not discipline should be imposed for a violation, and the severity of a sanction, depend on all the circumstances, such as the willfulness and seriousness of the violation, extenuating factors and whether there have been previous violations.

[20] Violation of a Rule should not itself give rise to a cause of action against a lawyer nor should it create any presumption in such a case that a legal duty has been breached. In addition, violation of a Rule does not necessarily warrant any other nondisciplinary remedy, such as disqualification of a lawyer in pending litigation. The rules are designed to provide guidance to lawyers and to provide a structure for regulating conduct through disciplinary agencies. They are not designed to be a basis for civil liability. Furthermore, the purpose of the Rules can be subverted when they are invoked by opposing parties as procedural weapons. The fact that a Rule is a just basis for a lawyer's self-assessment, or for sanctioning a lawyer under the administration of a disciplinary authority, does not imply that an antagonist in a collateral proceeding or transaction has standing to seek enforcement of the Rule.

[21] The Comment accompanying each Rule explains and illustrates the meaning and purpose of the Rule. The Preamble and this note on Scope provide general orientation. The Comments are intended as guides to interpretation, but the text of each rule is authoritative.

Rule 1.0. Terminology

(a) "Belief" or "believes" denotes that the person involved actually supposed the fact in question to be true. A person's belief may be inferred from circumstances.

(b) "Confirmed in writing," when used in reference to the informed consent of a person, denotes informed consent that is given in writing by the person or a writing that a lawyer promptly transmits to the person confirming an oral informed consent. See paragraph (e) for the definition of "informed consent." If it is not feasible to obtain or transmit the writing at the time the person gives informed consent, then the lawyer must obtain or transmit it within a reasonable time thereafter.

(c) "Firm" or "law firm" denotes a lawyer or lawyers in a law partnership, professional corporation, sole proprietorship or other association authorized to practice law; or lawyers employed in a legal services organization or the legal department of a corporation or other organization.

(d) "Fraud" or "fraudulent" denotes conduct that is fraudulent under the substantive or procedural law of the applicable jurisdiction and has a purpose to deceive.

(e) "Informed consent" denotes the agreement by a person to a proposed course of conduct after the lawyer has communicated adequate information and explanation about the material risks of and reasonably available alternatives to the proposed course of conduct.

(f) "Knowingly," "known," or "knows" denotes actual knowledge of the fact in question. A person's knowledge may be inferred from circumstances.
(g) "Partner" denotes a member of a partnership, a shareholder in a law firm organized as a professional corporation, or a member of an association authorized to practice law.

(h) "Reasonable" or "reasonably" when used in relation to conduct by a lawyer denotes the conduct of a reasonably prudent and competent lawyer.

(i) "Reasonable belief" or "reasonably believes" when used in reference to a lawyer denotes that the lawyer believes the matter in question and that the circumstances are such that the belief is reasonable.

(j) "Reasonably should know" when used in reference to a lawyer denotes that a lawyer of reasonable prudence and competence would ascertain the matter in question.

(k) "Screened" denotes the isolation of a lawyer from any participation in a matter through the timely imposition of procedures within a firm that are reasonably adequate under the circumstances to protect information that the isolated lawyer is obligated to protect under these Rules or other law.

(l) "Substantial" when used in reference to degree or extent denotes a material matter of clear and weighty importance.

(m) "Tribunal" denotes a court, an arbitrator in a binding arbitration proceeding or a legislative body, administrative agency or other body acting in an adjudicative capacity. A legislative body, administrative agency or other body acts in an adjudicative capacity when a neutral official, after the presentation of evidence or legal argument by a party or parties, will render a binding legal judgment directly affecting a party's interests in a particular matter.

(n) "Writing" or "written" denotes a tangible or electronic record of a communication or representation, including handwriting, typewriting, printing, photostating, photography, audio or video recording and e-mail. A "signed" writing includes an electronic sound, symbol or process attached to or logically associated with a writing and executed or adopted by a person with the intent to sign the writing.

Rule 1.1. Competence

A lawyer shall provide competent representation to a client. Competent representation requires the legal knowledge, skill, thoroughness and preparation reasonably necessary for the representation.

Rule 1.2. Scope of representation

(a) Subject to paragraphs (c) and (d), a lawyer shall abide by a client's decisions concerning the objectives of representation and, as required by Rule

1.4, shall consult with the client as to the means by which they are to be pursued. A lawyer may take such action on behalf of the client as is impliedly authorized to carry out the representation. A lawyer shall abide by a client's decision whether to settle a matter. In a criminal case, the lawyer shall abide by the client's decision, after consultation with the lawyer, as to a plea to be entered, whether to waive jury trial and whether the client will testify.

(b) A lawyer's representation of a client, including representation by appointment, does not constitute an endorsement of the client's political, economic, social or moral views or activities.

(c) A lawyer may limit the scope of the representation if the limitation is reasonable under the circumstances and the client gives informed consent.

(d) A lawyer shall not counsel a client to engage, or assist a client, in conduct that the lawyer knows is criminal or fraudulent, but a lawyer may discuss the legal consequences of any proposed course of conduct with a client and may counsel or assist a client to make a good faith effort to determine the validity, scope, meaning or application of the law.

Rule 1.3. Diligence

A lawyer shall act with reasonable diligence and promptness in representing a client.

Rule 1.4. Communication

(a) A lawyer shall:
(1) promptly inform the client of any decision or circumstance with respect to which the client's informed consent, as defined in Rule 1.0(e), is required by these Rules; (2) reasonably consult with the client about the means by which the client's objectives are to be accomplished; (3) keep the client reasonably informed about the status of the matter; (4) promptly comply with reasonable requests for information; and (5) consult with the client about any relevant limitation on the lawyer's conduct when the lawyer knows that the client expects assistance not permitted by the Rules of Professional Conduct or other law.

(b) A lawyer shall explain a matter to the extent reasonably necessary to permit the client to make informed decisions regarding the representation.

Rule 1.5. Fees - Omitted.

Rule 1.6. Confidentiality of information

(a) A lawyer shall not reveal information relating to the representation of a client unless the client gives informed consent, the disclosure is impliedly authorized in order to carry out the representation, or the disclosure is permitted by paragraph (b).

(b) A lawyer may reveal information relating to the representation of a client to the extent the lawyer reasonably believes necessary: (1) to prevent reasonably certain death or substantial bodily harm; (2) to prevent the client from committing a crime or fraud that is reasonably certain to result in substantial injury to the financial interests or property of another and in furtherance of which the client has used or is using the lawyer's services; (3) to prevent, mitigate, or rectify substantial injury to the financial interests or property of another that is reasonably certain to result or has resulted from the client's commission of a crime or fraud in furtherance of which the client has used the lawyer's services; (4) to secure legal advice about the lawyer's compliance with these Rules; (5) to establish a claim or defense on behalf of the lawyer in a controversy between the lawyer and the client, to establish a defense to a criminal charge or civil claim against the lawyer based upon conduct in which the client was involved, or to respond to allegations in any proceeding concerning the lawyer's representation of the client; or (6) to comply with other law or a court order.

COMMENT

[1] This Rule governs the disclosure by a lawyer of information relating to the representation of a client during the lawyer's representation of the client. See Rule 1.18 for the lawyer's duties with respect to information provided to the lawyer by a prospective client, Rule 1.9(c)(2) for the lawyer's duty not to reveal information relating to the lawyer's prior representation of a former client and Rules 1.8(b) and 1.9(c)(1) for the lawyer's duties with respect to the use of such information to the disadvantage of clients and former clients.

[2] A fundamental principle in the client-lawyer relationship is that, in the absence of the client's informed consent, the lawyer must not reveal information relating to the representation. See Rule 1.0(e) for the definition of informed consent. This contributes to the trust that is the hallmark of the client-lawyer relationship. The client is thereby encouraged to seek legal assistance and to communicate fully and frankly with the lawyer even as to embarrassing or

legally damaging subject matter. The lawyer needs this information to represent the client effectively and, if necessary, to advise the client to refrain from wrongful conduct. Almost without exception, clients come to lawyers in order to determine their rights and what is, in the complex of laws and regulations, deemed to be legal and correct. Based upon experience, lawyers know that almost all clients follow the advice given, and the law is upheld.

[3] The principle of client-lawyer confidentiality is given effect by related bodies of law: the attorney-client privilege, the work product doctrine and the rule of confidentiality established in professional ethics. The attorney-client privilege and work product doctrine apply in judicial and other proceedings in which a lawyer may be called as a witness or otherwise required to produce evidence concerning a client. The rule of client-lawyer confidentiality applies in situations other than those where evidence is sought from the lawyer through compulsion of law. The confidentiality rule, for example, applies not only to matters communicated in confidence by the client but also to all information relating to the representation, whatever its source. A lawyer may not disclose such information except as authorized or required by the Rules of Professional Conductor other law. See also Scope.

[4] Paragraph (a) prohibits a lawyer from revealing information relating to the representation of a client. This prohibition also applies to disclosures by a lawyer that do not in themselves reveal protected information but could reasonably lead to the discovery of such information by a third person. A lawyer's use of a hypothetical to discuss issues relating to the representation is permissible so long as there is no reasonable likelihood that the listener will be able to ascertain the identity of the client or the situation involved.

[5] *Authorized disclosure.* -- Except to the extent that the client's instructions or special circumstances limit that authority, a lawyer is impliedly authorized to make disclosures about a client when appropriate in carrying out the representation. In some situations, for example, a lawyer may be impliedly authorized to admit a fact that cannot properly be disputed or to make a disclosure that facilitates a satisfactory conclusion to a matter. Lawyers in a firm may, in the course of the firm's practice, disclose to each other information relating to a client of the firm, unless the client has instructed that particular information be confined to specified lawyers.

[6] *Disclosure adverse to client.* -- Although the public interest is usually best served by a strict rule requiring lawyers to preserve the confidentiality of information relating to the representation of their clients, the confidentiality rule is subject to limited exceptions. Paragraph (b)(1) recognizes the overriding value of life and physical integrity and permits disclosure reasonably neces-

sary to prevent reasonably certain death or substantial bodily harm. Such harm is reasonably certain to occur if it will be suffered imminently or if there is a present and substantial threat that a person will suffer such harm at a later date if the lawyer fails to take action necessary to eliminate the threat. Thus, a lawyer who knows that a client has accidentally discharged toxic waste into a town's water supply may reveal this information to the authorities if there is a present and substantial risk that a person who drinks the water will contract a life-threatening or debilitating disease and the lawyer's disclosure is necessary to eliminate the threat or reduce the number of victims.

[7] Paragraph (b)(2) is a limited exception to the rule of confidentiality that permits the lawyer to reveal information to the extent necessary to enable affected persons or appropriate authorities to prevent the client from committing a crime or a fraud, as defined in Rule 1.0(d), that is reasonably certain to result in substantial injury to the financial or property interests of another and in furtherance of which the client has used or is using the lawyer's services. Such a
serious abuse of the client-lawyer relationship by the client forfeits the protection of this Rule. The client can, of course, prevent such disclosure by refraining from the wrongful conduct. Although paragraph (b)(2) does not require the lawyer to reveal the client's misconduct, the lawyer may not counsel or assist the client in conduct the lawyer knows is criminal or fraudulent. See Rule 1.2(d). See also Rule 1.16 with respect to the lawyer's obligation or right to withdraw from the
representation of the client in such circumstances. Where the client is an organization, the lawyer may be in doubt whether contemplated conduct will actually be carried out by the organization. Where necessary to guide conduct in connection with this Rule, the lawyer may make inquiry within the organization as indicated in Rule 1.13(b).

[8] Paragraph (b)(3) addresses the situation in which the lawyer does not learn of the client's crime or fraud until after it has been consummated. Although the client no longer has the option of preventing disclosure by refraining from the
wrongful conduct, there will be situations in which the loss suffered by the affected person can be prevented, rectified or mitigated. In such situations, the lawyer may disclose information relating to the representation to the extent necessary to enable the affected persons to prevent or mitigate reasonably certain losses or to attempt to recoup their losses. Disclosure is not permitted under paragraph (b)(3) when a person who has committed a crime or fraud thereafter employs a lawyer for representation concerning that offense if that lawyer's services were not used in the initial crime or fraud; disclosure would be permitted, however, if the lawyer's services are used to commit a further

crime or fraud, such as the crime of obstructing justice. While applicable law may provide that a completed act is regarded for some purposes as a continuing offense, if commission of the initial act has already occurred without the use of the lawyer's services, the lawyer does not have discretion under this paragraph to use or disclose the client's information.

[9] A lawyer's confidentiality obligations do not preclude a lawyer from securing confidential legal advice about the lawyer's personal responsibility to comply with these Rules. In most situations, disclosing information to secure such advice will be impliedly authorized for the lawyer to carry out the representation. Even when the disclosure is not impliedly authorized, paragraph (b)(2) permits such disclosure because of the importance of a lawyer's compliance with the Rules of Professional Conduct.

[10] Where a legal claim or disciplinary charge alleges complicity of the lawyer in a client's conduct or other misconduct of the lawyer involving representation of the client, the lawyer may respond to the extent the lawyer reasonably believes necessary to establish a defense. The same is true with respect to a claim involving the conduct or representation of a former client. Such a charge can arise in a civil, criminal, disciplinary or other proceeding and can be based on
a wrong allegedly committed by the lawyer against the client or on a wrong alleged by a third person, for example, a person claiming to have been defrauded by the lawyer and client acting together. The lawyer's right to respond arises when an assertion of such complicity has been made. Paragraph (b)(5) does not require the lawyer to await the commencement of an action or proceeding that charges such complicity, so that the defense may be established by responding
directly to a third party who has made such an assertion. The right to defend also applies, of course, where a proceeding has been commenced.

[11] A lawyer entitled to a fee is permitted by paragraph (b)(5) to prove the services rendered in an action to collect it. This aspect of the rule expresses the principle that the beneficiary of a fiduciary relationship may not exploit it to the
detriment of the fiduciary.

[12] Other law may require that a lawyer disclose information about a client. Whether such a law supersedes Rule 1.6 is a question of law beyond the scope of these rules. When disclosure of information relating to the representation appears to be required by other law, the lawyer must discuss the matter with the client to the extent required by Rule 1.4. If, however, the other law super-

sedes this Rule and requires disclosure, paragraph (b)(6) permits the lawyer to make

such disclosures as are necessary to comply with the law. See, e.g., *29 DEL. CODE ANN. § 9007A(c)* (which provides that an attorney acting as guardian ad litem for a child in child welfare proceedings shall have the "duty of confidentiality to the child unless the disclosure is necessary to protect the child's best interests").

[13] Paragraph (b)(6) also permits compliance with a court order requiring a lawyer to disclose information relating to a client's representation. If a lawyer is called as a witness to give testimony concerning a client or is otherwise ordered

to reveal information relating to the client's representation, however, the lawyer must, absent informed consent of the client to do otherwise, assert on behalf of the client all nonfrivolous claims that the information sought is protected against disclosure by the attorney-client privilege or other applicable law. In the event of an adverse ruling, the lawyer must consult with the client about the possibility of appeal to the extent required by Rule 1.4. Unless review is sought, however, paragraph (b)(6) permits the lawyer to comply with the court's order.

[14] Paragraph (b) permits disclosure only to the extent the lawyer reasonably believes the disclosure is necessary to accomplish one of the purposes specified. Where practicable, the lawyer should first seek to persuade the client to take suitable action to obviate the need for disclosure. In any case, a disclosure adverse to the client's interest should be no greater than the lawyer reasonably believes necessary to accomplish the purpose. If the disclosure will be made in connection with a judicial proceeding, the disclosure should be made in a manner that limits access to the information to the tribunal or other persons having a need to know it and appropriate protective orders or other arrangements should be sought by the lawyer to the fullest extent practicable.

[15] Paragraph (b) permits but does not require the disclosure of information relating to a client's representation to accomplish the purposes specified in paragraphs (b)(1) through (b)(6). In exercising the discretion conferred by this Rule, the lawyer may consider such factors as the nature of the lawyer's relationship with the client and with those who might be injured by the client, the lawyer's own involvement in the transaction and factors that may extenuate the conduct in question. A lawyer's decision not to disclose as permitted by paragraph (b) does not violate this Rule. Disclosure may be required, however, by other Rules. Some Rules require disclosure only if such disclosure would be permitted by paragraph (b). See Rules 1.2(d), 4.1(b), 8.1 and 8.3.

Rule 3.3, on the other hand, requires disclosure in some circumstances regardless of whether such disclosure is permitted by this Rule. See Rule 3.3(c).

[16] *Acting competently to preserve confidentiality.* -- A lawyer must act competently to safeguard information relating to the representation of a client against inadvertent or unauthorized disclosure by the lawyer or other persons who
are participating in the representation of the client or who are subject to the lawyer's supervision. See Rules 1.1, 5.1 and 5.3.

[17] When transmitting a communication that includes information relating to the representation of a client, the lawyer must take reasonable precautions to prevent the information from coming into the hands of unintended recipients. This duty, however, does not require that the lawyer use special security measures if the method of communication affords a reasonable expectation of privacy. Special circumstances, however, may warrant special precautions. Factors to be considered in determining the reasonableness of the lawyer's expectation of confidentiality include the sensitivity of the information and the extent to which the privacy of the communication is protected by law or by a confidentiality agreement. A client may require the lawyer to implement special security measures not required by this Rule or may give informed consent to the use of a means of communication that would otherwise be prohibited by this Rule.

[18] *Former client.* -- The duty of confidentiality continues after the client-lawyer relationship has terminated. See Rule 1.9(c)(2). See Rule 1.9(c)(1) for the prohibition against using such information to the disadvantage of the former client.

Rule 1.7. Conflict of interest: Current clients

(a) Except as provided in paragraph (b), a lawyer shall not represent a client if the representation involves a concurrent conflict of interest. A concurrent conflict of interest exists if: (1) the representation of one client will be directly adverse to another client; or (2) there is a significant risk that the representation of one or more clients will be materially limited by the lawyer's responsibilities to another client, a former client or a third person or by a personal interest of the lawyer.

(b) Notwithstanding the existence of a concurrent conflict of interest under paragraph (a), a lawyer may represent a client if: (1) the lawyer reasonably believes that the lawyer will be able to provide competent and diligent representation to each affected client; (2) the representation is not prohibited by law; (3) the representation does not involve the assertion of a claim by one client against another client represented by the lawyer in the same litigation or other proceeding before a tribunal; and (4) each affected client gives informed consent, confirmed in writing.

Rule 1.8. Conflict of interest:

Current clients: Specific rules

(a) A lawyer shall not enter into a business transaction with a client or knowingly acquire an ownership, possessory, security or other pecuniary interest adverse to a client unless: (1) the transaction and terms on which the lawyer acquires the interest are fair and reasonable to the client and are fully disclosed and transmitted in writing to the client in a manner that can be reasonably understood by the client; (2) the client is advised in writing of the desirability of seeking and is given a reasonable opportunity to seek the advice of independent legal counsel on the transaction; and (3) the client gives informed consent, in a writing signed by the client, to the essential terms of the transaction and the lawyer's role in the transaction, including whether the lawyer is representing the client in the transaction.

(b) A lawyer shall not use information relating to representation of a client to the disadvantage of the client unless the client gives informed consent, except as permitted or required by these Rules.

(c) A lawyer shall not solicit any substantial gift from a client, including a testamentary gift, or prepare on behalf of a client an instrument giving the lawyer or a person related to the lawyer any substantial gift unless the lawyer or other
recipient of the gift is related to the client. For purposes of this paragraph, related persons include a spouse, child, grandchild, parent, grandparent or other relative or individual with whom the lawyer or the client maintains a close, familial relationship.

(d) Prior to the conclusion of representation of a client, a lawyer shall not make or negotiate an agreement giving the lawyer literary or media rights to a portrayal or account based in substantial part on information relating to the representation.

(e) A lawyer shall not provide financial assistance to a client in connection with pending or contemplated litigation, except that: (1) a lawyer may advance court costs and expenses of litigations, the repayment of which may be contingent on the outcome of the matter; and (2) a lawyer representing an indigent client may pay court costs and expenses of litigation on behalf of the client.

(f) A lawyer shall not accept compensation for representing a client from one other than the client unless: (1) the client gives informed consent; (2) there is no interference with the lawyer's independence of professional judgment or with the client-lawyer relationship; and (3) information relating to representation of a client is protected as required by Rule 1.6.

(g) A lawyer who represents two or more clients shall not participate in making an aggregate settlement of the claims of or against the clients, or in a criminal case an aggregated agreement as to guilty or nolo contendere pleas, unless each client gives informed consent, in a writing signed by the client. The lawyer's disclosure shall include the existence and nature of all the claims or pleas involved and of the participation of each person in the settlement.

(h) A lawyer shall not: (1) make an agreement prospectively limiting the lawyer's liability to a client for malpractice unless the client is independently represented in making the agreement; or (2) settle a claim or potential claim for such liability with an unrepresented client or former client unless that person is advised in writing of the desirability of seeking and is given a reasonable opportunity to seek the advice of independent legal counsel in connection therewith.

(i) A lawyer shall not acquire a proprietary interest in the cause of action or subject matter of litigation the lawyer is conducting for a client, except that the lawyer may: (1) acquire a lien authorized by law to secure the lawyer's fee or expenses; and (2) contract with a client for a reasonable contingent fee in a civil case.

(j) A lawyer shall not have sexual relations with a client unless a consensual sexual relationship existed between them when the client-lawyer relationship commenced.

(k) While lawyers are associated in a firm, a prohibition in the foregoing paragraphs (a) through (i) that applies to any one of them shall apply to all of them.

Rule 1.9. Duties to former clients

(a) A lawyer who has formerly represented a client in a matter shall not there-after represent another person in the same or a substantially related matter in which that person's interests are materially adverse to the interests of the former client unless the former client gives informed consent, confirmed in writing.

(b) A lawyer shall not knowingly represent a person in the same or a substantially related matter in which a firm with which the lawyer formerly was associated had previously represented a client: (1) whose interests are materially adverse to that person; and (2) about whom the lawyer had acquired information protected by Rules 1.6 and 1.9(c) that is material to the matter; unless the former client gives informed consent, confirmed in writing.

(c) A lawyer who has formerly represented a client in a matter or whose present or former firm has formerly represented a client in a matter shall not thereafter:
(1) use information relating to the representation to the disadvantage of the former client except as these Rules would permit or require with respect to a client, or when the information has become generally known; or (2) reveal information relating to the representation except as these Rules would permit or require with respect to a client.

Rule 1.10. Imputation of conflicts of interest: General rule

(a) Except as otherwise provided in this rule, while lawyers are associated in a firm, none of them shall knowingly represent a client when any one of them practicing alone would be prohibited from doing so by Rules 1.7 or 1.9, un-less
the prohibition is based on a personal interest of the prohibited lawyer and does not present a significant risk of materially limiting the representation of the client by the remaining lawyers in the firm.

(b) When a lawyer has terminated an association with a firm, the firm is not prohibited from thereafter representing a person with interests materially adverse to those of a client represented by the formerly associated lawyer and not currently represented by the firm, unless: (1) the matter is the same or substantially related to that in which the formerly associated lawyer represented the client; and (2) any lawyer remaining in the firm has information protected by Rules 1.6 and 1.9(c) that is material to the matter.

(c) When a lawyer becomes associated with a firm, no lawyer associated in the firm shall knowingly represent a client in a matter in which that lawyer is disqualified under Rule 1.9 unless: (1) the personally disqualified lawyer is timely screened from any participation in the matter and is apportioned no part of the fee therefrom; and (2) written notice is promptly given to the affected former client.

(d) A disqualification prescribed by this rule may be waived by the affected client under the conditions stated in Rule 1.7.

(e) The disqualification of lawyers associated in a firm with former or current government lawyers is governed by Rule 1.11.

Rule 1.11. Special conflicts of interest

for former and current government officers and employees

(a) Except as law may otherwise expressly permit, a lawyer who has formerly served as a public officer or employee of the government: (1) is subject to Rule 1.9(c); and (2) shall not otherwise represent a client in connection with a matter in which the lawyer participated personally and substantially as a public officer or employee, unless the appropriate government agency gives its informed consent, confirmed in writing, to the representation.

(b) When a lawyer is disqualified from representation under paragraph (a), no lawyer in a firm with which that lawyer is associated may knowingly undertake or continue representation in such a matter unless: (1) the disqualified lawyer is timely screened from any participation in the matter and is apportioned no part of the fee therefrom; and (2) written notice is promptly given to the appropriate government agency to enable it to ascertain compliance with the provisions of this rule.

(c) Except as law may otherwise expressly permit, a lawyer having information that the lawyer knows is confidential government information about a person acquired when the lawyer was a public officer or employee, may not represent
a private client whose interests are adverse to that person in a matter in which the information could be used to the material disadvantage of that person. As used in this Rule, the term "confidential government information" means information
that has been obtained under governmental authority and which, at the time this Rule is applied, the government is prohibited by law from disclosing to

the public or has a legal privilege not to disclose and which is not otherwise available to the public. A firm with which that lawyer is associated may undertake or continue representation in the matter only if the disqualified lawyer is timely screened from any participation in the matter and is apportioned no part
of the fee therefrom.

(d) Except as law may otherwise expressly permit, a lawyer currently serving as a public officer or employee: (1) is subject to Rules 1.7 and 1.9; and (2) shall not: (i) participate in a matter in which the lawyer participated personally and substantially while in private practice or nongovernmental employment, unless the appropriate government agency gives its informed consent, confirmed in writing; or (ii) negotiate for private employment with any person who is involved as a party or as lawyer for a party in a matter in which the lawyer is participating personally and substantially, except that a lawyer serving as a law clerk to a judge, other adjudicative officer or arbitrator may negotiate for private employment as permitted by Rule 1.12(b) and subject to the conditions stated in Rule 1.12(b).

(e) As used in this Rule, the term "matter" includes: (1) any judicial or other proceeding, application, request for a ruling or other determination, contract, claim, controversy, investigation, charge, accusation, arrest or other particular matter involving a specific party or parties, and (2) any other matter covered by the conflict of interest rules of the appropriate government agency.

Rule 1.12. Former judge, arbitrator, mediator

(a) Except as stated in paragraph (d), a lawyer shall not represent anyone in connection with a matter in which the lawyer participated personally and substantially as a judge or other adjudicative officer or law clerk to such a person or as an arbitrator, mediator or other third-party neutral, unless all parties to the proceeding give informed consent, confirmed in writing.

(b) A lawyer shall not negotiate for employment with any person who is involved as a party or as lawyer for a party in a matter in which the lawyer is participating personally and substantially as a judge or other adjudicative officer or as an arbitrator, mediator or other third-party neutral. A lawyer serving as a law clerk to a judge or other adjudicative officer may negotiate for employment with a party or lawyer involved in a matter in which the clerk is participating personally
and substantially, but only after the lawyer has notified the judge or other adjudicative officer.

(c) If a lawyer is disqualified by paragraph (a), no lawyer in a firm with which that lawyer is associated may knowingly undertake or continue representation in the matter unless: (1) the disqualified lawyer is timely screened from any participation in the matter and is apportioned no part of the fee therefrom; and (2) written notice is promptly given to the parties and any appropriate tribunal to enable them to ascertain compliance with the provisions of this rule.

(d) An arbitrator selected as a partisan of a party in a multimember arbitration panel is not prohibited from subsequently representing that party.

Rule 1.13. Organization as client

(a) A lawyer employed or retained by an organization represents the organization acting through its duly authorized constituents.

(b) If a lawyer for an organization knows that an officer, employee or other person associated with the organization is engaged in action, intends to act or refuses to act in a matter related to the representation that is a violation of a legal

obligation to the organization, or a violation of law which reasonably might be imputed to the organization, and is likely to result in substantial injury to the organization, the lawyer shall proceed as is reasonably necessary in the best interest of the organization. In determining how to proceed, the lawyer shall give due consideration to the seriousness of the violation and its consequences, the scope and nature of the lawyer's representation, the responsibility in the organization and the apparent motivation of the person involved, the policies of the organization concerning such matters and any other relevant considerations. Any measures taken shall be designed to minimize disruption of the organization and the risk of revealing information relating to the representation to persons outside the organization. Such measures may include among others: (1) asking for reconsideration of the matter; (2) advising that a separate legal opinion on the matter be sought for presentation to appropriate authority in the organization;
and (3) referring the matter to higher authority in the organization, including, if warranted by the seriousness of the matter, referral to the highest authority that can act on behalf of the organization as determined by applicable law.

(c) If, despite the lawyer's efforts in accordance with paragraph (b), the highest authority that can act on behalf of the organization insists upon action, or a refusal to act, that is clearly a violation of law and is likely to result in substantial injury to the organization, the lawyer may resign in accordance with Rule 1.16.

(d) In dealing with an organization's directors, officers, employees, members, shareholders or other constituents, a lawyer shall explain the identity of the client when the lawyer knows or reasonably should know that the organization's interests are adverse to those of the constituents with whom the lawyer is dealing.

(e) A lawyer representing an organization may also represent any of its directors, officers, employees, members, shareholders or other constituents, subject to the provisions of Rule 1.7. If the organization's consent to the dual representation is required by Rule 1.7, the consent shall be given by an appropriate official of the organization other than the individual who is to be represented, or by the shareholders.

Rule 1.14. Client with diminished capacity

(a) When a client's capacity to make adequately considered decisions in connection with a representation is diminished, whether because of minority, mental impairment or for some other reason, the lawyer shall, as far as reasonably
possible, maintain a normal client-lawyer relationship with the client.

(b) When the lawyer reasonably believes that the client has diminished capacity, is at risk of substantial physical, financial or other harm unless action is taken and cannot adequately act in the client's own interest, the lawyer may take reasonably necessary protective action, including consulting with individuals or entities that have the ability to take action to protect the client and, in appropriate cases, seeking the appointment of a guardian ad litem, conservator or guardian.

(c) Information relating to the representation of a client with diminished capacity is protected by Rule 1.6. When taking protective action pursuant to paragraph (b), the lawyer is impliedly authorized under Rule 1.6(a) to reveal information
about the client, but only to the extent reasonably necessary to protect the client's interests.

Rule 1.15. Safekeeping property - omitted

Rule 1.15A. Trust account overdraft notification - omitted

Rule 1.16. Declining or terminating representation

(a) Except as stated in paragraph (c), a lawyer shall not represent a client or, where representation has commenced, shall withdraw from the representation of a client if: (1) the representation will result in violation of the rules of professional conduct or other law; (2) the lawyer's physical or mental condition materially impairs the lawyer's ability to represent the client; or (3) the lawyer is discharged.

(b) Except as stated in paragraph (c), a lawyer may withdraw from representing a client if: (1) withdrawal can be accomplished without material adverse effect on the interests of the client; (2) the client persists in a course of action involving the lawyer's services that the lawyer reasonably believes is criminal or fraudulent; (3) the client has used the lawyer's service to perpetrate a crime or fraud; (4) a client insists upon taking action that the lawyer considers repugnant or with which the lawyer has a fundamental disagreement; (5) the client fails substantially to fulfill an obligation to the lawyer regarding the lawyer's services and has been given reasonable warning that the lawyer will withdraw unless the obligation is fulfilled; (6) the representation will result in an unreasonable financial burden on the lawyer or has been rendered unreasonably difficult by the client; or (7) other good cause for withdrawal exists.

(c) A lawyer must comply with applicable law requiring notice to or permission of a tribunal when terminating a representation. When ordered to do so by a tribunal, a lawyer shall continue representation notwithstanding good cause for terminating the representation.

(d) Upon termination of representation, a lawyer shall take steps to the extent reasonably practicable to protect a client's interests, such as giving reasonable notice to the client, allowing time for employment of other counsel, surrendering papers and property to which the client is entitled and refunding any advance payment of fee or expense that has not been earned or incurred. The lawyer may retain papers relating to the client to the extent permitted by other law.

COMMENT

[1] A lawyer should not accept representation in a matter unless it can be performed competently, promptly, without improper conflict of interest and to completion. Ordinarily, a representation in a matter is completed when the agreedupon assistance has been concluded. See Rules 1.2(c) and 6.5. See also Rule 1.3, Comment [4].

[2] *Mandatory Withdrawal.* -- A lawyer ordinarily must decline or withdraw from representation if the client demands that the lawyer engage in conduct that is illegal or violates the Rules of Professional Conduct or other law. The lawyer
is not obliged to decline or withdraw simply because the client suggests such a course of conduct; a client may make such a suggestion in the hope that a lawyer will not be constrained by a professional obligation.

[3] When a lawyer has been appointed to represent a client, withdrawal ordinarily requires approval of the appointing authority. See also Rule 6.2. Similarly, court approval or notice to the court is often required by applicable law before a lawyer withdraws from pending litigation. Difficulty may be encountered if withdrawal is based on the client's demand that the lawyer engage in unprofessional conduct. The court may request an explanation for the withdrawal, while the lawyer may be bound to keep confidential the facts that would constitute such an explanation. The lawyer's statement that professional considerations require termination of the representation ordinarily should be accepted as sufficient. Lawyers should be mindful of their obligations to both clients and the court under Rules 1.6 and 3.3.

[4] *Discharge.* -- A client has a right to discharge a lawyer at any time, with or without cause, subject to liability for payment for the lawyer's services. Where future dispute about the withdrawal may be anticipated, it may be advisable to prepare a written statement reciting the circumstances.

[5] Whether a client can discharge appointed counsel may depend on applicable law. A client seeking to do so should be given a full explanation of the consequences. These consequences may include a decision by the appointing authority that appointment of successor counsel is unjustified, thus requiring self-representation by the client.

[6] If the client has severely diminished capacity, the client may lack the legal capacity to discharge the lawyer, and in any event the discharge may be seriously adverse to the client's interests. The lawyer should make special effort to help
the client consider the consequences and may take reasonably necessary protective action as provided in Rule 1.14.

[7] *Optional Withdrawal.* -- A lawyer may withdraw from representation in some circumstances. The lawyer has the option to withdraw if it can be accomplished without material adverse effect on the client's interests. Withdrawal is also justified if the client persists in a course of action that the lawyer reasonably believes is criminal or fraudulent, for a lawyer is not re-

quired to be associated with such conduct even if the lawyer does not further it. Withdrawal is also permitted if the lawyer's services were misused in the past even if that would materially prejudice the client. The lawyer may also withdraw where the client insists on taking action that the lawyer considers repugnant or with which the lawyer has a fundamental disagreement.

[8] A lawyer may withdraw if the client refuses to abide by the terms of an agreement relating to the representation, such as an agreement concerning fees or court costs or an agreement limiting the objectives of the representation.

[9] *Assisting the Client upon Withdrawal.* -- Even if the lawyer has been unfairly discharged by the client, a lawyer must take all reasonable steps to mitigate the consequences to the client. The lawyer may retain papers as security for a fee only to the extent permitted by law. See Rule 1.15.

Rule 1.17. Sale of law practice - omitted

Rule 1.18. Duties to prospective client

(a) A person who discusses with a lawyer the possibility of forming a client-lawyer relationship with respect to a matter is a prospective client.

(b) Even when no client-lawyer relationship ensues, a lawyer who has had discussions with a prospective client shall not use or reveal information learned in the consultation, except as Rule 1.9 would permit with respect to information of a former client.

(c) A lawyer subject to paragraph (b) shall not represent a client with interests materially adverse to those of a prospective client in the same or a substantially related matter if the lawyer received information from the prospective client that could be significantly harmful to that person in the matter, except as provided in paragraph (d). If a lawyer is disqualified from representation under this paragraph, no lawyer in a firm with which that lawyer is associated may knowingly undertake or continue representation in such a matter, except as provided in paragraph (d).

(d) When the lawyer has received disqualifying information as defined in paragraph (c), representation is permissible if: (1) both the affected client and the prospective client have given informed consent, confirmed in writing, or: (2) the lawyer who received the information took reasonable measures to avoid exposure to more disqualifying information than was reasonably necessary to determine whether to represent the prospective client; and (i) the disqualified lawyer is timely screened from any participation in the matter and is apportioned no part of the fee therefrom; and (ii) written notice is promptly given to the prospective client.

Rule 2.1. Advisor

In representing a client, a lawyer shall exercise independent professional judgment and render candid advice. In rendering advice, a lawyer may refer not only to law but to other considerations, such as moral, economic, social and political factors, that may be relevant to the client's situation.

Rule 2.2. Intermediary (Deleted)

Rule 2.3. Evaluation for use by third persons - omitted

Rule 2.4. Lawyer serving as third-party neutral

(a) A lawyer serves as a third-party neutral when the lawyer assists two or more persons who are not clients of the lawyer to reach a resolution of a dispute or other matter that has arisen between them. Service as a third-party neutral may include service as an arbitrator, a mediator or in such other capacity as will enable the lawyer to assist the parties to resolve the matter.

(b) A lawyer serving as a third-party neutral shall inform unrepresented parties that the lawyer is not representing them. When the lawyer knows or reasonably should know that a party does not understand the lawyer's role in the matter, the lawyer shall explain the difference between the lawyer's role as a third-party neutral and a lawyer's role as one who represents a client.

Rule 3.1. Meritorious claims and contentions

A lawyer shall not bring or defend a proceeding, or assert or controvert an issue therein, unless there is a basis in law and fact for doing so that is not frivolous, which includes a good faith argument for an extension, modification or reversal
of existing law. A lawyer for the defendant in a criminal proceeding, or the respondent in a proceeding that could result in incarceration, may nevertheless so defend the proceeding as to require that every element of the case be established.

Rule 3.2. Expediting litigation

A lawyer shall make reasonable efforts to expedite litigation consistent with the interests of the client.

COMMENT

[1] Dilatory practices bring the administration of justice into disrepute. Although there will be occasions when a lawyer may properly seek a postponement for personal reasons, it is not proper for a lawyer to routinely fail to expedite litigation solely for the convenience of the advocates. Nor will a failure to expedite be reasonable if done for the purpose of frustrating an opposing party's attempt to obtain rightful redress or repose. It is not a justification that similar
conduct is often tolerated by the bench and bar. The question is whether a competent lawyer acting in good faith would regard the course of action as having some substantial purpose other than delay. Realizing financial or other benefit from otherwise improper delay in litigation is not a legitimate interest of the client.

Rule 3.3. Candor toward the tribunal

(a) A lawyer shall not knowingly: (1) make a false statement of fact or law to a tribunal or fail to correct a false statement of material fact or law previously made to the tribunal by the lawyer; (2) fail to disclose to the tribunal legal authority in the controlling jurisdiction known to the lawyer to be directly adverse to the position of the client and not disclosed by opposing counsel; or (3) offer evidence that the lawyer knows to be false. If a lawyer, the lawyer's client, or a witness called by the lawyer, has offered material evidence and the lawyer comes to know of its falsity, the lawyer shall take reasonable remedial measures, including, if necessary, disclosure to the tribunal. A lawyer may refuse to offer evidence, other than the testimony of a defendant in a criminal matter, that the lawyer reasonably believes is false.

(b) A lawyer who represents a client in an adjudicative proceeding and who knows that a person intends to engage, is engaging or has engaged in criminal or fraudulent conduct related to the proceeding shall take reasonable remedial measures, including, if necessary, disclosure to the tribunal.

(c) The duties stated in paragraph (a) and (b) continue to the conclusion of the proceeding, and apply even if compliance requires disclosure of information otherwise protected by Rule 1.6.

(d) In an ex parte proceeding, a lawyer shall inform the tribunal of all material facts known to the lawyer which will enable the tribunal to make an informed decision, whether or not the facts are adverse.

COMMENT

[1] This Rule governs the conduct of a lawyer who is representing a client in the proceedings of a tribunal. See Rule 1.0(m) for the definition of "tribunal." It also applies when the lawyer is representing a client in an ancillary proceeding conducted pursuant to the tribunal's adjudicative authority, such as a deposition. Thus, for example, paragraph (a)(3) requires a lawyer to take reasonable remedial measures if the lawyer comes to know that a client who is testifying in a deposition has offered evidence that is false.

[2] This Rule sets forth the special duties of lawyers as officers of the court to avoid conduct that undermines the integrity of the adjudicative process. A lawyer acting as an advocate in an adjudicative proceeding has an obligation to present the client's case with persuasive force. Performance of that duty while maintaining confidences of the client, however, is qualified by the advocate's duty of candor to the tribunal. Consequently, although a lawyer in an adversary proceeding is not required to present an impartial exposition of the law or to vouch for the evidence submitted in a cause, the lawyer must not allow the tribunal to be misled by false statements of law or fact or evidence that the lawyer knows to be false.

[3] *Representations by a Lawyer.* -- An advocate is responsible for pleadings and other documents prepared for litigation, but is usually not required to have personal knowledge of matters asserted therein, for litigation documents ordinarily present assertions by the client, or by someone on the client's behalf, and not assertions by the lawyer. Compare Rule 3.1. However, an assertion purporting to be on the lawyer's own knowledge, as in an affidavit by the lawyer or in a statement in open court, may properly be made only when the lawyer knows the assertion is true or believes it to be true on the basis of a reasonably diligent inquiry. There are circumstances where failure to make a disclosure is the equivalent of an affirmative misrepresentation. The obligation prescribed in Rule 1.2(d) not to counsel a client to commit or assist the client in committing a fraud applies in litigation. Regarding compliance with Rule 1.2(d), see the Comment to that Rule. See also the comment to Rule 8.4(b).

[4] *Legal Argument.* -- Legal argument based on a knowingly false representation of law constitutes dishonesty toward the tribunal. A lawyer is not required to make a disinterested exposition of the law, but must recognize the existence

of pertinent legal authorities. Furthermore, as stated in paragraph (a)(2), an advocate has a duty to disclose directly adverse authority in the controlling jurisdiction that has not been disclosed by the opposing party. The underlying concept is that legal argument is a discussion seeking to determine the legal premises properly applicable to the case.

[5] *Offering Evidence.* -- Paragraph (a)(3) requires that the lawyer refuse to offer evidence that the lawyer knows to be false, regardless of the client's wishes. This duty is premised on the lawyer's obligation as an officer of the court to prevent

the trier of fact from being misled by false evidence. A lawyer does not violate this Rule if the lawyer offers the evidence for the purpose of establishing its falsity.

[6] If a lawyer knows that the client intends to testify falsely or wants the lawyer to introduce false evidence, the lawyer should seek to persuade the client that the evidence should not be offered. If the persuasion is ineffective and the lawyer continues to represent the client, the lawyer must refuse to offer the false evidence. If only a portion of a witness's testimony will be false, the lawyer may call the witness to testify but may not elicit or otherwise permit the witness to present the testimony that the lawyer knows is false.

[7] The duties stated in paragraphs (a) and (b) apply to all lawyers, including defense counsel in criminal cases. In some jurisdictions, however, courts have required counsel to present the accused as a witness or to give a narrative statement if the accused so desires, even if counsel knows that the testimony or statement will be false. The obligation of the advocate under the Rules of Professional Conduct is subordinate to such requirements. See also Comment [9].

[8] The prohibition against offering false evidence only applies if the lawyer knows that the evidence is false. A lawyer's reasonable belief that evidence is false does not preclude its presentation to the trier of fact. A lawyer's knowledge

that evidence is false, however, can be inferred from the circumstances. See Rule 1.0(f). Thus, although a lawyer should resolve doubts about the veracity of testimony or other evidence in favor of the client, the lawyer cannot ignore an obvious falsehood.

[9] Although paragraph (a)(3) only prohibits a lawyer from offering evidence the lawyer knows to be false, it permits the lawyer to refuse to offer testimony or other proof that the lawyer reasonably believes is false. Offering such proof may reflect adversely on the lawyer's ability to discriminate in the quality of evidence and thus impair the lawyer's effectiveness as an advocate. Because

of the special protections historically provided criminal defendants, however, this Rule does not permit a lawyer to refuse to offer the testimony of such a client where the lawyer reasonably believes but does not know that the testimony will be false. Unless the lawyer knows the testimony will be false, the lawyer must honor the client's decision to testify. See also Comment [7].

[10] *Remedial Measures.* -- Having offered material evidence in the belief that it was true, a lawyer may subsequently come to know that the evidence is false. Or, a lawyer may be surprised when the lawyer's client, or another witness called by the lawyer, offers testimony the lawyer knows to be false, either during the lawyer's direct examination or in response to cross-examination by the opposing lawyer. In such situations or if the lawyer knows of the falsity of testimony elicited from the client during a deposition, the lawyer must take reasonable remedial measures. In such situations, the advocate's proper course is to remonstrate with the client confidentially, advise the client of the lawyer's duty
of candor to the tribunal and seek the client's cooperation with respect to the withdrawal or correction of the false statements or evidence. If that fails, the advocate must take further remedial action. If withdrawal from the representation is not permitted or will not undo the effect of the false evidence, the advocate must make such disclosure to the tribunal as is reasonably necessary to remedy the situation, even if doing so requires the lawyer to reveal information that otherwise would be protected by Rule 1.6. It is for the tribunal then to determine what should be done -- making a statement about the matter to the trier of fact, ordering a mistrial or perhaps nothing.

[11] The disclosure of a client's false testimony can result in grave consequences to the client, including not only a sense of betrayal but also loss of the case and perhaps a prosecution for perjury. But the alternative is that the lawyer cooperate in deceiving the court, thereby subverting the truth-finding process which the adversary system is designed to implement. See Rule 1.2(d). Furthermore, unless it is clearly understood that the lawyer will act upon the duty to disclose the existence of false evidence, the client can simply reject the lawyer's advice to reveal the false evidence and insist that the lawyer keep silent. Thus the client could in effect coerce the lawyer into being a party to fraud on the court.

[12] *Preserving Integrety of Adjunctive Process.* -- Lawyers have a special obligation to protect a tribunal against criminal or fraudulent conduct that undermines the integrity of the adjudicative process, such as bribing, intimidating or otherwise unlawfully communicating with a witness, juror, court official or other participant in the proceeding, unlawfully destroying or concealing documents or other evidence or failing to disclose information to the tri-

bunal when required by law to do so. Thus, paragraph (b) requires a lawyer to take reasonable remedial measures, including disclosure if necessary, whenever the lawyer knows that a person, including the lawyer's client, intends to engage, is engaging or has engaged in criminal or fraudulent conduct related to the proceeding.

[13] *Duration of Obligation.* -- A practical time limit on the obligation to rectify false evidence or false statements of law and fact has to be established. The conclusion of the proceeding is a reasonably definite point for the termination of
the obligation. A proceeding has concluded within the meaning of this Rule when a final judgment in the proceeding has been affirmed on appeal or the time for review has passed.

[14] *Ex parte Proceedings.* --] Ordinarily, an advocate has the limited responsibility of presenting one side of the matters that a tribunal should consider in reaching a decision; the conflicting position is expected to be presented by the opposing party. However, in any ex parte proceeding, such as an application for a temporary restraining order, there is no balance of presentation by opposing advocates. The object of an ex parte proceeding is nevertheless to yield a substantially just result. The judge has an affirmative responsibility to accord the absent party just consideration. The lawyer for the represented party has the correlative duty to make disclosures of material facts known to the lawyer and that the lawyer reasonably believes are necessary to an informed decision.

[15] *Withdrawal.* -- Normally, a lawyer's compliance with the duty of candor imposed by this rule does not require that the lawyer withdraw from the representation of a client whose interests will be or have been adversely affected by the lawyer's disclosure. The lawyer may, however, be required by Rule 1.16(a) to seek permission of the tribunal to withdraw if the lawyer's compliance with this Rule's duty of candor results in such an extreme deterioration of the client-lawyer relationship that the lawyer can no longer competently represent the client. Also see Rule 1.16(b) for the circumstances in which a lawyer will be permitted to seek a tribunal's permission to withdraw. In connection with a request for permission to withdraw that is premised on a client's misconduct, a lawyer may reveal information relating to the representation only to the extent reasonably necessary to comply with this Rule or as otherwise permitted by Rule 1.6.

Rule 3.4. Fairness to opposing party and counsel

A lawyer shall not:

(a) unlawfully obstruct another party's access to evidence or unlawfully alter, destroy or conceal a document or other material having potential evidentiary value. A lawyer shall not counsel or assist another person to do any such act;

(b) falsify evidence, counsel or assist a witness to testify falsely, or offer an inducement to a witness that is prohibited by law.

(c) knowingly disobey an obligation under the rules of a tribunal, except for an open refusal based on an assertion that no valid obligation exists;

(d) in pretrial procedure, make a frivolous discovery request or fail to make reasonably diligent efforts to comply with a legally proper discovery request by an opposing party;

(e) in trial, allude to any matter that the lawyer does not reasonably believe is relevant or that will not be supported by admissible evidence, assert personal knowledge of facts in issue except when testifying as a witness, or state a personal opinion as to the justness of a cause, the credibility of a witness, the culpability of a civil litigant or the guilt or innocence of an accused; or

(f) request a person other than a client to refrain from voluntarily giving relevant information to another party unless: (1) the person is a relative or an employee or other agent of a client; and (2) the lawyer reasonably believes that the person's interests will not be adversely affected by refraining from giving such information.

COMMENT

[1] The procedure of the adversary system contemplates that the evidence in a case is to be marshalled competitively by the contending parties. Fair competition in the adversary system is secured by the prohibitions against destruction or concealment of evidence, improperly influencing witnesses, obstructive tactics in discovery procedure, and the like.

[2] Documents and other items of evidence are often essential to establish a claim or defense. Subject to evidentiary privileges, the right of an opposing party, including the government, to obtain evidence through discovery or subpoena is an important procedural right. The exercise of that right can be frustrated if relevant material is altered, concealed or destroyed. Applicable law in many jurisdictions makes it an offense to destroy material for purpose of impairing its availability in a pending proceeding or one whose commencement can be foreseen. Falsifying evidence is also generally a criminal offense.

Paragraph (a) applies to evidentiary material generally, including computerized information. Applicable law may permit a lawyer to take temporary possession of physical evidence of client crimes for the purpose of conducting a limited examination that will not alter or destroy material characteristics of the evidence. In such a case, applicable law may require the lawyer to turn the evidence over to the police or other prosecuting authority, depending on the circumstances.

[3] With regard to paragraph (b), it is not improper to pay a witness's expenses or to compensate an expert witness on terms permitted by law. The common law rule in most jurisdictions is that it is improper to pay an occurrence witness any fee for testifying and that it is improper to pay an expert witness a contingent fee.

[4] Paragraph (f) permits a lawyer to advise employees of a client to refrain from giving information to another party, for the employees may identify their interests with those of the client. See also Rule 4.2.

Rule 3.5. Impartiality and decorum of the tribunal

A lawyer shall not:

(a) seek to influence a judge, juror, prospective juror or other official by means prohibited by law;

(b) communicate or cause another to communicate ex parte with such a person or members of such person's family during the proceeding unless authorized to do so by law or court order; or

(c) communicate with a juror or prospective juror after discharge of the jury unless the communication is permitted by court rule;

(d) engage in conduct intended to disrupt a tribunal or engage in undignified or discourteous conduct that is degrading to a tribunal.

COMMENT

[1] Many forms of improper influence upon a tribunal are proscribed by criminal law. Others are specified in the ABA Model Code of Judicial Conduct, with which an advocate should be familiar. A lawyer is required to void contributing
to a violation of such provisions.

[2] During a proceeding a lawyer may not communicate or cause another to communicate ex parte with persons serving in an official capacity in the proceeding, such as judges, masters or jurors, or with members of such person's family, unless authorized to do so by law or court order. Furthermore, a lawyer shall not conduct or cause another to conduct a vexatious or harassing investigation of such persons or their family members.

[3] A lawyer may not communicate with a juror or prospective juror after the jury has been discharged unless permitted by court rule. The lawyer may not engage in improper conduct during the communication.

[4] The advocate's function is to present evidence and argument so that the cause may be decided according to law. Refraining from abusive or obstreperous conduct is a corollary of the advocate's right to speak on behalf of litigants. A
lawyer may stand firm against abuse by a judge but should avoid reciprocation; the judge's default is no justification for similar dereliction by an advocate. An advocate can present the cause, protect the record for subsequent review and preserve professional integrity by patient firmness no less effectively than by belligerence or theatrics.

[5] The duty to refrain from disruptive, undignified or discourteous conduct applies to any proceeding of a tribunal, including a deposition. See Rule 1.0(m).

Rule 3.6. Trial publicity

(a) A lawyer who is participating or has participated in the investigation or litigation of a matter shall not make an extrajudicial statement that the lawyer knows or reasonably should know will be disseminated by means of public communication and will have a substantial likelihood of materially prejudicing an adjudicative proceeding in the matter.

(b) Notwithstanding paragraph (a), a lawyer may state: (1) the claim, offense or defense involved and, except when prohibited by law, the identity of the persons involved; (2) information contained in a public record; (3) that an investigation of a matter is in progress; (4) the scheduling or result of any step in litigation; (5) a request for assistance in obtaining evidence and information necessary thereto;
(6) a warning of danger concerning the behavior of a person involved, when there is reason to believe that there exists the likelihood of substantial harm to an individual or to the public interest; and (7) in a criminal case, in addition to subparagraphs (1) through (6): (i) the identity, residence, occupation and fam-

ily status of the accused; (ii) if the accused has not been apprehended, information necessary to aid in apprehension of that person; (iii) the fact, time and place of arrest; and (iv) the identity of investigating and arresting officers or agencies and the length of the investigation.

(c) Notwithstanding paragraph (a), a lawyer may make a statement that a reasonable lawyer would believe is required to protect a client from the substantial undue prejudicial effect of recent publicity not initiated by the lawyer or the lawyer's client. A statement made pursuant to this paragraph shall be limited to such information as is necessary to mitigate the recent adverse publicity.

(d) No lawyer associated in a firm or government agency with a lawyer subject to paragraph (a) shall make a statement prohibited by paragraph (a).

COMMENT

[1] It is difficult to strike a balance between protecting the right to a fair trial and safeguarding the right of free expression. Preserving the right to a fair trial necessarily entails some curtailment of the information that may be disseminated
about a party prior to trial, particularly where trial by jury is involved. If there were no such limits, the result would be the practical nullification of the protective effect of the rules of forensic decorum and the exclusionary rules of evidence. On the other hand, there are vital social interests served by the free dissemination of information about events having legal consequences and about legal proceedings themselves. The public has a right to know about threats to its safety and measures aimed at assuring its security. It also has a legitimate interest in the conduct of judicial proceedings, particularly in matters of general public concern. Furthermore, the subject matter of legal proceedings is often of direct significance in debate and deliberation over questions of public policy.

[2] Special rules of confidentiality may validly govern proceedings in juvenile, domestic relations and mental disability proceedings, and perhaps other types of litigation. Rule 3.4(c) requires compliance with such Rules.

[3] The Rule sets forth a basic general prohibition against a lawyer's making statements that the lawyer knows or should know will have a substantial likelihood of materially prejudicing an adjudicative proceeding. Recognizing that the public value of informed commentary is great and the likelihood of prejudice to a proceeding by the commentary of a lawyer who is not involved in

the proceeding is small, the rule applies only to lawyers who are, or who have been involved in the investigation or litigation of a case, and their associates.

[4] Paragraph (b) identifies specific matters about which a lawyer's statements would not ordinarily be considered to present a substantial likelihood of material prejudice, and should not in any event be considered prohibited by the general prohibition of paragraph (a). Paragraph (b) is not intended to be an exhaustive listing of the subjects upon which a lawyer may make a statement, but statements on other matters may be subject to paragraph (a).

[5] There are, on the other hand, certain subjects which are more likely than not to have a material prejudicial effect on a proceeding, particularly when they refer to a civil matter triable to a jury, a criminal matter, or any other proceeding that could result in incarceration. These subjects relate to: (1) the character, credibility, reputation or criminal record of a party, suspect in a criminal investigation or witness, or the identity of a witness, or the expected testimony of a party of witness; (2) in a criminal case or proceeding that could result in incarceration, the possibility of a plea of guilty to the offense or the existence or contents of any confession, admission, or statement given by a defendant or suspect or that person's refusal or failure to make a statement; (3) the performance or results of any examination or test or the refusal or failure of a person to submit to an examination or test, or the identity or nature of physical evidence expected to be presented; (4) any opinion as to the guilt or innocence of a defendant or suspect in a criminal case or proceeding that could result in incarceration; (5) information that the lawyer knows or reasonably should know is likely to be inadmissible as evidence in a trial and that would, if disclosed, create a substantial risk of prejudicing an impartial trial; or (6) the fact that a defendant has been charged with a crime, unless there is included therein a statement explaining that the charge is merely an accusation and that the defendant is presumed innocent until and unless proven guilty.

[6] Another relevant factor in determining prejudice is the nature of the proceeding involved. Criminal jury trials will be most sensitive to extrajudicial speech. Civil trials may be less sensitive. Non-jury hearings and arbitration proceedings may be even less affected. The Rule will still place limitations on prejudicial comments in these cases, but the likelihood of prejudice may be different depending on the type of proceeding.

[7] Finally, extrajudicial statements that might otherwise raise a question under this Rule may be permissible when they are made in response to statements made publicly by another party, another party's lawyer, or third persons, where a reasonable lawyer would believe a public response is required in or-

der to avoid prejudice to the lawyer's client. When prejudicial statements have been publicly made by others, responsive statements may have the salutary effect of lessening any resulting adverse impact on the adjudicative proceeding. Such responsive statements should be limited to contain only such information as is necessary to mitigate undue prejudice created by the statements made by others.

[8] See Rule 3.8(f) for additional duties of prosecutors in connection with extrajudicial statements about criminal proceedings.

Rule 3.7. Lawyer as witness
(a) A lawyer shall not act as advocate at a trial in which the lawyer is likely to be a necessary witness unless: (1) the testimony relates to an uncontested issue; (2) the testimony relates to the nature and value of legal services rendered in the case; or (3) disqualification of the lawyer would work substantial hardship on the client.

(b) A lawyer may act as advocate in a trial in which another lawyer in the lawyer's firm is likely to be called as a witness unless precluded from doing so by Rule 1.7 or Rule 1.9.

COMMENT

[1] Combining the roles of advocate and witness can prejudice the tribunal and the opposing party and can also involve a conflict of interest between the lawyer and client.

[2] *Advocate-Witness Rule.* -- The tribunal has proper objection when the trier of fact may be confused or misled by a lawyer serving as both advocate and witness. The opposing party has proper objection where the combination of roles
may prejudice that party's rights in the litigation. A witness is required to testify on the basis of personal knowledge, while an advocate is expected to explain and comment on evidence given by others. It may not be clear whether a statement by an advocate-witness should be taken as proof or as an analysis of the proof.

[3] To protect the tribunal, paragraph (a) prohibits a lawyer from simultaneously serving as advocate and necessary witness except in those circumstances specified in paragraphs (a)(1) through (a)(3). Paragraph (a)(1) recognizes that if the testimony will be uncontested, the ambiguities in the dual role

are purely theoretical. Paragraph (a)(2) recognizes that where the testimony concerns the extent and value of legal services rendered in the action in which the testimony is offered, permitting the lawyers to testify avoids the need for a second trial with new counsel to resolve that issue. Moreover, in such a situation the judge has firsthand knowledge of the matter in issue; hence, there is less dependence on the adversary process to test the credibility of the testimony.

[4] Apart from these two exceptions, paragraph (a)(3) recognizes that a balancing is required between the interests of the client and those of the tribunal and the opposing party. Whether the tribunal is likely to be misled or the opposing party is likely to suffer prejudice depends on the nature of the case, the importance and probable tenor of the lawyer's testimony, and the probability that the lawyer's testimony will conflict with that of other witnesses. Even if there is risk of such prejudice, in determining whether the lawyer should be disqualified, due regard must be given to the effect of disqualification on the lawyer's client. It is relevant that one or both parties could reasonably foresee that the lawyer would probably be a witness. The conflict of interest principles stated in Rules 1.7, 1.9 and 1.10 have no application to this aspect of the problem.

[5] Because the tribunal is not likely to be misled when a lawyer acts as advocate in a trial in which another lawyer in the lawyer's firm will testify as a necessary witness, paragraph (b) permits the lawyer to do so except in situations involving
a conflict of interest.

[6] *Conflict of Interest.* -- In determining if it is permissible to act as advocate in a trial in which the lawyer will be a necessary witness, the lawyer must also consider that the dual role may give rise to a conflict of interest that will require compliance with Rules 1.7 or 1.9. For example, if there is likely to be substantial conflict between the testimony of the client and that of the lawyer, the representation involves a conflict of interest that requires compliance with Rule 1.7. This would be true even though the lawyer might not be prohibited by paragraph (a) from simultaneously serving as advocate and witness because the lawyer's disqualification would work a substantial hardship on the client. Similarly, a lawyer who might be permitted to simultaneously serve as an advocate and a witness by paragraph (a)(3) might be precluded from doing so by Rule 1.9. The problem can arise whether the lawyer is called as a witness on behalf of the client or is called by the opposing party. Determining whether or not such a conflict exists is primarily the responsibility of the lawyer involved. If there is a conflict of interest, the lawyer must secure the client's informed consent, confirmed in writing. In some cases, the lawyer will

be precluded from seeking the client's consent. See Rule 1.7. See Rule 1.0(b) for the definition of "confirmed in writing" and Rule 1.0(e) for the definition of "informed consent."

[7] Paragraph (b) provides that a lawyer is not disqualified from serving as an advocate because a lawyer with whom the lawyer is associated in a firm is precluded from doing so by paragraph (a). If, however, the testifying lawyer would also be disqualified by Rule 1.7 or Rule 1.9 from representing the client in the matter, other lawyers in the firm will be precluded from representing the client by Rule 1.10 unless the client gives informed consent under the conditions stated in Rule 1.7.

Rule 3.8. Special responsibilities of a prosecutor

The prosecutor in a criminal case shall:

(a) refrain from prosecuting a charge that the prosecutor knows is not supported by probable cause;

(b) make reasonable efforts to assure that the accused has been advised of the right to, and the procedure for obtaining, counsel and has been given reasonable opportunity to obtain counsel;

(c) not seek to obtain from an unrepresented accused a waiver of important pretrial rights, such as the right to a preliminary hearing;

(d) make timely disclosure to the defense of all evidence or information known to the prosecutor that tends to negate the guilt of the accused or mitigates the offense, and, in connection with sentencing, disclose to the defense and to the tribunal all unprivileged mitigating information known to the prosecutor, except when the prosecutor is relieved of this responsibility by a protective order of the tribunal;

(e) not subpoena a lawyer in a grand jury or other criminal proceeding to present evidence about a past or present client unless the prosecutor reasonably believes: (1) the information sought is not protected from disclosure by any applicable privilege; (2) the evidence sought is essential to the successful completion of an ongoing investigation or prosecution; and (3) there is no other feasible alternative to obtain the information;

(f) except for statements that are necessary to inform the public of the nature and extent of the prosecutor's action and that serve a legitimate law enforcement purpose, refrain from making extrajudicial comments that have a substantial likelihood of heightening public condemnation of the accused and exercise reasonable care to prevent investigators, law enforcement personnel, employees or other persons assisting or associated with the prosecutor in a criminal case from making an extrajudicial statement that the prosecutor would be prohibited from making under Rule 3.6 or this Rule.

COMMENT

[1] A prosecutor has the responsibility of a minister of justice and not simply that of an advocate. This responsibility carries with it specific obligations to see that the defendant is accorded procedural justice and that guilt is decided upon the basis of sufficient evidence. Precisely how far the prosecutor is required to go in this direction is a matter of debate and varies in different jurisdictions. Many jurisdictions have adopted the ABA Standards of Criminal Justice Relating to the Prosecution Function, which in turn are the product of prolonged and careful deliberation by lawyers experienced in both criminal prosecution and defense. Applicable law may require other measures by the prosecutor and knowing disregard of those obligations or a systematic abuse of prosecutorial discretion could constitute a violation of Rule 8.4.

[2] In some jurisdictions, a defendant may waive a preliminary hearing and thereby lose a valuable opportunity to challenge probable cause. Accordingly, prosecutors should not seek to obtain waivers of preliminary hearings or other important pretrial rights from unrepresented accused persons. Paragraph (c) does not apply, however, to an accused appearing pro se with the approval of the tribunal. Nor does it forbid the lawful questioning of an uncharged suspect who has knowingly waived the rights to counsel and silence.

[3] The exception in paragraph (d) recognizes that a prosecutor may seek an appropriate protective order from the tribunal if disclosure of information to the defense could result in substantial harm to an individual or to the public interest.

[4] Paragraph (e) is intended to limit the issuance of lawyer subpoenas in grand jury and other criminal proceedings to those situations in which there is a genuine need to intrude into the client-lawyer relationship.

[5] Paragraph (f) supplements Rule 3.6, which prohibits extra judicial statements that have a substantial likelihood of prejudicing an adjudicatory proceeding. In the context of a criminal prosecution, a prosecutor's extrajudicial statement can create the additional problem of increasing public condemnation of the accused. Although the announcement of an indictment, for example, will necessarily have severe consequences for the accused, a prosecutor

can, and should, avoid comments that have no legitimate law enforcement purpose and have a substantial likelihood of increasing public opprobrium of the accused. Nothing in this Comment is intended to restrict the statements which a prosecutor may make which comply with Rule 3.6(b) or 3.6(c).

[6] Like other lawyers, prosecutors are subject to Rules 5.1 and 5.3, which relate to responsibilities regarding lawyers and nonlawyers who work for or are associated with the lawyer's office. Paragraph (f) reminds the prosecutor of the importance of these obligations in connection with the unique dangers of improper extrajudicial statements in a criminal case. In addition, paragraph (f) requires a prosecutor to exercise reasonable care to prevent persons assisting or associated with the prosecutor from making improper extrajudicial statements, even when such persons are not under the direct supervision of the prosecutor. Ordinarily, the reasonable care standard will be satisfied if the prosecutor issues the appropriate cautions to law-enforcement personnel and other relevant individuals.

Rule 3.9. Advocate in nonadjudicative proceedings - omitted

Rule 4.3. Dealing with unrepresented person

In dealing on behalf of a client with a person who is not represented by counsel, a lawyer shall not state or imply that the lawyer is disinterested. When the lawyer knows or reasonably should know that the unrepresented person misunderstands
the lawyer's role in the matter, the lawyer shall make reasonable efforts to correct the misunderstanding. The lawyer shall not give legal advice to an unrepresented person, other than the advice to secure counsel, if the lawyer knows or reasonably should know that the interests of such a person are or have a reasonable possibility of being in conflict with the interests of the client.

COMMENT

[1] An unrepresented person, particularly one not experienced in dealing with legal matters, might assume that a lawyer is disinterested in loyalties or is a disinterested authority on the law even when the lawyer represents a client. In order to avoid a misunderstanding, a lawyer will typically need to identify the lawyer's client and, where necessary, explain that the client has interests opposed to those of the unrepresented person. For misunderstandings that sometimes arise when a lawyer for an organization deals with an unrepresented constituent, see Rule 1.13(d).

[2] The Rule distinguishes between situations involving unrepresented persons whose interests may be adverse to those of the lawyer's client and those in which the person's interests are not in conflict with the client's. In the former situation, the possibility that the lawyer will compromise the unrepresented person's interests is so great that the Rule prohibits the giving of any advice, apart from the advice to obtain counsel. Whether a lawyer is giving impermissible advice may depend on the experience and sophistication of the unrepresented person, as well as the setting in which the behavior and comments occur. This Rule does not prohibit a lawyer from negotiating the terms of a transaction or settling a dispute with an unrepresented person. So long as the lawyer has explained that the lawyer represents an adverse party and is not representing the person, the lawyer may inform the person of the terms on which the lawyer's client will enter into an agreement or settle a matter, prepare documents that require the person's signature and explain the lawyer's own view of the meaning of the document or the lawyer's view of the underlying legal obligations.

Rule 4.4. Respect for rights of third persons

(a) In representing a client, a lawyer shall not use means that have no substantial purpose other than to embarrass, delay or burden a third person, or use methods of obtaining evidence that violate the legal rights of such a person.

(b) A lawyer who receives a document relating to the representation of the lawyer's client and knows or reasonably should know that the document was inadvertently sent shall promptly notify the sender.

COMMENT

[1] Responsibility to a client requires a lawyer to subordinate the interests of others to those of the client, but that responsibility does not imply that a lawyer may disregard the rights of third persons. It is impractical to catalogue all such
rights, but they include legal restrictions on methods of obtaining evidence from third persons and unwarranted intrusions into privileged relationships, such as the client-lawyer relationship.

[2] Paragraph (b) recognizes that lawyers sometimes receive documents that were mistakenly sent or produced by opposing parties or their lawyers. If a lawyer knows or reasonably should know that a such a document was sent inadvertently,
then this Rule requires the lawyer to promptly notify the sender in order to permit that person to take protective measures. Whether the lawyer is required

to take additional steps, such as returning the original document, is a matter of law beyond the scope of these Rules, as is the question of whether the privileged status of a document has been waived. Similarly, this Rule does not address the legal duties of a lawyer who receives a document that the lawyer knows or reasonably should know may have been wrongfully obtained by the sending person. For purposes of this Rule, "document" includes e-mail or other electronic modes of transmission subject to being read or put into readable form.

[3] Some lawyers may choose to return a document unread, for example, when the lawyer learns before receiving the document that it was inadvertently sent to the wrong address. Where a lawyer is not required by applicable law to do so, the decision to voluntarily return such a document is a matter of professional judgment ordinarily reserved to the lawyer. See Rules 1.2 and 1.4.

Rule 5.1. Responsibilities of Supervisors

(a) A partner in a law firm, and a lawyer who individually or together with other lawyers possesses comparable managerial authority in a law firm, shall make reasonable efforts to ensure that the firm has in effect measures giving reasonable assurance that all lawyers in the firm conform to the Rules of Professional Conduct.

(b) A lawyer having direct supervisory authority over another lawyer shall make reasonable efforts to ensure that the other lawyer conforms to the Rules of Professional Conduct.

(c) A lawyer shall be responsible for another lawyer's violation of the Rules of Professional Conduct if: (1) the lawyer orders or, with knowledge of the specific conduct, ratifies the conduct involved; or (2) the lawyer is a partner or has comparable managerial authority in the law firm in which the other lawyer practices, or has direct supervisory authority over the other lawyer, and knows of the conduct at a time when its consequences can be avoided or mitigated but fails to take reasonable remedial action.

Rule 5.3. Responsibilities regarding non-lawyer assistants

With respect to a nonlawyer employed or retained by or associated with a lawyer:

(a) a partner in a law firm, and a lawyer who individually or together with other lawyers possesses comparable managerial authority in a law firm, shall make reasonable efforts to ensure that the firm has in effect measures giving reasonable assurance that the person's conduct is compatible with the professional obligations of the lawyer;

(b) a lawyer having direct supervisory authority over the nonlawyer shall make reasonable efforts to ensure that the person's conduct is compatible with the professional obligations of the lawyer; and

(c) a lawyer shall be responsible for conduct of such a person that would be a violation of the Rules of Professional Conduct if engaged in by a lawyer if: (1) the lawyer orders or, with the knowledge of the specific conduct, ratifies the conduct involved; or (2) the lawyer is a partner or has comparable managerial authority in the law firm in which the person is employed, or has direct supervisory authority over the person, and knows of the conduct at a time when its consequences can be avoided or mitigated but fails to take reasonable remedial action.

Rule 5.4. Professional independence of a lawyer

(a) A lawyer or law firm shall not share legal fees with a nonlawyer, except that: (1) an agreement by a lawyer with the lawyer's firm, partner, or associate may provide for the payment of money, over a reasonable period of time after the lawyer's death, to the lawyer's estate or to one or more specified persons; (2) a lawyer who undertakes to complete unfinished legal business of a deceased lawyer may pay to the estate of the deceased lawyer that proportion of the total compensation which fairly represents the services rendered by the deceased lawyer; (3) a lawyer who purchases the practice of a deceased, disabled, or disappeared lawyer may, pursuant to the provisions of Rule 1.17, pay to the estate or other representative of that lawyer the agreed-upon purchase price; (4) a lawyer or law firm may include nonlawyer employees in a compensation or retirement plan, even though the plan is based in whole or in part on a profit-sharing arrangement; and (5) a lawyer may share court-awarded legal fees with a nonprofit organization that employed, retained or recommended employment of the lawyer in the matter.

(b) A lawyer shall not form a partnership with a nonlawyer if any of the activities of the partnership consist of the practice of law.

(c) A lawyer shall not permit a person who recommends, employs, or pays the lawyer to render legal services for another to direct or regulate the lawyer's professional judgment in rendering such legal services.

(d) A lawyer shall not practice with or in the form of a professional corporation or association authorized to practice law for a profit, if: (1) a nonlawyer owns any interest therein, except that a fiduciary representative of the estate of a lawyer may hold the stock or interest of the lawyer for a reasonable time during administration; (2) a nonlawyer is a corporate director or officer thereof or occupies the position of similar responsibility in any form of association other than a corporation; or (3) a nonlawyer has the right to direct or control the professional judgment of a lawyer

Rule 5.5. Unauthorized practice of law; multijurisdictional practice of law - omitted

Rule 5.6. Restrictions on right to practice - omitted

Rule 5.7. Responsibilities regarding law-related services - omitted

Rule 6.1. Voluntary pro bono publico service - omitted

Rule 6.2. Accepting appointments

A lawyer shall not seek to avoid appointment by a tribunal to represent a person except for good cause, such as:

(a) representing the client is likely to result in violation of the Rules of Professional Conduct or other law;

(b) representing the client is likely to result in an unreasonable financial burden on the lawyer; or

(c) the client or the cause is so repugnant to the lawyer as to be likely to impair the client-lawyer relationship or the lawyer's ability to represent the client.

Rule 6.3. Membership in legal services organization - omitted

Rule 6.4. Law reform activities affecting client interests - omitted

Rule 6.5. Non-profit and court-annexed limited legal-service programomitted

Rule 7.1. Communications concerning a lawyer's services - omitted

Rule 7.2. Advertising - omitted

Rule 7.3. Direct contact with prospective clients - omitted

Rule 7.4. Communication of fields of practice and specialization - omitted

Rule 7.5. Firm names and letterheads - omitted

Rule 8.1. Bar admission and disciplinary matters

An applicant for admission to the bar, or a lawyer in connection with a bar admission application or in connection with a disciplinary matter, shall not:

(a) knowingly make a false statement of material fact; or

(b) fail to disclose a fact necessary to correct a misapprehension known by the person to have arisen in the matter, or knowingly fail to respond to a lawful demand for information from an admission or disciplinary authority, except that this rule does not require disclosure of information otherwise protected by Rule 1.6.

Rule 8.2. Judicial and legal officials

(a) A lawyer shall not make a statement that the lawyer knows to be false or with reckless disregard as to its truth or falsity concerning the qualifications or integrity of a judge, adjudicatory officer or public legal officer, or a candidate for election or appointment to judicial or legal office.

(b) A lawyer who is a candidate for judicial office shall comply with the applicable provisions of the Code of Judicial Conduct.

Rule 8.3. Reporting professional misconduct

(a) A lawyer who knows that another lawyer has committed a violation of the rules of Professional Conduct that raises a substantial question as to that lawyer's honesty, trustworthiness or fitness as a lawyer in other respects, shall inform the appropriate professional authority.

(b) A lawyer who knows that a judge has committed a violation of applicable rules of judicial conduct that raises a substantial question as to the judge's fitness for office shall inform the appropriate authority.

(c) This Rule does not require disclosure of information otherwise protected by rule 1.6.

(d) Notwithstanding anything in this or other of the rules to the contrary, the relationship between members of either (i) the Lawyers Assistance Committee of the Delaware State Bar Association and counselors retained by the Bar Association, or (ii) the Professional Ethics Committee of the Delaware State Bar Association, or (iii) the Fee dispute Conciliation and Mediation Committee of the Delaware State Bar Association, or (iv) the Professional Guidance Committee of the Delaware State Bar Association, and a lawyer or a judge shall be the same as that of attorney and client.

Rule 8.4. Misconduct

It is professional misconduct for a lawyer to:
(a) violate or attempt to violate the Rules of Professional Conduct, knowingly assist or induce another to do so or do so through the acts of another;

(b) commit a criminal act that reflects adversely on the lawyer's honesty, trustworthiness or fitness as a lawyer in other respects;

(c) engage in conduct involving dishonesty, fraud, deceit or misrepresentation;

(d) engage in conduct that is prejudicial to the administration of justice;

(e) state or imply an ability to influence improperly a government agency or official or to achieve results by means that violate the Rules of Professional Conduct or other law; or

(f) knowingly assist a judge or judicial officer in conduct that is a violation of applicable rules of judicial conduct or other law.

-Notes-